POPULATION STUDIES:

Selected Essays and Research

POPULATION STUDIES:

Selected Essays and Research

Edited by
KENNETH C. W. KAMMEYER
University of Kansas

RAND McNALLY & COMPANY • CHICAGO

Rand McNally Sociology Series

Edgar F. Borgatta, Advisory Editor

Second Printing, 1970

PREFACE

I feel mildly defensive about preparing a book of readings. In the intellectual world the collection of readings is often the object of a looking-down-the-nose snobbism, if not open disdain. One has only to read the book-review sections of scholarly journals to see a manifestation of the generally negative critical response to this genre of book. Perhaps the task of providing a succinct evaluation of something as varied as a book of readings is so difficult and frustrating that it raises the aggression level of book reviewers, and thus accounts for their often critical assessments. However, I tend to reject the frustration-aggression hypothesis in favor of an anomie theory. The rules for evaluating a book of readings are not clear. Should one use the norms that apply to the more traditional book, or should an entirely new set of norms be applied to the book of readings? Exactly what is the reviewer to review? Should he review the contents of the selected papers, or the contributions of the editor, or both? If the book of readings is judged as a totality, should it be evaluated in terms of comprehensiveness, coherence, or usefulness, and if all three, what should be their order of importance?

My own feeling is that such works are best judged in terms of their usefulness. For I suspect that others like myself feel that when they work on a book of readings they are providing a service, and they have a fairly clear conception of the people who will be using that service. By contrast, the reviewer is only partially concerned with the users and the usefulness of the book, but is looking for other qualities that may or may not exist in the final product. In any case, let it be clear that my primary objective in preparing this book of readings is to provide a service for a particular audience.

The audience that remained foremost in my mind as I worked on this collection may be divided into two categories. In the first category there are the students who typically enroll in a college or university population course—a course that is almost always offered by the department of sociology. This course is generally taken by sophomores, juniors, or seniors, although one or two graduate students are also often enrolled. In my experience the backgrounds of these students, as indicated by major fields, are extremely varied. In my classes only a minority of the students are sociology majors; the rest come from a wide range of majors. The only common thread that runs through the student category is that in varying degrees they are interested in (or concerned about) population—usually phrased in terms of the "population problem." Indeed, one of the tasks of such a course is to emphasize that there is more to the study of population than simply the "population problem"—a task that is reflected in the papers selected for this book.

While I have observed a sizable number of population students over several years of teaching, and thus might claim to have some sampling of the universe, I am on no such solid empirical ground with respect to the second category of my audience: the teachers of population courses in the colleges and universities. Here I have largely relied upon a sample of one—myself—and some evidence indicating that I am not completely atypical.

For instance, Otis Dudley Duncan's study of the teaching of demography in the United States indicated that the typical population course is offered by a sociology department, and is taught by a sociologist.[1] The latter point is to be emphasized because its significance lies in the distinction between population courses taught by sociologists and population courses taught by demographers. While some might argue that population courses taught by sociologists rather than by demographers is a lamentable state of affairs, I'm not at all sure that I agree, and furthermore, whatever one's feelings on this issue, the empirical fact is that population courses are still most frequently taught by people whose primary disciplinary identification is with sociology and not demography. This latter assertion might be questioned, but Duncan found it to be true in 1951, and while graduate programs in demography expanded in numbers and enrollment during the 1950's and 1960's, I suspect that the change has not been great.

In summary, as I collected the papers for this volume, I had in

---

[1] Otis Dudley Duncan, "The Teaching of Demography in the United States of America," in *The University Teaching of Social Sciences: Demography*, ed. D. V. Glass (Deventer, Netherlands: United Nations Educational, Scientific and Cultural Organization, Ysel Press, 1957), pp. 162–93.

mind a very heterogeneous group of interested undergraduate and graduate students enrolled in sociologically oriented population courses. Secondly, I tried to collect papers that would be useful for the sociologist-demographer who introduces them to the study of population. If this book proves to be useful for these students and teachers, I will consider it a worthwhile effort.

My selection of articles is by no means definitive, nor is it meant to be. I was very consciously looking for certain kinds of papers and essays, and just as consciously avoiding others. I wanted papers that moved in some manner toward generalization or synthesis in some area of population study. In the case of data papers, they had to have a bearing on some issue or question that is of some consequence in the study of population. I did not want simple descriptive data papers, for while they are important, indeed essential, for the study of population, it did not seem to me that they would have the stimulating quality or the overarching importance that would warrant their inclusion in a collection.

It will be obvious from an examination of the selections that I tended toward the essay that explores and discusses some population question or theory. I have tried to select papers that will stimulate interest in the study of population.

The instructors who use this volume in a population course will see that the sections of the book are somewhat arbitrary, and represent only one of several possible ways in which the collection could have been divided. In my experience an instructor usually restructures a book of readings to suit his own teaching needs, and I invite those using this collection to do so. The arbitrariness of the sections is shown by the fact that there is no specific section devoted to population composition or structure, although at least two papers may be used in this area. The paper by Dorothy Good, "Questions on Religion in the United States Census," deals in part with the religious composition of the U.S. population. And the paper by Ansley Coale, "How a Population Ages or Grows Younger," is clearly concerned with the age composition of the population, but since it is primarily concerned with the manner in which changing mortality conditions influence age structure, I have chosen to include it in the section on mortality.

A considerable period of time has passed since the first moment when I thought about preparing this book of readings on population. During that time a large number of people have given me their help, cooperation, and encouragement, and I want to thank them. First, my thanks go to the authors of the papers in this collection. Since each individual paper is the end product of a great amount of research and thought, the total set represents a vast accumulation of experience and knowledge. I want to thank the authors collectively for generously allowing me to reprint their original works, and I want to acknowledge here that whatever quality this collection has is due to their scholarly efforts. I also want to thank the publishers of the original papers for their permissions to reprint the papers.

Over the period of time required to prepare this book I have been helped by a number of individuals, and for their help I am most grateful. Many of the tasks connected with preparing a book of readings are repetitive or routine, and certainly not too exciting, but the people who have worked with me have done so with enthusiasm. Among those who have worked with me during one stage or another of this project are: Fred Costello, Jeannie Farwell, Jeannie Freeman, Isao Horinouchi, Robin Pardini, Arthur St. George, and Kay Syverson. I want to thank all of these friends for their help.

CONTENTS

The Study
of Population

Introduction

Only a few years ago demographers and other scholars who were concerned about the rapidly increasing population of the world often had the feeling that their attempts to alert the public were not being heard, or, if heard, were not being heeded. Today the situation is quite different, for it seems that almost everyone is aware, at least to some degree, of the "population explosion." A public awareness of the "population problem" is certainly a very favorable sign, for we can now hope that this awareness means concern, and that concern will be translated into action; for concerted action is essential if we are to avoid the calamities of a too rapidly increasing world population.

The increasing awareness of and concern about the population problem has had the secondary effect of bringing more and more people to the study of population. While this newly burgeoning interest in population must surely be viewed very favorably, it is often the case that persons who are initially attracted by the population problem may have a narrow view of the study of population. There is frequently an initial lack of awareness of and interest in the long history of population study and the range of subjects it covers.

The historical and theoretical richness of population study is worthy of attention for two reasons. First, many population issues and questions are intrinsically interesting, and yet they do not have an immediate bearing on the problem of world population growth. For example, the many issues and problems related to migration within countries, and even population movements between countries, have little direct influence on the world's population growth, and yet there is much that is challenging and interesting about these questions. Second, an understanding of the broad scope of population study, both historically and substantively, can be of great value when one does consider the problem of population growth directly. Such an understanding provides the historical perspective for viewing the long-term trends and characteristics of world population. It may also provide a theoretical frame of reference that will aid in understanding the essence of complex demographic situations. Finally, it may provide greater awareness of the usefulness, as well as the inadequacies and shortcomings, of population data and the tools of demographic analysis.

One of the objectives of this volume is to illustrate the diversity of relevant population issues, but no claim is made that the papers selected cover the entire range of demographic analysis and inquiry. Many of the articles will show an affinity to the sociological perspective, in that they illustrate the influence of social organization and culture on demographic phenomena. In the first paper of this section, Philip Hauser's "Demography in Relation to Sociology," the author develops the distinction between demographic analysis and population study. He describes demographic analysis as "concerned with the statistical analysis of population size, distribution, and composition and with components of variation and change." According to Hauser, demographic analysis is characterized in part by the techniques of statistical analysis which are most commonly used, but more importantly by the notion that population characteristics are used as independent variables to explain variations in other population characteristics (viewed as dependent variables). In contrast, population study is "the interrelating of a set of dependent demographic variables with independent sets of social, economic, genetic, psychological, historical and other systems of variables." To put this distinction as clearly as possible, if one is examining the influence that one demographic characteristic may have on another demographic characteristic, this is demographic analysis. For example, in this collection we have included a paper by Ansley Coale in which he analyzes the relationship between the mortality rate and the age structure of a population ("How a Population Ages or Grows Younger," Section IV). Mortality rate is, of course, one of the basic dynamic characteristics of population (along with migration and fertility), while the age of a population is one of its structural or compositional characteristics, so we have in this paper a clear illustration of demographic analysis (some writers have called this formal demography).

By contrast, population studies are those that examine the influence of some nondemographic characteristic on a demographic variable (such as migration, mortality, fertility, age structure). As Hauser indicates, the nondemographic characteristics may come from a variety of other "systems of variables," so that two quite different independent variables might be employed to explain variations in the same demographic variable. As a simple illustration, differences in fertility or changes in fertility may be explained by differences in family structure or marriage customs (sociological variables), fears and stereotypes about birth-control techniques (psychological variables), differences in fecundity (a biological variable—fecundity is defined as the biological capacity to reproduce and is probably influenced by such things as diet, health, heredity, etc.).

Hauser, in this introductory paper, notes that nondemographers may also use demographic factors in their studies. The nondemographer may use a population factor as an independent variable to show the influence that it may have on a nondemographic variable. For example, a political scientist could examine the age structure of a population to determine what effect it might have on the voting behavior of the group. Strictly speaking, this is not demography, but for convenience we may consider it one kind of population study. We might then have population studies type I, where other systems of variables are used to explain variations in demographic variables, and population studies type II, where demographic variables are used to explain variations in other systems of variables.

Following these distinctions, it will be clear that we have tended toward the selection of those articles that would be labeled population study type I, and have chosen papers where the independent variables most often come from the social and cultural realms, sometimes from the psychological realm.

In his paper on the relationship between sociology and demography, Hauser goes on to emphasize "that there is no logical reason why demography should be more closely related to sociology than to any one of a number of other disciplines." He suggests that "the fact that demography has become largely a subfield of sociology . . . in the United States is more a matter of historical accident than of special affinity. The relationships between demographic and sociological sets of variables are not necessarily closed, more compelling, and more fruitful than similar relationships with economic, psychological, geographic, genetic, or other sets of variables."

This assertion raises two questions. First, is Hauser correct when he asserts that there is no special affinity between the study of population and sociology? Second, what are the historical conditions that led to the present situation, where the study of population is largely within the domain of sociology? The first of these two questions is worth considering, not because it contains the promise of a definitive answer, but because it will help to sensitize us to the nature of population study. Since the position that we might take on this issue is already indicated in the selections that have been made for this volume, and since taking an explicit position at this point might preclude further considerations by the reader, it might be most useful for us only to suggest some of the directions the discussion might take. It is to be hoped that this may help to ensure an ongoing consideration of the question as the reader continues through this book. While it could be argued that the question should not be considered at all until a person has developed an intensive and extensive familiarity with the study of population, we would suggest again that the sensitizing benefits of the question are most important.

A discussion of the special nature of the relationship between population study and sociology might include a consideration of the following kinds of questions: Can one advance a logical argument for the position that there *is* a special affinity between sociology and the study of population? Might it be possible to rank the various academic disciplines and sciences in order of their importance in the explanation of population phenomena? If so, where would sociology fall in the ordered ranking? Does sociology have a special or strategic position relative to the study of specific population phenomena? Consider, for example, that sociological variables might be of great importance in understanding migration, but of much less importance in explaining variations in mortality. These are only a few of the lines that a consideration of this issue can take, and although this volume will by its orientation and content imply that there is a special affinity between sociology and the study of population, each reader will have to draw his own conclusions on the basis of his continued and hopefully ever widening understanding of the subject.

Concerning the historical circumstances that have led to the inclusion of population study within the discipline of sociology, we may agree that some unique historical events played an important part in this process. One hypothesis might be developed around the strategic role played by the Reverend Thomas Malthus and his *Essay on the Principle of Population.* In the study of population the work of Malthus can be viewed as a turning point, or a time of redirection. Most of the writing on population previous to Malthus' essay is distinct from the major thrust of population study since.

The long history of population study prior to Malthus, who was writing in the early part of the nineteenth century, tended to focus on the size of the population of some nation or state or people as this population size related to the goals of the group. Thus the Greek philosophers Plato and Aristotle were primarily concerned with the ideal population size of the city-state and how that optimum might best be attained. Similarly the Roman writers were concerned with population size as it related to the resources and the power of the Roman Empire. The mercantilist philosophers of seventeenth- and eighteenth-century Europe were interested in the effect that population might have on the ability of a nation-state to accumulate wealth through a favorable balance of international trade. Now while it might be argued that Malthus' original reasons for writing his essay on population were also related to the national interests of his society, these purposes are overshadowed by the ultimate effect that his essay had on thinking about population matters. We may say that Malthus did two things with regard to the study of population: (1) he brought the study of population into the realm of empirical science, i.e., the testing of theory with data, while at the same time (2) he emphasized the vice and misery associated with excessive numbers of people, and thus made population a *social problem.* Since the main thrust of early sociology in the United States was a concern about social or societal problems, it was probably natural that some American sociologists should be attracted to the study of population. Twentieth-century sociology in the United States also became increasingly empirical and quantitative in character, so the study of population as it developed from Malthus' time had this similarity also.

We would suggest, then, that the character that Malthus gave to the study of population, emphasizing that it was a social problem and amenable to empirical scientific inquiry, is more responsible than any other single factor for the inclusion of demography within the discipline of sociology.

In this first section of the book we have a paper by Kurt Mayer, "Developments in the Study of Population," and a paper by Warren C. Robinson, "The Development of Modern Population Theory," presenting summaries and assessments of population theory and population study which provide sometimes contrasting, but often complementary, views of demography. Both of these papers open with discussions of Malthus which tend to deprecate his role in the development of modern-day demography, particularly in the area of empirical studies. This position, if valid, would, of course, weaken the contention above that it was the work of Malthus that advanced an empirically based scientific study of population. However, an analysis of the history of his famous *Essay on Population* supports our position, for while the first edition of the essay was primarily a political-philosophical polemic, the later editions were much more firmly based on the newly emerging data of population. The paper in this section on "Professor Malthus and His Essay" gives a much more detailed account of the nature and significance of Malthus' work and clearly indicates the empirical, quantitative aspects of the later editions of the *Essay*. This paper does, of course, indicate that the *Essay* provoked much argument and debate and "brought a new subject to the tireless pamphleteers of London and the universities." Thus while it is accurate to say, as both Mayer and Robinson do, that Malthus' theory of population prompted an abundance of population theory which dominated the literature during the nineteenth century, it cannot be concluded that the stimulus of the Malthusian controversy did not also lead directly to an empirically oriented study of population. The American demographer Warren Thompson has argued that Malthus' primary contribution to demography was exactly in this latter area. He has written:

> Malthus' primary contribution to the study of population, and one which in our opinion makes him the real father of modern population study, was his use of facts for the support of his general doctrine regarding the dynamics of population growth and change in relation to man's welfare. He is more responsible than anyone else for bringing population study within the field of social science.[1]

With regard to the polemic and controversy surrounding Mal-

---

[1] Warren S. Thompson and David T. Lewis, *Population Problems*, 5th ed. (New York: McGraw-Hill Book Co., 1965), p. 35.

thusian principles of population, none has been more durable than the controversy between the followers of Marx and Malthus. William Petersen's essay, "Marx versus Malthus: The Men and the Symbols," which concludes this section, is a detailed analysis of the similarities and differences between the two theoretical positions. In a very informed presentation Petersen demonstrates that there are more similarities, or at least parallels, in the writings of these two men than the impassioned controversies of their advocates would lead one to believe. It is instructive for the student of population to have the benefit of this scholarly analysis of two doctrines that have often been pitted against each other, and to see that some of the alleged differences are more imagined than real. Nevertheless, we must remember that the perceived differences between Marx and Malthus have been more important historically than these demonstrated similarities. The controversies that have gone on within socialist nations over the issue of population policy and Malthusian theory demonstrate that the label of "neo-Malthusianism" is still one of opprobrium for many followers of Marx. Perhaps nowhere has this been more evident than in mainland China since the Communist revolution there. The Chinese Communist leadership has had the dilemma of a large and growing population which threatens to outstrip the gains of the socialist economic system, and yet to admit this and call for population-control measures would seem to be "neo-Malthusian" and thus counterrevolutionary. This has resulted in rather abrupt changes in population policy as the Chinese government has vacillated between energetic birth-control programs and the complete abandonment of such programs.[2]

While the socialist position opposing population control has been an impediment to efforts to control population growth, there are now signs that even in the Communist world there is a recognition of the dangers of a rapidly growing world population. In particular the Soviet Union, which has tended to be underpopulated rather than overpopulated, shows signs of shifting from its long-standing and adamant anti-Malthusian position.[3] This is but one of many factors that will ultimately determine the population growth rate of the world in the future.

---

[2] H. Yuan Tien, "Birth Control in Mainland China: Ideology and Politics," *Milbank Memorial Fund Quarterly*, 41 (July, 1963), pp. 269–90.

[3] Population Reference Bureau, "Soviet Population Theory from Marx to Kosygin: A Demographic Turning Point?" *Population Bulletin*, 23 (October, 1967), pp. 85–115.

1

Demography in
Relation to Sociology[1]

Philip M. Hauser

ABSTRACT

Demography may be conceived as consisting of two facets, demographic analysis and population studies. The former is concerned only with the study of population size and composition and components of variation and change; the latter, with the interrelationships of population and other systems of variables of which the sociological constitute but one set. Population study affords the sociologist the opportunity to work with quantified variables which provide some benchmark against which to work with other sets of variables. Demography, although a multiscience discipline, can contribute to the central interests of sociology and, in return, gain from study of the interrelations of demographic and sociological variables.

With the encouragement of the National Science Foundation, a review was recently undertaken of the status of demography as a science. This paper is drawn largely from the volume which reports the results of this undertaking.[2] The investigation necessarily entailed consideration of demography in relation to a number of other disciplines, including sociology.[3]

Courses in demography in the United States, although offered in a number of disciplines, are primarily concentrated in departments of sociology. In fact, about three-fifths of the members of the Population Association of America, and about half of those in the International Union for the Scientific Study of Population, had their basic training in sociology. The modal demographer in the United States is a Ph.D. in sociology serving as

Reprinted from *American Journal of Sociology*, 65, no. 2 (September, 1959), pp. 169–73, by permission of the author and the University of Chicago Press. Copyright © 1959 by the University of Chicago.

a faculty member in a university or college; 26 per cent of the members of the Population Association of America are so described.

The extent to which sociology has "captured" demography in the United States is an interesting phenomenon. Especially is this so, when it is recalled that the study of population as a specialty probably antedated the emergence of sociology as a separate social science and that the close affinity between sociology and demography is largely a product of the last two or three decades.

It must be noted, however, that, although a large proportion of demographers are sociologists, only a small proportion of sociologists are demographers. Moreover, there would, in general, be agreement that most sociologists tend to ignore or to give scant attention to demographic considerations in their research and that some demographers have, on the whole, conducted their investigations without too much concern with, or attention to, problems of major sociological interest. In consequence, although demography in this country is primarily a subfield of sociology, the arrangement has been assumed to be more one of housekeeping convenience than of a fundamental theoretical, substantive, or methodological unity. By reason of these considerations it is appropriate to review the interrelationships of these fields and to explore the potentialities and prospects for their closer and more fruitful collaboration.

In the volume from which this paper is largely drawn, demography is conceived of as comprising two distinct facets, namely, demographic analysis and population studies.[4] The former is concerned with the statistical analysis of population size, distribution, and composition and with components of variation and change; the latter involves the interrelationships of demographic with other systems of variables. This distinction provides a logical framework for viewing the relationship of demography as a multiscience discipline to various disciplines, including sociology.

Scholars identified as "demographers," whether in sociology or other fields, have been primarily, although not necessarily exclusively, concerned with demographic analysis. Non-demographic scholars, however, also deal with demographic variables. For example, geographers, geneticists, ecologists, anthropologists, public health experts, psychologists, historians, economists, manpower specialists, and students of other disciplines, as well as sociologists, frequently consider population variables in the conduct of their research.

The demographer, whatever his training may be, is characterized by a major interest in demographic phenomena as dependent variables. He is concerned with accounting for the variability in demographic behavior, with the object of achieving predictability and control or explanation. In research designed to achieve this objective the demographer may use as independent variables either population or other phenomena. When the research of the demographer is confined to the interrelating of a set of dependent demographic variables with independent demographic factors, it is "demographic analysis"; when the research involves the interrelating of dependent demographic variables with independent sets of social, economic, genetic, psychological, historical, or other systems of variables, it is an example of "population studies." In the pursuit of such an interest the individual demographer is apt to work with the subject matter of the discipline in which he has been trained, as, for example, sociology, economics, psychology, genetics, or geography. Whatever may be their disciplinary origin, demographers have in common an interest in demographic analysis and are equipped, therefore, with a common body of theory, knowledge, and method for achieving it. In addition, they usually have general training in a social or natural science with departmental standing in academic organization.

The non-demographer, whether sociologist, geneticist, economist, or whoever else, who utilizes demographic variables to account for variability in sets of dependent variables in which he is interested, is also engaged in population studies. His interest may differ from that of the demographer, however, in that he is more likely to treat population phenomena as independent, rather than as dependent, variables in his effort to achieve predictability and explanation of his non-demographic phenomena.

Within this framework it is clear that there is no logical reason why demography should be more closely related to sociology than to any one of a number of other disciplines.[5] The fact that demography has become largely a subfield of sociology for instructional and academic housekeeping purposes in the United States is more a matter of historical accident than of special affinity. The relationships between demographic and sociological sets of variables are not necessarily closer, more compelling, and more fruitful than similar relationships with economic, psychological, geographic, genetic, or other sets of variables. Each of these configurations of interrelationships could conceivably make some contribution to achieving predictability and explanation of population phenomena considered as dependent variables. Conversely, population variables, considered as independent variables, could help to explain the behavior of the other sets of variables. But they have no closer relationship to the explanation of sociological than of other phenomena of social or natural science. There exists then as much justification for relating demography to any one of a number of natural as well as social sciences as there is for the relationship between demography and sociology.

These considerations are presented as a basis for neither the secession nor the expulsion of demography from sociology. On the contrary, a better understanding of the interrelations of these disciplines could conceivably lead to more fruitful research in both. It is with this objective in mind that exploration is made in the paragraphs which follow of the potentialities and prospects for closer and more productive research involving demographic and sociological variables.

The exploration of such potentialities may be considered from two standpoints: first, the possible gains to demography and, second, the possible gains to sociology.

GAINS TO DEMOGRAPHY

In respect to the possible gains to demography, there is evidence that the demographer is increasingly turning to studies involving sociological variables in his effort to predict and explain demographic phenomena. This is particularly true, as might be expected, of the demographer who has been trained in sociology. It is perhaps most evident in research concerned with fertility and migration.

Although the demographer has learned much about changes in fertility and about differential fertility and has developed methods for comparative study of fertility in time and space, he is far from having achieved a high order of predictability and explanation of fertility behavior. This is perhaps most strikingly manifest in the preparation of population projections, in which relatively wide ranges in the course of birth rates are usually involved. The demographer's projection of birth rates is generally tied to explicitly stated assumptions, usually based on previously observed "high" or "low" birth rates. But the demographer does not know which, if any, of the assumptions will hold, because little is known about the relation between fertility behavior as a dependent variable and the sociological and social-psychological factors which may affect it. Demographers interested in predicting and explaining fertility behavior have increasingly been turning to research in which sociological and social-psychological variables, among others, are related to fertility behavior in the hope of achieving improved understanding and predictability. A number of major studies of this type have been undertaken or are now in process.[6] Similarly, although the demographer has achieved some understanding of international and internal migration, the ability to predict and explain migratory behavior still awaits a better understanding of the role, among other things, of various cultural and psychological factors in migration.[7]

Although the course of mortality in the economically more advanced countries can be predicted with greater precision than that of fertility or migration (if there is no war), even here gains would undoubtedly be possible if a better understanding were achieved of the relationship between various sociological factors and death rates. Moreover, with the increasing availability of data and the increasing interest of demographers in morbidity, important new areas of research are opening in the relating of sociological to general health phenomena. The increasing interest in medical sociology may, among other things, contribute to a better understanding of both population and social phenomena.[8]

A better understanding of population composition and changes may also be expected from population studies relating compositional data to various types of sociological data. Certainly, characteristics such as marital status, education, labor-force status—including occupation—require much more exploration than they have yet received in relation to various types of sociological variables.[9]

In general, the demographer interested in an understanding of population phenomena beyond that which can be achieved through demographic analysis has much to gain from the pursuit of research concerned with the interrelations of demographic with sociological sets of variables. For there can be little doubt that the three major frameworks and methods of approach which sociology has to offer—namely, the culturological, the social-psychological, and the ecological—can be expected materially to contribute to a better understanding of various aspects of demographic behavior.

GAINS TO SOCIOLOGY

Of greater concern to the sociologist, not demographer, is the consideration of the gains which may be expected in sociology from increased research relating demographic to sociological variables. The interest of the non-demographer–sociologist in population phenomena is likely to be an interest in such phenomena as independent variables.

To begin with, demography has a special place in sociology, arising from its relations with human ecology as a subfield of sociological interest. The ecological and demographic approaches in sociology, although closely interrelated, have often been separate areas of activity, both in instructional and in research activities. In a fundamental sense, however, a case can be made, and Duncan is among those who have done so effectively,[10] for considering population as a subarea of human ecology, whether conceived of broadly and comprehensively or as a subarea of sociology. For human ecology as delineated by Duncan, population is one of the four key elements in the "ecological complex," the others being environment, technology, and organization.

The relation between ecology and demography and other interests in sociology emerged early in the history of sociology and occupied a central place in its development. It was formally and explicitly stated by Durkheim in his concern with "social morphology," and it was further explicitly treated by Halbwachs.[11]

Study of the social order necessarily involves concern with population as an organization rather than as an aggregate. Indeed, one of the major conceptualizations which has emerged in sociology hinges around demographic-ecological considerations. Durkheim's differentiation of "mechanical" and "organic" solidarity is explicitly tied to such considerations. Tönnies' distinction between *Gemeinschaft* and *Gesellschaft* and Redfield's and Wirth's treatment of the "folk" and "urban" societies are founded largely on population and ecological differences, although this has not always been made clear.

Wirth, in his synthesis of this literature, related the basic characteristics of "urbanism as a way of life" to population size, density, and heterogeneity of population.[12] Further exploration of the relation between differences in social organization and population factors is indicated and may add to both demographic and sociological knowledge: differences in urbanism as a way of life in Asian and Western cities offer one such area of research.

Moore stresses functional theory in sociology as most relevant to demography and envisages population as an "endogenous variable" in the analysis of the social system.[13] Population phenomena, like other human relations, may be considered from the standpoint of its "structural suitability" to specific societies, or in general terms. Population may also be considered in relation to various social functions such as rites of passage or the maintenance of a system of stratification. Moore takes the position that the functional approach in sociology "explicitly brings demographic variables into the scheme of sociological theory." He also leaves room, however, for the relating of demographic to sociological phenomena by means of other approaches in sociology including "the 'relativistic' position that emphasizes 'cultural' differences and attempts to establish detailed connections between structural elements in particular social systems and the demographic characteristics of such systems." Moore sees much to be gained from the interrelating of demographic to sociological variables in increasing understanding of both.

Sociology also has much to gain from demography in a methodological way. Demography, compared with other branches of sociology, has harder, that is, quantitative, data with which to work and more rigorous methods, including special demographic techniques, in addition to general statistical methods for the analysis of data. Demographers, although they make up a relatively small proportion of all sociologists, comprise a much larger proportion of sociologists trained in quantitative research. Sociology stands to gain from closer relations with demographic research not only in the acceptance and adapting of demographic research methods to other sociological uses, but also in the utilization of demographic variables as benchmarks against which to achieve better metrics of sociological phenomena. In using demographic data as independent variables, the sociologist has at least one set of variables with, generally, relatively high validity, reliability, and precision. Working with demographic phenomena thus enables the sociologist to avoid the frustration he all too frequently encounters when neither his independent nor his dependent variables are sufficiently well measured to permit the observation of possible relationships. In having population data as independent variables, he is in a position to experiment to obtain metrics for his dependent variables with some basis for evaluating his success.

NOTES

1. Prepared for annual meeting of American Sociological Society, Seattle, 1958.

2. Philip M. Hauser and Otis Dudley Duncan (eds.), *The Study of Population: An Inventory and Appraisal* (Chicago: University of Chicago Press, 1959).

3. Explicitly treated were: "Ecology and Demography," chap. xxvii, by Peter W. Frank; "Human Ecology and Population Studies," chap. xxviii, O. D. Duncan; "Geography and Demography," chap. xxix, Edward A. Ackerman; "Physical Anthropology and Demography," chap. xxx, J. N. Spuhler; "Genetics and Demography," chap. xxxi, Franz J. Kallman and John D. Rainer; "Economics and Demography," chap. xxxii, Joseph J. Spengler; and "Sociology and Demography," chap. xxxiii, Wilbert E. Moore.

4. Hauser and Duncan, *op. cit.*, chap. i.

5. See also George A. Hillery, Jr., "Toward a Conceptualization of Demography," *Social Forces*, XXXVII, No. 1 (October, 1958), 45–51.

6. E.g., the Study of Fertility under way by the Office of Population Research, Princeton University, and the Study of Growth of American Familes, soon to ap-

pear, by Ronald Freedman, P. K. Whelpton, and Arthur Campbell. See also N. B. Ryder, "Fertility," chap. xviii in Hauser and Duncan, *op. cit.*

7. Donald J. Bogue, "Internal Migration," chap. xxi, and Brinley Thomas, "International Migration," chap. xxii, *ibid.*

8. Harold F. Dorn, "Mortality," chap. xix, *ibid.* See also Jacob J. Feldman, "Barrier to the Use of Health Survey Data and Demographic Analysis," *Milbank Memorial Fund Quarterly*, XXXVI, No. 3 (July, 1958), 203–21.

9. Amos H. Hawley, "Population Composition," chap. xvi, *ibid.*

10. O. D. Duncan, "Human Ecology and Population Studies," chap. xxviii, *ibid.*

11. Maurice Halbwachs, *Morphologie sociale* (Paris: Librairie Armand Colin, 1946); Émile Durkheim, "Morphologie sociale," *L'Année sociologique*, II (1897–98), 520–21.

12. Louis Wirth, "Urbanism as a Way of Life," in *Community Life and Social Policy* (Chicago: University of Chicago Press, 1956).

13. Wilbert E. Moore, "Sociology and Demography," chap. xxxiii, in Hauser and Duncan, *op. cit.*

2

Developments in
the Study of Population[1]

Kurt Mayer

In recent years there has been widespread concern with population questions. Stagnation and impending population decline, the popular clichés of
the thirties, have been replaced by population explosion and urban sprawl
as slogans of the fifties and sixties. Unfortunately, the bewildered layman
finds little relief by turning to the demographers, because the professional
students of population problems have been notoriously unsuccessful not
only in predicting future population growth, but even in explaining past
population changes. These shortcomings of a discipline that ostensibly
deals with hard, quantifiable data may seem surprising at first glance, but
an examination of the development of population studies may reveal some
of the reasons for their predicaments and permit some assessment of their
future progress. For this purpose it is useful first to distinguish between two
aspects of population studies, demography and population theory, which,
though equally indispensable, have often traveled along different roads.[2]

Demography is concerned with three main tasks: ascertaining the
numbers, the characteristics, and the distribution of people in a given
area; determining changes in numbers, characteristics, and distribution
over time; and explaining the major factors accounting for these changes.
The explanation of population changes relies on three basic variables—
fertility, mortality, and migration (the latter will not be discussed in this
article)—for any factors affecting the numbers and distribution of people
must operate through one or more of these variables; a population cannot
change in any other way. The statistical measurement of fertility, mortality,
and migration forms the core of formal demographic analysis. Formal
demography stands out among the social sciences in its strong emphasis

Reprinted from *Social Research*, 29, no. 3 (Autumn, 1962), pp. 293–320, by permission of the author and the publisher. Footnotes have been renumbered.

on quantification and its persistent use of precise mathematical models and various statistical techniques.

However, the study of population is not confined to measuring, counting, collecting, and analyzing statistical data. For it is evident that fertility, mortality, and migration are not independent variables; they are to a large extent socially and biologically determined. The numbers of births, deaths, and migrants are affected by a whole host of physical, biological, social, and psychological factors. In turn, population changes have far-reaching effects on the social organization and the economic system of the societies in which they occur. Any meaningful interpretation of the causes and effects of population changes must therefore extend beyond formal statistical measurement of the components of change, and draw on the theoretical framework of several other disciplines for assistance. This analysis of the causal determinants and consequences of population changes forms the subject matter of population theory. Demography thus deals with the inner or formal variables in the population system, while population theory is concerned with the outer or ultimate variables, which are biological, economic, and sociological.

Despite their logical interdependence, formal demography and population theory have not developed at an even pace historically. The progress of demographic measurement has depended partly on the evolution of mathematical statistics, and to a large extent on the supply of basic demographic statistics, which are collected at great public expense, often primarily for administrative rather than for scientific purposes. The development of population theory, on the other hand, has been conditioned not only by the availability of demographic data, but also by the growth of other sciences, some of which are of fairly recent origin, like sociology and psychology. Moreover, determining which of the sciences could provide the most suitable frame of reference for the causal analysis of demographic events posed a thorny question, which has found varying answers in the course of time. As a result of their uneven rates of progress, the relations between demography and population theory have often been tenuous. At times the formal analysis of demographic variables developed along strictly empirical lines, with little reference to causal interpretations. The development of population theory, however, was influenced by shifting interests and by preoccupations with the changing economic, social, and political problems of the day. Its progress has been marked by constant controversy, often taking a purely speculative and deductive turn, with only slight and casual references to empirical demographic phenomena. The study of population phenomena has thus been retarded by the disjointed way in which population theory and demography have often developed. Fortunately, there is some evidence of the emergence at long last of a modern population science in which formal demographic analysis and causal interpretation appear better integrated and more closely interrelated. However, we cannot properly understand recent developments in this complex field—the main concern of this paper—without a brief survey of historical origins.

EARLY DEVELOPMENTS

The origins of formal demography antedate the development of a systematic population theory by a full century. The latter did not develop until late in the eighteenth century, when lively controversies about national population trends broke out both in England and in France. The first empirical investigations of demographic data, on the other hand, date back to the seventeenth-century mercantilist and cameralist writers, who called their studies "political arithmetic." In 1662 John Graunt published his *Natural and Political Observations . . . Made upon the Bills of Mortality.* These "bills of mortality" were weekly reports of buryings and christenings occurring in the London area. Analyzing these materials, Graunt observed the numerical regularity of deaths and births; calculated mortality rates, fertility ratios, sex ratios; classified deaths and death rates by cause; and constructed a London life-table in skeleton form. His work greatly influenced Sir William Petty, who published similar *Observations* on the Dublin mortality bills in 1676 and 1683; the astronomer Halley, who in 1693 calculated a much more detailed life-table; and Johann Peter Suessmilch, who in 1742 wrote the first complete treatise on population, *Die Göttliche Ordnung in den Veränderungen des menschlichen Geschlechts aus der Geburt, dem Tode und der Fortpflanzung desselben erwiesen [The Divine Order in the Changes of the Human Race Shown by Its Birth, Death and Reproduction].* Yet, as the title of Suessmilch's volume so clearly indicates, while the demographic measurements of these writers were scientific, their causal interpretations were not. They interpreted the uniformity and the predictability of demographic phenomena as manifestations of the divine ordering of human events. This naïve theological approach inhibited the further development of the new discipline. The discovery of previously unknown quantitative relations in the processes of life and death was considered an end in itself; since they represented the will of God, it was superfluous to search for causal interpretations.

Lacking an adequate theory, political arithmetic could not burgeon into a full-fledged science. Its methods of empirical inquiry were further developed only along one fairly narrow line: the analysis of mortality and the formulation of life expectancies, both propelled by the demand of insurance companies for more accurate actuarial values and by the increasingly scientific approach of public-health authorities in the control of diseases.

Systematic causal interpretations of population change began to develop when the Enlightenment replaced Christian metaphysics, and when theological explanations of demographic phenomena no longer appeared satisfactory in an age of rationality. Instead, population processes were now interpreted as determined by natural laws that rest on biological factors. Population dynamics were explained as the result of fixed universal relationships between man's biological nature and the physical environment. Although he was not the first proponent of this doctrine, Malthus, in his *Essay on the Principle of Population*, first published in 1798, became the most famous and the most influential expositor of the biological thesis. Postulating that man's powers of procreation are always and everywhere greater than nature's ability to produce food, Malthus asserted that man can increase means of subsistence only in arithmetic progression, whereas population tends to grow in a geometric ratio. Therefore population always tends to outgrow the limit of subsistence, but is contained within the limit by the operation of positive checks like famine, war, and disease, which raise the death rate, and by preventive checks operating through deferment of marriage and abstinence within marriage, which lower the birth rate.

Malthus' *Essay* aroused a storm of controversy that dominated the literature throughout the nineteenth century and has not yet completely diminished. Actually many, though by no means all, of Malthus' opponents shared the biological point of view. Although they violently attacked his pessimistic conclusions, they substituted other biological explanations, claiming that advancing civilization leads to a reduction of natural fecundity. The argument varied, but the different writers—like Spencer, Doubleday, and Sadler—shared the underlying causal assumption that population changes are determined by the relation of the human species to its physical environment.

Although the biological approach predominated in nineteenth-century population writings, the Malthusian debate also brought forth other theories, which drew on sociological and economic frames of reference rather than biological ones. One of the first to categorically reject the existence of any universal laws of population was Marx, who stated that every historic mode of production has its own laws of population, historically valid only within that period. Marx and his followers acknowledged the existence of population pressure on resources, but attributed its causes to the characteristics of the capitalistic mode of production, not to man's biological proclivities.

It is remarkable that the Malthusian controversy, which produced an abundance of theoretical writings, had comparatively little direct influence on the development of formal demography. The bulk of the many books, pamphlets, and articles on "the population question" which were published during the middle decades of the nineteenth century contained only slight and casual references to any empirical demographic data. Only a few of the scholars who engaged in the theoretical discussions undertook any serious empirical studies.

This does not mean, of course, that formal demography made no headway at all during this period. Indeed, a large measure of progress was made during the nineteenth century in developing population censuses and vital statistics. But the development of these basic sources of demographic data was stimulated only very indirectly by the debate on the population question. It was caused primarily by the administrative requirements of national governments that needed increasingly detailed information for the fulfillment of their rapidly expanding functions. The first reliable, periodic census count continuing into present days was instituted in Sweden in 1749, in the United States in 1790, and in both England and France in 1801. Thereafter the practice of taking regular national census counts was adopted by a steadily increasing number of nations. At the same time, the scope of the enumerations expanded and their accuracy increased. But even today there are large underdeveloped areas where reliable counts have never been made and where we must still rely on very rough estimates.

Systematic records of births, deaths, and marriages date back to the fifteenth and sixteenth centuries, when clergymen in most European countries were required to keep registers of all weddings, baptisms, and burials at which they officiated. In England and Ireland the ecclesiastical records were supplemented by the independently collected and published "bills of mortality." As pointed out before, these bills provided the basic sources for the "political arithmetic" of the seventeenth and early eighteenth centuries. The church registers laid the foundation for the subsequent development of national civil registration systems, although this transformation took considerable time. It was achieved first in Sweden, where a continuous series of national vital statistics has been available since 1748. In England and Wales a national system of civil registration was established in 1837; other European countries followed suit somewhat later in the nineteenth century. In general, the development of vital statistics had advanced in step with the development of census enumerations, with the notable exception of the United States, where more than a century elapsed between the inauguration of a periodic census program and the establishment of a nationwide vital-statistics system.

DEVELOPMENTS SINCE 1870

Beginning with the 1870s, a combination of factual events and scientific developments opened up a new era of progress for both population theory and formal demography. First, a rapid expansion of economic production in manufacturing and extractive industries greatly improved conditions in Western countries. In the West, therefore, Malthus' positive checks lost their significance and the previous preoccupation of theorists with the relation of population to the means of support no longer seemed relevant. Second, in some of the economically most advanced countries the birth rate began to decline in the 1870s; in other countries a precipitate drop began around the turn of the century. This was brought about through the spreading use of birth control after marriage, a factor that neither Malthus nor Marx had taken into consideration. Third, the great improvement and extension of census and registration statistics had made available a vast body of appropriate and relatively accurate data, which now permitted new refinements in the methods of analyzing demographic statistics.

Social and Cultural Theories of Declining Fertility

The events and discoveries that rendered the Malthusian fears obsolete, at any rate for the West, led many contemporary students of population to concentrate their attention on the decline of the birth rate. The causes of this decline became the subject of considerable conjecture and controversy, while its effects were viewed with a good deal of alarm. Interest centered particularly on the phenomenon of differential fertility. Differences in the fertility of social classes had long existed in the Western world, but these differences had been relatively small and quite stable. The general decline in the birth rate, however, greatly increased the existing group differentials. While all occupational and economic groups were eventually affected by the general fertility decline, it was evident that the groups of the highest socio-economic status were the leaders. Numerous statistical investigations undertaken from the 1890s onward came to essentially similar conclusions, an almost universal inverse relationship between social status and fertility: the more fortunate and favorable the social and economic circumstances of a group or class, the lower was its fertility.

Most of the various theories that attempted to provide a causal explanation of the general decline of the birth rate and the widening fertility differentials advanced some sort of sociological interpretation, although their proponents were often economists by profession rather than sociologists or demographers. Among the most prominent explanations for a time was the theory of increasing prosperity, which attracted much attention, first in France, the classical country of declining fertility, and later on also in Germany. In the late nineteenth century French scholars like Leroy-Beaulieu, Bertillon, Levasseur, and others advanced the thesis that the desire for a high standard of living or wealth motivates couples to limit the number of their offspring: the greater the family's prosperity, the smaller its size. A more sophisticated attempt to explain fertility differentials also originated in France. In 1890 Dumont pointed out that there is no direct causal relationship between declining fertility and increasing prosperity; instead, both must be viewed as products of an underlying common cause, the striving of individuals to move up in the prestige hierarchy of their society. Dumont compared the individual's drive for social recognition to the capillarity of fluids: wherever there is a social hierarchy, the individual aspires to move up. Social capillarity is most effective in the open-class societies, where obstacles to movement from class to class are comparatively few. Here the acquisition of wealth tends to be the most important avenue of social mobility. At the same time children are encumbrances that retard or prevent the individual's struggle for advance. Therefore, Dumont concludes, prosperity varies directly, whereas fertility varies inversely, with social capillarity.

Along with social mobility and increasing wealth, urbanization has often been considered a major factor influencing the attitude of individuals toward parenthood. The decline in fertility was preceded and accompanied in all Western countries by a massive shift of the population from the country to the cities. Leroy-Beaulieu, Dumont, and many others suggested, therefore, that the rapid increase in the proportion of the population living in the cities is causally connected with the decline in fertility. It had long been known that urban populations are generally less fertile than rural populations. Urban-rural fertility differentials existed in many countries long before the onset of the decline in the birth rate. But as in the case of class differentials, the general decline of the birth rate increased the existing fertility differences between town and country, because fertility declined more rapidly at first in the urban areas. This evidence was cited by many observers who analyzed various aspects of urban life which they believed to be particularly favorable to family limitation. First, the upbringing of children is more expensive in the city. Second, family life is less cohesive and plays a smaller role in the city. The urban adult tends to be involved in a broad range of outside interests and activities that draw him away from home; a large family would interfere with these varied urban pursuits. Third, as Dumont pointed out in his discussion of social capillarity, opportunities to gratify status aspirations are more plentiful in the cities, but those who wish to take advantage of them find children a liability in their upward struggles.

As time went on, it became increasingly evident that the decline in fertility was not confined to the upper classes and the urban population. By the second and third decades of the twentieth century, family limitation had spread widely among the working classes and the farm population in many Western countries. It appeared obvious, therefore, that theories that had sought to attribute the decline exclusively or primarily to such factors as urban residence, increasing wealth, or competition from social advancement could not adequately explain a phenomenon that was affecting very different population groups. A workable theory needed to explain not only the low fertility of the upper classes, but also the recent fertility decline among the proletariat and the farmers. Hence some authors developed theories attributing the cause of the overall fertility decrease to the spread of a rationalistic mentality, a specific product of capitalism, inherent in the spirit of striving which started with the urban bourgeoisie but eventually permeated all classes of society: the proletariat now imitates the behavior of the upper classes, adopting their rationalistic attitude toward life and a correspondingly rationalistic reproductive-behavior pattern. Others, however, have warned against exaggerating the connection between capitalism and the motives in the minds of modern couples which guide their reproductive behavior, and some writers have rejected altogether the invocation of any unquantifiable "spirit" to explain historical changes in fertility patterns.

Despite considerable differences in emphasis, the various theories reviewed above generally agree that the explanation of the fertility decline must be sought in an interplay of various social and economic factors and their effects on the attitudes of individual couples. As to the causal connection between social factors and individual attitudes, most theories could offer no more than plausible inferences. There was no lack of empirical investigations that discovered and confirmed statistical relationships between fertility and socio-economic factors. Usually, however, the data of these studies were primary population statistics of the census type. That is, the data had been collected for other purposes, and the theories advanced to explain the statistical relationships discovered were developed ex post facto.

In the early 1930s a series of studies was undertaken in which data were specially collected to investigate the role of contraception in bringing about class differences in fertility. These studies furnished strong evidence that class fertility differentials can be accounted for almost entirely by differences in the prevalence and effectiveness of contraceptive practices; but they did not inquire into the causes underlying these differences. Obviously, contraception is the immediate means of family limitation; the causes are the factors that encourage or discourage its practice. In 1938, however, a committee of demographers, sociologists, and psychologists was organized in the United States for the specific purpose of undertaking a field study of the social and psychological factors underlying reproductive behavior. This research, popularly known as the Indianapolis Study, was the first major empirical investigation designed to test causal hypotheses, by inquiring directly into the motivations and attitudes of married couples regarding the planning and having of children, and the factors responsible for differences in fertility. For various reasons the committee decided to restrict the study to native-born white, urban, Protestant couples, married from twelve to fifteen years, living in the city of Indianapolis.

The Indianapolis Study clearly confirmed both the importance of contraception in the general reduction of fertility and the key role of socio-economic status in the effectiveness of contraceptive practices. Some form of contraception was practiced by virtually every couple in the sample; nevertheless, slightly over half of all the pregnancies occurred while birth control was being practiced. As expected, the effectiveness of contraceptive practices varied inversely with socio-economic status: the higher the income, occupational status, education, and the like, the greater was the proportion of couples practicing contraception effectively. Of special significance, however, was the finding that among those couples who had exercised complete and effective fertility control and therefore had no unplanned pregnancies, there obtained a *direct* relationship between fertility and socio-economic status: the higher the income, occupation, and education, the larger the size of the planned families.

Although the Indianapolis Study was a pioneer attempt to go beyond the collection of primary population statistics in order to investigate some of the complex causal factors underlying reproductive behavior, its success was limited. Because of a variety of weaknesses in conceptualization, limitations in the sample, and deficiencies in the data, most of the hypotheses that attempted to unravel the social and psychological variables underlying fertility differences were neither adequately confirmed nor decisively refuted. The Indianapolis Study thus adds comparatively little to the various theories that have attempted to explain the general decline in fertility. The same is true of another major study of family limitation undertaken in Great Britain in 1946, on behalf of the Royal Commission on Population. This investigation was based on interviews with 10,297 female patients in general hospitals, widely distributed throughout the country. The findings clearly demonstrate the continuously increasing usage of birth control in Britain since the early years of this century. They also show the familiar inverse relationship of birth-control practice and social class, but give some indication that these differences are narrowing as knowledge and practice of contraception are increasing in all social classes. Although particularly valuable for international comparative purposes, the research was sheerly empirical and adds nothing new to the existing theories of declining fertility.

Most of these theories suffer from the same major limitation: they are all ad hoc theories, dealing only with one specific historical phenomenon, the decline of the birth rate and of family size in the Western world during the nineteenth and twentieth centuries. Limited in time and space, these theories do not meet the exacting qualifications of a comprehensive theory of population change, which must provide causal explanations also of the population dynamics of other societies and of different historical epochs. But though only small progress has been made to date toward the elaboration of a truly comprehensive sociological theory of population change, there has been no dearth of attempts to find universally valid laws of population growth outside the sociological frame of reference. While sociologically oriented theorists have focused their attention mainly on the phenomenon of overall decreasing fertility and fertility differentials, biologists and economic theorists have developed some ambitious theories of considerably wider scope. At the same time considerable progress has been made in the development and further refinement of formal demographic models.

Biological Theories of Population Change

The search for biological laws of population growth, which had dominated the early Malthusian controversy, had a vigorous though fairly brief revival during the present century. In the 1920s the biometrician Raymond Pearl stirred up considerable excitement by reasserting the hypothesis of biological determinism and advancing a mathematical formula of population growth. Like other biological theorists, Pearl contended that the law of human population growth is fundamentally the same as that which regulates the growth of plants and animals: all living organisms increase in size in cyclical fashion, growing rapidly at first, slowly thereafter, until the organism finally dies. Arguing by analogy, Pearl assumed that the growth of collectivities like entire populations resembles that of individual organisms. Population growth, too, occurs in cycles consistent with the observed rhythm of growth characteristic of all living matter. Since populations always grow in a finite area, they must have an upper limit, but in the case of human populations several successive growth cycles can occur in the same area, which reflect changes in the economic organization of society. Thus the transition from an agricultural to an industrial society, for example, creates the possibility of additional population growth in a new cycle. In the early stages of each growth cycle, population increases at an accelerating rate, until the midpoint is reached; thereafter the growth rate decreases. Represented graphically, population growth cycles form an elongated S-shaped curve, which in mathematical terminology is known as the logistic curve, discovered in 1838 by Verhulst.

Comparison of the calculated values of the curve with the actual census data of several countries resulted in a remarkably good fit. Pearl therefore assumed that future population growth could be predicted with some confidence. He was not satisfied, however, with the purely empirical nature of the logistic formula, and attempted to explain the causal mechanism underlying it: the reason why population increases logistically in a spatially limited area is that fertility correlates inversely with population density, that is, as density increases, fertility declines. Pearl proclaimed this to be a biological principle that universally regulates the growth of all living matter throughout nature, adducing experimental evidence from the behavior of yeast cells and fruit flies in a bottle. However, this altogether too simple analogy was clearly refuted by Pearl's own later empirical investigations of contraceptive practices, which he had undertaken with the expectation of proving that variations in social conditions other than density have only a negligible influence on human fertility. As a result, the excitement about the logistic formula has subsided; it is now generally recognized that with respect to human populations the logistic curve is a purely empirical formula, which sometimes accurately describes the past course of population growth of a given area but does not necessarily predict its future development.

The evidence provided by Pearl's study, as well as by other investigations of the prevalence and nature of contraceptive practices, also contradicts the theories of those contemporary writers who have argued on various grounds that increasing prosperity tends to decrease the reproductive capacity of human beings. First advanced during the Malthusian controversy, such ideas were revived by some twentieth-century authors, especially Gini, who attributed the fertility decline and the widening of group fertility differentials to decreases in reproductive capacity, allegedly induced by the strains and stresses of social mobility, which lead to the physical exhaustion of the upper classes. However, the accumulating evidence about the extent of contraception has documented rather decisively the lack of class differences in physiological capacity to reproduce. The Indianapolis Study, for example, found approximately the same proportion of sterile couples in each socio-economic status group, and among the fecund couples the fertility rates during periods of noncontraceptive exposure were strikingly similar, regardless of social class. In view of such evidence, Gini partly shifted his ground. Accepting the fact that the major part of the fertility decline is the result of contraception, he held that the spread of contraceptive practices is itself the result of biological decadence, an assertion that neither he nor anyone else has ever been able to prove.

The Concept of the Optimum Population

In contrast to the exponents of the biological approach, many of the professional economists who have contributed to population theory have been less concerned with finding and expounding the *causes* of population change than with assessing its *results*. They have been interested in the economic and social effects of population growth or decline on natural resources, labor supply, levels of consumption and production, and so forth, rather than in the mode or rate at which population changes. In attempting to analyze the complex and intricate interrelationships between population and the economy, certain economists have raised the intriguing question: "What size of population is economically most advantageous in given circumstances?"

The theory of an optimum population size is the outgrowth of the synthesis of two different bodies of generally accepted economic theory. On the one hand there is the notion that a growing population results in an enlarged market and a greater division of labor, and consequently brings about an increase in productivity per capita. On the other hand there is the doctrine of diminishing returns, which holds that if other factors are held constant, productivity per capita will diminish if the number of people working given resources increases beyond a certain point. From a combination of these two doctrines, it logically follows that there must be a point at which the two opposing tendencies are in equilibrium: an optimum point at which a given (optimum) size of population results in maximum productivity per capita. Two further concepts follow from this premise: if the size of the population exceeds the (optimum) point that provides the highest possible level of per capita output, the area is overpopulated; and conversely, if population size is below the optimum, the area is underpopulated.

It has also been pointed out that the optimum point is never static but continually shifts, because the quantity and quality of resources and technology are constantly changing. It is clear, therefore, that empirical measurement of the optimum population presents enormous difficulties, and it is not surprising that to date no satisfactory statistical indicators of overpopulation or underpopulation have been devised, in spite of frequent attempts to do so. The theory of the optimum population is an ideal-typical construct that enables us to understand hypothetically the influence of population size on economic productivity. At the present state of knowledge, however, the optimum concept cannot be translated into empirical terms of any precision, and therefore it does not lend itself as an instrument of practical population policy, despite the tempting policy implications inherent in its very terminology.

Formal Demography

During the last thirty years considerable progress has been made in the development of a different body of abstract and logically interrelated principles which appears to be more fruitful as a guide in the examination and interpretation of empirical population data. The theory concerns the universal relationships that always obtain between the basic components of population change—fertility, mortality, and migration. It has variously been called analytical theory, pure demography, or formal demography. The fact that a population consists of organisms that are subject to the inescapable biological processes of birth, maturation, and death makes it possible to view any human population as a sex and age structure that is determined by the vital processes and migration. Leaving migration out of account, the age and sex structure of a "closed" population at any given time is the result of the operation of specific mortality and fertility frequencies in the past. In turn, this structure influences and sets limits for future variations in fertility and mortality. It is therefore possible to establish deductively a series of mathematical theorems, much like geometrical axioms, which define the relationships between sex and age composition and the vital rates.

Pure demographic theory involves as a central core the concept of the "stable population," a hypothetical model of a particular age and sex structure that would ultimately develop in any population subject to age-specific fertility and mortality rates continuing unvaried for an extended period of time, if there were meanwhile no migration or other disturbing influences. The population that would eventually result from the long-time operation of constant vital rates is called "stable" because the proportion of the population in each age group will not vary in time, even though the size of the population as a whole might increase or decrease. In a stable population, the birth rate, death rate, and rate of natural increase remain constant and can be computed mathematically.

Although the basic principle of a stable population dates back to the development of Halley's life-table in 1693, the theory was not fully developed until 1925, when Lotka and Dublin introduced the idea of the reproduction of generations into the analysis of the stable population. They proved that the stable age distribution and the net reproduction rate are both the result of the same conditions, that is, of a long-time regime of constant age-specific fertility and mortality rates. A net reproduction rate is a measure of the number of daughters that one cohort of newborn girls would bear *if* the age-specific fertility rates and mortality rates of the current life-table were to continue unchanged to the end of their childbearing period. A net reproduction rate is thus an estimate of the extent to which a cohort of women of an actual population will replace itself, *provided* current fertility and mortality conditions continue unchanged. Therefore the net reproduction rate represents not only a replacement index of an actual population, but also the ultimate rate of increase of the stable population. If now this rate of increase is expressed per annum instead of per generation, it corresponds to the intrinsic or "true" rate of natural increase of an actual population. The corresponding intrinsic or "true" birth and death rates of the actual population (which are also at the same time the crude death and birth rates of the stable population) can be calculated easily. Since in all three of the intrinsic rates the effect of age is controlled, these rates can be used for comparing the reproductive activities of actual populations regardless of differences in their age and sex composition. Intrinsic rates, like the net reproduction rate, measure correctly the current reproductive activity of an actual population, but since current conditions rarely remain unchanged, they have no predictive power and should not be used to forecast future population change, as has frequently been done with disastrous results.

The stable-population model, the net reproduction index, and the intrinsic vital rates are used in demographic research to discover relationships underlying actual vital processes but not visible in the observed crude rates of birth, death, and natural increase—just as geometrical models are used in engineering to measure concrete relations. Major interest attached to the indexes of reproductivity, especially during the 1920s and 1930s. It appeared at that time that the decline in the birth rate had temporarily inflated the proportion of persons in the childbearing ages. Consequently the crude rate of natural increase seemed to be spuriously high in Western nations, presenting a picture of continued population growth. At the same time, however, calculations of the intrinsic rates showed the "true" death rate exceeding the "true" birth rate, and the net reproduction rate well below unity in many countries, thus indicating that the current cohorts of women were not then giving birth to enough daughters to replace their numbers. Demographers therefore concluded that the observed vital rates were actually concealing a trend toward incipient decline, and did not hesitate to forecast the end of population growth and even population decline in the foreseeable future.

However, the unanticipated postwar upsurge of the birth rate brought massive population growth to most of the countries that had been labeled as those of "incipient decline," especially the United States and Canada. This made it painfully clear that net reproduction and intrinsic rates cannot serve as predictive instruments, because fertility and mortality are assumed constant in their computation. A further difficulty lies in the fact that the net reproduction rate is computed by the summation of age-specific fertility rates of all women in the childbearing ages during a *single year*. The net reproduction rate thus gives a cross-sectional view of the reproductive activity of a hypothetical generation, an artificial cohort. It cannot, therefore, measure the basic changes in the fertility behavior of real cohorts over time. This limitation very clearly indicates the need for longitudinal analysis of reproduction in terms of real cohorts of women; for example, all women in the population born in the same year or married in the same year. The reproductive behavior of any given cohort is determined not only by conditions of the moment, but also by past circumstances and by anticipation of future conditions. The fertility history of every real cohort is thus shaped by many factors, which do not necessarily operate the same way on different cohorts. It is imperative, therefore, to study fertility behavior over time if one wants to detect genuine trends.

Intensive efforts to study fertility and reproduction from the real cohort or longitudinal point of view were first begun in the 1940s, and this type of work continues prominently in the forefront of formal demographic endeavors at the present time. The substantive findings of these studies indicate, first, that most of the sharp fluctuations of the crude birth rate in the 1930s and 1940s reflect changes in the timing of family-building behavior of different cohorts; depression, war, and postwar prosperity caused a great deal of postponing, making up, and moving ahead of births. The findings show, second, that over and above such changes in the timing of births, a definite change in the long-time downward trend of fertility is evident. For example, in the United States the total number of children per 1,000 women born to each cohort of native white women declined continuously from the 1875 to the 1909 cohort, the total drop amounting to one-third. However, the cohorts of women born in 1910 and later give definite indications of having reversed the trend. It is too early as yet to gauge the extent of the change in fertility trends with any precision, but it does appear that the long-term trend toward smaller family sizes has been halted in practically all countries of "incipient decline." In the countries of northwestern Europe, fertility seems to be stabilized for the time being at slightly above prewar levels, while in the United States and in the British Dominions a trend toward larger families is unmistakable.

Current Fertility Research

In the United States the unanticipated upturn in fertility, which clearly demonstrated the urgent need for improved measures of replacement and forecasting, has stimulated two major new field researchers of fertility behavior and the social and psychological factors that affect it. The first of these studies, undertaken jointly, in 1955, by the Scripps Foundation for Research in Population and the Survey Research Center of the University of Michigan, involved interviews with 2,713 married white women, aged 18–39 years, selected through a national area probability sample, including all religious groups.[3] The women were questioned about the following topics: socio-economic status, marital history, pregnancy history, physical impairment of fertility, birth-control practices and attitudes toward birth control, expectations about the number and birth dates of additional children and the reasons for these expectations, attitudes toward children, and beliefs about what constitutes the "ideal" family size.

The results indicate three main conclusions. First, family limitation is now almost universally approved in the United States, and is practiced widely and effectively by white couples. Second, women of all social classes are largely agreed on the number of children wanted and expected. The average number of expected children is approximately three and, with the exception of religion, the traditional fertility differentials appear sharply reduced if not eliminated. Catholics desire and expect more children than Protestants and Jews, but the difference lies within the range of two to four children generally accepted as the norm. Third, if the present family growth plans are continued and actually realized, the American population will continue to grow rapidly. Although fecundity impairments are widespread, they will not materially reduce the rate of population growth. Since all conclusions were based on expectations only, the study was repeated in 1960, albeit with a different sample, in order to ascertain how expectations reported in 1955 compared with actual performance during the ensuing five-year period. Preliminary indications are that although there were numerous differences between expectations and performance, these differences canceled out, so that the aggregated number of children born by 1960 approximated closely the number expected in 1955.[4]

The other project, a successor to the Indianapolis Study, was undertaken by the Office of Population Research of Princeton University, and is designed in longitudinal form. It is based on interviews and questionnaires obtained in 1957 from a sample of 1,165 native-born couples, selected at random in seven large metropolitan areas and including all religions. All of these couples had a second child in September 1956. The data gathered initially relate to the pregnancy and contraceptive histories, socioeconomic status and related attitudes, personality characteristics and marital adjustment, aspirations with respect to having a third child, and the total size of family desired. The couples were reinterviewed after about thirty months to ascertain how the actual fertility situation had developed. This study is therefore a prediction study of a metropolitan sample of couples with two children, which attempts to isolate factors associated with future childbearing, especially with respect to the timing of a third child. Inherent in the research design are provisions for testing the correctness of the prediction.

To date only the findings of the first round of interviews have been published.[5] They strongly corroborate the conclusions of the Michigan-

Scripps study. Only 11 per cent of the couples were not using contraception after a second birth. Family sizes of two, three, and four children were equally popular, and accounted for 90 per cent of the reported preferences. While class differentials were negligible, religion exerted a strong influence on fertility, with Catholics desiring larger families than Protestants, and Jews wanting the smallest number of children. Preliminary reports from the second phase of the survey show that the religious differences were clearly manifested in actual fertility behavior. Three-fifths of the Catholic, one-half of the Protestant, but barely more than one-fourth of the Jewish couples actually had additional pregnancies in the two-and-one-half-year interval between the first and second interviews.[6]

Perhaps the most interesting aspect of current American fertility research is the virtual disappearance of the traditional class differences in the number of children American couples desire and expect. Moreover, the remarkable convergence on an average of three children means that fertility will be high enough to maintain a rapid rate of population increase in the foreseeable future. This represents a definite change from the prewar situation. However, the basic causes that have brought about this change cannot possibly be ascertained by interviewing methods. Field research in fertility behavior has definite limitations. It may reveal the shifts in attitudes and motivations which directly result in fertility "fashion changes." Yet shifts in motivation and corresponding changes in fertility behavior are themselves but reflections and symbols of underlying long-term changes in social structure and economic systems of human societies. Such basic factors cannot be studied by means of attitude and opinion surveys; they require comprehensive analysis of social structure and cultural norms in historical depth.

Comprehensive Structural Population Theories

The lack of an adequate frame of reference that would permit us to understand the fundamental social changes behind major shifts in reproductive behavior, not only in Western but also in many other societies, has recently prompted renewed attempts to formulate comprehensive sociological theories of population change. One such theory, which has been developed during the last thirty years, especially by American and British demographers, is known in the literature as the theory of the demographic transition. Briefly described, this theory explains the rapid growth of the world's population during the last three hundred years as the result of a transition from high to low birth and death rates which societies undergo in the process of industrialization and modernization. This growth began with reductions in mortality in Europe, caused by increases in food supply brought about by agricultural innovations and improved transportation, followed later by spectacular sanitary and medical advances. Fertility, less responsive to the processes of modernization, declined less rapidly at first. The widening gap between the two rates provided the tremendous growth of the European population and caused its swarming overseas. Eventually, however, the new urban-industrial conditions of life provided strong incentives to couples to limit their fertility through birth control, until finally a new demographic balance of low mortality plus low fertility was achieved, resulting in approaching population stability and possible decline.

Different countries reach different stages of the demographic cycle at different times. It is therefore possible to divide the world's population into three categories, according to the stages reached in the transition cycle. First, there are the countries of "incipient population decline," which have nearly completed the transition. This category includes the populations of northwestern and central Europe, North America, Australia, and New Zealand. Second are the countries in the stage of "transitional growth," where mortality is declining sharply and fertility has begun to decline but is still lagging behind, with the result that these populations are now experiencing very rapid growth. The nations in this stage include Eastern Europe, the Soviet Union, Japan, and parts of Latin America. Finally, we have the countries of "high growth potential," which have not yet begun the transition or are only on the verge of it. Here births and deaths are still high and growth is slow, but it could become explosive if and when the characteristic gap between mortality and fertility decline develops. Most of Africa, Asia, the Middle East, and much of Latin America belong in this category.

Although widely acclaimed for a time, the validity of the transition theory has been severely questioned in recent years. Examination of the demographic experience of several Western countries shows considerable variations in their history of population growth which do not fit the postulated three stages. Thus in France and in North America the decline in the death rate began early, preceding modernization, while in England and the Netherlands fertility increases preceded the decline in mortality and accounted for the population growth in the eighteenth and through most of the nineteenth century. The accuracy of the theory as a description of past demographic history in the Western world is therefore in doubt. Moreover, major questions have been raised about its predictions of future population growth and the assumed sequences on which they are based. Analysis of recent population trends in underdeveloped countries leads to serious question whether the countries now assumed to be in the "transitional growth" stage will actually recapitulate either the demographic or the industrial experiences of the West. Furthermore, the strong postwar fertility upsurge in some of the countries in "incipient decline" casts doubt about the predictive aspects of the theory even if it is limited to the West. Some critics have therefore suggested that further stages should be added to the transition theory or that the United States and the British Dominions represent a special case where low mortality and moderately high fertility have resulted in a substantial rate of population increase.

Such modification and revisions reduce the status of the demographic transition concept to that of yet another ad hoc theory, limited in time and space, valid only for specific historical situations. Thus it would appear reasonable for population theorists and demographers to be finally willing to learn the lesson taught by two centuries of continued failures: there simply is no universal law of population change; therefore attempts to develop general theories designed to explain population changes occurring under widely differing social and cultural conditions by the same set of causal factors must necessarily be futile. This does not mean, however, that population theory must be confined to purely empirical generalizations or ad hoc hypotheses. On the contrary, there is urgent need for comprehensive sociological analyses of population dynamics, but such theories must clearly recognize the cultural relativity of demographic phenomena. Sociologically adequate theories must show how variations in the social structure and the cultural context produce differences in population structure. They will not imply a single or uniform factor as the cause for varying rates of population change. Instead, they will identify distinctive types of causal factors which operate differently in different social contexts.

Although an adequate conceptual framework for an acceptable structural population theory is still lacking, it is encouraging to note that real progress is now being made. Some preliminary steps in this direction have recently been taken in the United States by Lorimer and by Kingsley Davis, who have employed a structural-functional approach in analyzing specific aspects of social organization and cultural norms that are functionally related to fertility and mortality controls in different societies.[7] Their work illustrates what may be called a cross-cultural approach leading to a comparative sociology of population dynamics. It lacks, however, the historical depth that some recent European theories attempt to supply.

A sociologically and historically sophisticated theory has been advanced in Germany by Mackenroth, and his work has inspired a brief but excellent analysis by the Swiss economist and demographer Bickel.[8] Departing from the insight originally provided by Marx, that every historical epoch has its own laws of population, Mackenroth proceeds to trace the historical development of different European populations from mediaeval days to the present, relating in each instance the specific features of the changing social structure to the reproductive-behavior pattern typical of the particular historical context. Extending this analysis also to European settlements overseas and to non-Western societies, Mackenroth distinguishes typical demographic patterns, or population dynamics, as Bickel calls them, each of which is historically unique, depending on the reciprocal relationship between social structure, culture, and reproductive behavior.

As Mackenroth points out, however, the analysis of this relationship is complicated by two factors. Since every society is socially differentiated and stratified, its demographic pattern is not uniform; rather, every major social group has its own patterns of reproductive behavior, which must be identified separately. Moreover, since neither social structures nor population patterns are static, there is rarely a perfect synchronization between them. On the contrary, the reproductive behavior of a given group or of a society as a whole frequently overlaps different historical epochs, causing time lags and survivals to arise. For example, time lags tend to develop between changes in the social structure and the fertility behavior of different social groups whose population dynamics can often be understood only by reference to past rather than present conditions. At the same time the presence of group differences facilitates both statistical analysis and causal interpretation. Mackenroth interprets as lag phenomena not only class fertility differences but also the rapid population growth of Western nations during the nineteenth century. He attributes the latter to the overlapping of fertility mores and ethics typical of pre-industrial conditions into the epoch of urbanization and industrialization, where they were no longer appropriate. The subsequent decline in fertility can then be understood as an adaptation of reproductive behavior to changed social conditions.

Although neither Mackenroth nor Bickel offers an analysis of the postwar changes in fertility trends, this mode of analysis can be extended to include the most recent developments. For example, analyzing the American experience, this writer has recently argued that basic changes in the social structure cause large swings in reproductive-behavior patterns.[9] The decline of American fertility below the replacement level in the 1930s represents the extreme point in a long swing that occurred as a reaction to the fundamental transformation from an agricultural to an urban-industrial society. Once the structural transformation was completed, the pendulum swung back, and the current convergence of fertility differentials marks the adaptation of the reproductive behavior of different population groups to an increasingly homogeneous social structure. To be sure, such hypotheses require rigorous testing, but it would seem that only systematic historic-structural analyses can ultimately lead to adequate interpretations.

NOTES

1. This is a revised and abbreviated version of an article contributed to a German symposium, edited by René König, *Handbuch der empirischen Sozialforschung*, vol. 1 (Stuttgart 1962), pp. 453–79, under the title "Bevölkerungslehre und Demographie."

2. Two recent works present extensive accounts of the historical development of population theories and of the current status of demography: *The Determinants and Consequences of Population Trends*, published by the Population Division of the United Nations (New York 1953); and Philip M. Hauser and Otis Dudley Duncan, eds., *The Study of Population: An Inventory and Appraisal* (Chicago 1959). Instead of presenting a copious apparatus of footnotes, I refer the reader to the extensive bibliographies contained in these works. Only a few recent publications will be cited here.

3. Ronald Freedman, Pascal K. Whelpton, Arthur A. Campbell, *Family Planning, Sterility and Population Growth* (New York 1959).

4. P. K. Whelpton, Arthur Campbell, Richard Tomasson, "Preliminary Results from the 1960 Study of Growth of American Families," unpublished paper presented at the annual meeting of the Population Association of America, New York, May 5, 1961.

5. Charles F. Westoff, Robert G. Potter, Jr., Philip C. Sagi, and Elliot G. Mishler, *Family Growth in Metropolitan America* (Princeton 1961).

6. Charles F. Westoff, Robert G. Potter, Jr., and Philip C. Sagi, "Preliminary Results from the Study of Family Growth in Metropolitan America," unpublished paper presented at the annual meeting of the Population Association of America, New York, May 5, 1961.

7. Frank Lorimer *et al.*, *Culture and Human Fertility*, Unesco (Paris 1954); Kingsley Davis and Judith Blake, "Social Structure and Fertility: An Analytical Framework," in *Economic Development and Cultural Change*, vol. 4 (April 1956), pp. 211–35; see also Kingsley Davis, *Human Society* (New York 1949), Chapters 20–21.

8. Gerhard Mackenroth, *Bevölkerungslehre: Theorie, Soziologie und Statistik der Bevölkerung* (Berlin 1953); Wilhelm Bickel, "Bevölkerungsdynamik und Gesellschaftsstruktur," in *Schweizerische Zeitschrift für Volkswirtschaft und Statistik*, vol. 92 (September 1956), pp. 317–28. The interesting recent publication by Andreas Miller, *Kultur und menschliche Fruchtbarkeit* (Stuttgart 1962), which presents a sophisticated equilibrium theory of population developments, was received too late to be considered in this article.

9. Kurt Mayer, "Fertility Changes and Population Forecasts in the United States," in *Social Research*, vol. 26 (Autumn 1959), pp. 347–66.

3

The Development of
Modern Population Theory

Warren C. Robinson

I. INTRODUCTION

Recent discussions of the population "explosion" have focused public and scholarly attention on the question of population change to a greater degree than at any time since the high point of the Victorian controversies over birth control propaganda culminating in the Besant-Bradlaugh trials. Contemporary interest stems from the postwar upsurge in the birth rate in this country as well as the population problems of the emerging areas of Asia and Africa.

The best-known theory of population growth is that which was first expounded in 1798 by T. R. Malthus, and it still provides the starting place for most popular discussions of the subject of population change.[1] The Malthusian formula pictures a grim life cycle. The birth rate remains high, at the biological limit or close to it, and the death rate is the regulator of the size and rate of increase of the population, the rate rising as population becomes too numerous relative to resources, and falling as population is thinned out by disease and starvation and resources are freed from the press of excess people. Population changes consist, for the most part, of fluctuations around an upper limit.[2]

Malthus' neat, almost syllogistic formulation, coupled with the strong plausibility of his basic premises, has combined to make his theory extremely popular and persistent. Indeed, it seems a common belief that modern population experts, who call themselves demographers, are still merely engaged in refining and validating the work of the master.

Nothing could be farther from the truth. Malthus is, and has been

Reprinted from *American Journal of Economics and Sociology*, 23, no. 4 (October, 1964), pp. 375–92, by permission of the author and the publisher.

for a good, long time, in poor repute as a demographer among professional demographers. The whole focus of demographic research has shifted since his time, away from theory and toward empirical research. Kingsley Davis was speaking for the last several generations of demographers when he noted:

> It is difficult to avoid the conclusion that the major advances in the science of population have come from improvements in the sources of information and in the techniques of analysis, rather than from the broad interpretations. Ironically, the interpretive literature on population probably exceeds by many times (if not in pages, certainly in readers and attention) the amount of empirical publication. The discrepancy was already clear with Malthus. He did not fully understand the progress in systematic demography that had been made by this time, yet it was his work that captured most attention, and it is his work that is still debated today in general population theory. Despite the outpouring of books, pamphlets, and articles on population theory— *Bevoelkerungslehre*—it is hard to cite a single scientific advance since Malthus' day that this literature has contributed to the subject.[3]

Notestein puts it equally bluntly:

> . . . there is considerable warrant for the view that much of the progress made during the past two or three decades is due to the fact that demographers at long last managed to rid themselves of the preoccupation with the over-arching theories which dominated so much of the nineteenth century work in the field. It seems likely that for the foreseeable future any such intellectual construct will have more the character of an ideology than a means of submitting reason to the test of experience.[4]

In spite of this emphasis on empirical research, theoretical innovations have also occurred.[5] Modern, non-Malthusian theory is much more firmly rested in empirical and historical research than were the propositions of Malthus or his predecessors; in turn, hypothesis and low-level theory are necessary forerunners to empirical research.

This relative disinterest in theorizing has had an unfortunate result: the lineage and development of modern theories have remained obscure and undocumented. This essay makes at least a beginning toward supplying such a documentation.

II. THE BACKGROUNDS TO MODERN THEORIES

Throughout the nineteenth century Malthusianism dominated population theorizing. Fertility was high and virtually constant, while fluctuations in mortality occurred, thus leading alternately to periods of population growth and decline. Mortality rates were falling in Europe in the late nineteenth century, but this was seen as only a temporary phenomenon which would inevitably reverse itself when population grew so large as to press against resources again. It was against this intellectual background that the birth control movement in England was launched.

Around the turn of the century, however, population analysts discovered that birth rates in most Western European nations were declining. Fertility was not as constant as had been assumed and, indeed, for many nations could not even be described as high.[6]

Kuczynski observed:

> With a fertility and mortality as they prevailed in Western and Northern Europe forty or fifty years ago, the population would have doubled in three generations. With a fertility and a mortality as they have prevailed for some years, the population of Western and Northern Europe is bound to die out . . . The process . . . can be stopped by an essential change in mortality and fertility. But the future reduction of mortality in those ages which are the only decisive ones, that is, those under fifty years, cannot be very great after all that has already been accomplished. The future then depends mainly on the trend of fertility.[7]

These trends were simply not compatible with the Malthusian system. New theories capable of explaining the new facts were required, and several quite distinct new schools of thought took shape. Many of these had their roots in much earlier theories by contemporaries and even predecessors of Malthus. Most, however, continued the Malthusian methodological tradition of explaining population change in terms of a relatively small number of variables, related one to another in rigid, nearly mechanical fashion, operating as general if not universal principles. These theories were, in the meanings suggested by Warren Thompson, "natural" rather than "social" in content.

> The former [natural theories] are based on the belief that there is something inherent in the nature of man, or of the world in which he lives, that determines his growth at a rate and in a direction largely or wholly beyond his control . . . It is not surprising that wherever and whenever men have thought about population, many have been eager to find the natural law of its growth for this would give them a sure basis for reasoning on many related social problems. In the social theories of population growth, on the other hand, the underlying assumption is that population growth is not subject to any immutable natural law but is rather the resultant of the social conditions (social here is used to include economic) in which a people finds itself. To one who accepts this view it would appear to be folly to search for a simple natural law of population growth; what should receive attention is

rather the factors which determine its growth in a particular community at a particular time.[8]

As we shall see, the evolution of post-Malthusian population theory has been from the "natural" toward the "social." The rigidly deterministic relationships originally postulated in order to explain the declines in the birth rate have gradually taken on almost purely social and economic colorations.

III. NATURAL THEORIES

Cyclical Theory

One of the first and most important of the modern "natural" theories to receive clear formulation was the cyclical theory, propounded by Corrado Gini beginning in the early Nineteen Twenties and still associated with his name.

> . . . the cyclical theory, which goes by our name, is often opposed to that of Malthus. This theory holds that independently of external circumstances, and as the result of internal factors, populations tend to follow a course analogous, from many points of view, to that of the life course of individual organisms, passing through successively the stages of development, maturity, and involution.[9]

Gini's emphasis is on the fecundity of the populations; "demographic metabolism" is the key variable in his theory, and it is changes in this biological, inherent quality which explain changes in total population and in growth rates.[10]

At times in his argument Gini seems to suggest that the biological decay of nations may also involve an increase in the susceptibility of nations or peoples to diseases of various sorts. But this is not elaborated upon. In the main, he dwells on the change in fecundity and, consequently, fertility as the cause of the cyclical movements in total population which he argues take place.

The cyclical theory has not gained too many adherents. Gini's biology is speculative and on some especially crucial points his theory is wholly non-quantitative. The theory is at least as philosophical as it is scientific and entails almost a whole theory of history as well as a theory of population change.

A few quotations will suffice to illustrate these aspects of his work.

> We must therefore conclude that the primary cause of the evolution of nations must be sought in biological factors.
>   The biological theory of the evolution of nations also explains why the rise, the arrest, and the fall of populations are either accompanied or

followed, at no great distance, by the expansion, the stoppage, or the decline of other national manifestations in the military, economic, political and scientific fields. The fact is that those same genetic forces which determine a rapid growth of population cause at the same time a notable flowering of robust and daring individuals of keen, prompt, and adaptable intelligence.

All these circumstances contribute to determine the golden age of a nation. It is no mere chance, therefore, that in periods of rapidly expanding population the nations find the great captains who lead them to victory, the industrial geniuses who provide them with the arms required for the needs of war and peace, the great poets who idealize their aspirations and electrify their enthusiasm, the great thinkers who systematize their conceptions of life and of the universe, and the great historians who transmit their deeds to posterity.

As far as metabolism is concerned, there is no doubt that its intensification, more especially when marked differentiation reduces the fertility of those who rise or who hope to rise, hastens the demographic exhaustion of the nation. It is also certain that when the social metabolism becomes too rapid and intense, the individuals who rise to the upper classes are often lacking in that intellectual and moral preparation for occupying positions of responsibility which can only be supplied by a long family tradition.[11]

The introduction to this same volume discusses the "slow exhaustion of the reproductive powers of human population and of animal species, that is to say, of their germinal cells . . ."[12]

The Periodic

A variation of the cyclical theory has come to be called the periodic. It differs from cyclical in that it explains movements in population by reference to an exogenous variable, the growth of some other population which "devours" the population in question. This is the cats-and-mice theory applied to humans and the growth, perhaps, of bacteria which slay humans, with the human population bearing an inverse relationship to the bacteria population, rising as the latter falls, and falling when it rises. Here the key factor for the human population is the death rate, which is, in turn, dependent on the growth rate in the bacteria population. The periodic theory, in other words, assumes levels of fertility and then makes the changes in death rates the dynamic factor.[13]

The Logistic

Perhaps almost as well known as the Malthusian theory itself is the proposition that population growth curves follow a logistic function, gradually but asymptotically approaching an upper limit. Credit for the modern formulation must go to the biologist Raymond Pearl, although the roots of the theory are much older.[14]

> Almost half a century later than that of Malthus, and now a popular one in scientific circles, is the theory . . . that while population tends indeed to increase in geometrical progression with a constant coefficient, it is, from a certain point onwards, increasingly hindered by obstacles which lower that coefficient in a degree proportionate to the increase already realized, from that point onwards, in the size of the population. The combined effects of the force of growth and of the obstacles in its way give rise to the so-called "logistic" curve of growth, which tends asymptotically to attain a maximum . . . or rather a condition of stationary equilibrium.[15]

Pearl at first offered evidence to support his contention that populations tended to level off as they approached some upper limit without offering any logical scheme for explaining why this should be the case. He compared his results to Kepler's Law of the motion of the planets or Boyle's Law before they had been reinforced with Newtonian and Maxwellian theory, respectively.[16] However, he did argue that, since his "law" seemed to hold for the non-human population too, the logical, or theoretical, explanation must not be couched in terms of social or economic institutions. He said:

> . . . these causes are not peculiar to human beings, such as the economic or social structure or organization of human society . . . This means that the search must be thrown back to more fundamental natural causes, biological, physical or chemical.[17]

Very early, Pearl made at least a beginning in presenting these fundamental causes, and not all of them were biological, physical or chemical.

> Fourth, that rate of reproduction or fertility is negatively correlated with density of population . . . This evidence indicates that in the direct and indirect biological effects of density of population upon reproduction exists one *vera causa* for the damping off of the growth of population as the upper limit of the logistic curve is approached . . . Fifth, that birth rate is negatively correlated with wealth (or positively correlated with poverty) . . . Sixth, that the indirect psychological and social effects of relative poverty as contrasted with relative wealth express themselves . . . in the sexual activity of human beings, and through sexual activity to birth rates.[18]

In later works, Pearl moved even farther away from his earlier biological determinism.

This chart of factors affecting population increase, in common with most succinct classifications of complex human phenomena and relationships, falls short of logical perfection or completeness. But, perhaps it will in some degree serve two purposes: first, help to clarify and unite in a single view some of the more significant elements in an extremely complex matter; and, second, to get into the record, as the legal phrase has it, a formal statement of the fact that the writer is not unaware of the great importance of the influence of social and economic variables upon human fertility. Perhaps this chart will be permitted to take the place of tiresome reiteration of this awareness every time specifically biological aspects of fertility are discussed in the remainder of the book.[19]

And he then listed economic circumstances as being an indirect factor of the same sort as density of population.

Pearl allowed for the chance that his theory might be very wrong in times of great upheaval. The growth of the population as described by the curves always assumed that "no fundamentally new factor or forces influencing the rate of population growth different from those which have operated during the historical period of this population's growth shall come into play."[20] And the forces he listed include great changes in the culture of nations, wars, famines, mass emigration and other catastrophes. Thus, Pearl perhaps would have argued that in normal times it is changes in fertility (because of changes in density) which are the dynamic factors, although he does not seem to have attempted to supply his own counterpart of Newtonian or Maxwellian theory to go with his empirical law.

Yule attempted to interpret the logistic theory in terms of the vital rates. Insofar as the modern period is concerned, he said:

... all the facts seem consonant with the view that in recent historical times and in civilized States, it is the birth rate that must be regarded as the regulating factor in population; no other view seems possible.[21]

If Pearl had stuck to his original contention that the cause of the empirical law was not to be found in human institutions or habits, and accepted also Yule's contention, which indeed seems impossible not to accept, he would have been led to something very like Gini's notion of a decline in ability to reproduce as an explanation for the upper asymptote of his curve, and, in fact, in his early work he seemed to be moving in this direction.

The logistic gained wide currency in this country and abroad. Many of its advocates, however, have been even farther from purely biological in their interpretation of the factors underlying the curve—that is, in explaining what causes the changes in births and deaths which are observed in the population. Knibbs, for example, while accepting the validity of the law of growth, listed seven factors which affect population growth, including such things as social tradition, political and economic security and customary age at marriage.[22]

Reed likewise seems to have been willing to admit that social and economic factors may be important and suggested that such things be considered as parameters of the curve; he suggested fitting population growth curves to as many populations as possible and then seeing to what extent divergencies of the actual from the expected could be correlated with differences in these parameters.[23]

Thus, in its modified statements the logistic had nearly become a "social" rather than a "natural" theory.[24]

IV. OPTIMUM POPULATION THEORY

Another important part of the gradual shift toward economic and social causation was the body of ideas and propositions which rose to popularity in the late Nineteen Twenties and early Thirties under the name "optimum population" theory.

Robbins has described the optimum population as "a point at which population is neither too great nor too small, but is just such as to secure a maximum return per head, under the given conditions of production."[25]

Generally speaking, the factors determining the optimum population were: (a) natural resources available, (b) the skill, endowment, knowledge and habits of the population, (c) the opportunities for economic activity.[26] Given these factors, then, there would exist one "right" population to maximize per capita output and income. In essence, this is a variation on the economist's problem of factor proportions. The optimum population was that population which when combined with the given social capital stock yielded the highest marginal product per capita.[27]

Now, strictly speaking, this is not a theory at all. It is nothing but a description of what most people would view as a desirable situation for a society.

The entire question of population optimums was in great vogue in the decade of the Thirties, a time when falling growth rates seemed to presage stationary or even declining populations for most of the countries of the West. The optimum could, of course, be deliberately pursued for society by social engineers. It provided a target. Indeed, from its very inception this approach was policy-oriented. But even as a policy directive it is static in nature. That is, only given a certain social capital stock can population be thought of as approaching an optimum. And once one admits the difficulties of imagining a constant stock of social capital, including human knowledge, then the meaning of the optimum as a real goal of policy becomes less and less clear.[28]

In order truly to be a theory of how population actually behaves, this approach would also have to describe some social or biological mechanisms whereby the birth rate and/or the death rate were affected so as to lead population to the optimum. Few writers argued that any such mechanism or tendency existed.

In retrospect, much of the discussion of population optimums which consumed so much time strikes one as an interesting, often ingenious, but altogether sterile exercise.[29]

V. THE SOCIAL THEORY OF POPULATION CHANGE

The Background to the Theory

As the decline in the birth rate in the Western countries continued into the Thirties, more and more attention was given to the factors underlying this decline.[30]

Increasingly, the weight of evidence suggested that the decline in the birth rate was due to human volition; that is, it was the result of conscious and deliberate efforts by married couples to limit the size of their families.

Pearl, writing as a biologist rather than theorist, stated:

> All the evidence that has been accumulated by the work of the last quarter of a century on the subject agrees with cumulative force in showing that among civilized populations of the western world the main factors leading to group or class differential fertility are (non-genetic) in nature and that any group differences in innate biological (genetic) fertility, if they exist at all in such populations, play a small role in producing group differences in expressed fertility.[31]

And Carr-Saunders observed: "So far as we have taken the matter, birth-control can be held to explain sufficiently the facts of the decline of the birth-rate within the sphere of European civilization."[32]

Thus, a "social" theory rather than a "natural" theory seemed to be required. As seen above, the logistic in its later variations was very close to a social theory. The last step toward a completely social theory capable of explaining the observed histories of Western populations and capable also of being applied to other populations was taken with the development of what has come to be called Theory of the Demographic Transition, or, more simply, Transition Theory.

Instead of focusing on one or a few variables, such as demographic metabolism, rate of growth of agricultural output, or population density, as an explanation of population change, it takes into account a great many social and economic factors. It says that changes occur in fertility and mortality because of complicated processes not to be explained easily or neatly by any system.

The Theory Stated

Coale and Hoover write:

> In barest outline the sequence of events, according to the theory of the demographic transition, can be summarized as follows: The agrarian low-income economy is characterized by high birth and death rates— the birth rates relatively stable, and the death rates fluctuating in response to varying fortunes. Then as the economy changes its form to a more interdependent and specialized market-dominated economy, the average death rate declines. It continues to decline under the impact of better organization and improving medical knowledge and care. Somewhat later the birth rate begins to fall.
>
> The two rates pursue a more or less parallel downward course with the decline of the birth rate lagging behind. Finally, as further reduction of the death rate becomes harder to attain, the birth rate again approaches equality with death rate and a more gradual rate of growth is re-established, with, however, low risks of mortality and small families as the typical pattern. Mortality rates are now relatively stable from year to year and birth rates—now responsive to voluntary decisions rather than to deeply imbedded customs—may fluctuate from year to year. This short description fits the experience of most countries whose economies have undergone the kind of reorganization we have been calling economic development.[33]

The essence of the theory, then, is that the "transition" in fertility is from control by environment to control by calculated individual choice. Changes in mortality continue to be the result of social decisions and habits, but the "transition" implies an increasingly effective control.[34]

First Statements of the Theory

The transition approach is derived from the actual experience of the countries of the European sphere of civilization. It is a description of what has happened to these nations during the course of their economic and demographic development in approximately the last century.

Warren Thompson made one of the earliest attempts to generalize the demographic experience of Europe into a theoretical frame of reference which could apply to other areas as well. He grouped the nations of the world into three categories according to the level of their birth and death rates.

Briefly stated, the characteristics of these groups from the standpoint of their vital statistics are: Group A: Very rapidly declining birth-rate and death-rate with the former declining more rapidly than the latter so that the rate of natural increase is also declining. Group B: Evidence that decline in both birth-rate and death-rate is under way in certain classes, but that the death-rate is declining as rapidly or even more rapidly than the birth-rate with the result that the rate of natural increase will probably remain for some time as great as now, or even become larger in the near future. Group C: Both birth-rates and death-rates are less controlled than in either A or B. But, in some of these countries . . . there is some indication that death rates are coming under control faster than birth rates . . . there is likely to be a very rapid increase in numbers during the next few decades.[35]

A decade or so later, Willcox noted the fundamental differences in the age structures of the "occidental-type" and "oriental-type" (*i.e.*, the larger percentage of the total made up of infants and children in the latter) populations and marked those populations in between as "transitional."[36] This seems to have been the first use of the word "transitional" in this connection. At about the same time the term "vital revolution," now often used as a synonym for "demographic transition," was coined by Himes. He defines it as "stabilization of population at a more economical level, *i.e.*, with low birth and death rates instead of high birth and death rates."[37]

Causes of Fertility Declines

Within the general framework of Transition Theory some debate occurred over the causes of the fertility declines which the theory described. All agreed that the causation was "social" rather than "natural," but the agreement ended there.

Carr-Saunders, Fairchild and others believed that modern contraceptive methods were responsible for a large part of the decline in the birth rate. They argued that only after the invention and mass availability of "appliance" techniques of contraception did widespread interest in family limitation arise and did effective human control over the birth rate become possible.[38]

This view was, however, disputed by Notestein and Stix, who pointed out that some form of birth limitation seems to have always existed in society and that sometimes relatively crude, non-appliance methods (notably coitus interruptus) proved quite effective.[39] They also pointed out that the decline in most Western nations began well before modern contraceptive techniques and appliances were widely known or used. They concluded that "the rapid decline in birth rates may be attributed in part to a rapid extension in the use of folkway contraception . . . New patterns of living and new values brought growing interest in family limitation that spread the use of known methods and stimulated the development of new ones. In a real sense, modern birth control is as much the result of new interest in family limitation as its cause."[40]

The Stix-Notestein position was supported by the findings of the Royal Commission on Population published in 1949. The commission reported that, in marriages occurring in England prior to 1910, 80 per cent of all contraception practiced was of the "non-appliance" type; moreover, it also reported that only in marriages occurring in the middle Thirties or later was "appliance" contraception more widespread than "non-appliance" methods. This lent strong support to the contention that the decline in the birth rate was caused by a rise in the desire of couples to limit family size with whatever techniques were available—in the earlier period of the late nineteenth century and early twentieth century with coitus interruptus, and in the more contemporary period with mechanical or chemical means.[41]

Other studies have also supported this approach, and the socio-economic interpretation put on "transition" by Notestein and Stix has gained general acceptance. Davis, for example, writes: ". . . some of the most important developments (in the European transition) were doubtless intangible—the growth of democratic institutions, scientific ideals, humanitarian sentiments."[42] And this is the interpretation of the transition taken in the numerous writings on the subject in the last two decades by Thompson, Notestein, Davis, Landry, Kirk and many others.[43]

The Transition Theory has gained wide acceptance in the last two decades. It would scarcely be an exaggeration to call it *the* modern population theory. As has been seen, it is based on the actual history of Europe and America and is a purely social theory. It is at the same time a very general theory, lacking in rigorous formulations or neat, concise answers to complex questions on population change. Seen in context, it is also a logical outgrowth and modification of the earlier work of such post-Malthusian determinists as Pearl and Gini.

The Present Status of the Theory

So much for the nature and development of Transition Theory. Dominant though it has been, this theory has by no means settled all questions of population growth. In the last decade, several developments have called into question the validity of the theory and led to renewed theoretical speculations. These developments have been: first, the postwar fertility upsurge in the United States; and, second, the rapid growth of population in the lesser-developed areas of the world.

(a) Population Growth in Lesser-Developed Areas. The emerging Asian, African and Latin American countries are experiencing what Europe

experienced a century or two ago—a period of falling death rates coupled with fairly constant birth rates, resulting inevitably in rapid growth. To be sure, the time scale of these changes is different in these areas than it was in Europe. Death rates have been halved in a matter of years, not centuries or decades, and that is why the growth in these areas has been an explosion. But the basic cause of the growth—a growing social control over death rates—is the same in both cases. And the other stage of "transition"—control over birth rates—may ultimately be achieved in these areas too. The exact mechanisms of this control are far from clear to us today, but that is hardly surprising. The precise manner in which the "transition" to controlled fertility was to occur in Europe eluded Malthus and most other demographers even while this transition was taking place.[44] But the fact of this growth is not at all incompatible with Transition Theory.

(b) The Postwar Resurgence of Fertility in the United States. Some critics have interpreted the postwar upsurge in birth rates in the United States as disproof of Transition Theory. The failure of virtually all forecasts of postwar United States population is attributed to the widespread belief among demographers that the United States had reached the final evolutionary "stage" of growth characterized by a near equality between low death rates and low birth rates.[45]

To the extent that the completed "transition" does imply a forecast of ultimate stability in total population, then the postwar upsurge in United States and other Western populations would constitute a disproof of the theory. It seems clear that no balance of birth rates with death rates in this country is in the offing for the foreseeable future.

On the other hand, Notestein has answered this criticism of Transition Theory as follows:

> I have not been able to see that the current resurgence in the birth rates of the United States, Canada, Australia and New Zealand, for example, has any real bearing on the transitional argument. To repeat somewhat we may view the heart of transition theory as being based on two propositions:
>
> 1. The reduction of mortality can be rather quickly achieved because the necessary techniques can be borrowed and their application involves only slight adjustment in the existing value structures.
>
> 2. The reduction in fertility in modern times has come as the controls of fertility have been shifted from factors that were mainly institutional to factors that were mainly individual and rational.
>
> Nothing in the above gives us clues to the rate of population growth after the transition has taken place. At least nothing suggests that the rate of growth is necessarily slow. At the heart of the theory is the presumption that individually and rationally controlled fertility

will be much lower than the high rates of the peasant societies, but with low death rates even moderate fertility rates can give high rates of population growth. I see no reason to suppose that fertility in the United States is not mainly under individual and rational control, and yet no reason to suppose that within the framework of the 2 to 4 child family, rational choice may not yield a distribution which continues to give us high rates of population increase.[46]

Crucial to this argument is what is meant by equilibrium. Ordinary usage defines the word as absence of change, but it is not clear whether this means stability in total numbers of population, stability of the growth rate over time, stability in the underlying vital rates, or something different from any of these. In any case, it seems clear that equilibrium does not necessarily and in all cases mean stability of total numbers. The pre-transitional equilibria in the Western nations almost certainly did not involve any long-term stability in total numbers. But there was a stability in the social, economic and psychological environment which acted upon the vital rates. There was, in short, an equilibrium of the forces governing population change, and the breakdown of this equilibrium launched the "transitional" era. Now it is possible that a new equilibrium has been reached in the United States, one in which there is again an underlying stability in the social and psychological forces governing the vital rates but one which implies continued growth in total population.[47]

Thus, if one ignores total numbers and concentrates instead on the processes of movement from one equilibrium to another, in the above sense, then the postwar developments in Western fertility are quite compatible with the theory of the demographic transition. Admittedly, this interpretation marks a change of emphasis from some of the earlier formulations of the theory (including some of those cited earlier in this paper), but no useful, empirically based theory is ever a finished body of doctrine allowing no changes or amendments.[48]

VI. SUMMARY AND CONCLUSIONS

This paper has presented some of the highlights of population theorizing in the last half century. This has not been a thorough survey of all writings on the subject and, indeed, has not even covered all the major schools of thought. Most notable among the omissions are the whole body of Catholic Church writings on the subject,[49] as well as Marxist and neo-Marxist thought.[50]

The presently dominant theory is that commonly called the Theory of Demographic Transition. This body of general propositions, which explains population change in terms of a battery of complex social, economic and psychological factors, continues to provide what theoretical foundations exist for the diverse empirical researches under way into demographic behavior. As a frame of reference for understanding the major population changes occurring abroad and also in this country, Transition Theory is useful and important.

On the other hand, population theory is once again being discussed. Transition Theory is ultimately subject to the test of its ability to explain observed events and facts. Considering the fate of many other theories, there seems little room to doubt that ultimately it too may be replaced by some presently totally unsuspected view of why population growth occurs.

NOTES

1. Thomas Robert Malthus, *An Essay on the Principle of Population* (London: 1798). A total of seven revised editions were issued between 1803 and 1834.

2. For modern formal presentations of the Malthusian system, see Harvey Leibenstein, *A Theory of Economic-Demographic Development* (Princeton: Princeton University Press, 1954); D. V. Glass, *Introduction to Malthus* (London: 1952).

3. "The Sociology of Demographic Behavior," *Sociology Today,* ed. by Robert K. Merton, Leonard Broom, and Leonard S. Cottrell, Jr. (New York: Basic Books, 1959), pp. 313–4.

4. Comment by Notestein on "Population Theory," essay in *Survey of Contemporary Economics,* Vol. II, ed. by B. F. Haley (Homewood, Ill.: Irwin, 1952), p. 129.

5. By a "theory of population" is understood an attempt to elucidate the major factor or factors determining population growth. (*Cf.* Sydney Coontz, *Population Theories and the Economic Interpretation* [London: Routledge and Kegan Paul, 1957], p. 13.) We use this definition since it follows "ordinary" usage and in spite of obvious shortcomings. Hauser and Duncan *(The Study of Population: An Inventory and Appraisal* [Chicago: Chicago University Press, 1959], p. 13) offer a more precise definition, as follows: "What may be properly called a 'theory' of population consists of a body of interrelated principles which has at least some degree of empirical support, which affords an explanation or

prediction of observed and observable relationships and which has heuristic implications in suggesting hypotheses for investigation." These authors make clear that their definition is framed purposely to "exclude from consideration both the purely speculative exposition of laws of population growth and the construction of minuscule models of relationships, whether hypothetical or empirical, without systematic relevance to other sets of hypotheses" (p. 13). They also refer to "empirical regularities" (for example, "the volume and rate of internal migration tends to fall off with increasing distance") which they do not consider theories.

6. The economist Cannan was one of the first to notice and comment on this development. See "The Probability of the Cessation of the Growth of Population in England during the Next Century," *Economic Journal,* Vol. V (December, 1895), pp. 505–15.

7. R. R. Kuczynski, *The Balance of Births and Deaths* (New York: Macmillan, 1928), Vol. I, p. 62. Kuczynski goes on to point out that, while increases in the birth rate had occurred before, they had always reversed themselves after a decade or so. The downturn in the birth rate which started in the last quarter of the nineteenth century had, he maintained, continued.

8. Warren S. Thompson, *Population Problems,* 4th ed. (New York: McGraw-Hill, 1953), p. 45.

9. Corrado Gini, "A Coordination of the Different Population Theories," *Revue*

de l'Institut International de Statistique, Vol. 11, Nos. 1–2 (1943), pp. 37–8.

10. See the above-cited 1943 article and "The Cyclical Rise and Fall of Population," Population, Harris Foundation Lectures for 1929 (Chicago: Chicago University Press, 1930), pp. 1–140. Gini has written extensively, but these sources contain good summaries of his theory as well as references to his other writings.

11. Ibid., pp. 26, 28, 28–9, and 31, respectively.

12. Ibid., p. 9.

13. This approach has been traced to Darwin. More recently, see V. Volterra, "Fluctuations dans la lutte pour la vie. Leur leis fondamentales et de réciprocité," Réunion Internationale des Mathématiciens (Paris, 1937–38). See also Gini's previously cited 1943 article, and Coontz, op. cit., Chap. II.

14. Raymond Pearl, The Biology of Population Growth (New York: Alfred Knopf, 1925). See also United Nations, The Determinants and Consequences of Population Trends, pp. 41ff.

15. Corrado Gini, "A Coordination of Different Population Theories," loc. cit., pp. 37–8.

16. Raymond Pearl, Studies in Human Biology (Baltimore: Williams and Wilkins Co., 1924), p. 585.

17. Ibid., p. 585.

18. Raymond Pearl, The Biology of Population Growth, op. cit., p. 209. The entire last half of this book, from p. 126 on, is devoted to discussing these causes.

19. Raymond Pearl, The Natural History of Population (London: Oxford University Press, 1939), p. 95.

20. Ibid., p. 587.

21. G. Yule, "The Growth of Population and the Factors Which Control It," Journal of the Royal Statistical Society, Vol. 86 (1925), p. 33. Pearl quoted from this article by Yule at length and with obvious approval in the Biology of Population Growth.

22. Sir George H. Knibbs, Shadows of the World's Future (London: 1928), pp. 36ff.

23. Lowell J. Reed, "Population Growth and Forecast," Annals of the American Academy of Political and Social Science, Vol. 188 (November, 1936), p. 166.

24. Criticisms of the logistic have been numerous, mostly on the count of its early biological formulations. See A. B. Wolfe, "The Population Problem since the War: A Survey of Literature and Results," in Hauser and Duncan, op. cit. [sic], p. 65; D. O. Cowgill, "The Theory of Population Growth Cycles," The American Journal of Sociology, Vol. 55, No. 2 (September, 1949), pp. 163–77; T. D. Hiller, "A Cultural Theory of Population Trends," Journal of Political Economy, Vol. 38 (October, 1930), pp. 523–50; and G. A. Lundberg, "The Biology of Population Cycles," Social Forces, Vol. 9, No. 3 (March, 1931), pp. 401–8.

25. Lionel Robbins, "The Optimum Theory of Population," London Essays in Economics in Honor of Edwin Cannan (London: Routledge, 1927), p. 114.

26. Sir A. M. Carr-Saunders, World Population: Past Growth and Present Trends (Oxford: Clarendon Press, 1936), p. 330.

27. For a development of this point, see A. B. Wolfe, "The Theory of Optimum Population," Annals of the American Academy of Political and Social Science, Vol. 188 (October, 1936), p. 243. See also A. B. Wolfe, "On the Criterion of Optimum Population," American Journal of Sociology, Vol. 39, No. 5 (March, 1934), pp. 585–99.

28. Among the variants to this theory was the "optimum of welfare" theory, authored by Penrose and described as follows: "The per capita welfare optimum population for any area is that population in which per capita income stands at a maximum when it is spent in the consumption of the composite commodity that, in the light of existing scientific knowledge, makes a greater contribution to welfare than, in the existing state of the arts, can be made by any alternative composite commodity." E. F. Penrose, Population Theories and Their Application (Stanford: Food Research Institute, 1934), p. 84.

29. Osborn writes of the optimum: "We conclude then that the concept of optimum size is hard for the scientist to handle, impractical for the politician or statesman, and does not interest the people who make the actual decisions as to size of family. The concept is likely to remain . . . a rather vague and theoretical objective." Frederick Osborn, "Optimum Rates

of Population Growth," in *The Population Ahead*, ed. by Roy G. Francis (Minneapolis: University of Minnesota Press, 1958), p. 43. Osborn likens optimum population to the ideal of feminine beauty—a thing which continues to fascinate men but which is incapable of precise definition.

30. See Roderich von Ungern-Sternberg, *The Causes of the Decline in Birth-Rate within the European Sphere of Civilization*, Eugenics Research Association Monograph No. 4 (Cold Spring Harbor, L.I., N.Y., 1931), Parts IV and V.

31. Raymond Pearl, *The Natural History of Population* (Oxford University Press, 1939), p. 24.

32. Sir A. M. Carr-Saunders, *World Population* (Oxford: Oxford University Press, 1936), p. 105.

33. A. J. Coale and E. M. Hoover, *Population Growth and Economic Development in Low Income Countries* (Princeton: Princeton University Press, 1958), pp. 12–3. See also N. Ryder, "The Conceptualization of the Transition in Fertility," Cold Spring Harbor Symposia on Quantitative Biology, Vol. XXII, *Population Studies: Animal Ecology and Demography*, 1957.

34. For other statements of the theory, see F. W. Notestein, "The Population of the World in the Year 2000," *Journal of the American Statistical Association*, Vol. 45 (September, 1950), pp. 335–45; "Population Theory," in *A Survey of Contemporary Economics*, Vol. II, *op. cit.*, p. 95. See also Joe S. Davis, "Population and Resources," *Journal of the American Statistical Association*, Vol. XLV, No. 251 (September, 1950); C. P. Blacker, "Stages in Population Growth," *The Eugenics Review*, Vol. 39 (October, 1947), pp. 81–101; D. O. Cowgill, "Transition Theory as General Population Theory," *Social Forces*, Vol. 41, No. 3 (March, 1963), pp. 270–74.

35. "Population," *American Journal of Sociology*, Vol. 34 (March, 1929), pp. 961–2.

36. "The Length of Life in the Early Roman Empire." *Démographie Historique*, Vol. II of the proceedings of Congrès International de la Population (Paris, 1937), pp. 20–2. A revised version of this paper appears as Chap. III. of Willcox's *Studies in American Demography* (Ithaca: Cornell University Press, 1940).

37. Norman E. Himes, *Medical History of Contraception* (Baltimore: Williams and Wilkins Co., 1936), p. 391.

38. Henry P. Fairchild, *People* (New York: Holt & Co., 1939), Chap. VII. See also A. M. Carr-Saunders, *World Population, op. cit.*, pp. 105ff.

39. Frank W. Notestein and Regine K. Stix, *Controlled Fertility* (Baltimore: Williams and Wilkins Co., 1940), Chap. XV and especially pp. 148ff.

40. *Ibid.*, pp. 149–50.

41. E. Lewis-Faning, *Report on an Enquiry into Family Limitation and Its Influence on Human Fertility During the Past Fifty Years*, Papers of the Royal Commission on Population, Vol. I (London: H.M.S.O., 1949).

42. Kingsley Davis, "The World Demographic Transition," *World Population in Transition, Annals of the American Academy of Political and Social Science*, Vol. 237 (January, 1945), pp. 4–5.

43. Warren S. Thompson, *Population and Peace in the Pacific* (Chicago: University of Chicago Press, 1945), Chap. II; *Plenty of People*, rev. ed. (New York: Ronald Press, 1948), Chap. VI; *Population Problems*, various editions (New York: McGraw-Hill), pp. 267–72 of the 4th ed. (Notestein, *op. cit.*, p. 335, and Paul K. Hatt, Nellie L. Farr and E. Weinstein, "Types of Population Balance," *American Sociological Review*, Vol. 20 [February, 1955], pp. 14–21, agree in crediting the 1929 Thompson article with being the first generalized statement of Transition Theory.) Notestein, "Economic Problems of Population Change," *Proceedings of the Eighth International Conference of Agricultural Economists* (London: Oxford University Press, 1953), pp. 13–31; *The Future Population of Europe and the Soviet Union* (New York: League of Nations, 1944), Chap. II. Adolphe Landry, *Traité de démographie* (Paris, 1945), Chap. IX. (Landry refers to the stages as "regimes," but they are substantially the same as those outlined by Thompson and Notestein.) Dudley Kirk, *Europe's Population in the Interwar Years* (Princeton: League of Nations, 1946), pp. 36ff.

44. For a penetrating discussion of the applicability of Transition Theory to the lesser-developed areas, see Irene B. Taeuber, "The Future of the Transitional

Areas," in *World Population and Future Resources*, ed. by Paul Hatt (New York: American Book Co., 1952). There has also been a renewal of interest in the Malthusian model. See, for example, R. R. Nelson, "A Theory of the Low-Level Equilibrium Trap in Underdeveloped Countries," *American Economic Review*, Vol. 46 (December, 1956), pp. 894–908; E. E. Hagen, "Population and Economic Growth," *American Economic Review*, Vol. 49, No. 3 (June, 1959), pp. 310–27.

45. Kurt Mayer, "Fertility Changes and Population Forecasts in the United States," *Social Research*, Vol. 26, No. 3 (Autumn, 1959), pp. 347ff.

46. Letter from Frank W. Notestein to the author, December 8, 1958.

47. Mayer, *loc. cit.*, argues that fairly accurate forecasts are again possible by focusing on completed generation fertility and that there exists a long-term stability in the average size of family. This same assumption is made by the population forecasts made in the recent Scripps Foundation–Survey Research Center Study. See Ronald Freedman, Pascal K. Whelpton, and Arthur A. Campbell, *Family Planning, Sterility and Population Growth* (New York: McGraw-Hill, 1959), pp. 367ff.

48. Some recent authors have stressed the more purely economic factors affecting fertility changes and variations. See Robert A. Easterlin, "The Baby Boom in Perspective," *American Economic Review*, Vol. 51, No. 5 (December, 1961), pp. 869–911. See also Gary S. Becker, "Economic Aspects of Fertility," in *Demographic and Economic Change in Developed Countries*, Universities–National Bureau of Economic Research Conference (Princeton, 1960). These works would still appear to be operating within the general structure of Transition Theory.

49. John A. Ryan, "Population," *The Catholic Encyclopedia*, Vol. 12, pp. 276–80.

50. Coontz, *op. cit.*, argues a neo-Marxist position and explains population growth in terms of the response of the supply of labor function to changes in real wages. He also reviews and summarizes Marxist population literature since Marx, almost none of which is in English.

4

Professor Malthus
and His Essay

Judy K. Morris

I think I may fairly make two postulata.

First, that food is necessary to the existence of man.

Secondly, That the passion between the sexes is necessary, and will remain nearly in its present state.

Assuming, . . . my postulata as granted, I say, that the power of population is indefinitely greater than the power in the earth to produce subsistence for man.—Robert Malthus, 1798

The Reverend Robert Malthus (Malthus preferred to drop the "Thomas"), Professor of History and Political Economy at East India College, Hailey-bury, England, was not a man one would expect to stir up controversy. He took religious orders, according to the head of his college, because "the utmost of his wishes was a retired living in the country."

In an age when prolonged public debate was a major British pastime, Malthus avoided the game. Eager for discussion with the economist David Ricardo, he "took the liberty of introducing himself," hoping that, "as we are *mainly* on the same side of the question, we might supersede the necessity of a long controversy in print respecting the points in which we differ, by an amicable discussion in private."

The first edition of Malthus's famous work, *An Essay on the Principle of Population,* was published anonymously.

But this reticent man, when quite young, stumbled upon a subject which dominated his life and caused his name to be very much on the public tongue: his controversial "principle of population." The essential concept of the principle lay in what Malthus saw as a tendency toward imbalance between the rates of growth of a population and its food supply. To balance

Reprinted from *Population Bulletin,* 22, no. 1 (February, 1966), pp. 7–27, by permission of the publisher, Population Reference Bureau, Inc., Washington, D.C.

the two, Malthus said, nature used both "preventive" and "positive" (war, plague, famine, and the ubiquitous "vice") checks to population.

Interest generated by his pronouncements, as well as a flow of new information, led Malthus to revise and republish his *Essay* five times. Malthus's principle of population appears to be as relevant today—200 years after his birth—as it was in 1798, when the *Essay* first appeared. That Malthus's views remain controversial is perhaps symbolic of the confusion in which the population problem is cast, even in this assumedly enlightened age.

Even today Malthus is still coolly dismissed or roundly denounced in some quarters. But, while population is growing as never before, in most of the world it does not thrive. The number of people now on the verge of falling victim to what Malthus saw as the ultimate check to population—famine—*is twice the total population of the world when he wrote his* Essay.

Malthus's fundamental concept remains unchallenged: *Unchecked population growth accelerates faster than the greatest increases of food that man is able to wrest from the earth on a sustained basis.*

The controversy which this idea engendered has had such wide-ranging consequences that Malthus stands as one of the select few who have made unique and enduring contributions to man's understanding of himself and of his place on this planet.

THE MISUNDERSTOOD MAN

Any controversial figure is subject to rumor, innuendo, and misunderstanding, and Malthus was no exception. For example, he has come to be known as the "gloomy parson."

Actually, he was rather a cheerful person. It is true that he was not one to gloss over the grim realities of life, as in this statement:

> It has appeared, that from the inevitable laws of our nature, some human beings must suffer from want. These are the unhappy persons who, in the great lottery of life, have drawn a blank.

But he also called life "a blessing." In his introduction to the *Essay*, he attempted to forestall a "gloomy" view of his personality by denying he had "a jaundiced eye, or an inherent spleen of disposition."

Technically, Malthus was a "parson." In 1803, he was appointed to a rectory in Haileybury, a position he held the rest of his life. Actually, he left his parish in the charge of a succession of curates. His real vocation was as a professor of political economy. No less an authority than John Maynard Keynes has given him the highest marks in economics:

> If only Malthus, instead of Ricardo, had been the parent stem from

which nineteenth-century economics proceeded, what a much wiser and richer place the world would be today!

A more serious misconception links Malthus with the movement promoting the use of birth-control devices. In fact, he abhorred even the idea of contraception, which he referred to delicately as "improper arts." As will be noted later in this discussion, he paradoxically advocated large families at the same time forecasting the imminence of mass famine.

Perhaps most surprising, Malthus thus by no means frowned on large and growing populations. On the contrary, he said:

> That an increase of population, when it follows in its natural order, is both a great positive good in itself, and absolutely necessary to a further increase in the annual produce of the land and labour of any country, I should be the last to deny. The only question is, what is the order of its progress?

Malthus wanted men to "unite the two grand *desiderata*, a great actual population and a state of society in which abject poverty and dependence are comparatively but little known." In the appendix to the third edition of his *Essay*, he complained of criticism which proceeded:

> . . . upon the very strange supposition that the *ultimate* object of my work is to check population, as if anything could be more desirable than the most rapid increase of population, unaccompanied by vice and misery. But of course my ultimate object is to diminish vice and misery, and any checks to population which may have been suggested are solely as means to accomplish this end.

Malthus was concerned with nature's often cruel ways of eliminating "redundant" populations. He never referred to a "population problem," only to the problems of misery and vice, of poverty and labor surpluses, resulting from too-rapid growth.

He frequently discussed the application of his "principle of population" as it related to social conditions in England. His conviction—shocking to many then and now, but based for Malthus on the feudal antecedents of his society—was that the poor, through overbreeding, were largely responsible for their condition. He said, in effect, those who have ceased to have the power to eat or to live, ceased to have the right: that there is no inherent right to sustenance. By pretending otherwise, society misleads and cruelly disappoints the poor. He advised the poor to forgo marriage until they could support their offspring, thus limiting their numbers, tightening the labor market, and raising wages.

Malthus was not a prudish person who disapproved of sex. The *Essay* contains occasional hymns to "virtuous love":

Virtuous love, exalted by friendship, seems to be that sort of mixture of sensual and intellectual enjoyment, particularly suited to the nature of man, and most powerfully calculated to awaken the sympathies of the soul, and produce the most exquisite gratifications. Perhaps there is scarcely a man, who has once experienced the genuine delight of virtuous love, however great his intellectual pleasures may have been, who does not look back to that period as the sunny spot in his whole life . . .

He regarded "the passion between the sexes" as mankind's unique characteristic and a great force for potential good:

. . . we appear to have under our guidance a great power, capable of peopling a desert region in a small number of years; and yet, under other circumstances, capable of being confined by human energy and virtue to any limits however narrow, at the expense of a small comparative quantity of evil.

Malthus was indebted to the work of many other men for ideas which contributed to the development of his theories. Conversely, others were indebted to him. For instance, Charles Darwin found the inspiration for his law of evolution by natural selection in the *Essay:*

I happened to read for amusement Malthus on Population, and being well prepared to appreciate the struggle for existence which everywhere goes on, from long-continued observation in the habits of animals and plants, it at once struck me that under these circumstances favourable variations tend to be preserved, and unfavorable ones to be destroyed. The result of this would be the formation of new species. Here then I had at least got a theory by which to work.

Alfred Russel Wallace, who simultaneously and independently arrived at an identical theory, also found his inspiration in the *Essay.* As the crucial spark for this epochal idea alone, Malthus's place in history is secure.

CURRICULUM VITAE

Depending upon the source one chooses, Thomas Robert Malthus was born either on St. Valentine's Day, February 14, 1766, or on the 13th. In any case, according to a brief biography of the essayist by Lord Keynes, Jean Jacques Rousseau and David Hume visited Malthus's father three weeks after his son's birth. Keynes suggests these "two fairy godmothers . . . may be presumed to have assigned to the infant with a kiss diverse intellectual gifts." The baby was not so lucky in another respect: Malthus had a harelip which rendered his speech defective throughout his life.

Malthus was born into a middle-class family at a small but elegant mansion in farming country near Dorking, just south of London. Among his forebears were the Vicar of Northolt, the apothecary to King William, and a director of the South Sea Company. Malthus's father, Daniel, was an Oxford-educated country gentleman, who led an earnestly intellectual life. Daniel corresponded with Rousseau and, according to family legend, with Voltaire. Young Robert was brought up in a world of very advanced ideas.

James Bonar, a late 19th-Century biographer, described the England of Malthus's youth:

> The early life of Malthus . . . coincides of necessity with the accomplishment of England's greatest industrial revolution. Malthus was born in 1766, three years after the Peace of Paris. There was an end, for the time, to foreign wars; and trade was making a brave start. The discoveries of coal and iron in northern England, going hand in hand with the inventions of cotton-spinning and weaving, were beginning to convert the poorest counties into the richest, upsetting the political balance. The new science of chemistry had begun to prove its usefulness. Wedgwood was perfecting his earthenware, Brindley cutting his canals, Telford laying out his roads, Watt building his steam-engines. England in Roman days had been a granary; in later ages she had been a pastureground; she was now becoming the land of machinery and manufacture, as well as the centre of foreign trade.

Malthus was tutored at home during his early years, then went to Jesus College, Cambridge, which was then becoming a center of intellectual ferment. He took his Holy Orders about 1788, but spent little time at his ecclesiastical post.

He married in 1804, the year after the second edition of the *Essay* was published. Of his three children, two were daughters, one of whom died young. According to Lord Keynes, Malthus has no descendants today.

In 1805, Malthus was appointed to the college established by the East India Company for the training of young men entering its service. He apparently enjoyed teaching, for he remained in his Chair at Haileybury for the rest of his life. And his students apparently enjoyed him, for they called him "Pop." A Whig, he was by no means isolated from current political and economic ideas and Mrs. Malthus's evening parties drew the elite of the London scientific world.

His duties as a professor included occasional preaching, frequently on the benevolence of God. His continuing religious dedication is obvious, particularly in the conclusion of the first edition of his *Essay*, where he defends God against those who complained that He brought misery, the "checks" to population, into man's life. Even in the more worldly second edition, he saw the Creator's plan thus:

> . . . we can have no reason to impeach the justice of the Deity because his general laws make this virtue [restraint from marriage] necessary

and punish our offences against it by the evils attendant upon vice, and the pains that accompany the various forms of premature death. A really virtuous society, such as I have supposed, would avoid these evils. It is the apparent object of the Creator to deter us from vice by the pains which accompany it, and to lead us to virtue by the happiness that it produces.

Malthus produced so many books, articles, and papers in his field of political economy as to suggest that early 19th-Century academe had its own version of the "publish or perish" dictum. Perhaps his greatest legacy in the field is the long series of letters exchanged during his friendly debate with David Ricardo. Their friendship, begun with Malthus's hesitant self-introduction in 1811, lasted until Ricardo's death in 1823. Malthus said of Ricardo:

> I never loved anybody out of my own family so much. Our interchange of opinions was so unreserved, and the object after which we were both enquiring was so entirely the truth ... that I cannot but think we sooner or later must have agreed.

In his biography, Lord Keynes described the varying approaches of Malthus and Ricardo, and then cast his own vote:

> Here indeed, are to be found the seeds of economic theory, and also the divergent lines—so divergent at the outset that the destination can scarcely be recognised as the same until it is reached—along which the subject can be developed. Ricardo is investigating the theory of the *distribution* of the product in conditions of equilibrium, and Malthus is concerned with what determines the *volume* of output day by day in the real world. Malthus is dealing with the monetary economy in which we all happen to live; Ricardo with the abstraction of a neutral money economy. ...
>
> One cannot rise from a perusal of this correspondence without a feeling that the almost total obliteration of Malthus's line of approach and the complete domination of Ricardo's for a period of a hundred years has been a disaster to the progress of economics. Time after time in these letters Malthus is talking plain sense, the force of which Ricardo with his head in the clouds wholly fails to comprehend.

Applying his "plain sense" to another field, Malthus believed that authors who were proclaiming the perfectibility of man and society could not ignore the tendency of population to outgrow food supplies. The down-to-earth scholar took on the idealists in 1798, with the publication of the first edition of his *Essay*. He was 32.

His concern for getting to the truth of the human condition led him into extensive research and travel to find evidence to corroborate his theories. His findings and expanded thought led to the second edition in 1803. He continued to expound his themes in additional revised editions, the last in 1826, and in an article for the 1824 supplement to the *Encyclopaedia Britannica*. Malthus died at age 68 in 1834.

THE BEST OF TIMES, THE WORST OF TIMES

Like the rumblings of the scientific revolutions, those of the American and the French revolutions promising universal equality were heard in all Western nations at the turn of the 19th Century. Charles Dickens was to call this "the best of times . . . the worst of times." Liberals dreamed of drastic changes in the social order which would enable man to achieve his potential best. Those in power had nightmares of mass uprisings which would sweep away their established rule. The English Poor Laws—in effect since the time of Queen Elizabeth—quite obviously were not alleviating the lot of the poverty-stricken; rather, the poor grew in number. The English aristocracy feared any worsening of conditions might well trigger a revolution.

It was a time when theories abounded—aired in multitudinous pamphlets and shouted in the public houses. An idea was advanced and immediately answered, often with a volley of tracts. Everyone, it seemed, had his own intellectual foxhole. In Malthus's opinion:

> The late rage for wide and unrestrained speculation seems to have been a kind of mental intoxication, arising perhaps from the great and unexpected discoveries which had been made in various branches of science. To men elate and giddy with such successes, everything appeared to be within the grasp of human powers; and under this illusion they confounded subjects where no real progress could be proved with those where the progress had been marked, certain, and acknowledged.

It was a time of war and uneasy peace. Perhaps the radical concepts in Malthus's *Essay* were as widely accepted as they were, despite much dissent, because England was in and out of war, and the island nation could well imagine the horrors of food shortages. Five years of poor harvests preceded the publication of the first edition; severe food shortages continued through the first quarter of the 19th Century.

England's population was growing rapidly, although the surprising dimensions of the growth were not then known. The first British census (1801) was not taken until three years after the *Essay* first appeared. Compulsory registration of births and deaths did not begin until 1837, three years after Malthus died. Until then, church records of baptisms and burials served as the vital statistics of the realm. Nevertheless, with his acute interest in the economic situation, Malthus recognized that the poor were increasing with a consequent growth in unemployment.

Demographers have established that England's death rate began a long and steady decline in 1740, whereas the birth rate remained fairly high until the last quarter of the 19th Century. Offhand references in Malthus's *Essay* bring home sharply what a high death rate meant: "One out of five children is a very unusually small proportion to lose in the course of ten years," he said. And later, "The average age of marriage will almost always be much nearer to the average age of death than marriage is to birth . . ."

In 1740 both birth and death rates were about 36 in England and Wales; in 1840, the birth rate was 37, the death rate was down to 23. In the half century before Malthus wrote his *Essay*, England's population grew sizeably. And, during the years he was revising it, the population took on a new pattern of very rapid growth. England and Wales had an estimated population of about 6 million in 1700; the 1801 Census counted 8.6 million; the 1901 Census counted a fourfold increase to 32.5 million. This rapid growth occurred despite massive emigration. Farming techniques improved, industry demanded more people to man its factories, industrial England traded with the world and was able to support her additional millions partly by increased agricultural production but mainly by food imports. Although poverty was not banished, the population of England boomed.

Amid the turmoil of ideas, Malthus's were not new. Forty years earlier, Dr. Robert Wallace mentioned excessive population growth as an obstacle to a more perfect human society. In his first preface, Malthus described his debt to, and differences from, earlier writers:

> It is an obvious truth, which has been taken notice of by many writers, that population must always be kept down to the level of the means of subsistence; but no writer, that the Author recollects, has inquired particularly into the means by which this level is effected; and it is a view of these means, which forms, to his mind, the strongest obstacle in the way to any very great improvement of society.

THE SIX EDITIONS, AND HOW THEY GREW

Malthus wrote his *Essay on the Principle of Population* to put in order thoughts roused in continuing discussion with his father, Daniel, over the "future improvement of society." The seed of the argument lay in some proposals by William Godwin, a utopian anarchist, political philosopher, and sometime novelist.

Godwin's treatises criticizing established society and proposing a system based on reason and innate human justice rather than on law had attracted a substantial and vociferous following, including the poet Percy Bysshe Shelley. . . .

Daniel Malthus supported Godwin's convictions. His son Robert thought Godwin, and others who postulated ideal societies, made a fatal error in ignoring population growth and the forces which checked it. If ideal societies were established, he reasoned, hunger, jealousy, and antagonism would soon mar these perfect states and restore the familiar competitive world.

His *Essay* held that the various proposals for the perfectibility of society had not been subjected to careful and dispassionate scrutiny. This first edition presented an untypically abstract formulation of Malthus's understanding of population growth and checks, with brief references to existing and former societies. It was marked by a philosophic, even theological, acceptance of the demographic situation as Malthus saw it.

The full title of the first edition was: *An Essay on the Principle of Population as it affects the Future Improvement of Society, with remarks on the Speculations of Mr. Godwin, M. Condorcet, and other writers*. The concluding chapter heading suggested a somber outlook indeed: "Moral evil probably necessary to the production of moral excellence."

The second edition took a more hopeful view. It was entitled: *An Essay on the Principle of Population or, A view of its past and present effects on Human Happiness; with an enquiry into our prospects respecting the future removal or mitigation of the evils which it occasions*. The final chapter heading carried a definite banner of hope: "Of our rational expectations respecting the future improvement of society."

Fully half the second edition was devoted to a detailed examination of how the principle of population worked and identification of the checks which operated in past and contemporary societies. In this extensive revision, Malthus adjusted and fleshed out his basic theory. His approach, this time, was altogether worldly. The second edition was cast in the terms of politics, economics, and history.

He refuted the systems of equality suggested by Godwin *et al.*, and applied his own analysis to the economic and political problems of contemporary England: the Poor Laws, the Corn Laws, the optimum proportions of agriculture and commerce for a national economy. For instance, Malthus warned England that the new nation, America, would soon be setting up mills and factories and processing its own raw materials. England, he said, must be prepared to cease counting on America both as a supplier of raw goods and as a buyer of finished goods.

The last quarter of the book introduced his most important new principle: the possibility of encouraging moral restraint as a means of checking population growth with a minimum of human unhappiness.

Between the first (1798) and second (1803) editions, Malthus developed—from a reading of history, from current records, and from first-hand observations—the factual basis and substantive analysis he preferred to his first rather abstract approach. Among the sources cited are Robertson's *History of America* (1780), *Voyage dans l'Intérieur de l'Afrique*, Cook's accounts of his three voyages, Hume's *Essays*, the Bible, Tacitus's *De Moribus Germanorum*, Gibbon's *Decline and Fall of the Roman Empire*, Tooke's *View of the Russian Empire*, and Plato's *The Republic*.

More current sources included parish registries, scientific papers, transactions of meetings, population abstracts, and bills of mortality. While, as Malthus noted, the first edition was written "on the impulse of the occasion, and from the few materials which were then within my reach in a country situation," he completely overcame this deficiency. The second edition—almost 600 pages of small type in the *Everyman* edition—is about four times the length of the first.

In his research on population growth, he found "much more had been done than I had been aware of . . . and the most violent remedies proposed, so long ago as the times of Plato and Aristotle." Many of his contemporaries, he reported, had treated the subject "in such a manner . . . as to create a natural surprise that it had not excited more of the public attention."

Some of the information he gathered during two European tours was too subjective to be of scientific value. About Norway—the country to which he gave highest marks for a robust economy and an awareness of the dangers of rapidly growing population—he said:

> I particularly remarked that the sons of housemen and the farmers' boys were fatter, larger, and had better calves to their legs than boys of the same age and in similar situations in England.

Why the great variation in tone and content between the first two editions? Bonar suggested the "happy coincidence" that England was at war when the first was written and at peace five years later. Whatever the reason, one critic said that Malthus's changes, particularly the advocacy of moral restraint, indicated the essayist had abandoned his original argument. Another suggested it was Godwin himself, in a letter to Malthus (now lost), who recommended prudence to circumvent the dreadful checks.

As new information accumulated, and in order to respond to criticism and questions stirred by his work, Malthus revised and added to his *Essay* through a total of six editions. However, the later editions (1806, 1807, 1817, 1826) differed little from the second.

Joseph J. Spengler, Professor of Economics at Duke University, found increasingly in later editions the assertion that population growth depends on the availability of employment. In Malthus's *Principle of Political Economy* (1820), Spengler found this idea most fully developed: that the availability of sustenance determines the upper bound of population size, but within this limit the amount of available and prospective employment conditions the rise and fall of population.

THE PRINCIPLE OF POPULATION

Malthus's principle is succinct. After stating that "the power of population is indefinitely greater than the power in the earth to produce subsistence for man," he continued:

> Population, when unchecked, increases in a geometrical ratio. Subsistence only increases in an arithmetical ratio. A slight acquaintance with numbers will show the immensity of the first power in comparison of the second.
>
> By that law of our nature which makes food necessary to the life of man, the effects of these two unequal powers must be kept equal.
>
> This implies a strong and constantly operating check on population from the difficulty of subsistence. This difficulty must fall somewhere; and must necessarily be severely felt by a large portion of mankind. . . .
>
> Among plants and animals [the effects of this great restrictive law] are waste of seed, sickness, and premature death. Among mankind, misery and vice. . . . This natural inequality of the two powers of population, and of production in the earth, and that great law of our nature which must constantly keep their effects equal, form the great difficulty that to me appears insurmountable in the way to perfectibility of society. . . . I see no way by which man can escape from the weight of this law which pervades all animated nature. No fancied equality, no agrarian regulations in their utmost extent, could remove the pressure of it even for a single century.

In addition to the "positive" population checks (the "misery and vice" of famine, war, pestilence; "vicious customs with respect to women, great cities, unwholesome manufactures, luxury"), Malthus also noted the "preventive" check of restraint from early marriage during hard times, which tended to lower the number of births.

He cited the known doubling of the population in 25 years in the United States of America as proof that such a rate of increase was possible, though perhaps near a maximum.

Malthus said that, with great effort, a country might double its agricultural production in 25 years, but that it was impossible to double production again, to four times the original output, in the succeeding 25 years. The utmost one could hope for, he surmised, was an increase again equal to the original production: an arithmetical increase.

If, to begin with, the food supply met the needs of the population, it would again be sufficient after both had doubled in the first 25-year interval. If, during the succeeding 25 years, population again doubled but food only increased by the original amount, the food available per capita would be reduced by a fourth. With numbers pressing on marginal subsistence Malthus saw the positive and preventive checks rigidly limiting further population growth.

Malthus was positive that in the end the checks would come into action:

> The different modes which nature takes to prevent, or repress a re-
> dundant population, do not appear, indeed, to us so certain and regular;
> but though we cannot always predict the mode, we may with certainty
> predict the fact. If the proportion of births to deaths for a few years in-
> dicate an increase of numbers much beyond the proportional increased
> or acquired produce of the country, we may be perfectly certain, that
> unless an emigration takes place, the deaths will shortly exceed the
> births. . . .

Actually, this tendency to geometric increase is a property of all living things. The *potential* for rapid increase is much greater in agricultural crops and herds than in human populations. Crop plants have a potential doubling time of less than one year, a fact which is utilized by plant breeders to multiply new strains with fantastic speed.

In agricultural practice, however, making two blades of grass or two bushels of wheat or rice grow where one grew before is no easy matter. Most of the good agricultural land in the world is already under cultivation. The land available for crops remains effectively constant from year to year. It is being farmed by methods—and with resources—which change very slowly. There is no question that improved techniques, better varieties, and increased use of fertilizer could provide an adequate diet for all the world's people. Agricultural production, world-wide, is currently increasing by about 1 per cent a year, which will double production in 75 years. By that time, at the present rate of increase, the number of people would have grown to over 13 billion, four times the present population.

In the second edition, Malthus conceded that "the comparison between the increase of population and food . . . had not perhaps been stated with sufficient force and precision." He made less of the ratios and relied more heavily on his many examples of populations which grew when food was plentiful, only to suffer cruel ravages when supplies were scarce.

Malthus held that food scarcity was the ultimate barrier against which population growth faltered. The action of both the preventive and positive checks he related to the food supply.

For instance, as people weakened from hunger, they were more vulnerable to plagues. Thus sickness actually caused death, although scarcity of food had paved the way. (WHO has recently stated that in Latin America "among the children aged 1 to 4 about half the deaths are attributable to malnutrition.") The quantity of employment, he said, while related to food production, did not vary as much from year to year as did food supplies. Therefore, it was a much steadier check, and, since it encouraged or discouraged marriage, acted as a preventive, rather than a harsher, positive check.

Malthus dramatically described the awesome power of famine in proscribing man's increase in one of the few highly colored passages in his generally restrained prose:

> Famine seems to be the last, most dreadful resource of nature. The power of population is so superior to the power in the earth to produce subsistance for man, that premature death must in some shape or other visit the human race. The vices of mankind are active and able ministers of depopulation. They are the precursors in the great army of destruction; and often finish the dreadful work themselves. But should they fail in this war of extermination, sickly seasons, epidemics, pestilence, and plague, advance in terrific array, and sweep off their thousands and ten thousands. Should success be still incomplete, gigantic inevitable famine stalks in the rear, and with one mighty blow, levels the population with the food of the world.

MALTHUS'S HOPE: MORAL RESTRAINT

In the first edition, Malthus's proposals for limiting the misery resulting from overpopulation were little more than recommendations of various new measures for dealing with the poor. Not until the second edition did he declare that moral restraint from imprudent marriage should be encouraged in order to stave off, not population growth, but the vices and miseries which are the natural checks to population growth.

He did note, in the first *Essay*, that a preventive check existed in England and in "all old states," when some individuals chose to put off marriage because of financial hardship or the exigencies of social ambition.

Malthus was distressed to note that restraint from marriage, "almost necessarily, though not absolutely," resulted in vice. Although he frowned on imprudent early marriage, he had compassion for those who,

> . . . guided either by a stronger passion or a weaker judgment, break through these restraints; and it would be hard indeed if the gratifications of so delightful a passion as virtuous love, did not sometimes more than counterbalance all its attendant evils.

He was certain, however, that the consequences of imprudent marriages usually justified his forebodings.

Moral restraint, as introduced in the second *Essay*, was no haphazard natural check but a carefully defined series of stages which Malthus hoped would comprise a program to be generally encouraged, especially among the poor. He called it "a restraint from marriage from prudential motives, with a conduct strictly moral during the period of this restraint."

First, then, moral restraint demanded the postponement of marriage until the individuals were sure of sufficient income to support a family without relying on the state for aid. Malthus here meant a purposeful, knowledgeable decision by the parties involved, rather than the preventive check of the first edition, where restraint from marriage was "unconnected with its consequences."

Second, moral restraint imposed complete sexual continence before the postponed marriage. The probability that this requirement would not be met Malthus allowed to be the only plausible objection to his plan. Curiously, he countered this objection by saying that sexual vices were not

> . . . the only vices which are to be considered in a moral question; [nor are they] . . . even the greatest and the most degrading to the human character. They can rarely or never be committed without producing unhappiness somewhere or other, and therefore ought always to be strongly reprobated: but there are other vices the effects of which are still more pernicious . . . Powerful as may be the temptations to a breach of chastity, I am inclined to think that they are impotent in comparison of the temptations arising from continued distress.

Malthus did not believe the greatest threat to chastity came from a code of celibacy before marriage:

> . . . marriage has been found to be by no means a complete remedy. . . . Add to this, that abject poverty, particularly when joined with idleness, is a state the most unfavourable to chastity that can well be conceived. The passion is as strong, or nearly so, as in other situations: and every restraint on it from personal respect, or a sense of morality, is generally removed.

The third aspect of moral restraint is most surprising: that within marriage there should be no restriction on family size. While this was not part of the definition first given in the *Essay*, scholars accept it as part of Malthus's thought. In the *Essay* he referred to contraceptives as "improper arts," and in the appendix to the 1817 edition made his position completely clear:

> . . . I should always particularly reprobate any artificial and unnatural modes of checking population, both on account of their immorality and their tendency to remove a necessary stimulus to industry. If it were possible for each married couple to limit by a wish the number of their

children, there is certainly reason to fear that the indolence of the human race would be very greatly increased, and that neither the population of individual countries nor of the whole earth would ever reach its natural and proper extent.

Malthus's enthusiasm for the efficacy of moral restraint was unbounded: "the only line of conduct approved by nature, reason, and religion."

He built what looks suspiciously like an entire war on poverty on the single pillar of moral restraint:

> The operation of the preventive check in this way, by constantly keeping the population within the limits of the food, though constantly following its increase, would give a real value to the rise of wages and the sums saved by laborers before marriage . . . all abject poverty would be removed from society; or would at least be confined to a very few.

The chances for establishing a general practice of moral restraint, he felt, were fair. He acknowledged that moral restraint

> . . . does not at present prevail much among the male part of the society . . . [but] it can scarcely be doubted that in modern Europe a much larger proportion of women pass a considerable part of their lives in the exercise of this virtue than in past times and among uncivilised nations.

SOCIAL IMPLICATIONS: HARDHEARTED OF HARDHEADED?

Although Malthus believed the government had a "very considerable" obligation "in giving the best direction to those checks which in some form or other must necessarily take place," his conclusion was that the poor themselves must accept responsibility for their condition.

With typical bluntness, he said it was necessary to

> . . . impress as strongly as possible on the public mind that it is not the duty of man simply to propagate his species, but to propagate virtue and happiness; and that, if he has not a tolerably fair prospect of doing this, he is by no means called upon to leave descendants.

He condemned the Poor Laws for removing any need for prudent doubts among those poor who might otherwise hesitate to marry. By providing precious food for the poorest, least industrious citizens, the laws deprived those who were more industrious of their just share and thus were likely to push more people into dependence on the state.

"Fortunately for England," said Malthus, "a spirit of independence still remains among the peasantry. The poor-laws are strongly calculated to eradicate this spirit." The laws, he said, diminished "both the power and the will to save, among the common people, and thus to weaken one of the strongest incentives to sobriety and industry, and consequently to happiness."

But it was not only as a weapon against poverty and hunger, or as an incentive to sobriety and industry, that Malthus recommended the practice of moral restraint. He thought it could be a strong buffer to the tide of revolution which many feared would shortly sweep across the Channel. He believed that:

> A mob which is generally the growth of a redundant population goaded by resentment for real sufferings, but totally ignorant of the quarter from which they originate, is of all monsters the most fatal to freedom.

The poor, who quite rightly disliked their position, tended to blame the government in power, and this was the seed of revolution. The prevention, Malthus said, was to teach the poor the true cause of their condition—imprudent marriage—and explain to them that "the withholding of the supplies of labour is the only possible way of really raising its price, and that they themselves, being the possessors of this commodity, have alone the power to do this."

He stated further:

> If these truths were by degrees more generally known . . . the lower classes of people, as a body, would become more peaceable and orderly, would be less inclined to tumultuous proceedings in seasons of scarcity, and would at all times be less influenced by inflammatory and seditious publications, from knowing how little the price of labour and the means of supporting a family depend on a revolution.

Malthus's theories, and the political and social views he derived from them, fully supported the *status quo*. He had no doubt that he was revealing a "natural law" of society. He was very skeptical about inherent "natural rights":

> Nothing would so effectually counteract the mischiefs occasioned by Mr. Paine's Rights of Man as a general knowledge of the real rights of man. What these rights are it is not my business at present to explain; but there is one right which man has generally been thought to possess, which I am confident he neither does nor can possess—a right to subsistence when his labour will not fairly purchase it. Our laws indeed say that he has this right, and bind the society to furnish employment and food to those who cannot get them in the regular market; but in so doing they attempt to reverse the laws of nature; and it is in consequence to be expected, not only that they should fail in their object,

but that the poor, who were intended to be benefited, should suffer most cruelly from the inhuman deceit thus practised upon them.

In another statement he recognized that "social laws" did enhance the "right to subsist," but that this right appears not to be divinely ordained:

> The Abbe Raynal has said that "Avant toutes les loix sociales l'homme avoit le droit de subsister" ["Before all social laws, man has the right to survival"]. He might with just as much propriety have said that, before the institution of social laws, every man had a right to live a hundred years. Undoubtedly he had then, and has still, a good right to live a hundred years, nay a thousand *if he can,* without interfering with the right of others to live; but the affair in both cases is principally an affair of powers not of right. Social laws very greatly increase this power, by enabling a much greater number to subsist than could subsist without them, and so far very greatly enlarge *le droit de subsister;* but neither before nor after the institution of social laws could an unlimited number subsist, and before as well as since, he who ceased to have the power ceased to have the right.

Obviously, Malthus would stand aghast at the modern welfare state— whose existence has been made possible by the remarkable increases in productivity since his time.

Perhaps in answer to the charges of social injustice, Malthus occasionally stressed his liberal persuasion. For all his claim that imprudent marriage is an "immoral act," for instance, he stated firmly that the nation could not take away a man's right to marry whenever he chooses.

And Malthus wanted to improve the social status of single women, not only so that women would feel less compelled to marry, but also in deference to "the plainest principles of equity." Malthus was for a general system of public education, as a means of teaching the poor his own ideas of "the real nature of their condition," and also to render them less vulnerable to the spell of "interested and ambitious demagogues."

Even his suggestion for reducing population growth was basically democratic—if somewhat naïve: give the poor the facts and they will surely act wisely in their own best interests.

REACTIONS: RUMPUS AND RESPECTABILITY

Reaction to the *Essay* was instinctively violent. Lord Keynes describes the magnitude of Malthus's suggestion that man restrain his procreative powers:

> The voice of objective reason had been raised against a deep instinct which the evolutionary struggle has been implanting from the com-

mencement of life; and man's mind, in the conscious pursuit of happiness, was daring to demand the reins of government from out of the hands of the unconscious urge for mere predominant survival.

The public returned a volley of outraged protest. Typical of the sniping was this comment by William Hazlitt, a combative critic and essayist in London's literary and political world, who said Malthus had produced:

> . . . a complete theory of population, in which it is clearly proved that the poor have no right to live any longer than the rich will let them. . . . Is it an argument that because the pressure of a scarcity does not fall directly upon those who can bear it best, viz. the very rich, that it should therefore fall upon those, (sic) who can bear it least, viz., on the very poor? Unless Mr. Malthus can contrive to starve someone, he thinks he does nothing.

Malthus had brought a new subject to the tireless pamphleteers of London and the universities, a subject relatively unexplored, with overtones of philosophy and politics, and—though who was to say it then—an undertone of psychology. Comments and protests appeared in letters, humor magazines, parliamentary speeches, and scholarly and popular journals. Many responses showed careless reading of Malthus, or no reading at all; some were fanciful exaggeration. Others constituted thoughtful, well-founded criticism.

Opponents attacked Malthus's rather loose and arbitrary exposition of the geometrical and arithmetical growth ratios of food and population. The seeming precision and authority, critics felt, helped popularize his theory. In Hazlitt's opinion: "Mathematical terms carry with them an imposing air of accuracy and profundity, and ought, therefore, to be applied strictly, and with greatest caution, or not at all."

Some dismissed Malthus's argument as a truism. Obviously there can be no more people than the food to feed them; obviously population stays within bounds. Samuel Taylor Coleridge, who attended Cambridge when Malthus was in a position of some authority there and apparently had reason to resent the essayist, made this marginal note on his copy of the *Essay:*

> Are we now to have a quarto to teach us that great misery and great vice arise from poverty, and that there must be poverty in its worst shape wherever there are more mouths than loaves and more Heads than Brains?

For all the barrage, the *Essay* gathered more and more adherents. By 1820, the nay-sayers had been so ineffectual that William Godwin himself felt called upon to publish a lengthy refutation. The good standing of Malthus's theory can be surmised from the fact that the self-aggrandizing Godwin took pains to remind his readers that it was his own work which stimulated Malthus's original effort.

Malthus lived to see the revision of the English Poor Laws in the direction he had suggested. The stern new laws would not encourage anyone to marry out of a certainty that his children would be raised by the state. According to D. V. Glass, Professor of Sociology at the London School of Economics, Malthus's views colored British attitudes towards social services for a century or more.

The reaction in America was preponderantly negative, although far less attention was paid the *Essay*—a scattering of brief comments, mostly in journals. The first American edition, reprinted from the third London edition, was published in 1809. Commentators in the young and optimistic nation simply felt there was no shortage of land. If there ever should be? Well, a man's ingenuity and a little sweat could make the earth yield twice as much and twice as much again.

The *Essay* was translated into German and French during Malthus's lifetime. In Germany, hard times brought on a short-lived and inconclusive government-ordained Malthusian regime of restrictions on marriage.

In England, arguments about the principle of population raged long after Malthus's death in 1834. By the last half of the 19th Century, the brunt of public attack had moved to the neo-Malthusian proposal that births should be controlled within marriage by what Malthus had once decried as "improper arts."

The manifold developments of the 19th Century had the greatest bearing on the long-term reaction to Malthus's theory. Cities sprang up and spread. Power, production, and transportation facilities were invented and put to use everywhere. By the end of that century, the major checks to population—famine, plague, and war—had been greatly mitigated for that part of mankind living in Europe.

The new inventions and machines led to an outpouring of industrial production which not only revolutionized life at home, but also prodded the major European nations to seek foreign colonies as consumers and to supply raw materials. These colonies shipped a continuing stream of foodstuffs. New methods applied to domestic agriculture greatly increased yields. It seemed that Europe need never again fear empty larders.

Developments in medicine and public health paralleled gains in industry and agriculture. Together with the sustained adequate food supplies, these innovations led to rapid declines in mortality. However, birth rates remained high, and population grew rapidly. Although there was some unemployment and working conditions were horrendous, most of the additional people either were absorbed into the new industrial plants or migrated to the colonies.

While war was not eliminated on the continent in the 19th Century, the almost continuous clashes of the 18th Century were over.

In the second half of the century individuals began to limit the size of their families and national birth rates slowly dropped. The gloomy spectre of masses of starving people receded. Malthus was "proved" a false prophet.

Nevertheless, Malthus remained an important figure in economic history. In 1921, The Macmillan Company of New York and London published parallel chapters from the first and second editions in its *Economics Classics* series. In 1926, the Royal Economic Society reproduced the first edition:

> . . . with the least possible change, preserving its features not only in the lines, pages, and spellings but, it is hoped with fair success, in colour of paper and style of binding.

A unique example of the spontaneous application of moral restraint was Ireland. Contrary to the popular view, it was well before the terrible potato famine of 1848–1852 that the Irish people evolved a custom of late marriages which has continued for over a century. Prophetically, Malthus had warned of the dangers of adopting the potato as a one-crop basic staple:

> In Ireland, or in any other country, where the common food is potatoes, and every man who wishes to marry may obtain a piece of ground sufficient, when planted with this root, to support a family, prizes may be given till the treasury is exhausted for essays on the best means of employing the poor. . . . When the commons were all divided, and difficulties began to occur in procuring potato-grounds, the habit of early marriages, which had been introduced, would occasion the most complicated distress; and when, from the increasing population, and diminishing sources of subsistence, the average growth of potatoes was not more than the average consumption, a scarcity of potatoes would be, in every respect, as probable as a scarcity of wheat at present; and, when it did arrive, it would be beyond all comparison more dreadful.

This is almost an exact description of what was to happen in Ireland. The people of Ireland drastically modified their traditional pattern of early marriage. They adopted, whether or not purely by coincidence, the "preventive checks" which Malthus advocated. Ireland's population has declined from 8 million in 1846 to less than 3 million today. As far as many individuals are concerned, this has definitely been a painful and frustrating solution of the population problem. That it is infinitely better than famine can hardly be gainsaid.

The controversy centering around Malthus's views continues. A recent critique of Malthus by a British economist, Kenneth Smith, notes that the world has been unfair to those critics of Malthus who "forecast that population would both grow, and grow richer. . . ." This did indeed happen for a time, and in certain fortunate areas.

Smith's disdain of Malthus leads him to posit a principle of indefinite growth which is as naïve in its way as some of Malthus:

> Man and his food supplies are governed by similar principles of growth, and which can outstrip the other will depend on the relative rates of growth of each. With regard to minerals, which have been laid down once and for all, the annual produce is great or small according to the effort put forth and the skill with which it is applied. The limit in regard to plants and animals is space; in regard to minerals the exhaustion of the deposits. But these are long-run positions. In the short run no principle emerges which makes it impossible for man to cater for his growing numbers.

Smith did see another check beginning to operate:

> In the days when Malthus wrote, space was not a limiting consideration. It is possible that it now is; that the long-run position is being reached; that the world is full.

Writing only 15 years ago, Smith cited populations, such as some in Asia and Latin America, which grew enormously (after medical science reduced the incidence of disease), without having increasing backlogs of food to encourage such growth.

Today the food crisis is engulfing these very populations which obviously did not grow beyond the point of minimal subsistence, but which are now confronting—*in the short run*—the action of the primary checks envisioned by Malthus.

Malthus's ideas of the dynamics of population change were elementary, and his suggestions for checking multiplication of people were naïve. Yet the continuing controversy which has centered around his name has highlighted a problem which is central in world affairs today, and for which a solution has not yet been found.

SOURCES

Bonar, James. *Parson Malthus.* Glasgow: James Maclehouse, 1881.

———. *Malthus and His Work.* New York: Harper and Brothers, 1885.

Brown, Lester R. *Increasing World Food Output: Problems and Prospects,* U.S. Department of Agriculture Foreign Agricultural Economic Report No. 25. Washington, April 1965.

Carr-Saunders, A. M. *World Population*. Oxford: Clarendon Press, 1936.

Glass, D. V. *Introduction to Malthus*. London: Watts and Company, 1953.

Keynes, John Maynard. "Robert Malthus" in *Essays in Biography*. New York: W. W. Norton & Company, Inc., 1963. (Note: First published in Great Britain in 1933.)

Malthus, T. R. *An Essay on the Principle of Population*. (Parallel chapters from the First and Second Editions.) New York: The Macmillan Company, 1921.

————. *An Essay on Population*. Volume One. London: J. M. Dent and Sons, Ltd., and New York: E. P. Dutton and Company, no date.

————. *An Essay on Population*. Volume Two. London: J. M. Dent and Sons, Ltd., and New York: E. P. Dutton and Company, no date.

Smith, Kenneth. *The Malthusian Controversy*. London: Routledge and Kegan Paul, 1951.

5

Marx versus Malthus:
The Men and the Symbols

William Petersen

I

In a number of recent discussions of how to cope with population pressure in underdeveloped countries, Malthus and Marx have been taken as symbols of the two principal alternatives open to policy-makers.[1] A compilation of Marx's own writings on Malthus, thus, was introduced with the assertion that "if the social struggles of the early nineteenth century were essentially summed up in the controversy between Malthus and Ricardo, those of our own times are perhaps not unfairly summed up in that between Malthusians and Marxists."[2] ...

The common designation of Malthus as a "reactionary"—that is, the other pole from a Marxian "progressive"—ignores important parallels between the two men, not only in their economic analyses but even in their social philosophies. Specifically, when Marx's criticisms of Malthus's principle of population are examined, it becomes evident that neither Marx himself nor any Marxist has developed a population theory to replace the Malthusian one they rejected. The appealing simplicity of a Marx-Malthus axis as a framework for population analysis has been achieved by amalgamating divergent and even contradictory theories and policies into "Malthus" and into "Marx"; so that once the two names have recalled to progressives their faith that social planning is superior to a *laissez-faire* system, "Malthusian" proponents of family-planning are attacked by "Marxians" who believe that the rational control of human fertility is iniquitous.

Reprinted from *Population Review*, 1, no. 2 (July, 1957), pp. 21–32, and William Petersen, *The Politics of Population* (Garden City, N.Y.: Anchor Books, Doubleday & Co., 1965), by permission of the author and the publisher. Footnotes have been renumbered because of deletion of a portion of the original text.

II

That Malthus wrote his *Essay on the Principle of Population* in a political context is a commonplace. In its very title, the first edition was directed against two of the more extravagant of the eighteenth-century perfectibilists—Condorcet, who foresaw not only the complete abolition of war and disease but the indefinite prolongation of human life, and Godwin, who looked forward to the wholly rational society where no one would work more than a half-hour a day. In any case, the dispute would have probably been largely in political rather than scientific terms; for Malthus's "principle of population" was both a convenient rationalization for resolute defenders of the status quo and a block to the facile millennium of the Jacobins. "It is only to be expected that the early socialists would be hostile to the Malthusian theory. From Dr. Charles Hall . . . to Marx, there is a clear-cut repudiation. At bottom they have a different rating of humanity and human institutions, different social and political aims, and a different expectation of the future."[3]

The division along political lines was not, however, either necessary or complete. Even Cobbett, who later termed Malthus's population theory "infamous and really diabolical," a "mixture of madness and blasphemy," began by endorsing it—before it had been used in the debate over the poor law.[4] And on the other side, Nassau Senior, whom Marx attacked in language as strong as his usual epithets to characterize Malthus, was also among the first to challenge the *Essay*.

In any case, Marx might well have stood above the usual political division. He did not typically defend the views of the men he and Engels dubbed "utopians"; and the theory of such an economist as Ricardo, Malthus's good friend, he treated with respect. His total rejection of Malthus is remarkable, moreover, for on some fundamental issues the difference between these two was smaller than that between Marx and the classical school as a whole. This is particularly so on the key question of whether a general glut can develop in a capitalist economy. By the classical theory of the market, the very production of goods distributes the power to purchase them; and local disturbances, the consequence of having produced particular goods for which there is no demand, are adjusted automatically through a change in prices and so do not accumulate into an overall disruption of the system. A general crisis, which for Marx was capitalism's inevitable end, was thus impossible. The only thinker in the main line of nineteenth-century economics who recognized the possibility of general underconsumption was Malthus; and Keynes, who brought the principle of effective demand back into twentieth-century theory, fully acknowledged his debt to him.

"It is a most important error," Malthus wrote, "to couple the passion for expenditure and the passion for accumulation together, as if they were of the same nature." Manufacturers and merchants "produce very largely and consume sparingly," for their whole way of life induces them to live ascetically and to accumulate more capital. But if luxuries are manufactured and not consumed, then the workers who produce them will be thrown out of work and will be unable to buy even necessities; and the underconsumption will become general. To prevent this, "there must be a considerable class of persons who have both the will and the power to consume more material wealth than they produce, or the mercantile classes could not continue profitably to produce so much more than they consume." These unproductive consumers are the landlords and their servants of various types, and this seemingly parasitic class is thus seen to serve the function of keeping the economy in a healthy state. "A country such as our own, which has been rich and populous, would, with too parsimonious habits, infallibly become poor and comparatively unpeopled."[5]

How important underconsumption is in Marx's theory of capitalist crises is a matter of dispute even among Marxian economists,[6] but all agree that, while less important in his system than the long-run fall in the rate of profit, the tendency to produce more than could be consumed was also a significant factor in his view of capitalist development. For orthodox Ricardians, on the contrary, the continuous accumulation of capital was an unmixed good, leading only to a higher standard of living for all. However, in the few places where he discussed Malthus's concept of effective demand, Marx gave him scant praise for having abrogated Say's law. On the contrary, his economic theory was interpreted as a rationalization of this reactionary politics:

> Malthus represents the interest of the industrial bourgeoisie only to the extent that it is identical with the interest of the landlords, the aristocracy—that is to say, against the mass of the people, the proletariat. But when these interests diverge and are opposed to one another, then he puts himself on the side of the aristocracy against the bourgeoisie, as in his defense of the "unproductive worker."[7]

Malthus's defense of the unproductive consumer derived indeed from a fundamentally different appreciation of the role of the aristocracy in English society, but it derived also from a significant improvement—in Marx's view—of the classical theory of the market. But for Marx it was less important that Malthus had analyzed the working of the economy "correctly" than that he had drawn "reactionary" political conclusions from this analysis.[8]

The difference between Malthus and Marx is not that one accepted misery and vice as inevitable and the other railed against it; the difference lies in the means by which they believed misery might be overcome. According to Marx, the industrial workers would acquire from their common way of life an awareness of their common interest and, strong in this knowledge, would overthrow the capitalist system and establish a more or less unspecified substitute called "socialism." According to Malthus, on the contrary, society could be improved only by the development of individual responsibility, and he judged specific institutions according to whether or not they tended to foster such a sense of responsibility.

This was true in particular of his stand on the poor law, which excited more scurrilous comment than even his principle of population. The Speenhamland system, which assured a minimum family income to the poor irrespective of their earnings, had eventually obliterated the distinction between worker and pauper, and the ostensible production of labor had become synonymous with its utter subordination. Malthus argued for the Poor Law of 1834, which by a surgical operation on sentimentality transferred to each worker the responsibility for his own welfare. It would be difficult to overstate the importance, whether actual or theoretical, of this shift. Family allowances like those paid under the Speenhamland system are not only a social welfare measure but very often a good index of what Karl Mannheim has termed the "basic intention" of the state. There is hardly a better bolster to conservatism than to strengthen the family, for so long as the older generation is able to set the thought and behaviour patterns of the younger generation, social change is likely to be slow. Socialist parties have usually opposed family subsidies or, at most, halfheartedly supported them; for such a policy, while it does distribute aid to the poor and is therefore good, also contradicts the fundamental trade-union tenet of equal pay for equal work.[9] Socialists have seldom noted, however, that the political effect of revoking the Speenhamland system was similarly ambiguous. The workers, told to depend on themselves, suffered for it; but this shift to a free labour market was a prerequisite to the later development of a self-conscious working class and the trade-union movement. Only when the feudalistic paternalism had been ended by emphasizing the self-dependence of the common people could they indeed become self-reliant.[10]

Another important indication of Malthus's reactionary tendencies, according to Marx, was the fact that he was a curate of the Church of England, "Parson Malthus."[11] The point would be relevant if Marx had attempted to show that Malthus's ecclesiastical background introduced a consistent bias into his non-theological writings. Actually, many clergymen found his interpretation of Providence not to their liking, and one went so far as to charge Malthus with atheism.[12] The population theory appropriate to a "parson," they felt, was something along the line of Luther's adage, "*Gott macht Kinder, der wird sie auch ernahren*" ["God makes children, and He will also nourish them"]. The principle of population, on the contrary, brought man fully into nature, one species among others. As Darwin himself remarked, his casual reading of the *Essay*, "for amusement," furnished the first clue out of which the theory of evolution developed. Thus, in the dispute between evolutionists and traditionalist theologians, a momentous struggle that set the tone of intellectual life during the whole second half of the nineteenth century, the role of Malthus was not that of a theologian but rather a forerunner to scientific biology. When Marx wrote that "an abstract law of population exists for plants and animals only,"[13] he unwittingly set the minimum level at which a Malthusian approach must be taken as valid. If much of Malthus is as unacceptable as the work of any pioneer, he remains worth studying just because of his emphasis on the fact that man *is* an animal, living in a finite world.

If Malthus's social philosophy does not mark him a reactionary, neither do his more specific policy recommendations. He is notorious for having opposed a poor law that had reduced free workers to pauperdom; but he is less well known as the advocate of free universal education, free medical aid to the poor, state assistance to emigrants, and even direct relief to families of more than six children, or as the opponent of using minors in cottage industry, and of free trade when it benefited the traders but not the public.[14] The advocacy of free education for all was especially significant and, for his day, most unusual. Malthus did not see the gap between the social classes as innate; it could be bridged by the development of a sense of responsibility among the common people. And the upper classes were not automatically right by reason of their social position; if they did not fulfill their duty toward the lower classes and assist them in becoming self-reliant, they were thereby censurable. In contrast, *laissez-faire* liberalism, as it was developed during Malthus's lifetime, demanded of each man only that he seek his own self-interest.

Malthus's main reaction to the French Revolution and especially to some of its perfectibilist ideologues was negative; and such a political sentiment, personified best in England by Burke, has ordinarily been used to define modern conservatism. On the other hand, in several respects Malthus was markedly unconservative. The answer to this contradiction, perhaps, is that for figures as complex as Malthus or Marx the usual one-dimensional continuum from left to right is not a useful analytical model. This point can be illustrated by making use of one of the richest and most stimulating efforts to define one end-point of this continuum, namely, Mannheim's essay on conservative thought in the early nineteenth century.[15] One important difference between progressives and conservatives, Mannheim writes, is the way they experience time: "the progressive experiences the present as the beginning of the future, while the conservative regards it simply as the latest point reached by the past. But the whole thrust of Malthus's arithmetic and geometric progressions was to the future; and Marx, though he hypothesized the extrapolation of present trends to a future utopia, concentrated in his writing on connecting the capitalist system with its historical past. Or: "The conservatives replaced Reason with concepts such as History, Life, the Nation." Malthus, on the contrary, extended the legitimate use of reason to the family, that sanctum of traditionalist norms; while for Marx reason was indeed subsumed in an irrepressible History. Or: The conservative "starts from a concept of a whole which is not the mere sum of its parts . . . The conservative thinks in terms of 'We' when the liberal thinks in terms of 'I.' " Marxist analysis is wholly in terms of social classes, wholes greater than the sum of the individuals that make them up; and Malthus, like all who participated in developing the theory of market relations, began his analysis with the individual consumer or individual parent.

These paradoxes could be continued, but the point has been made. Political reality ordinarily has more than one dimension. This is true of the differences between Marx and Malthus and, *a fortiori*, of those between Marxists and Malthusians. In the radical-liberal heyday, "left" meant toward increased personal freedom; and then it acquired the additional meaning of toward increased state control over the economy. It is now apparent, however, that these two goals do not always lie in the same direction. With respect to population control, on the contrary, the right of individual parents to decide on the size of their family, established during one of the momentous struggles of the liberal era, is now often challenged because of the state's obsessive desire for more manpower.

III

In spite of these parallels between the two men, Marx rejected Malthus and his works, and did so in language strong even by his standards—"the contemptible Malthus," a "plagiarist," "a shameless sycophant of the ruling classes," who perpetrated a "sin against science," "this libel on the human race." The constant hyperbole suggests a polemical weakness: vituperation is no more a sign of strength with Marx than with any other social analyst. In order to preserve his faith in the inevitability of the socialist society, Marx found it necessary to discard Malthus's principle of population,[16] but he was not able to fashion a demographic theory to take its place.

Marx's main objection to the principle of population can be stated in a single sentence: "every special historic mode of production has its own special laws of population, historically valid within its limits alone."[17] With the proviso, already noted, that man is an animal and that at one level of analysis biological generalizations are therefore relevant, this is certainly a valid criticism. Indeed, the demographic cycle hypothesis, one might say, is a specification of Malthusian theory in the sense that Marx suggested, since it divides the human species into three stages related to their "modes of production." Marx himself, however, had nothing to say of what governed the population growth of primitive, feudal, or socialist societies, and what he termed his law of population for capitalist society was markedly incomplete.

According to Marx's theory, the competition in a capitalist economy drives all entrepreneurs to increase their efficiency to the utmost by installing more and more machinery. "Accumulate, accumulate! This is Moses and the prophets!"[18] The growing stock of capital goods that results, by the very fact of its greater efficiency, tends to displace some of the workers that had been employed at a lower technological level. "The labouring population therefore produces, along with the accumulation of capital produced by it, the means by which [it] itself is made relatively superfluous, is turned into a relative surplus population; and it does this to an always increasing extent."[19] Moreover, the composition of the employed force steadily deteriorates: the capitalist "progressively replaces skilled labourers by less skilled, mature labour-power by immature, male by female, that of adults by that of younger persons or children."[20] No amelioration is possible under capitalism, for the capitalist mode of production depends on this "industrial reserve army" of the technologically unemployed; employers, if they are to remain in business, must respond promptly to the state of the market and cannot afford to adjust their production also to the supply of laborers.

This line of reasoning, a generalization from Ricardo's demonstration that mechanization *may* lead to unemployment, cannot be regarded as one of Marx's successful prophecies.[21] Since machines and labor are interchangeable to some degree, the increase in the stock of capital did mean that fewer workers were required to produce the same amount of goods. The general consequences of this greater efficiency, however, were the higher standard of life, the shorter work week for the industrial labor force, and the development of tertiary services. And in presently underdeveloped countries, where the surplus agrarian population—what Marx termed the latent industrial reserve army—is often large, the consequent very low wage standard is ordinarily not the stimulus to capital accumulation it should be by Marx's analysis but a serious impediment to it.

But even if Marx's main point is granted—that with increasing mechanization there is a long-term trend toward an ever larger number of unemployed—it still does not follow that this trend operates "independently of the limits of the actual increase of population."[22] Marx's theory of the industrial reserve army pertains not to population as such but to the labor force; and while the two are related, they are not identical. Given the state of the market, the proportion of the labor force able to find work depends —as one of the important variables—on the number of new workers seeking jobs.[23] According to Marx, if wages rise because of a relative shortage of labor, the rate of capitalization will increase and the labor surplus will thus be reestablished.[24] But Marx's analysis began, it will be recalled, with the thesis that every capitalist is driven to accumulate at the highest possible rate under all conditions; and it was illogical—to put it no stronger—to develop the argument with an assertion that under certain conditions the rate of mechanization will be accelerated.

If Marx freed Ricardo's theory of the effect of capital growth on employment from a "fatal dependence on the Malthusian population dogma," as Sweezy declares,[25] this "great accomplishment" was at the cost of taking the essence of Malthusianism for granted. In the 1930's, demographers generally forecast that the population of the West would soon decline, but for Marx this was not even a hypothetical contingency. In this respect, his usual historical perspective failed him: he took the rapid population increase typical of the nineteenth century as the norm and built his system around it—and without even so imperfect a theory as Malthus's principle to account for this increase. If the population were to decline at the same rate as machines displaced workers, then there would be no industrial reserve army, no "immiseration," no Marxist model altogether. Such an extreme example illustrates strikingly how completely dependent Marx's system can be on the unanalyzed variable of population growth, and this dependence exists to one degree or another, no matter what the rate of growth.

As with their general theories, so with their analyses of population movements, there are many parallels between Marx's system and what Spengler has termed Malthus's total population theory,[26] which was developed in both the *Essay* and the *Principles*. The effect of the economic system on employment and thus on population growth, the problem with which Marx was mainly concerned, Malthus analyzed at length only in the *Principles;* and many of Marx's criticisms of the *Essay,* in any case rather casual, are less cogent when applied to the argument of both works together.

In Malthus's system, the psychological base of any human society consists in the opposed drives of man's natural sloth and the passion between the sexes, the first inductive to stagnation and the second to progress. (Marx's reply to this, as we have noted, was to deny the relevance of such psychological universals to a social analysis at any level whatever.) The balance between the two drives in any specific society, Malthus continues, is set by its institutions. While the "struggle for existence" is viewed in the first instance as that of man against nature, the character of this struggle and its probable success depend on the social order.[27] Here the divergence from Marx is no longer absolute.

That is to say, according to Malthus, the growth of a population depends not only on the resources available to it (in a biological-geographical context) but also on the effective demand for labor (in an economic-cultural context). "An increase of population, when an additional quantity of labour is not required, will soon be checked by want of employment and the scanty support of those employed."[28] These two determinants, moreover, need not operate in the same direction. For example, a population can be too great with respect to job openings and yet smaller than the available resources make possible; Marx's industrial reserve army is thus a special case in Malthus's broader analysis. On the other hand, if the effective demand for labor remains greater than the supply, the consequent growth of population will be brought to an end ultimately by the limit of the resources available (exploited with whatever technical efficiency a particular society may have) and, short of this ultimate point, by its consumption standards—a cultural rather than an economic factor. The lowest point at which real family income can be stabilized, as with Marx, is the minimum cost of producing another generation. According to Marx, there was a long-term tendency for wages to fall to this level; but with Malthus this minimum could be raised by an increase in "the amount of those necessaries and conveniences, without which [the workers] would not consent to keep up their numbers to the required point." When Gunnar Myrdal wrote that the conscious limitation of family size is a powerful lever with which to force governments to enact social legislation, he was expressing a point of view whose germ is to be found in Malthus.

This point is important enough to deserve some amplification, and this can be given it in a passage from Sidney and Beatrice Webb, who had a juster appreciation of Malthus's social philosophy than probably any other socialist writer.

> No argument could be founded on the "principle of population" against Trade Union efforts to improve the conditions of sanitation and safety, or to protect the Normal Day. And the economists quickly found reason to doubt whether there was any greater cogency in the argument with regard to wages. . . . From the Malthusian point of view, the presumption was, as regards the artisans and factory operatives, always in favour of a rise in wages. For (as Malthus had written in the *Principles*) "in the vast majority of instances, before a rise of wages can

be counteracted by the increased number of labourers it may be supposed to be the means of bringing into the market, time is afforded for
the formation of . . . new and improved tastes and habits . . . After the
laborers have once acquired these tastes, population will advance in
a slower ratio, as compared with capital, than formerly." . . . The ordinary middle-class view that the "principle of population" rendered
nugatory all attempts to raise wages, otherwise than in the slow course
of generations, was, in fact, based on sheer ignorance, not only of the
facts of working-class life, but even of the opinions of the very economists from whom it was supposed to be derived.[29]

Thus, the person the Webbs designated, somewhat inappropriately,
as "the fanatical Malthusian" was mistaken in his fear of "the devastating
torrent of children," mistaken because Malthus had been correct in his
theory that a rising standard of living would tend to reduce the birth rate.

For Marx, the overthrow of the system was both inevitable and the
prerequisite to all social betterment; and the solution of the population
problem would be so automatic under socialist institutions that he did not
find it useful to sketch in how this would be achieved. For Malthus, as we
have noted, social betterment was defined as the increase in individual responsibility[30] or, specifically with respect to population, in the wider practice of moral restraint. While such social changes as the extension of free
education to the poor would foster this sense of responsibility, and were
thus defined as good, the moral differentiation already existing in any
society made a gradual improvement possible for some.

It is not required . . . to pursue a general good which we may not distinctly comprehend, or the effect of which may be weakened by
distance and diffusion. The happiness of the whole is to be the result
of the happiness of individuals, and to begin with the first of them. No
cooperation is required. Every step tells. He who performs his duty
faithfully will reap the full fruits of it, whatever may be the number
of others who fail.[31]

Compared with a view of the future that declared the perfect society to be
inescapable, Malthus's admonitions are more than a bit astringent, particularly since "few of my readers can be less sanguine than I am in their
expectations of any sudden and great change in the general conduct of
men on this subject."[32] That the course of action he advocated was not
wholly fanciful is suggested by the one example of Ireland, where the dramatic stimulus of the famine and the strict regulation of morals by the
church have resulted in the control of population growth by institutionalized late marriage.

More generally, neither Malthus nor Marx can be regarded as having forecast the future of the Western world with any accuracy. Dogmatists of either school find it difficult to cope with the fact that the marked rise in the working-class living standard was within the capitalist system, on the one hand, and was concomitant with an unprecedented increase in the population, on the other. If we include in Marx's foresight the improvements within the capitalist system effected by the rise of trade unions and the consequent change in power relations, and in Malthus's the reduction in average family size by contraceptives rather than by postponement of marriage —common extensions of their views that do violence to the essential ideas of the two men—then both can be said to have been partly correct.

To my knowledge, Marx himself never commented on the birth-control movement so active in England during the last years of his life, particularly from the Bradlaugh-Besant trial (1876) to his death (1883). The Marxist views of the good society, as expressed in such classic documents as *The Communist Manifesto* and Engels' *Origin of the Family,* included the emancipation of the woman from household drudgery as a main feature; but whether she should also be emancipated from bearing many children was not made explicit. In a letter to Kautsky, Engels spoke of the "abstract possibility" that the number of persons in a communist society might have to be limited by conscious control, but he declined to discuss the matter further.[33] By such a reply, Engels avoided having to discuss in any detail either the economic significance of population growth or the moral system of the socialist society he was advocating.

In summary, both Malthus and Marx welcomed the new capitalist era,[34] but both with important reservations. Neither saw the market as a perfect instrument for translating the self-interest of individuals into the optimum social policy, and they both, though to different degrees, therefore, rejected the *laissez-faire* norms of liberal industrialism. Neither was a sentimentalist: when they thought it necessary Malthus was willing to advocate the abrogation of a bad poor law and Marx to call for revolution. But both offered these programs in a rational effort to establish similiar humanitarian values. As against Economic Man, both stressed to some degree the whole man, Malthus in part by seeking to preserve a portion of pre-industrial tradition and in part by espousing certain fundamental reforms, Marx by seeking to establish a new society with an industrial-agrarian balance. Marx's concept of democracy, while it laid a basis for present theories of social control by planning boards, also had a community of socially responsible persons as its fundament. The working class would lead the world to a better state because workers, unlike peasants, had been disciplined by their style of life; of the undisciplined irresponsible mass, the "Lumpenproletariat," Marx had the same horror and the same fear as Malthus.

NOTES

1. For example, Alfred Sauvy, the dean of French demographers, has used the opposition between these two historical figures to structure his analysis of under-developed countries; see his *Théorie générale de la population*, Vol. I: *Économie et population* (Paris: Presses Universitaires de France, 1952), chap. xviii: "Les pays sousdeveloppés: Marx ou Malthus?" Raymond Aron has written a stimulating popular article on the same subject under the title "Asia—Between Malthus and Marx" (*Encounter*, August, 1954). For other confrontations of the two theories, see James Bonar, *Malthus and His Work* (New York: Macmillan, 1924), pp. 388 ff.; Samuel M. Levin, "Marx vs. Malthus," *Papers of the Michigan Academy of Arts and Letters* (Ann Arbor: University of Michigan Press, 1937), Vol. XXII, pp. 243–258; Joe Banks, "Neither Malthus nor Marx," *Socialist Commentary* (London), XIX (January, 1955), 12–14.

2. Ronald L. Meek (ed.), *Marx and Engels on Malthus: Selections from the Writings of Marx and Engels Dealing with the Theories of Thomas Robert Malthus* (London: Lawrence and Wishart, 1953; New York: International Publishers, 1955), p. 47.

3. H. L. Beales, "The Historical Context of the Essay on Population," D. V. Glass (ed.), *Introduction to Malthus* (New York: Wiley, 1953), pp. 1–24. For further evidence that pre-Marxist socialists generally repudiated Malthus, see United Nations, *The Determinants and Consequences of Population Trends*, Population Study No. 17 (New York, 1955), pp. 32–33.

4. See Herman Ausubel, "William Cobbett and Malthusianism," *Journal of the History of Ideas*, XIII:2 (April, 1952), 250–256.

5. Malthus, *Principles of Political Economy*, 2nd ed., Book II, Chapter I, Sections 3 and 9 (New York: Kelley, 1951).

6. Sweezy writes, concerning this: "It could be maintained that Marx regarded underconsumption as one aspect, but on the whole not a very important aspect, of the crisis problem. This appears to be the opinion of Dobb, and there is no doubt much to back it up. Another view

is possible, however, namely, that in these scattered passages [which Sweezy had analyzed in detail] Marx was giving advance notice of a line of reasoning which, if he had lived to complete his theoretical work, would have been of primary importance in the overall picture of the capitalist economy; . . . and, on the whole, it seems to me the more reasonable of the two alternatives" (Paul M. Sweezy, *The Theory of Capitalist Development: Principles of Marxian Political Economy* [New York: Oxford University Press, 1942], p. 178). *Cf.* Maurice Dobb, *Political Economy and Capitalism* (London: Routledge, 1937), pp. 118–121; and *Studies in the Development of Capitalism* (London: Routledge, 1947), chapters 6–8.

7. Marx, *Theorien über den Mehrwert*, 3rd ed. (Stuttgart: Dietz, 1919), II:1, 306–307.

8. Inevitably, a Marxist has gone beyond Marx and declared that since Malthus was right for the wrong reason, he was not right. In his attack on Ricardo's theory, according to Erich Roll, Malthus insisted on "the possibility of economic dislocations for reasons inherent in the capitalist system." The "main purpose" of that attack, however, "was to defend the unproductive consumer. Historically, therefore, it was reactionary. Malthus . . . seems to have aspired to a sort of balance between Whig-aristocrat and primitive industrial-bourgeois elements at a time when a complete victory of the latter was already inevitable. For this reason, Ricardo's theory was clearly superior because it was appropriate to the direction of contemporary economic development" (*A History of Economic Thought* [London: Faber and Faber, 1938], p. 203).

9. See William Petersen, "Family Subsidies in the Netherlands," *Marriage and Family Living*, XVII:3 (August, 1955), 260–266.

10. Compare the following passage from Karl Polanyi: "As long as a man had a status to hold on to, a pattern set by his kin or fellows, he could fight for it, and regain his soul. But in the case of the laborer this could happen only in one way: by his constituting himself the member of a new class. Unless he was able to make a living

by his own labor, he was not a worker but a pauper. To reduce him artificially to such a condition was the supreme abomination of Speenhamland. This act of an ambiguous humanitarianism prevented laborers from constituting themselves an economic class and thus deprived them of the only means of staving off the fate to which they were doomed in the economic mill" (*The Great Transformation* [New York: Rinehart, 1944], p. 99).

11. Indeed, according to Marx, "most of the population-theory teachers are Protestant parsons . . . —Parson Wallace, Parson Townsend, Parson Malthus and his pupil, the arch-Parson Thomas Chalmers, to say nothing of the lesser reverend scribblers in this line." However, in contrast to other Protestant clergymen, who "genererally contribute to the increase of population to a really unbecoming extent," Malthus "had taken the monastic vow of celibacy" (*Capital* [Chicago: Kerr, 1906], I, 675–676). That Marx did not know Malthus was a married man and the father of three children indicates that he knew rather little about the man whose character and motives he impugned.

12. *Cf.* Bonar, *op. cit.*, p. 365.

13. Marx, *Capital*, I, 693. But according to Engels, offering his final tribute to his lifelong collaborator at the latter's graveside, Marx's prime virtue had been that he stressed man's biological necessities as basic: "As Darwin discovered the law of evolution in organic nature, so Marx discovered the law of evolution in human history: the simple fact, previously hidden under ideological growths, that human beings must first of all eat, drink, shelter and clothe themselves before they can turn their attention to politics, science, art and religion" (Franz Mehring, *Karl Marx: The Story of His Life* [New York: Covici Friede, 1935], p. 555).

14. *Cf.* Bonar, *op. cit.*, p. 343, where citations are given to the passages in Malthus's works expressing these opinions.

15. Karl Mannheim, "Conservative Thought," *Essays on Sociology and Social Psychology* (New York: Oxford University Press, 1953), pp. 74–164.

16. "If Malthus's theory of population is correct," Marx wrote, "then I can *not* abolish this [iron law of wages] even

if I abolish wage-labor a hundred times, because this law is not only paramount over the system of wage-labor but also over *every* social system. Stepping straight from this, the economists proved fifty years ago or more that Socialism cannot abolish poverty, which is based on nature, but only *communalise* it, distribute it equally over the whole surface of society!" (Marx, *Critique of the Gotha Programme* [New York: International Publishers, 1933], p. 40).

17. Marx, *Capital*, I, 693.

18. *Ibid.*, p. 652.

19. *Ibid.*, p. 692.

20. *Ibid.*, p. 697.

21. As Professor Meek remarks in an article in *Science and Society*, "Marx's basic 'law of population' (like a number of his other laws) will have to be worked out more fully and adapted to the new conditions before it can be safely employed in the analysis of the present situation" (Meek, "Malthus—Yesterday and Today," *Science and Society*, XVIII:1 [Winter, 1954], 21–51). The reason given for this remarkable judgment, however, is not that Marx lacked total prescience but that conditions have changed: "capitalism is now in its imperialist stage of development."

22. Marx, *Capital*, I, 693.

23. As Marx points out in a different context, "the demand for labourers may exceed the supply and, therefore, wages may rise" (*ibid.*, p. 672); and one of his examples when this happened is the fifteenth century, after the extraordinary mortality of the Black Death had reduced the population, and thus the labor force, by a considerable proportion.

24. "A limitation of the increase in the working population, through diminishing the supply of labor and hence through raising its price, would only accelerate the use of machinery and the transformation of circulating [capital; that is, labor] into fixed capital and in this fashion would create an artificial surplus population" (Marx, *Theorien über den Mehrwert*, II:2, 373; cited in Sweezy, *op. cit.*, p. 223). Sweezy comments as follows: "From this it is but a short step to the conclusion that any slowing down in the rate of population growth not only has the paradoxical effect of

creating unemployment but also strengthens the tendency to underconsumption." This may be a short step, but it takes one outside a Marxian framework. The large increase in population did help, as Sweezy points out, to keep the nineteenth-century capitalist world in a healthy state, but only because the increasing "immiseration" of the masses, which Marx had postulated as the necessary consequence of the inevitable fall in the rate of profit, was nowhere to be observed.

Compare Malthus: "Almost universally, the actual wealth of all the states with which we are acquainted is very far short of their powers of production; and among these states, the slowest progress in wealth is often made where the stimulus arising from population alone is the greatest. . . . Population alone cannot create an effective demand for wealth" (*Principles*, Book II, Chapter 1, Section 2).

25. Sweezy, *op. cit.*, p. 89.

26. See Joseph J. Spengler, "Malthus's Total Population Theory: A Restatement and Reappraisal," *Canadian Journal of Economics and Political Science*, II:1 (February, 1945), 83–110; II:2 (May, 1945), 234–264.

27. Analyses of Malthus based on the *Essay* alone typically reach just the opposite conclusion. Bowen, for example, concludes his discussion of the theory with the statement that "the clear alternative to Malthus's theory is the hypothesis that economic as well as social conditions affect the growth and size of populations, and that sexual passions operate only within the restrictions or stimuli imposed by these conditions" (Ian Bowen, *Population* [London: Nisbet, 1954], p. 111).

28. *Principles*, Book II, Chapter I, Section 2.

29. Sidney and Beatrice Webb, *Industrial Democracy* (London: Longmans, Green, 1919), pp. 632–635. The quotation from Malthus's *Principles* is from Part III, Section 7.

30. This criterion was applied even to social changes as thoroughgoing as the French Revolution: "The effect of the revolution in France has been to make every person depend more on himself and less upon others. The labouring classes are therefore becoming more industrious, more saving and more prudent in marriage than formerly; and it is quite certain that without these effects the revolution would have done nothing for them" (Malthus, *An Essay on the Principle of Population*, 7th ed. [London: Reeves and Turner, 1872], Book III, Chapter VII, p. 320).

31. *Ibid.*, Book IV, Chapter III, p. 404.

32. *Ibid.*, p. 403. He adds: "The chief reason . . . I allowed myself to suppose the universal prevalence of this virtue [of moral restraint] was that I might endeavour to remove any imputation on the goodness of the Deity, by showing that the evils arising from the principle of population were exactly of the same nature as the generality of other evils which excite fewer complaints, that they were increased by human ignorance and indolence, and diminished by human knowledge and virtue."

33. "It is for the people in the communist society themselves," Engels wrote, "to decide whether, when, and how this is to be done, and what means they wish to employ for the purpose. I do not feel called upon to make proposals or to give them advice about it. These people, in any case, will surely not be any less intelligent than we are" (letter of Engels to Kautsky, February 1, 1881; cited in Meek, *Marx and Engels on Malthus*, p. 109).

34. Marx, however, in more glowing terms than Malthus. Consider this passage from *The Communist Manifesto*: "The bourgeoisie has played a most revolutionary role in history . . . It has been the first to show what man's activity can bring about. It has accomplished wonders far surpassing Egyptian pyramids, Roman aqueducts, and Gothic cathedrals; it has conducted expeditions that put in the shade all former migrations of nations and crusades . . . The bourgeoisie has through its exploitation of the world market given a cosmopolitan character [not yet a pejorative term] to production and consumption in every country . . . The bourgeoisie, by the rapid improvement of all instruments of production, by the immensely facilitated means of communication, draws all nations, even the most barbarian, into civilisation . . . The bourgeoisie . . . has created enormous cities, has . . . rescued a consid-

erable part of the population from the idiocy of rural life . . . The bourgeoisie, during its rule of scarce one hundred years, has created more massive and more colossal productive forces than have all preceding generations together." (Marx and Engels, *The Communist Manifesto* [New York: International Publishers, 1948], pp. 11–14).

The Data
of Demography

Introduction

Demography, or the study of population, is an empirical science. It is the goal of every science to describe, explain, and predict the occurrences connected with some particular phenomena, so demography must fulfill these tasks with regard to aggregates of human organisms. In order to achieve these general goals of science it is necessary to have data or facts, and in the case of demography the facts that are needed are about human populations.

Demography has been labeled an "observational science," in contrast to the "experimental sciences."[1] The observational sciences are those whose data are produced primarily by records that are made of naturally occurring events. By contrast, the experimental sciences are those in which the data are generally produced by experiments conducted in the laboratory under conditions that are greatly controlled by the experimenter. While demography is an observational science, this does not mean that experimental procedures cannot be and have not been used to acquire knowledge that is useful for an understanding of population phenomena. It simply means that on balance the demog-

---

[1] Philip M. Hauser and Otis Dudley Duncan, eds., *The Study of Population* (Chicago: University of Chicago Press, 1959), pp. 4–5.

rapher is more likely to get his data from some process other than the laboratory experiment.

Hauser and Duncan have pointed out that demography is an observational science because the data are "spread out."[2] The data are spread out in two senses: in time and in space. The events that interest the demographer—births, deaths, migration—are spread out over vast geographical areas, and go back in time to the beginning of man's existence. The primary implication of the spread-out nature of population data is that a single demographer can gather only a very small proportion of the data that are necessary when he wants to describe population phenomena, to test population hypotheses, or to build generalizations about population.

Now the work of the demographer can be only as good as the quality of the data he uses, and yet the demographer uses data that are gathered by others, and under circumstances over which he has little or no control. Furthermore, the very facts that are to be gathered are often decided upon by individuals other than the demographer.

Whenever a scientist does not have personal control over the data-gathering process, he must be on guard against the errors and inadequacies in the data he is using. It is for this reason that this section is devoted to several articles that focus on the data used by demographers. Each of the papers in this section relates to some of the events, issues, or problems connected with population data.

The paper by Ian Sutherland on John Graunt describes the work of one of the first and probably the most prominent of a group of seventeenth- and eighteenth-century scholars who have been labeled the "political arithmeticians." The political arithmeticians of England and the European continent were often men who had been trained in the natural sciences, or else, as in the case of Graunt, men who recognized the possibilities of applying the observational techniques of the natural sciences to political and social phenomena. It can be argued that the political arithmeticians were the first real demographers, and thus it would follow that they should be given credit for stimulating and initiating the study of population as an empirical science. However, this latter assumption is not too well founded in fact, because it is difficult to establish a continuous scholarly lineage from the political arithmeticians to the demographers of the nineteenth century. The only appar-

---

[2] *Ibid.*, p. 5.

ent exception is in the analysis of mortality, especially the construction of life-expectancy tables, which started with the political arithmeticians and has proceeded in a fairly unbroken line since their time. The reason for the continuing interest in and development of life tables appears to have been the growing need of insurance societies for ever better actuarial data.

There were two major factors that seemed to motivate the political arithmeticians of the seventeenth century. First, for many of them the basic reason for gathering data on population (and other resources as well) was better to assess the resources of the nation, particularly as these were vested in the royal family. Second, the political arithmeticians accepted the intellectual challenge that was inherent in any attempt to describe the size and characteristics of the population in an era when the data had to be extracted from whatever records were at hand.[3]

With the advent of the modern census, beginning at the end of the seventeenth century, the data on population became much more available, and one would guess that the intellectual challenge that motivated the early political arithmeticians no longer existed. Thus, as suggested above, the intellectual line of the political arithmeticians appears to have waned, except in the area of mortality.

It is beneficial to read an account of the life and work of one of the political arithmeticians, such as we are able to do in Sutherland's tribute to John Graunt, because it reminds us that only 300 years ago in one of the most advanced countries of the world there was scarcely any knowledge of some of the most elementary population facts. In our age, when statistical data seem to exist on all aspects of life, it is difficult to imagine an England in which such data were not available. It also brings into focus again the spread-out character of population data which we described above. In this case we see more clearly that historical population data, even for European countries, is likely to be very limited for any current-day researcher who might want to reconstruct the demographic past.

Philip Hauser's paper in this section, titled "Statistics and Society," provides an excellent summary of the history of statistical data, with a special emphasis on population data. Hauser presents an interesting

---

[3] Some additional details on the political arithmeticians were presented in Kurt Mayer's paper "Developments in the Study of Population" in Section I.

chronicle of the collection of population statistics, with particular reference to the history of the United States census. He provides this detailed historical information within a discussion of the hypothesis that there is a concomitance, or perhaps causal relationship, between the emergence of urban and metropolitan patterns of living and the increasing volume of statistical data. The United States Census Bureau, which has throughout its history increased the amount of information gathered and reported on the population, is a prime illustration of Hauser's general hypothesis.

But, while the census of the United States has been improved greatly since its beginnings in 1790, and while the present census provides an indispensable fund of knowledge for the demographer, it may still have inadequacies and shortcomings. One type of inadequacy exists when certain items of information which might be useful for research purposes are not included among those asked by the census taker. For example, many social researchers, and particularly demographers, deplore the lack of a question on religion in the United States census. The paper by Dorothy Good, "Questions on Religion in the United States Census," provides a detailed discussion of this often argued issue. Good presents some of the available data on the religious composition of the United States, and then presents a list of the arguments for and against the inclusion of a religious question on the census. It is, of course, true that many special-interest groups are trying regularly to have questions placed on the census form that would be useful to them, and some selectivity must be exercised by the Bureau of the Census. Nevertheless, since religion is such an important characteristic of a population, and in some instances an influential determinant of population behavior (e.g., fertility), the demographer cannot but wish that a question on religion be asked on the U.S. census form.

The other kind of inadequacy or shortcoming of the census is much more far-reaching and significant, for it has to do with the general validity and accuracy of census data. This issue, of prime importance to the demographer using census data, is discussed in great detail by Donald Bogue in his paper "The Pros and Cons of 'Self-Enumeration.'" Using as his reference the basic change in the census-taking method between 1950 and 1960 from the "canvasser" method to the "householder" method, Bogue describes current census procedures and analyzes the degree of error in the census reports.

The "canvasser" method of census taking is the procedure whereby the census taker interviews a member of the family and records the data, while the "householder" method is largely a method of self-enumeration. Bogue lists the advantages of each method, and in these lists it is possible to discern two underlying values: efficiency and data quality. Most of the advantages can be classified under one of these two rubrics, and it is of some importance to note that in Bogue's list of advantages the value of efficiency is most often met by the householder method, while improvement in data quality is more often achieved by the canvasser method. It is probably obvious to the reader which of these two values is ranked highest by demographers, for while demographers, like most Americans, are interested in achieving efficient methods of data gathering, the fact that the quality of their research is dependent upon the quality of the data makes them much more concerned about the latter.

The final article in this section, by Mortimer Spiegelman, is concerned with vital statistics and health statistics. While our federal system of government provided for a census at regular ten-year intervals (so that the House of Representatives could be properly apportioned on the basis of state populations), the Constitution did not provide for a system of collecting data on the vital events of population, such as births, deaths, marriages, divorces, etc. In fact, at the same time that our federal system of government ensured that we would have a continuing and ever improving body of population data collected by the Census Bureau, it also had in it the seeds of a rather poor system for collecting vital statistics. The federal system of government that we have gives a great deal of autonomy and responsibility to the individual states of the Union. Thus each state may decide *if* it will collect data on vital events, and it may decide *how* it will collect such data. As a result of this state freedom, widely varying and inconsistent methods of collecting vital statistics have been characteristic of the United States. Such variety in the collection of vital statistics has made the task of accumulating data for the entire country difficult, and in some instances impossible. Persistent efforts to standardize the methods of recording vital events have eventually led to an adequate and fairly consistent system, particularly with regard to births and deaths, but compared to the census system it has been very late in coming. Spiegelman reviews this point and then goes on to discuss some of the most important current problems that must be solved and the needs that must be met if we are to improve our system of vital and health statistics.

6

John Graunt:
A Tercentenary Tribute

Ian Sutherland

SUMMARY

John Graunt was a London draper who, three hundred years ago, published some "Natural and Political Observations on the Bills of Mortality." These observations represent the first, and an extremely competent, attempt to draw scientific conclusions from statistical data. The present study illustrates Graunt's careful scientific approach, his ability to extract the essence from what by modern standards are distinctly untrustworthy demographic data, and his intuitive appreciation of the amount of interpretation his findings would stand. Graunt's analysis was largely based upon ratios and proportions of vital events and consideration of the way in which these altered in different circumstances, and is remarkably free of major statistical errors. His statistical understanding was considerable; for example, we owe to him the first scientific estimates of population size, the concept of the life table, the idea of statistical association, the first studies of time series, and a pioneer attempt to draw a representative sample. Graunt's book is well worth reading today, not only for entertainment and instruction, but because it laid the foundations of the science of statistics.

1. INTRODUCTION

Just 300 years ago, in 1662, a small book was published under the title "*Natural* and *Political* OBSERVATIONS Mentioned in a following INDEX, and made upon the Bills of Mortality." The author was "*JOHN GRAUNT*, Citizen of LONDON." A celebration of the tercentenary of publication of

Reprinted from the *Royal Statistical Society Journal*, Series A, 126 (1963), pp. 537–56, by permission of the author and the publisher.

a small seventeenth-century book by a little-known author requires some initial justification, and this is perhaps best provided by a nineteenth-century inscription in a copy in the library of our Society. "Captain John Graunt of London merits the high honour of being the founder of Statistics. His natural & political Observations on the Bills of Mortality ... first directed public attention to the important inferences that might be deduced from correct registers of Births, deaths, & marriages." This is indeed a high claim; we may be prepared to concede that he was the first to study *medical* statistics, but to attribute the beginnings of the whole scientific discipline to him may sound a little extravagant. I hope to show, however, in the course of what follows, that the claim is justified, and that we are really celebrating the tercentenary of statistics as well as that of Graunt's book. . . .

2. A BIOGRAPHICAL SKETCH

John Graunt was born in London on April 24th, 1620, to Henry and Mary Graunt, and was christened a week later at St. Michael, Cornhill. His father was a draper who had moved to London from Hampshire, and carried on his business in Birchin Lane. John was the eldest of a large family and, after serving an apprenticeship, took up and eventually succeeded to his father's business, as a "Haberdasher of small-wares," which he carried on in the family house for the greater part of his life. He became a Freeman of the Drapers' Company ("by Patrimony") at the age of 21, was granted the Livery of the Company when he was 38, and rose to the distinguished position of Renter Warden three years before his death at the age of 53. In this and other ways Graunt became a respected London citizen. He passed through the various ward offices of the city and was eventually elected to the common council for two years. He was a captain in the (military) trained band for several years and a major for two or three more. Even before he was 30 his influence was sufficient to procure the professorship of music at Gresham College for his friend Dr. William Petty.

From the comments of those who knew him we can tell that he must have been an unusually likeable person. Aubrey describes him as "A man generally beloved; a faythfull friend. Often chosen for his prudence and justnes to be an Arbitrator." He was "very facetious and fluent in his conversation" and "very hospitable." In addition he was a man of some accomplishment and taste. He was, to his friend Richard Smyth, "an understanding man of quick witt and a pretty schollar," to Aubrey a "very ingeniose and studious person" who "rose early in the morning to his Study before shop-time. He understood Latin and French." He "wrote Shorthand dextrously," and "had an excellent working head." He was acquainted with Samuel Cooper, the miniaturist, and John Hales, also a portrait painter, and had both professional and social dealings with Samuel Pepys, who, on a visit to Graunt's house, much admired his collection of prints—"indeed . . . the best collection of anything almost that ever I saw, there being the prints of most of the greatest houses, churches and antiquitys in Italy and France, and brave cutts." Despite these links with the arts, however, there is unfortunately no known portrait of Graunt.

Graunt's house, and presumably much of the contents, was burnt down in the Fire of London in 1666, and was rebuilt with financial assistance from Petty. Graunt's business probably suffered too, but it seems that his financial position did not become acute until shortly before his death. He had been brought up a Puritan and was throughout his life deeply religious, using his shorthand to make notes on the many sermons he went to hear. For several years he adhered to Socinian, that is unitarian, beliefs, but eventually turned Catholic, giving up his civil and military offices on this account. This doubtless played a major role in his change of fortune, but the full reasons are obscure; the family house passed to Petty, and Graunt moved into Bolt Court, in the parish of St. Dunstan-in-the-West, Fleet Street. He died in poverty on April 18th, 1674, of jaundice, and was buried in St. Dunstan's church on the 20th; later in the year his widow was granted an annual pension of £4 by the Drapers' Company "in regard of her low condition." Aubrey gives us details just where in the church John Graunt was buried, and comments "what pitty 'tis so great an Ornament of the Citty should be buryed so obscurely!" If it was obscure then, it is more so now, as the church was rebuilt in about 1830 on a rather different site, and neither the old church nor the new had any monument to Graunt. Graunt's best monument, however, is undoubtedly his *Observations,* and no apology is needed for celebrating the tercentenary of its publication rather than any other event in Graunt's life. Although he also wrote some "Observations on the Advance of Excise," these were not published and the manuscript has not come down to us.

3. THE "OBSERVATIONS"

This distinctly unusual tradesman, at the age of 41, published a distinctly unusual book. One of the dedicatory epistles is dated the 25th of January, 1662; on February 5th, 50 copies of the book were presented by Graunt to the Royal Society of Philosophers, and he was proposed as a candidate for membership. A Committee was appointed to examine the book and reported favourably; on February 26th, only a month after publication, Graunt was elected to the Royal Society. He continued as a Fellow for some years, and was a member of the Council of the Society from November 1664 until April 1666.

The admission of Graunt to so distinguished a gathering may have surprised some people, but it was approved by King Charles II. Sprat (1667, p. 67) describes "the recommendation which *King* himself was pleased to make, of the judicious Author of *the Observations on the Bills of Mortality:* In whose Election, it was so farr from being a prejudice, that he was a Shop-keeper of *London;* that His Majesty gave this particular charge to His Society, that if they found any more such Tradesmen, they should be sure to admit them all, without any more ado." Indeed, the Society was able to follow this precept in Charles's lifetime, and elect not merely another distinguished shopkeeper, but another draper; Anthony Leeuwenhoek, of Delft, was elected a Fellow in 1679, in recognition of his pioneer microscopical discoveries.

The *Observations* evidently made an impact elsewhere too. Samuel Pepys (who did not become a Fellow until later) bought a copy in March 1662, commenting that the observations "appear to me on first sight to be very pretty," and later in the year a new edition was printed. In 1665, in the early months of the Great Plague, a third and fourth edition appeared. These are described as "much enlarged," but the only important additions are a fairly short appendix and some related tables. The fifth edition was published in 1676, two years after Graunt's death, probably having been seen through the press by Sir William Petty; it contains a very few "further observations."

4. GRAUNT'S SCIENTIFIC APPROACH

The first point that strikes one on reading the book is the modesty of the author. This appears not merely in the dedications at the beginning—where it might be only false modesty—but underlies much of the text. The preface affords a particularly good example:

> Having been born, and bred in the City of *London,* and having always observed, that most of them who constantly took in the weekly Bills of *Mortality,* made little other use of them, then to look at the foot, how the *Burials* increased, or decreased; And, among the *Casualties,* what had happened rare, and extraordinary in the week currant: so as they might take the same as a *Text* to talk upon, in the next Company; and withall, in the *Plague-time,* how the *Sickness* increased, or decreased, that so the *Rich* might judge of the necessity of their removall, and *Trades-men* might conjecture what doings they were like to have in their respective dealings:
>
> 2. Now, I thought that the Wisdom of our City had certainly designed the laudable practice of takeing, and distributing these Accompts, for other, and greater uses then those above-mentioned, or at least, that some other uses might be made of them: And thereupon I

casting mine Eye upon so many of the General *Bills*, as next came to hand, I found encouragement from them, to look out all the *Bills* I could, and (to be short) to furnish my self with as much matter of that kind, even as the Hall of the *Parish-Clerks* could afford me; the which, when I had reduced into Tables (the Copies whereof are here inserted) so as to have a view of the whole together, in order to the more ready comparing of one *Year, Season, Parish,* or other *Division* of the City, with another, in respect of all the *Burials,* and *Christnings,* and of all the *Diseases,* and *Casualties* happening in each of them respectively; I did then begin, not onely to examine the Conceits, Opinions, and Conjectures, which upon view of a few scattered *Bills* I had taken up; but did also admit new ones, as I found reason, and occasion from my *Tables.*

3. Moreover, finding some *Truths,* and not commonly-believed Opinions, to arise from my Meditations upon these neglected *Papers,* I proceeded further, to consider what benefit the knowledge of the same would bring to the World; that I might not engage my self in idle, and useless Speculations, but like those Noble *Virtuosi* of *Gresham-Colledge* (who reduce their subtile Disquisitions upon Nature into downright Mechanical uses) present the World with some real fruit from those ayrie Blossoms.

4. How far I have succeeded in the Premisses, I now offer to the World's censure. Who, I hope, will not expect from me, not professing Letters, things demonstrated with the same certainty, wherewith Learned men determine in their *Scholes;* but will take it well, that I should offer a new thing, and could forbear presuming to meddle where any of the Learned Pens have ever touched before, and that I have taken the pains, and been at the charge, of setting out those *Tables,* whereby all men may both correct my *Positions,* and raise others of their own: For herein I have, like a silly Schole-boy, coming to say my Lesson to the World (that Peevish, and Tetchie Master) brought a bundle of Rods wherewith to be whipt, for every mistake I have committed.

It is clear from this that Graunt was, quite understandably, conscious of his lay status; he was no doctor, no mathematician, no politician, but an enquiring citizen who rated his efforts no higher than to "offer at a new thing," and took pains to tabulate his basic material so that his readers could check his deductions and add others he had overlooked (I do not believe that any of them have been able to). It seems to me that Graunt's lay status may have been an advantage in his enquiries rather than the reverse, by encouraging a degree of detachment from, and modesty towards, the handling of his data. These qualities are just as essential for an effective statistician today as they were in Graunt's time, but a statistician must now learn to combine them with an extensive knowledge of his particular field of application.

Secondly, Graunt shows a methodical tidiness throughout the book. *"THE Observations, which I happened to make (for I designed them not) upon the* Bills of Mortality, *have fallen out to be both* Political, *and* Natural, *some concerning* Trade, *and* Government, *others concerning the* Air, Countries, Seasons, Fruitfulness, Health, Diseases, Longevity, *and the proportions between the* Sex, *and* Ages *of* Mankinde." Since his observations fall into these two distinct classes, there are two dedications in the book, one of the political observations to the Lord Privy Seal, and one of the natural observations to the President of the Royal Society. This is perhaps a trivial example. The preface, quoted above, gives a better illustration of Graunt's methodical approach; it is as good a statement as one could hope to find, in any age, of the reasons for undertaking a scientific enquiry, of the thorough collection of relevant data, of the need to check first impressions against more extensive facts, and of the drawing of practical conclusions from the findings. This careful logical approach pervades the book, as you will see from my later examples.

Thirdly, Graunt devotes much space to a description of the bills of mortality, explaining how they were compiled and in what way they had developed. A lesser man would have thought this unimportant, or would not have bothered on the grounds that most of his readers would know it all already. As it is, his modern readers are in as good a position as Graunt's contemporaries were to understand the basis for his deductions. Moreover, and this is crucial, having described his sources, Graunt does not accept the information they contain without further question; he is critical both of their completeness and of their accuracy. Indeed, such appraisal of the data is often an integral part of his argument, affecting his deductions and conclusions, and giving them a validity they could not otherwise possess. Again, I shall be illustrating this below.

These three points I have touched upon, namely a humility of approach, a tidiness born of logic, and a critical appraisal of the basic data, are fundamental to any scientific enquiry. To find them adopted and pursued, at the very beginnings of serious scientific research, by a London draper, is a further justification for this celebration. Even though his scientific approach may have been intuitive rather than conscious, we can recognize in Graunt a pioneer of scientific method, quite apart from his contribution to statistics. . . .

5. THE BILLS OF MORTALITY

At some time early in the sixteenth century, a system arose whereby the totals of burials in each London parish, distinguishing deaths from the plague, were collected each week. It is likely that these weekly "bills of mortality" were at first prepared only during times of plague, but from about 1563 onwards they appear to have become a regular manuscript series. The earliest printed bills date from the first years of the seventeenth century, and in this form eventually became available to the public.

The weekly totals of christenings in each parish were included with those of burials from an early date, and causes of death other than plague were first recorded in about 1604, although not included in the printed bills until 1629.

Graunt gives us an excellent description of the way in which the bills of mortality for London were compiled during the seventeenth century.

> When any one dies, then, either by tolling, or ringing of a Bell, or by be-speaking of a Grave of the *Sexton*, the same is known to the *Searchers*, corresponding with the said *Sexton*.
> 11. The *Searchers* hereupon (who are antient Matrons, sworn to their Office) repair to the place, where the dead Corps lies, and by view of the same, and by other enquiries, they examine by what *Disease*, or *Casualty* the Corps died. Hereupon they make their Report to the *Parish-Clerk*, and he, every *Tuesday* night, carries in an Accompt of all the *Burials*, and *Christnings*, hapning that Week, to the *Clerk* of the *Hall*. On *Wednesday* the general Accompt is made up, and Printed, and on *Thursdays* published, and dispersed to the several Families, who will pay four shillings *per Annum* for them.

From about 1604 onwards, these weekly bills were consolidated at the end of December, and a general bill for the year was published. . . .

Graunt's statistical data for London were drawn almost exclusively from the series of annual bills from 1604 to 1660—although he turns to the weekly bills in connection with some of his observations on plague, and includes annual and some weekly figures for years up to 1665 in later editions of the book. Essentially his data consisted of the annual numbers of christenings and burials for the above period, subdivided by parish, and, from 1629 onwards, by sex. He also had statements of the causes of death under a large number of headings (not subdivided by sex or age) from 1629 until 1660; deaths from "that extraordinary and grand *Casualty* the *Plague*," however, had been shown separately since the beginning of the period.

Graunt's table of the annual deaths by cause, taken from the annual bills, is qualified by the following note: "Memorandum, *That the 10 years between 1636 and 1647 are omitted as containing nothing Extraordinary, and as not consistent with the Incapacity of a Sheet.*" It is sad that Graunt did not use a less incapacious sheet for his table, as no annual bills for the omitted years appear to have survived the Fire of London, and Graunt's table is the sole authority for nearly all the other years included on it. One might think that after such an interval this does not matter much, but the bills are still studied today; a recent historical study of attitudes to suicide in England contains the annual series of proportionate mortality rates from suicide in London from 1629 to 1800—complete apart from these 10 years (Sprott, 1961, p. 159).

In addition to these data from the London bills, Graunt had some statistics for the country parish of Romsey in Hampshire, namely the annual numbers of weddings, and the christenings and burials by sex, from 1569 to 1658. For later editions this was supplemented with corresponding information for Tiverton in Devon and Cranbrook in Kent.

6. GRAUNT'S ARGUMENTS AND METHODS

From this very limited material, for he had no information, when he first wrote, on the size of London's population, and never had any on its age-distribution, Graunt discovered a surprising amount about the vital statistics and demography of seventeenth-century England. Amongst other things, he was the first to direct attention to the extremely high rates of mortality in infancy, and to the higher rate of mortality in London than in the country. He made the first realistic estimates of the size of the population of London, and of the country as a whole, showed that the populations of both were increasing, and that there was a steady migration into London from the country. He even made something of the extremely rudimentary data on causes of death, for example, distinguishing between endemic and epidemic diseases, noting for the first time the stability from year to year of accident and suicide rates, arguing cogently that rickets was an increasing disease and syphilis an under-recorded one, and demonstrating that the causes of death in infancy were often confused. He showed, too, that plague was under-recorded by about a quarter as a cause of death, examined which of the plague years had the greatest mortality, discovered the extent to which London depopulated itself in plague years, and then found how rapidly it repopulated itself.

But interesting though these conclusions are (and I have given only a selection), the arguments by which Graunt reached them are even more interesting. He had a remarkable and enviable facility for handling numerical data of mixed reliability and drawing valid conclusions from them, and in the process he founded a methodology of descriptive statistical analysis. One of the best examples of his approach is his discussion on rickets.

> 19. My next Observation is, that of the *Rickets* we finde no mention among the *Casualties*, untill the year 1634, and then but of 14 for that whole year.
> 20. Now the Question is, whether that Disease did first appear

about that time; or whether a Disease, which had been long before, did then first receive its Name?

21. To clear this Difficulty out of the Bills (for I dare venture on no deeper Arguments:) I enquired what other Casualties before the year 1634, named in the Bills, was most like the *Rickets;* and found, not onely by Pretenders to know it, but also from other Bills, that *Liver-grown* was the nearest. For in some years I finde *Liver-grown, Spleen* and *Rickets,* put all together, by reson (as I conceive) of their likeness to each other. Hereupon I added the *Liver-growns* of the year 1634, *viz.* 77, to the *Rickets* of the same year, *viz.* 14, making in all 91, which Total, as also the Number 77 it self, I compared with the *Liver-grown* of the precedent year, 1633, *viz.* 82. All which shewed me, that the *Rickets* was a new Disease over and above.

This, the reader may think, is not very convincing, being based on a rise from 82 to 91. Graunt did not think so either.

22. Now, this being but a faint Argument, I looked both forwards and backwards, and found, that in the year 1629, when no *Rickets* appeared, there was but 94 *Liver-growns;* and in the year 1636, there was 99 *Liver-grown,* although there were also 50 of the *Rickets:* onely this is not to be denyed, that when the *Rickets* grew very numerous (as in the year 1660, *viz.* to be 521) then there appeared not above 15 of *Liver-grown.*

23. In the year 1659 were 441 *Rickets,* and 8 *Liver-grown.* In the year 1658, were 476 *Rickets,* and 51 *Liver-grown.* Now, though it be granted that these Diseases were confounded in the judgment of the *Nurses,* yet it is most certain, that the *Liver-grown* did never but once, *viz. Anno* 1630, exceed 100, whereas *Anno* 1660, *Liver-grown,* and *Rickets* were 536.

24. It is also to be observed, That the *Rickets* were never more numerous then now, and that they are still increasing; for *Anno* 1649, there was but 190, next year 260, next after that 329, and so forwards, with some little starting backwards in some years, untill the year 1660, which produced the greatest of all.

Here is another, less frequently quoted, example of Graunt's understanding of his material, which has a number of points of interest.

11. The *Lunaticks* are also but few, *viz.* 158 in 229250, though I fear many more then are set down in our *Bills,* few being entred for such, but those who die at *Bedlam;* and there all seem to die of their *Lunacie,* who died *Lunaticks;* for there is much difference in computing the number of *Lunaticks,* that die (though of *Fevers,* and all other Diseases, unto which *Lunacie* is no *Supersedeas*) and those, that die by reason of their *Madness.*

The wording is perhaps a little strange to our ears, but there is no doubt that Graunt had a clear grasp of the distinction between mortality

and morbidity from a specific disease; the difficulty of making this distinction in practice has bedevilled official mortality statistics in all countries
ever since. I find the ensuing paragraph very entertaining.

> 12. So that, this *Casualty* being so uncertain, I shall not force my
> self to make any inference from the numbers, and proportions we finde
> in our Bills concerning it: onely I dare ensure any man at this present,
> well in his Wits, for one in the thousand, that he shall not die a *Luna-
> tick* in *Bedlam*, within these seven years, because I finde not above one
> in about one thousand five hundred have done so.

Graunt evidently knew just how one might run an insurance business.
He allows himself some leeway from the risk of 1 in 1,500 to a premium of 1
in 1,000 and then slips in a couple of extra clauses about "well in his Wits"
and "within these seven years," to "make assurance double sure." He was
writing just 100 years before the first commercial life office (the Equitable)
was opened in London.

7. POPULATION MOVEMENTS

Graunt, having no direct information on the size of the population of London, uses the information on christenings and burials most ingeniously, to
study the movements and other characteristics of the population. I shall
now outline some of these arguments in the sequence in which they occur,
because they illustrate not only the variety of conclusions he is able to draw
from his data, but the careful logical structure of the book. Graunt proceeds
deliberately from one topic to another, and has frequent occasion to build
his earlier findings into his later arguments.

His first mention of the numbers of christenings is when he relates the
numbers of abortions and stillbirths to the christenings, this incidentally
being just the form of stillbirth rate adopted by the World Health Organization for international use nowadays. He immediately comments that between 1629 and 1659 either the stillbirth rate must have increased or the
christenings must have decreased; he prefers the latter explanation, because
the numbers of christenings, having been almost equal to the burials from
1603 to 1642, had by 1659 become less than half the burials; and this he
attributes principally to increasing religious dissension during the Common-
wealth period. He notes that, if the stillbirth rate had been the same at the
end of this period as at the beginning, the number of births in 1659 (as
distinct from the number actually christened) would have been about
three-quarters of the number of burials. He then points out that a better
account is kept of women dying in child-bed than of abortions and stillbirths
and so prefers instead to base his calculations on a constant maternal
mortality rate. This gives him an estimate of the number of births in 1659

which is much closer to the number of burials, a most satisfying conclusion.

Graunt then uses the christenings explicitly as an indicator of changes in size of the population in London in times of plague, in preference to burials, "because few bear children in *London* but *Inhabitants*, though others die there." He concludes that two out of five expectant mothers died, fled or miscarried during years when plague was epidemic (notably 1603 and 1625), but found that christenings, and by implication the population, returned on each occasion to their former level within two years.

Graunt next compares the numbers of burials and christenings, deliberately restricting his comparison to the period 1604–43, for which he trusted the figures of christenings. He finds more burials than christenings in London, but rejected one obvious conclusion, that this implied a decline in the population, because he had other evidence that the population of London was increasing (as we have today), namely the "daily increase of Buildings upon new Foundations, and . . . the turning of great Palacious Houses into small Tenements. It is therefore certain, that *London* is supplied with People from out of the Countrey, whereby not onely to repair the overplus difference of *Burials* above-mentioned, but likewise to increase its *Inhabitants* according to the said increase of housing."

Next, he has figures to show that in the country the reverse applies, namely, that there were more christenings than burials. He estimates, in three ways, that the population of England and Wales was about 6,440,000, namely about fourteen times that of London, which he estimates elsewhere (also in three ways) to have been about 460,000. This enables him to show, in a rather intricate but quite valid argument, assuming his country area to be typical, that the excess of christenings over burials in the whole country was about three times as many as would provide London with an influx of population large enough to account for the observed excess of burials, the remainder either making the country more populous, or emigrating. He concludes "That the People of the whole Nation do increase, and consequently the decrease of *Winchester, Lincoln,* and other like places, must be attributed to other Reasons, then that of refurnishing *London* onely."

Once Graunt comes to deal with the numbers of the two sexes in the population he immediately extends his data to include figures after 1643, noting in justification that the general decrease in christenings has not affected the relative proportions of the sexes. He finds more male christenings than female, and more male burials than female, each in the proportion fourteen to thirteen; from this he concludes that there were more males alive than females. This would be a fair conclusion if age-specific death rates for males and females were equal, but is not necessarily correct otherwise. (Similar excesses of male over female births and male over female deaths are found in England and Wales today, but because age-specific death rates are uniformly higher among males than females, there are fewer males than females living.) Unfortunately Graunt, who had no data which would permit a statistical examination of the point, leaves us in some uncertainty whether he regarded male and female death rates as equal or not. On the one hand, he suggests "that men, being more intemperate then women, die as much by reason of the Vices, as the women do by the Infirmitie of their *Sex*, and consequently, more *Males* being born, then *Females*, more also die." On the other hand, he implies a differential death rate, at least among young adults, in a famous statement which eventually influenced Malthus: "that although more men die violent deaths then women, that is, more are *slain* in Wars, *killed* by mischance, *drowned* at *Sea*, and die by the *Hand of Justice*. Moreover, more men go to *Colonies*, and travel into foreign parts, then women. And lastly, more remain unmarried, then of women, as *Fellows* of *Colleges*, and *Apprentises*, above eighteen, &c. yet the said thirteenth part difference bringeth the business but to such a pass, that every woman may have an Husband, without the allowance of *Polygamy*." Apparently Graunt realized that a differential mortality rate would affect the relative numbers of adult males and females, but missed the corollary, that his conclusion (of more males alive than females) was unlikely to be valid unless the age-specific death rates of males and females were closely similar. This is one of the very few places in the book where one can legitimately criticize the logic of one of Graunt's deductions.

The final item in this sequence consists of Graunt's assessment of the increase in London's population. Here he wishes to deal with the whole period from 1593 to 1659, and so has to rely upon the burials as his indicator of the population rather than christenings. But he uses these data with his customary instinct for a correct statistical approach. He subtracts plague deaths from the total deaths throughout, he leaves out the years when plague was epidemic and those immediately following, because of the exodus of the population, and to make the comparisons more reliable he bases them on averages of two years rather than on single years. He concludes that the total population of London had increased from "two to five" in 54 years (1605–59), the greatest increases being in the parishes outside the walls of the city, and "That the City of *London* gradually removes *Westward*." This last observation is not original, having been made by Evelyn the previous year in "Fumifugium," the famous first treatise on atmospheric pollution in London, but Graunt was the first to demonstrate it statistically.

8. ESTIMATES OF THE SIZE OF THE POPULATION

I referred above to Graunt's estimates of population size, and in this field too his approaches are most instructive. He tells us that his interest in estimating the population of London was aroused by hearing an assertion that there were 2 million more people in London in 1661 than before the plague in 1625. He begins, characteristically, by pointing out that this would imply a total population of about 6 or 7 million in London in 1661, which, from the deaths recorded in the bills, would mean that the annual mortality would have been less than 1 in 400. He next shows that another popular belief, "That it is esteemed an even Lay, whether any man lives ten years longer," when applied to an estimate of the adult deaths, led to a figure for the total population which he clearly regards as much too small.

Graunt then describes three ways in which he "endeavoured to get a little nearer" the truth; each involved estimating the number of families in London, and multiplying this by the average size of family, which Graunt took to be eight, made up of a man and his wife, three children, and three servants or lodgers. Graunt's estimates of the number of families were made respectively via births, deaths and houses.

> 4. I considered, that the number of *Child-bearing women* might be about double to the *Births:* forasmuch as such women, one with another, have scarce more then one Childe in two years. The number of *Births* I found, by those years, wherein the *Registries* were well kept, to have been somewhat less then the *Burials.* The *Burials* in these late years at a *Medium* are about 13000, and consequently the *Christnings* not above 12000. I therefore esteemed the number of *Teeming women* to be 24000: then I imagined, that there might be twice as many Families, as of such women; for that there might be twice as many women *Aged* between 16 and 76, as between 16 and 40, or between 20 and 44. . . .

This gives him 48,000 families, and a population of 384,000.

> 5. Secondly, I finde by telling the number of Families in some Parishes within the walls, that 3 out of 11 families *per an.* have died: wherefore, 13000 having died in the whole, it should follow, there were 48000 Families. . . .
>
> 7. And lastly I took the Map of *London* set out in the year 1658 by *Richard Newcourt,* drawn by a scale of Yards. Now I guessed that in 100 yards square there might be about 54 Families, supposing every house to be 20 foot in the front: for on two sides of the said square there will be 100 yards of housing in each, and in the two other sides 80 each; in all 360 yards: that is 54 Families in each square, of which there are 220 within the Walls, making in all 11880 Families within the Walls. But forasmuch as there dy within the Walls about 3200 *per Annum,* and in the whole about 13000; it follows, that the housing within the Walls is ¼. part of the whole, and consequently, that there

are 47520 Families in, and about *London,* which agrees well enough
with all my former computations: the worst whereof doth sufficiently
demonstrate, that there are no Millions of People in *London,* which
nevertheless most men do believe.

Graunt's estimate of 460,000 for the population of London, which I
mentioned earlier, arises by the addition of one-fifth to the figure of 384,000
to encompass *"Westminster, Stepney, Lambeth,* and the other distant
Parishes."

Graunt's first argument "that *England* hath fourteen times more People" than London is that *"London* is observed to bear about the fifteenth
proportion of the whole Tax." His second is based upon a computed density
of population of 220 to the square mile in his country parish (Romsey),
"of which I abate ¼ for the overplus of People more in that Parish, then in
other wilde Counties"; this leads him to the figure quoted earlier of 6,440,000
persons in the whole country (including London), which has an area of
39,000 square miles. The third estimate, of 6 million, is based upon a suggested average population of 600 in each of the 10,000 parishes in the
country.

It is, of course, easy to criticize individual items in the edifice of assumptions and approximations behind each of these estimates, but to do this is
to miss the point. The importance of these paragraphs is that they represent
the earliest attempts to estimate population size scientifically, and the results show very clearly how much a scientific guess is to be preferred to an
unscientific guess. By using a variety of approaches to each population figure Graunt shows that he is well aware of the shortcomings of the data, and
at the same time the consistency of the various estimates (even though it
may be in part artificial) is at least confirmation that Graunt's orders of
magnitude are likely to be correct.

It is of especial interest that, after making these estimates, Graunt
was able to apply a check to his figure for London. An enumeration of the
population of the city and liberties of London had been made in 1631 for
taxation purposes, but the findings were not generally available, and Graunt
was clearly unaware of their existence when he first published the *Observations.* He later obtained the figures and included them with the appendix in
the third and later editions of the book. When scaled up in accordance with
his own estimate of the population increase in the city and liberties in the interval of 30 years, and again in accordance with his estimate of the relative
populations of all London, and the city and liberties, in 1661, the total figure
Graunt obtains is 403,000; from which "it will appear, that I computed too
many rather than too few, although the most part of men have thought
otherwise."

9. THE FIRST LIFE TABLE

I turn to what is commonly regarded as Graunt's masterpiece, the first life table.

> 9. Whereas we have found, that of 100 quick Conceptions about 36 of them die before they be six years old, and that perhaps but one surviveth 76, we, having seven *Decads* between six and 76, we sought six mean proportional numbers between 64, the remainder, living at six years, and the one, which survives 76, and finde, that the numbers following are practically near enough to the truth; for men do not die in exact Proportions, nor in Fractions: from whence arises this Table following.

Viz. of 100 there dies within the first six years	36
The next ten years, or *Decad*	24
The second *Decad*	15
The third *Decad*	09
The fourth	6
The next	4
The next	3
The next	2
The next	1

> 10. From whence it follows, that of the said 100 conceived there remains alive at six years end 64.

At Sixteen years end	40
At Twenty six	25
At Thirty six	16
At Fourty six	10
At Fifty six	6
At Sixty six	3
At Seventy six	1
At Eighty	0

There has been much speculation how Graunt derived his column of survivors—indeed the production of rival explanations seems to have become almost a statistical parlour-game in the nineteen-twenties and thirties. More recently, Glass (1950) suggested that Graunt used a method of diminishing differences for distributing the deaths, and this appeals to me more than the earlier efforts because it involves an arithmetical approach more likely to have occurred to Graunt.

This life table is derived from a distribution of deaths by age, and not, as a modern one would be, from mortality rates based on the population. Greenwood (1948) pointed out that as a consequence this table would be valid as a description of the dying-out of the population only if the population were stationary (which, Graunt had shown, was not so) and discusses whether Graunt realized this. I find it hard to convince myself that Graunt would have appreciated so abstruse a point. Greenwood appears to assume tacitly that Graunt approached the problem of compiling his table from the standpoint of a modern actuary or statistician, and this I am sure he did not. Thus, Greenwood refers to Graunt's "great achievement, the estimation of rates of mortality at ages when the numbers and ages of the living were not recorded." But this is not what Graunt set out to achieve; he had, as I suggest below, a much more practical aim. Nor, in this context, was the lack of information on the living his problem; it was the lack of information about the dead. He had estimated—and estimated is here the right word—that of 100 children born alive 36 would die before they were six years old, and it would naturally occur to him to wonder when the remaining 64 would die. He had no information on ages at death from which to estimate this and so he fell back on a piece of arithmetical guesswork; he distributed the 64 deaths into a diminishing series which would link smoothly with the initial figure of 36 and leave the last of his deaths to occur at a suitably advanced age. If his procedure was that suggested by Glass this would lead him to a final death at an age exceeding 76, and this may be the origin of Graunt's otherwise unsupported suggestion "that perhaps but one surviveth 76." Graunt then built up the column of survivors.

Now Graunt introduces his table just after estimating London's population to consist of 199,000 males and 185,000 females. His reason for introducing it is to compute how many of the 199,000 are "fighting Men," and he does this by deriving from the column of survivors the proportion of the population aged between 16 and 56, applying this to the total of 199,000. But at this point he commits an important statistical error. What he derives from the column of survivors and uses in his calculation is not the proportion living at ages 16 to 56, but the proportion *dying* between those ages. No one appears to have noticed this error for more than 250 years (Westergaard, 1932, p. 23), so Graunt may perhaps be excused for having made it. Nevertheless, as Greenwood said, "Graunt was not at all clear in his mind as to how to use a life table."

Graunt, having introduced the table for a specific purpose, and having, as he thought, achieved this, makes no further reference to it; he gives no sign of having perceived its actuarial uses. Nor does Petty, who made a similar table (Hull, 1899, 1, 144), and committed the same error, at a later date (although Petty did indicate in a different context that, if certain information were available for the population, one could calculate mortality rates at ages and put these to actuarial use—see Greenwood, 1948, 15). It was left to Halley (1693a, b) to derive a realistic age-distribution of a stationary population from records of ages at death, and to describe its actuarial uses. It seems to me that unless Graunt had first realized the actuarial potentialities of *his* table, the point discussed by Greenwood would certainly not have occurred to him.

If this account of the origins of Graunt's table is correct, he retains the honour of making the first attempt to describe the dying out of a population cohort, but cannot be regarded, actuarially speaking, as having compiled the first life table. The distinction may seem a fine one, but I believe that it is historically correct.

10. FURTHER STATISTICAL APPROACHES

Most of Graunt's arguments, as we have seen, are based upon the study of ratios, differences between ratios and time-trends in ratios. But what Graunt describes as "*the* Mathematiques *of my Shop-Arithmetique*" extended further than that. He knew how to study associations, to "counterpoise the Opinion of those who think great *Plagues* come in with *Kings* reigns, because it hapned so twice, *viz. Anno* 1603, and 1625, whereas as well the year 1648, wherein the present *King* commenced his right to reign, as also the year 1660, wherein he commenced the exercise of the same, were both eminently healthful, which clears both *Monarchie,* and our present *King's Familie* from what seditious men have surmised against them." Two against two may not wholly convince a modern statistician, but there is nothing wrong with the approach. Again, Graunt noted an inverse association between christenings and burials, both in London and in the country, years with the more burials having the fewer christenings, and vice versa.

He made a rational attempt to study time-series, defining a sickly year as one in which there were not more than 200 deaths from plague and in which the burials exceeded those of the preceding and succeeding year. He even touched upon the classic problem of epidemiology, the course of an epidemic, noting, among other characteristics, that plague took longer to rise to its peak than to decline from it, in the proportion of three to two.

He was also interested in geographical variations, particularly in the relative numbers of male and female births, and this led him to attempt what can only be described as the first sample survey. "I have here inserted two other Countrey Bills, the one of *Cranbrook* in *Kent,* the other of *Tiverton* in *Devonshire*, which with that of *Hantshire*, lying about the midway between them, give us a view of the most Easterly, Southerly, and Westerly parts of *England*: I have endeavoured to procure the like account from *Northumberland, Cheshire, Norfolk* and *Nottinghamshire*; Thereby to have a view of seven Countries most differently situated, from whence I am sorry to observe that my Southern friends have been hitherto more curious and diligent than those of the North."

11. THE LIMITS OF GRAUNT'S STATISTICAL PERCEPTION

Perhaps the main single impression which Graunt leaves with a modern statistical reader is one of his sure-footed progress through a mass of untidy numerical data, apparently instinctively keeping clear of that which was unanalysable and extracting the maximum of information from the rest; he seems, too, to have had an intuitive appreciation of just how much interpretation his findings would stand, and takes care not to exceed this.

I have referred to Graunt's two major statistical errors, in connection with the relative numbers of the two sexes and in using his life table. I do not consider that these detract from Graunt's achievement. A pioneer must be judged by the amount of new ground he explores, not by the fact that he is eventually brought to a halt. Graunt's errors both arise at the extreme limits of what he might have been expected to appreciate. In a situation in which no ages at death were recorded, and there was no prospect of information about the numbers and ages of the living, it is not surprising that Graunt should have failed to appreciate the subtle interplay between birth-rates, age-specific death-rates and the size of the living population. Even today a student of demography may pause at the apparent paradox of more male than female births and more male deaths, and yet fewer males than females alive; and may make the mistake of regarding a column of survivors at various anniversaries as if it represented an age-distribution of a living population.

In one section of the book, Graunt emphasizes the much greater proportionate variation from year to year in the numbers of births and deaths in his small country parish than was found in London. He has consequently been criticized (Hull, 1899, 1, p. lxxvi) for failing to appreciate that the smaller numbers would be inherently more variable. But surely he did appreciate this—otherwise why should he have combined the burials for consecutive years when studying the trends in size of London's population over a period of years? Moreover, as Greenwood (1948) showed, the variations in the country districts were substantially greater than would be expected from chance alone, and he suggested that Graunt might have recognized this intuitively.

12. THE AUTHORSHIP OF THE "OBSERVATIONS"

I have deliberately left until now a matter on which some comment might have been expected earlier. It concerns the allegation that Graunt never wrote the *Observations* at all, these being the work of his friend Sir William Petty. This allegation was not made, as far as we know, until after Graunt's death, but it has persisted in some quarters until the present day. It would, unfortunately, take too long even to outline the arguments on the two sides (see Hull, 1899, 1, p. xxxix; Willcox, 1937 or 1939; Greenwood, 1948, p. 36), but it is sufficient, in the present context, to say that statisticians have never been in any serious doubt that Graunt wrote his own book. Assessing them as statisticians, there is no comparison between the two men. There is sufficient evidence above of the validity of Willcox's (1937 or 1939) comment that "To the trained reader Graunt writes statistical music," and there is little difficulty in verifying the antithesis, that "Petty is like a child playing with a new musical toy which occasionally yields a bit of harmony."

There can, however, be little doubt that the two men, who were then close friends, discussed the book while it was in preparation, and Petty may well have suggested additions and perhaps even supplied some draft. But by far the greater part of the text, and certainly all the statistically important parts, could never have come from Petty. This is not to deny Petty's many other merits. He was an inventive man, and full of good ideas, even though they did not all come to fruition as fast or as successfully as he wished. In particular, he advocated, in detail, the setting up of a General Register Office in this country more than 150 years before it was achieved, and it was he who was responsible for carrying forward Graunt's isolated statistical effort into the beginnings of political arithmetic, or, as we now call it, demography. . . .

ACKNOWLEDGEMENTS

It is a pleasure to thank Professor E. S. Pearson for allowing me to consult the manuscripts of Karl Pearson's lectures on the history of statistics, and Professor D. V. Glass for keeping me informed of his own recent discoveries about Graunt. I am indebted to Mr. E. C. Chamberlain, Fitzwilliam Museum, Cambridge, and to Mr. R. Williams, British Museum, for their efforts to locate a portrait of Graunt, and to Dr. H. Campbell for pointing out the parallel between Graunt and Leeuwenhoek.

REFERENCES

Glass, D. V. (1950), "Graunt's life table," *J. Inst. Actu.*, **76**, 60–64.

Greenwood, M. (1948), *Medical Statistics from Graunt to Farr*. Cambridge University Press.

Halley, E. (1693a), "An estimate of the degrees of the mortality of mankind, drawn from curious tables of the births and funerals at the city of Breslaw; with an attempt to ascertain the price of annuities upon lives," *Phil. Trans.*, **17**, 596–610.

————— (1693b), "Some further considerations on the Breslaw bills of mortality," *Phil. Trans.*, **17**, 654–656.

Hull, C. H. (Ed.) (1899), *The Economic Writings of Sir William Petty together with the Observations on the Bills of Mortality more probably by Captain John Graunt.* (Including a reprint of the fifth edition, 1676.) Cambridge University Press.

Royal Statistical Society (1934), *Annals of the Royal Statistical Society, 1834–1934.* London.

Sprat, T. (1667), *The History of the Royal Society of London, for the Improving of Natural Knowledge.* London.

Sprott, S. E. (1961), *The English Debate on Suicide from Donne to Hume.* La Salle, Illinois: Open Court.

Todhunter, I. (1865), *A History of the Mathematical Theory of Probability from the Time of Pascal to That of Laplace.* London: Macmillan.

Tukey, J. W. (1962), "The future of data analysis," *Ann. math. Statist.*, **33**, 1–67.

Westergaard, H. (1932), *Contributions to the History of Statistics.* London: King.

Willcox, W. F. (1937), "The founder of statistics," *Rev. Inst. int. Statist.*, **5**, 321–328.

————— (Ed.) (1939), *Natural and Political Observations made upon the Bills of Mortality by John Graunt.* (A reprint of the first edition, 1662.) Baltimore: Johns Hopkins Press.

7

Statistics
and Society

Philip M. Hauser

Some years ago, in helping to present the budget of the Bureau of the Census to a Sub-Committee of the House Appropriations Committee, I was asked by a Congressman strategically placed to influence the course and development of government statistics—"If American business has been able to get along for 150 years without statistics, why does it need them now?" [8, p. 1]. It is of crucial importance, not only to statisticians as a professional group, but to all other segments of contemporary society to face and to attempt to answer this question. It is even more important to attempt to answer the broader question: Why does society now need a vast array of statistical activities when in prior centuries it was able to get along with little or virtually none? . . .

Permit me to begin with an elementary perspective. Man has inhabited this globe for a minimum of 200,000 years and, perhaps, as long as two million years or more. Recent finds by the British anthropologist Leakey [11] indicate that close relatives of man wandered over the earth as long as 14 million years ago. Over almost all of this vast span of time there was no field of statistics and, perhaps happily, there were no statisticians.

For most of the time that man has been on this earth he has been a nomad. Permanent human settlement was not possible until after the great advances of the Neolithic Revolution some 10,000 years ago. These included the domestication of plants and animals, which made it unnecessary for man to chase his food supply, and the elaboration of the crafts [15, pp. 51–67]. Moreover, in addition to these and other technological developments, man, over the years, achieved cultural, intellectual, and moral ad-

Reprinted from the *Journal of the American Statistical Association*, 58, no. 301 (March, 1963), pp. 1–12, by permission of the author and the publisher.

vances which were also preconditions for permanent human settlement—manifest in various forms of social organization and social control.

The size that a human settlement could reach was a function of three major factors—environment, technology, and social organization. The Neolithic village never achieved a size of more than a few hundred persons at most. In Europe the largest pre-historic village yet known—Barkaer in Jutland—had only 52 small one-room dwellings. Sixteen to 30 houses were the more usual, setting an upper limit to population varying from about 200 to some 400 persons [2, p. 6]. The small size of the Neolithic village arose from the need for people to live within easy walking distance of areas under cultivation with primitive agricultural methods. Thus, when population growth exceeded the capacity of the land within ready walking distance, the village grew through fission—a new settlement had to be formed.

At the outset all members of the peasant Neolithic village were primarily cultivators. Non-agricultural specialists were not possible until the combination of technological and social organizational developments resulted, on the one hand, in a food surplus and, on the other, in some method of effecting an exchange relationship between the cultivator and the non-agricultural specialist. Among the early specialists were the ruler, the priest, and the craftsman. Some of these experts could not be supported at the outset by any one village alone. They could make a living, apparently, only by travelling a circuit; and indeed this pattern of activity has been observed among the Maori in more recent times [2, p. 7].

Continued technological and organizational developments made possible the city—a population clumping many times the size of any known Neolithic village. The city first appeared about 5500 years ago. Turner traces some of the highlights of its emergence from the peasant-village of the Neolithic period in Mesopotamia, India, Egypt, and Crete [15, Chs. II–VI]. The city may be distinguished from the village by its relatively large size, the full-time specialist freed from food production, and the presence of organizational development which permitted the storing and allocation of food surplus [2, pp. 12 ff.]. For storage and allocation of surplus, record keeping was necessary. Hence, the early civilizations in which the city first appeared developed systems of writing and of numerical notation. These inventions in turn contributed greatly to the growth of larger cities.

Systems of writing and numerical notation were a pre-condition for science and its auxiliaries—arithmetic, geometry, and mathematics in general. Numerical notation made possible measurement with scales other than the nominal scale. Continued developments in mathematics and in measurement played a major role in advances in knowledge and in the invention of science—physical, biological and, more recently, social. The development of writing and numerical notation, essential to the keeping of records for the storing and allocation of food surpluses, had far-reaching consequences.

The collection and allocation of food surpluses were accomplished through the ruler, who in ancient times often combined with his temporal powers the authority of the supernatural, as in ancient Egypt. Record keeping, which facilitated the performance of this function, also contributed to other important governmental activities for domestic and foreign purposes [2, pp. 12 ff.]. It made possible the count, recruitment, organization and utilization of able-bodied men for police and military purposes and also for the levying and collection of taxes.

The emergence of systems of writing and of numerical notation antedated by far the appearance of statistics and statisticians. Literacy and counting ability for most of the time that man has lived in cities were in themselves forms of specialization. This is apparent even as recently as in our own national history. In a memorial to the Congress which reached the Senate on January 10, 1800, the American Philosophical Society, through its President, Thomas Jefferson, petitioned for the expansion of census statistics and included reference to the need for occupational information. Jefferson wrote:

> . . . in order to ascertain more completely the causes which influence life and health, and to furnish a curious and useful document of society in these States, and of the conditions and vocations of our fellow citizens . . . [a table was to specify] the number of free male inhabitants, of all ages, engaged in business, under the following or such other descriptions as the greater wisdom of the legislature shall approve, to wit: (1) men of the learned professions, including clergymen, lawyers, physicians, those employed in the fine arts, teachers, and *scribes in general* [20, p. 19; italics added].

Jefferson then continued to list eight other categories of occupations. Thus, to read and write in the United States in 1800 was to have a "learned profession." Men of letters, those who could write, read, and reckon, were in their origin associated with the aristocratic ruling group. The term "statistics" referred to "matters of state," reflecting the early relationship between record keeping and the performance of state functions. The term "statists" was, in fact, sometimes used for statisticians during the 19th century. The Statistical Society of London in 1884 for its Jubilee Session asked that the views of "foreign statists" be ascertained [13, p. 5].

It took the same social, economic, and political developments that led to the undermining of the feudalistic and aristocratic orders and the emergence of a democratic society for the skill of the scribe to become widely diffused through the general population. Moreover, it took the complex developments, technological and social, which make up the agricultural, commercial, industrial, and scientific revolutions to produce the mammoth cities and metropolitan areas of the contemporary world, and, with them, the greatly increased specialization, including considerable differentiation of "scribes in general." The statistician may be regarded as one of the forms of specialization of the general function of the scribe.

This is neither the time nor the place to attempt the full tracing of events which produced the statistician, but I should like to present some highlights of these developments and a framework born of "human ecological" considerations for understanding them. For purposes of exposition, I shall use the phrase "social morphological revolution" to stand for what I am about to describe. This is in keeping with the best academic traditions, for scholars, seeking a short descriptive phrase for a chapter title or book title, are, after all, responsible for the invention of the various "revolutions" —the "agricultural revolution," the "commercial revolution," the "industrial revolution," the "scientific revolution" and the like. I cannot claim complete credit for this neologism, for it was Emile Durkheim writing in the 19th century who made much of "social morphology'" as a key to understanding the nature of society and social behavior [4, Bk. II, Ch. II]. The "social morphological revolution," as I am using the term, refers to the basic changes in the size and density of human settlement over time and the consequences of these changes. It is a way of summarizing quantitatively the transition from nomadic existence to neolithic village living to town life and, finally, to urban and metropolitan patterns of living.

Durkheim has stated that:

> Social life rests on a substratum whose size as well as its form is determined. This substratum is constituted by the mass of individuals who make up society, the way in which they are distributed on the soil, and the nature and configuration of all sorts of things that affect collective relationships. The social substratum differs according to whether the population is large or small and more or less dense, whether it is concentrated in cities or dispersed over the countryside, how cities and houses are constructed, whether the area occupied by the society is more or less extensive, and according to the kind of boundaries that delimit it [3, pp. 9–10].

In elaboration of this keen observation of Durkheim's, let us consider the differences in potential social interaction in a community with a fixed land area but varying population density. Let the land area be that which lies within a circle with a 10-mile radius, namely, 314 square miles. In such an area the size of the population under different density conditions is shown below [10, pp. 100 ff.]:

Population Density (Population per Square Mile)	Number of Persons Circle of 10-mile Radius
1	314
50	15,700
8,000	2,512,000
17,000	5,338,000
25,000	7,850,000

The density of one person per square mile is not too far from the density of the United States when occupied by the Indians. The density of 50 is approximately that of the United States today, and also of the world as a whole. The density of 8,000, in round numbers, was that of central cities in metropolitan areas in 1950, the density figure of 17,000 was that of Chicago in 1950, and the 25,000 density figure that of New York .

Thus, in aboriginal America the person moving about within a circle of 10-mile radius could potentially make only 313 different contacts. In contrast, the density of the U.S. as a whole today would make possible well over 15,000 contacts in the same land area; the density of central cities in the U.S., in 1950, would permit over 2.5 million contacts; the density of Chicago over 5.3 million contacts; and the density of New York City about 7.9 million contacts. These differences in density and therefore in potential social interaction necessarily affect the nature of collective activity and social organization.

This simple way of presenting the implications for interaction of differences in size and density of populations underlies and portrays a mutation in social organization and, consequently, in human behavior and thought. The increasing size and concentration of population are responsible for the social mutation—the equivalent of a genetic mutation—represented by the felicitous phrase of my late colleague Louis Wirth "urbanism as a way of life" [18, Part II, Ch. 1].

It is my thesis that the social morphological revolution culminating in urbanism as a way of life has, among other things, produced both statistics and statisticians. For the social morphological revolution has produced the "mass society"—a society in which the nature of human nature and the nature of social organization has been profoundly altered. The multiplier effect of increasing size and density of population on social interaction has produced contacts which are "secondary" rather than "primary"—that is, distant rather than face to face, segmental rather than integral, utilitarian rather than sentimental [18, ibid.]. Under these conditions, human behavior has tended to become rational rather than traditional, and social control has tended to become formal, effected through law and regulation, rather than informal, operating through the constraint of the folkways and mores. In the mass society, social institutions have become increasingly "enacted" rather than "crescive," that is, they are more invented and created by deliberate design rather than the product of gradual development in the history of a culture [14, pp. 53 ff.]. In the mass society, "bureaucracy" has become a necessity. "Bureaucracy" used in the Weberian sociological sense [17, Ch. VIII] does not refer to government bureaus and "tax eaters" as elements in the prevalent stereotype of "big government." In its sociological connotation, "bureaucracy" is a form of indispensable organization in a mass society. Bureaucracies are formal organizations designed to achieve specific objectives. Bureaucracy is not confined to the political or governmental. There are no sectors of the mass society in which bureaucratic organization does not appear. It is evident in business, in labor, in education, in religion, and in civic, fraternal, recreational, and other voluntary organizations. The essential characteristics of a bureaucracy are contained in four elements: one, in a division of labor and specialization; two, in a hierarchy of authority —a well-structured system of superordination and subordination; three, in an explicit system of fixed rights and obligations; and, four, in consequence of these elements, in an aura of impersonality.

Although government bureaucracy is but one facet of bureaucratic organization in the mass society, it is a facet of great general significance and, also, of considerable import in the development of statistics and the emergence of the statistician. Big government has, as we are all aware, become a matter of basic political cleavage on both the international and the domestic scenes. But the proliferation of government functions and the increased number of government bureaus and employees cannot be regarded as the result of victories or defeats in the political process in accordance with opposing ideologies in respect to the role of government. Big government is rather a product of the social morphological revolution—an inevitable concomitant of the evolution of the mass society. The record shows, for example, that the functions of American government have continuously expanded in the course of our history; and that the expansion has been largely without regard to the political complexion of the party in power or the philosophy of the administration in regard to the role of government [19, Ch. XXV; 7, pp. 3–28].

A simple example of this proposition is to be found in the changed role and function of government in respect to the automobile. Even if the automobile had been available in colonial America, it is unlikely that local government would have included the contemporary complex of functions relating to it. With the size and density of population in colonial America, it is unlikely that local government would have had to provide for traffic signals, traffic policemen, traffic tickets, traffic courts, and parking meters; let alone off-street parking facilities, expressways, and institutions for dealing with traffic accidents—ambulance services, emergency medical centers, hospital wards, and morgues. The proliferation of government functions and personnel necessitated by the automobile is a clear-cut and by no means unique example of the changes resulting from increased size and density of the population and advancing technology.

A few additional examples may serve further to clarify the transformation in the role and function of government in the mass society. Certainly there is more than a casual connection between the inability of the family in the contemporary urban order to cope with the problems of urban health hazards, industrial accidents, and unemployment, and the expansion of government functions in the field of public health, workmen's compensation, and unemployment insurance benefits. Similarly, the creation of the Interstate Commerce Commission, the Federal Trade Commission, the Securities and Exchange Commission, the Council of Economic Advisors, the Atomic Energy Control Commission, the Department of Health, Education and Welfare, and the Urban Renewal Administration, are but a few examples, on the Federal level, of new government agencies which have been created to perform functions never anticipated by the founding fathers.

The expansion of government functions has inexorably led to increased record keeping and to greater need for facts as a guide to policy and action. Government agencies have thus played a prominent part in the collection, tabulation, dissemination and use of statistics—facts in quantified and organized form.

Early in the history of the United States, the volume and flow of statistical data were relatively small and there was no or little need for the personnel dealing with statistics to become specialist-statisticians. Yet by the time the Federal government was established in 1789, statistics had already become useful in the conduct of government.

To begin with, the Federal government inherited an accumulation of statistics from Colonial times. For during the Colonial period, statistics on population became available from 1610; on the slave trade from 1619 (Virginia); on daily wages of workmen from 1621, on weekly basic diets from 1622, on exports and imports from 1697, on bills of credit and treasury notes from 1703. Indexes of wholesale prices can be calculated from 1720 and tax collections from 1765. Statistics on private insurance date from 1759 [16, Ch. Z].

Of the greatest significance, however, is the fact that the very organization of the Federal government was made dependent on a statistical operation—a census of population as required decennially by Article 1, Section 2, of the Constitution of the United States. Moreover, from the beginning of the activity of the new government, statistics were maintained on such matters as government finances, military personnel, elections, foreign trade, water transport, balance of international payments, postal services, patents, and membership in religious bodies. Early in the life of the Federal government statistical series began to multiply. Data on hay, cotton, and cottonseed acreage production and prices became available from 1790; on gold and silver production from 1792; on iron ore and pig iron production from 1799; on currency stock and currency in circulation from 1800; on public land sales from 1800; on medical schools and dentists from 1810; on banking from 1811; and on immigration from 1820 [16, Ch. Z].

The development of statistics as a function of advancing technology is evident in the data relating to transport in the U.S. Data on water transport are available from 1789, on railroads from 1830, on highways from 1890, on scheduled air transport from 1926. The story is paralleled in the field of communication. Postage statistics have been available since 1789, data relating to telegraph and cables from 1866, to telephones from 1876, to radio from 1921, and to television from 1941 [16, Ch. Z].

Perhaps the best single operation in which the expansion of statistics can be traced as a function of social change—the increased complexity and interdependence of the social order—is in the decennial census of the U.S. The first census, in 1790, was entirely restricted to population and contained only 6 inquiries, including the names of heads of families and items relating to age, sex, and free or slave status. The number of inquiries by 1800 had doubled, although they were still restricted to the same topics—age, sex, and free or slave status. By 1820, the inquiries included new topics, indicating the new problems engaging the attention of the Congress—questions relating to naturalization and to workers in agriculture, commerce, and manufacture. By 1830, the schedule required the reporting of the deaf and dumb and also the blind. In 1840, seven categories of work activity were called for and also information on pensions for "Revolutionary or military services" [20, pp. 12–39]. Incidentally, the 1840 census was the first for which the newly formed American Statistical Association (1839) presented a memorial to the U.S. Congress [5, pp. 15–6].

In 1850, with the accelerating tempo of technological and social change, there was a major expansion in census inquiries. The Congress required six schedules to be used of which Schedule No. 1, relating to free inhabitants, was an expanded population schedule. It included questions requiring detailed occupational returns for all males over 15 years of age, the value of real estate owned, place of birth, whether married within the year, school attendance, literacy, and an elaboration of information on physical disabilities. Schedule No. 2 related to slave inhabitants and called for the names of slave owners and the number of slaves, as well as for information on the characteristics of slaves. Schedule No. 3 related to mortality, requiring information on the characteristics of all persons who died during the year. Schedule No. 4 was an agricultural schedule, calling for detailed returns on agricultural production and related items. Schedule No. 5 was an industrial schedule applying to manufacturing, mining, fisheries and all kinds of "mercantile, commercial or trading business." Schedule No. 6 called for "social statistics" for each political subdivision, including such items as valuation of estate; annual taxes; colleges, academies and schools; seasons and crops; libraries; newspapers and periodicals; religion; pauperism; crime and wages. The Census of 1850 may well be regarded as the first U.S. Census attuned to the statistical needs of the emerging mass society. It, by the way, in addition to greatly broadening the scope of census inquiries, introduced important changes in census procedures to improve the quality of the data [20, pp. 39–50].

The Censuses of 1860 and 1870, in the main, followed the outlines of the Census of 1850. But important modifications were made in the 1870 Census schedules at the initiative of the Superintendent of the Census, General Francis A. Walker. He, by the way, was President of the American Statistical Association from 1883 to 1896. Five new inquiries were added to the population schedule, two on place of birth of foreign parents, two on "constitutional relations" following the 14th Amendment to the Constitution (right to vote and its abridgement) and a question on month of birth for persons born during the year. Other modifications were made in the census schedules by way of refining the inquiries and dropping or adding questions in accordance with the experience gained in the Censuses of 1850 and 1860 [20, pp. 50–7].

The first effort to achieve a quinquennial census was made during the 1870's—for a census in 1875. Even then, as once again in the present decade, it was felt that census statistics were needed more often than decennially; and, in addition, a Census of 1875 would have recorded the centennial of Independence. But President Grant's recommendation for such a census at the suggestion of Superintendent Walker was rejected by the Congress [20, p. 58].

The Census of 1880 employed five schedules, as in 1870, relating to population, agriculture, manufacturers, mortality, and social statistics. Population schedule additions included questions on relationship to head of household, marital status, illness as well as disability, and unemployment (months unemployed during the census year). Noting only the most important population census changes since, ability to speak English, immigration, tenure of home and veteran status appeared in 1890; farm residence, duration of marriage and fertility in 1900; mother tongue in 1910; value of home and radio set in 1930; internal migration, years of school completed, labor force including employment status, income, usual occupation and social security number in 1940. More detailed income questions were added in 1950; and questions relating to place of work, means of transportation to work, and length of residence in same dwelling unit, in 1960 [20, pp. 58 ff. to Census of 1890 and census schedules thereafter].

In addition to these developments in the Census of Population, provision was made for separate new censuses. The schedules relating to industry, agriculture, and commerce introduced in 1850 may be regarded as the precursors of the Census of Manufactures initiated in 1904, the quinquennial Census of Agriculture in 1925, the Census of Distribution in 1930. The Census of Religious Bodies, not without earlier precedent, was provided for in 1906. The newest of the censuses, in response to a chronic urban plant problem, is the Census of Housing, first taken in 1940, and a Census of Transportation [which was] taken in 1963.

The full story of the elaboration of the statistical activities of the Bureau of the Census cannot be related here. But at least mention must be made of the growing importance and greatly expanded size of the current statistical program of the Bureau, signaling the increasing recognition of the role of statistics as a form of knowledge for current use, rather than for the historical record.

Needless to say, the expansion of census activities was paralleled by the elaboration of statistical activities throughout the Federal government. In the Department of Agriculture, the U.S. Public Health Service, and the Federal Reserve Board, highly significant statistical agencies were developed; and, in virtually all Departments, statistical activities of some sort were originated or expanded. The need to control, to coordinate, and to integrate Federal statistics led to the Committee on Government Statistics in 1933, and, eventually, to the Federal Reports Act in 1941 and to the creation of the Office of Statistical Standards in the Bureau of the Budget in the Executive Office of the President of the United States [9, v ff. and p. 1 ff.].

Nor was the increase in statistics restricted to government alone. There is practically no collective activity in our mass society which does not maintain records from which statistics are a by-product. The proliferation of statistics in business has certainly matched that in government, and for similar reasons. Highly important private statistical data collecting and publishing efforts include those of the National Bureau of Economic Research, the National Industrial Conference Board, the Dodge Corporation, Standard and Poor's, Dun and Bradstreet, and McGraw-Hill. In the field of market statistics and sample surveys, the operations of Gallup, Roper, Audit & Surveys, National Analysts, the University of Michigan Survey Research Center, and the University of Chicago National Opinion Research Center loom large.

The financial and other pages of the daily newspaper trace some of this development. Important areas in which the mushrooming of statistics in the business community is evident include the stock exchanges, the bond market, banking and financial institutions, insurance, trade associations, advertising and market research, and public opinion polls. Relatively recent and spectacular expansion of statistics in the private as well as the public sector is afforded by the rapid growth of quality control and operations research methods and their application. Space does not permit even the outlining of the ways in which statistics have become important elements in policy formation and program administration in the private sectors of the American economy and society—not only in business, but also in other areas such as labor, religion, recreation, health, education, and science.

The evolution of statistics in the United States in response to the changing social order was, of course, paralleled on the world scene. Internationally comparable statistics were compiled in systematic form during the 19th century; and are even now gaining great momentum in the post-World-War-II world under the aegis of the United Nations and the Specialized Agencies. Just as national statistics developed in response to the need for sound facts in the more complex and interdependent mass society in the U.S., so the evolution of international statistics reflects the growing need for comparable data in the shrinking, and ever more interdependent, world. The U.N. *Statistical Yearbook*, the *Demographic Yearbook*, and its current publication series, as well as the statistical publications of the Specialized Agencies [9, Ch. 14], will, over time, trace not only the expansion of international statistics, but also the emergence of a world order.

This brief overview of the evolution of statistics emphasizes the expanding volumes *per se* of statistical data collected and utilized in answer to the needs of society. It was with the swelling in the volume of statistical data and the increasing need to effectively and efficiently use them that statistical technology was born and has developed to the point where today we use the term "method" to characterize the central core of statistics. And it was these statistics, both as data and method, that, in turn, contributed to the evolving technology and forms of social organization which accelerated the development of the mass society. That is, statistics was not only a by-product of the social morphological revolution, but also an essential ingredient of it. . . .

REFERENCES

1. American Statistical Association and Institute of Mathematical Statistics, *Careers in Statistics*. Washington, D.C., 1961.

2. Childe, V. Gordon, "The Urban Revolution," *Town Planning Review*, 21 (1950), 3–17.
3. Durkheim, Emile, "Morphologie Sociale," *L'Année Sociologique*, Volume II (1897–1898), as quoted from translation in Maurice Halbwachs, *Population and Society*. Glencoe, Illinois: The Free Press, 1960.
4. Durkheim, Emile, *The Division of Labor in Society*. Glencoe, Illinois: The Free Press, 1947.
5. Fitzpatrick, Paul J., "Statistical Societies in the United States in the Nineteenth Century," *The American Statistician*, Volume 11, No. 5 (December, 1957), 13–21.
6. Haggard, Howard Wilcox, *Devils, Drugs & Doctors*. London: W. Heinemann, Ltd., 1929.
7. Hauser, Philip M., *On the Impact of Population and Community Changes on Local Government*. Pittsburgh: Institute of Local Government, University of Pittsburgh, 1961.
8. Hauser, Philip M., and Leonard, William R., *Government Statistics for Business Use*. New York: John Wiley & Sons, 1946 (First edition).
9. Hauser, Philip M., and Leonard, William R., *Government Statistics for Business Use*. New York: John Wiley & Sons, 1956 (Revised edition).
10. Hawley, Amos H., *Human Ecology*. New York: The Ronald Press Company, 1950.
11. Leakey, Louis Seymour Bazett, as reported in *The New York Times*, March 23, 1962, p. 1, col. 1.
12. Miksch, W. F., "The Average Statistician," *Collier's*, June 17, 1950, p. 10.
13. Nixon, J. W., *A History of the International Statistical Institute: 1885–1960*. The Hague: International Statistical Institute, 1960.
14. Sumner, William Graham, *Folkways*. Boston: Ginn & Company, 1907.
15. Turner, Ralph, *The Great Cultural Traditions*, Vol. 1, *The Ancient Cities*. New York: McGraw-Hill Book Co., Inc., 1941.
16. U.S. Bureau of the Census, *Historical Statistics of the United States, Colonial Times to 1957*. Washington, D.C.: Government Printing Office, 1960, Ch. Z, "Colonial Statistics."
17. Weber, Max, "Bureauracy," in H. H. Gerth and C. Wright Mills, *From Max Weber: Essays in Sociology*, Translated Edition. New York: Oxford University Press, 1946.
18. Wirth, Louis, *Community Life & Social Policy*. Chicago: University of Chicago Press, 1956.
19. Wooddy, Carrol H., "The Growth of Governmental Functions," *Recent Social Trends*. New York and London: McGraw-Hill Book Co., 1933, Volume 1, Ch. XXV.
20. Wright, Carroll D., *The History and Growth of the United States Census*. Washington: Government Printing Office, 1900.

8

Questions on Religion
in the United States Census

Dorothy Good

For some time empirical studies of limited scale in this country and on a national scale in foreign countries have appeared to indicate a highly significant relation between religious preference and behavior affecting demographic change. Most of these studies have been concerned with behavior affecting fertility, but mortality and migration have not been altogether neglected.[1]

For the fertility studies the information on religious preference has been obtained either by direct interrogation of the subjects selected for field survey or indirectly. Among those using the first method, such as the Indianapolis Study in 1941, the Detroit Area Study in 1952, the nation-wide study of the Growth of American Families in 1955, and the study of two-child families in seven metropolitan areas being conducted in Princeton, little difficulty was encountered in obtaining what the investigators considered accurate information on religious preference by broad religious groups (Protestant, Catholic, Jewish, Other).[2]

Studies getting at religious classifications indirectly have used a variety of methods. Stouffer in 1935 divided birth registration data obtained by the Wisconsin State Board of Health into Catholic and non-Catholic according to whether the marriage had been performed by a Catholic priest or by another person, and followed up the records of subsequent confinements in Wisconsin cities between 1919 and 1933.[3] Jaffe in 1939 obtained a rough classification from U.S. census data on country of origin of foreign born by equating Italian, Irish, and Polish origin with Catholic preference, Russian with Jewish, English, Welsh, Scots, and Scandinavian with non-Catholic, and German and Canadian with mixed religions.[4] Kirk in 1955 employed

---

Reprinted from *Population Index*, 25, no. 1 (January, 1959), pp. 3–16, by permission of the author and the publisher.

critically data available in the published statistics of the Roman Catholic Church.[5]

Although the sample surveys and the analyses using defective data agree in finding important fertility differences among the broad religious groups, the extent and trend of such differences remain uncertain. For the United States as a whole there is no basis for comparison with studies of differential fertility in countries that possess census data on religious preference, for example, Canada, Western Germany, the Netherlands.[6]

Among the countries with 500,000 or more inhabitants for which censuses have been published in recent years . . . about half have included at least one question on religion.[7] By continental divisions these totaled seven in North America, three in South America, twelve in Europe (including all the German governments as one), sixteen in Africa, and two in Oceania. Although, as the editors of the United Nations *Demographic Yearbook* remark,[8] the lack of comparability in census practice prevents quantitative summary even for this portion of the world, the material for some degree of national analysis is present. In some of the countries national series of long duration, such as Canada's since 1861 and Switzerland's since 1860, permit longitudinal studies of considerable scope.

Although the proposal that the United States include a question or questions on religion in the decennial census is far from new, demographers have recently been pressing it more urgently, especially in connection with plans for the 1960 census. It will be our purpose here to examine the proposals and some of the factors that the Bureau of the Census must presumably have had to take into account in reaching an adverse decision.

THE BACKGROUND AND CONTENT
OF RECENT PROPOSALS

At no time since 1790 has the decennial census included a question on religious preference or affiliation directed to individuals, nor have any questions on political belief ever been asked. Although the opponents of the proposal to ask religion have frequently cited the stipulation of the First Amendment that "Congress shall make no law respecting an establishment of religion, or prohibiting the free exercise thereof; or abridging the freedom of speech, or of the press," there has been no reference to this in census legislation, nor has a judicial interpretation of its applicability been handed down.

From the beginning, questions on some social and ethnic characteristics have been included on the enumeration schedule.[9] In the first five censuses, few details other than sex and age group were to be reported; among these few was a question on condition of personal servitude. There was some expansion of the questions in 1840, and in 1850 a section on churches and church accommodation appeared for the first time. This latter information was reported to the federal marshals in each judicial district by the local administrative officers of the religious bodies. Figures by county, not only for church accommodation but for religious newspapers and periodicals, Sunday schools and church libraries, were published. In 1860 similar questions were asked, but because of the war, only a brief summary was published.

In 1870 not only were full details by counties again published, but elaborate analyses and diagrams accompanied the tables.[10] For each denomination appeared a textual summary of the statistics supplied and a brief statement of the church's chief tenets and form of organization. This census also published statistics of school attendance and illiteracy, libraries, newpapers and periodicals, pauperism and crime, as well as the continuing data on color, nationality, sex, age, and occupation. Similar data on churches were obtained and published as parts of the censuses of 1880 and 1890, but only those for the latter date were tabulated and published, including for the first time data on church membership.

Then it was decided that instead of including church data in the decennial censuses, a special census on religious bodies should be held in the sixth year of each decade, continuing the inquiry on an institutional basis. These special censuses were taken in 1906, 1916, 1926, and 1936.[11] In 1946 and 1956 Congress failed to make the necessary appropriations, and apparently efforts by such groups to revive the Census of Religious Bodies have been unavailing.

This was the situation in 1956 when plans for the decennial census of 1960 began to take shape. The Population Association of America's Committee on the 1960 Census was one of several groups, advising the Bureau of the Census, to submit proposals on a religious question. The text of the recommendation presented by the majority of the Work Group on the Religious Question and adopted by the full Committee has already appeared in *Population Index*.[12]

SAMPLE SURVEYS OF RELIGIOUS PREFERENCE
BY GOVERNMENTAL AND PRIVATE AGENCIES

As tests of the public's willingness to respond to religious queries, the results of a variety of surveys are at hand.

Primarily for this purpose the Census Bureau conducted its own pretest of questions on religion and comparable matters in Milwaukee in November 1956. Of 837 persons, 14 years old and over, the enumerators asked as the last question on the schedule whether the respondent would voluntarily state which of four broad classifications was "his religion" and also for the Protestant respondents which was his denomination. Of this sample 95.5 per cent gave a codable answer immediately, 1.3 per cent gave an ambiguous answer not codable, and 3.2 per cent refused or replied that they had no religion or known preference. These results represented a higher response than was obtained on similar tests of questions on income.

In March 1957 the Bureau of the Census included similar questions on the Current Population Survey, covering 35,000 households in 330 sample areas across the nation. As a follow-up, the Census Bureau asked one enumerator in four the reaction to the question on religion. On the basis of these reports it appeared that an even higher proportion than in the pretest replied without hesitancy; less than three per cent expressed mild resentment; and less than one per cent strong resentment.

For many years public opinion polls have been asking questions on religious preference and practice. According to the records centralized at the Roper Public Opinion Research Center at Williams College, Elmo Roper and Associates included a question on religious preference at least seventeen times in the eleven-year period 1946–1956. The usual wording is, "What is your religon?" and replies are classified as Catholic, Protestant, Jewish, Other, None. In only two cases were Protestant denominations specifically listed. During the same period the Gallup organization, American Institute of Public Opinion, included such a question on 77 of their surveys, and in the eleven years 1947–1957 the *Minneapolis Tribune's* Minnesota Poll asked such a question 39 times.

Evidently this kind of question was more frequent than questions on religious practice, such as: "About how often do you go to church as a usual thing?" (Roper, 1948); "Do you ever go to church?" and "If Yes, about how often do you go as a usual thing?" (Minnesota Poll, 1949).[13] The American Institute of Public Opinion has periodically asked samples of civilian adults whether they had attended church during the week preceding the interview. During the eleven years indicated above, this question was asked four times (May 1947, April 1950, July 1954, December 1955), as well as on other occasions, both earlier and more recently.[14]

When sample surveys of communities have been conducted by social scientists or by church bodies for the measurement of religious affiliation and its correlates, the surveyors have had, as a preliminary, to examine the distribution of religious preference in the total population of the community. No particular resistance to this type of questioning is recorded in the reports of a number of such surveys, representing urban and rural communities, differing geographical areas, and all three of the leading religious groups.[15]

TABLE 1. Estimates of Distribution of Religious Preference, 1957, and of Religious Affiliation, Mainly for 1956, United States

Religion	Individuals Indicating Preference (Aged 14 and Over)		Church Membership	
	Numbers (1,000's)	Per Cent	Numbers (1,000's)	Per Cent
Protestant	78,952	66.2	60,149	58.3
Baptist	23,525	19.7	19,439	18.8
Lutheran	8,417	7.1	7,280	7.1
Methodist	16,676	14.0	11,924	11.6
Presbyterian	6,656	5.6	3,959	3.8
Other Protestant	23,678	19.8	17,547	17.0
Roman Catholic	30,669	25.7	34,564	33.5
Jewish	3,868	3.2	5,500	5.3
Other religion	1,545a	1.3	3,012c	2.9
No religion	3,195b	2.7		
Religion not reported	1,104	0.9		
Total population aged 14 and over	119,333	100.0		
Total church membership			103,225d	100.0
Total U.S. population, Jan. 1, 1957			169,800	

a"The group 'other religion' consists largely of persons reporting such organizations as the Eastern Orthodox Churches, the Polish Catholics, and the Old Catholics. It also includes the relatively few persons who are Buddhists, Moslems, and other non-Christians." Source, pp. 3–4.

b"The group 'no religion' includes persons who reported that they were atheists, agnostics, or said they had no religion." Ibid., p. 4.

cIncludes Buddhists, Old Catholics and Polish National Catholics, and Eastern Churches. Numbers of Muslims are unreported.

dThis compilation excludes numerous small local bodies and the Christian Science Church, which in 1936 reported 268,915 members.

Sources: Data of first two columns from U.S. Bureau of the Census, Current Population Reports, Series P-20, No. 79, p. 6. Data of third column from National Council of Churches of Christ in the United States of America, Yearbook of American Churches 1958, pp. 258, 259, 262–264. This is a compilation of reports on church membership received from official statisticians of religious bodies. Estimate of total U.S. population from U.S. Bureau of the Census, Current Population Reports, Series P-25, No. 173, p. 3. Data of last column computed at the Office of Population Research.

ESTIMATES OF RELIGIOUS DISTRIBUTIONS
AS SUBSTITUTES FOR CENSUS DATA ON RELIGION

In Table 1 are summarized recent estimates of religious distributions on a national scale. To serve as a satisfactory substitute for a complete census enumeration on religious preference, estimates based on sample surveys or other methods would have at least to equal the census enumerations in accuracy, completeness, internal comparability, continuity, and availability of correlative information on demographic and socio-economic characteristics.

The first set of estimates in the table, those based on the Current Population Survey,[16] pass the first three of these tests for reasons that have already been sufficiently indicated. If the religious questions are repeated at intervals on future Current Population Surveys, comparisons over time will gradually become available. It is in the availability for comparison with other characteristics that the estimates, especially in the form so far published, are mainly deficient.

On the positive side, the report does give some analysis on broad geographical distribution, urban-rural residence, age, sex, and marital status for persons 14 years old and over, plus information on relation to household head for children under 14. Total numbers by age and sex, but no other breakdowns, are supplied for the four largest groups of Protestant denominations. On the negative side, data collected but not published include the above information for the separate Protestant denominations and all information and analysis on other cross-classifications.

Sampling surveys such as those represented by the Current Population Survey cannot by their nature give data cross-classified for states and smaller areas. As for other characteristics, the situation is different. This survey, it will be recalled, was based on information collected in March 1957. The first report, entitled "Religion Reported by the Civilian Population of the United States: March 1957," was released on February 2, 1958, as No. 79 of Current Population Reports, Series P-20. On page 3 of that report is the statement "Other reports presenting results of this survey are being prepared." Although at least one other report, presenting cross-classifications with income and education, was prepared, none has appeared. On July 23, 1958, Mr. Frederick H. Mueller, then Assistant Secretary and now Under-Secretary of Commerce, in reply to a request from the Chairman of the Social Statistics Committee of the American Sociological Association, wrote that "we have examined [the matter] carefully and come to the conclusion that it is most consistent with the public interest to make no further publication of data on this subject at this time."[17]

On the whole the conclusion must be that while the Current Population Survey reports on religious preference would in any case fail to provide the full range of information that could be obtained if religion were on the decennial census, they do now provide important information on religion that can be obtained in no other way, and they might provide much more than has yet been released.

The other estimates summarized in Table 1 differ from those of the CPS, not only in being estimates of affiliation rather than of preference, but in being supplied by a variety of bodies each with its own definition of membership. No checks of accuracy or completeness for the list as a whole are offered. On the contrary, the compilers of the estimates have regularly called attention to the immense discrepancies in the definitions and the methods of data collection.[18] The succession of censuses of religious bodies and the figures issued by constituent groups since 1936 provide continuity of a sort, but shifts in definition are so numerous as largely to invalidate comparison. Correlations with data on other characteristics are generally lacking, though one detailed set of nationwide estimates, compiled by the National Council of the Churches of Christ in the U.S.A., gives denominational statistics by regions, divisions, states, counties, and standard metropolitan areas in 1952 and also tabulates socio-economic characteristics for those areas as given in the 1950 census.[19]

Although the official estimates of affiliation do not give data on age-sex structure, unofficial estimates by various indirect methods have given rough indications for particular denominations or groups. Examples are the application of fertility ratios to data on Catholic baptisms described by Mulvaney and a number of methods of gauging Jewish population described by Horowitz.[20] All of these, however, must rest heavily on assumptions. For a few church communities age distributions have been obtained through direct enumeration.[21]

OPINIONS EXPRESSED ON THE PROPOSALS

The arguments most often put forward in favor of asking individual religious preference on the decennial census stress the need for quantitative data, cross-classified with that on other characteristics, for empirical studies or for practical purposes.

(1) The studies of differential fertility, mortality, and migration already referred to are not the only types of study suffering from underdevelopment because of starvation rations of basic data on religion. For the demographer, however, these are one of the most pressing needs of social analysis. The knowledge that one of the most significant social variables exists and might be quantified if the right questions were asked in the right places spurs him to seek the experiment.

(2) The adjoining province of the sociology of religion[22] is, from the empiricist's point of view, still in a defective state as long as most hypotheses are largely untestable by inductive methods. The clash of competing theories, he will grant you, may never be resolved, but the problem could be clarified if elementary data were assembled. In their absence not even the validity of occasional observations can be solidly established.

(3) Basic problems of the definition of cultures and the shaping of measures for aggregative statistics of social change wait on solutions of such nearer problems as those of the definitive description of religious differences.

(4) Of quite different nature are the immediately practical ends that other proponents of the religious question on the census cite as reasons for advocating it. Religious bodies with areal programs, commercial enterprises

supplying their equipment, planning bodies concerned with community programs, with school construction, and with health insurance, governmental and other agencies charged with the prevention of discriminatory practices, all, it has been pointed out at one time or another, would benefit from the publication of specific information on religious preference by small local units cross-classified with data on other social and economic characteristics.

On the other hand, arguments against religious enumerations by the government and against the publication of even such results as have been obtained bring forward criteria pertaining to political considerations, considerations of the quality of the data, and questions of church policy.

(1) It is argued that the recording of a person's religion on his census schedule might become the entering wedge for the kind of secret governmental files on individual characteristics that were detested features of the Nazi and Fascist regimes. Collectively, too, it is said, the dangers of discrimination would increase if the publication of data on income and literacy, whether for small communities or large, revealed characteristics of a religious group that might make it a tempting target for the demagogue or that might tempt the religious organizations themselves to enter politics as clerical partisans.

(2) On political grounds also, it is argued that there is an infringement of the individual's right of privacy in asking the proposed questions. Not only should the constitutional guarantees secure him against intimidation on the score of his beliefs, it is urged; they should secure him from the necessity of stating what these are, except in a time of clear and present danger.

(3) Critics of the proposals also see them as contravening the principle of the separation of church and state. The frequent association in Europe of the taking of census data on religion with the collection of church taxes by the state is cited as a logical development that might happen here.

(4) Among other critics, to whom the political dangers may not seem serious, the question of quality weighs against the proposals. While not disregarding the demographer's and the sociologist's need for quantitative data, this kind of critic fails to see that the crude information obtainable from the proposed questions would actually mean much without additional information on belief and practice. He feels that the risks of misinterpretation would hardly be worth the equivocal knowledge gained.

(5) As matters of church policy, some sects object either to the principle of enumeration or to the publication of statistics of membership.

All these arguments for and against the proposals have their rebuttals.

To the arguments that stress the need for data in sociological research, it is answered that the purpose of the census is not to supply statistics for researchers, but, as stated in the Constitution, to establish the basis for the apportionment of representation in Congress. Similarly, the answer is given to those who stress the practical advantage of the desired information for special groups that that is not the proper purpose of the census. On the basis of this criticism, however, one may doubt whether most of the information collected by the census in past years was appropriate.

In refutation of the arguments on the dangers of increasing discrimination, it is pointed out that the law provides penalties for the wrongful disclosure of information and that individual schedules are to be treated as confidential, with certain exceptions.[23] On the collective basis, the reply goes, first, the publication of accurate information on the characteristics of religious groups would be less harmful to them than surmise and wrongful allegation have been; second, the possession of the census data would be an aid in the enforcement of anti-discrimination measures; and, third, at best the implied assumption that in any sensitive area risks are to be avoided by cultivating ignorance rests on dangerous grounds.

To the argument against the invasion of privacy, it is replied that while the individual should be permitted reasonable privacy as to his beliefs, he cannot be granted it absolutely if the public interest demands otherwise. In this connection, it has been proposed that the law be amended to permit a refusal to reply to the proposed religious question by individuals with private objections.

To the arguments on the threat to the separation of church and state, the answer is given that analogies with foreign countries that have established churches are irrelevant and that the administrative separation of church and state does not involve non-recognition the one of the other.

To those opposing the religious question on the census because of defects in the information obtainable, the advocates reply that the first step to more adequate data is the collection and critical analysis of empirical evidence as broadly based as possible. Dangers of misinterpretation are always present, but should decrease with more accurate information. Much would depend on the way in which the question was presented to the public and the way in which the results were analyzed.

Finally, objections on the score of church policy could be met, the defenders of the proposals point out, by the existing laws, which provide for exemption from replying on the ground of membership in bodies having conscientious scruples. The numbers affected would probably not be large on the national scale.

Since there has been no polling of attitudes on the specific proposals for the decennial census, the estimate of the weight of opinion for and against must depend largely on the assessment of spontaneously initiated or formally organized expressions of views. The principal media for these have been letters and articles in the metropolitan daily and church periodical press, the presentation of committee reports and the adoption of resolutions by interested bodies, public utterances of various kinds by individual spokesmen, and individual correspondence with and deputations to the officers of the Bureau of the Census. In the alignment of groups that support the proposals are the relevant committees of the Population Association of America, the American Sociological Association, the American Statistical Association, the Catholic Hierarchy of the United States, the Catholic Press Association, the National Council of the Churches of Christ in the U.S.A., and the Association of Statisticians of Religious Bodies. Among those opposed are the American Civil Liberties Union, the Anti-Defamation League of B'nai B'rith, the American Jewish Congress, the Union of American Hebrew Congregations, the Jewish Statistical Bureau, and individual Protestant and Catholic churchmen.

THE MAKING OF THE DECISION

The enabling legislation now in force to carry out the Constitutional mandate for the holding of a decennial census consists of the basic law of 1902, frequently amended and substantially recodified in 1954. According to it, the responsibility for executing the census is vested in the Secretary of Commerce, and delegated by him to the Director of the Bureau of the Census, both appointed by the President. Appropriations from the Treasury must be authorized by Congress annually, though the decennial census is granted a three-year appropriation for the census period beginning January 1, 1960.

The law specifically provides that "The Secretary may collect decennially statistics relating to religious bodies."[24] With regard to the census of 1960, it states that "The censuses provided for by sections 141 and 142 of this title shall be restricted to inquiries relating to population, to agriculture, to irrigation, to drainage, to unemployment, and to housing."[25] Reports on the inquiries included in the censuses must be completed within the three-year decennial census period.

No such stipulation attaches to the surveys, such as the Current Population Survey, for which it is merely provided that "The Secretary may make surveys deemed necessary to furnish annual and other interim current data on the subjects covered by the censuses provided for in this title."[26] The surveys also lack the powers of compulsion that fortify the decennial census, for which the law provides penalties of fines or imprisonment, varying in amount, for refusal or neglect to answer questions, giving false answers, and giving suggestions or information with intent to cause inaccurate enumeration of population.

Within the Bureau of the Census the Director receives the advice and consultation of his professional staff officers, and, periodically, that from permanent or *ad hoc* advisory groups of census users. The Bureau, the largest of the statistical and fact-finding agencies in the Federal Government, must coordinate its activities with those of the other agencies through specially constituted bodies, such as the Office of Statistical Standards of the Bureau of the Budget and various interdepartmental subcommittees.

In this complex of considerations and pressures the decisions on the religious question are made. As of December 1, 1958, two have apparently been reached.

First, in the matter of the decennial census, a press release by the Bureau of the Census in December 1957 states that a question on religion will not be included in the decennial census of 1960. The release specifically adds, however, that this decision relates only to the 1960 census and not to future decennial censuses or to voluntary surveys conducted by the Census Bureau (i.e., the Current Population Survey and the Post-Enumeration Survey).

Second, in the matter of the reports of the Current Population Survey dealing with religion, no official release has enunciated the administrative decision to suppress further reports on the data collected in March 1957. Protests against that decision are continuing.

The American Sociological Association at its annual meeting in August passed a resolution in which it "protests this suppression of reliable statistical information secured in the course of a competent survey conducted by the Bureau of the Census." In a letter conveying this resolution to the then Secretary of Commerce, the Honorable Sinclair Weeks, the Chairman of the Social Statistics Committee set forth the reasons for the protest:

> I would respectfully submit that it is a dangerous principle for the government to suppress statistical information because it might reflect unfavorably in the public eye on the occupational, income or educational characteristics of any particular group. It is our belief that prejudiced persons do not have to find statistics to bolster their prejudices. In the absence of facts they will manufacture extravagant assertions that are likely to go unchallenged and do much more damage than the factual information itself. We would like to believe that the American public is not afraid of facts and that all groups in the population will in the long run be benefited by more accurate information.[27]

In the matter of repeating the religious question on future Current Population Surveys, decision appears to hinge on what is decided about further publication of the reports on the March 1957 data.

So the problem stands at the moment. The basic issues remain to be resolved.

NOTES

1. Some of the fertility studies are listed below. The first of a varied group of studies of the mortality of religious groups is described in: Vance, Rupert B., and Madigan, Francis C. Differential mortality and the "style of life" of men and women: a research design. Pp. 150–163 in: Milbank Memorial Fund. Trends and differentials in mortality. New York, 1956. 166 pp. Differential migration is briefly considered in such studies as: Houtart, Fr. A sociological study of the evolution of the American Catholics. Social Compass (The Hague) 2(5/6):189–216. [1955]

2. Whelpton, P. K., and Kiser, Clyde V. Social and psychological factors affecting fertility. Vol. I. New York, Milbank Memorial Fund, 1946. VIII, 137 pp. See pp. 132–133.

Freedman, Ronald, and Sharp, Harry. Correlates of values about ideal family size in the Detroit Metropolitan Area. Population Studies 8(1):35–45. July 1954.

Whelpton, P. K., and Freedman, Ronald. A study of the growth of American families. American Journal of Sociology 61(6):595–601. May 1956.

Westoff, Charles F., et al. A new study of American fertility. Social and psychological factors. Eugenics Quarterly 2(4):229–233. Dec. 1955.

3. Stouffer, Samuel A. Trends in the fertility of Catholics and non-Catholics. American Journal of Sociology 41(2):148–166. Sept. 1935.

4. Jaffe, A. J. Religious differentials in the net reproduction rate. Journal of the American Statistical Association 34: 335–342. June 1939.

5. Kirk, Dudley. Recent trends of Catholic fertility in the United States. Pp. 93–105 in: Milbank Memorial Fund. Current research in human fertility. New York, 1955. 164 pp.

6. Langlois, Conrad. La chute de la natalité dans la province de Québec [The drop in natality in the province of Quebec]. L'Actualité Economique (Montreal) 33(2):225–241. July–Sept. 1957.

Freudenberg, Karl. Methodik und Ergebnisse der Fruchtbarkeitsstatistik [Methods and results of fertility statistics]. Schmollers Jahrbuch (Berlin) 75(6):43–65. 1955.

Germany. Federal Republic. Statistisches Bundesamt. Die Geburtenhäufigkeit nach der Religionszugehörigkeit [Fertility according to religion]. By Henriette Peters. Wirtschaft und Statistik 10(1): 24–25. Jan. 1958.

Heek, F. van. Roman-Catholicism and fertility in the Netherlands: demographic aspects of minority status. Population Studies 10(2):125–138. Nov. 1956.

Wolff, P. de, and Meerdink, J. La fécondité des mariages à Amsterdam selon l'appartenance sociale et religieuse [Marital fertility in Amsterdam, according to social class and religion]. Translated and edited by Jacques Zajicek and Roland Pressat. Population (Paris) 12(2):289–318. April–June 1957.

7. United Nations. Statistical Office. Demographic yearbook 1956. Eighth issue. Special topic: Ethnic and economic characteristics. Annuaire démographique 1956. Huitième édition. Sujet special: caractéristiques ethniques et économiques. Sales No.: 1956.XIII.5. New York, 1956 [i.e. 1957]. viii, 744 pp. Table 8. Population by religion and sex: each census, 1945–1955. Pp. 267–281. Data on religion are given for 90 countries as compared with the 267 listed in Table 1, Geographic distribution. Further data compiled by the Statistical Office since 1956 are included in the totals by continental divisions given here.

8. Ibid., Description of tables . . . Table 8. P. 33. "Limitations: The nature of statistics on religion makes them basically non-comparable. As has been pointed out above, it is known that the data represent—in unknown proportions—religious belief or religious affiliation; the latter may be of recent origin or dating from childhood. If a specific church membership is of recent origin, it has little significance as an ethnic factor. No criterion is used by the enumerator to determine church 'membership' and none is possible to verify 'belief.' Moreover, there is a definite tendency for this question to remain unanswered on a large number of schedules. Therefore, these statistics in Table 8 must be used only as rough indicators of the distribution of populations by broad religious designations."

9. Wright, Carroll D. The history and growth of the United States Census, prepared for the Senate Committee on the Census by . . . , Commissioner of Labor, assisted by William C. Hunt, Chief Statistician, Twelfth Census. Washington, Government Printing Office, 1900. 967 pp.

10. U.S. Census Office. Ninth census. Volume I. Washington, 1872. xlix, 805 pp. and 7 folding maps. Table XVII (A) and (B), Table XVIII.

U.S. Census Office. Statistical atlas of the United States based on the results of the ninth census of 1870 with contributions from many eminent men of science and several departments of the government. Compiled under the authority of Congress by Francis A. Walker, Superintendent of the Ninth Census. [Washington], Julius Bien, Lith., 1874. Plate XXXI.

11. U.S. Bureau of the Census. Religious bodies: 1936. Washington, Govt. Printing Office, 1941. Vol. I. Summary and detailed tables. VIII, 943 pp. Vol. II. Separate denominations: Statistics, history, doctrine, organization, and work. [In two parts.] Part 1—Denominations A to J; Part 2—Denominations K to Z. XIV, 797 pp.; XIV, 799–1695 pp. See Vol. I, p. 3.

12. Duncan, Otis Dudley. Report of the Committee on the 1960 Census, Population Association of America. Population Index 23(4):293–305. Oct. 1957. "(7) *Religion.* The work group points out that a majority of countries include a question on religion in their censuses. It indicates that census information on this subject would serve a wide variety of important research uses, and that both foreign census experience and American survey experience show the feasibility of collecting such information. Considering the need for religious data to be well established, the work group recommends (a) that an inquiry on religion be included among questions addressed to the proposed 25 per cent sample; (b) that an inquiry on religion in the Current Population Survey not be regarded as an effective substitute for a census enumeration; (c) that if only one question is asked, first consideration be given to a question on religious preference, second consideration to a question on membership in religious bodies; (d) that if more than one question is asked, the additional ones be designed to ascertain membership or affiliation; (e) that no question be included on subjective religious belief, religious practice, or extent of religious observance; (f) that the respondent be given the option of indicating no preference, of declining to state a preference, or of stating it in a general category such as 'Protestant'; (g) that tabulations be presented for small areas in terms of major groups (e.g., Protestant, Catholic, Jewish, other, and no preference), that demographic composition of major groups be given for cities and metropolitan areas, and that detailed cross-tabulations of fertility and marital status by religion be given at the national level. One member of the work group (Lorimer), while endorsing the group's 'review of relevant objective conditions,' abstained with respect to its recommendations 'for reasons outside the purview of the report.' "

13. Information from the Roper Public Opinion Research Center, Williamstown, Mass.

14. National Council of the Churches of Christ in the United States of America. Yearbook of American Churches. . . . 27th issue, annual edition for 1959. Edited by Benson Y. Landis. New York, 1958. vi, 334 pp. Reference on p. 297.

15. Bultena, Louis. Church membership and church attendance in Madison, Wisconsin. American Sociological Review 14(3):384–389. June 1949.

Freedman, R., and Axelrod, M. Who belongs to what in a great metropolis? Adult Leadership 1(6):6–9. Nov. 1952. [Detroit Area Study.]

Garnett, William E. The Virginia rural church and related influences, 1900–1950. Virginia Agricultural Experiment Station Bulletin 479. Blacksburg, Virginia Agricultural Experiment Station, Virginia Polytechnic Institute, 1957. 88 pp.

Obenhaus, Victor, et al. Church participation related to social class and type of center. Rural Sociology 23(3):298–308. Sept. 1958.

Massachusetts Council of Churches. Haverhill, Massachusetts; a study of church and community. Haverhill, Dept. of Research and Strategy, Massachusetts Council of Churches, 1953. 58 + 10 leaves, processed.

Kelly, George A. Catholics and the practice of the faith: a census study of the diocese of Saint Augustine. Catholic University of America School of Social Science, Studies in Sociology, Vol. 19. Washington, The Catholic University of America, 1956. viii, 224 pp.

Bigman, Stanley K. The Jewish population of Greater Washington in 1956. Report on an interview survey of size, social characteristics, residential mobility, community participation, and observance of some traditional practices. Washington, D.C., The Jewish Community Council of Greater Washington, 1957. [x], xx, 174 pp., processed, and specimen form.

16. U.S. Bureau of the Census. Current Population Reports. Series P-20. Population characteristics. Washington, 1947–. No. 79. Religion reported by the civilian population of the United States: March 1957. Feb. 2, 1958. 8 pp.

17. Personal communication from Dudley Kirk.

18. U.S. Bureau of the Census. Religious bodies: 1936. Vol. I. P. 50.

19. National Council of Churches of Christ in the United States of America. Churches and church membership in the United States. Enumeration and analysis by counties, states, and regions [80 Bulletins]: Series A, Major faiths by regions, divisions and states; Series B, Denominational statistics by regions, divisions and states; Series C, Denominational statistics by states and counties; Series D, Denominational statistics by standard metropolitan areas; Series E, Analyses of socio-economic characteristics. New York, 1956–1958.

20. Mulvaney, Bernard G. Catholic population revealed in Catholic baptisms. American Ecclesiastical Review 133(3): 183–193. Sept. 1955.

Horowitz, C. Morris. Demographic techniques and Jewish education. Jewish Education 26(2):17–23. Fall 1955.

21. For example, the Haverhill and St. Augustine studies cited in Footnote 15.

22. For a review of recent trends, see: Glock, Charles Y. Sociology of religion, 1945–1955. Pp. 84–86 in: Zetterberg, H., Editor. Sociology in the United States, a trend report. Documentation in the Social Sciences. Paris, Unesco, 1956. 156 pp.

23. United States. Statutes at large containing the laws and concurrent resolutions enacted during the second session of the eighty-third Congress of the United States of America 1954 . . . Vol. 68. Part 1. Public laws and reorganization plans. Washington, Govt. Printing Office, 1955. 282, CXVI pp. Public Law 70—Aug. 31, 1954. Chapter 1, Administration, Subchapter I—General provisions, Paragraph 8, states, on p. 1013, "(a) The Secretary may, upon a written request, and in his discretion, furnish to Governors of States and Territories, courts of record, and individuals, data for genealogical and other proper purposes, from the population, agriculture, and housing schedules prepared under the authority of subchapter II of chapter 5, upon the payment of the actual, or estimated cost of searching the records and $1 for supplying a certificate. (b) The Secretary may furnish transcripts or copies of tables and other census records and make special statistical compilations and surveys for State or local officials, private concerns, or individuals upon the payment of the actual, or estimated cost of such work. (c) In no case shall information furnished under the authority of this section be used to the detriment of the persons to whom such information relates."

24. Ibid. Chapter 3—Collection and publication of statistics, Subchapter III—Miscellaneous, Paragraph 102. P. 1018.

25. Ibid. Chapter 5—Censuses, Subchapter II—Population, housing, agriculture, irrigation, drainage and unemployment, Paragraph 144. P. 1020.

26. Ibid. Subchapter IV—Current interim data, Paragraph 181, Surveys. P. 1021.

27. Personal communication from Dudley Kirk.

9

The Pros and Cons
of "Self-Enumeration"

Donald J. Bogue

I. HOUSEHOLDER VERSUS ENUMERATOR
COLLECTION OF DATA

Two alternative procedures are available for the collection of population data: the "householder" approach and the "canvasser" approach.[1] Using the first, the information required by the census is recorded by the household head or someone he designates. Using the second procedure, the recording is made by an enumerator who visits each house, asks the questions printed on the census schedule, and records the information as it is provided by a respondent who is deemed to be qualified.

Both systems have been in use for many years. The householder approach has been used primarily in European countries. Until the 1960 census the canvasser approach was used by the United States Census; in 1960 an approach was substituted that relied primarily upon the householder to provide the required data. The new procedure, widely but incorrectly termed "self-enumeration," is almost certain to be used in the 1970 and other future censuses of the United States. Inasmuch as the Bureau of the Census tends to set statistical styles, there is a growing trend for other data collection operations to use "self-enumeration" in conducting household surveys.

The present paper seeks to promote wider research and discussion of a question which deserves international as well as internal discussion: *"What are the pros and cons of the householder versus the canvasser approach to the collection of population data?"* It will try to present the hypotheses that are involved, to summarize the arguments favoring each, and

Reprinted from *Demography*, 2 (1965), pp. 600–25, by permission of the author and the publisher. Footnotes have been renumbered.

to review some of the evidence available from the 1960 census and other sources. The conclusion will be reached that, although the question is a highly important one, the data needed to test many of the basic hypotheses either are not available or else yield results that are inconclusive—as of right now there is insufficient scientific or economic basis for clearly preferring one approach over the other. An evaluation of the results obtained by the two alternative approaches indicates that neither mode of enumeration yields sufficiently precise data to meet the current needs of scientific demography. It is hoped that demographers all over the world will become increasingly sensitive to the problem of data quality and will keep an open mind on the problem, continuing to explore it by pooling their findings—irrespective of the particular procedures they may be using to collect their data at the present time.

II. THE QUALITY OF CENSUS DATA: FACT AND NEED

The question of how to collect census data cannot be answered without considering two questions: "How precise do we think census data need to be for the conduct of contemporary demographic research?" and "How precise, for purposes of demographic research, are the data of past censuses taken by the enumerator and the householder approach?" No census organization in the world has equalled the United States Census for concern over these questions. It is only because this staff of outstanding technicians has been so sensitive to the needs and desires of its "customers" that it is possible to discuss the topic in more than academic terms. On the one hand, panels of advisors have been organized by the Census in order to learn more about the needs of those who use census data in their professional work, and, on the other, panels of technical advisors have been organized and encouraged to promote a continuous critical evaluation of the results of past censuses and of procedures proposed for future ones. Meanwhile, task forces of census statisticians have been assigned to study and report on the quality of census data. The appended bibliography of their published writings is most impressive; no other national census has been so completely and publicly critical of its own work.

A very large share of the empirical data we have with which to study these problems has been created by the United States Census as part of a long-term program to collect special data concerning census errors. Two ambitious research programs, following the 1950 and the 1960 censuses, have produced a large quantity of data. Research on the problems of data collection is becoming in itself an important subfield of demography as a result.

The appropriate perspective from which to view the problem of census data quality was succinctly stated more than a decade ago by Morris Hansen, Director of the Census Division for Research and Development and leading architect in the search for facts about census errors, and two of his collaborators in this sustained program, William N. Hurwitz and Leon Pritzker:

> We should like to call attention to a major change in attitude with respect to census taking. Until recently, the emphasis in census taking has been primarily on producing the most accurate census possible, without any particular attention being given to the question of the required accuracy and to what extent it is worth an additional cost to increase the accuracy. [Instead] . . . emphasis has been placed on achieving results of needed accuracy at minimum cost and on attempting to consider the overall accuracy required in relation to the costs and the purposes to be served. . . . Instead of striving for perfection, we view the task as that of balancing the costs of producing statistics against the losses from errors in the statistics.
>
> What is the significance of census errors? . . . We believe that a solution of the problem calls for, among other things, recognition of the principle that considerations of accuracy and of utility are inseparable. We have been forced to this recognition by having to view the Bureau of the Census as a factory engaged in the production of statistical tables. In the management of that factory, just as in the management of any other factory, . . . management is required to examine the costs of production and relate them to the value of what is produced. The value of our product depends on the uses that are made of it and, depending on the use and the risks and losses associated in making a mistake in the use, the allowable tolerances of error may vary. Instead of the principle of highest possible accuracy, then, this view substitutes the principle of determining the level of accuracy that is optimum by balancing the losses due to errors against the costs of greater accuracy.[2]

Every census in the world needs to seek an answer to the Hansen-Hurwitz-Pritzker question, "How serious is the loss in terms of opportunity costs now being incurred because of inadequacies in census data?" Demography, as a profession, should help to supply a sincere and honest reply to it. A complete answer would require a thorough canvass of research demographers. It would be presumptuous for any one person to try to speak for the profession. The present writer seeks only to utter an opinion, based on the experience of having made extensive research use of 1940, 1950, and 1960 censuses, at the national, state, and micro-demographic level. This opinion is one which he believes is shared by many if not most statisticians who make intensive use of census data—that these losses are substantial and serious. *Despite the valiant and heroic efforts of the world's leading group of census experts, the research needs of demographers appear to be running ahead of the quality (precision) of the available data, and the gap between present quality of data and the quality needed by the research is widening instead of lessening. In fact, the research demands are so varied, so detailed, and backed by such important considerations for public welfare as well as academic "theory" that they drive the "needed" level of precision much nearer the old-fashioned ideal of census perfection than many may realize.* In other words, it may now be desirable to think of an acceptable level of error for a census as being not significantly lower than that now being achieved by the best of the national sample surveys, and that achieving it should be the goal in planning future censuses. The evidence now available suggests that the modern demographer, by the uses he attempts, implicitly desires and is asking for nothing less. It is to be hoped that demographic and statistical ingenuity and research all over the world will accept this need for precision as a challenge and will unite their talents and redouble their research endeavors in a drive to achieve it.

If such high precision is accepted as the standard, then the choice of the appropriate method for collecting the data for any census should be that method which offers the best hope for ultimately achieving the hoped-for precision. It would be short-sighted to adopt a procedure that is no worse than any other if it later proves to reach a barrier of imprecision through which it cannot pass on the way to achieve the necessary.

III. THE NEED FOR PRECISION

The above strong assertions about the need for precision in census data require documentation. Below are identified twelve distinctive types of common research situations, found either singly or in combination with each other, that require high precision in population data. Space permits only a brief statement and illustration of each.

1. *Detailed Classifications Involving Fine Discrimination.* Demographers increasingly find need for tabulations of age in terms of single years for studies of fertility, nuptiality, and migration. Users of economic data find much use for the detailed classifications of occupation (297 categories) and of industry (149 categories) instead of the dozen general categories that have formerly been used. All branches of the study of population composition press for more refined categories: Education is needed in terms of single grades and separately for public and private schools. Family and household status is needed in full detail to show the relationship of every member to every other. Marital status must separate persons who are married into three groups—living together, separated for reasons of estrangement, and separated for other reasons. Migration researchers press hard for

a more detailed classification of type of area of origin. Labor-force experts press for refinements of the classification of reasons for not being in the labor force or for being unemployed. Along all fronts the research calls for the making of finer distinctions and the use of more complex and lengthy systems of classification. The limit to this refinement is not lack of ingenuity of the researchers or the unwillingness of census designers to oblige. Instead, it usually is a frank assessment that as yet census procedures are not sufficiently precise to make fine discriminations of the type desired.

2. *Multiple-Variable Cross-Classifications.* Each census is coming to be more elaborate than the preceding because of the increased amount of cross-tabulations. Some of these involve cross-tabulation of one detailed characteristic by another (as detailed occupation by detailed industry). Others may involve the cross-tabulation of as many as six or seven variables simultaneously. Demographers have come to regard the *Special Reports,* tabulated after the "regular" reports, as the rich ore of the census. For the testing of hypotheses of the type now being studied, it is not at all unusual to need a tabulation such as the following: women by children ever born, by age, color, education, migration status, occupation of husband, urban-rural residence, region of birth, and region of present residence. Since such tabulations are made from a sample, the average cell density becomes very small for certain critical categories, and it is highly important that the cases found in each cell be measured with a minimum of error. For example, if the number of categories in the above examples were $7 \times 11 \times 10 \times 2 \times 6 \times 3 \times 3 \times 4 \times 4$, there would be an average of only 2.4 cases per cell in the 5 percent sample used for such tabulations in 1960, and the average density in the cells for nonwhite, rural-farm, the migrants, those with unusually high or low education, and the childless would be much below this.

3. *Studies of Small Areas.* The areas of micro-demography, micro-economics, and micro-sociology are expanding rapidly; research is focusing increasingly upon adopting small spatial units of population as units of observation and analysis. Demands for data for small individual communities, for townships, census tracts, and city blocks are increasing, both in variety of data wanted and the amount of detailed categories and cross-classification of data. The programs to fight poverty, to rebuild slums, and to aid depressed areas are augmenting this development, because such programs require exact information about local problems and situations. The need is not only for reliable population and reliable economic information for small areas, but to unite several varieties of information in order to deal with these problems in all of their aspects.

4. *Studies Where the Dependent Variable Is a Residual.* Many phenomena cannot be measured directly but can be studied indirectly by eliminating all other plausible factors and identifying "what is left" as the

topic of analysis. A well-known example is the estimation of net migration by the survival ratio method, wherein the natural increase is subtracted from total growth in order to permit the assumption that the residual is an estimate of net migration.[3] An equally important class of problems is the exploration of all classes of *differentials*, such as differentials in fertility, mortality, nuptiality, or migration by race, educational attainment, socio-economic status, and so forth. The measurement of intercensal change itself is a residual—the difference between two censuses. Hence, *many, if not most, variables in demography are not derived directly from census data but are residuals or differences between two or more census counts.* As was pointed out by Dr. Leon Truesdell several years ago,[4] all the errors of coverage and classification made by a census are also included in such residuals. Therefore, a residual is measured much less accurately than the trait itself. In fact, errors of 50 or 100 percent in the measurement of residuals are not at all uncommon, especially when the residuals being measured are comparatively small.[5] Inasmuch as the study of differences, change, and net residuals comprise a very large part of demographic research, this is perhaps the single strongest argument for high precision in the basic data.

5. *Studies of Small Groups with Special Combinations of Characteristics.* Many research hypotheses refer only to a small segment of the population (perhaps widely dispersed in space) that has some unique trait. Quite often, for "critical tests" of an hypothesis it is only a small group with an extraordinary combination of traits that can provide the data. For example, we may ask the question, "Which is more influential in promoting school attendance, the level of education of the father or the level of education of the mother?" In this example we need data on the school attendance of children 14–17 years of age by sex, educational attainment of father, educational attainment of mother, family income, urban-rural residence, and perhaps nativity and region of birth. For such studies, only highly detailed and accurate data can provide valid information about such special groups. The "crucial data" in such a table would be the cells for mothers with college education married to husbands with only a grade school education and for well-educated men married to poorly educated women. It is highly important that such data arise from events as they exist in the population, not contaminated by errors occurring during the process of enumeration and tabulation.

The number of such special subgroups which have particular interest is large and increasing. Some examples follow:

1. Women who have borne an extraordinarily large number of children or those who are childless or with only one child, though married for several years.

2. Child marriages: children 15–17 years of age who have married—or unusually late marriages: age at first marriage 35 years or older.
3. Early motherhood—girls 15–18 who have borne children.
4. Misfits in the labor force—persons with prolonged unemployment, extraordinarily low pay or high education for given occupations, or part-time workers.
5. Men 25–49 years of age who are not in the labor force.
6. Small ethnic groups—American Indians, Chinese, Japanese, Filipinos, foreign-born Negroes, and so forth.
7. Employed women living with husband and with numerous children of school age in the home.
8. Women in occupations usually held only by men.
9. College graduates with low incomes, in low-skill occupations.
10. Uneducated persons with high incomes, high-skill occupations.
11. Persons who journey extraordinarily great distances to work.
12. Persons past age 30 who are still in school.
13. Persons aged 14–19 who are employed full time or persons this age who are not in school and not in the labor force.
14. Households in which the head is an employed mother with small children.
15. Migrants who have made extraordinarily long or unusual journeys.
16. Persons who have been married two or more times.
17. Widows of less than 40 years of age.
18. Children who are retarded or accelerated in school.
19. Elderly persons of low income living alone.
20. Lodgers in the homes of others.
21. Homes in which there is a grandchild but no child of the head.

Much of the research that is needed for the making of policy decisions about these problems requires valid data for such groupings. Because there is no alternative source, more and more reliance is being placed upon the census to provide such information, at least once per decade.

6. *Studies of the Incidence of Events in the Absence of Registration Data.* By appropriate demographic techniques it is possible to estimate the rates at which events are occurring in a population from census data. The articles by Mertens and by Grabill-Cho in the present issue of *Demography* are pioneering methodological statements in this tradition.[6] By using two or more consecutive censuses, it is sometimes possible to calculate a wide variety of rates by such procedures, as fertility, mortality, nuptiality, social mobility, marital dissolution, retirement, raises in pay, promotion in school, intermarriage of ethnic groups, and others. The validity of all such measures is greatly affected by the quality of the data, for they constitute a special class of residuals. Although in many cases the data can be smoothed and graduated to correct obvious errors, only precise data can successfully

duplicate the results that would be given by a registration system. As Grabill-Cho point out in their article, this line of study permits the calculation of rates for special subgroupings of the population (income, ethnicity, etc.) for which no registration system anywhere can provide information. This line of research is therefore not one confined only to "underdeveloped countries": it is destined to become a very large and important segment of routine demographic analysis.

7. *Studies of Cohort Changes Over Time.* As the number of successive censuses becomes greater and as the comparability of data from census to census improves, more and more refined cohort studies will be undertaken, covering a wider variety of topics. Cohort analysis is no longer confined to fertility studies of a very general nature. Instead, we have cohort studies of migration, education, marriage, labor mobility, income, home ownership, and so forth.[7] Such studies require not only higher precise data with respect to age (single years) in order to preserve the integrity of the cohorts, but also exact data on other characteristics in order to calculate comparative rates of change in the various cohorts.

8. *Studies Where the Tabulations Are Based on Small Samples.* Unfortunately, a great amount of the census tabulations that are of greatest research interest is based on comparatively small samples (have low average cell density). The average cell density in the special reports tabulations of the United States Census has been surprisingly small in all censuses for which they have been performed—1940, 1950, and 1960. The fact that most population characteristics now are collected for only a 25 percent sample introduces rather great relative sampling variability into data for city blocks and census tracts, with consequently greater need that the data be more precise. The inferences that can be drawn from such tabulations are greatly influenced by the amount and pattern of error in the data. The greater the precision, the greater the reliability of the findings based upon small samples.

9. *Studies Where the Variable Is Not Measured Directly but Is Inferred Indirectly.* Demographers and economists are highly adept at devising special indexes to measure indirectly variables for which data were not explicitly collected by the census. For example, by taking the percentage of children of grammar school age attending private schools and expressing it as a percentage of all children of these ages in school, it is purportedly possible to identify areas of concentration of population of Roman Catholic faith. Combinations of items from housing censuses have been used to identify "slum," "blighted areas," and "upper class neighborhoods." Data on living arrangements have been combined with other items to identify Skid Rows, "rooming house areas," "areas of social disorganization," and so forth in the city. The intensity of racial segregation and of segregation

of residence on the basis of occupation and income has been measured by such indirect means. Census data are used to estimate the "economic base" of a community—the types and amounts of goods it exports or exchanges with other communities as its function in the national division of labor— and the number of persons engaged in such work. Similarly, the economic dependency of a community upon the rest of the economy has been measured by the same procedure. Census data play a central role in the construction of the components of national accounts, and census data are used in the derivation of the equations that express the flows of commodities in input-output analysis. The refinement of economic and demographic models depends to no small degree upon refinement of the basic data from which these numerous indirectly inferred variables are estimated.

10. *Studies of Phenomena Where Judgment or Evaluation Is Required.* In the data collection enterprise there is a move to rely upon the field worker to make judgments and evaluations that otherwise would be difficult to quantify. A well-known example is the evaluation of housing as "dilapidated," "deteriorated," or "sound." When armed with comparatively simple instructions and uniform training, interviewers can collect with usable validity data for a variety of pathological or unusual conditions that may be of interest but available only through observation.

Together these ten types of research situations emphasize the need for precision in population data. Moreover, these suggest that the need for precision is increasing rapidly, so that merely by staying the same, censuses of the future will become progressively less adequate.

The electronic computer has enabled researchers to pose highly sophisticated and highly complex questions—and for very small populations delimited either in terms of combinations of traits or of residence in a particular area. Because they lack data from other sources, they turn to the census for information.

It is possible to react to this need in two ways. One could assert, "The census was never intended for such purposes and researchers have no right to expect such high precision." Alternatively, it is possible to accept this need as a census goal in the spirit of the Hansen-Hurwitz-Pritzker quotation given above. The "losses" that are being suffered and will be suffered increasingly from insufficient precision, as mentioned in this quotation, are difficult to assess, but estimates suggest that they are tremendous. To reduce them to tolerable limits, the nation could well be justified in tripling or quadrupling the budget for the decennial census and adopting procedures far more elaborate and costly than any heretofore envisaged, if by doing so it could accomplish the level of precision needed for both scientific and public welfare purposes. If this philosophy prevails, then the needs of research, not past performance, will set the goals for future censuses and define their nature. Procedures for collecting the tabulating data will then be established in the light of efforts to attain those goals.

IV. ADVANTAGES OF CANVASSER ENUMERATION: THE FUNCTIONS OF THE ENUMERATOR

Before considering empirical evidence it may not be inappropriate to review the functions which an interviewer (in theory) is supposed to perform if he or she is doing a good job. It is possible to identify at least ten such functions.

1. *Minimize refusal and noncompliance.* A certain percentage of respondents is hostile to the idea of being interviewed, while an even larger percentage is adamant or negligent. It is widely believed by "survey researchers" that both groups would not comply with the request for information if the interviewer did not intercede to explain the purpose of the survey and by personal contact facilitate getting the information—or that if they did comply the response would be minimal. Most questionnaires mailed to the general population have only a return of 30–50 percent because of this phenomenon. Although the census has a legal status which a private survey lacks, it has long been presupposed that an interviewer's presence would have a beneficial effect upon the full compliance of a substantial percentage of the population. At the time of the census the interviewer is a personification of the national government, and his very presence (if he is a person worthy of respect) is a genial but nevertheless legal summons to furnish information. Long-term census employees who have worked in the field have many anecdotes to illustrate the point that, with his portfolio under his arm, the census taker is Uncle Sam himself to the unwilling as well as the willing respondents.

2. *Enforce honesty and minimize falsification.* Many persons dislike to report their age, their marital status, their income, or to admit that they have little education or a poor job. Others may want to understate or hide their socio-economic status. The fact that an interviewer is present to observe the approximate age, to gauge the approximate income level from the location, size, and furnishings of the dwelling unit, has been thought to be a curb to misrepresentation. It has been supposed that the official nature of his visit, backed by the census law, gives the census interview a testimony-taking flavor that would minimize falsification.

3. *Explain concepts, clarify misunderstandings, and answer questions.* Many of the concepts used by the Census are quite complex. A significant share of the respondents may get confused about the objectives of some

questions and give responses that are irrelevant or at best only partly correct. Each of the recent censuses has had a 100-page *Enumerator's Reference Manual*, cataloguing the many unusual types of situations that arise and giving instructions on how each situation is to be handled in order to minimize bias in the data. A householder respondent has only a very brief instruction at most to guide him, and if he falls into one of the very numerous ambiguous situations, he must guess his way out of it as best he can or omit it altogether and thereby create bias. Many a babysitter or other part-time worker could honestly wonder whether she or he is unemployed or not in the labor force; others may fail to grasp the distinction between occupation and industry. Traveling salesmen, circus troupes, and inmates of institutions will have complex questions about their mobility status. The high school graduate may report attendance at a business college, beautician school, or apprenticeship as a part of "years of schooling completed." In reporting children ever born, many women will report only legitimate children or children by the present marriage, and the childless married woman may simply ignore the question. Should family income include the earnings of a nephew paying board and room or a tuition scholarship to college won by a child? The interviewer who has been carefully coached on these definitions and their fine points should be prepared to explain what they mean, define terms, and answer questions. The more ambitious in scope a census becomes, the more its concepts become complex, with need for clarification.

4. *Detect inconsistencies, incomplete responses, and unintentional errors, and, by probing, correct them on the spot.* Many erroneous answers are given innocently, either from a low level of intelligence, faulty memory, temporary confusion, or giving a stereotyped response that really does not answer the question. An alert interviewer is expected to perform an editorial function as he records; incongruities and apparent impossibilities or improbabilities get his attention and he makes inquiries about them. The correct age of an elderly grandmother may be revised downward by comparison with the age of the respondent; forgotten dates necessary to record migration status accurately may be recalled with interviewer assistance, and so forth. In theory, at least, the interviewer is prepared to raise the performance of such persons to an acceptably high level by means of patient explanation and probing. The statistics of the prevalence of persons of borderline intelligence, extreme neurosis, and low level of initiative to perform tasks which are onerous but which carry no reward suggest that a low level of performance may be expected by a highly unrepresentative but not small fraction of householders. If this editorial function is performed in an office, it is too late to do much by way of detecting and correcting

the work of incompetents. Contacting a person by telephone to ask him to clarify an apparent inconsistency requires much more initiative and may be much more challenging than a simple friendly query from an on-the-spot interviewer. To the extent that there is a tendency for office personnel to falsify the returns *ex post facto* by "writing in what the respondent obviously meant," errors from staff editing may be quite substantial with householder enumeration.

5. *Prevent nonresponse to particular items.* When people do not wish to supply a particular item of information on a self-enumeration form but do not wish to be uncooperative altogether, they simply may omit answering the single items to which they object. With householder enumeration there is little to prevent this. When perfectly usable schedules with minor omissions arrive at the census office, the Census is given a most uncomfortable choice. Shall the person be called on the telephone and asked to supply it? If he has no telephone, should an interviewer go to his residence and obtain it? Or should it be supplied by machine guessing, allocating a characteristic on the basis of the characteristics of other persons who have similar traits? With a well-designed enumeration form and good enumerators, this situation should be minimized.

6. *Enumeration by observation.* Some items of census data require only that the interviewer observe and record, without asking questions. Examples are race and condition of dwelling unit. Before 1960, Negroes scarcely knew that the question on race was being asked, because it was simply observed by the interviewer and recorded. By the householder method they are forced to certify their race in writing. The current drive by civil rights groups to get the race item removed from all data collection forms may be greatly intensified by this forced self-registration of race. It is not improbable that a racist organization will inspire its members either to refuse to answer this question at future censuses or else encourage them to falsify their responses. Self-enumeration makes each series of data vulnerable to refusal to cooperate by one or more groups most unique or deviant from the population average.

7. *Obtain a legible record.* A very substantial share of the population writes illegibly. The writing instruments used by many households are of very smeary, smudgy, blotty, and scratchy quality. Self-enumeration produces a great quantity of illegible marks on paper, and a poorly written record is typical rather than exceptional. This problem has been serious enough in previous censuses, where interviewers were screened for their ability to write legibly and instructed to do so. Persons who must transcribe self-enumeration records find themselves guessing whether given symbols are 5 or 2, 3 or 8, 7 or 4, and so forth, and whether the state of birth or

place of last residence were Mississippi, Michigan, Minnesota, or Wisconsin. Errors of transposition, of making incorrect and misleading abbreviations, of placing answers in the wrong boxes, and so forth, almost certainly must be higher among the general population than among a corps of trained enumerators who must pass an examination to be hired.

8. *Assure transmission of each question in full.* An interviewer is instructed to read each question aloud *in full* and to read it in exactly the same way to each respondent. This is done in an effort to assure that every respondent gets the same stimulus. In filling out enumeration forms, many impulsive householders may look only at the caption heading and insert what they think ought to go there, without "reading the fine print" that gives extra information or instructions. Thus, many persons do not get the question presented in full and experience a different stimulus from that given by the interviewer. Moreover, hearing a question read aloud with proper phrasing and intonation may convey clearer comprehension than a quick reading by a person not accustomed to reading and comprehending factual questions of this type.

9. *Build rapport and maintain good public relations during the census.* At the time of the census a great many public issues get tied to the census. Salesmen pose as enumerators; zealots condemn certain items or otherwise try to benefit from the situation. Even the neighborhood hothead, an irresponsible disc jockey or news commentator, or a radical newspaper or pamphleteer can create substantial mass anti-enumeration unrest and anti-census feeling. The more urban we become, the greater are the potentialities for mass media campaigns against the census or particular parts of the census. Canada's recent experience with counting ethnic origin is an example. A friendly, well-mannered interviewer, circulating in each neighborhood, armed with counter-arguments given him as a part of his training, is expected to be an antidote to such temporary hysteria. Under a scheme of householder enumeration, rumors can be fabricated and spread with almost no counter-information except that which is put through formal channels, which most rumor-believers may not trust. The census enumerator hopefully is a force for maintaining stability and public calm and trust while the count is on. The fact that enumerators are spread uniformly throughout the entire population means that counter-information is never far from the source of rumor.

10. *Obtain information about hard-to-reach persons.* Persons who are hard to reach because they are away from home and not receiving mail and are likely not to be enumerated often can be contacted and enumerated at least approximately by contacting neighbors. With a system of mail enumeration, this is more difficult to accomplish. When self-enumeration is

combined with sampling, as in the 1960 census, failure to obtain any information about persons in sample households can be a substantial source of bias.

V. THE ADVANTAGES OF HOUSEHOLDER ENUMERATION

There are no less than nine arguments in favor of the householder approach to enumeration which, if valid, are very powerful.

1. *Each person has an opportunity to report for himself,* or at least to have an opportunity to review the information concerning himself before it is forwarded to the census office. The enumerator calling at each house usually must accept the replies of a single informant and cannot wait to have ambiguous answers clarified by a family caucus in the evening. If each person describes his job, reports his own income, birth date, employment status, and so forth, to the person completing the report, it would seem plausible that the total amount of error could be much smaller than under a system whereby the enumerator must accept the answers given by a single adult informant who happens to be home at the time. The enumeration of lodgers and more distant relatives of the head might be thought to benefit especially from this procedure.

2. *It reduces bias and variance in enumeration.* It has now been demonstrated beyond any doubt that enumerators do inject a significant amount of bias and variance into census data, and that particular enumerators exhibit particular patterns of error.[8] The article by Powell and Pritzker[9] presents a carefully reasoned presentation of the theory and some empirical results which demonstrate not only that it is *possible* for this undesired source of difficulty to arise, but that in fact it *does* occur. Similar results have been measured in the Canadian census.[10] This research indicates that this bias and variance are contributed by a comparatively small group of interviewers; the majority do work that is reliable, but a small minority creates problems by systematically mishandling particular questions. Although there is a tendency for persons who mishandle one question also to mishandle others, unfortunately the tendency is only a general one.[11] Although substantial reductions in errors could be made by a policy of early detection and discharge of error-prone enumerators, as of right now it appears that this could only alleviate but not wholly resolve the problem. *It is firmly established that under the programs of recruitment, training, supervision, and quality control of field work thus far employed, data collected by enumerators fail to measure up to the standards of precision outlined in Section II.* (Documentation of this assertion will be given below.) Does householder enumeration materially improve the quality of the data collected by re-

ducing bias and variation? In theory, allowing each person to "speak for himself" should solve the problem completely, unless errors of householder-reporting outweigh those of enumerator-reporting.

3. *It reduces the amount of time required to take a census.* By mailing out the forms, everyone can enumerate himself on a single day. In fact, where a *de facto* census is taken, in some nations only the householder system can hope to achieve the ideal of one-day counting. Enumerators require more than one day to complete an assigned enumeration district. Some enumerators fail and their unfinished assignments must be taken over by others. Where insufficient enumerators can be hired, some districts must wait until an enumerator has finished his first assignment before work can begin.

4. *It provides time for compiling correct answers.* The enumerator is paid according to the number of people he enumerates. In order to maximize his pay he must spend a minimum amount of time at each house. He is in no mood to encourage a wife to locate last year's tax return in order to report income more accurately or otherwise to consume time in compiling precise answers. Errors that otherwise would occur because of haste, carelessness, or lack of immediate access to the correct information are reduced.

5. *It is cheaper.* If every household head would report accurately and completely for all members of his dwelling unit, there would unmistakably be a great saving in interviewing costs. The major costs of the fieldwork in previous censuses has been the salaries of enumerators and supervisors. If this cost could be eliminated, it would be a major economy.

6. *It simplifies fieldwork.* At first thought one might presume that householder enumeration would greatly reduce the complexity of the fieldwork. It would be necessary only to mail out the forms, collect them, and mail them to the census office. If this proved to be true, it would eliminate the process of recruiting, training, and supervising large numbers of enumerators, and the large census offices that must be opened up and then dismantled after the enumeration.

7. *It requires less skilled personnel.* To be effective, enumerators must be superior persons—in terms of education, integrity, drive, and perseverance. It is possible that under self-enumeration the job can be done with a few highly talented people with administrative skills and a corps of persons of very modest experience and ability.

8. *It preserves confidentiality.* Canvassers are recruited from the local area and often are known to the persons whom they are enumerating. There may be more reluctance or resentment at having to report income or other private information to such a person than reporting it on a form that is mailed to a central office.

9. *It creates greater public interest and sense of responsibility for the*

success of the census. The fact that each household shares a part of the responsibility for the census creates greater public awareness and interest and sense of involvement.

VI. VIEWS OF DEMOGRAPHERS BEFORE 1960 VIS-A-VIS HOUSEHOLDER ENUMERATION

Discussions of the respective merits of the two systems of collecting data are not new. Before 1960 the problem had been reviewed by experts on both sides of the Atlantic, and from it had emerged a consensus which may be summed up in the following principle:

For speed and acceptable precision in taking a simple census among a literate and favorably disposed population, use the householder method; for high quality data where the concepts are more complex, the list of questions is long, the population is of low education or is indifferent or negative, use the canvasser approach.

Three illustrations of this view follow:

> The advantages of the householder method are that there is ample time to fill in the details of the schedule and also that there is a smaller chance of missing members of the household who are temporarily absent. However, since the burden of completing the return falls upon the household, the questions asked must necessarily be simple and few in number. Even so, many errors in reporting may be made due to misunderstanding of the questions on the part of the respondent, to a lack of interest, and to a dilatory attitude.
>
> The method of direct interview has the advantage that the enumerators can be trained to secure more accurate reporting, more elaborate questions can be asked, and the results will be fairly uniform in quality.[12]

While endorsing the householder approach as used in England and Wales, because it permits rapid enumeration as of a given date, Peter Cox observes:

> It might be thought that more and more information about the population of a country could be gained simply by adding to the number of questions asked on the census ·schedule. It is generally considered, however, that if this process is pursued far enough a point will be reached where public indifference or inability fully to understand what is required can give rise to such a degree of inaccuracy that doubt is thrown on the validity of the results of the whole enumeration. The limit to the number of questions to be asked was considered by the authorities in England and Wales to have been approached in 1911,

since when little or no increase has been made in the complexity of the schedule of that country. If canvassers are used it should be possible to explain the more difficult questions and so help to improve the accuracy of the answers.[13]

Essentially the same position is reached by Wolfenden:

It is stated on pp. 13–14 of the "General Report of the Census of England and Wales, 1911" that "the transfer to the householder of the duty of record can be regarded as advantageous, if at all, only provided that the scope of the census inquiry is to be severely restricted," because "the census schedule is an elaborate and in the nature of things a difficult form to fill in, and the average householder is a person without much clerical or literary training, and quite unaccustomed to the formidable form with which he is confronted." . . . The "canvasser" method, however, notwithstanding its higher cost and its dependence on the efficiency of the enumerators, is justified by the more elaborate enquiries which can be made when the information, as in that system, is obtained directly by officials who are familiar with the requirements of the schedule, and by the fact that it secures more reliable information from colored and foreign-born populations among whom the percentage of illiteracy is genuinely high.[14]

The principle stated above seems to have been accepted around the world. As reported by the United Nations, censuses taken between 1945–54 used the canvasser method uniformly where literacy was low.[15] In Africa, South America, and Asia the canvasser method has been employed almost exclusively. It has also been employed in part in Europe by Denmark, France, and Norway. (In France, if the householder expressed the wish to complete the questionnaires himself, he was permitted to do so. In Norway and Denmark the canvasser method was used in rural areas only and the householder method was used in urban areas.)

All the remaining nations of Europe used the householder approach. Among the family of nations, the United States is clearly in an anomalous position—it has a highly literate and generally favorably disposed population, yet it has the longest and most complex census questionnaire, with much evidence that in future years the scope and complexity will increase even more. It also outstrips all other nations in having a corps of professional demographers ever demanding greater detail and precision as outlined above. What course should it follow?

Admittedly, most of the judgments held before 1960 were arrived at on the basis of general observation and experience rather than on the basis of formal research investigations. What light can be thrown on this problem by the comprehensive evaluation studies of the 1950 and 1960 censuses of the United States?

VII. EVIDENCE FROM THE POST-ENUMERATION EVALUATION OF UNITED STATES CENSUSES

The amount of material available for analysis in this area is very large, and the picture that is built up may well reflect the bias of the analyst. The present article was prepared with the explicit advance understanding that, if it so chose, the United States Bureau of the Census would append its own evaluation and reaction to the selection and interpretation made by the author. The Census was also invited to summarize its own evaluation of its experience with self-enumeration and its future potential. Unfortunately, direct answers are not available for many of the questions asked, and it is necessary to reason indirectly, using the principle that the 1950 census was a canvasser census and the 1960 census was primarily a householder census. Such comparisons are, of course, biased against the canvasser approach, becaused many administrative and procedural refinements not directly related to either approach were added to the 1960 census as a result of experience with the 1950 census. Nevertheless, if caution is used, much can be learned by this line of reasoning.

A. Coverage

The 1960 census had as one of its objectives the improvement of coverage. Of the several measures taken to improve coverage, two involved householder enumeration directly or indirectly—the advance census report and two-stage enumeration.

Advance Census Reports. "An advance census report was mailed to households on a nationwide basis so that written information for household members would be available when the enumerator called. This advance report contained instructions as to who was to be included; and, since it was available prior to the enumerator's visit, it permitted the members of the household to develop a correct list of persons to be enumerated in the housing unit. It also served to focus attention on questions related to coverage during the interview conducted by the enumerator. Not all householders filled out the advance report; but many did, and the net effect of the whole procedure was to add to the enumeration situation another factor calculated to increase the completeness of enumeration above that achieved in previous censuses."

Two-Stage Enumeration. "In areas covering approximately 82 percent of the total 1960 population, the 1960 census was conducted in two stages. In the first stage, the enumerator visited each household in his enumeration district and collected the relatively small amount of information—name, household relationship, sex, race, birth date, and marital status—which, along with some limited housing information, was obtained on a complete-count basis. He left a sample schedule with additional questions at every fourth household, with the request that it be filled out and mailed to the census office. This procedure meant that the first-stage enumerator needed training only on the relatively few 100 percent items; and, therefore, relatively more emphasis could be placed on coverage in his training. Likewise, in the actual canvass, more attention could be given to coverage and the canvass could be completed more rapidly."[16]

To the extent that householders did fill out the advance census reports and enumerators accepted them without repeating the entire enumeration process for households that had filled out the forms, there was householder determination of the persons to be included or excluded.

The evidence available from the experience suggests two hypotheses: (a) The net overall gains in coverage with householder participation in enumeration in 1960 as contrasted with canvasser enumeration in 1950 were negligible and (b) the proportion of persons within each household who were erroneously included or erroneously omitted did not decrease and possibly may have increased substantially.

Evidence on the first point is furnished by Taeuber and Hansen.[17] They report that the program of coverage improvement yielded an improvement of 277,000 persons with an estimated 3,438,000 persons left unenumerated by the 1960 procedure. Thus, only 7.5 percent of the coverage problem appears to have been solved, leaving 92.5 percent untouched. The advance census reports must share this small gain with the use of listing books, improved control and checking of coverage, the two-stage procedure, and heavy emphasis on improving coverage given during training of enumerators.

Evidence concerning the second hypothesis is ambiguous. The postenumeration survey following the 1950 and the 1960 censuses yielded estimates of percentage error as shown in the accompanying tabulation.[18]

	1960	1950
Omissions of persons	3.0	2.3
In missed living quarters	1.6	1.6
In enumerated living quarters	1.4	0.6
Erroneous inclusions of persons	1.3	0.9
Net undercoverage of persons	1.7	1.4

These data make the 1950 canvasser census look much better than the 1960 householder census. In presenting these figures, Taeuber and Hansen cast doubt on the estimates for 1950 and attribute the poorer showing of the 1960 census to a more effective re-enumeration procedure used in 1960.[19] (The specific changes that would account for these differences are not cited.) The alternative hypothesis—*that these are exactly the results that would materialize if householders interpreted the coverage rules less adequately than do enumerators*—should not be completely rejected without further evidence.

B. Nonresponse

A major difference between the 1960 and the 1950 and earlier censuses was a substantially higher rate of nonresponse in 1960—for almost all characteristics. Table 1, reported by Taeuber and Hansen, illustrates the change.

TABLE 1.   Percent of Nonresponse (NA's) for Selected Characteristics: 1960 and 1950

Selected Characteristics	Percent 1960	Nonresponse 1950
Age	1.7*	0.2
State of birth	2.7	1.0
School enrollment (persons 5–34 years old)	8.3	5.9†
Highest grade completed (persons 25 and over)	4.9	4.6
Employment status (persons 14 and over)	3.1	1.0
Occupation (employed persons)	4.9	1.3
Children ever born (to women ever married)	6.0	9.0
Income (persons 14 and over)	6.2	6.7

*Year or decade of age not reported. The 1.7 figure is based on Stage I or 100-percent enumeration. In Stage II, the corresponding nonresponse figure was 1.0 per cent.

†Enrollment data available only for persons 5–29 years old in 1950.

Source: Conrad Taeuber and Morris H. Hansen, "A Preliminary Evaluation of the 1960 Census of Population and Housing," *Demography*, I (1964), 6.

Two hypotheses may explain this change: (1) The 1960 census instructed enumerators who were collecting data to obtain information only from an acceptable respondent in the household, and, if three call-backs failed to produce the needed information, to close it out as a nonresponse. In contrast, in 1950 and earlier censuses enumerators were permitted to make inquiries from neighbors. This tended to produce a higher percentage of nonresponse in 1960. (2) The "self-enumeration" procedure (the second stage of the two-stage enumeration) resulted in a very substantial percentage of forms being mailed in with nonresponse to one or more items. Special corps of follow-up workers, using telephones and making field revisits, were needed to shrink this nonresponse to tolerable levels. The level finally achieved represented the best that could be done with the budget and personnel available within the allotted time.

There is clear evidence that *both* these explanations are valid. On the one hand, the number of households known to be occupied, but for which no enumeration was made, was larger in 1960 than in 1950; this is proof that the closeout procedure tended to boost nonresponse statistics. On the other hand, there is substantial evidence that householder enumeration itself created an increase in nonresponse rates: (1) A comparison of nonresponse rates in selected cities of the 18 percent of the population enumerated by the householder method, made by Shryock and Greene, indicated a higher rate of nonresponse in the "self-enumeration" areas.[20] (2) Examination of householder returns when first received in the mail showed that a significant proportion lacked information on multiple items to the extent that they would have been considered clearly deficient if performed by an enumerator. (3) The rate of nonresponse reported in 1960 is much higher for some items than for others. If the difficulty were due solely to the problem of obtaining a qualified informant, the nonresponse rate would tend to be of the same general magnitude for all characteristics, unless the householder enumeration procedure had already created a willful tendency to omit responses to particular items. (4) The rate of nonresponse is especially high among populations of low socio-economic status, low education, living in slum areas, in foreign-language communities, and so forth. Persons with these characteristics would be expected to have difficulty in filling out the forms properly and in having sufficient knowledge of the purpose and importance of the census to be motivated to comply. For example, Shryock and Greene found that occupation was not reported for 4.4 percent of the nonwhite population in cities enumerated by direct enumeration, but, in a corresponding sample of cities with self-enumeration, 10.1 percent of the nonwhite employed persons failed to report their occupation.

Taken together, these shreds of evidence indicate that the householder approach yields a higher rate of nonresponse, especially for complex items such as occupation, education, income, and so forth, than would be obtained by enumerators.

The exact extent of the increase in nonresponse due to householder enumeration is difficult to estimate. When allowance is made for the effects of improvement in questions and general enumeration procedures of 1960 and even if the more stringent closeout rules are allowed to share in the responsibility for the increase in nonresponse, it is difficult to avoid the conclusion that the increase was sizable—perhaps as much as 50 percent in nonresponse rates for the more complex census items and 100 percent for the nonwhite population. This is only a very crude and impressionistic estimate.

Given that "householder enumeration" does increase the nonresponse rate, is this necessarily bad? Many times it is preferable to accept a nonresponse in lieu of bad information. The usual procedure in such cases is to make an imputation, either directly or by assuming the NA's are distributed like the knowns. For several items in the 1960 census, imputation for nonresponses was done by computer, attributing characteristics that were consistent with the other facts known for the individual. Whether this procedure is preferable to accepting information provided by neighbors is highly debatable and should not lightly be assumed to be so. The computer-imputation procedure merely substitutes an average value for each unknown. The unknowns, in a disproportionately large share of the cases, tend to be deviant in some way. In the self-enumeration procedure the very fact that the information was omitted (either intentionally or by oversight) and then subsequently could not be obtained readily because of lack of a telephone or persistent failure to be found at home creates the presumption that the nonresponse items accumulated by the householder approach may be deviant cases in a disproportionately large percentage of instances and as a consequence would be very inadequately represented by computer imputation. In fact, the approach may well have the tendency to "chop off the tails" of the distributions for most characteristics, especially at the lower end of the socio-economic scale, and produce a bias for overstating the welfare of the population. It is quite possible that information on occupation, educational attainment, employment status, and so forth, provided for such extraordinary people by their neighbors, may be superior to imputation by the computer. This is a problem for research and one that is of crucial importance before making a decision concerning the comparative precision that is obtained by the two methods of enumeration.

Another hypothesis that should be mentioned here, but for which no data are available to the writer's knowledge, may be stated as follows: The extra work required to obtain missing information on mailed-in census returns invites false enumeration in a context where quality control checks are difficult to impose. For example, instead of making a third telephone call after two "no answer" attempts or of assigning a householder report for reinterview, it may be found easier simply to write in an "educated guess" in the field office. Enumerators who are assigned to clean up problem cases may do much more of their interviewing at home than is suspected, unless strict quality controls are established. It is more difficult to establish quality control over such operations than is the case with canvasser enumeration.

C. Errors of Classification

Did householder enumeration succeed in reducing the very substantial rate of misclassification that characterized the 1950 (and presumably earlier) censuses? The evidence available suggests that for several characteristics the rates of misclassification were somewhat lower in the 1960 census than in 1950.[21] The extent to which householder enumeration was responsible for this is debatable. In some cases the improvement seems to have resulted primarily from improvement in the formulation of the questions and layout of the schedule to increase clarity and to facilitate correct recording. Also, in some cases, at least a part of the improvement appears to be linked to the higher rate of nonresponses in 1960; by refusing to accept approximations by neighbors, the census tended to have fewer errors of classification in the group for which information was obtained. (See example of education, below.) Thus, instead of a complete overall gain, there may have been an exchange of one type of deficiency for another, with the total overall effect not known.

The data to be presented below run counter to the thesis that there was an improvement in classification between 1950 and 1960. Instead they appear to justify the following hypothesis: "The reduction in misclassification in the 1960 householder census, in comparison with the 1950 canvasser census, is disappointingly small. In fact, on balance it appears that the effect of householder enumeration may have been to *increase* misclassification."

A particular difficulty arises in testing this hypothesis because of differences of opinion concerning the appropriate measurement of misclassification that should be used. The rate of misclassification may be measured in several different ways, and the various alternatives do not all give the same verdict. A measure which is believed to be at least as adequate as any other in assessing the overall quality of census data for making statistical inferences (and possibly the best) is the proportion of population found to be in a given category at the post-censal follow-up re-enumeration that was *not* classified in that particular category by the census.[22] In other words, it is the proportion of each post-enumeration category that falls "off the diagonal" but in the same row when the results of the post-enumeration survey are cross-classified (in rows) against the matching census returns (in columns). A preferable measure would be one that summarizes the *magnitudes* of the deviations from the diagonal.[23] The measure $b/a + b$ proposed here is useful because it indicates the proportion of observations upon which a given statistic is based that are erroneous, and which in cross-tabulations may be interacting in unknown ways with similar errors in other variables to vitiate the inferences that would be arrived at by cross-classifying without error two or more variables simultaneously.

Table 2 reports such data for both 1960 and 1950 for three of the more complex census concepts: occupation, income, and education.

Occupation.[24]   Errors of classification of occupation clearly seem to be more serious in 1960 than in 1950, as measured by the indexes of Table 2. This is indeed a surprise, because it was believed that one of the major gains to be made from householder enumeration was permitting the breadwinners to report their work activities for themselves instead of permitting their spouses to report to the enumerator for them while they were away at work. The increase in misclassification appears to have affected all occu-

TABLE 2.   Percent of Census Respondents Not in Same Classification in Comparison with Post-enumeration Survey: 1960 and 1950

Characteristic	Percent Not in Same Class as Post-enumeration Survey		
	1960	1950	Change[a] 1950–60
Occupation			
Total	20.98	17.00	3.98
Professional, technical, and kindred workers	12.13	11.05	1.08
Farmers and farm managers	13.91	7.55	6.36
Managers, officials, and proprietors exc. farm	32.84	19.95	12.89
Mgr., off., prop. (n.e.c.) salaried	32.83		
Other	45.51		
Clerical and kindred workers	22.62	17.63	4.99
Clerical and kindred workers (n.e.c.)	37.92		
Other	29.14		
Sales workers	16.93	15.15	1.78
Salesmen and sales clerks (n.e.c.)	22.09		
Other	13.58		
Craftsmen, foremen, and kindred workers	20.37	17.36	3.01
Operatives and kindred workers	20.23	17.47	2.76
Operatives and kindred workers (n.e.c.)	36.57		
Other	22.06		
Private household workers	36.37	17.24	19.13
Service workers, exc. private household	13.32	12.84	0.48
Farm laborers and foremen	24.49	24.37	0.12
Laborers, exc. farm and mine	39.59	29.46	10.13
Laborers (n.e.c.)—manufacturing	42.75		
Other	40.52		
Total Personal Income, Males			
Total	41.30	41.62	−0.32
$1–$499 or loss	45.77	37.95	7.82
$500–$999	45.37	42.39	2.98
$1,000–$1,499	54.10	46.22	7.88
$1,500–$1,999	53.51	46.75	6.76
$2,000–$2,499	60.61	45.21	15.40
$2,500–$2,999	59.84	41.60	18.24
$3,000–$3,499	53.34	32.40	20.94
$3,500–$3,999	54.16	39.48	14.68
$4,000–$4,499	45.77	42.00	3.77
$4,500–$4,999	40.90	46.94	−6.04
$5,000–$5,999	32.89	38.42	−5.53
$6,000–$6,999	37.65	56.85	−19.20
$7,000–$9,999	22.23	44.66	−22.43
$10,000 or over	16.59	35.23	−18.64
Educational Attainment			
Total	25.78	37.09	−11.31
Elementary, total (not in the same specific class)	31.48	40.06	−8.58
1–2 years	59.62	54.58	+5.04
3–4 years	35.83	40.36	−4.53
5–6 years	33.14	43.84	−10.70

TABLE 2.   Percent of Census Respondents Not in Same Classification in Comparison with Post-enumeration Survey: 1960 and 1950—Cont.

Characteristic	Percent Not in Same Class as Post-enumeration Survey		
	1960	1950	Change[a] 1950–60
7 years	38.74	55.33	−16.59
8 years	23.79	30.25	−6.46
High school, total (not in the same specific class)	23.56	35.64	−12.08
1 year	34.80	50.68	−15.88
2 years	35.88	53.27	−17.39
3 years	41.39	56.48	−15.09
4 years	14.39	20.39	−6.00
College, total (not in the same specific class)	19.09	30.53	−11.44
1 year	29.80	49.90	−20.10
2 years	27.40	41.18	−13.78
3 years	35.60	49.95	−14.35
4 years or more	5.48	13.03	−7.55

aMinus sign denotes an improvement in 1960 Census as compared to 1950.

pational groups but was especially serious among managers, laborers, and private household workers. The overall increase between 1950 and 1960 in proportion of misclassification, as measured by this index, was 20 percent. It must be kept in mind that these data refer to the broad *major* occupational categories, in which one entry in five was estimated to have been an error. *That the rate would be very much higher for the 297 detailed occupational categories is certain.* No evaluation of quality of data for these detailed categories has been attempted. The statistics for the broad categories hint that, if this were to be done, it would show that for many detailed occupation categories the data are worthless.

Income.   With respect to income, the change in misclassification between 1950 and 1960 was mixed. Errors of classification were much greater in 1960 than in 1950 at the *lower* end of the income scale but correspondingly less at the *upper* end of the income scale, with little overall change. This would be consistent with the hypothesis that wealthy people dislike to report their income to an enumerator and poor people (with less education) tend not to comprehend the concepts if required to report for themselves without help. It is generally believed that the system of questions devised for asking income in 1960 was superior to that of 1950 and that a part of the improvement at the upper end of the scale must be attributed to this. Also, at the time of the 1950 census there had been a rebellion against the income question, led by influential politicians, openly encouraging citizens to refuse to report their incomes. The appeals of this group were primarily to the wealthy. The fact that resistance of this type was much reduced in 1960 may also help account for the 1950–60 improvement at the upper income ranges. Taking all of these factors into consideration, we conclude that the 1960 census data on income appear to be inferior to those for 1950 for studying the prevalence and correlates of poverty and that perhaps householder enumeration increased misclassification at the lower end of the scale. (It should be noted here that we are dealing with *gross* errors of classification, because it is such errors that can potentially affect inferences concerning relationships and differences. It is true that 1960 *net* errors in income appear to be smaller than in 1950).[25]

Education. Statistics for education appear to be clearly subject to less error in 1960 than in 1950;[26] however, it is doubtful whether householder enumeration can be credited with much of the gain. First, there was a major improvement in the educational level of the population during the decade; a substantial proportion of the very poorly educated (elderly) population died and was replaced by a generation of much more adequately educated persons. This alone would have tended to improve the quality of reporting. In addition there was a major change in office procedure between 1950 and 1960 in the handling of this item that would have the effect of reducing errors of classification. This is explained by the census as follows:

> In 1950, persons for whom highest grade attended was reported but for whom no report was made on finishing the grade were assumed not to have finished the grade if they were at the compulsory school ages but to have finished the grade if they were not at those ages. In 1960, nonresponse on both highest grade attended and completion of grade were eliminated by the procedure described in the section on "editing of unacceptable data."[27] [This is a procedure of editing by computer and imputing a value.]

In other words, the 1950 procedure accepted without question the response of the individual and treated all errors in such a way that there would be an upward bias in classification, whereas the 1960 procedure subjected the responses to an edit that would remove a certain fraction of more conspicuous errors and eliminate at least some if not all of the upward bias. Had this same procedure been followed in 1950, errors of classification would have been fewer. In addition, formulation and layout of the 1960 questions were greatly improved over 1950. When allowance is made for these factors, the improvements in classification which almost certainly may be traced to these other procedures, little remains that could be claimed for self-enumeration. Moreover, a careful examination of Table 2 reveals *that most of the reported improvements occurred at the upper educational levels, and at the lowest levels there was less than average improvement.*

These results would be consistent with the hypothesis that a general over-all improvement was achieved by the other programs, while self-enumeration caused a deterioration in quality among the less educated segments of the population.

All of the data pertaining to classification errors examined thus far hint at an hypothesis suggested in the quotations above from Cox, Spiegelman, and Wolfenden:

> Populations lower in the socio-economic scale are much less able to participate in a householder enumeration than are persons higher in the scale, and errors of classification rising from use of the householder approach would tend to show a much wider differential by socio-economic status than corresponding errors of data collected by enumerators.

Evidence with which to test this hypothesis directly is not available. However, Tables 3 and 4, showing indexes of misclassification for several census traits separately for the white and nonwhite population, reveal differences that are in the direction of supporting the hypothesis. For each variable, errors of classification for the nonwhite population are much greater than for the white. Unfortunately, comparable data are not available to permit a determination whether the differential was less in 1950. It is clear, however, that among the nonwhite population householder enumeration in 1960 permitted errors of very substantial magnitude to occur. It is not at all uncommon to find categories in which errors of classification outnumber correct entries. As has been discussed elsewhere, the fact that these errors tend to cancel each other is no argument that they do not affect research.[28]

D. Summary of Evidence from United States Experience

Taken together, the evidence cited above tends toward the conclusion that *neither the householder approach nor the canvasser approach to enumeration is succeeding in producing data of the precision needed and expected by modern demographic research, and both are falling short by a wide margin of the standards outlined in Section I.*

Our review of the evidence from the United States experience led to the following opinions concerning the apparent effect of self-enumeration:

a) Coverage was not improved and possibly was worsened by larger gross errors caused by an increase in omissions balanced by double enumeration.

b) Nonresponse was increased.

c) Errors of classification were not less and perhaps were greater, especially among low socio-economic groups.

TABLE 3.   Estimated Percent of Census Respondents Not in Same Classification in Comparison with Post-enumeration Survey for Selected Social and Economic Characteristics, by Sex and Color, 1960

Characteristic	White		Nonwhite	
	Male	Female	Male	Female
Relationship to Household Head[a]				
Head	0.92	7.77	2.55	4.89
Primary family head	1.16	16.71	3.13	12.19
Primary individual	5.73	3.66	16.97	5.42
Child	1.64	1.15	4.54	0.58
Other relative	16.37	12.71	32.61	19.50
Nonrelative	19.31	25.33	35.21	16.67
Marital Status				
Married	1.23	1.46	6.08	3.12
Excluding separated	0.60	0.90	1.97	1.94
Separated	56.55	34.20	62.89	22.94
Widowed	12.68	7.11	20.50	12.94
Divorced	36.38	17.88	50.00	27.23
Single	1.92	1.22	2.11	2.82
Employment Status				
Employed in agriculture	23.94	57.03	29.13	69.12
Wage and salary workers	35.46	56.20	42.24	66.67
Self-employed workers	25.99	52.28	38.25	79.17
Unpaid family workers	63.78	69.24	61.82	50.00
Employed in nonagricultural industry	4.46	10.35	9.42	19.88
Wage and salary workers	6.18	9.45	9.28	19.18
Self-employed workers	22.01	48.92	35.14	46.67
Unpaid family workers	—	56.92	—	00.00
Unemployed	46.13	69.24	59.22	67.35
Not in labor force	9.66	5.55	10.20	12.40
Occupation				
Professional, technical, and kindred workers	12.23	7.36	9.29	32.00
Farmers and farm managers	12.51	68.19	29.48	00.00
Managers, officials, and proprietors, exc. farm	32.55	49.57	47.96	34.05
Clerical and kindred workers	21.70	7.05	34.24	9.22
Sales workers	16.37	15.95	64.29	34.79
Craftsmen, foremen, and kindred workers	19.84	38.62	36.07	00.00
Operatives and kindred workers	18.81	8.32	32.53	9.10
Private household workers	48.00	6.86	00.00	7.54
Service workers, exc. private household	12.45	15.50	16.83	8.64
Farm laborers and foremen	22.02	25.74	31.03	35.90
Laborers, exc. farm and mine	38.92	88.24	41.70	65.22

[a]Reported for total and nonwhite population only.

Source: U.S. Bureau of the Census. "Accuracy of Data on Population Characteristics as Measured by CPS-Census Match." Evaluation and Research Program of the U.S. Census of Population and Housing, Series ER 60, No. 5.

Contrary to what many hoped, the introduction of householder enumeration did not seem to lead to a significant improvement in the precision of population statistics. The best that can be said is that quality remained about the same, with perhaps some rather serious deterioration for data for Negroes and other lower status groups. It is even possible that entrusting the enumeration to householders led to an overall decline in the self-enumeration census of 1960, in comparison with the canvasser census of 1950, but that this deterioration was offset and partially hidden by other

TABLE 4.   Estimated Percent of Census Respondents Not in Same Classification in Comparison with Post-enumeration Survey for Selected Economic Characteristics, by Sex and Color, 1960

Characteristic	White		Nonwhite	
	Male	Female	Male	Female
Industry				
Agriculture, forestry, and fisheries	7.04	15.24	14.24	00.00
Mining	21.50	57.70	00.00	—
Construction	18.98	35.08	28.91	—
Manufacturing	8.12	7.08	18.55	4.09
Durable goods	10.23	10.31	22.08	14.29
Nondurable goods	12.81	9.26	20.92	6.43
Transport., commun., & other				
pub. util.	9.11	6.74	12.45	24.14
Transportation	9.02	9.18	9.56	30.44
Commun., utilities, & san. serv.	9.87	5.60	30.16	00.00
Wholesale and retail trade	18.16	9.74	21.28	7.53
Wholesale trade	40.90	37.64	44.63	56.25
Retail trade	18.95	10.05	20.68	3.81
Finance, insurance, and real estate	12.90	6.36	00.00	00.00
Business and repair services	36.33	31.23	21.32	50.00
Personal services	14.82	10.81	24.64	10.07
Private household	68.27	9.65	75.00	7.42
Other	7.17	17.36	15.43	30.51
Entertainment and recreation				
services	13.34	7.06	13.80	00.00
Professional and related services	9.20	4.42	18.70	6.66
Public administration	6.60	5.06	6.56	00.00
Income				
$1 to $499 or loss	37.31	16.99	32.92	27.64
$500 to $999	36.40	28.83	52.28	36.37
$1,000 to $1,999	44.01	29.57	44.31	42.00
$2,000 to $2,999	46.21	29.59	59.35	49.39
$3,000 to $3,999	43.78	32.73	38.05	36.03
$4,000 to $4,999	42.15	29.01	52.64	8.34
$5,000 to $5,999	38.45	39.97	44.92	00.00
$6,000 to $6,999	40.85	38.12	42.38	—
$7,000 to $9,999	26.85	32.37	77.20	—
$10,000 and over	23.81	34.10	00.00	—

improvements, such as better question design, machine editing and correction of obvious errors of recording, and improved quality control.

VIII. HOW DO ENUMERATION ERRORS ARISE?

Two good interviewers assigned to enumerate a given population should get identical results. They should deliver for their employer all ten of the benefits listed in Section IV above, without introducing error into the results because of their own unique personalities and traits. This ideal is very nearly achieved by sample survey organizations and by the Bureau of the Census for its *Current Population Survey*.[29] But at the time of the decennial census a great deal of variance, attributable solely to the enumerators, manifests itself. Why should this be? There must be highly specific and discoverable explanations for this; it would be illogical to view it simply as some mysterious inherent and irradicable trait of decennial censuses. Once explanations are made, programs to deal more effectively with the problem can be devised.

Also, we must learn why and how the equally large errors of classification arise in householder enumeration.

In other words, it would appear that the next phase of study in problems of data quality is to research the enumeration process step-by-step to discover exactly how and why enumerators and householders make their errors and thereby introduce needless variance and bias into the results.

It is quite possible that if the conditions that permit enumeration error are identified, the most serious ones can be controlled at a cost that can be afforded.

Perhaps we may begin by hypothesizing that the following "explanations of enumerator failure" are simultaneously at work during any data-gathering operation carried out by canvassers and must be minimized if maximum precision is to be achieved:

1. *Idiosyncratic prejudice.* Emotional reaction against particular questions or instructions so that they are omitted altogether, are reworded, and are asked in an incomplete, improper, or biasing way, or not asked but an answer is presumed and recorded by the enumerator.[30]

2. *Incompetence.* Lack of intelligence, education, and work experience necessary to comprehend the study, undergo training, and make necessary decisions in the field.

3. *Carelessness.* Disinterest, poor morale, lack of concentration.

4. *Laziness.* Desire to obtain full pay while doing only a part of the work.

5. *Dishonesty.* Deliberate falsification or omission in order to minimize effort needed to get full pay.

6. Inadequate training. Failure to comprehend the goals of the items, misunderstandings concerning definitions and instructions, lack of familiarity with the forms, lack of skill in conducting an interview, ignorance concerning record keeping procedures.

7. Physical incapacity. Poor eyesight, palsy, inability to climb stairs, obesity, and other conditions that slow down or hamper enumeration.

8. Poor mental health. Unpleasant disposition, offensive manners or mannerisms, neurotic personality traits, poor interpersonal relations with others.

9. Poor supervision. Vague instructions or assignment, incorrect interpretation of procedures, failure to check first few interviews to assure procedure is understood, infrequent contacts between interviewer and supervisor. Lazy, incompetent, or dishonest supervisors who set a bad example.

10. Less than desired effectiveness in quality check on each phase of the fieldwork. During the data-gathering phase processes may be pyramided on each other with incomplete checks on quality. There may be too much reliance on the honesty, drive, and ability of the average interviewer.

11. "Human error." Oversights, transpositions, recordings in improper place by occasional accident—created by fatigue, haste or inexperience.

12. Memory failures. Lack of planning and foresight, failures to check maps, callback records, and so forth. Failure to apply specific instructions to the situations to which they refer.

If one examines the above list carefully, an important discovery emerges: *The householder is subject to making exactly the same errors, or analogous ones, as the census canvasser.* A person reporting for himself and family can be unintelligent, careless, lazy, cheating, misunderstanding, forgetting, with an idiosyncratic reaction to particular questions, neurotic, misinformed, undertrained, or subject to human error and failures of memory. *Shifting the responsibility for reporting from a corps of selected, trained, and paid enumerators to a cross-section of householders with no possibility of selecting, only little possibility of training, and who furthermore are asked to work without pay, is trading one set of "employees" for another.* The householder enumeration may be expected to reduce error only if the performance of an average paid canvasser is worse than the performance of an average unpaid householder.

Moreover, the reduction of enumerator variance by eliminating the canvasser may be largely illusory. We could imagine, for instance, that a national census taken by the householder method is really an enumeration by about a dozen or so enumerators, each with his own particular response variance pattern to particular items on the census and each with a varying but huge field assignment. These persons, by name, might be:

Mr. Carefully Competent
Mr. Subnormal Intelligence
Mr. Lick and a Promise
Mr. Ego Inflator
Mr. Little Fib
Mr. Minority Group
Mr. Very Busy
Mr. Smart Alec
Mr. Neurotic Personality
Mr. Illegible Writer
Mr. Low Education
Mr. Error Prone
Mr. Can't Quite Remember
Mr. Computer Imputed

It is not at all impossible that "enumerator variance" associated with each of these types of householder is equal to or greater than that found for individual enumerators. In the selection of canvassers, most of these objectionable types of persons can be eliminated. The fact that response variance for each class of householder extends to the entire national census, instead of being canceled out at the enumeration district level, may result in a far greater effect upon the data than could realistically exist in a canvasser census. All of this is only conjecture, however. Thus far, we know even less about the errors made by householders than we do about the errors made by enumerators.

IX. IMPLICATIONS

Recognition that both the canvasser and householder approaches to data collection as practiced in the past fail to meet the needs of today's highly specific hypotheses, mathematical models, and micro-population analysis is an important first step in making the decision whether to use householder or canvasser enumeration in future censuses. It might be argued that the choice should be based upon an estimate of which method offers the greater promise of eventually attaining the desired level of precision, instead of deciding which is least inadequate now.

A second important step is recognition that the difficulties of enumerating the United States population appear to be highly concentrated in the lowest two socio-economic quartiles. Data of acceptable quality can very probably be obtained for the upper one-half by either method using the best practices now known. It might be argued that the choice of householder versus canvasser enumeration should be based upon an estimate of which method offers the greater possibility of obtaining minimum error for the poorest and least educated one-half of the population.

Combining these two points leads to the formulation of the problem in the following terms: Which method, householder or canvasser enumeration, offers the greater promise of eventually obtaining, for the lower socioeconomic strata of the United States population (especially poor nonwhite), data that are precise enough to meet the needs of modern demographic research and current social action programs concerning population problems?

Too little is known about the causes of the errors made by householders to do much more than speculate upon what courses of action might be taken to reduce them. Mass instruction via television and cinema immediately prior to the enumeration is one possibility. Experts in communication would warn that those who need instruction most (least educated and poor) would be instructed least by such a procedure. It is possible that the reduction of errors made by householders will prove to be a very much more difficult task than reducing the errors made by canvassers. If true, continued use of householder enumeration simply because it is no worse and involves less elaborate advance organization may be taking a short-run rather than long-run view.

One avenue of approach that has some plausibility would be to maintain a persistent program of experimenting with the canvasser approach with the goal of ultimately learning how to take a decennial census with essentially the same precision as now achieved by the *Current Population Survey*. It is not difficult to develop a list of hypotheses for trial in such a program. Among them are the following:

1. Experiment with new procedures, for enumerating problem areas, such as slums, ethnic ghettos, and so forth, more effectively. This includes programs to recruit enumerators from among the residents of such areas. (Census tract data indicate that an ample supply of persons qualified to be enumerators actually resides in each such problem area.)

2. Abandon the political patronage system of recruiting field personnel, and experiment with building semi-permanent civic organizations to recruit enumerators at the time of the census. "Political referral" in employing census personnel is an anachronism which thus far census bureau technicians apparently have not been permitted to bring under their research searchlight. Despite assertions that this time-honored procedure of filling all field census posts first with candidates recommended by the local political machine (even if such candidates must take entrance tests) does not damage the census, objective experiments in eliminating it should be tried. Some observers believe it has the pernicious effects of discouraging the participation in the census operation of many nonpartisan civic organizations

and tends to place marginally competent persons in supervisory and teaching roles at all levels.

3. Experiment with devising improved diagnostic and testing procedures for rejecting error-prone candidates for positions as enumerators.

4. Experiment with devising diagnostic and testing procedures for rejecting inadequately trained candidates after training, before giving them a field assignment.

5. Development of new techniques for making field assignments to minimize the effect of enumerator variance. This could include reducing the size of the enumerator's assignment and making more assignments per enumerator, not permitting the same person to have two assignments in the same census tract.

6. Experiment with increasing the pay given to enumerators in order to attract more qualified applicants for the posts.

7. Re-evaluate past methods of training, and experiment with new training procedures to overcome enumerator resistance to particular items on the census. Develop tests to detect this reaction among enumerators.

8. Experiment with various systems of quality control in the field, to reduce error at acceptable cost.

9. Experiment with combinations of householder and canvasser collaboration in enumeration.

10. Experiment with various systems for organizing and supervising the work of canvassers.

These, however, are only superficial suggestions with little specific programmatic content. The United States Bureau of the Census already is working at most, if not all, of them. Effective solutions to the problem of data quality will be devised only after much more is known about the processes by which errors are generated: "Who makes them?" "Under what conditions are they made?" "How are they made?" and "What causes or permits them to occur?"

The United States Bureau of the Census has taken the lead in revealing the shortcomings of its own data. A semi-critical paper, by a "semi-discontented customer," such as the present one, is possible only because of this courageous and praiseworthy policy. It might not be unduly speculative to assert that all of the population data—social and economic—collected by all private survey and other research organizations suffers from deficiencies equal to or greater than those revealed by the Census. The problem of how best to collect data is, therefore, one that is shared by many and worthy of a many-faceted research attack. If the many ingenious mathematical models and elegant statistical procedures currently being made available are to realize their full potential contribution, the whole of social science must follow the lead of the Census (suggested by Deming more than two decades ago)[31] in taking the lid off this Pandora's box and facing up to the contents.

NOTES

1. For a full description and discussion of each, see United Nations, *Handbook of Population Census Methods*, I, *General Aspects of a Population Census* (New York, 1958), pp. 88–98.

2. Morris H. Hansen, William N. Hurwitz, and Leon Pritzker, "The Accuracy of Census Results," *American Sociological Review*, XVIII (1953), 416–17, 421–22.

3. Horace C. Hamilton and F. M. Henderson, "Use of the Survival Rate Method in Measuring Net Migration," *Journal of the American Statistical Association*, XXXIX (1944), 197–206.

4. Leon E. Truesdell, "Residual Relationships and Velocity of Change in the Field of Statistical Forecasting," *Journal of the American Statistical Association*, XXXIII (June, 1938).

5. Daniel O. Price, "Examination of Two Sources of Error in the Estimation of Net Migration," *Journal of the American Statistical Association*, L (1955), 689–700.

6. Walter Mertens, "Methodological Aspects of the Construction of Nuptiality Tables," *Demography*, II (1965), 317–48; Wilson H. Grabill and Lee Jay Cho, "Methodology for the Measurement of Current Fertility from Population Data on Young Children," *Demography*, II (1965), 50–73.

7. For example, see Hope T. Eldridge, "A Cohort Approach to the Analysis of Migration Differentials," *Demography*, I (1964), 212–20.

8. See references below to Stock and Hochstim (1951); Gray (1956); Gales and Kendall (1957); Hanson and Marks (1958); Eckler and Hurwitz (1958); Kish and Slater (1960); Hansen, Hurwitz, and Bershad (1960); Kish (1962); and Fellegi (1964).

9. Barbara A. Powell and Leon Pritzker, "Effects of Variation in Field Personnel on Census Results," *Demography*, II (1956), 8–32.

10. See reference to Fellegi (1964).

11. Powell and Pritzker, *op. cit.*

12. Mortimer Spiegelman, *Introduction to Demography* (Chicago: Society of Actuaries, 1955), pp. 10–11.

13. Peter R. Cox, *Demography* (London: Cambridge University Press, 1959), p. 25.

14. Hugh J. Wolfenden, *Population Statistics and Their Compilation* (Chicago: University of Chicago Press, 1954), pp. 12–13.

15. United Nations, *op. cit.*, pp. 34–35.

16. U.S. Bureau of the Census, *U.S. Census of Population, 1960: Introduction to Number of Inhabitants, United States Summary* (Final Report, PC 1-1A; Washington, D.C.: U.S. Government Printing Office, 1961), p. xi.

17. Conrad Taeuber and Morris H. Hansen, "A Preliminary Evaluation of the 1960 Censuses of Population and Housing," *Demography*, I (1964), 2.

18. *Ibid.*, p. 4.

19. *Ibid.*, pp. 4–5.

20. Cited in *ibid.*, p. 6.

21. L. Pritzker and R. H. Hanson, "Measurement Errors in the 1960 Census of Population," *Proceedings of the Social Statistics Section* (American Statistical Association, 1962), pp. 80–90. See also Charles B. Nam, "Some Comparisons of Office of Education and Census Bureau Statistics on Education," *Proceedings of the Social Statistic Section* (American Statistical Association, 1962), pp. 258–69; Taeuber and Hansen, *op. cit.*, p. 12.

22. In the familiar schematic representation of the census used in all the introductions to the ER 60 Reports (see References) this measure is b divided by $a + b$ or 1.00 minus the Census "percent in CES class identically reported."

23. This alternative was advanced and its possibilities illustrated by Donald J. Bogue and Edmund M. Murphy in "The

Effect of Classification Errors upon Statistical Inference: A Case Analysis with Census Data," *Demography*, I (1964), 42–56.

24. Editor's note: The validity of this section on occupation has been questioned in a paper by Taeuber and Hansen. They present data refuting Bogue's contention that errors of classification of occupation were more serious in 1960 than in 1950 (Conrad Taeuber and Morris H. Hansen, "Self-enumeration as a Census Method," *Demography*, III [1966], 289–95). While there may be some inaccuracy in this part of the analysis, there seems to be no question about the remaining data in Bogue's analysis, and certainly no question about the validity of his general point regarding the high amount of classification error in the 1960 census data. For a more recent consideration of the same issue, see "The Census—What's Wrong with It, What Can Be Done?" *Trans-Action*, V (May, 1968), 49–56.

25. See Herman P. Miller, "New Evidence Regarding Errors in Income Size Distributions" (processed paper presented at annual convention of the American Statistical Association, 1962).

26. See Charles B. Nam, *op. cit*, pp. 258–69.

27. U.S. Bureau of the Census, *U.S. Census Population, 1960: Detailed Characteristics, U.S. Summary* (Final Report PC [1]), p. xv.

28. Bogue and Murphy, *op. cit.*

29. Evidence that the canvasser approach, when carried out under the highest skill and best knowledge, is capable of accomplishing very high levels of precision is demonstrated in at least two highly important studies in this area worthy of very careful study by those interested in this problem. They are U.S. Bureau of the Census, *The Current Population Survey Reinterview Program: Some Notes and Discussion* (Technical Paper No. 6, Washington, D.C.: Government Printing Office, 1963); and Leslie Kish, "Response Variance and Its Estimation," *Journal of the American Statistical Association*, LIX (1964), 1016–41. The Census article shows that by careful selection and training of data-gatherers errors of classification can be reduced to very low levels, and the Kish article suggests that enumerator (interviewer) variance can be greatly reduced even for highly subjective and emotion-laden attitude questions.

30. An outstanding example of the type of research which is needed in this area is the article by Robert H. Hanson and Eli S. Marks, "Influence of the Interviewer on the Accuracy of Survey Results," *Journal of the American Statistical Association*, LIII (September, 1958), 635–55. Hanson and Marks find evidence that particular interviewers develop a more or less irrational "resistance" to given questions, with a consequent tendency to alter the wording of the question or to omit it altogether. It is the discovery and detailed study of mechanisms such as this that offer hope for eventually achieving greater precision in all social science data.

31. W. E. Denning (see References).

REFERENCES

Akers, Donald S. "Estimating Net Census Undercount in 1960, Using Analytical Techniques." Presented at the Annual Population Association of America meetings in May, 1962.

Bogue, Donald J., and Murphy, Edmund M. "The Effect of Classification Errors upon Statistical Inferences: A Case Analysis with Census Data," *Demography*, I (1964), 42–56.

Bradshaw, Benjamin S., and Akers, Donald S. "Age Heaping in the 1960 Census of Population." U.S. Bureau of the Census (processed), 1962.

Deming, W. E. "On Errors in Surveys," *American Sociological Review*, IX (1944), 359–70.

Eckler, A. Ross, and Hurwitz, William N. "Response Variance and Biases in Censuses and Surveys," *Bulletin of the International Statistical Institute,* XXXVI, No. 2 (Stockholm, 1958), 12–35.

Fasteau, Hermann H.; Ingram, Jack; and Mills, Ruth H. "Study of the Reliability of Coding of Census Returns," *Proceedings of the Social Statistics Section* (American Statistical Association, 1962).

Fellegi, I. P. "Response Variance and Its Estimation," *Journal of the American Statistical Association,* LIX (1964), 1016–41.

Gales, Kathleen, and Kendall, M. G. "An Inquiry Concerning Interviewer Variability," *Journal of the Royal Statistical Society,* Ser. A, CXX (1957), 121–47.

Gray, Percy G. "Examples of Interviewer Variability Taken from Two Sample Surveys," *Applied Statistics,* V (1956), 73–85.

Hansen, M. H.; Hurwitz, W. N.; and Bershad, M. A. "Measurement Errors in Censuses and Surveys," *Bulletin of the International Statistical Institute* (32d Sess., Part II), XXXVIII (1960), 359–74.

Hanson, Robert H., and Marks, Eli S. "Influence of the Interviewer on the Accuracy of Survey Results," *Journal of the American Statistical Association,* LIII (1958), 635–55.

Kish, Leslie. "Studies of Interviewer Variance for Attitudinal Variables," *Journal of the American Statistical Association,* XLIX (1954), 520–38.

Kish, Leslie, and Lansing, John B. "Response Errors in Estimating Value of Homes," *Journal of the American Statistical Association,* LVII (1954), 520–38.

Marks, Eli S., and Mauldin, Parker W. "Response Errors in the Census Research," *Journal of the American Statistical Association,* XLV (September, 1950), 424–38.

Miller, Hermann P. "New Evidence Regarding Errors in Income Size Distributions." U.S. Bureau of the Census (processed), 1962.

Nam, Charles B. "Some Comparisons of Office of Education and Census Bureau Statistics on Education," *Proceedings of the Social Statistics Section* (American Statistical Association, 1962), 258–69.

Pritzker, L., and Hanson, R. H. "Measurement Errors in the 1960 Census of Population," *Proceedings of the Social Statistics Section* (American Statistical Association, 1962), 80–90.

Pritzker, Leon, and Hansen, Morris H. "The Post-enumeration Survey of the 1950 Census of Population: Some Results, Evaluation, and Implications," U.S. Bureau of the Census (processed), 1956.

Rice, Stuart A. "Contagious Bias in the Interview," *American Journal of Sociology,* XXXV (1929), 420–23.

Steinberg, Joseph; Gurney, Margaret; and Perkins, Walter. "The Accuracy of the 1960 Census Count," *Proceedings of the Social Statistics Section* (American Statistical Association, 1962), 76–79.

Stock, J. S., and Hochstim, J. R. "A Method of Measuring Interviewer Variability," *Public Opinion Quarterly*, XV (1951), 322–34.

Taeuber, Conrad, and Hansen, Morris H. "A Preliminary Evaluation of the 1960 Census of Population and Housing," *Demography*, I (1964), 1–14.

U.S. Bureau of the Census. *Evaluation and Research Program of the U.S. Censuses of Population and Housing*, 1960 (Series ER60, Washington, D.C.); No. 1, *Background, Procedures, and Forms* (1963); No. 2, *Record Check Studies of Population Coverage* (1964); No. 3, *Accuracy of Data on Housing Characteristics* (1964); No. 4, *Accuracy of Data on Population Characteristics as Measured by Re-interviews* (1964); No. 5, *Accuracy of Data on Population Characteristics as Measured by CPS–Census Match* (1964).

————. *The Current Population Survey Re-interview Program: Some Notes and Discussion* (Technical Paper No. 6; Washington, D.C.: Government Printing Office, 1963).

————. *The Post Enumeration Survey: 1950* (Technical Paper No. 4, 1960).

————. *Procedural Studies of the 1950 Censuses*, No. 1: *Infant Enumeration Study, 1950*.

————. *U.S. Census of Population, 1960: Number of Inhabitants, United States Summary* (Final Report PC [1]-1A; Washington, D.C.: Government Printing Office, 1961), p. 11.

Veroff, J.; Atkinson, J. W.; Feld, S. C.; and Gurin, G. "The Use of Thematic Apperception to Assess Motivation in a Nationwide Interview Study," *Psychological Monographs: General and Applied* (Fall, 1960), 1–32.

Zelnik, Melvin. "Errors in the 1960 Census Enumeration of Native Whites," *Journal of the American Statistical Association*, LIX (June, 1964), 437–59.

10

The Realm of Vital
and Health Statistics

Mortimer Spiegelman

Nothing is so personal as one's health and the vital events of birth, marriage, and death. Although some individual records were kept in family Bibles and parishes, compulsory registration of such vital events with civil authorities is a rather recent development. Massachusetts, the first state to provide for mandatory reporting of vital events, began its system in 1842, but it was not until 1933 that each state had developed a system satisfactory to the federal government for the compilation of national statistics. Even so, that stage has been reached only for birth and death statistics; in the case of marriage and divorce, many states are still lacking the requirements for acceptance into a national system for compilation of data. Health statistics present an entirely different situation. Few individuals can recite fully and accurately their own health history, and the compilation of centralized statistics from individual records is adapted largely to meet the needs of specific problems.

DEFINITIONS OF VITAL AND HEALTH STATISTICS

A handbook of the United Nations states that "Vital records may be defined as those concerned with live births, deaths, fetal deaths (stillbirths), marriages, divorces, adoptions, legitimations, recognitions, annulments, and separations; in short, all the events which have to do with an individual's entrance into or departure from life, together with the changes in civil status which may occur to him during his lifetime." A smaller scope of events is included in the latest (1959) revision of the Model Vital Statistics Act approved and recommended by the United States Public Health Serv-

Reprinted from *The American Behavioral Scientist*, 6, no. 9 (May, 1963), pp. 18–23, by permission of the author and the publisher, Sage Publications, Inc.

ice and two non-governmental professional associations for the consideration of the states in the revision of their vital statistics laws.

The purpose of the Model Vital Statistics Act is to set forth the minimum principles, policies, and practices regarded as essential for a uniform vital statistics system in the United States, and the individual states are free to enlarge upon it. According to the minimum in this model, *"Vital Statistics* means records of birth, death, fetal death, marriage, divorce, and data related thereto."* Also a *"System of Vital Statistics* includes the registration, collection, preservation, amendment, and certification of vital statistics records, and activities related thereto, including the tabulation, analysis, and publication of statistical data derived from such records." Several terms within these statements of particulars require definition in themselves, notably *live birth* and *fetal death,* but these will not be pursued further here. For the most part, the events included within the scope of vital statistics are clearly recognizable, definitive, and objective.

It is usual to find that health statistics refer not to data descriptive of a state of well-being, but rather to data relating to a morbid state and the health services and medical care involved. The United States National Health Survey says that "Morbidity is basically a departure from a state of physical or mental well-being, resulting from disease or injury, of which the affected individual is aware. It includes not only active or progressive disease but also impairments, that is, chronic or permanent defects that are static in nature, resulting from disease, injury, or congenital malformation." Since this concept relates only to conditions "of which the affected individual is aware," its subjective nature is apparent.

It is possible that a person may have a morbid condition, but be unaware of it and so fail to report it upon inquiry. Another person with the same morbid condition may consider it insignificant and so neglect to refer to it, while still another may be overwhelmed by that morbid state and make it widely known. Personal attitudes toward a morbid state may also be influenced by the economic climate. For example, when times are hard, there may be some hesitancy in reporting a morbid condition if it may result in loss of a job. On the other hand, in some instances there may be an incentive to exaggerate a morbid condition, as when an insurance income benefit may be derived that is high in relation to the wage loss involved. Accordingly, disability resulting in some limitation of usual activity as a result of a morbid condition requires careful definition for the purpose at hand. The definition for insurance purposes will differ from that for a general population health survey, and both will differ from that used for entitlement to benefits under our social security program.

Reference is often made to *acute* and *chronic* conditions, as if their meanings were generally understood. However, for data compilation some precision in definition is necessary, since no convention has been reached, and each investigator will adopt a definition suited to his purposes. The National Health Survey regards as chronic any condition that lasted more than three months or was contained on a check list of conditions. All other conditions are regarded as acute.

At this point, it may be asked whether there is or can be any generally acceptable concept of "health needs." Casual questioning of physicians usually leads to vague or rambling accounts, but further discussion occasionally leads to an expression of ideas similar to those in a statement by the National Health Survey: "Needed medical care may be described as that care (in the broadest sense) which a person would seek, if it were available, if he knew it was available, if he were well-informed as to what was considered desirable medical care, and if there were no important economic or other barriers to his obtaining it." How to measure the need for medical care in a community raises complex issues. The National Health Survey expresses a preference for a morbidity survey, based upon a representative sample of the population, in which all services, including diagnostic, needed by both the sick and apparently well would be appraised by experts. Reference is also made to data reflecting the experience of groups presumably in receipt of "good" medical care and to the study of claimed shortages of facilities and personnel.

The second phase of health statistics relates to health services, medical care, and expenditures on these items. Such expenditures may be considered from the viewpoint of the individual and his family, and thus in relation to income and savings, and also from the community, state, and national viewpoints. In any case, problems of definition arise which require careful consideration. A particular point at issue in definition is that of the expenditures to be regarded as insurable for the sake of comparison with insurance benefits paid. With regard to health and medical services, it becomes necessary to distinguish betweeen services available and those rendered, and the relationship between availability and utilization. Some agreement on the content and scope of health and medical care services is needed for purposes of comparison among communities and among health insurance plans and also for the study of trends.

The importance of definition in the study of vital and health statistics cannot be over-stressed. These data cannot be accepted at their face value nor in their popular sense. For example, the term "expectation of life" is sometimes considered applicable to an individual, overlooking the fact that it refers to an average for a prescribed category of individuals. Also overlooked is the fact that the usual figures given for expectation of life are based upon mortality data for a current period and generally do not take likely improvements into account. The careful student of vital and health statistics will always examine the definitions underlying his data, and their changes.

PURPOSES OF VITAL AND HEALTH STATISTICS

Vital and health records and statistics serve a wide variety of purposes for the individual; for government at the federal, state, and local levels; for many facets of business, particularly life and health insurance; and for students of social and economic trends. They play an essential role in the wide range of public health and medical care services under the auspices of governmental and voluntary agencies.

Vital and health statistics are fundamental in the work of the life insurance actuary and their study is included in his training. He is concerned primarily with the mortality, morbidity, and medical care experiences under the various insurance programs of his own institution, but also has a keen interest in the corresponding experiences of other insurers. However, the actuary frequently finds it useful to have access to comparable data for the general population and from other specialized sources to confirm or supplement his own findings. In fact, he expresses a particular need for such data when he is faced with a problem for which insurance data are lacking. In this case, he takes special caution in adapting data from non-insurance sources to meet problems which arise in the selection and classification of risks. The evaluation of estates, a function often undertaken by the consulting actuary, may require the use of rates of birth, marriage, remarriage, divorce, and death.

To the demographer, for example, vital statistics are a basic component in his studies of population characteristics and trends. Both mortality and morbidity statistics are used by the epidemiologist in his studies of the patterns of disease in the community, and their changes; however, he uses medical care data with some caution since they are affected by the availability of medical care facilities and personnel, and by the health attitudes of the population. These attitudes form part of the statistical analyses of the medical sociologist; they encompass such topics as self-appraisal of health status, health expectations, attitudes toward maintenance of health, and attitudes toward utilization and financing of health services. The economist uses certain facets of health statistics in his studies of the living conditions of populations and includes such data among the components in the construction of price indices. The medical economist has a special interest in analyses of the sources of funds for health and medical care, and of the expenditure of these funds for facilities and services.

COLLECTION OF VITAL AND HEALTH STATISTICS

Although the National Center for Health Statistics, an agency within the United States Public Health Service, has broad responsibilities in the collection and analysis of vital and health statistics, specialized types of such data also emerge variously from other agencies of federal, state, and local government, from studies by private insurers, from surveys by academic institutions, and from many voluntary health and welfare agencies.

For the most part, the trails leading from the origin of the birth, fetal death, and death certificates to the tabulation of national vital statistics follow common paths. In the case of the death certificate, the physician has the responsibility of entering the particulars relating to the cause of death. The character of the medical detail entered on this form depends much upon his training, his acuity, and his attitude toward this responsibility. The funeral director, who completes such details on the death certificate as name, age, sex, race, and marital status, files the form with the local registrar whose jurisdiction extends over some defined civil unit. A course very similar is followed for the fetal death certificate. In the case of the birth certificate, the form is completed by the physician in consultation with the parents, and this also is filed with the local registrar.

From the local registrar, the birth, fetal death, and death certificates, or copies of them, reach the state office of vital statistics where statistical tabulations are prepared. Copies of these certificates are sent by the state to the National Vital Statistics Division, a part of the National Center for Health Statistics, where tabulations are made for both the states and the nation as a whole; these data, and rates based upon them, are published in reports.

A national system for the collection of adequate marriage and divorce, including annulment, statistics is still in the course of development, for not all states have yet met the basic requirements of the National Vital Statistics Division. Many problems arise in a national compilation of marriage and divorce statistics. For example, the determination of the usual place of residence of one or both of the parties may be difficult. In place of the actual date of the marriage, the record may enter in state files according to the date of issuance or of filing of a marriage license; or, in place of the actual date of divorce, the court record may be filed by date of the decree. Among other sources of error in marriage records are statements of age, particularly on the part of those under a legal minimum age, and statements of occupation.

In addition to the wide variety of studies and analyses possible from statistical tabulations of information contained in the individual birth, death, and fetal death certificates, and marriage and divorce reporting forms, a very broad range of research and investigation is opened up by the use of these documents in conjunction with other individual records of the parties concerned. One technique recently put into use is the follow-back device whereby the individual vital statistics documents, or a sample of them, serve as a starting point in a search for further information. Thus, in the case of the death certificate, further information regarding the deceased may be sought from the funeral director, the certifying physician, the hospital or other institution of death, and the informant (most likely a relative) on the personal detail of the deceased for the certificate. This device may also be used for studies of the composition and characteristics of families with a recent birth and for studies of child-spacing. Applied to marriage and divorce records, the technique opens up a great breadth of social and economic investigation. In the case of marriage, studies might be possible of the educational and work experience of the partners and of their family backgrounds; a better insight into the family history leading to marital disruption and the role of their children might be obtained from the recently divorced.

A second technique involving the use of vital records for a broad scope of study is that of record linkage. For example, by bringing together the birth and death record for individual infants, a study was made of mortality in very early life in relation to birth weight, a fact recorded on the birth certificate but not on the death certificate. In other instances, the marriage records and birth records were linked for a study of child-spacing. Another example is the case in which individual records of marriages, first births, and divorces were linked for a study of premarital pregnancy. A still different approach is that in which the death records for a short period following a census date are linked to the census returns for the deceased, thereby enlarging the details on the death certificate by the wealth of demographic, social, and economic information entered in the enumeration. A study of this kind, using the 1960 census of population, is being conducted at the University of Chicago.

In a third technique, the death certificate is used as the end point in a study of the mortality experience of a defined cohort of lives observed over an extended period. This technique is commonly employed in medico-actuarial studies of the experience of insured lives who show a medical history or physical impairment of some significance at the time of their application. Large-scale examples of this approach are the 1951 Impairment Study and the Build and Blood Pressure Study by the Society of Actuaries. Among other examples that may be cited are the investigations of the Veterans Administration and the many specialized follow-up studies of persons with a history of heart disease, diabetes, cancer, and other conditions. The latter are sometimes made from the records of clinics or of private practitioners.

Within the relatively short period since it was authorized by Congressional legislation in 1956, the National Health Survey Division, another part of the National Center for Health Statistics, has become a leading source of morbidity and medical care data. This division takes three lines of approach in its operation. First, using a sample representative of the non-institutional population of the nation, it conducts a continuing survey through health interviews; for this, the program of questioning is varied in the course of time to cover a wide range of health problems. Second, with the use of mobile units equipped for specific health examinations and traveling teams of physicians, dentists, and nurses, it carries on a nation-wide sample survey of health examinations. Its third approach is to conduct health-records surveys from hospital and other medical care institutions. By these means, a large body of morbidity and medical care data are being accumulated that provide opportunity for studies in relation to many demographic, social, and economic characteristics of the population.

Space limits to very brief mention the many agencies other than the federal government engaged in the collection and analysis of vital and health statistics, generally with regard to social and economic implications. Thus, California conducted a statewide health survey during May 1954—April 1955. Prominent among the academic agencies is the National Opinion Research Center at the University of Chicago, whose nationwide surveys on medical care expenditures and health attitudes have added substantially to the field of health statistics. Local surveys are conducted occasionally by universities, but since no common pattern has developed among them, the results are hardly comparable. Only infrequently do records of health insurance plans, physical examinations in schools, and absenteeism reports from industry yield health statistics suited for research purposes. Data from these sources are usually compiled for administrative purposes, but there are a few notable exceptions. Surveys under non-governmental auspices are providing a valuable insight into patterns of human reproductivity. These surveys are concerned not only with patterns of human fertility in relation to demographic, social, economic, and geographic factors, but also with regard to social and psychological factors affecting fertility. Investigations in the postwar years have shown the importance of studying human fertility in a generation of women traced over their reproductive cycle during marriage, rather than making observations on various ages within a short calendar period.

THE INTERPRETATION OF VITAL AND
HEALTH STATISTICS

In order to grasp the essentials from the great mass of individual vital and health records that are continuously arising, some conventions are needed not only for processing the returns but also in the summary statistical measures used for their interpretation. Possibilities for error lie not only in the responses and entries made on the original record, but also in the several stages in which they are compiled and processed. Furthermore, the statistical measures proposed for the interpretation of the final tabulations must be so designed as to yield meaningful and unambiguous results. In the case of data obtained by a sampling procedure, the methods used must be theoretically sound and there should be an indication of the sampling variability of the results. Only a few highlights of the problems in each of these areas can be mentioned here.

In completing any return, the chance of error is, of course, greater when someone else is reporting for the party concerned. And even when an individual reports for himself, he may be ignorant of some facts (such as his age), he may have forgotten them (as some details in his medical history), or he may misrepresent them (some divorced claim to be single). As already indicated, much of the quality of the report on cause of death depends upon the physician. Although the compiling and processing of vital and health records may seem straightforward for the most part, special problems arise in the classification of verbal items, such as occupation, industry, morbid condition, and cause of death. For each of these, a great variety of statements is reported on the original form and the problem is to devise a classification system which would encompass these within fairly homogeneous groups and yet serve many different purposes. The classification systems that have been devised undergo continued study and are subject to occasional revision in the light of new developments. New occupations and industries come into being and old ones lose importance or disappear; new medical concepts and improved diagnostic techniques have brought new disease entities and changes in medical terminology. For purposes of tabulation, the practice has been to select, from among the morbid conditions listed on the death certificate, that considered by the reporting physician as the underlying cause of death; all others are lost in the statistical presentation.

With the large-scale control of acute conditions and the aging of the population, the chronic and degenerative diseases have come to lead among the causes of death. These diseases are usually of unknown origin and may possibly be due to more than one factor or, perhaps, a combination of several. Since a large proportion of death certificates list more than one morbid condition, further opportunities for study of the complex of morbid conditions leading to death would be opened by tabulations of multiple causes in place of a single selected cause.

For purposes of comparing vital and health statistics among communities, or for study of trends within a community, account must be taken of differences in their numbers of population. Thus, it is common practice to speak of birth rates or death rates per 1,000 population, or of infant deaths (under one year of age) per 1,000 live births, or of physician visits per capita per year, or of average days of hospital stay per hospital admission per year, and so forth. However, comparison based upon such rates, ratios, or averages have little meaning unless account is also taken of differences in the demographic, social, or economic structures of communities being compared. Thus, the death rate per 1,000 population in a community with a large population of elders may be expected to be greater than that for a community with most of its people at the prime of life. The issue becomes, then, one of comparing the two communities on the basis of death rates specific for age; for example, deaths at ages 65 and over per 1,000 population at ages 65 and over, and similarly for any other age groupings.

In like manner, the level of the marriage rate for a community is affected not only by the proportion of its population who are unmarried and at the marriageable age, but further by the ratio of the sexes among these unmarried. Also, the level of the birth rate in any year is influenced by the proportion of the population who are married women at the main reproducing ages, and the distribution of these women according to duration of marriage and interval since birth of the last previous child. Only a gross picture is obtained by computing a divorce rate per 1,000 population, for the rate will be low with a small proportion of married in the community. An erroneous picture is also produced by relating annual divorces to annual marriages for the same year, since the two are unrelated for the most part and the ratio may leave the impression that a large proportion of current marriages end in divorce. A more meaningful ratio is that of annual divorces per 1,000 married couples at the midyear, since the latter approximates the average number of couples subject to the risk of divorce during the year. Further comparable examples may be cited in the case of rates, ratios, and averages computed for morbidity and medical care statistics.

In summary, the careful interpretation of vital and health statistics requires an insight into the circumstances surrounding the origin of the individual records or observations, the procedures in their compilation and processing, the statistical measures used to compare communities or trends within a community, and the qualifications to such comparisons. An insight is also required into the sampling procedures, if such were used.

THE VITAL AND HEALTH STATISTICS
MONOGRAPH SERIES

In contrast to the long history of censuses in the United States, that for vital and health statistics is relatively short. Census monograph series containing analytical treatments have been published on the basis of the censuses of 1920 and 1950, and another series is planned for the 1960 census. Although there have been many significant studies on special facets of vital and health statistics, and a few summary treatments of the subject, no comprehensive analysis was considered until the 1960 census came into view. The proposal for a vital and health statistics monograph series was accepted by the Statistics Section of the American Public Health Association in the fall of 1958, and a committee was organized to explore the situation and develop the program if feasible. The committee decided to go ahead and secured initial support from the Rockefeller Foundation, the Milbank Memorial Fund, and the Health Information Foundation.

The objective, as contained in a statement designed to solicit support, is: "Using the opportunity provided by the 1960 census of population for a close examination of current vital and health statistics, the purpose of this proposal is to produce a series of monographs based on specific and general topics which will not only present analyses of these current findings but also discuss trends and bring into evidence whatever data from local surveys or clinical experience, in this country or elsewhere, are pertinent." Authors were recruited for the following monograph topics:

A
Accidents and homicide
Arthritic and rheumatic
  conditions
Cardiovascular-renal diseases
Diabetes mellitus
Diseases of digestive system
Infectious diseases (including
  respiratory system, but not
  tuberculosis)
Mental and psychoneurotic
  diseases and suicide
Neoplasms

Neurological diseases
Perinatal mortality, mortality in
  infancy and childhood,
  maternal mortality
Tuberculosis
Venereal disease

B
Dental health
Social and economic factors in
  morbidity and mortality
Fertility
Marriage and divorce

A grant, with support indicated for a five-year period beginning May

1, 1961, has been received from the National Institutes of Health (RG 8262) for topics listed under "A," and application for a supplemental grant has been submitted for the topics under "B." It is expected that there will also be a review volume. Conferences of authors were held in 1960 and 1961 to exchange views and explore common problems.

The planning and coordination of special vital statistics tabulations for 1959–61, according to indications provided by the authors, are being performed within the National Center for Health Statistics under contract with the American Public Health Association. The National Center for Health Statistics has also contracted for the tabulations and computations of rates. Negotiations for publication of the monographs are under way between the Harvard University Press and the American Public Health Association. The monographs are expected to be useful to social scientists, schools of medicine and public health, life and health insurance organizations, medical care program workers, research workers, students, practicing physicians, drug houses, and market analysts.

Migration

Introduction

Migration, the movement of members of a population from one place of residence to another, is one of the three dynamic aspects of population, the other two being fertility and mortality. Like fertility and mortality, migration may be examined from a societal perspective. If the migration occurs between societies we speak of emigration and immigration, and among other things we can ask why people move from one society to another, what effect the emigration from a society has had on that society, and what effect the arrival of the immigrants has had on the receiving society. In a general way this latter question has received the most attention in American society, particularly from sociologists studying the urban places into which most American immigrants settled. When one examines the migration that occurs within a society (internal migration), a nearly parallel set of questions may be asked. We may ask why people move from one community to another, what impact their moving has had on the communities they have left and the communities they have entered, and finally what effect this general population movement has had on the total society. Answers to at least some of these questions will be found in the papers that follow. The papers that we have selected for this section focus almost exclusively on internal migration within the United States, but the questions they deal with are often applicable to immigration as well.

One perspective on population migration may be generally labeled a functional perspective. This perspective allows us to view migration as a process of population adjustment within a society. Following this point of view, we may first note that within any nation or society some imbalances are likely to develop with regard to economic or population resources. For example, some segments or regions of a society are likely to have higher birth rates than other segments or regions. It also happens that some regions or communities of the society may have expanding economic opportunities while others have contracting economic opportunities. The changing economic condition of a community or region may have a variety of causes. It may be due to a change in technology, as when there was a decline in the use of coal with the advent of the diesel locomotive, or it may be due to the depletion of some natural resource, such as the soil, a mineral, or a forest. Whatever the reasons, the important point is that when a region or a community in a society does experience economic decline, the migration of the native population out of that area and into a more prosperous or promising one serves to improve the economic and social balance of the society. There are many concrete examples of this phenomenon, but perhaps the most general and most persistent has been the migration of rural people to urban places during our history. Although the movement of young people from rural to urban areas is often viewed with alarm, particularly by rural people, it is largely a necessary adjustment to a changing agricultural technology (which needs fewer and fewer workers), coupled with a historically higher rural birth rate.

The first paper in this section, "Occupation and Patterns of Migration," by C. T. Pihlblad and C. L. Gregory, is based on a large study of rural-to-urban migration. While the time period covered by this study now goes back two decades, it still stands as one of the more solid pieces of empirical research done on the factors that influence the migration patterns of rural youngsters. In an earlier research report on this study the same authors had reported that the migration patterns of rural and small-town Missouri high school graduates were related to their scores on a standard intelligence test. They had found that students with higher intelligence-test scores were more likely to migrate, to move longer distances, and to settle in larger towns and cities. The authors say, "In our earlier paper we suggested that the tendency for those with higher abilities to move disproportionately toward larger cities and to make longer moves was probably the result of occupational choice." In the present report the authors demonstrate the validity of that hypothesis.

The major conclusion of the Pihlblad and Gregory study is this: "emigration from the small towns of Missouri has been selective of the professions, students—most of whom are probably embarking on professional careers—and skilled workers." This conclusion appears paradoxically to run counter to much of the discussion in the paper "Adjustments to the New Institutional Environment," by Lee G. Burchinal and Ward W. Bauder, which also appears in this section. In discussing the adjustment of the migrant to his new environment, Burchinal and Bauder refer to the sizable amount of research that has been done on rural migrants to urban places. Among other things they note that the rural-reared migrant living in an urban place often has a lower social status (as measured by education, income, occupation, etc.) than the urban native. The apparent contradiction of this fact to the findings of the Pihlblad and Gregory study is easily resolved if it is recognized that the perspective one uses to view the facts is all-important. From the perspective of the rural communities, they are losing disproportionately more of their more talented youngsters, but from the point of view of the urban communities, while they are receiving many of the most able of the rural youngsters, they are at the same time receiving, in absolute numbers, a great many rural youngsters in unskilled occupations. A careful examination of Table 1 of the Pihlblad and Gregory paper reveals that in this particular sample, while the urban places are receiving about 113 professional males (77.9 percent of 145), they are also receiving 176 unskilled male morkers (56.9 percent of 309). And the Pihlblad and Gregory study covers only high school graduates; it is probably safe to assume that overall the ratio of unskilled to professional workers that had to be absorbed into the life of the city was even higher.

One additional word on the Burchinal and Bauder paper: This paper represents one of the best efforts that we have found in spelling out the theoretical and substantive dimensions that must be considered in a detailed analysis of the adjustments of migrants in their new place of residence. A careful reading of this paper can be rewarding if one wants to know the boundaries and dimensions of this important population question. The authors also provide a considerable amount of substantive material on the important questions of migrant adjustment.

The study by Brown, Schwarzweller, and Mangalam, "Kentucky Mountain Migration and the Stem-Family: An American Variation on a Theme by Le Play," illustrates again the societal adjustment function of migration. The eastern Kentucky area has been in a considerable economic decline for several decades, and in the words of the authors, "surplus population has been drained off which if allowed to 'dam up' might well have brought such strain that this society dominated by the family-kinship system would have broken up completely." The most important focus of this paper is upon the important role that the extended or "stem" family plays in the migration process and the adjustment of individuals within a migration system. The authors present data to support their hypothesis that kinship ties influence the destination of migrants, and then go on to argue that the nature of the eastern Kentucky "stem-family" aids the migrant in his adjustment to the new environment. The stem-family also provides a haven for the returning migrant in the event that adjustment to or articulation with the urban-industrial place is not successful.

Perhaps the most important point the authors make is that the family in its stem form is supportive of migration, and thus even the extended family structure can be consonant with the needs of an urban-industrial society. This is, of course, only one case study of the relationship between family structure and migration, and since we would expect the traditional extended family to be more manifest in the Appalachian country (and also the Ozark region studied by Zimmerman and Frampton, whose work is cited by Brown, Schwarzweller, and Mangalam), we might be skeptical about the general applicability of the findings. In any case, this paper adequately demonstrates that there can be a general relationship between kinship structure and the process of migration.[1]

While the title of the paper by Lewis M. Killian which closes this section, "The Adjustment of Southern White Migrants to Northern

---

[1] For another study of the same relationship, see Felix M. Barardo, "Kinship Interaction and Migrant Adaptation in an Aerospace-Related Community," *Journal of Marriage and the Family*, 28 (August, 1966), pp. 296–303. Barardo focused on the effect of kinship on the social integration of migrants to the Cape Kennedy missile complex, and his results do not support the contentions of Brown, Schwarzweller, and Mangalam that the kinship group facilitates adaptation to the new place. The contradictory conclusions may mean that important regional and occupational differences exist and must be further specified, but this will remain uncertain until we have had more research on the relationship between kinship and migration.

Urban Norms," suggests that it is concerned with essentially the same issue as some of the other papers in this section, this study is directed toward a much broader question. Briefly, the question is this: In a heterogeneous or regionally diversified society, will internal migration be an effective instrument of cultural diffusion and social integration? In our own society there are fairly pronounced cultural differences from one region to another. When people from different cultures (or sub-cultures) interract with one another, there is usually some degree of mutual exchange of cultural elements. Such a mutual exchange should result in decreasing cultural diversity and thus in greater social integration. Killian's paper is one of the few studies bearing on the role that migration plays in changing cultural norms.

Killian describes southern whites who have migrated to a northern city where the social norms governing the treatment of Negroes differ from those they knew in the South. Killian concludes that although southern migrant whites may overtly conform to the northern urban norms governing race relations, their internal feelings have not been greatly modified. Killian does report a slight tendency for the southern migrants to see the southern patterns as "unusual" after their northern urban experience. Perhaps this presages a change in attitudes too. Of course, it is equally possible that southern culture patterns of race relations are diffused into northern places by migration, and one could cite instances where this interpretation of current events might be valid (for example, when people in northern cities and states vote for legislation that tends to perpetuate racial segregation in housing).

The relationship between migration and societal integration is another instance of a migration question that is greatly in need of more social research. The selections that follow raise only a few of the many questions that might be considered with regard to the movement of people from one place to another.

11

Occupation and
Patterns of Migration

C. T. Pihlblad
C. L. Gregory

This paper is one of a series in which we have attempted to analyze the selective processes involved in migration and occupational choice among a sample of Missouri high school students. We have demonstrated that there is a significant tendency for students with superior test scores to be more migratory, to move longer distances, and to settle disproportionately in larger communities.[1] We have also shown that test intelligence is related to occupational choice; that teaching, the other professions, and clerical work tend to attract disproportionately from among those with higher scores while those with lower aptitudes show a tendency to gravitate toward less prestigeful occupations in farming and manual work.[2]

In our earlier paper we suggested that the tendency for those with higher abilities to move disproportionately toward larger cities and to make longer moves was probably the result of occupational choice. Occupations which tend to attract superior individuals offer their best opportunities largely in larger communities. For the most part, these were located at some distance from the small communities in which our subjects attended high school. To test the hypothesis that migration is selective of occupation we will present in this paper an analysis of the relation between the vocations followed by our subjects ten years after they had completed high school and the size of the communities in which they were residing at time of report, as well as the distances of migration, and the communities or areas in which they had settled. Since Missouri has two large metropolitan centers, St. Louis and Kansas City, it will be of interest to note the degree of

---

Reprinted from *Social Forces*, 36, no. 1 (October, 1957), pp. 56–64, by permission of the authors and the publisher, the University of North Carolina Press.

attraction which these centers have for Missouri youth as well as the extent to which out-of-state migration may be selective of occupation.

The proposition that migration is primarily motivated by the search for occupational opportunity and that its volume and direction are primarily influenced by job opportunity has been shown in many studies. Stouffer has attempted to state this quantitatively in his theory of intervening opportunities,[3] and others have also tested it empirically.[4] Recent reports on population mobility by the Census Bureau have likewise shown that both migration rates and distance moved are related to occupation.[5] To follow the professions—law, medicine, journalism, or scientific pursuits—or to obtain training in these fields, migration from the small town to the city is almost necessary. On the other hand, jobs in unskilled work are likely to be closer at hand. Even for certain other occupations, as in skilled work, job restrictions and union requirements are likely to interpose obstacles just as certification requirements tend to limit opportunities for teachers to certain communities. Thus migration in these occupational categories may be channeled away from larger cities and limited to shorter distances.

THE MATERIAL

The material for this study consists of reports on the residence and occupation in 1950–1952 of 1,553 males and 1,862 females who completed their high school education in 116 Missouri small communities about ten years earlier, 1939 to 1940. The towns and villages selected for the study varied in population from crossroads hamlets with less than 100 people to county-seat towns with more than 5,000. One small city of 10,000 was included. Three-fourths of the sample (75.3 percent) came from places with populations in 1940 of less than 2,500, about one-tenth (12.8 percent) from towns of 2,500 to 5,000, and one-tenth from small cities over 5,000 in population. The communities were selected to be representative of Missouri rural social areas as defined by C. E. Lively and C. L. Gregory.[6] Data concerning the current (1950) residence and occupation of each of our subjects were obtained from parents, relatives, friends, and former teachers of the subjects. Since most students complete their high school education at about 18, their age at time of report was approximately 28. Roughly, a ten-year interval covering World War II and the postwar period had intervened between date of high school graduation and the date when the data were gathered.

OCCUPATION AND SIZE OF COMMUNITY

In 1950 about two-thirds of the subjects were no longer residing in the community of their school attendance ten years earlier. If we define as migrants those who had moved beyond the county of their 1940 residence, then approximately 55 percent of the males and 60 percent of our female subjects could be so classified. Let us turn attention first, then, to the size of the communities toward which our subjects had been attracted. These data are presented separately for each sex in Tables 1 and 2.

In the tables we have shown the subjects classified by occupational categories with a percentage distribution according to residence in 1950–52. For the male group we have omitted those who were occupied in farming since nearly all such subjects resided on farms. In the female group we have included only those who were reported as gainfully occupied. These include both single and married women. The omission of the nongainfully occupied housewives reduces the size of the sample so that comparisons tend to become somewhat doubtful.

Although in 1939–1940 three-fourths of our subjects had attended school in communities of less than 2,500 population, nearly two-thirds of the men and 70 percent of the women resided in 1950 in urban communities. In large cities (over 100,000) were one-fourth of the men and 30 percent of the occupied women. In general, women appear to have settled in large cities with greater frequency than have the men, although, as we shall see, this tendency is largely due to the different occupational composition of the two sexes.

Differences in residential distribution between the various occupational categories are quite clear. Urban settlement was most marked for the professional group excluding teachers, with about four out of five of each sex group residing in cities and approximately 40 percent in cities with 100,000 or more population. Professional male workers resided in cities from 20 to 30 percent more frequently than did the sample as a whole and with a frequency 60 percent greater than the total sample in Class III cities. The tendency for professionals to reside in large cities was a little more marked among males than among females, although the number of professional women was so small as to make comparisons doubtful. The somewhat different residential distribution of the professionally occupied women is probably due to differences in the specific occupations within the professional category followed by each sex.[7] Few professional women were to be found in medicine and law, while the nursing profession had attracted a substantial portion of the women.[8] An occupational category closely related to the professional was the students, all of them males, and nearly all pursuing graduate and professional studies beyond the A.B. degree. In light of the concentration of Missouri institutions for advanced study in cities of Class I and II, their distribution is not surprising.

The residential pattern of teachers is strikingly different from that of the other professional category. Nearly 40 percent of the male teachers

TABLE 1.   Percentage Distribution of Residence for 1,165 Males Classified by Occupation, 1950–1952

Residence	Total (N = 1,165)	Professional (N = 145)	Teachers (N = 73)	Clerical (N = 56)	Business (N = 327)	Skilled (N = 218)	Unskilled (N = 309)	Student (N = 37)
Total	100.0	100.0	100.0	100.0	100.0	100.0	100.0	100.0
Farm	3.0	4.1	5.5	0.0	2.4	3.2	2.9	0.0
Village	33.0	17.9	38.3	35.7	32.4	34.4	40.1	10.2
Urban	64.0	77.9	56.2	64.2	65.1	62.3	56.9	83.7
I. 2,500–10,000	18.0	17.2	15.1	7.1	29.1	11.9	14.6	10.8
II. 10,000–100,000	21.1	20.7	31.5	28.6	17.4	23.9	16.8	43.2
III. 100,000 plus	24.8	40.0	9.6	28.6	18.6	26.6	25.6	29.1

Chi-square tests at the 5 percent level show significantly different residence patterns for the following occupational categories when comparisons are made with the remainder of the sample: Professional, Teachers, Business, Unskilled. Other occupational categories are not significant at the 5 percent level.

TABLE 2.   Percentage Distribution of Residence for 470* Females Classified by Occupations, 1950–1952

Residence	Total (N = 470)	Professional (N = 45)	Teachers (N = 76)	Clerical (N = 189)	Business (N = 59)	Skilled (N = 17)	Semi & Unskilled House-keeper (N = 84)
Total	100.0	100.0	100.0	100.0	100.0	100.0	100.0
Farm	2.5	2.2	7.9	0.5	0.0	0.0	3.5
Village	28.2	13.3	50.0	19.6	28.8	29.4	35.7
Urban	69.3	84.4	42.1	79.9	71.1	70.5	60.7
I. 2,500–10,000	17.6	20.0	13.1	16.9	27.1	5.9	17.9
II. 10,000–100,000	22.3	28.8	18.4	22.8	23.7	29.4	19.0
III. 100,000 & over	29.4	35.5	10.5	40.2	20.2	35.2	23.8

*Includes only females reported as gainfully occupied.

Chi-square tests at the 5 percent level show significantly different residence patterns for the following occupational categories when comparisons are made with the remainder of the sample: Teachers, Clerical. Other occupational categories are not significant at the 5 percent level.

and 50 percent of the women were village residents as compared with one-third of all men and less than 30 percent of all women. An additional 5 percent of the men and 8 percent of the women were on farms. Unlike the other professional group, teachers had not settled in the expected proportions in larger cities of Class II and III. For each sex one teacher out of ten resided in large cities, while about one-third of the men and about one-fifth of the women lived in medium-sized urban communities (Class II). The differences between the sexes in the distribution of the teaching profession probably lie in the different vocational aspirations in the profession as between men and women. For women, teaching is often a temporary interlude before marriage. Hence there is not the same incentive to obtain advanced training and to meet the higher certification required of the urban teacher. Aspiration to an administrative position in a larger school system requiring more formal training and experience is reflected in the concentration of male teachers in small and medium-sized cities. At the same time these small-town-bred and -educated subjects rarely achieve positions in metropolitan school systems, which more commonly recruit their staffs from locally reared and educated candidates.

The residential distribution of the male clerical workers closely resembles the total sample with a slight tendency toward concentration in Class II and III cities. The number of males in this category, however, is too small to warrant generalization. Among the women, however, the clerical group contains nearly one-half of all gainfully occupied. This is largely an urban group with 40 percent of the total residing in metropolitan centers. The somewhat generally greater mobility of women and their greater tendency to settle preponderantly in large cities is probably the result of their concentration in clerical pursuits, for which the best job opportunities are to be found in metropolitan communities. It might be remarked, at this point, that the tendency for the larger cities to attract the relatively superior young people (in terms of test score) is the product of the tendency for the professions and clerical pursuits to recruit disproportionately from those with higher test intelligence.

Compared to the professional and clerical groups, persons who had entered business and sales occupations tended to be a village and small-town group. In their distribution they closely resembled the sample as a whole. Among the men there was a tendency for over-representation in small cities and under-representation in metropolitan areas. This group includes a large number who own small business enterprises or were employed by such organizations. The group comprises, as we shall see, a disproportionate number of short-distance migrants who appear to have settled in or close to the communities in which they attended school. Many of them have followed the paternal occupation or inherited the business.

The strong influence of paternal occupation has been demonstrated in an earlier study.[9] The young women in this group were somewhat more urban than the men and were found more frequently in Class II and III cities. Although, occupationally, they probably did not differ greatly from the clerical category, they did not show quite the same concentration in larger urban centers as did the latter.

In their residential distribution manual workers appear to fall somewhere between the professional and clerical on the one hand and the business and sales people on the other, less urbanized than the former but more so than the latter. Differences between the skilled and unskilled were not statistically significant except for the tendency of the unskilled to show a little greater concentration in the village category and a somewhat smaller proportion in the medium-sized cities (Class II). The skilled and unskilled had moved to large cities in almost exactly the same proportions.

There is nothing particularly new or striking in the results described. They are about what one would expect. Nevertheless, the role of occupation in determining residential and migration patterns needs to be kept in mind when generalization about sex differences in migration or the tendency for migration to be selective in other respects is analyzed. Certainly many of the differences between migrants and nonmigrants grow out of occupational choice.

By far the greater proportion of our subjects have been reared on farms or in small towns in rural districts in an area of generally declining economic opportunity for youth. With a few exceptions the counties from which they stem have been losing population steadily for the past several decades except perhaps during the 1930's. Lively and Bright have shown that farming, the major industry, has been steadily losing its capacity to absorb the youth who reach the labor market each year.[10] Those who have left their home communities have done so largely in search of job opportunity, and the distance and direction of their migration have been dictated largely by actual or purported economic opportunity. Attention will next be directed to the relation between occupation and distance migrated.

OCCUPATION AND RANGE OF MIGRATION

For purposes of classification a scheme of concentric zones has been used. Subjects have been classified as residing in one of six zones as follows: zone one, same address as that of their school attendance; zone two, same county but at different address; zone three, adjoining county; zone four, other county in Missouri; zone five, state adjoining Missouri; zone six, other state. This classification scheme is similar to that used by the Census Bureau and gives a rough picture of the distances involved in mobility. The relationship

TABLE 3. Percentage Distribution According to Range of Migration of 1,591 Males Classified by Occupation, 1950–1952

Range of Migration	Total (N = 1,591)	Professional (N = 154)	Teachers (N = 76)	Clerical (N = 58)	Business & Sales (N = 340)	Skilled (N = 226)	Unskilled (N = 309)	Students (N = 42)	Farmers (N = 386)
Total	100.0	100.0	100.0	100.0	100.0	100.0	100.0	100.0	100.0
Same address	36.0	11.7	7.9	32.8	38.8	30.5	34.9	9.5	56.0
Same county	10.0	1.3	9.2	1.7	5.9	4.9	9.7	2.4	22.5
Adjoining county	10.6	7.1	19.7	6.9	12.4	8.9	9.4	2.4	12.2
Other county in Mo.	19.7	39.6	27.6	24.1	18.8	22.6	21.4	52.4	3.9
State adjoining Mo.	10.9	14.3	21.1	15.5	10.6	12.8	13.6	16.7	3.4
Other states	12.8	26.0	19.0	18.9	13.5	20.4	11.0	16.7	2.1

Chi-square tests at the 5 percent level show significantly different patterns of migration for the following occupational categories when comparisons are made with the remainder of the sample: Professional, Teachers, Skilled, Students, and Farmers. Other occupational categories are not significant at the 5 percent level.

TABLE 4. Percentage Distribution According to Range of Migration of 1,962 Females Classified by Occupation, 1950–1952

Range of Migration	Total (N = 1,962)	Professional (N = 46)	Teachers (N = 76)	Clerical (N = 193)	Business & Sales (N = 60)	Skilled (N = 19)	Unskilled (N = 50)	Personal Service (N = 31)	Housewives (N = 1,487)
Total	100.0	100.0	100.0	100.0	100.0	100.0	100.0	100.0	100.0
Same address	28.6	15.2	30.3	29.0	28.3	26.3	40.0	22.6	28.7
Same county	10.5	6.5	11.8	5.2	8.3	5.3	8.0	9.7	11.5
Adjoining county	10.3	2.2	14.5	5.8	10.0	5.3	8.0	6.5	11.2
Other county in Mo.	20.9	19.6	21.0	35.8	28.3	10.5	16.0	22.6	19.0
State adjoining Mo.	13.1	17.4	14.5	10.4	15.0	15.8	12.0	19.4	13.1
Other states	16.5	39.2	7.9	14.0	10.0	36.7	16.0	19.4	16.5

Chi-square tests at the 5 percent level show significantly different patterns of migration for the following occupational categories when comparisons are made with the remainder of the sample: Professional, Clerical, Business, Skilled, Unskilled. Other occupational categories are not significant at the 5 percent level.

between occupation and range of migration is shown separately for each sex in Tables 3 and 4.

In terms of the proportion migrating and in distance moved the professional group was the most mobile. While nearly one-half the entire male sample was still residing in the same county as that of their school attendance, only one person out of eight of the professionals was a resident of his home county. At the other extreme about 40 percent of the professional men had moved beyond the state boundaries as compared with one-fourth of all male subjects. Among the women the distribution is somewhat different, with a tendency toward concentration at the two extremes of the distance continuum, larger proportions than among the men remaining in their home county and also moving out of the state, and with a somewhat smaller proportion migrating to other counties of the state. Among men the largest numbers were those settling in other counties in Missouri, while among women the largest group (two out of five) were out-of-state migrants. Perhaps the tendency for lawyers and doctors to settle in county-seat towns and in larger cities of the state accounts for this concentration of male professionals in other counties of the state. The disproportionate loss to the state of professional people, however, is one of the significant aspects of the selectivity of migration.

Although a professional group, the distribution of the teachers showed quite a different pattern from the other professionals. Among the male teachers, less than one-fifth were residents of their home county, while another fifth had moved to a contiguous county. The same proportion as among other professionals had moved outside the state, although there was less tendency among teachers to move toward far distant states. Among women the teachers were distinctly a stay-at-home group, a larger proportion of them residing at their original address than was true for the sample as a whole. Only half as many women teachers moved outside the state as was the case with men. Again, as discussed in our analysis of the relation between occupation and type of residence, certification requirements and the large number of women who stay in teaching for only a short period before marriage act as deterrents toward long-distance migration, and probably account for the difference in the migration patterns between the two sexes. Women teachers belong distinctly to the "home guard."

Clerical workers, relatively unimportant among the men, make up 40 percent of all the occupied women (excluding housewives). These have been less migratory than have professional women but more so than teachers. Their concentration in "other Missouri counties" (zone 4) probably reflects the attraction for the secretary and stenographer of the larger cities of the state, which, for most of these people, lie in zone 4. Distinctly fewer of them than among the professionals have moved outside Missouri. The small number of cases of men in this group does not justify extended analysis.

The business and sales class show a distribution pattern not greatly different from the group as a whole, if we except the farmers, and are considerably less mobile than either the professional or the clerical categories. With the exception of the unskilled workers and the farmers, a larger proportion of the business and sales group is to be found in the home community than is the case for any other vocational classification. In an earlier paper we have shown that there is a strong tendency for this group to follow the paternal occupation, undoubtedly in many cases taking over the father's business.[11] Perhaps this explains why nearly 40 percent of these subjects still resided in their home community ten years after graduating from high school. Less than one-fourth had left the state, a considerably lower proportion than was true of the other white-collar groups. The young women of this class were somewhat more migratory than the men and showed the same tendency as the clerical group to settle in Missouri counties at some distance from their homes.

The skilled workers were more migratory than the unskilled. A significantly larger proportion of the former still resided in their home county than among the latter, while fewer of the unskilled than of the skilled had left the state. Among the women the small number of cases makes doubtful any generalization.

Least mobile of all occupational classes were those engaged in farming. Well over half the farmers had remained in their own community, and nearly four out of five were residents in their home county. Less than 10 percent had moved beyond zone 3. The large number of farmers in our sample (25 percent) tends to influence the distribution of the whole and to make it less migratory than it would be if this group had been excluded. The stability of farmers also accounts for the greater migration rate among women than among men. If the farm group had been excluded, the mobility pattern of the two sexes would be much alike.

Among the women in our group we have said little about the housewives, who make up 1,487 cases out of the total of 1,962 women (almost 80 percent of the total). Obviously their distribution largely determines that of the total group. For the most part the residence of a married woman is likely to be determined more by the occupational choice of her husband than by her own. If the comparison of mobility patterns had been made between married women, gainfully occupied women, and all men, the married women would resemble more the male distribution pattern than it would that of gainfully occupied women. Let us turn now to an examination of the specific cities and areas in which our subjects had settled.

TABLE 5. Percentage Distribution According to Area of Destination of 1,606 Males Classified by Occupation, 1950–1952

Area of Destination	Total (N = 1,606)	Professional (N = 154)	Teachers (N = 76)	Clerical (N = 58)	Business & Sales (N = 342)	Skilled (N = 228)	Semi & Unskilled (N = 310)	Student (N = 42)	Farmer (N = 396)
Total	100.0	100.0	100.0	100.0	100.0	100.0	100.0	100.0	100.0
Missouri	76.5	59.7	64.4	65.5	76.0	67.1	75.4	66.7	94.6
Nonmigrants	45.5	12.9	17.1	34.4	44.4	35.0	44.5	11.9	76.5
St. Louis	5.0	9.7	1.3	10.3	4.9	5.7	8.3	7.1	0.0
Kansas-City	5.1	11.6	2.6	5.1	4.9	6.5	8.3	9.5	0.0
Other Mo. counties	20.6	25.3	43.4	15.5	21.6	19.7	14.2	38.0	18.1
Outside Missouri	23.5	40.2	35.6	34.4	24.0	32.9	24.6	33.3	5.3
North East	1.8	7.1	1.3	3.4	2.0	1.7	0.6	2.3	0.0
Middle States	8.0	11.0	15.7	12.0	8.7	10.5	13.8	6.9	3.1
South	4.7	9.1	10.5	12.0	4.6	4.8	3.5	6.9	0.7
West	7.0	12.9	7.8	6.8	8.4	15.7	6.4	16.6	1.5

Chi-square tests at the 5 percent level show significantly different destination patterns for the following occupational categories when comparisons are made with the remainder of the sample: Professional, Teacher, Skilled, Unskilled, Farmer. Other occupational categories are not significant at the 5 percent level.

TABLE 6.   Percentage Distribution According to Area of Destination of 1,988 Females Classified by Occupation, 1950–1952

Area of Destination	Total (N = 1,988)	Professional (N = 47)	Teachers (N = 78)	Clerical (N = 193)	Business & Sales (N = 60)	Skilled (N = 19)	Semi & Unskilled (N = 50)	Personal Service (N = 32)	Housewives (N = 1,509)
Total	100.0	100.0	100.0	100.0	100.0	100.0	100.0	100.0	100.0
Missouri	70.8	44.6	78.2	75.6	75.0	47.4	72.0	62.5	70.8
Nonmigrants	38.6	21.2	41.0	34.2	36.6	31.6	48.0	31.3	39.6
St. Louis	5.7	8.5	3.8	12.9	1.7	10.5	4.0	9.4	5.0
Kansas City	6.4	0.0	2.5	14.7	8.5	0.0	6.0	9.4	5.8
Other Mo. counties	19.9	14.8	30.7	13.9	28.3	5.3	14.0	12.5	20.5
Outside Missouri	29.2	55.3	21.7	24.4	25.0	52.6	28.0	37.5	29.2
North East	1.8	6.3	0.0	5.2	0.0	5.3	0.0	0.0	1.5
Middle States	11.4	10.6	15.3	10.4	15.0	10.5	18.0	15.6	10.9
South	4.9	10.6	1.3	3.1	3.3	0.0	4.0	3.1	5.4
West	11.1	27.7	5.1	5.7	6.6	36.7	6.0	18.8	11.4

Chi-square tests at the 5 percent level show significantly different destination patterns for the following occupational categories when comparisons are made with the remainder of the sample: Professional, Clerical, Business, Skilled, Housewives. Other occupational categories are not significant at the 5 percent level.

OCCUPATION AND DESTINATION

In Tables 5 and 6 we have attempted to present a picture of the direction of migration taken by our subjects by showing for each occupational category the general location, both inside and outside the state, of their 1952 residence. Residents of Missouri have been classified into those residing in their home county, those residing in the two metropolitan areas of the state, and residents elsewhere within Missouri. Those migrating beyond the borders of the state have been subdivided on the basis of their 1952 residence into four broad regions of the United States.

Although not striking, some differences appear between the two sex groups. A somewhat larger proportion of women seem to have been attracted by opportunities outside Missouri while their home state had held a little larger proportion of the men. The differences, however, are probably more apparent than real, since the relatively large number of farmers among males, of whom over 95 percent were Missouri residents, tends to overbalance the influence of more migratory groups. The difference between the sexes also is obscured by the influence of the large "housewife" group, who migrate with their husbands and hence tend to have a distribution pattern similar to the total male group. Considerable differences appear between the two sexes if one compares specific occupational categories.

The attraction of the home community, other sections of Missouri, and regions outside the state differed considerably for different occupational groups. In the professional group disproportionate numbers, for both sexes, had been attracted toward communities outside the state, especially toward the West. Less than one-fourth of all men had migrated outside Missouri but two-fifths of all professional men resided outside the state. The corresponding percentages for women were 30 percent and 55 percent. The West exerted almost twice the influence on professional men that it had for men in general. The difference was even greater in the case of women. The Northeast also had disproportionate influence on professionals of both sexes. St. Louis and Kansas City as well as other counties of the state appeared to have offered more occupational opportunity to professional men than was to be found in their home neighborhoods. This does not appear to have been as true for professional women. The student group also had sought educational opportunity outside the state in disproportionate numbers, with one-third pursuing their advanced education in other states, especially in the western region. Nearly all of this group were graduate or professional students. Perhaps the tendency for advanced students to seek their professional training outside Missouri explains in part why those engaged in professional activity do not settle in the expected proportions within the state.

Clearly home communities tend to lose the services of their professionally trained people although it may be true that this loss is counterbalanced by the movement into the state of professional workers from ouside Missouri.

Teachers show quite a different residential pattern from other professionals. Relative occupational opportunities seem to have been greater within the state, although the middle states have had a somewhat disproportionate attraction for this profession. Women in the profession, however, tended to stay in their home community while men tended to find jobs in the "other counties" in the state. Probably the explanation for the residential pattern of teachers lies in the point alluded to earlier, namely the restrictions imposed on mobility by certification requirements for teachers and the tendency of the young women to regard teaching only as a temporary interlude between completion of minimum educational requirements for teaching in the home school and marriage. Most male teachers, however, move on to other communities but not to the larger cities.

Clerical workers make up the largest occupational group among women but are less important among the men. Three-fourths of the women in this category had found work within the state, and about one-third in their home community. St. Louis and Kansas City had disproportionate attraction for women in clerical pursuits, stronger than for any other occupational class in either sex. Well over one-fourth of the clericals as compared with a little more than a tenth of all women had been attracted to the two large Missouri cities. Outside Missouri, the middle states had exerted the strongest pull on this group. The relatively small number of men reported in clerical occupations makes any discussion of doubtful value except, perhaps, to remark that they seem to have found work at greater distances than did the corresponding class of women.

Of all the white-collar groups, those engaged in business and selling were the most stable and tended to find vocational outlets locally. Nearly half were engaged in business in their home community and another fifth in "other Missouri counties." In spite of the great expansion of trade and commerce in the two large cities, surprisingly only one in ten had been attracted to these centers. As compared with opportunities for professional workers, business in other states had held less attraction. As suggested earlier, it seems probable that the business and sales group was predominantly engaged in small business enterprise in close proximity to their homes and not employed by large corporations in Missouri metropolitan centers or in the cities of other states.

Of the manual workers, the skilled group has felt strongest the pull of industrial expansion outside their home state, particularly in the middle states and in the West. For both men and women the West has had the strongest attraction for skilled workers in spite of the distance involved in the move. Semi-skilled and unskilled workers have been attracted outside Missouri in considerably smaller proportions. The difference between the two groups who have moved toward the West is particularly significant.

As might be expected, opportunities for those engaged in agriculture had been found largely in the community in which the subjects had been reared. Few of the farmers had been attracted outside the state. Three-fourths of them were non-migrants while less than a fifth had settled in other Missouri counties.

If we view migration from the point of view of the attraction which various regions of the country had for our young people, the situation can be summarized briefly. A little more than half of our subjects who were migrants had been attracted outside the state. The middle states seem to have received the larger proportion of them, although it must be kept in mind that these are states bordering Missouri, and the factor of distance probably explains the larger share. In light of the long-distance moves, the West held disproportionate promise for our migrants. Their home communities tended to hold larger numbers of farmers, unskilled workers, and business and sales people, as well as women in teaching. The large cities of Missouri had the strongest attraction for professional and clerical workers but not for male teachers, who had been drawn to other Missouri counties and toward neighboring states. Communities outside the state had drawn heavily from among professional people, somewhat less from teachers, with the West and the Northeast exerting the strongest attraction. Regions outside the state, and especially the West, also had attracted skilled workers. The middle states held stronger attraction for unskilled workers. Certainly the data indicate that variations in occupational opportunity in the home state as compared with other regions have exerted considerable selective influence on migration of high school graduates in Missouri.

SUMMARY

The results of our analysis point to the general conclusion that emigration from the small towns of Missouri has been selective of the professions, students—most of whom are probably embarking on professional careers— and skilled workers. A larger proportion of these categories have left the state of Missouri, with a distinct tendency to move toward the western states, than was true for the business groups, the unskilled workers, or the farmers. Since it seems to be true that a higher order of ability and talent is necessary for entrance into the professions and related white-collar occupations than seems to be the case for common labor and farming, the process of occupational selection is largely responsible for the tendency of those with higher intelligence as measured by a standard test to migrate more frequently, to move longer distances, to be attracted more by the larger than the smaller cities, and to move toward certain regions of the country rather than toward others. It may be the case that a counter movement of those in the higher status occupations from other states into Missouri compensates for this apparent loss. Similar studies in other states and regions would help to throw light on this question.

NOTES

1. C. T. Pihlblad and C. L. Gregory, "Selective Aspects of Migration among Missouri High School Graduates," *American Sociological Review*, 19 (June 1954), pp. 312–24.

2. C. T. Pihlblad and C. L. Gregory, "Occupational Selection and Intelligence in Rural Communities and Small Towns of Missouri," *American Sociological Review*, 21 (Feb. 1956), pp. 192–99. Also, "The Role of Test Intelligence and Occupational Background as Factors in Occupational Choice," *Sociometry*, XIX (Sept. 1956), pp. 192–99. Also, "Changing Patterns in Occupational Choice," *Journal of Teacher Education*, VI (Dec. 1955), pp. 286–92.

3. S. A. Stouffer, "Intervening Opportunities: The Theory Relating Mobility and Distance," *American Sociological Review*, 5 (1940), pp. 845–67.

4. Margaret L. Bright and D. S. Thomas, "Interstate Migration and Intervening Opportunities," *American Sociological Review*, 6 (1941), pp. 773–83; F. L. Strodtbeck, "Equal Opportunity Intervals," *American Sociological Review*, 14 (1949), pp. 490–97.

5. *Current Population Reports*, Series P-20, No. 14, "Internal Migration in the United States" (April 1940–1947).

Also, "Economic Characteristics of Migrants" (April 1949), Series P-50, No. 20.

6. C. E. Lively and C. L. Gregory, *Rural Social Areas in Missouri*, University of Missouri, Agricultural Experiment Station, Research Bulletin 414 (April 1948).

7. The number of cases in each specific occupation makes a further breakdown unprofitable.

8. It must also be kept in mind that some of the occupied women were married and may have been influenced in their choice by the occupation of the husband. Certainly their residence is more likely to be determined by their husband's occupation than by their own choice.

9. "The Role of Test Intelligence and Occupational Background as a Factor in Occupational Choice," *Sociometry*, XIX (Sept. 1956).

10. Charles E. Lively and Margaret L. Bright, *The Rural Population Resources of Missouri*, University of Missouri, Agricultural Experiment Station, Research Bulletin 428 (Nov. 1948).

11. This has been brought out in a paper by the authors entitled "Occupational Inheritance and Occupational Shifting" (unpublished).

12

Adjustments to the New Institutional Environment

Lee G. Burchinal
Ward W. Bauder

Residential mobility is a basic part of the American scene and is an experience common to most of us. Statistical data are hardly needed to remind us of the frequency and the ease with which our restless population moves about the nation and, increasingly, the world. Residential movement is the norm: in a given year approximately one-fifth of the population moves. In any three- to five-year period many of our colleagues, friends or relatives will have changed their residences. Adults who have lived all or most of their lives in the same dwelling or neighborhood are fast becoming the deviant minority.

Despite the massive magnitude of residential mobility, there has been relatively little research on post-movement adjustments of individuals and families. And despite the near-universal frequency of this phenomenon, there still remain cautious or, perhaps as often, negative views of the consequences of uprooting oneself and family and becoming reintegrated in a new community. These views stem partly from the high value placed on stability ("Lived here all my life—there's no place like it") and those community-bound views so highly treasured in rural nostalgia.

Concerns about the effects of residential mobility on the migrant also arise from erroneous conceptions of the importance of the local "neighborhood" or "community" in contributing to one's security or the need for close geographical proximity to ensure continued functional relationships among kin-related nuclear families.[1]

Also, our guarded apprehension about the effects of residential mobility probably reflects broader negative attitudes toward social change in general. Usually social changes are slowly and only partially accepted. For instance, recent research shows that the working mother still unnecessarily carries extra burdens of guilt and anxiety regarding the development of her children and the preservation of marital roles.[2] Mention of divorce almost always evokes concern for the children involved, often justifiably. But seldom and only very reluctantly do persons grant that some children may not be adversely affected or may even benefit from the divorce of their parents.[3] Discussion of farm-to-urban migration frequently includes greater emphasis on the social and personal costs involved as compared with social and personal advantages of higher levels of living, more efficient utilization of labor and greater opportunities for personal growth and development.

Lack of enthusiastic acceptance of residential mobility is inconsistent with its massive proportions. While the ideology favoring intergeneration geographical stability may have been well suited for the age of the yeoman farmer and the settled burgher and may still bring peace and comfort to some, it is far removed from the reality of a mass society with a highly urbanized and mobile population. When matters really count, however, we are cognizant of reality and act accordingly—we move. And, we hypothesize, most families and persons adapt reasonably well to new circumstances. This optimistic view is the major working hypothesis of our discussion: Residential mobility is a response by which individuals and families expect to, and generally do, succeed in better meeting important housing and other personal and family needs.

This hypothesis is based on the fact that most moves involve short distances, impose few disruptions in major systems of social roles and occur as a result of voluntary decisions—for the most part due to increases in family size and desires to adapt housing to one's improving social position. Otherwise, as outlined in Figure 1, the ease and completeness of adjustment to residential mobility varies with a large number of factors.

CONCEPTUALIZATION OF ADJUSTMENT
TO RESIDENTIAL MOBILITY

Figure 1 represents a tentative model for analyzing adjustments following residential mobility. No cluster of factors is intended to be exhaustive, and no doubt some may wish to add, delete or substitute clusters of factors or individual factors included in the clusters.

Despite its initial apparent complexity, Figure 1 is basically a simple flow diagram. It contains three interrelated time periods which, starting from the top, include (1) a cluster of factors preceding residential mobility but which by interacting with (2) a set of intervening factors influence (3) the kinds of post-movement adjustments made by individuals and families. In short, adjustments following residential changes cannot be understood apart from the previous patterns of individuals and families and the degree to which the moves provide opportunities for or require changes in these patterns of living, both within the family and in various community roles.

Reasons for Moving

Most moves are voluntary, some are clearly imposed upon individuals and families, and many involve mixtures of choice and compulsion. Three sets of factors strongly influence voluntary moves: upward status aspirations or upwardly mobile career patterns,[4] position in the family cycle[5] and familism.[6] Many studies agree in finding that residential mobility is greatest when families are experiencing their greatest growth.[7] Upward social mobility based on career movement of the male head and more recently expedited by employment of wives provides a second powerful inducement to residential mobility. Overlapping these motivations are those associated with familism. Moves to be nearer immediate family members or the rush to the suburbs "for the sake of the children" are clearly familistic in character. Because these three factors often are interrelated, reasons for moving frequently may include aspects of all three. Finally, we include "nomadism," coined by Goldstein to describe the large volume of moves made by a small proportion of families.[8] Moves by this minority do not fit any of the current conceptualizations. Some people seem to change residence fairly regularly largely for the sake of change.

Examples of involuntary moves include evictions; inability to maintain a style of life with attendant housing due to declining income; destruction of housing because of urban renewal, highway construction or other public works; moves necessitated by family disruption following death, divorce or separation; and moves required because of employment, such as job transfers or the search for employment. Precise distinctions between voluntary and involuntary moves break down for those associated with employment. Some jobs, especially certain managerial ones and many of the ones in the armed forces, require considerable geographical mobility, often with no status mobility. Hence they impose moves on individuals whether they want them or not. In other cases job transfers may be voluntary and frequently are rewarded with status enhancement. Attainment of better employment by millions of unemployed or underemployed persons also includes varying degrees of choice or compulsion. Much of the rural-to-urban movement has stemmed historically and currently from the search for economic opportunities. Sometimes it involves desperate desire for any kind of employment; at other times it involves a choice between low incomes in rural areas and hopes for higher incomes in urban areas.

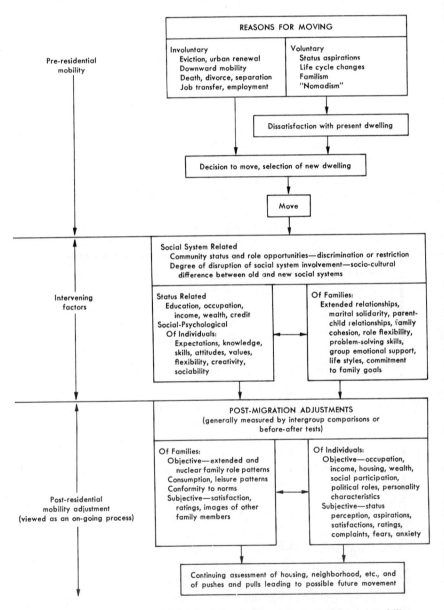

FIGURE 1. Tentative Model for Studying Adjustments to Residential Mobility

Forced moves probably involve more post-migration adjustments than moves undertaken voluntarily. This hypothesis, however, is difficult to test because circumstances forcing a change in residence are also likely to make it difficult to resume role patterns after making a move. After some forced moves, adjustments may be complicated by losses in roles. Examples are situations involving divorce or the death of a spouse or losses in work roles.

Intervening Factors

The three sets of intervening factors are listed as sociological, status-related and social-psychological. The combinations of solid lines and arrows in Figure 1 are meant to show the interrelationships among the three factors as well as their separate and joint influences on the kinds or levels of adjustments made following residential change.

Post-movement adjustments are greatly influenced by the status and role structures of the communities into which persons have moved. Large metropolitan areas, for instance, include a wide range and great number of status positions and associated roles as well as a large number of informal organizations and special interest groups. By contrast small towns and rural communities generally offer considerably fewer such opportunities for social participation. Discrimination limits opportunities for some persons (notably Negroes, Spanish-Americans and Puerto Ricans) in relation to housing, education, jobs and participation in the social life of the community. Availability of specialized social roles and freedom to participate in them obviously condition adjustments to residential changes.

The two remaining sociological factors are closely linked to the distance moved. In the city, moving down the street, over several blocks or from one neighborhood to another generally imposes only slight changes on the role patterns of the individuals and families. Family wage earners generally keep the same jobs, adults maintain their activity in formal and informal social organizations, and visiting patterns are unbroken. Some new friendships may be substituted for previous ones; the children may have to change schools and develop new friendships; but by and large there is no great disruption in participation in various social systems.

The social and cultural homogeneity of most metropolitan and even smaller urban centers in the United States also allows long-distance moves without major disruption in social roles associated with community institutional structure. Individuals participate in different social systems, but in our mass society these systems closely resemble the ones the individuals had known in their previous communities. Except for moves necessitated by death, divorce or separation, nuclear family structure remains intact and the family system continues as a functional set of relationships, despite long-distance migration.[9] Occupational roles are transferred readily or, put more precisely, the ease of movement within or among occupational roles permits widespread geographical mobility. Interurban migration also need not disrupt participation in civic, service, social, religious, political, recreational or other specialized interest groups. Most urban centers are replete with their local associations of national bodies. For example, lodges, service clubs, PTA's, religious organizations, children's organizations, many recreational groups and all the other minutiae of social life are replicated in cities and suburbs, metropolitan centers and larger towns throughout the United States.

Disruption of social roles following residential movement frequently is associated with conflicts arising from socio-cultural differences between old and new social systems. Prominent among moves giving rise to socio-cultural conflicts is the migration of poorly educated, low-status, "culturally different" people—largely from rural areas to metropolitan areas. Racial minority status[10] or inferior social status[11] further complicates urban adjustment problems.[12] Rapid upward or downward social mobility frequently gives rise to residential mobility. Socio-cultural conflicts arising from differences which exist between old and new housing, neighborhoods, acquaintances and roles and which result from social mobility undoubtedly complicate associated post-movement adjustments.

When marked changes in social status levels are not involved, the ease and success of post-movement adjustments are assumed to be directly related to status. That is, persons and families having more education, higher incomes, higher prestige occupations, more wealth and greater access to credit are better able to dictate or control the conditions arising from residential mobility. They find it less necessary to adapt their expectations, adjust their behavior and fit their life styles to limits presented to them. We also hypothesize that higher status persons and families require less time to re-establish their style of life following moves than do persons of lower status. This is partly because of the greater financial resources of higher status persons, but also because of their greater nonmaterial assets (illustrated by social-psychological characteristics in Figure 1). Of course this hypothesis has certain limits. Persons of extremely low status may have little to gain or lose following residential mobility. Because they have virtually no organizational affiliations, they establish in the immediate community only a limited set of social roles, if any.

We have now anticipated our next set of factors—social-psychological characteristics. These factors are considered separately for individuals, each of whom must come to terms with situations presented in the new social systems, and for families, each of whom must maintain or redefine both extended and nuclear family relationships. We refer to relationships both of individuals and of family groups, although each set of adjustments influences the other. Family behavior represents the crystallization of individual abilities, attitudes, goals, values, flexibility, interpersonal skills, etc. Individual functioning, in turn, is influenced by family structure and role patterns, emotional support received from family members, and other types of group factors listed in Figure 1.

Post-Residential Mobility Adjustment

Finally, post-movement adjustment can be considered separately for individuals and family groups. Moreover, each set can be considered in terms of two broad categories of data, which we arbitrarily designate as "objective" and "subjective." Objective data include directly observable role patterns or other behavioral characteristics; subjective data include perceptions, satisfactions and evaluations inferred from what individuals say about themselves and their situations.

Numerous hypotheses can be derived from the interrelationship suggested in Figure 1. Some specific hypotheses have been presented. Others can be developed.

One final point needs to be made: adjustment to moving is a continuing process, as suggested by the notation in the extreme lower right-hand portion of Figure 1. At any point after a given move, the factors listed under post-migration adjustments become push-pull factors for the next move or become intervening factors or variables which help determine adjustment to subsequent moves. . . .

RESEARCH ON ADJUSTMENTS
TO RESIDENTIAL MOBILITY

The literature on migration is immense, but most of it deals with rates of migration and population changes by various geographical areas.[13] There has been comparatively little research on adjustments to residential change. The greatest amount of such research, strangely enough, is based upon a type of residential change involving only a minority of the population— movement from farms or rural areas to urban centers. Fortunately, such movement offers a theoretically and substantively significant area for discussion of adjustment to residential changes.

Rural to urban migration studies assume that some important rural-urban differences still exist. While the general status of such differences is not known and while it is clear that many differences between rural and urban social systems have declined greatly or disappeared altogether, some large and important sociocultural differences probably remain between the social systems of larger urban centers and those of more isolated rural communities in the United States. Moreover, organizations such as the Center for Agricultural and Economic Development and many state and federal agencies are vitally interested in rural-urban movement. Therefore, partly due to availability of data and partly due to current interests, discussion of adjustments to residential mobility is limited largely to data from rural-urban studies.

In addition to the scarcity of data, we must note several additional limitations of this body of knowledge. Migration studies typically have not measured family factors. Attention has been given to various individual characteristics such as occupation, education, income, attitudes, goals, values and aspirations. Generally, we can speak only of individual adjustments to movement, many of which, however, are influenced by unmeasured or ignored family structural and relationship factors. Also, none of the rural-urban investigations yet published have studied carefully the process of urban adjustment of newly arrived migrants. Cross-sectional survey techniques have predominated in these studies. Moreover, data often have been obtained long after rural migrants first entered the urban scene. Because of these limitations, we shall not pursue discussion of detailed findings; rather, we focus on several areas of broad substantive and theoretical import.

SUBSTANTIVE CRITERIA FOR MEASURING URBAN ADJUSTMENTS OF RURAL MIGRANTS

The many factors that have been used in studies of urban adjustments of persons with rural backgrounds may be organized into three categories:

1. Occupation and related measures of social status have been employed as broad measures of assimilation into urban social systems.

2. Social participation indexes, including visiting with friends and relatives, have been used as measures of integration of newcomers into community social systems apart from the economic system with its occupational role systems.

3. Various measures of values, attitudes, goals and aspirations have been used as measures of normative integration.

In addition to these three categories of data, we briefly discuss relationships between migration, familism and post-migration adjustments.

The Overriding Influence of Social Status

Levels of social status, both before and after movement, go to the heart of any discussion of adjustments following residential change, regardless of the methods or criteria used to assess adjustment. Status is a particularly crucial factor in analyzing urban adjustments of rural in-migrants. All of us are familiar with rural-urban differences in levels of education and income, with or without controls for race, and with differences in occupational distributions between rural and urban populations. Although in recent years the occupational structure of the rural labor force has begun to approximate that of the nation as a whole, the rural labor force still contains a large proportion of farm jobs, as would be expected. Moreover, both the rural and rural-nonfarm labor forces contain a smaller proportion of white-collar jobs than does the urban labor force.

There is some evidence that greater proportions of the better educated persons leave rural areas, but care should be used in interpreting such comparison when age differences are not taken into account. Nevertheless, in study after study, the farm or rural migrants to the city are less well educated than their urban-reared neighbors. It is not surprising, therefore, that in comparison with urban-reared persons, there also are proportionately more rural migrants in the lower status occupations. Moreover, rural migrants have lower incomes and more frequently view themselves as members of the lower or working classes.[14]

Two questions arise from this well-established generalization:

1. How much of the differences in status achievement between rurally reared and urban-reared persons is due to differences in formal education and how much is due to a residual rural socialization effect?

2. How much of the difference in other measures of adjustment, such as social participation, visiting, voting, etc., is due to status differences between the in-migrants from rural areas and urban-reared persons and how much is due to a residual rural socialization effect?

It is helpful to consider the "educational effect" and the "residual rural socialization effect" as separate influences, although we readily admit they are not independent influences on adult social roles.

The answer to the first question is not clear. Inadequate data are available, and among the few studies in which education, residence during socialization and present occupational achievement in the urban setting are interrelated, inconsistent research results have occurred. For instance, Lipset found that education accounted for much of the occupational achievement difference between rural migrants and urban-reared persons in his sample. However, even with groups of comparable education the superiority of the urban-reared was still evident. Similar results were obtained in an investigation in Cedar Rapids, Iowa.[15] In contrast, age and educational level explained all significant differences in occupational achievement among three samples of men studied in Des Moines, Iowa—those reared on farms, those who had moved to Des Moines from other urban areas, and those who had always lived in Des Moines. Of the two factors, age was less closely related to occupational achievement than was education. In this investigation the occupational achievement differences originally thought to be related to the community backgrounds of the men in fact primarily reflected differences in education and secondarily differences in age.

In the Cedar Rapids study differences in the men's occupational achievement levels varied more with differences in education than with differences in community backgrounds. However, differences in education did not fully explain differences in occupational achievement between the farm- and urban-reared men. More than sheer numbers of years of education was involved. We can only conjecture about these other factors. They may include the quality of education received, the amount and accuracy of information about jobs, knowledge of where to secure information about better jobs, willingness to move to a new community where there are better jobs available, and other value and attitudinal factors.[16]

Data are not available for explaining the lack of agreement between the Des Moines and Cedar Rapids studies. Differences in the characteristics of the two metropolitan areas, especially in their occupational structures, probably contributed to the lack of agreement. Des Moines has a greater proportion of its labor force in clerical and other white-collar jobs, reflecting the insurance industry and state government located in that city. Cedar Rapids has a larger proportion of its labor force in skilled and semi-skilled occupations, reflecting a wider range and greater concentration of manufacturing jobs. Very likely the two metropolitan areas attract and retain different proportions of rural migrants in the varying educational and skill levels.

This finding has considerable theoretical meaning. In addition to considering characteristics of migrants and urban-reared persons, some of whom are interurban migrants, this finding suggests that attention must also be given to the sociological characteristics of the metropolitan areas being studied.

The large and persistent differences in status between rural and urban persons indicates the necessity of accounting for the influence of this factor in studying urban adjustments of rural newcomers. For instance, where the effect of educational and occupational status was eliminated there was no significant difference in what farm–Des Moines migrants, urban–Des Moines migrants and those who always have lived in Des Moines considered their level of social status to be. Results from a study of eastern Kentucky migrants living in Cincinnati confirmed the necessity of controlling socioeconomic status when comparing persons from the southern Appalachian region with those who had grown up elsewhere.[17] Numerous differences between the Appalachian newcomers and others largely disappeared when differences in socioeconomic status were accounted for. On the other hand, when community background was ignored, large and significant differences were found between lower and higher social status levels for a wide range of parent-child relations and of characteristics of parents and children. The few significant differences which did occur between newcomers and others were observed in low-status comparisons. Comparable tests for the two high-status groups generally yielded no significant differences.

These results suggest that persons with more resources—material as well as nonmaterial resources such as education, skills and resourcefulness—generally made the transition more easily and quickly, with greater likelihood of either maintaining or enhancing their previous levels of participation in group activities. Newcomers having lower levels of resources more likely failed initially to match their previous levels of integration in community systems and required a longer time to match or exceed their previous levels of association. Higher status persons are more likely to have the skills to penetrate and to be accepted into the social systems of a new community, especially when these are more complex than the community which they left. Lower status persons more frequently are baffled, confused or frustrated by their experiences in the new setting.

These data support one of the hypotheses advanced earlier, that adjustments to residential changes are directly related to social status. However, some qualifications must be recognized. In the Cincinnati study, higher status in-migrants with Appalachian backgrounds probably differed from lower status Appalachian newcomers in one of several ways: (1) The higher status in-migrants may have lived in Cincinnati longer, and, therefore, had a greater opportunity for upward mobility; (2) they may have been better educated or had other upward mobility advantages at the time they originally came to Cincinnati; or (3) some combination of the preceding factors affected the situation. Regardless of the reasons, the results underscore the necessity of assessing post-migration movement adjustments in terms of criteria appropriate to the status levels of the migrants. Otherwise, for rural-urban migrants, who generally are represented to a greater extent among lower status levels, less participation in formal social organizations, greater political apathy or other social characteristics typical of lower status could be erroneously interpreted. Such behavior could spuriously be interpreted as lack of adjustment to urban social systems when, in fact, such behavior may closely match that of other lower status urban residents.

The poorer urban occupational achievement among males with rural backgrounds is based upon studies using the comparative group design. When before-after tests are used, however, a different picture is seen. If the rural migrant to the city is as deprived of many of the more visible marks of successful adjustment to urban life, notably occupational achievement, as he is generally believed to be, he is often unaware of it. Shannon noted:

. . . much of the concern over the "plight" of the Mexican-Americans (in Racine, Wisconsin) revolved around the *apparent* lack of concern over their own sorry state of affairs evidenced by the Mexicans. This in itself was cause for great alarm on the part of middle-class persons. Knowledge of the environment from which the Mexicans came might have tempered local concern over the attitude of the Mexicans toward their present living conditions.[18]

Most measures of adjustment are urban-oriented; they rank performance in occupational or organizational activity in terms of an urban standard instead of the standard of the migrant's rural community of orientation. The rural migrant may not, therefore, fully accept the urban standard in evaluating his own performance. In fact, by urban standards, he may be relatively unsuccessful in his occupational pursuit and associated income and material benefits, but from a rural frame of reference he may have improved his lot immensely. For the same reasons, southern rural Negro migrants to northern cities also may report more favorable reactions to urban life than southern rural whites.[19]

Farm-reared migrants, like urban-reared migrants, move primarily for economic reasons, and the majority report that their economic position has improved as a result of moving. In Des Moines about the same percentage of farm-reared as urban-reared migrants listed economic reasons—better job, higher wages—as the cause of their migration—88 and 83 percent, respectively.

In general, approximately equal proportions of the two Des Moines migrant groups felt their family welfare had been improved because of their move to Des Moines—and that their welfare had been improved in about the same ways. These ways included having a better job with more regular hours, higher pay or better working conditions, having more friends, having a better social life, having better schools for the children, and feeling more settled. However, about twice as large a proportion of farm migrants (48 percent) as urban migrants (26 percent) reported having better living conditions or a nicer home.

Social Participation Including Visiting Patterns
as Measures of Adjustment

Omari found that the rural-reared were slower to enter formal associations and took longer to adjust to them than urban migrants. He found that the latter typically made a rapid adjustment, soon approximating and frequently exceeding the participation rates of urban natives.[20] In contrast, Zimmer found that given enough time in the city, many of the farm-reared equalled the participation rates of urban natives. Furthermore, differences that remained after a period of time were largely related to socioeconomic status.[21] On the other hand, in Wilmington, Delaware, the rise in social participation levels among rural-urban migrants was not very great and was more dependent on factors such as occupational status than on community of orientation. For example, recent white-collar migrants from rural areas were more active socially than their blue-collar counterparts who had been there longer.[22] Lower status southern Appalachian newcomers to Cincinnati also were less active in social organizations than other lower status residents, but differences in social participation rates between high-status southern Appalachian newcomers and other high-status residents were nonsignificant.[23]

In Des Moines, social participation scores were determined in six categories of voluntary association: religious, occupational, educational, social-recreational, civic-service and political. Differences in scores between farm-reared migrants, urban-reared migrants and Des Moines natives were nonsignificant in all categories. With one exception—the total social participation scores of wives—differences also were nonsignificant for total organizations belonged to and for total social participation scores. However, the higher the occupational status of the husbands, the higher the social participation scores of both husbands and wives.

What generalizations can be drawn from this smattering of data? The results are inconsistent. Thus there can be no general statement summarizing relative rates of social participation between rural migrants and other city residents. Some studies indicate that rural-urban migrants have lower social participation rates than urban-reared persons but that with increasing opportunity to become familiar with urban social systems differences between the two groups disappear. These studies show that at any given time differences between social participation rates of rural newcomers and others are principally dependent on status differences between the two groups. However, other studies (Des Moines) indicate that a group of farm-reared persons with considerable urban experience participates in social organizations with approximately equal frequency as urban-reared persons.

Analysis of political behavior of urban residents with farm-versus-urban backgrounds does not clear up these inconsistencies. Political activity and voting behavior may be used as a measure of the degree to which persons feel they are part of a community and behave as if they believe that they can influence major policy decisions affecting them. However, comparisons of voting behavior between farm-reared or rural-reared persons and other residents also reveal lack of agreement among findings. For instance, farm-reared urban migrants included in a national urban sample were politically less active in 1952 than were urban-reared persons. This relationship held when allowances were made for differences in income, region, age, sex and size of residential community.[24] Data from the Cincinnati and Des Moines studies, however, do not agree with these results. When an allowance was made for differences in status, the proportions of persons registered or who recently voted were similar for southern Appalachian newcomers and other Cincinnati residents. In Des Moines nonsignificant differences in several measures of voting occurred among the three samples used and for both men and women. It is not easy to reconcile differences between the results based on the national sample and those derived from the two community studies. Obviously the national data provide the widest basis of generalization—if voting behavior can be generalized from one national election to another. But the results of the two community studies remind us that the national data do not apply equally well to all metropolitan areas.

Beyond the matter of validity of generalizations there lies a more important question: so what? What if social participation rates of rural migrants are lower than those of other urban residents of comparable status? How valid or important a measure of urban adjustment is social participation? Studies of urban social participation generally show that most persons belong to only a few organizations—typically church, work-related groups such as a union, business or professional organization, and, for those having children, the P.T.A. or other school-related organization. Furthermore, these studies show that most urban residents attend these organizations relatively infrequently. Often the difference between social participation of rural migrants and others, where such exists, smacks of a difference between a little and virtually nothing rather than differences which are theoretically and substantively important.

Moreover, variations in social participation rates invariably are more closely related to status than to region of origin.[25] For example, the median number of organizations to which men in the three Des Moines samples belonged ranged from 2.4 to 2.7; for women, the range was from 1.9 to 2.5. Larger variations, however, were observed among persons in each of three status levels within each migration category, from 1.9 to 3.7 for men and from 1.7 to 3.4 for women.

The Des Moines data illustrate the point raised earlier about the substantive importance of differences in social participation scores. How important is a median difference of 0.3 or 0.6 in numbers of organizations belonged to? (Incidentally, for both men and women the highest medians occurred among urban–Des Moines migrants. Medians for farm–Des Moines migrants and natives to the city were the same.) Could differences of these sizes be interpreted as differences in integration into social systems of Des Moines? Hardly. Because their social participation rates are lower than urban migrants, are we to conclude that the Des Moines natives are less well adjusted to Des Moines? The answer is that generally lower status levels prevailed among the Des Moines natives and farm migrants as compared with the urban migrants.

Lower urban social participation by rural newcomers is lamented by some because they believe lack of such participation limits the newcomers' opportunities for learning the ways of urban living and for availing themselves of widened opportunities in the city.[26] We have probably revealed enough to indicate that we cannot agree with this interpretation. First, we doubt that participation in the usual variety of religious, social, political, recreational, educational and other organizations really provides newcomers an opportunity for learning urban norms, roles and values. Most social interaction in these formal organizations is too fleeting and superficial to permit learning to occur. Moreover, participation in most urban social organizations is much more status guided than in typical rural or small communities. As a result of the urban stratification system, newcomers would most likely be exposed only to a limited set of norms, values and attitudes—those typical of the status level occupied by the newcomers and ones which may not be markedly different from their previous patterns. However, programs specifically designed to reach low-income, poorly educated and normally somewhat alienated newcomers may aid them considerably in making more successful adjustment to city life. Reorganization of programs in schools, churches, unions, recreational groups and neighborhood associations offer such opportunities.

Normative Measures of Urban Adjustment

Attitudes, values, perceptions, satisfactions, aspirations, etc., have been used least frequently as measures of urban adjustment of rurally reared persons. Data have been given for ways in which farm migrants and urban migrants reported they were better off since moving to Des Moines. In general, the majority of both groups felt they had improved their way of life, particularly economically. In contrast, the two migrant groups differed in some of their evaluations of ways in which they felt they were less well off as a result of having moved to Des Moines. Slightly over 47 percent of the farm-migrant wives disliked the traffic congestion, dirt, noise and pace of city life compared with 5 percent of the urban-migrant wives. On the other hand, a greater proportion of urban migrants (32 percent) than farm migrants (19 percent) missed their close friends. Also, urban migrants more frequently complained of higher taxes and expensive housing (27 percent compared with 11 percent for farm migrants). Otherwise, roughly equal proportions of respondents in both groups complained of an unfriendly atmosphere, not feeling safe, poor recreational facilities, difficulties in rearing children, husbands being dissatisfied with their work, children's unhappiness at school or that the families just did not like Des Moines.

Important differences existed between the two samples for parents' aspiration levels for their children.[27] Lower educational and occupational aspirations persisted among parents in the farm-migrant sample, even after the parents had lived there for an average of almost 11 years. Urban-reared parents had higher educational and occupational aspirations for their young sons than rural-reared parents. Also, the mature sons of urban-reared parents were better educated and had higher levels of occupational achievement records than the mature sons of rural-reared parents. Many of the differences in educational and occupational aspirations or achievements, where these existed among the three migration groups in the Des Moines study, were accounted for by the lower educational and occupational levels of the parents in the farm-reared sample. Lower achievement begets low aspirations for children, which beget low achievement. And so goes the vicious cycle. How many generations this pattern will persist among the descendents of rural migrants is an important question.

Familism and Post-Migration Adjustments

A number of interesting hypotheses have been developed for relationships among familism, migration and subsequent adjustment. Among persons from the Kentucky hills the potential insecurity of leaving the home area is lessened by the prospect of joining family members who moved out earlier.[28] Joining other family members in northern cities undoubtedly is one of the major reasons for the stability of certain migrant streams, as for example from eastern Kentucky into southern Ohio. In addition to encouraging migration from the Kentucky hills and other areas of Appalachia, familism also aids migrants in becoming established in the urban center to which they go. But how broadly can these findings be generalized?

The critical factor is the degree of familism. Few other areas of the country, perhaps only the Ozark area, match or approach the familistic characteristics of the more isolated sections of the southern Appalachian region. Otherwise there is much assertion about greater familism among rural and especially farm families as compared with urban families, but the few studies that have tested this hallowed generalization fail to support it.[29] Recent studies of urban family systems also question this generalization.[30]

Familism, as a system of beliefs, status and role relationships which make the family unit more important than individual members or other social groups, probably is not characteristic of all rural areas generally and certainly has little vitality in most urban areas. But kinship relationships, now organized as a set of somewhat obligatory and often mutually beneficial relationships, may influence migration and subsequent adjustments.

Aside from the description of the influence of family relationships upon the migration of members from southern Appalachian regions into southern Ohio, there are little systematic data on how relatives influence persons' decisions to move. The meager data available, however, suggest that the picture drawn by Brown for southern Appalachian migrants cannot be generalized broadly; it may apply only to certain ethnic groups who also have low levels of education, skills and minority status.

For instance, urban-reared migrants in Des Moines were less likely than farm-reared migrants to be preceded by relatives. Almost half of the farm migrants had relatives in Des Moines at the time they moved there compared with almost one-third of the urban-migrant families. On the surface these data appear to support the hypothesis of greater familistic ties among migrants who came largely from Iowa farms. But other data show that the farm migrants more frequently had always lived in Iowa, whereas a greater proportion of urban migrants came from out of the state. The data also show that a greater proportion of the farm migrants than urban migrants or natives had relatives living close to Des Moines. These additional data suggest that farm migrants simply are less geographically mobile than urban migrants.

More important than having relatives in or near Des Moines prior to moving there is whether those relatives influenced the migrants' decisions to move to Des Moines. About one-quarter (26 percent) of both farm migrants and urban migrants reported their relatives had influenced their decision to move to Des Moines. Hence, in this Iowa study, the influence of relatives was relatively minor in decisions to move and reflected equal importance among both farm and urban migrants.

Other data from the Des Moines investigation belittle the greater importance of kinship relationships among farm-urban migrants in comparison with urban-reared migrants.

Familism scores for the three samples of families varied only slightly.

Percentages of families reporting large family gatherings were virtually similar for farm-migrant families (85 percent) and for families who always had lived in Des Moines (83 percent), both exceeding the 71 percent for families of urban migrants.

Visits with relatives living in Des Moines, on a per relative basis, did not vary greatly among the three samples of families.

The greater frequency of visiting with relatives living outside Des Moines reported by farm-migrant families as contrasted with the other two groups of families was related to the closeness of the farm migrants' relatives to Des Moines. A larger proportion of the relatives of the farm-migrant families than of the relatives of the other families lived in Polk County or counties adjacent to Des Moines.

What then is the effect of kinship ties on adjustment to urban life? Kinship ties, we argue, do not influence the decision to move for the majority of families, except those occupying particular status positions or coming from certain regions of the country. Where they exist, however, these ties are no doubt useful in initial stages of adjustment to the city. But what are the long-term effects of kinship ties on the adjustment of rural migrants? Rose and Warshay[31] found evidence that migrants with already existing primary group contacts in their new community are more likely to remain isolated from the rest of the community and to remain isolated longer than migrants without such contacts. Rural-urban differences in migrants' backgrounds were related less to various measures of adjustment than was the presence of friends or relatives in the new community.

At least two other factors, however, must be considered in evaluating the effects of relatives upon longer-term adjustments of newcomers. These are the educational levels and social status of migrants. Admittedly these two factors are interrelated, but they need to be considered separately.

For some migrants, particularly ones from more isolated rural regions, familism may promote and facilitate migration, but it is chiefly through their skill levels that persons are sorted into jobs. And skill level is primarily determined by education. It may be, therefore, that kinship influences are more instrumental in securing unskilled or semi-skilled employment and consequently in influencing adjustments to other social systems as well, primarily because these less well-educated migrants are restricted to a narrower range of employment. With increased education we might expect changes in the paths of migration and in the influences that determine job selection. Fewer migrants will be guided to their destination areas primarily because family members are there; instead, migration will become more sensitive to labor-market conditions covering a wider geographical area.

Data from a study conducted in Wilmington, Delaware, is predictive of changes we have suggested. Migrants with urban backgrounds coming to Wilmington tended to migrate by means of a relatively impersonal contact through the labor market and to bring with them significant amounts of knowledge about cities in general and Wilmington in particular. Migrants with rural backgrounds were more likely to use personal ties in the decision to move and brought little knowledge of the city with them. Migrants with an urban background retained much of their way of life, even if they cut many of their personal ties; the rural migrants retained personal ties, even if they changed much of their way of life.[32]

Another aspect of family-related migration is reminiscent of the problems encountered by foreign-born migrants in American cities. Apart from levels of education and jobs, some migrants are accorded an inferior social status. Examples are Negroes, Appalachian migrants in midwestern cities and Spanish-Americans in cities of the Southwest and California. Under the conditions of social stigmata migrants so affected insulate themselves from the hostile and alien urban environment by developing their own communities. They create a little bit of Kentucky or West Virginia in the slum areas of Cincinnati or Detroit, part of the rural South in Atlanta or Washington and something of "Old Mexico" in Los Angeles or Santa Fe. Living primarily with their own group enhances the role of familism in migration and adjustment to urban life. If they enjoyed equal social status with other whites we can only surmise that the self-imposed segregation among southern Appalachian newcomers and other whites and nonwhites, for that matter, would be considerably less. For instance, rural migrants from the Great Plains or areas of the Midwest adjacent to cities generally do not form identifiable neighborhoods, except those having general characteristics corresponding to the socioeconomic status of the migrants.

In most circumstances family aid generally should help in making initial urban adjustments such as becoming acquainted with shopping areas and service facilities, developing new acquaintances, becoming familiar with recreational facilities and generally becoming familiar with the city. But continuous and near exclusive interaction with relatives, especially under conditions of insulated community life, can only accentuate inferior social status and probably retard the assimilation of migrants.

NOTES

1. See Marvin B. Sussman and Lee G. Burchinal, "Kin Family Network: Unheralded Structure in Current Conceptualizations of Family Functioning," *Marriage and Family Living*, 24:231–40; and Marvin B. Sussman and Lee G. Burchinal, "Parental Aid to Married Children: Implications for Family Functioning," *Marriage and Family Living*, 24:320–32.

2. F. Ivan Nye and Lois W. Hoffman, *The Employed Mother in America*, Rand McNally, 1963. This volume contains 27 chapters devoted to research, analysis, discussion and integration of theory and data pertaining to the employed mother in America.

3. For data showing no major differences between children from broken and unbroken homes, see: Paul H. Landis,

"The Broken Home in Teenage Adjustment," Washington Agr. Exp. Sta. Bul. No. 542, June, 1953; William J. Goode, *After Divorce*, The Free Press, Glencoe, Ill., 1956, pp. 307–29; F. Ivan Nye, "Child Adjustment in Broken and Unhappy Unbroken Homes," *Marriage and Family Living*, 19:356–61, 1957; J. Louise Despert, *Children of Divorce*, Doubleday and Co., 1962; Lee G. Burchinal, "Characteristics of Adolescents from Unbroken, Broken and Reconstituted Families," *Marriage and Family Living*, forthcoming.

4. Two recent studies supply data and review previous studies supporting the relationship between status mobility and geographical mobility. See Gerald R. Leslie and Arthur H. Richardson, "Life-Cycle, Career Pattern, and Decision to Move,"

Amer. Soc. Rev., 26:894-902, 1961; Vincent H. Whitney and Charles M. Grigg, "Patterns of Mobility among a Group of Families of College Students," Amer. Soc. Rev., 23:643–52, 1958.

5. Leslie and Richardson, op. cit.; Peter H. Rossi, Why Families Move: A Study in the Social Psychology of Urban Residential Mobility, The Free Press, Glencoe, Ill., 1955.

6. E. Gartly Jaco and Ivan Belknap, "Is a New Family Form Emerging in the Urban Fringe?" Amer. Soc. Rev., 18:551–57, 1953; Wendell Bell, "Familism and Suburbanization: One Test of the Social Choice Hypothesis," Rural Sociology, 21: 276–83, 1956; Ernest R. Mowrer, "The Family in Suburbia," in William A. Dobriner, ed., The Suburban Community, G. P. Putnam's Sons, New York, 1958, pp. 147–64; Eugene Litwak, "Occupational Mobility and Extended Family Cohesion," Amer. Soc. Rev., 25:9–21, 1960; Eugene Litwak, "Geographical Mobility and Extended Family Cohesion," Amer. Soc. Rev., 25:385–94, 1960.

7. Rossi, op. cit., pp. 9, 178.

8. Sidney Goldstein, Patterns of Mobility, 1910–1950, The Norristown Study, University of Pennsylvania Press, Philadelphia, 1958.

9. See Litwak, "Geographical Mobility and Extended Family Cohesion," op. cit.; Sussman and Burchinal, op. cit.; and Ward W. Bauder and Lee G. Burchinal, "Adjustments of Rural-Reared Young Adults in Urban Areas," Background Paper No. 35 for the Conference on Problems of Rural Youth in a Changing Environment, Oklahoma State University, Sept. 22–25, 1963, conducted by the National Committee for Children and Youth, Washington, D.C.

10. As in the case of Neogres.

11. As in the case of Puerto Ricans, Spanish-Americans and white newcomers from isolated, depressed rural areas such as many Appalachian, Ozark, Cascade, or northern Great Lakes communities.

12. Mel Ravitz, "Rural In-Migration and Urban Assimilation," Background Paper No. 32 for the Conference on Problems of Rural Youth in a Changing Environment, Oklahoma State University, Sept. 22–25, 1963, conducted by the National Committee for Children and Youth, Wash-

ington, D.C.; and Oscar Handlin, The Newcomers; Negroes and Puerto Ricans in a Changing Metropolis, Doubleday and Co., 1962.

13. George L. Wilber and James S. Bang, "Internal Migration in the United States 1940–1957: A List of References," Mississippi State University Agr. Exp. Sta., Sociology and Rural Life Series No. 10, Oct., 1958; Vera J. Banks, "Migration of Farm People—An Annotated Bibliography," 1946–1960, Economic Research Service Miscellaneous Publication, USDA, forthcoming. See also G. Beijer, Rural Migrants in Urban Setting, Martinus Nijhoff, The Hague, 1963, for an analysis and review of studies of rural-urban migration in 12 European countries, with a bibliography of 1,300 titles.

14. Lee G. Burchinal, with A. O. Haller and Marvin Taves, "Career Choices of Rural Youth in a Changing Society," North Central Regional Publication No. 142, Minnesota Agr. Exp. Sta., Nov., 1962; Bauder and Burchinal, op. cit.

15. Lee G. Burchinal and Perry O. Jacobson, "Migration and Adjustment of Farm and Nonfarm Families and Adolescents in Cedar Rapids, Iowa," Iowa Agr. and Home Econ. Exp. Sta. Res. Bul. No. 516, June, 1963.

16. Bauder and Burchinal, op. cit.

17. Roscoe Griffin, "Appalachian Newcomers in Cincinnati," in Thomas E. Ford, ed., The Southern Appalachian Region, A Survey, University of Kentucky Press, Lexington, 1962, pp. 79–84.

18. Lyle W. Shannon, "Occupational and Residential Adjustment of Rural Migrants," in Labor Mobility and Population in Agriculture, Iowa State University Press, Ames, 1961, p. 130.

19. Eldon D. Smith, "Migration and Adjustment Experiences of Rural Migrant Workers in Indianapolis," unpublished Ph.D. thesis, University of Wisconsin, 1953.

20. Thompson P. Omari, "Factors Associated with Urban Adjustment of Rural Southern Migrants," Social Forces, 35:47–53, 1956.

21. Basil Zimmer, "Participation of Migrants in Urban Structures," Amer. Soc. Rev., 20:218–24, 1955.

22. Charles Tilly, "The Assimilation of Rural and Urban Migrants to Wilming-

ton, Delaware," a paper presented at the Rural Sociological Society Meeting, Washington, D.C., Aug., 1962.

23. Griffin, *op. cit.*

24. Ronald Freedman and Deborah Freedman, "Farm Reared Elements in the Nonfarm Population," *Rural Sociology,* 21:50–61, 1956.

25. Griffin, *op. cit.;* Bauder and Burchinal, *op. cit.*

26. Griffin, *op. cit.*

27. Bauder and Burchinal, *op. cit.*

28. James Brown, "The Family Group in a Kentucky Mountain Farming Community," Kentucky Agr. Exp. Sta. Bul. No. 588, 1952.

29. Robert O. Blood and Donald M. Wolfe, "The Division of Labor in City and Farm Families," *Marriage and Family Living,* 20:170–74, 1958; see also Blood and Wolfe, *Husbands and Wives,* The Free Press, Glencoe, Ill., 1949, pp. 44–45; Lee G. Burchinal and Ward W. Bauder, "Comparisons of Family Authority and Role Patterns between Farm and Nonfarm Families," Iowa Agr. and Home Econ. Exp. Sta. Res. Bul., forthcoming.

30. Litwak, *op. cit.;* Sussman and Burchinal, *op. cit.*

31. Arnold M. Rose and Deborah Warshay, "The Adjustment of Migrants to Cities," *Social Forces,* 36:63–76, 1957.

32. Tilly, *op. cit.*

13

Kentucky Mountain Migration and the Stem-Family: An American Variation on a Theme by Le Play[1]

James S. Brown
Harry K. Schwarzweller
Joseph J. Mangalam

ABSTRACT

In studying Kentucky Mountain migration, the authors found Frédéric Le Play's *famille-souche* or "stem-family" concept useful in understanding the functions of the kinship structure in (a) the processes of migration and (b) the adjustment of individuals within a migration system.

Case study of three Eastern Kentucky neighborhoods (Beech Creek) over a period of twenty years shows that (a) members of the same extended family in 1942 tend to migrate to the same places, (b) migrants from these neighborhoods now living in a given town are almost all related by close kinship ties, and (c) migration destination appears to be social class oriented (closely related to kinship structure).

We conclude that the consistency of the directional pattern of Eastern Kentucky's out- and in-migration may well be due to kinship relationships.

Finally, many Beech Creek families, like Le Play's stem-family, facilitate and encourage migration and provide in crises "havens of safety." Furthermore, "branch-families" in the new communities provide a socio-psychological "cushion" for the migrant during the transitional phase.

Reprinted from *Rural Sociology*, 28, no. 1 (March, 1963), pp. 48–69, by permission of the authors and the publisher. Footnotes have been renumbered.

INTRODUCTION

In this paper we are concerned with functions performed by kinship groups in the migration of persons from the rural areas of Eastern Kentucky to the more urbanized, industrial areas of Ohio, Indiana, and elsewhere.[2]

Though this exploratory attempt to indicate functional connections between kinship structure and migration process in the case of Eastern Kentucky migration will not, of course, be wholly applicable to studies of migration in all other areas, the frame of reference developed in this paper, which systematically links kinship structure and migration process, suggests, we believe, a conceptual approach that has wider application. Almost by definition folk cultures are characterized by strong familistic bonds that unite kin members in cohesive family groups and fit individual desires into a framework of family needs.[3] The Eastern Kentucky subculture, a part of the Southern Appalachian regional complex, has been, and still is, an area dominated by traditionally sanctioned particularistic value orientations; even today, in Eastern Kentucky, the *extended family* plays a highly functional role. Understanding the functions performed by kinship groups in the process of migration in the case of Eastern Kentucky migration should be useful in understanding the pattern of migration and the transitional adjustments of persons who move to urban areas of industrial opportunity from similarly strong familistic folk cultures in other parts of the world.[4] Furthermore, the general problem with which this paper is concerned arises from a serious deficiency in studies of migration elsewhere, namely, the superficial treatment of the part played by the family structure in migration and in the adjustment phase of the migration process.[5]

In this article we will be concerned with:

(1) The pattern of migration of Eastern Kentuckians, reviewed briefly to establish the general demographic characteristics and to put the problem in its broader setting.

(2) Various aspects of migration during a twenty-year period from a three-neighborhood cluster in Eastern Kentucky, described as a case example of the part played by kinship in migration.

(3) Finally, certain modifications of Frédéric Le Play's conceptualization of family types, especially that of the stem-family *(famille-souche)*, which we have found useful in studying the functions of kinship structure both in (a) the processes of migration and (b) the adjustment of individuals within a migration system.

(1) THE PATTERN OF MIGRATION
OF EASTERN KENTUCKIANS

Without going into extensive detail, let us draw from more complete demographic analyses of regional population trends a few pertinent observations about the patterns of Eastern Kentucky migration:[6]

(a) In the last twenty years the population of the part of Eastern Kentucky which is primarily a subsistence-agricultural area and in which our case-study area lies (State Economic Area 8) declined 19 percent, largely due to heavy migration from the area. During the 1940's the net loss

TABLE 1.   Out-Migration: Intra-area and to Contiguous and to Noncontiguous Areas, 1935–40 and 1949–50, Eastern Kentucky[a]

	1935–40		1949–50	
	Number of Migrants[b]	Percent	Number of Migrants[b]	Percent
Total	107,477	100.0	50,445	100.0
Intra-area	37,524	34.9	17,615	34.9
Contiguous area	32,741	30.5	12,500	24.8
Noncontiguous area	37,212	34.6	20,330	40.3

[a]"Eastern Kentucky" in 1935–40 included Kentucky State Subregions 5 and 9. For the counties included, see Donald J. Bogue, Henry S. Shryock, Jr., and Siegfried A. Hoermann, *Streams of Migration between Subregions*, Volume I of *Subregional Migration in the United States, 1935–40*, Scripps Foundation Studies in Population Distribution—Number 5, Oxford, Ohio: Miami University, 1957.

"Eastern Kentucky" in 1949–50 included Kentucky Metropolitan Area C and State Economic Areas 5, 8, and 9. For the counties included, see Donald J. Bogue, *State Economic Areas*, U.S. Bureau of the Census, Washington, D.C.: U.S. Government Printing Office, 1951.

[b]A "migrant" is defined as a person who has moved his residence across county lines. Intra-area migration is migration among the counties of Eastern Kentucky. Contiguous area migration is migration to areas adjacent to Eastern Kentucky. Noncontiguous area migration is migration to areas not adjacent to Eastern Kentucky.

through migration was the equivalent of 34 percent of the 1940 population, and during the 1950's the equivalent of 25 percent of the 1950 population.

Eastern Kentucky is a chronically depressed area with limited economic opportunities for its people. From 1940 to 1960 many more economic opportunities were available in the more prosperous urban areas nearby, and tens of thousands of Kentucky Mountain people have moved to take advantage of these opportunities.

(b) The pattern of the streams of migration from the area has been remarkably consistent over the years.

For example, the proportions of migrants moving (1) within Eastern Kentucky (that is, to other counties within State Economic Areas 5, 8, and 9), (2) to contiguous areas, or (3) to noncontiguous areas are very similar for both the periods 1935–40 and 1949–50 (Table 1), though there is a discernible trend for a higher proportion to go longer distances and for a lower proportion to go to contiguous areas.

(c) The great stream of out-migration from the subsistence-agricultural area of Eastern Kentucky (SEA 8) to noncontiguous areas has been to areas in Ohio and secondarily to areas in Indiana. Out-migration from Eastern Kentucky other than in these well-established streams has been to widely scattered destinations (Table 2).

TABLE 2. Percentage of Out-Migration to and In-Migration from State Economic Areas Not Contiguous with Kentucky State Economic Area 8, 1949–50

	Out-Migration[a]		In-Migration[b]	
	Number	Percent	Number	Percent
Total number of migrants to and from noncontiguous areas	6,130	100.0	4,410	100.0
Kentucky, total	590	9.6	330	7.5
Kentucky A (Louisville)		3.3		1.9
All other Kentucky		6.3		5.6
Ohio, total	2,410	39.3	1,800	40.8
Ohio C		10.0		6.8
D		6.4		6.5
K		6.8		9.0
3		5.4		2.8
4		4.5		4.2
All other Ohio		6.3		11.6
Illinois, total	150	2.4	90	2.0
Indiana, total	945	15.4	540	12.2
Michigan, total	305	5.0	355	8.0
All others	1,690	27.6	1,295	29.4

[a]The total number of out-migrants during this period was 10,815, of whom 43.2 percent moved to contiguous areas.

[b]The total number of in-migrants during this period was 8,115, of whom 45.6 percent came from contiguous areas.

(d) Countercurrents of in-migration, which generally accompany all streams of migration out of an area, exhibit a pattern almost identical with that of the out-migration. In other words, the proportion moving *to* a particular area "outside" is practically the same as the proportion coming *from* that specific area, although more people move from than move to the Eastern Kentucky area during a specified time period (Table 2).

These data from demographic studies of Eastern Kentucky migration have led us to some basic questions, in the answering of which we find knowledge of the kinship structure relevant:

First of all, why has the directional pattern of out-migration from Eastern Kentucky been so consistent over the years that we could almost say the streams of out-migration were running in well-worn riverbeds?

Certain widely accepted factors are important in understanding these streams of migration: Eastern Kentucky is an area of underemployment, and its people tend to migrate toward areas where more job opportunities are available. This generalization, that labor tends to flow in the direction of greater economic opportunity, is well founded.[7] However, geographical, historical, and other factors must be considered too. Stouffer's hypothesis of "intervening opportunities"[8] helps explain certain deviations from what might be considered a "normal" pattern for this area, e.g., the "leap" over the largely agricultural counties of Central and Northern Kentucky to the industrial counties of Southern Ohio.

But we believe that kinship also is a factor of some importance in the explanation of this consistency in the directional pattern of out-migration. For, as Lively and Taeuber point out, the "evaluation of relative opportunities is essentially a subjective matter."[9]

The kinship structure provides a highly persuasive line of communication between kinsfolk in the home and the new communities which channels information about available job opportunities and living standards directly, and most meaningfully, to Eastern Kentucky families. Thus, kinship linkage tends to direct migrants to those areas where their kin groups are already established.[10]

This effective line of communication among kin (which is, in our experience, overwhelmingly more important than that of state employment offices) helps also to explain the fact that the rate of out-migration is so immediately responsive to fluctuations in the rate of unemployment in migratory target areas.[11]

Because of ascribed role obligations, kinship structure also serves a protective function for new migrants to an area—a form of social insurance and a mechanism for smoother adaptation during the transitional phase of adjustment.

Secondly, why do streams of in-migration exhibit patterns that are practically identical to the patterns of out-migration from this area?

Individuals' reasons for moving back are of many kinds, as Peter Rossi observed in his study of "Why Families Move."[12] Knowing that Eastern Kentucky has long been an area with heavy net losses through migration, that it has not, especially in the last two or three decades, attracted many outsiders, and knowing also from much observation over more than twenty years that most persons migrating into the area are former residents, we can assume, until more systematic data are available, that most in-migrants to Eastern Kentucky are former residents and their spouses. Some of them could not adapt themselves to "outside" circumstances and decided to move back to their "home" areas. Others are persons who are of retirement age or are drawing pensions of one sort or another and feel they can live better and at less expense in their "home" areas. Most persons who migrate into the area, then, have "roots" in Eastern Kentucky, among which kinship ties are very important.[13] This suggests that kinship ties attract former residents to a specific area from areas to which they migrated in approximately the same proportions as have migrated to these outside areas.

These questions, posed by the analyses of demographic data, suggest a specific problem for research:

What influence do kinship ties have on the destination of migrants? Although our case study of an Eastern Kentucky neighborhood will focus primarily on this problem, the more general (and certainly the more theoretically significant) problem is:

What function does the kinship structure perform in the process of migration? In the exploration of the specific problem we shall attempt to shed some light also on the general problem. However, the latter, more fundamental problem obviously requires far more attention than we can give it either in this paper or in any one research project. Perhaps some indications of how we conceptualize various facets of the general problem may help to point out its theoretical significance as well as its scope and potential for students of migration.

Does, for example, the particular kinship structure characteristic of Eastern Kentucky encourage heavy out-migration? We believe it does, and have found Habakkuk's discussion of the effects of rules of succession upon population growth in nineteenth-century Europe suggestive. Habakkuk points out that "the single-heir system tended to retard population growth and [the system of equal] division to promote it."[14] Eastern Kentucky has had a system of equal division of property among heirs, and here too this system seems to have promoted great population growth, so much so, indeed, that equal division of land seemed to be becoming somewhat less common and alternative plans were becoming more widespread (e.g., one heir's buying the shares of other heirs or of all the heirs giving up their shares to one, often the youngest child, on condition that he take care of the old parents until they died).

Another of Habakkuk's findings is pertinent to this discussion—the rules of equal division of property in Europe tended to promote long-distance migration for seasons or short periods, such migration being

> not an escape from the peasant family but a condition of its survival. The peasant went, not to acquire a new occupation in a different society, but to improve his position in the old. . . . [But] the inhabitants of division areas were not likely in the absence of . . . severe pressure to respond readily to demands for permanent industrial labor in regions distant from their homes.[15]

From a study of the history of an isolated neighborhood cluster in the Eastern Kentucky Mountains and less systematic observations of Eastern Kentucky's agricultural areas as a whole, this same pattern seems to have been common until recently when pressure became so great as to sweep out whole families and almost whole neighborhoods. The earlier pattern of a man's leaving his family in the home neighborhood while he worked in "public works" out in Ohio has become much less common as whole families have migrated.

Another function or set of functions performed by the kinship structure in the process of migration is that surplus population has been drained off which if allowed to "dam up" might well have brought such strain that this society dominated by the family-kinship system would have broken up completely. Actually the gradual migration characteristic of Eastern Kentucky for decades has led to the formation of patterns enabling it to absorb the shock even of very heavy loss. The situation is similar to that Arensberg and Kimball found among the small farmers in Ireland, where

> . . . the forces operative within that structure are of such a nature as to allow the society of which they are a part to continue to function in essentially similar fashion through the welter of economic, political, and other events which have impinged upon the human beings who have successively filled the structure. Likewise, the structure is capable of continued and virile existence in the present, governing the lives of its component individuals and modifying itself to take in "new influences."[16]

A crucial aspect of the Eastern Kentucky situation, confronting any student of this social and cultural area, is the importance attached to kinship relations in the everyday life of its people. Since familism, as a value-orientation, permeates the society and stamps all institutions with its mark,[17] to know the significant effects of heavy out-migration on the social institutions in the area, one would certainly want to begin by exploring the influence of out-migration on the family.

(2) BEECH CREEK MIGRATION AND KINSHIP

Let us turn, now, to a case study that permits us to examine, in greater detail, the relationship of the kinship structure to the process of migration. Throughout this paper, we shall mean by "Beech Creek" a three-neighborhood cluster located in a relatively isolated area of Eastern Kentucky that was studied intensively in 1942, with family, class, and value patterns as the main foci.[18] We have the unique opportunity, then, of using our knowledge of Beech Creek to interpret the migration pattern from that area since 1942.

Beech Creek was, and still is, a family-centered neighborhood. Kinship units tend to be culturally insular groups, kinship relationships the most meaningful interactional patterns, and familistic norms the most important mechanisms of social control. In the sociocultural system of Beech Creek, familism as a traditional value-orientation has been, and still appears to be, dominant.

Loss through migration is an old pattern for the Beech Creek area. During the last two decades, however, the loss has been unusually heavy.[19] Of the persons living in the Beech Creek area in 1942, 318 are still living (as of July 1, 1961), but only 25 percent presently reside in the original neighborhoods. About 17 percent have moved to nearby neighborhoods. Fifty-seven percent have established residence outside of Eastern Kentucky (Table 3).[20] About three-fourths of the migrants to areas outside of Eastern Kentucky now live in Ohio (Table 3).

TABLE 3.   Persons Living in Beech Creek Area on July 1, 1942, by Residence on July 1, 1961

	Number of Persons	Percent
Total Beech Creek residents 1942 still living July 1, 1961	318	100.0

Residence as of July 1, 1961	Number of Persons	Percent of Total		
A. In Kentucky, total			156	49.1
1. Beech Creek area	80	25.2		
2. Nearby neighborhoods	54	17.0		
3. Other parts of Eastern Kentucky	2	0.6		
4. Kentucky outside of Eastern Kentucky, total	20	6.3		
B. Outside Kentucky, total			162	50.9
5. Ohio, total	133	41.8		
6. Indiana, total	17	5.3		
7. All other states, total	8	2.5		
8. Armed forces	4	1.3		

Two Southern Ohio towns (here referred to as X-town and Y-town) which are close to each other and their immediate vicinity have drawn about 42 percent of the Beech Creekers who have migrated from Eastern Kentucky; about 16 percent live in a big city nearby (referred to as City A) and another 16 percent are residents of a smaller city (referred to as City B). The rest of the migrants tend to form smaller clusters in rather widely scattered towns in the Ohio Valley.

These data show the tendency of out-migrants from Beech Creek to cluster in certain areas of destination. Now, let us explore the part that kinship ties have in this clustering. We will do this in several ways:

(a) *Members of the same family group in 1942 tended to migrate to the same places.*

The earlier study of Beech Creek (1942) established the existence of "family groups" in these neighborhoods.[21] The concept "family group" as used here is roughly synonymous with the concept "extended family." In the main, "family groups" consisted of families of old parents and their adult children or of adult siblings and their grown children's families. The composition of these groups was determined, however, not merely by ascertaining kinship relationships, but by considering also the groups of kin which had the closest social relationships.[22] Thus, a conjugal family related by blood to a number of other families in the neighborhood was considered

TABLE 4.   Persons Who Constituted the Andrews-Barnett Family Group in Beech Creek on July 1, 1942, by Residence on July 1, 1961

		Number
Total, of the 58 persons in the Andrews-Barnett family group 1942 still living July 1, 1961		53
Residence as of July 1, 1961		
A. In Kentucky, total		35
1. Beech Creek area		23
2. Nearby neighborhoods		4
3. Kentucky, outside Eastern Kentucky		8
B. In Ohio, total		15
1. City A		2
2. City B		12
3. X-town		1
C. All other states, total		3

to belong to that family group with which it, as a family, had the strongest social bonds.

Of the 58 persons who in 1942 were in the Andrews-Barnett family group, 5 had died and 53 were still living as of July 1, 1961. About one-half of the original members of this family group still live in the old neighborhood or in nearby neighborhoods. The out-migrants, as our data show, clearly tend to concentrate in two specific areas: (1) City B, a small city in Southern Ohio, has drawn 12 members, or nearly half of the migrants, and (2) a small metropolitan area in Kentucky has drawn 6, all members of one family (Table 4).

Similarly, other examples can be noted of this tendency for migrants of the same family group to cluster. Our analysis of the migratory distribution of five family groups revealed: (1) Of the 76 living members of these five family groups as originally delineated, 32 still live in Beech Creek or nearby neighborhoods, (2) 36 now live in "X-town," a small town in Southern Ohio, and (3) only 8 live elsewhere. (See Summary Statement A.)

(b) *Another way of showing the clustering of migrants who are kin is to analyze the kinship relationships of migrants in a given town or city.*

We find, for example, that Beech Creek migrants in City B (a small city in Southern Ohio) were predominantly from two family groups, the Andrews-Barnetts and the Preston Johnsons. Only 5 of the 24 Beech Creek migrants in this smaller city were *not* members or had not married members of the original family groups. And of these 5, only 2 were *not* attached to these families by close kinship ties.

TABLE 5.   Out-Migrants: Persons in Designated Social Class Positions, Beech Creek Neighborhoods, 1942, by Residence Outside Eastern Kentucky, as of July 1, 1961

| | Total Out-Migrants Still Living July 1, 1961 (N = 182) | | | | | | | |
| | High Class | | Intermediate | | Low Class | | Unranked | |
	No.	%	No.	%	No.	%	No.	%
Total, all residence categories	38	100.0	72	100.0	53	100.0	19	100.0
Residence as of July 1, 1961:								
A. Kentucky, outside Eastern Kentucky	9	23.7	4	5.6	6	11.3	1	5.3
B. Ohio								
1. City A, a big city in Southern Ohio	3	7.9	8	11.1	12	22.6	0	0.0
2. City B, a smaller city in Southern Ohio	19	50.0	4	5.6	1	1.9	0	0.0
3. City C, northern smaller city	0	0.0	2	2.8	5	9.5	2	10.5
4. Two smaller towns in Southern Ohio (X-town and Y-town)	1	2.6	34	47.2	20	37.7	10	52.6
5. Other Ohio	1	2.6	7	9.7	3	5.7	1	5.3
C. Indiana	1	2.6	7	9.7	4	7.5	5	26.3
D. All other states	4	10.6	2	2.8	2	3.8	0	0.0
E. Armed forces	0	0.0	4	5.6	0	0.0	0	0.0

In X-town, Ohio, the situation, though somewhat more complicated, reveals a similar pattern. Of the 35 Beech Creek migrants now living there, 22 are members, or have married members, of two family groups, the Lambert-Snows and the Barnetts. Nearly all of the other 13 Beech Creek people there are related in some way to the Barnetts or to the Lambert-Snows, and, in a number of cases, to both.

Here we are perhaps being a bit "archeological," sticking too closely to statistical bones. For actually we *know* from many observations that members of a family "peel off" as they get old enough and join their kinsfolk who have previously migrated.

(c) *Finally, we observe the same clustering phenomenon when we analyze the distribution of out-migrants by present residence and according to their 1942 social class positions*[23] *in Beech Creek (Table 5).*

Summary Statement A.   Examples of the tendency of members of the same family group to cluster when they migrate.

(Based on persons who constituted five family groups in Beech Creek on July 1, 1942, by residence on July 1, 1961)

1. The Barnetts (16 still living):
    5 in Beech Creek and nearby neighborhoods
    10 in "X-town," a small town in Southern Ohio
    1 elsewhere

2. The Carters (15 still living):
    5 in Beech Creek
    7 in "X-town," a small town in Southern Ohio
    3 elsewhere

3. The Cundiffs (10 still living):
    5 in Beech Creek
    5 in "X-town," a small town in Southern Ohio
    0 elsewhere

4. The Lambert-Snows (22 still living):
    7 in Beech Creek and nearby neighborhoods
    11 in "X-town," a small town in Southern Ohio
    4 elsewhere

5. The Smiths (13 still living):
    10 in Beech Creek
    3 in "X-town," a small town in Southern Ohio
    0 elsewhere

Total, of all five family groups (76 still living):
    32 in Beech Creek and nearby neighborhoods (42.1%)
    36 in "X-town," a small town in Southern Ohio (47.4%)
    8 elsewhere (10.5%)

Half of all the "high-class" out-migrants now live in and around City B, a small city in Southern Ohio. Only one "high-class" out-migrant lives in X-town.

On the other hand, nearly half (48.6%) of all those out-migrants previously designated as "intermediate class" live in X-town while only four live in City B.

The "low-class" pattern is much the same as that of the "intermediate" except that "low-class" migrants tend to concentrate less in any one area.

These observations are in the expected directions when one recognizes that class lines in Beech Creek tend to follow kinship lines very closely. To a great extent, the family group is the basic social class unit in the stratification system of Beech Creek, as is the conjugal family in American society.[24] Furthermore, inter-class marriages are not common in Beech Creek, especially between persons of the "high" and "low" strata; the social classes, therefore, tend to be networks of kinship relations. Thus, the available migration data reveal a pattern that is probably more a kinship than a social class phenomenon.

(3) LE PLAY'S STEM-FAMILY[25]

On the basis of these exploratory efforts discussed above, we conclude that kinship ties do, indeed, influence the destination of migrants from Beech Creek.

For a long time we have been aware of the similarity of Eastern Kentucky and the Ozark Mountain area, as reported by Zimmerman and Frampton.[26] In particular, the structure of the Ozark family, which the authors call "an uncodified variety of the stem-family,"[27] resembles in many respects the structure of the Beech Creek (Eastern Kentucky) family, as described by Brown.[28]

Their imaginative use of Le Play's model in studying the Ozark family has increasingly influenced our thinking and has led us to consider carefully Le Play's discussion of the stem-family *(famille-souche)* and its pattern of emigration as well as other aspects of his work.[29]

Let us, then, note briefly some of the main features of Le Play's conceptual model of the *famille-souche*, the stem-family, emphasizing of course what has been most useful to us.

Le Play considers the family the elementary and basic social unit.[30] He held that there was only one general family type though fluctuations in the strength of the main form accounted for three major subtypes of families—the patriarchal, the unstable, and the *famille-souche* or stem-family.

The *patriarchal type* has as its theme the principle of continuity; emphasis is on keeping the family group intact and preserving traditional family boundaries rather than on encouraging individual initiative. Members are loyal to family tradition and the established social order; strong familistic, religious, and moral beliefs are maintained. All property and savings in this type of family are controlled by the household head. Married children reside near the parental homestead and remain under the dominance of the family. If, however, economic conditions become difficult, the patriarchal family either migrates *as a unit* or begins to break up under the strain.

The *unstable type* of family, on the other hand, has as its theme the principle of change; a high degree of individualism is encouraged by freeing children from family obligations. Members of the family have no particular attachment to the parental homestead; family history and traditions have little importance. This type, according to Le Play, is found primarily in new, growing, and unstable industrial orders. The individual member of an unstable family, write Zimmerman and Frampton, "depends more upon himself for a standard of living, and, in case of serious accidents, unemployment, or other calamities, he suffers unless some extra-family agency, such as the government, takes care or him, or unless he has accumulated sufficient property to take care of himself."[31] Cyclical periods of unemployment and economic recession can, therefore, cause much physical and psychological hardship.

Finally, the *famille-souche,* which Le Play conceived as the type *best* able to adjust to the changing conditions of an industrial society, incorporates some of the characteristics of both the patriarchal and unstable types, emphasizing both the principles of change and of continuity within the same structural framework. Zimmerman and Frampton describe this type as follows:

> This stem-family consisted of a parent household *(the stem)* which preserved the organic basis of society, and of a number of individuals *(the branches)* who leave the parent household in order to fit into industrial organizations and urban environments where high but fluctuating money incomes were produced. The stem of the family helps to preserve the society and to insure that the branches which fail in their adaptations to contractual relations have havens of safety to which they may return. Thus, the stem part of the family reduces to a minimum the needs for public charity for the unemployed. At the same time, the successful branches contribute to the embellishment of society by their rapid adjustment to new opportunities, by the development of industrial areas, and by the increase in new types of production.[32]

In his conceptualization of the structure and functions of the *famille-souche,* Le Play, we must emphasize, was describing an "ideal type," deriving this abstraction from his studies of concrete families. Zimmerman and Frampton note this in saying, "The stem-type form is only a common manifestation of many strong families and does not necessarily appear in all or in most families of an area predominantly familistic. In the Ozarks it is far from being manifested in all families."[33] Consequently, we would not expect all Beech Creek families to manifest the characteristics of the stem-family form.

Though our purpose here is not to examine exhaustively the *famille-souche* type, in order to show its usefulness we will discuss certain essential elements of Le Play's conceptual model in relationship to what we have learned about the Beech Creek migrants and migration.

The *famille-souche,* as described by Le Play, maintains a homestead for its immediate members and sends other members elsewhere to make their own living. The ancestral home, built by the founder, is maintained by an heir, thus guaranteeing a continuous head to the family and assuring the preservation of family traditions. In the case of Beech Creek, a family homestead ("the homeplace") in the very broad sense of the term is maintained by the family. This is usually the parental household. However, often it may be simply a piece of land, a presently abandoned or temporarily rented house, or close kinsfolk in the old neighborhoods who offer migrants a "haven of safety" in time of need. The Le Play *homestead concept* appears in the Beech Creek case as a configuration of elements blending land, neighborhood, parental household, kinsfolk, and the like into, as one Ohio migrant put it, "a place to go back to if things get rough out here." Zimmerman and Frampton hint at this point when they suggest, "It seems that the spirit and not the form, the strength and not the mould, is the dominating characteristic of this family."[34]

Family headship in this Beech Creek case, however, is *not* automatically ascribed to an heir who maintains the ancestral home. Nor is there a formal pattern of succession of the family leadership role, although on an informal level family leaders can be identified. Migration from the area has been so great over the years that family leadership is often held by one of the branches rather than by the stem. In this respect, the branches may, then, have as much to do with preserving family traditions and continuity as does the stem.

In case of misfortune, according to Le Play, the branches may secure temporary subsistence and aid from the stem or may draw back to the protective cover of the parental homestead. Thus, serving as a "haven of safety," the stem-family reduces to a minimum the need for public charity for the unemployed. Numerous examples from the Beech Creek case suggest this protective function of the kinship structure during the process of migration. Often migrants who have lost their jobs in Ohio, for instance, move back to their home neighborhoods until employment opportunities are again favorable in the Ohio area. Le Play, however, could not foresee such broad governmental programs of assistance for the unemployed as we have in the U.S. today, and these programs have done much to modify the stem-family form as found in Eastern Kentucky.[35]

Le Play's central concern was with the stem of this type of family and what it does for its branches in two ways: on the one hand facilitating and encouraging migration when conditions demand it, and on the other hand providing "havens of safety" to which the branches could return during crises such as unemployment. *This is our point of departure from Le Play's model,* though we should note at once that the variation described here is implicit in Le Play's schema.

The stability of the directions of migratory streams from Eastern Kentucky, discussed in Part I, and the clustering of class-oriented family groups in certain areas during migration, described in Part II, are *both* suggestive of the supportive role played by the "branch-families" (that is, the migrants' family and kin in the new communities) within the migration system. Numerous researchers have noted that the new migrant is not necessarily alone or a stranger in the new community,[36] and indeed most Beech Creek migrants have many kinsfolk in the communities to which they go. To extend Le Play's model, these kinsfolk form a network of "branch-families" which serves important supportive functions during the transitional period of adjustment. Our preliminary field observations of the Beech Creek migrants indicate, for example, that kinsfolk in the areas of destination often provide the newcomers with temporary housing, help in finding jobs, and assistance of many other sorts during difficult times.[37] Furthermore, it seems reasonable to expect that these networks of branch-families function as a sociopsychological "cushion" for the migrants during the transitional phase, and it is this cushioning function of the branch-families that will be our concern during the remainder of this paper.

For purposes of clarity, let us briefly explain two notions that we have used in the body of this paper without elaborating their meanings, first, our use of "migration system," and secondly, our use of "adjustment."

A migrant[38] is here defined as a person who has moved spatially from one system of interaction to another. This interaction system in which a migrant originates is called his "donor subsystem." The implication is that the two subsystems (the donor subsystem and the recipient subsystem) together form the interaction system in which we wish to consider the adjustment of a given group of migrants, individually and collectively. As presented in our preceding discussions, we have then *one migration system* to consider, namely the Beech Creek–Ohio migration system.[39]

Secondly, what do we mean by "adjustment"?[40] From our definition of a migrant it follows that migration means the shifting of an individual, or a group of individuals, from one relatively stable set of normative patterns of behavior (norms governing institutionalized ways of acting in a given specific social situation) to another. This shift necessarily entails stresses on individuals and on groups. The strains thus produced have psychological, sociological, and cultural dimensions. The resolution of these strains in a manner that enables individuals and groups to function adequately in terms of the demands of the interaction (migration system) is what we are calling adjustment, without restricting its meaning to any *one* of the three dimensions. As we conceptualize it, it is a holistic notion, defined as "a dynamic state in which individuals in a given society are able to live in relation to the members of their significant membership groups, satisfying their basic needs, fulfilling the responsibilities of their major roles, and maintaining the identity and integrity of their individual selves."

Having thus somewhat clarified the notions of "migration system" and "adjustment," let us return to consider the relationship between our modified notions of Le Play's *famille-souche* and adjustment in the migration system.

According to Le Play, the stem-family encourages individual initiative while at the same time exerting moral control over its members. The individual who is unhappy with his present circumstances and wishes to advance socially and economically is offered an "escape mechanism" through the family structure.[41] He is assisted in his quest for opportunity, and also encouraged to go out "on his own." Further, branches that are already established in the areas of destination, as well as the stem at "home," provide a supportive structure and socializing agency for the individual during the process of migration. This support facilitates his adjustment to new circumstances in the migration system and helps to stabilize the migrant, in whom two interactional subsystems meet during the process of migration.

The foregoing arguments have led us to an over-all working hypothesis as the basis for our study of the Beech Creek migrants out of Eastern Kentucky:[42]

The greater the functional adequacy of the stem-family (modified to include the network of the associated "branch-families") of the Beech Creek sociocultural system in responding to the changing needs of the Beech Creekers, the more adjusted the migrants will be, both as individuals and as families, under certain conditions.

In conclusion, let us put the whole problem which we have been discussing in a somewhat larger setting of social and cultural change.

Bell and Vogel have made the helpful suggestion that in analyzing family functions and changes in family functions it is necessary to make clear whether, for instance, the reference point is the nuclear family or the extended family. As they point out:

> In some primitive and agrarian societies, the family is said to have (or have had) major economic, political, religious and educational duties, but in many cases these are (or were) functions of the extended family, not the nuclear family. In more complex societies, these functions are performed not by the extended family, but by specialized institutions organized on other bases than kinship; the nuclear family's relationship with these institutions has become more important, while the relationship with the extended family has been less important.[43]

Obviously when we have been saying that kinship ties have much to do with a Beech Creek migrant's destination, his ways of finding a job and a place to live in the new community, and his general social and personal adjustment, we have been emphasizing the continuing importance of the extended family. As time goes on the importance of the extended family will probably decrease and the broader pattern of the American kinship structure will be approximated both in Eastern Kentucky and in the areas to which the migrants go, notably in that the nuclear family will be much more emphasized. This change, the strains and stresses connected with it, and the process of change in the stem-family itself form another major focus of the Beech Creek Study.

As a subsidiary point we should say that though our general hypothesis is that extended family relationships help cushion the shock of moving from Eastern Kentucky to Ohio, for example, and thus help the migrant to make a better personal and social adjustment in the new community, we recognize that the kinship structure may also be an actual deterrent to more rapid assimilation. In the "little Kentuckies," e.g., migrants' social relationships tend to be exclusively among themselves. This limits their contacts with native Ohioans and lessens their opportunity to learn and accept new patterns.

Finally, Parsons points out that it

> is above all the presence of the modern occupational system and its mode of articulation with the family which accounts for the difference between the modern, especially American, kinship system and *any* found in non-literate or even peasant societies. . . . This means essentially that as the occupational system develops and absorbs functions in the society, it *must* be at the expense of the relative prominence of kinship organization as a structural component in one sense, and must also be at the expense of many of what previously have been functions of the kinship unit.[44]

The general American family type, it should be noted, has gradually changed to meet the changing needs of the occupational and other institutions (and of course has changed these other institutions too). The Beech Creek family has remained much more of an extended family, not the least reason being that it met the needs of that society better than other familial forms. Now that the mountain family has been more or less abruptly moved into modern American society, it will be interesting to see how and how fast it is changed by (and perhaps changes) the "outside world."

NOTES

1. Paper prepared for the annual meeting of the American Sociological Association, St. Louis, Missouri, September 1, 1961. This is the first of a series of working papers from the Beech Creek Study which is sponsored by the National Institute of Mental Health in cooperation with the Kentucky Agricultural Experiment Station.

2. This paper is based on materials from: (1) demographic studies of the entire Southern Appalachian Region, of which Eastern Kentucky is a part; (2) a number of studies of migrants from Eastern Kentucky; (3) an intensive study of a three-neighborhood cluster (Beech Creek) by the senior author in 1942–43; (4) continuous field observations of migration from these neighborhoods during the last twenty years; (5) preliminary field work this past year in preparation for an intensive follow-up study (called The Beech Creek Study) of people who have migrated from these three neighborhoods; and (6) a series of discussions of the adjustment of migrants from Eastern Kentucky involving professional sociologists, economists, psychologists, anthropologists, and extension workers.

3. See, for example, Pitirim A. Sorokin, Carle C. Zimmerman, and Charles J. Galpin, A Systematic Source Book in Rural Sociology, Minneapolis, The University of Minnesota Press, 1931, vol. I, ch. 4, pp. 186–259.

4. For example, in India thousands of Malayalees, caught by very high population density and limited employment opportunities, migrate from their homes in Kerala (Malabar Coast) to such urban areas as Bombay and New Delhi. They live in these cities in close proximity to one another, forming a cultural island within the local society. Their interaction with life in New Delhi, for example, is only segmental, being primarily in their occupational roles. The rest of the time they live a life of their own, their conduct being governed by the norms of the local world of their origin. They send money "home" for the support of their stem-families; they go "home" for marriage; and they are instrumental in bringing streams of Malayalees to New Delhi and in performing supportive functions for the newly arrived Malayalees, both as individuals and as families. This is a pattern very similar to the pattern of out-migration from Eastern Kentucky to Ohio.

5. One notable exception is found in Conrad M. Arensberg and Solon T. Kimball, Family and Community in Ireland, Cambridge, Massachusetts: Harvard University Press, 1940. They discuss the relationship of family structure and migration as follows:

"Viewed in the light of this family structure, the decline of population becomes interpretable not as a flight from intolerable conditions, though economic distress had a powerful effect, not as a political gesture, though political disturbance took its toll, but rather as a movement arising from the effect of all these causes upon a family system whose very nature predisposed it to disperse population and which could, therefore, accommodate itself to that dispersal when it occurred. Emigration, no new thing in 1845, appears as the logical corollary of this dispersal. It derives much of its character, such as assisted passages and remittances, from the social forces at work in the family" (pp. 155–156).

Another exception, which will be discussed more fully later, is the Zimmerman and Frampton study of the Ozark Mountain family. (Carle C. Zimmerman and Merle E. Frampton, *Family and Society: A Study of the Sociology of Reconstruction*, New York: D. Van Nostrand Co., 1935.)

6. See James S. Brown and George A. Hillery, Jr., "The Great Migration: 1940–1960," a chapter in *The Southern Appalachian Region: A Survey*, now in press, University of Kentucky Press; see also George A. Hillery, Jr., and James S. Brown, "Some Conclusions on Migratory Streams from a Study of the Southern Appalachians," a paper presented at the annual meeting of the Population Association of America, May, 1961.

7. One might begin with this thesis as developed by Goodrich and his colleagues. See: Carter L. Goodrich, *et al.*, *Migration and Economic Opportunity*, University of Pennsylvania Press, Philadelphia, 1936.

See also:

(a) Donald J. Bogue, Henry S. Shryock, Jr., and Siegfried A. Hoermann, *Subregional Migration in the U.S., 1935–40, Volume I, Streams of Migration between Subregions*, Scripps Foundation Studies in Population Distribution No. 5, Miami University, Oxford, Ohio, 1957.

(b) Donald J. Bogue, *Components of Population Change, 1940–50: Estimates of Net Migration and Natural Increase for Each Standard Metropolitan Area and State Economic Area*, Scripps Foundation Studies in Population Distribution No. 12, Miami University, Oxford, Ohio, and Population Research and Training Center, University of Chicago, Chicago, 1957, especially pp. 24–29.

(c) Donald J. Bogue, *The Population of the United States*, The Free Press, Glencoe, Illinois, 1959, ch. 15: "Internal Migration and Residential Mobility," pp. 375–418, especially pp. 416–418.

(d) Everett S. Lee et al., *Population Redistribution and Economic Growth U.S., 1870–1950, Volume I; Methodological Considerations and Reference Tables*, The American Philosophical Society, Philadelphia, 1957.

(e) K. M. George, *Association of Selected Economic Factors with Net Migration Rates in the Southern Appalachian Region, 1935–1957*. Unpublished M.A. thesis, University of Kentucky, June, 1961.

8. See Samuel A. Stouffer, "Intervening Opportunities: A Theory Relating to Mobility and Distance," *American Sociological Review*, vol. V, 845–867.

9. C. E. Lively and Conrad Taeuber, *Rural Migration in the United States*, Research Monograph XIX, Works Progress Administration, U.S. Government Printing Office, Washington, D.C., 1939, p. 79.

10. Bogue and Hagood note in their study of differential migration in the Corn and Cotton Belts that: "This examination of the household status of migrants of each age group in comparison with the household status of the populations of the same ages in the area of origin and of destination yields indirect evidence that the detailed form which migration takes is a response to a wide variety of factors many of which are only incidentally economic. Rural youth may choose a particular destination because they have relatives living there rather than because it offers the most opportunities" (Donald J. Bogue and Margaret Jarman Hagood, *Differential Migration in the Corn and Cotton Belts: A Pilot Study of the Selectivity of Interstate Migration to Cities from Nonmetropolitan Areas*, Scripps Foundation Studies in Population Distribution, No. 6, Miami University, Oxford, Ohio, 1953, p. 37).

(They also say that "streams of migration between two particular points tend to be self-perpetuating by virtue of the fact that the first migrants to arrive influence their relatives to migrate to that place, and provide housing and other assistance to the relatives who follow them. This appeared to have been particularly true of migrants whose origin had been in a rural area," pp. 28–30.)

In their valuable study of rural migration in the 1930's Lively and Taeuber found: ". . . In the Kentucky areas more moved to adjoining states than to counties adjoining the survey areas. . . . Actually selective forces, such as the location of relatives and friends and employment opportunities, were active in determining the distribution of the migrant children" (Lively and Taeuber, op. cit., pp. 99–100).

11. T. W. Schultz notes that the "post-war behavior of the economy clearly indicates that the *rate* of off-farm migra-

tion is highly sensitive to changes in unemployment that have characterized these post-war booms and recessions in business. . . . When 5, 6 or 7 percent of the labor force is unemployed, the adjustment process under consideration is brought to a halt; on the other hand, when unemployment declines to 3 or 4 percent off-farm migration becomes large" (T. W. Schultz, "A Policy to Redistribute Losses from Economic Progress," University of Chicago Office of Agricultural Economics, Research Paper No. 6008, October 31, 1960, pp. 13–14).

12. An excellent abstract of Rossi's study of residential mobility is found in: Peter H. Rossi, "Why Families Move," Section V, ch. 8, in *The Language of Social Research*, edited by Paul F. Lazarsfeld and Morris Rosenberg, The Free Press, Glencoe, Ill., pp. 457–468.

13. In this sense, we would also regard individuals whose parents, in-laws, spouse, children, or other close kin are or have been residents of that area as having "roots" there.

14. H. J. Habakkuk, "Family Structure and Economic Change in Nineteenth-Century Europe," ch. 13 in Norman W. Bell and Ezra F. Vogel, A *Modern Introduction to the Family*, Glencoe, Ill.: The Free Press, 1960, p. 167.

15. *Ibid.*, p. 168.

16. Arensberg and Kimball, *op. cit.*, pp. 156–157.

17. Sorokin *et al.*, vol. II, p. 41.

18. See James S. Brown, *The Social Organization of an Isolated Kentucky Neighborhood*, Ph.D. thesis, Harvard University, 1950.

James S. Brown, *The Family Group in a Kentucky Mountain Farming Community*, Kentucky Agr. Exp. Sta., University of Kentucky, Bulletin 588, June, 1952.

James S. Brown, *The Farm Family in a Kentucky Mountain Neighborhood*, Kentucky Agr. Exp. Sta., University of Kentucky, Bulletin 587, August, 1952.

19. The migration data reported here were obtained as the first phase of a 1961 follow-up study of those who in 1942 were living in the Beech Creek area. During the summer of 1961, these people were interviewed at their present residences or, in the case of migration to areas too distant for field interviewing, their present residences were verified by interviews with close kin.

20. If we define migration as the ecological movement of people, involving residential changes that (1) remove them from the immediate interactional systems of which they have been a part and to which they are accustomed and (2) places them in new interactional systems with which they are not accustomed, then those Beech Creekers who have moved to places outside Eastern Kentucky are the "true" out-migrants.

21. See Brown, *The Family Group in a Kentucky Mountain Farming Community, op. cit.*

22. Pearsall made a similar observation in her study of a small isolated neighborhood in the Tennessee area of the Southern Appalachians: "An important feature of the kinship structure is the sense of closeness not only between a couple's family of procreation and their families of orientation, but also between these and all collateral lines. In other words, Parsons' 'inner circle' combines with his 'outer circle' to form one large kinship group—this is reminiscent of the early American family." (See Marion Pearsall, *Little Smoky Ridge*, University of Alabama Press, 1959, p. 94.)

23. For a definition of the "class schema" employed and a description of the class structure in Beech Creek (1942), see: James S. Brown, "Social Class, Intermarriage, and Church Membership in a Kentucky Community," *American Journal of Sociology*, LVII (3) (Nov., 1951), 232–242.

24. Talcott Parsons, "An Analytical Approach to the Theory of Social Stratification," *Essays in Sociological Theory*. The Free Press, Glencoe, Illinois, 1949, p. 173.

25. The following sources will be helpful for further study: Frédéric Le Play, *Les ouvriers européens*, 2nd ed., 6 volumes, Paris: Tours A. Mame et fils, 1878.

Frédéric Le Play, *The Organization of Labor*, translated by G. Emerson, Philadelphia: Claxton, Remsen & Haffelfinger, 1872.

Carle C. Zimmerman and Merle E. Frampton, *Family and Society*, New York, D. Van Nostrand Co., Inc., 1935.

Pitirim A. Sorokin, *Contemporary Sociological Theories*, Harper and Brothers, New York and London, 1928, ch. 2 on "Frédéric Le Play's School," pp. 63–98.

For Le Play's biography, see: Dorothy Herbertson, "The Life of Frédéric Le Play," Le Play House Press, Ledbury, Herefordshire, England, 1950, which is a reprint of Section 2, vol. XXXVIII (1946), of the *American Sociological Review*.

26. Zimmerman and Frampton, *op. cit.*

27. *Ibid.*, p. 272.

28. Brown, *op. cit.*

29. Though Le Play's contributions to social science were many and important and the interplay of Le Play's inquisitive mind, his many interests, and the social and historical circumstances in which his ideas evolved is fascinating, we will discuss only a few of his ideas which are most relevant. We should, however, emphasize that Le Play lived in a period when urbanization and industrialization were bringing about great social changes (born 1806, died 1882). Both the period of transition in which Le Play lived and his attempts to understand the social and economic phenomena of his day make his work particularly relevant to the problems undertaken in this paper.

30. Sorokin, *op. cit.*, p. 39, notes that Le Play realized "an isolated individual cannot constitute a social phenomenon." This is precisely why we contend that a great deal more could be learned about the process of migration if we focus our attention on the family as a basic social unit in that process.

31. Zimmerman and Frampton, *op. cit.*, p. 98.

32. *Ibid.*, p. 47.

33. *Ibid.*, p. 286.

34. *Ibid.*, p. 286.

35. Nevertheless, although the protective function of the stem-family system so far as the economic aspects are concerned may not be as important as during Le Play's time, the social-psychological aspects, especially in terms of the migration process in a complex society, may be even more important.

36. Bogue and Hagood, *op. cit.*, p. 37, note: "This concept of the lonely migrant in the city, living in a single room in a large rooming house and slowly suffering personality deterioration because of isolation, could apply to only a very small part of the migrant population, and probably to rather a select part. If the data for the present study are at all typical of migration generally, the much more usual pattern is that the young migrant sets up his own household at an earlier age than non-migrants of his own age, both in the population at the place of origin and at the destination, that he lives with a relative, or that he is a lodger in a private home."

In support of this conclusion, see also Albert J. Reiss, Jr., "Rural-Urban and Status Differences in Interpersonal Contacts," *The American Journal of Sociology*, LXV (2) (Sept., 1959), 182–195, and Lyle W. Shannon, "Effects of Occupational and Residential Adjustment of Rural Migrants," a paper read at the Conference on Labor Mobility and Population in Agriculture, November 8–10, 1960, Iowa State University, Ames, Iowa, p. 7.

37. Sharp and Axelrod, for instance, found that mutual aid among friends and relatives is widespread in Detroit and, though there is a difference in this phenomenon between natives and migrants, 66 percent of their migrant sample reported help given or received from friends or relatives. Harry Sharp and Morris Axelrod, "Mutual Aid among Relatives in an Urban Population," in *Principles of Sociology*, Freedman, *et al.*, New York: Henry Holt, 1956, pp. 433–439.

Smith, in his study of migrants in Indianapolis, concludes that "one of the primary functions performed by friends and relatives involves the dissemination of information about urban opportunities." Eldon D. Smith, "Migration and Adjustment Experiences of Rural Migrant Workers in Indianapolis," unpublished Ph.D. thesis, University of Wisconsin, 1953, p. 284.

This observation has been made also about southern white migrants in Chicago. See: William R. Simon, "The Southern White Migrant in the Metropolis," a paper read at the Social Science Research Institute, University of Chicago, May, 1961.

38. See footnote 20.

39. We recognize that Beech Creek itself is comprised of a number of interaction subsystems and so, even more obviously, is Ohio (or Indiana or some other

place of destination). The point we are trying to make, however, is that we are not dealing with the adjustment of a given group of migrants, just in the place of destination; instead we are also concerned with the adjustment of a given group of migrants, collectively and individually, in relation to two subsystems of interaction in which they are forced to participate in the normative sense.

40. A second working paper for our study will deal with this concept and will advance arguments in support of the definition that we merely present in this paper.

41. It has been suggested by Slotkin and others that a necessary precondition for migration to occur is a "cultural inadequacy" of the source culture. Slotkin emphasizes the idea of migration as an "escape valve" for those individuals who find their own sociocultural system inadequate for their own role expectations. With this perspective, we tend to look upon migration as an "unnormal" event—that is, the deviant behavior of an individual relative to the normative structure of his society. However, regional migration statistics and an examination of the pattern of migration from the Beech Creek area lead us to believe that the migration process is an adaptive mechanism somehow tied in with the sociocultural system, and functional in maintaining the Beech Creek family structure. James Sydney Slotkin, *From Field to Factory*, The Free Press, Glencoe, Ill., 1960.

42. Migrants, that is, to such places as listed in Table 5.

43. Bell and Vogel, *op. cit.*, p. 6.

44. Talcott Parsons and Robert F. Bales, *Family, Socialization and Interaction Process*, Glencoe, Ill.: The Free Press, pp. 11–12.

14

The Adjustment of
Southern White Migrants
to Northern Urban Norms

Lewis M. Killian

Human migration and its concomitants have long been subjects of major interest to sociologists. Important theories in the fields of human ecology, social change, social disorganization and intergroup relations have been derived from migration studies. *The Polish Peasant* was an early indication that immigrant groups would constitute a rich source of data for social psychologists.[1] Significant insights into the process of attitude change, the diffusion of attitudes, the formation of new social norms, and the development of new conceptions of self and role have stemmed from "immigrant studies." Furthermore, the physical movement has important implications for reference group theory, involving, as it does, changes of milieu, conflicts of norms, and opportunities for the development of new reference groups.

The tide of immigration to the United States from abroad has long since decreased from its former volume. Such studies as *The Polish Peasant*,[2] *The Ghetto*,[3] and *Old World Traits Transplanted*[4] have been relegated to the dubious status of "classics." Yet opportunities to study the effects of migration, in the context of reference group theory, are still abundant. The migration of people within our borders goes on apace. Since it is the role of the migrant as a newcomer, as well as his particular cultural or racial characteristics, which determines his behavior, the native-born, internal migrant constitutes a profitable subject for research.

During the lush years of high industrial productivity, which began about 1940, there has been a fairly steady flow of workers from the rural South to the industrial centers of the North, such as Chicago and Detroit.

Reprinted from *Social Forces*, 32, no. 1 (October, 1953), pp. 66–69, by permission of the author and the publisher.

Between 1947 and 1949 the writer studied certain aspects of the adjustment of a group of rural, southern, white laborers to life in the Near West Side of Chicago. The central questions in this research were: 1) Do these native white migrants come to constitute, to any extent, a distinct sub-group in the area of settlement in Chicago? and 2) To what extent, and in what ways, are they able to resolve the conflict between their "southern" attitudes towards Negroes and northern, urban norms and patterns of Negro-white relations?

During the period of field research, 150 southern white migrants were interviewed and the actual behavior of these and many other southern whites was observed. Non-southerners and Negroes who were part of the social world of the migrants, including plant managers, foremen, policemen, teachers, bartenders, and other workers, were also interviewed.

The southern whites were members of many small "clusters" of migrants concentrated in an ethnically heterogeneous portion of the Near West Side. The majority of them came from farms and small towns in the South Central States, especially northwestern Tennessee. Although these people were known as "hillbillies" in Chicago, few of them came from mountainous areas and they regarded the name as a misnomer.

The pattern of settlement of the southern whites suggested that they constituted, to some extent, a definite sub-group in the population of the area. Ecological factors partially accounted for their concentration. The Near West Side is an area characterized by the availability of cheap, furnished flats and easy access to industrial plants, and hence is attractive to in-migrants seeking "blue collar" work. In-group ties, carried over from southern communities of origin, also contributed to the development of spatial concentration, however. Newcomers from the South consistently tended to settle near relatives or friends who had migrated earlier. Often one of the important motives for migration itself was encouragement from earlier migrants.

The fact that the somewhat derogatory and often much-resented group label, "hillbilly," was applied to the migrants also pointed to their existence as a distinct group, even as a quasi minority. It was found that a vague, but recognizable, stereotype of the southern white migrant was held by many non-southerners, and that the so-called "hillbillies" were regarded as a distinct, cohesive, ethnic group. While little hostility toward them was discovered, they were generally regarded by non-southern whites as a culturally inferior group. This was especially true in the case of some employers who consciously avoided hiring "hillbillies."

In turn, the southern whites themselves exhibited definite group consciousness. This group consciousness was manifest not only in verbalizations but in the selection of associates. Patronage of the "hillbilly tavern," a gathering place for southern whites during hours of leisure, constituted a form of voluntary segregation.

Of most significance in the context of reference group theory was the "hillbillies'" conception of their own status in the Near West Side. This conception clearly reflected the subjects' comparison of their position in Chicago with the one which they had enjoyed in the South.

Contrary to many stereotyped conceptions of the southern rural migrant, these people were not indigent "po' white trash." They defined themselves, and were regarded in their home communities, as respectable, honest, "working class people." More important, they were members of the dominant ethnic group in a system organized along one axis—white and Negro. Finally, they were established members of small, relatively friendly and intimate communities.

In Chicago, they found themselves only one group in a mosaic of diverse ethnic groups—Old Americans, Irish, Italians, Mexicans, and Negroes. The fact that they were white, native-born, and Protestant lost some of its prestige value in an area dominated culturally and politically by Italian-Americans, most of them Catholic and many of them foreign-born. Negroes, while subject to many subtle forms of discrimination in Chicago, still possessed far more freedom and power than they could enjoy in the rural South. Comparing their position *vis-à-vis* "foreigners" and Negroes in Chicago and in the South, the southern whites felt a relative loss of status which intensified their defensive group consciousness.

The impersonality and anonymity of many types of social relationships in the northern city stood in sharp contrast to the friendly intimacy of the small southern town. As a result, the *laissez-faire* attitude of the city folk was interpreted by the "hillbillies" as evidence of hostility. The term "hillbilly," even when used in jest, was often perceived as a derogatory group label, a slur. Individual altercations between southerners and members of other ethnic groups were frequently perceived as intergroup conflicts. To the feeling that they, as southern whites, were a disadvantaged group was thus added the belief that they were a disliked group. This was true in spite of the fact that only slight hostility to the southern whites as a group was discovered even among the Italians, identified by the "hillbillies" as their worst enemies.

This defensive group consciousness did not, however, result in the development of in-group organization of a formal type. But the "hillbillies," preoccupied with making a living, regarding the South as home, and suspicious of non-southerners, constituted a marginal and unstable element in the institutions and associations of the area. The city church did not perform the social function of community integration for them that the rural church did, and they tended to develop a "vacation attitude" towards church participation. Church leaders who expected these white Protestants to be a source of new strength for their churches were disappointed and bewildered by the failure of the southern whites to continue their church participation after migration. In the schools, the "hillbilly" children constituted an identifiable group but presented no special problems other than that of mobility. The reputation of the "hillbillies" for instability, more than for lack of education or industrial experience, caused them to be regarded by employers as a marginal group of laborers who were conveniently available when there was a shortage of other labor, but who were not as desirable as local workers. On the other hand, the defensive group consciousness of the southerners, and their desire to feel superior to "foreign" workers, combined perhaps with a suspicion that they did not occupy a superior status, led them to create an entirely unrealistic picture of their position in industry. Rather than recognizing their marginal position, they conceived of themselves as a highly desirable and superior type of labor, and prided themselves on the very traits of mobility and independence which employers found most objectionable.

Thus it may be said that the southern whites felt themselves to be in, but not of, the Near West Side community. The southern community of origin continued to be home and its norms were still praised as the best, even when they could not be followed. Yet, despite this transient psychology and the persistent loyalty to the home community, few "hillbillies" actually returned to the South to stay; instead, irregular going back and forth, regulated by employment opportunities in Chicago, was the pattern. Detached from their native milieu but imperfectly assimilated in their new membership groups, these people were truly marginal.

The relationship of the southern whites to Negroes in Chicago revealed not only the persistence of old group norms but the development of new patterns of behavior in response to new situations. The "hillbillies" constantly praised the southern pattern of racial segregation and deplored the fact that Negroes were "taking over Chicago." In most of their behavior, however, they made a peaceful, if reluctant, accommodation to northern urban patterns.

This is not to imply, however, that this accommodation necessarily involved a reduction of prejudice. It involved, instead, substitution of the private, informal, and indirect techniques of discrimination, characteristic of race relations in the North, for the public, formal, and direct manifestations of prejudice found in the South.[5] The southern white who moves to the northern city does not move from a prejudiced society to an unprejudiced society; rather, he moves from one pattern of discrimination into another. Furthermore, in the transition from one milieu to another he becomes a different person. In the words of B. Schrieke:

However much a paradox it may seem, the foreigner outside of his traditional environment is not a typical member of his group. . . . The traveller is not a normal specimen of his group, for he is without the typical social control, i.e., the inner compulsion to conform to the prevailing standards of his community.[6]

Because of the existence of informal but effective techniques of segregation in Chicago, the problem of adjusting to the new pattern of race relations was alleviated for the southerners. Yet the great majority of them still felt that the northern pattern was one of the features of living in Chicago which they disliked the most. There were still many situations in which segregation and white supremacy could not be maintained. In such situations the "hillbillies" usually acquiesced, although not without some reluctance. The reasons for this accommodation show clearly the conflict of group norms which confronts the migrant.

A common explanation of the fact that the southern white could not act towards the Negro in Chicago as he did in the South was that different customs prevailed in the North and that they could not be changed by the southern white. This did not mean that the "hillbillies" had come to like the customs, or that they would modify their behavior in the South when they returned. But that they did accept the northern way is shown in statements such as the following one:

One thing I don't like about Chicago is the colored. I don't want to do anything mean to them, but I want to be able to let them alone. But you can't do that up here. When you're in Rome you have to do as the Romans do. I've kind of got used to sitting next to 'em and eating in resturants with 'em, but I don't like it. I wouldn't expect to do it in the South, but up here you have to.

There was also the feeling that Chicago was not "our city" and that it was not incumbent upon the individual southerner to support and enforce an etiquette of race relations. A woman who had lived in Chicago for twenty years said:

There's nothing you can do about the way the niggers are up here. We're up here in their country and we can't do anything. We have to do what these people up here do, even if we don't like it.

Moreover, the "hillbillies" were quick to perceive the different legal status of the Negro in Chicago and in the South. Many things which they noted were interpreted as evidence that the Negro had equal rights with the white man, or that he even had a preferred status before the law, such as the fact that police protection was sometimes afforded Negroes moving into white neighborhoods. Hence fear of running afoul of the law was the principal deterrent to starting trouble with Negroes.

Another deterrent to forthright adoption of a southern attitude towards Negroes was fear of physical retaliation. The Negro population of Chicago is concentrated in large population aggregates massed in "Black ghettoes." Many Negroes in Chicago will protest assertions of white supremacy, sometimes with violence. As a result, the "hillbillies" not only felt that it was unsafe to assert their ideas of superiority; some felt insecure in the presence of large numbers of Negroes.

Part of the feeling of lack of power to control the Negroes was based on the southerners' perception of the impersonality and heterogeneity of the white population and the lack of consensus regarding "the Negro's place." These factors are made explicit in the following statement.

> I can't see that you can do anything about the niggers up here. You see, in the South you can count on collaboration. You know that other people feel like you do, and if you start anything you can count on them. But up here you can't depend on that. You can't be sure that people will back you up, and you might even get hurt if you started something.

While the southern whites protested against the necessary compromises with southern norms, the changes in overt behavior were sometimes accompanied by changes in attitude. These changes were slight, it is true, and did not indicate a general reorientation towards Negroes. But they did occur, as is shown in these somewhat paradoxical remarks:

> There's niggers living in the house with us now—we're the only white family there. The landlady has tried to get us out, but she ain't give us no eviction notice and I ain't fixing to move. She wants to put niggers in my place, but my money is just as good as theirs. I can't find me another place to live. But it ain't so bad. Some of those niggers are better than some of the white people that used to live there. Hell, I got out my knife and started to kill the first one that moved in there, but then I found out he was a nigger I knew. He's a good southern nigger and he stays in his place. You know, in the South we make 'em stay in their place.

It is significant that such changes were, however, almost always specific to a particular situation, or area of contact, and did not lead directly to changes in attitudes concerning contact with Negroes in other situations. Eighteen southern whites out of the 150 interviewed were actually living in close physical proximity to Negroes—three of them living in the same house with them. Yet 15 of the 18 still tried to avoid contact with Negroes in at least one type of situation—work, school, or in the "hillbilly taverns." The writer knew many "hillbilly" men who were regular patrons of a "hillbilly tavern" in which a Negro was more likely to be beaten up than served, but who regularly ate lunch in a non-segregated restaurant next door.

In summary: lacking leadership, organization, and consensus in an area where life is highly impersonal and individualistic, the southerners saw no effective way of giving overt expression to their dissatisfaction with the pattern of race relations. The absence of legal sanctions for segregation and other assertions of white supremacy, and an exaggerated conception of Negro strength and unity over against white "weakness" and disunity, constituted powerful deterrents to overt and aggressive action in distasteful situations. While there were some indications of a slight shift of attitudes in the direction of greater friendliness towards Negroes in specific situations, this did not constitute a general reorientation towards Negroes as a group, nor were these new attitudes necessarily carried over into other situations of contact. Necessary, but distasteful, compromises with the cherished reference group norms were usually rationalized with the idea, "Chicago is not our home—when in Rome we must do as the Romans do."

Yet we may suspect that, in spite of themselves, the "hillbillies" were gradually developing new reference groups as they conformed more and more to northern urban patterns of behavior. An unconscious revelation of this process may be seen in the rather amusing comment of a southern woman:

> You know, the last time I was in Tennessee I went to a restaurant. They served colored, but they made 'em go in the back door and eat in the kitchen. I said to my husband, "That sure does look funny after you've lived in Chicago, doesn't it?"

NOTES

1. W. I. Thomas and Florian Znaniecki, *The Polish Peasant in Europe and America* (Boston: Richard G. Badger, 1920).

2. *Ibid.*

3. Louis Wirth, *The Ghetto* (Chicago: University of Chicago Press, 1928).

4. Robert E. Park and Herbert A. Miller, *Old World Traits Transplanted* (New York: Harper and Brothers, 1921).

5. Louis Wirth, "The Price of Prejudice," *Survey Graphic*, XXXVI (January 1947), 19.

6. B. Schrieke, *Alien Americans* (New York: The Viking Press, 1936), p. 73.

Mortality and Morbidity

Introduction

With regard to the three dynamic aspects of population it is probably
accurate to assert that sociologists and other social scientists have
tended to focus most of their attention on migration and fertility, while
giving much less attention to mortality. This relative lack of attention
to mortality is probably best understood if we recognize at the outset
that death (and ill health) are influenced most immediately and
directly by biological or medical factors. If we consider the major decreases in the death rates of most societies through the last century, it
appears that the single most important factor producing these decreases
has been the application of advancing medical knowledge. It might be
added, somewhat parenthetically, that there is some evidence that longevity (or length of life) is related to inherited genetic characteristics,
thus introducing another important nonsocial variable.

It seems, then, that the principal factors that explain variations in
the death rate are in the biological/medical realm rather than in the
social or cultural realm. This places many questions relating to mortality
and morbidity outside of the natural domain of the social scientist,
whose special competence is studying the effects of social organization
and culture.

Despite these qualifying remarks, there are some cultural and social factors that appear to be clearly related to death rates. Consider that, historically at least, rural people have enjoyed a greater life expectancy than urban people. The underlying reason for the higher mortality of the city probably lies in the high density of the urban population, with its accompanying unsanitary and unhealthful living conditions. Perhaps the higher death rate in cities could also be related to the increased tension and pressure that presumably characterize urban life, but this interpretation is speculative and is not based on firm evidence.

More recent evidence on rural-urban mortality differentials indicates that in modern industrial societies the city may actually have an advantage in controlling the death rate up to the ages of thirty to thirty-five.[1] However, the advantage shifts back to the rural areas after thirty-five. The etiology of this difference must await further research on the subject.

One of the more interesting social characteristics related to the death rate is that of marital status. This relationship seems to have an exceptional persistence and consistency, being found in all countries where such data are available. Married persons have lower death rates than single persons, who in turn have lower rates than widowed or divorced persons. This relationship holds, of course, even when age is held constant.

The interpretation of the relationship between marital status and death rate is open to some discussion. Probably the most important explanatory factor lies in the fact that the selection of a marriage partner is not a random matter, but is rather a selective process in which people choose from among alternatives. Thus it would seem that those people in the population who are socially and physically less acceptable would have a smaller chance of being selected for marriage. One of the factors that is likely to contribute to a person's acceptability as a marriage mate is good health. Thus those people in the population who have poorer health are less likely to enter into marriage, so it would follow that the single, never-married group will have a higher proportion of people in poorer health, which would lead to a higher mortality rate. As an additional factor contributing to the greater longevity of the

---

[1] Warren S. Thompson and David T. Lewis, *Population Problems*, 5th ed. (New York: McGraw-Hill Book Co., 1965), p. 364.

married, it has been suggested that they are better cared for and probably live more regular and healthful lives. Aside from the single, never-married group, there are the widowed and divorced, who have even higher death rates, with the divorced having a higher rate than the widowed. Both widowhood and the divorced status probably are indicative of some kind of instability and possibly also physical ill health. One indication of poorer physical and mental health among the widowed and divorced would be their higher suicide rate—which, of course, at the same time increases their general death rate. Probably even more significant is the fact that both divorce and widowhood are not evenly distributed in the population, but are found disproportionately among the lower socioeconomic classes. There are more marriage-partner deaths and more separations and divorces among the lower social classes, and as we will indicate in more detail below, the lower social classes have a higher death rate than the upper classes. It follows, then, that the widowed and divorced would have higher death rates simply by virtue of their socioeconomic status.

Without a doubt the single most important social factor related to mortality is social class, or an individual's socioeconomic status. Social classes may be thought of as segments or strata of the population of a society having different amounts of economic goods and political power and different life styles. It has been said that one indication of the presence of social classes is that people in the different classes do not have the same "life chances." Life chances may be such things as the chance to enjoy comfortable living, good health, and the greatest of life chances, life itself. There is ample evidence that people in the different classes of our society do have different life chances, including a different chance for life itself. When sociologists carry out social-class analysis they typically use some convenient measure of class level such as occupation or income, or, as in one study that we shall describe below, the average (median) rental value or family income of city census tracts. There are of course complicating factors such as race which are also related to social class, and thus we often examine the effect of social class for the different racial groups (white and nonwhite).

Sociologists at the University of Chicago have been studying the mortality (and fertility) rates in that city for a number of decades, and their research provides a convenient illustration of how much social class and race influence the mortality rate. The study we draw on here is a summary report by Evelyn M. Kitagawa and Philip M. Hauser titled "Trends in Differential Fertility and Mortality in a Metropolis—Chicago,"[2] which analyzes mortality data for the city of Chicago from 1930 to 1950 by socioeconomic status, sex, and race. Socioeconomic status was indicated by the median rental for 1930 and 1940 and median family income for 1950. For this analysis the 935 census tracts of Chicago were divided into five socioeconomic categories. Some of the generalizations following from their analysis are:

1. For each racial group and each sex group in all three census periods—1930, 1940, and 1950—there was a consistent relationship between socioeconomic class and expectation of life. As the socioeconomic level of census tracts went down, the life expectancy of the residents diminished. There were no exceptions, and in fact an earlier paper, published some years previously, which had taken the analysis back to 1920, showed the same results. In 1930 the white males and females in the highest socioeconomic group had a life expectancy eleven to twelve years longer than the lowest status white group, and twenty-three to twenty-four years longer than the lowest status nonwhite group —nearly a quarter of a century difference in life expectancy! In 1950, the life expectancy of the white males and females in the highest status group exceeded that of the white males and females in the lowest status group by eight and six years respectively, and exceeded that of the lowest status nonwhites by thirteen and fourteen years.

2. Infant mortality rates also varied by socioeconomic status. In 1930 the infant mortality rate for white babies in the lowest status group was 125 percent higher than that for babies in the highest status group. By 1950 this difference had decreased, with the low-status whites having infant mortality rates about 40 percent higher. It is of interest to note that for the nonwhites the differences in infant mortality for the high- and low-status groups were not so pronounced or consistent. This inconsistency may reflect another feature of urban social life: racial segregation. At least one study of infant mortality has implicated the segregation of Negroes in black ghettos as a factor contributing to infant mortality.[3]

3. When one considers the total effect of socioeconomic and racial differences on mortality rates in the city of Chicago, the results are

---

[2] In *Contributions to Urban Sociology*, edited by Ernest W. Burgess and Donald J. Bogue (Chicago: University of Chicago Press, 1964), pp. 59–85.

[3] Alfred Yankauer, "The Relationship of Fetal and Infant Mortality to Residential Segregation," *American Sociological Review*, 15 (October, 1950), pp. 644–48.

astounding. In order to demonstrate the impact that race and social-class position have on a person's life chances, one may ask the following question: How many deaths would not have occurred if the death rates of the highest status group of whites had prevailed in the total population? In 1950 one-third of all deaths in Chicago would not have occurred if all people had had the same death rate as the highest status white groups. In 1930, 41 percent of the deaths in Chicago would have been avoided. If one examines what would have happened if the non-whites in Chicago had had the same death rates as the highest status white group, the results are startling. As late as 1950, *50 percent of all nonwhite deaths would not have occurred if they had had the death rates of the high-status white group. In 1930 more than two-thirds of the nonwhite deaths would not have occurred.*[4]

The data from the study by Kitagawa and Hauser are drawn from only the single city of Chicago, and while social-class data are not available for the entire U.S. population, there are U.S. data on race and mortality which indicate that nonwhites continue to have a distinctly higher death rate than whites. At all ages and for both sexes the death rate for nonwhites exceeds that for whites. In 1965 the average life expectation at birth for whites was 71.0 years, while for nonwhites it was 64.1 years.[5]

In this section on mortality the first two papers illustrate primarily how the culture of a group or subgroup may influence mortality. In the first of these papers, "An Approach to the Cultural Base of Infant Mortality in India," Dr. Alfred Yankauer begins by discussing the significance of infant mortality, particularly as it relates to technological development, and then goes on to discuss the factors in the material and nonmaterial culture which influence infant mortality. Of great interest in Dr. Yankauer's discussion is the variety of nonmaterial cultural elements found in India which have at least the potential of influencing the infant mortality rate. Focusing on the processes of "the ingestion of nutrients, the egestion of wastes, and the reproduction of the species," the author specifies a number of attitudes, opinions, and behavioral practices existing in the Indian culture which are very likely to have

---

[4] Burgess and Bogue, eds., *Contributions to Urban Sociology,* p. 81.

[5] U.S. Bureau of the Census, *Statistical Abstract of the United States: 1967,* 88th ed., prepared under the direction of Edwin D. Goldfield (Washington: U.S. Government Printing Office, 1967), p. 53.

an influence on infant mortality, particularly postneonatal mortality—deaths occurring between one month and one year of age. Although the author offers some general suggestions for making changes in the non-material culture, it is difficult to escape the feeling that many of these beliefs and practices will be difficult to change. On the other hand, one of the most significant factors that may contribute to changing cultural values is the fact that there is a nearly universal positive value placed on life itself. If in educational programs the cultural practices (representing beliefs and values) can be placed in juxtaposition to the value of life, then some changes may take place in Indian culture. While it may seem that people in other cultures should be "rational" about these matters, perhaps as Americans we might recognize that we retain in our culture a positive valuation of such things as fast and highly powered automobiles even in the face of the mortality that frequently results from their use. Perhaps the use of tobacco and its relationship to mortality is too obvious an example of nonrationality in our own culture, but it certainly makes the point clear that cultural values have a tenacity that makes them difficult to change, even in the face of objective evidence.

The second paper in this section deals with some of the objective evidence relating cancer to smoking, but more important for our interests is the fact that the paper by Saxon Graham, "New Clues to the Causes of Cancer," demonstrates again how mortality and morbidity vary among social and ethnic groups. Using an epidemiological approach, Graham reviews how some of the different kinds of cancer are found disproportionately in certain ethnic and nationality groups, thus suggesting that some cultural practice of that group is influencing their mortality.

The final paper in this section, "How a Population Ages or Grows Younger," by Ansley Coale, begins from a perspective that is quite different from the other two. In this paper mortality is viewed as an independent variable and the author asks, "What effect does a decrease in the mortality rate have on the age composition of the population?" It may be noted here again that this paper is an example of demographic analysis, as defined in Section I, and it is as much concerned with population composition as with mortality.

Because the principal point being made by Coale in this paper is somewhat contrary to what common sense would suggest, it deserves some special mention. What Coale is saying is that the prolongation of life by the reduction of death rates may have the effect of making the population younger rather than older. In the case of the United States, if the risks of death that prevailed in 1900 had continued unchanged, the average age of the population would be greater today than it is— the proportion of children would be less, and the proportion of persons over sixty-five would be greater.

Coale provides a detailed explanation of why this would be so, and we will not repeat the entire discussion here. But the key to understanding his discussion depends upon a clear recognition that whenever the death rate of a society goes down, it is primarily because changes in mortality have occurred at two quite different points in the life cycle: at infancy and at advanced ages. Changes in U.S. mortality (life expectation at birth) have taken place to a great extent because of improvements in our infant mortality rates. The point is most easily grasped if one remembers that any baby that lives when it previously would have died is the same as another conception and birth. Furthermore, within twenty years that child will be likely to be producing babies (under still better infant mortality conditions), thus adding again to the younger ages in the population. It is in this manner that the population typically gets younger as the mortality rate goes down.

15

An Approach to
the Cultural Base of
Infant Mortality in India

Alfred Yankauer, M.D.

Not you alone proud truths of the world,
Nor you alone ye facts of modern science,
But myths and fables of eld, Asia's, Africa's fables,
The far darting beams of the spirit, the unloos'd dreams,
The deep diving bibles and legends . . .
  —*Passage to India*
  WALT WHITMAN

In 1909, at a time when the infant mortality rate in England and Wales was above 120 and some forty years after William Farr had demonstrated that tremendous variations in infant mortality were directly related to urban socio-economic differentials, Sir Arthur Newsholme wrote: "Infant mortality is the most sensitive index we possess of social welfare and sanitary administration, especially among urban conditions."[1] These are words which have been quoted often and thoughts which have been enshrined in textbooks. Not only medicine and public health but allied disciplines have been taught to think in these terms. Yet there are good reasons today to take a longer and harder look at them—first to be sure that their meaning is clear, and secondly to qualify their dogmatic assertions in the light of more recent observations on mortality rates and other indices of technological development.

The concept of "social welfare" is value laden. Therefore it takes on different shapes in the minds of men depending upon the values transmitted to them by their different cultures. Such shapes may not only differ,

Reprinted from *Population Review*, 3, no. 2 (July, 1959), pp. 39–51, by permission of the author and the publisher.

but may even diametrically oppose each other, as, for example, the shape of the central institution of human social life, the family, in India and in the U.S.A. Who is to say whether "social welfare" is better served by the human closeness and sense of duty engendered by growing up as a member of a large, joint, kinship-rooted family than by the individual freedom and the stress on initiative which are more characteristic of the small companionship family of the West? Or, in converse, that "social welfare" is worse served by the dependency and the intense but narrow social obligations that appear to be associated with the joint family than by the restlessness, tensions and hurry that seem to characterize the Western family?

This report will point up ways in which social institutions (such as the family), patterns of behaviour, and ways of thinking are etiologically related to infant mortality in India (as in all other countries). Therefore, it is important to recognize that the values of culture in their higher sense, the contributions made toward fulfillment, purpose and contentment in life, are not the subject of discussion. Infant mortality is no measure of social welfare in this sense. What Newsholme meant by social welfare is more comparable to what is now called technological development, or material prosperity, or social welfare services. This is but one expression of the Western industrialized, materialistic society of the twentieth century. There are many other expressions of this same society which can be judged inimical to social welfare, the most insistent and threatening of these being its propensity for self-destruction in a cloud of atomic dust. However, this same society has thus far succeeded in preventing premature death—particularly in infancy and early childhood—to an extent undreamed of by any previous order of civilization. The characteristics which have enabled it to do so are both physical, in the sense of a favourable balance of natural resources, scientific knowledge and population, and mental, in the sense of a culture or way of behaviour and human interrelationships which could develop such resources and apply such knowledge efficiently and rapidly.

Whether the infant mortality rate is the most sensitive index of this type of technological development, however, is open to question. A number of observers in recent years have pointed out the key position of the 1–4-year age mortality rate in this connection.[2] Table 1 compares current mortality rates of different age groups from birth through 14 years of age in Madras City and in the U.S.A.[3] It will be observed that the greatest contrast in rates is in the 1–4-year age group, followed by the 1–11-month segment of infant mortality rather than its total. There are other vital statistics which are sensitive indices of technological development: weight at birth, the ratio of neonatal to post-neonatal mortality, the average expectation of life at birth, even the age distribution of the population and the age distribution of its deaths. There is probably little point in arguing as to which of these indices is the most sensitive. All are useful reflections of differences and contribute to a description of a nation's health problems.

TABLE 1.   Age-Specific Mortality Rates in U.S.A., 1954,
and in Madras City, 1954–1956

Age Group	Madras City	U.S.A.	Ratio: Madras/ U.S.A.
Under 1 month*	55	19.1	3.5
1–11 months*	87	7.5	11.5
Total under 1 year	142	26.6	5.4
1–4 years†	47	1.2	42.0
5–14 years†	4.6	0.5	9.2

*Rate per 1,000 live births may be considered fairly accurate for both U.S.A. and Madras City.
†Rate per estimated 1,000 children. Population estimate for Madras City based on age distribution of 10% sample of Madras State (1951 census) applied to estimated city total population, 1954–1956. Accuracy questionable.

THE INFANT MORTALITY RATE

The really compelling characteristic of infant mortality is its size, for more deaths occur during this first year than at any other equivalent period of time of the human life span. Although this is characteristic of nations in all stages of technological development, the contrast is vastly greater in underdeveloped areas. Thus, in Madras City, infant deaths in 1956 formed 28% of all deaths, while in New York State they formed only 5.3% of all deaths. This striking contrast is a reflection of the higher birth rate and the lower expectation of life, as well as the higher mortality in infancy in Madras.

It is conventional and convenient to separate the components of infant mortality into two parts: those whose origin lies in the natal, pre-natal or pre-conception period, and those which act upon the infant only after its birth. In general, deleterious pre-natal or natal forces cause death soon after birth so that even though medical certification of death may be incomplete or inaccurate, some insight into the relative importance of these components is obtained by examining the time of death in infancy. The most striking change which has occurred in these components in Western countries is the sharp decline in mortality after one month of age, a change which has not been paralleled in India nor in other nations whose technological development has remained under-privileged. This is illustrated in Figure 1, which compares the trend of infant mortality above and below one month of age in the U.S.A. for whites (relatively privileged class) and non-whites

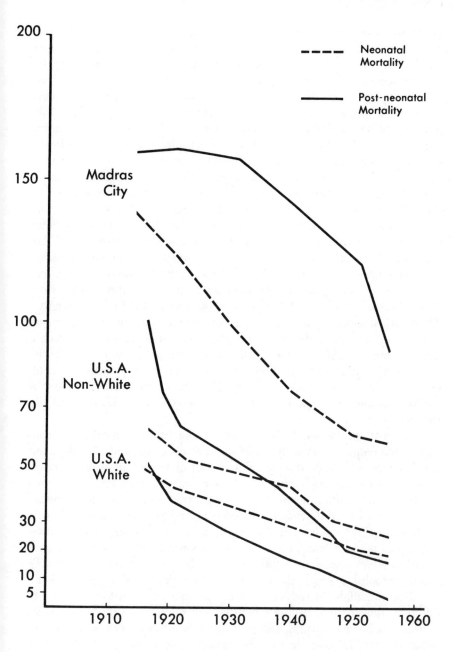

**FIGURE 1.   Neonatal and Post-neonatal Mortality Rates
per 1,000 Live Births in U.S.A. (White and Non-White)
and Madras City, 1915–1955**

(a relatively under-privileged class) with that of Madras City for the past 40 years. It will be observed that the decline in neonatal mortality is comparable for all three groups; the decline in post-neonatal mortality for American non-whites parallels that for whites, indicating that they have shared equally in the benefits of material prosperity, although their relative status is unchanged. (A precisely similar effect has been noted in the U.K. in trends of neonatal and post-neonatal mortality for social classes during the present century.[4]) In contrast, the post-neonatal mortality in Madras City has fallen no faster than its neonatal mortality and exceeds it to the same extent that it did forty years ago, so that, in a comparative sense, ground has actually been lost. The total infant mortality rate in Madras was thrice that of the U.S.A. in 1915. It was almost six times that of the U.S.A. in 1954. The fall in post-neonatal mortality since 1950 in Madras is of interest, but too short a time period is involved to know whether this trend will continue. From the point of view of rates, the situation in Madras today is comparable to that in England and Wales at the beginning of the twentieth century. During the nineteenth century infant mortality and the ratio of neonatal to post-neonatal deaths in Britain remained virtually stationary.[5] The drastic decline in post-neonatal deaths did not begin until 50 years ago.

Causes of infant deaths, although inaccurately reported, reflect a similar picture. In Madras these causes are reported today in virtually the same relative proportion as they were forty years ago,[6] whereas in all technologically developed countries the relative proportion of deaths ascribed to infections (particularly gastro-intestinal) has been drastically reduced.

In the West, the twentieth century has sometimes been called the century of the child. In the early 1900s social reform, economic development and the free milk and educational activities of the infant welfare movement supplemented each other to relieve poverty, hunger and overcrowding and to substitute rational infant care for traditional practice. Together with advances in the science of medicine and public health and their application, this combination of circumstances accounts for the precipitous fall in post-neonatal mortality in Western countries. All these factors were interdependent and cross-fertilized each other to such an extent that it would be foolish to emphasize the exclusive importance of any one of them.

The potentials for reducing infant mortality in India today are quite different from those of Britain fifty years ago. Quite apart from differences in tradition, history, natural resources, and relationships with other nations, influences hard to compare, two obvious differences exist. In the first place there is more knowledge about the cause, cure and prevention of disease to apply; and in the second place the government is in a stronger position to form policy and program and to translate it into action. This last difference has come about because of the increasing growth and acceptance of the idea of "the welfare state" which has accompanied technological development all over the world. In India this is manifest not only in the deliberate planning and controls of the Central Government, but in the stated objectives of the controlling Congress Party and its leaders. Although there may be some disadvantages to such a role for government, the potential for more rapid change which this role offers far outweighs them. In fact, one may with some legitimacy ask why improvement in infant mortality has not been more striking and rapid up to the present time. The remainder of this discussion will focus primarily on the post-neonatal segment of infant mortality, since it is this segment which has shown the least tendency to change in India.

Basically the causes of the excess infant post-neonatal mortality in India are to be found in the nutritional status of its infants and in their over-exposure to large doses of pathogenic micro-organisms. This is obvious to the most casual observer and needs no special survey to substantiate it. These two basic causes of death supplement and reinforce each other. Nutritional privation lowers resistance to infection and infection accentuates nutritional privation.

Purely medical methods and means, of course, have no bearing on the prevention, and little relevance to the permanent cure, of nutritional privation. With respect to infant deaths due to infections, the situation is more complicated. Immunizing agents against a number of specific diseases exist: pertussis, poliomyelitis, diphtheria, tetanus, tuberculosis, and small-pox. Mass immunization will effectively prevent deaths from these diseases and is economically sound. Malaria eradication is also economically sound. However, the number of infant deaths that would be prevented as a result of immunization and mosquito-killing campaigns is relatively small (except in areas of high malarial endemicity). The vast excess of deaths due to the common diarrheal and respiratory infections would remain untouched by such campaigns.

Early, thorough and adequate treatment of these common infections could theoretically prevent most fatal outcomes. However, the expense of facilities, drugs, and other therapeutic agents and the enormous numbers of trained personnel needed to carry out such a program would be beyond the dreams of the wildest planner. Furthermore, it is unsound to concentrate energy on repair work if there are ways of avoiding damage in the first place.

The application of modern methods of sanitary science to water supply, human waste disposal and food production would surely prevent many of these excess deaths. However, such application is also hampered by the inordinate expense of facilities, the shortage of trained personnel and traditional modes of behaviour which militate against the use of facilities even when provided. It would, however, be most useful to be able to establish priorities in the approach to disease control by sanitation. These could be set up if modern epidemiologic and bacteriologic methods were applied to the study of the cause, source and spread of infections in India. Such studies have not been carried out and one can only guess at the nature of the infecting agent and speculate about which of its several possible channels of spread are most important. The experiences of other countries cannot be drawn upon except as methodological models.

CULTURAL FACTORS

If medical and sanitary approaches to reducing infant mortality are of limited value, other approaches must be sought. When viewed broadly, the basic causes of the excess infant deaths in India, under-nutrition and over-infection, possess a material and a non-material component. The material component exists because of Indian shortages in resources, capital and technological know-how. The non-material component exists because of the human behaviour, human relationships, motivations and values which compose India's culture. From the material point of view the problem of under-nutrition exists because there is not enough food produced and distributed, not enough money to invest or enough technological know-how to apply modern methods of food production and distribution, not enough income per family to permit purchase of an adequate diet, etc. From the non-material point of view, however, both the producer and the consumer of food have a choice even within the restricted economic range imposed upon them. The choice they make is not calculated to get the most nutritional value out of a product of comparable cost or availability. It is based purely and simply upon traditionally learned behaviour and the symbolic significance of particular kinds of food in the Indian scale of values. Considerable thought and attention have been given to the material components of these bases of disease and death in infancy and to the development of programs which seek to eliminate them. In contrast, relatively little attention has been paid to the non-material components and to the deliberate development of a program to modify them in such a way that they no longer contribute to disease and death. Although in this discussion attention is devoted mainly to cultural factors affecting post-neonatal deaths, the same reasoning and approach could also be applied to neonatal deaths, but the specific examples and operational effects might differ.

It is significant that the cultural values and practices of India which (whatever their other significance) contribute to infant disease and death center around the three primal characteristics of all living matter: the ingestion of nutrients, the egestion of wastes, and the reproduction of the species. This is an indication of the deep-seated holds, their roots in early childhood experience, and their resistance to change. It is relatively easy to point out what they are, but relatively difficult to know how to change them. Yet change is occurring and will continue to occur in these cultural values and practices. Such change can be hastened by community action, and planning such action could well receive as much attention as planning to raise the material level of living.

Any discussion of the relationship of culture to health in India is necessarily limited by the fact that cultural variations exist in different parts of the country and different segments of the population. Most of the features to be discussed have been observed in Madras. However, many, if not most of them, are common to other parts of India, and to all segments of the population as evidenced by a number of written reports.[7] The discussion is also handicapped by the author's limited period of observation and limited ability to observe, understand and interpret. This is a more serious criticism. It can only be hoped that the discussion will stimulate further study and work in this important field. The details presented (whether accurate or inaccurate) are less important than the point of view they are used to illustrate.

FOOD

Cultural values and practices related to the ingestion of nutrients bear upon infant deaths by influencing the amount of a nutrient ingested and its absorption (thus affecting body needs directly) and by causing food to become a channel for the introduction of pathogens. The amount of nutrients ingested and absorbed is influenced by the following practices:

1. *The custom of introducing solid foods at a relatively late age.* Breast milk contains relatively little Vitamin D, insufficient Vitamin C and virtually no iron. Beyond the age of six months the quantity of breast milk is generally insufficient to meet the infant's caloric and protein needs. The scarcity and high cost of cow's milk (the most desirable major additional source of protein at this age) make it all the more important that solid foods containing protein, iron and vitamins be started at the very latest by six months of age. In Madras such a practice is quite uncommon. Prior to their first birthday only one out of two children will generally have received any food other than breast or cow's milk. Even at a year and a half a few children will have not yet been introduced to other foods.

2. *Practices which dilute or destroy nutrients.* Milk is commonly diluted when given to infants and children, and the degree of dilution is

great and bears little relationship to age. This practice is harmful insofar as it deludes mothers into equating quantity with quality, a delusion most commonly encountered when the expensive, well-advertised proprietary baby milk mixtures or food are being used. The practice of diluting milk may be economically rather than culturally determined, but this is by no means always true. Occasionally an artificially fed infant is being given a formula so dilute that he cannot possibly take it all and the full food value of the milk is lost to him. The prolonged cooking of food, often long before its consumption, tends to destroy its accessory food values, although without effect on other elements. Most children under two years of age receiving foods other than milk are fed out of the family pot, rather than given food especially prepared for them. Thus this is a relevant factor. The precise importance of these particular practices is difficult if not impossible to measure.

3. *Practices which interfere with the absorption of nutrients in food.* Practices which hasten bowel evacuation are the routine administration of castor oil and the use of irritating spices, chillies and peppers in food offered to children. The administration of castor oil daily or bi-weekly is quite common in Madras, and, as previously mentioned, feeding children from the family pot is customary. Like the previous factors of dilution and destruction, the importance of these practices is purely conjectural, although not illogically so.

4. *Customs, beliefs and practices influencing the choice of foods.* These constitute a wide and relatively unexplored spectrum of factors, whose details seem to vary (often to conflict with each other) according to geography, caste, and family. Sometimes even individuals of the same family will fail to agree upon them. Although details (such as the classification of a particular food) may vary, these factors do possess a number of common denominators:

(a) The system of classifying foods as "hot" or "cold," a practice prevalent in the folk belief of many parts of the world and incorporated in *Ayurveda*, influences choice not only because of the avoidance of certain "very hot" or "very cold" foods (particularly in babies) or the avoidance of too much of a series of hot or cold foods, but also because illnesses and their cures are also classified in terms of "hot" and "cold." Thus the presence of a mild diarrhea will tend to make for avoidance of "hot" and consumption of "cold" foods. Because of the enormous burden of illness in infancy, this latter practice has frequent scope for operation, even if other factors are considered less important. Children admitted to hospital for severe protein deprivation (kwashiorkor) have often been deliberately deprived of protein-containing foods because of some illness which by itself would not have been serious.

(b) Certain foods are apparently avoided because of what seems to be an imitative relationship to illness. In Madras, for example, it is commonly believed that ripe bananas cause diarrhea and that drinking water enhances diarrhea.

(c) Certain foods are deemed harmful only to particular classes of people, among whom lactating women and nursing infants are probably the most outstanding. Thus, meat or fish, although eaten by all other members of the family, will often not be given to the infant or young child.

(d) Although probably of relatively little significance, since it is practiced only by a small portion of the population, vegetarianism based on family tradition, religious custom, or moral conviction should also be listed as a factor influencing food choice. Of more significance is the religio-cultural status of cattle, a status which conflicts with their potential as a food source (beef) and a food producer (milk).[8]

(e) In almost every society certain foods are invested with a high degree of emotional and social significance whose meaning derives from early childhood experience and links closely with fundamental personality determinants. The strength and meaning may be very great and influence food choice proportionately, particularly when economic factors operate as well. In South India rice and rice eating must exist not only because of custom and the nature of the agricultural economy, but also because rice itself is invested with emotional values, associations and meanings. When the family budget permits, other foods will be consumed along with rice as part of a balanced diet. When the budget is limited, however (as is the case in the vast majority of families), foods other than rice will be sacrificed, regardless of their relative cost and nutritional value, in order to procure enough rice to achieve some degree of satisfaction from eating.

Food may also serve as a carrier of pathogenic micro-organisms. The manner in which food is prepared, stored, served and eaten has obvious relationships to the presence or absence of such organisms. In general, existing practices of food preparation tend to eliminate micro-organisms (viz., boiling of milk, customary purchase and storage of only small quantities of food, etc.). These practices also promote food preservation under tropical conditions. However, the use of fingers as eating utensils may facilitate the spread of micro-organisms in infants and children. This practice is undoubtedly less significant for adults, since what contaminates an individual's fingers is likely to enter his mouth regardless of how he eats. However, when combined with the fact that many adults and older siblings may feed the same child and that children are fed by others rather than allowed to feed themselves for a very much longer period of their life than in Western cultures, it seems possible that this custom may make some contribution to the excessive infections of infancy. Hands, banana leaves and tumblers are often rinsed with water before food contacts them. However, the extent of rinsing is unlikely to eliminate many micro-organisms. The practice of rinsing seems part of a larger trait, that of avoiding, eliminating or hiding from view the obviously offensive. Since it is not based upon an understanding of the germ theory of disease, it may sometimes do more harm than good. Thus the mother who boils milk before giving it to her baby may (after boiling) contaminate the milk by straining it through an unsterile rag to remove scum particles.

A final cultural factor which may affect infant mortality by way of food and infection is the method of feeding fluids to small infants. The Western observer cannot help but be impressed by the contrast between the infant held closely in arms, head up and comfortable, to suck freely at the breast, and the infant laid flat on its back, helplessly restricted by its mother, while she pours milk or other fluids into its crying mouth. Apart from the psychological trauma of this common feeding practice, the possibility of its contributing to respiratory infections because of the aspiration of milk or other food cannot be ignored. Unfortunately no postmortem studies specifically searching out aspiration pneumonia are available to test this hypothetical point.

HUMAN WASTES

Urinary wastes rarely are carriers of micro-organisms, whereas respiratory and gastro-intestinal waste products frequently carry pathogens. The spread of disease through such channels depends partly upon how these wastes (sputum and faeces) are disposed of and partly (since air is the only repository of expiration) upon how closely people live together. Closeness of living, to take the last factor first, is not determined solely by economic necessity. The joint family itself groups many under one roof and brings many adults in contact with one single infant, increasing the infant's exposure to germs. Some desire or need to live closely with others must account for the presence of densely packed village settlements in a rural economy which could as easily support isolated homes nearer the fields to be worked. In this sense culture contributes to overcrowding; the overexposure to infection in rural India is greater than in Western countries where families are small, infants are handled almost exclusively by their mothers, and individual dwelling units are occupied by fewer people in spite of the overwhelming urbanization of society.

Few could deny that promiscuous defecation and (to a lesser extent) expectoration, with the subsequent migration of pathogens to a new host via flies, water, dust, or food, constitute an important channel of disease spread in India. Although this chain can be broken at several places, the most obviously vulnerable point of attack is the behaviour of the human being himself. Mere provision of sanitary latrines is no solution to this problem, as field experience has shown.[9] For latrines to be used, traditional behaviour and attitudes must change as well.

The subject of defecation is not a topic of polite conversation. As an intimate body function, its discussion is apt to cause embarrassment. This is reflected by a general neglect of the human attitudes, motivations and associations with this act in medical, public health and social science literature. Even descriptive analyses of the act as it is followed by a community are singularly absent. Yet it would be useful to know something factual about place, time, efforts to cleanse or cover, if they are made, and other ascertainable details, and to relate actual practice to ancient ritual prescriptions or to expressed ideals. Casual observation in Madras City reveals that open places near water seem preferred; even when a segregated common spot that is cleansed out daily is used as a repository, faeces are rarely deposited in a covered pot or covered with earth, although either precaution would be quite feasible and desirable.

Far less is known about bowel attitudes and personality formation in India, although Carstairs[10] has some interesting things to say on this score. Yet if change in behaviour is sought it might be important to know more about these deeper associations also. One of the things which strikes a Western observer most forcibly is the "permissiveness" of toilet training in children, an attitude that can be characterized as psychologically healthy compared to the obsessional rigidity and emotional horror with which the Western parent generally approaches the subject. The relationship of this permissive attitude and the community personality which it expresses to the maintenance of community physical health and the spread of faecal-borne disease in India is worthy of further exploration.

SEX

Sexual intercourse is also taboo to polite discussion, although in recent years the urgent need to control population growth has caused medical and social science to focus attention on it. The act itself will not be considered here as it relates to spreading disease (venereal disease), but rather the organization and attitudes of society which have been built around the act in India.

High fertility and large family size must be considered an important contributory cause of infant mortality in the light of the under-privileged social and economic circumstances prevailing in India today. With a more favourable balance of material goods and habitable lands, these factors might be of negligible importance. As it is, in addition to other effects, they intensify (by dilution) the mass malnutrition and magnify (by concentration) the mass over-infection of infants and children. Cultural factors affecting fertility and family size in India have been discussed by others in more authoritative fashion than can be done here. Chandrasekhar,[11] for example, has pointed out that among other things, early and universal marriage, the banning of remarriage, the inferior position of women in society, and the difficulty of practicing contraception within joint family living conditions, all contribute to the problem.

One other factor which seems to have received relatively little attention in the literature is the relationship of the culturally defined purpose of the sexual act itself to fertility and family size. In Western society today sexual intercourse, by and large, is apt to be consciously seen as the culmination of deeply felt love between two human beings and as an emotional experience whose achievement is an end in itself, even though some segments of society would consider such a purpose immoral. In India, its purpose, as formulated by the culture in which it exists, appears to be more directly related to the production of children, so that it is not as apt to be viewed as an experience valuable in itself. The expressed desire of many Indian families to limit the number of children they produce, a fact revealed by various surveys,[12] is in seeming conflict with such an observation. However, if this observation is correct, it would merely point up an ambiguity in motivation and add another cultural factor to the list of those interfering with a program of population control.

In India the joint family and caste system are the cultural institutions within which sexual intercourse is permissible and desirable. Although these institutions may be fast changing, they have certainly not disappeared so that their possible relationships to infant mortality (apart from their contribution to high fertility and large family size) are worth considering. One contribution, the assemblage of many relatives in one household unit and the resultant overcrowding and facilitation of disease spread, has already been mentioned. A second, the custom of intracaste and subcaste marriage, may also contribute by producing more defective foetuses than would be produced by more exogamous mating. No data are available on this point, however, and it must remain conjectural. A final and equally conjectural point is the set of values and the view of life and interpersonal relationships which are transmitted to the growing Indian child through family, clan and (their extension) religion. In many small but obvious ways these values may affect infant mortality: by giving the purchase of a marriage gift for a relative a higher priority than purchasing needed medicine or food; by valuing the ritual purification of a dead body above the performance of a postmortem examination; by rendering performance of unplanned social obligations more important than the keeping of a planned medical appointment, etc. In a larger way, the disintegrating effect in today's world of the heritage of joint family, caste and religious philosophy on interpersonal relationships and the functioning of the adult Hindu personality and thus on infant mortality, as on all else, is perhaps less obvious. Among others, Carstairs, Panikkar, and Narain[13] have commented on this point, and it deserves notation at least in any discussion of the subject.

This brief catalogue of culturally conditioned practices and attitudes which of themselves contribute to infant mortality has necessarily accentuated the negative. Cultural practices and attitudes which favor infant survival, such as the almost universal breast feeding, the inevitable boiling of animal milk, the affection lavished on most children, etc., have not been discussed. It is important to bear this point in mind lest the impression be gained that all cultural attitudes and practices in India contribute to infant mortality. It should also be pointed out that Western medical practice is as capable of creating and perpetuating its own unscientific rituals and superstitions as any society. It is recognized today that beliefs once firmly preached, such as feeding by the clock and early toilet training, belong in the realm of prejudice rather than science. In the same way, some of the suggestions made earlier but unsupported by scientific observation, such as the harmfulness of castor oil and chillies or the practice of hand eating, may arise from unfounded prejudice.

CULTURAL CHANGE

The social institutions and the patterns of learned behaviour, attitude and feeling to which we give the name culture are as inseparable from the physical or material aspects of a society as the psyche and the soma of the individual man. Teleologically man's culture is a tool that enables him to extend his individual biological mastery of environment, but as his expenditure of energy for survival, food and shelter becomes less, the environment itself is altered and this in turn affects the pattern of culture. This has occurred most strikingly in Western society since the advent of mechanization and industrialization, with the result that the culture of the Western world has also become a tool that enables man to use and live with the machines he has created to master the physical aspects of his environment. Sometimes these machines themselves become a hazard to him, as with the automobile. Sometimes, when viewed from a universal frame, the cuturally transmitted behaviour of machine-centered man may seem ridiculous, as for example the compulsive need of a suburbanite to catch a train, to be at the office on time, to keep each appointment on schedule. Yet it is this same compulsive perfectionism that keeps the wheels of a complex industrial society moving smoothly and that motivates a mother to prepare artificial foods for her baby which are as free from contamination as human breast milk. Sometimes the driving competitiveness of the Westerner seems excessive, yet it is this same source of energy which causes mothers to vie with each other to feed solids to their infants and have them immunized at the earliest possible age.

These interrelationships between the physical and cultural aspects of man's environment are worth bearing in mind. They point up the difficulty of isolating and modifying one small aspect of culture, such as an infant feeding practice considered harmful, without also changing the physical environment or, more significantly, without also changing the underlying personality traits which this one small practice reflects. But if these considerations point up difficulties, they also emphasize the necessity of viewing economic and social man together. If the physical and cultural aspects of his environment cannot be compartmentalized, neither can any approach to the prevention of disease and death to which these two aspects of his environment contribute.

It is far easier to catalogue aspects of culture that may influence infant mortality than it is to suggest ways of modifying them. Indeed, any serious approach to this subject necessarily verges into realms of religious thought and philosophies of governmental action. Rather than attempting to treat it in detail, some general principles will be discussed, out of which a program to reduce infant mortality by changing culturally conditioned practices and attitudes could grow.

There seem to be three ways of hastening the change in human behaviour and attitude that occurs naturally with growth and experience. Mass behavioural or cultural change can be effected in the same ways. The first way, by exhortation, persuasion and reward or promise of reward, is most often associated with religion, but it is also used a great deal by medical practitioners. This is the method of "shoulds," and its effectiveness is directly related to the prestige and status of the preacher or doctor. To the Western observer this method seems to be used more often in Indian social, business and political life than it is in the West. When applied to Indian child-rearing methods and attitudes its effectiveness may well be related to the status and prestige of grandmother or mother-in-law as compared to doctor, nurse or political and religious leader. The more Westernized and urbanized the family, the greater the chance for its success.

The second way of change, by compulsion, regulation, punishment or threat of punishment, is most often associated with a martial existence and government by dictatorship. However, every society regulates its own welfare by a system of formal sanctions or laws as well as by the informal sanctions of its culture. It is only by the degree of regulated action and thought and in the thoroughness of regulatory enforcement that army and civilian life and governments differ. Laws can be a force for changing culture as well as for retaining its status quo. Unless the rationale of a law is understood and generally accepted by the people, however, its enforcement becomes either a mockery or a butchery.

If a given regulation will improve health and if it can be enforced without great difficulty, there is no reason why any government as well as any army should not adopt it. Thus in the early part of the present century in the U.S.A. legal measures and public opinion united to virtually eliminate the fairly common practice of indiscriminate expectoration in public places; remnants of this campaign can still be seen in the signs on New York City subways notifying passengers that spitting is punishable by severe fine and imprisonment. This campaign was successful because public opinion supported it. It should be contrasted with the failure of legal measures to affect the indiscriminate elimination of human wastes in a city such as Madras. This failure cannot rightly be ascribed to a lack of sanitary facilities, because even the simplest of sanitary precautions are ignored; it cannot be ascribed to a lack of law-enforcement officers, because the prohibited acts sometimes occur in their presence. It can only be ascribed to the observable fact that these illegal acts do not arouse in the people or police officers of Madras the same outraged sense of personal indignation that expectoration in the subways aroused in the people of New York City.

Other practices affecting infant mortality may yield more readily to the regulatory approach. The rationing of food, for example, was practiced during the last war in India with some degree of acceptance. Whether food rationing or subsidies as a means of favourably affecting food choice in India today is feasible or not would probably depend upon the educational efforts which accompanied it and its acceptance by the people as a drastic but necessary step for the welfare of all.

The third way of change, by insightful decision based on clarified understanding, is most often associated with psychoanalytic therapy. It is a way of change that can be used effectively with small groups as well as with individuals. Although this approach, if used on a mass scale, could also be labeled educational, it is education in a much deeper sense than imparting knowledge alone. It is not enough for man and wife to know how to practice contraception; the nature of their understanding of method must be fervent and large enough to guarantee that the method will be applied whatever the existing circumstances.

How can motivation of this nature be produced in an entire society as well as in individuals and small groups? This is a question which the advertising merchant, the political leader and the public health official all ask themselves for their own reasons and purposes. If there were any single or easy answer in a society whose government is not totalitarian, it would be well known.

Western experience does, however, offer a way to find out what these answers might be in a given society and to validate the answers in practice. This is the scientific method of research. Social science is young compared to physical science and the body of knowledge and research method it possesses might well be called immature. This is all the more reason to cultivate rather than ignore it. Its promise of holding a rational solution to man's human problems is the one constructive contribution of Western civilization to the problems it has created through its technology. Appreciation of the significance of social science research in public health is of relatively recent origin.[14] Almost unknown is the idea of taking official government cognizance of the relationship of cultural factors to health and assigning consultant missions to social scientists. A conspicuous example of this was the appointment and mission of the Committee on Food Habits of the National Research Council (U.S.A.) during the late war.[15] This committee of distinguished scientists initiated studies and made recommendations to government agencies concerning government policy which opened up entirely new vistas of thought and which were eminently practical. Unfortunately, the passing of the war emergency meant the termination of the Committee's work.

In many respects India's situation today has the character of an emergency. It would be salutary indeed if the problem of infant mortality were boldly faced as one reflecting primarily the economic and cultural development of the country, rather than as something to be shouldered by a public health program expected to work in isolation with nothing but medical or sanitary tools. If it were so faced, ways to reduce it by changing culturally conditioned behaviour could be sought and applied in a thorough and scientific manner. The listing of cultural factors given earlier can be reevaluated in such a light. Some of them, as noted in the listing, are still conjectural, as, for example, the effect of finger feeding or force feeding in a supine position—for these, studies to establish or disprove their significance are needed. Others (both medical and anthropological) are not conjectural at all, as, for example, the late age at which solids are introduced and practices associated with the elimination of wastes. Studies (primarily social science based) could be designed on a broad scale to learn more about what these customs mean to people and what methods might be expected to change them. Later the actual results of the application of proposed methods could be evaluated as a scientific study. It is of vital importance, however, that these studies and the development of methods for cultural change should not be conducted within the narrow planes of medical and paramedical action, nor even within the conventional confines of what is called health education. They should embrace the whole potential range of man's economic and social life, including government policy, regulation, and service, and the action of other societal groups and individuals. The potential use of all methods of behavioural change: exhortation, compulsion, mass media or decision making by small groups, needs to be explored scientifically—indeed, they might be applied in various combinations. The application must be thorough and many-pronged, not, as so often occurs in health education efforts, an isolated, undermanned sortie that merely forms one pressure among the many that impinge on a community and seek to modify its behaviour.

Something like this research approach to the solution of a problem is now being carried out in the "research cum action" programs designed to promote the use of latrines in villages.[16] However, the amount and scope of these efforts are pitiably small when viewed against the background of need.

In summary, the excess infant (post-neonatal) mortality in India, when compared to technologically more developed countries, has been viewed as a product of the cultural as well as material factors of the Indian environment. Attention has been focussed on the nature of the cultural factors and they may operate to help produce disease and death. The factors discussed centered around primal biological functions, ingestion of food, egestion of wastes and reproduction of the species, an indication of their deep-seated holds. The concept of planning to reduce infant mortality by deliberately seeking to modify cultural practices and attitudes considered harmful and doing so within the framework of current economic development was presented. Exhortation, compulsion and the educational process of insightful change are potential methods of change, but the important factor is the application of studies to learn more about the relationship of culture and health, followed by the planned evaluation of considered action. This action must be part of a deliberate and total program rather than an isolated pitch.

This is an approach which has been pointed out by Western social science, but never utilized by Western society except in times of disaster. It can be adopted in India today with far more justice and urgency than in Western countries. To execute it, the problem of infant mortality must be viewed boldly and broadly as the product of both material and non-material aspects of a total society and not merely as the product of a group of diseases which require only medical treatment and medically trained personnel for their prevention and cure. Remedial or preventive measures must be devised which are more far reaching and pervasive than health and welfare services in the usual sense of these terms—measures which will invest the day-to-day living and thinking of people with an ardour for progressive change.

NOTES

1. Newsholme, A., Report by the Medical Officer on Infant and Child Mortality, Supplement to the 30th Annual Report of the Local Government Board, London, 1910.

2. Verhoestraate, Z., International Aspects of Maternal and Child Health, *Amer. J. Pub. Health,* 46:19, 1956; Williams, C. D., Social Medicine in Developing Countries, *Lancet,* 1:863, 1958.

3. In this report statistics and experiences from Madras City, New York State (excluding New York City) and the continental U.S.A. will be drawn upon because they are readily available to the writer. It is believed that they are fairly illustrative of India as a whole and its contrasts with the West.

4. Morris, J. N., and Heady, J. A., Social and Biological Factors in Infant Mortality, *Lancet,* 1:343, 1955.

5. Charles, J., in *Diseases of Children,* Pt. I, Vol. I, Chap. I, Moncrieff, A., and Evans, P., eds., Edward Arnold Co., London, 5th ed., 1953.

6. Yankauer, A., unpublished data.

7. Williams, C. D., Social Medicine in Developing Countries, *Lancet,* 1:863, 1958; Jelliffe, D. B., Cultural Variation and the Practical Pediatrician, *J. of Ped.,* 49: 661, 1956.

8. *Report on India's Food Crisis and Steps to Meet It,* Agricultural Production Team (Ford Foundation), Govt. of India, New Delhi, 1959.

9. Baskharan, T. R., Environmental Sanitation in NEFA, *Swasth Hind,* 2:226 (Sept.), 1958.

10. Carstairs, M. A., *The Twice Born,* Hogarth Press, London, 1957.

11. Chandrasekhar, S., *Population and Planned Parenthood in India,* Geo. Allen & Unwin, London, 1955.

12. Panikkar, K. M., *Hindu Society at Cross Roads,* 2nd ed., Asia Pub. House, Bombay, 1956.

13. Carstairs, M. A., *Twice Born;* Panikkar, K. M., *Hindu Society at Cross Roads;* Narain, D., *Hindu Character,* University of Bombay Publications, Sociology Series, No. 8, 1957.

14. Paul, B. D., Social Science in Public Health, *Am. J. Pub. Health,* 46: 1390, 1956.

15. *The Problem of Changing Food Habits,* Bull. Nat. Research Council (U.S.A.), 108 (Oct.), 1943.

16. Neurath, P., Research-cum-Action as a Method in Public Health Work, *Swasth Hind,* 2:224 (Sept.), 1958.

16

New Clues to the
Causes of Cancer

Saxon Graham

Fifteen years ago, when evidence linking smoking and lung cancer was based mainly on studies of mice, apologists for the tobacco companies asserted that this evidence had proved only one thing—that mice shouldn't smoke. Today there are many studies on human beings as well, and all show that people who smoke run increased risk of lung cancer. Even though the biochemistry of lung cancer is still not understood, these studies comparing the incidence of lung cancer among smokers and nonsmokers give us what we need to know to begin preventing lung cancer. We need to alter a behavioral pattern; in this case, to stop people from smoking.

This same line of attack—comparing incidence rates among various groups—is now being applied to the study of other types of cancer as well. The *social epidemiological* approach, as it is called, traces the distribution patterns of various types of disease among different national, religious, racial, class, occupational, residential, and other social groups. The findings help narrow the search for the causes of disease—by informing the investigators which groups they should study further. Of course, groups with very low incidence rates, such as Jewish women with their low rates of cervical cancer, are just as significant as those with very high rates. In the one case, researchers look for behavior patterns that promote disease; in the other, for habits that prevent disease.

In searching for the cause of lung cancer, researchers had a logical candidate to investigate. Clinicians had noticed that lung cancer rarely develops in a nonsmoker; that chronic cough and bronchitis are characteristic of smokers; and that over several decades the growth in the incidence

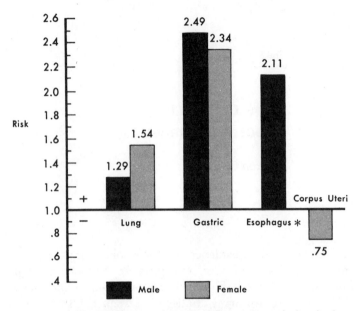

* Number of cases of cancer of the esophagus in females is
too low to calculate relative risks.

**FIGURE 1.   Relative Risk of Developing Cancer,
Males Compared to Females**

of lung cancer paralleled the growth of cigarette smoking among the
population.

In other types of cancer, the epidemiological correlates have been
more obscure. Researchers, however, have already uncovered some of them.
A very early example of this strategy was Sir Percival Pott's discovery, in
1775, of the chain of events leading to cancer of the scrotum. Pott's initial
observation—the one that put him on the right track to find the more
specific causes of the disease—was that scrotal cancer occurred most
frequently among working-class city dwellers. He also observed that a
disproportionate number of the victims were chimney sweeps. Having nar-
rowed down the field by class, residence, and occupation, Pott was able to
pinpoint the disease-causing agent—soot.

In sociological terms, this chain of events can be summarized this way:
An environmental need for heated dwellings led to the widespread installa-
tion of home space-heaters. The fuel for these heaters produced so much
soot that exhaust passages had to be cleaned frequently. Thus, the occupation of chimney sweep developed. The chimney sweep's work put him into

close and frequent contact with soot, and in susceptible individuals this contact caused scrotal cancer.

GENETIC AND SOCIAL FACTORS

But what makes one individual, and not another, susceptible? This may depend on his genetic makeup, his previous exposure to the disease, and his general physical and mental state. And all of these factors may, again, be strongly influenced by the social situation. For example, the ubiquitous tubercle bacillus is more likely to produce disease in a lower-class person than in a person of higher socioeconomic status. The higher-class person, because of his income, enjoys better nutrition, better medical attention, less crowding, and a more hygienic environment.

Of course, nonsocial environmental factors (like sunlight) and genetically determined individual characteristics (like fair coloring) may also figure importantly in the chain—as in the case of skin cancer. But even here, it is clear that social factors, such as the prevalence of occupations (like farming) that involve exposure to the sun, or the percentage of fair-skinned people in the population, may significantly alter group-incidence rates.

As Pott found when he prescribed bathing to remove soot as a preventive for scrotal cancer, the chain of events may be interrupted at almost any stage and the disease rate reduced. One does not even have to know all the links in the chain in order to bring about this reduction. The real agents in soot and in tobacco smoke are still obscure, for example, but the incidence of scrotal and lung cancer can be reduced by changing behavior patterns—taking baths and not smoking.

Socioeconomic status has been found to be a factor in conditions ranging all the way from pellagra to poliomyelitis. Incidence studies in Copenhagen, New Haven, and Buffalo show higher risk of cancer of the lung, stomach, and cervix for lower-class people, and higher risk of cancer of the breast and body of the uterus for the upper classes. Further inquiry has uncovered other facts, consistent with these socioeconomic distributions, that give us more clues to the origins of these diseases. Breast cancer, for example, has been found to be less frequent in women who have had many pregnancies, have nursed many children, and have had early menopause by virtue of hysterectomy or ovariectomy. And all of these characteristics are more typical of lower-class rather than upper-class women.

Religion is also significantly related to disease patterns. Incidence studies in the United States and Israel confirm that Jewish women are much less likely than non-Jews to have cancer of the cervix. Medical sociologists have considered a number of Jewish folkways as possible explanations for

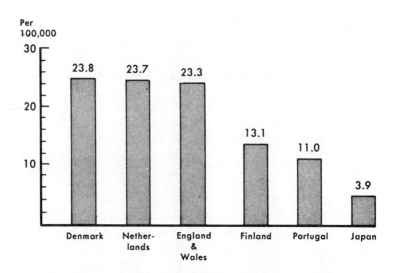

FIGURE 2.   Mortality from Cancer of the Breast in Females

this difference—among them, the practice of male circumcision and the Old Testament's prohibition against sexual intercourse for a certain number of days after the menstrual period.

Attempts to study circumcision directly, however, have yielded inconclusive results. The effect of of circumcision has always been studied by asking cervical-cancer victims and those without the disease whether their husbands were circumcised. One such study showed only a small relationship between circumcision and low cancer rates; the other two studies showed no relationship at all. But these results may have been due to errors in the wives' reports about their husbands. In a recent survey on circumcision, comparison of men's verbal reports about themselves with the results of physical examinations showed that over one-third of the men questioned were mistaken! Whether their wives' reports would be any more accurate is certainly open to doubt. As for the sexual abstinence prescribed in Leviticus, Jews stoutly assert that this rule is rarely observed.

Other research suggests that the following factors are directly related to cervical cancer: having many children, having first coitus early in life, having coitus frequently, and having many sex partners, either extramaritally or intramaritally. Supporting evidence includes the fact that nuns have a very low rate of cervical cancer; that prostitutes have an unusually high rate; and that lower-class and Negro women, with typically earlier marriages and more children, have higher rates than the rest of the population and far higher rates than Jews in particular.

Just as researchers have compared smokers who do develop lung

cancer with smokers who escape the disease, Clyde Martin has compared
the sexual habits of Jewish women who do develop cervical cancer with
the habits of Jewish women who don't. His findings indicate that there is a
higher risk for Jewish women who have many sex partners, particularly
if some of these men are not Jewish. Martin, stressing that his research
is not conclusive, proposes a theory that is both sociological and virological:
Cervical cancer is caused by a virus that only certain men carry, and the
uncircumcised non-Jew is more likely than the Jew to harbor this virus.
Thus, as the number of men with whom a woman has intercourse increases,
so does the possibility of her exposure to the virus and the risk of her developing cervical cancer.

In addition, whether Martin's theory is correct or not, researchers must
consider the possibility that Jews have certain genes in common that protect
against cervical cancer. There is, after all, some genetic evidence of an
aggregation of physical traits in Jews (such as fingerprint whorls), so we
cannot rule out the existence of a gene that protects against cervical cancer.

The World Health Organization's data on cancer of the cervix show
the United States' nonwhite population has the highest rate; the Japanese
and Israeli rates are conspicuously low. Israel's low rate is reminiscent of
the previous findings on American Jews as compared with other Americans.
And it is noteworthy that groups with high or low mortality from cancer of
the cervix have correspondingly high or low rates of cancer mortality in
another sexual site, the prostate.

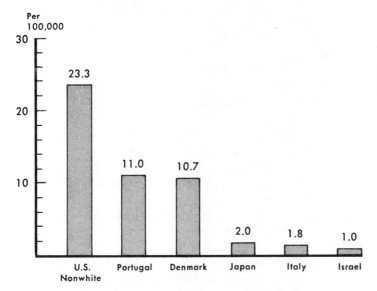

FIGURE 3.   Mortality from Cancer of the Cervix

Using the virus hypothesis already described, we could speculate that this virus is transferred from one sex to the other—that is, that the same virus responsible for cervical cancer in women could also figure in cancer of the prostate in men. The agent carrying the virus to the susceptible tissues might be smegma, the fatty secretion that accumulates under the foreskin in uncircumcised males. Smegma produces cervical cancer in some strains of mice, and it could possibly have the same effect in human beings.

Lack of circumcision and poor penile hygiene—as well as venereal infections—may also be related to cancer of the penis, and *may* partly explain why this form of cancer is more frequent, in the United States, among nonwhites than among whites. In fact, the cancer rates in *all* of the sexually related sites discussed—the cervix, the prostate, and the penis—are significantly higher for nonwhites than for whites.

LEUKEMIA AMONG JEWS

We have seen that the Jews seem to enjoy relative immunity to sexually related cancers. On the other hand, they seem especially susceptible to another type of cancer—leukemia (cancer of the blood). Brian MacMahon was the first to suggest this relationship. And in upstate New York recently, my associates and I ran a comparative study of leukemia rates among Jews and non-Jews, with these results: The expected relationship between leukemia and religion did not hold for children, but for adults there was a higher risk of leukemia among Jews than among non-Jews.

The origins of leukemia are not fully known, but there are some clues. Because exposure to irradiation can alter cell structure, undergoing X rays may—in part—account for the white blood cell deterioration that is characteristic of leukemia. And not only does direct irradiation increase risk, but—equally important—irradiation of the pregnant mother, as studies in England and Buffalo suggest, raises the risk in the child. Moreover, our study indicates that irradiation of a woman *before* she conceives will increase the risk of leukemia in any subsequent offspring. While we cannot conclude that irradiation is the sole cause of leukemia—or even that irradiation alone can produce the disease without other contributing factors—these results certainly indicate *some* relation between irradiation and this usually fatal malignancy.

A few researchers have suggested that the high risk of leukemia among Jews may be related to their getting better medical care and hence more X rays. However, the results of our study hold *regardless* of X-ray history. The relationship may also be partly a product of national background, but only partly. Foreign-born Jews have higher leukemia rates than native-born Jews, and Eastern Europeans generally have higher rates than other foreign-born. But the Jews among the East Europeans *still* have much higher rates than the non-Jews in the same nationality groups. This suggests the possibility of some cultural or genetic predisposition to leukemia among Jews —a predisposition that may be enhanced by exposure to X rays and by certain behavior patterns that are associated with East European culture.

The fact that there is a higher risk of leukemia among foreign-born adults than among the native-born is consistent with a larger pattern of cancer incidence in the United States. Even when factors such as age, occupation, class, urban-rural residence, and smoking behavior are controlled, foreign-born Americans have higher risks of cancer of the stomach, lung, and esophagus. The foreign-born are a heterogeneous group, however. In narrowing the search for behavioral factors, we need to compare risks among the specific nationality groups that make up the foreign-born.

NATIONAL DIFFERENCES IN CANCER RATES

In Buffalo and surrounding counties, most of the foreign-born population is made up of the Irish, the Germans, the Italians, and the Poles. Here the Polish-born have rates of lung and esophageal cancer almost twice as high as the rates for the other three nationality groups. The German and the Irish rates run very near the foreign-born averages for all types of cancer. And the Italians, who run a significantly low risk of lung cancer, are 2.4 and 2.7 times as likely as the other foreign-born to develop cancers of the bladder and the colon. The Italian-born also run a higher risk of cancer of the pharynx.

Another part of the throat—the larynx, or voice box—is a high-risk site not only for Italians, but for people of other Latin countries as well. France, for example, reports about 9 deaths for cancer of the larynx per 100,000, whereas Norway reports only 0.40. Because of diagnostic and treatment differences among countries, it is often dangerous to use mortality data. But where case-fatality rates are high (as in most cancers) and differences great (as in those cited below), they warrant consideration. France's rate is 22.5 times that of Norway. The four countries reporting the highest rates of larynx cancer—France, Portugal, Italy, and Belgium—are all Latin or (in the case of Belgium) partially Latin in background.

Among the many habits these Latinate countries have in common is wine-drinking. Both Ernest Wynder in the United States and Daniel Schwartz in France found an increased risk of cancer of the larynx among heavy drinkers of alcohol, particularly wine, even after the rates were adjusted for smoking. Evidently, wine-drinking patterns in these countries should be investigated further. It is interesting, on the other hand, that three of the four countries with the lowest reported rates of larynx cancer—Denmark, Sweden, and Norway—are Scandinavian. Explanations for such uniformly low larynx-cancer rates in countries that are abstemious of wine but not of other alcohol might furnish additional clues as to the causes of the disease.

One of the most interesting cancer sites, as far as ethnic and cross-cultural distributions are concerned, is the stomach. We have already noted that, in the United States, cancer of the stomach is linked with low socioeconomic status. But it is also linked with foreign birth and, among women in particular, Polish birth. Incomplete data on Poland are corroborative. Figures for other countries show that the highest male mortality rates are reported by Japan, Finland, and Austria. The lowest are reported by Canada, Australia, New Zealand, and United States whites. The fact that the countries with lowest rates are all English in origin suggests a common protective shield—a shield that may be cultural, genetic, or both.

Japan's mortality from stomach cancer is five times higher than that of the country reporting the lowest mortality, the United States. R. L. Smith, studying mortality among Japanese in Japan, Hawaii, and the West Coast of the United States, found a lower rate in Hawaii than in Japan, and a lower rate on the West Coast of the United States than in Hawaii. West Coast Japanese still had much higher rates than Caucasians. Since all these groups are full-blooded Japanese and probably genetically similar, there may be a sociological factor that explains the differences—perhaps some dietary custom that is abandoned as Japanese move east to Hawaii or the United States and adopt American culture. It is possible, of course, that migrating Japanese are different genetically from nonmigrating ones, but cultural factors would seem to provide a more likely explanation.

Mitsu Segi, for example, studying Japan, found that two habits seemed to carry an especially high risk of stomach cancer—drinking alcohol and eating at irregular intervals. Research on patients in Buffalo reinforced the finding about irregular eating, and tentatively implicated two foods frequently found in Polish diets: cabbage and potatoes. In addition, there is some evidence that the Polynesian peoples, such as the Maori and the Hawaiians, have higher rates than the whites in New Zealand and Hawaii. The Polynesian diet, like the Polish, is apparently low in ascorbic acid and very high in starch, and this may account for these differences.

The dramatic international differences between Japanese and American rates of stomach cancer are reversed for cancer of the prostate. Here the Japanese have a distinct advantage. The highest rate reported in international studies, that of the U.S. nonwhite, is 16 times the rate of the Japanese. W. B. Quisenberry, studying Hawaii, also found low rates from the resident Japanese there as compared with the white population. The country with the third lowest rate is Israel—a finding consistent with the low rates of prostate cancer found among Jews in the United States.

According to these same international statistics, the Japanese also enjoy the lowest rate of breast-cancer mortality among the score of countries studied. Denmark, with the highest rate, reports a mortality six times that of the Japanese. The Netherlands, and England and Wales, follow Denmark in mortality figures. Of the nine countries having the highest mortality rates from cancer of the breast, six were settled by people of predominantly English stock (England and Wales, Scotland, Canada, South Africa, New Zealand, and Ireland). Furthermore, William Haenszel's studies of breast-cancer mortality in the United States show a rate among English-born Americans that is higher than that of the general population. One implication of these figures is that people of Northwestern European birth or descent may harbor some special genetic susceptibility to cancer of the breast.

But the genetic explanation may be too simple. Other studies indicate the importance of social factors such as marriage, family, and child-care customs. We have already seen the class differences in breast-cancer rates within the United States alone: Low-status women in the breast-cancer age group are much more likely to have married early, to have many children, and to have breast-fed these children—and these low-status women are also much *less* likely to develop breast cancer. These same factors may also apply on an international scale. Very generally, "low economic status" countries seem to have low breast-cancer rates, and "high economic status" countries high rates.

The Danes and the Dutch, as well as most people living in countries of historically English origin, enjoy a high standard of living. And a high standard of living is associated with deferred marriage, limited family size, and the abandonment of traditional child-care practices such as breast-feeding —precisely the factors found to be related to high breast-cancer rates among women in the United States. In this case, the familiar social-scientific strategy has been applied. Research of one sort, demographic, has yielded results consistent with that of another: The socioeconomic finding jibes with those on nursing and family size.

MENSTRUAL ACTIVITY AND BREAST CANCER

The demographic finding is not important in and of itself, but rather because it is consistent with findings on items of behavior that may be much more closely related to the disease. The observation that nursing and family size were related to breast cancer was consistent with the socioeconomic finding. It also suggested that something associated with nursing and fertility might be related to the disease. A logical factor was menstrual function —because with each period of pregnancy and nursing, menstruation (and concomitant hormonal function) is temporarily halted. Another piece of data pointing to menstrual function was the reduction in breast-cancer risk for women who had had early menopause because of surgical removal or irradiation of the ovaries. Early menopause would also reduce one's total lifetime menstrual activity. The implication, then, was that perhaps lifetime menstrual activity might be inversely related to breast cancer. We examined this in a series of breast-cancer and control patients by subtracting months pregnant plus months spent nursing babies from the total time between onset of menstruation and menopause. We found that risk of breast cancer decreases as menstrual activity decreases.

This study needs doing again and again on other series of patients. But so far, as in the other forms of cancer we have discussed, research points to an intricate complex of sociological and biological conditions that may be related to the development of disease. This complex may explain hitherto odd findings, such as the low breast-cancer incidence among the Japanese: Japanese women of the breast-cancer age group frequently have had many pregnancies and, as Ruth Benedict pointed out long ago, frequently nurse each child for a long period of time. Or the complex of relationships may suggest avenues for further inquiry: Animal experiments focusing on short and long periods of menstrual activity could furnish important evidence from another field for or against the hypothesis.

When more complete, such social epidemiological information can be very useful. First—and even before we understand the biochemical processes underlying cancer—it can aid in prevention. In the case of lung cancer, we don't need to know *why* smoking contributes to the disease to know that not smoking will increase the chances of avoiding it. Second, such information can also help us pin down the disease processes themselves. If we can systematically find out which groups of people get certain forms of cancer, then by examining their genetic makeup and their customs—dietary, sexual, hygienic, and so forth—we may begin to form more specific ideas of where the causes lie. In this way, medical sociological research can make its own unique contribution to the control of some forms of cancer.

FURTHER READING SUGGESTED BY THE AUTHOR

Because social epidemiology is a new—some would say nonexistent—field, there are no books specifically concerned with it. However, appropriate chapters of the following volumes may shed some additional light.

Handbook of Modern Sociology by Robert E. L. Faris (Chicago, Ill.: Rand McNally & Co., 1964). Chapter 9.

Handbook of Medical Sociology by Howard Freeman, Sol Levine, and Leo G. Reeder (Englewood Cliffs, N.J.: Prentice-Hall, 1963). Chapters 3–6.

Patients, Physicians and Illness by E. Gartley Jaco (New York: Free Press–Macmillan, 1968).

Epidemiologic Methods by Brian MacMahon, Thomas F. Pugh, and Johannes Ipsen (Boston: Little, Brown and Co., 1960). The social dimension is apparent throughout this methodologic review.

Sociology in Medicine by M. W. Susser and W. Watson (New York: Oxford University Press, 1962). Chapters 1–4.

Smoking and Health, Advisory Committee of the Surgeon General of the Public Health Service, U.S. Government Printing Office, 1964. A complete critical review of research by a panel of experts approved by scientists as well as tobacco companies.

17

How a Population Ages
or Grows Younger

Ansley J. Coale

The age of the whole human population could, I suppose, be measured from the moment the species originated, and the age of a national population could be measured from the country's "birthday." The age (in this sense) of the human population has been estimated as at least 100,000 and no more than a million years, and the age of national populations ranges from several thousand years for Egypt or China to a year or so for some of the emerging nations of Africa.

In this chapter, however, when we speak of the age of a population we refer to the age of its members, and to be precise we should use the term *age distribution* of a population—how many persons there are at each age— rather than the age of a population. The only way a single age can be given for a group of persons is by using some sort of average. A *young* population, then, is one that contains a large proportion of young persons, and has a low average age, while an *old* population has a high average age and a large proportion of old people.

The ages of various national populations in the world today are very different, and in many countries the present age distribution differs markedly from the past.

The oldest populations in the world are found in Northwestern Europe. In France, England and Sweden, for example, 12 per cent of the population is over sixty-five, and half of the population in these countries is over thirty-three, thirty-six, and thirty-seven respectively. The youngest populations are found in the underdeveloped countries—those that have not incorporated modern industrial technology in their economies—the populations of

Reprinted from *Population: The Vital Revolution,* ed. Ronald Freedman (Garden City, N.Y.: Anchor Books, Doubleday & Co., 1964), pp. 47–58, by permission of the author and the publisher.

HOW A POPULATION AGES OR GROWS YOUNGER   299

Asia, Africa and Latin America. Half of the population of Pakistan is under eighteen years, of the Congo under twenty years, and of Brazil under nineteen years. The proportion over sixty-five in Brazil is less than one fourth what it is in France. The proportion of children under fifteen is twice as great in Pakistan as in England. Paradoxically enough, the oldest nations— China, India and Egypt—have very young populations.

The highly industrialized countries all have older populations than the underdeveloped countries, and also older populations than they did fifty to a hundred years ago. Since 1900 the median age has risen in England from twenty-four to thirty-six, in the United States from twenty-three to thirty, in Japan from twenty-three to twenty-six, and in Russia from twenty-one to twenty-seven. In the underdeveloped countries, however, the age distributions have changed only slightly, and they have, if anything, become slightly.younger. In Taiwan, for example, the median age has declined from twenty-one to eighteen since 1915.

What accounts for these differences and these trends in the age distribution of populations? One obvious factor to consider is migration. A famous spa has an old population because old people come there for the cure, and university towns like Princeton have young populations because young people come there to study. But the age distribution of most national populations is not much affected by migration, especially today when almost everywhere international migration is restricted.

Whether a national population is young or old is mainly determined by the number of children women bear. When women bear many children, the population is young; when they bear few, the population is old.

The effect of fertility (as the rate of childbearing can be called) on the age distribution is clearest when a population continuously subject to high fertility is compared to one continuously subject to low fertility. The high-fertility population has a larger proportion of children relative to adults of parental age as a direct consequence of the greater frequency of births. Moreover, by virtue of high fertility a generation ago, today's parents are numerous relative to *their* parents, and hence the proportion of old people is small. Conversely, the population experiencing a prolonged period of low fertility has few children relative to its current parents, who in turn are not numerous relative to *their* parents. Prolonged high fertility produces a large proportion of children, and a small proportion of the aged—a population with a low average age. On the other hand, prolonged low fertility produces a small proportion of children and a large proportion of the aged—a high average age.

It is the small number of children born per woman that explains the high average age now found in industrialized western Europe, and the high birth rate of the underdeveloped countries that accounts for their young populations. The increase in average age and the swollen proportion of old people in the industrialized countries are the product of the history of falling birth rates that all such countries have experienced.

Most of us would probably guess that populations have become older because the death rate has been reduced, and hence people live longer on the average. Just what is the role of mortality in determining the age distribution of a population? The answer is surprising—mortality affects the age distribution much less than does fertility, and in the opposite direction from what most of us would think. Prolongation of life by reducing death rates has the perverse effect of making the population somewhat younger. Consider the effect of the reduction in death rates in the United States, where the average duration of life has risen from about forty-five years under the mortality conditions of 1900 to about seventy years today. Had the risks of death prevailing in 1900 continued unchanged, and the other variables—rates of immigration and rates of childbearing per mother—followed the course they actually did, the average age of the population today would be greater than it is: the proportion of children would be less and the proportion of persons over sixty-five would be greater than they are. The reduction of the death rate has produced, in other words, a younger American population.

These statements seem scarcely credible.

Does not a reduction in the death rate increase the average age at death? Are there not more old people as a result of reduced mortality than there would be with the former high death rates? How then can it be said that a reduction in the death rate makes a population younger?

It is true that as death rates fall, the average age at which people die is increased. But the average age of a population is the average age of living persons, not their average age at death. It is also true, as we all immediately realize, that as death rates fall, the number of old persons in a population increases. What we do not so readily realize is that reduced mortality increases the number of *young* persons as well. More survive from birth to ages one, ten, twenty, and forty, as well as more living to old age. Because more persons survive to be parents, more births occur.

The reason that the reduced death rates, which prolong man's life, make the population younger is that typical improvements in health and medicine produce the greatest increases in survivorship among the young rather than the old.

There is one kind of reduction in death rates that would not affect the age distribution of the population at all, that would lead to the same proportion of population at every age as if mortality had not changed. This particular form of reduced mortality is one that increases the chance of surviving one year by a certain amount—say one tenth of 1 per cent—at every age. The result would be one tenth of a per cent more persons at age one, five, ten, sixty, and eighty—at every age—than there would have been had death rates been unaltered. Because there would be one tenth per cent more parents, there would also be one tenth per cent more births. Therefore the next year's population would be one tenth per cent larger than it would otherwise have been, but the proportion of children, of young adults, of the middle-aged, and of the aged would not be altered—there would be one tenth per cent more of each.

Reductions in mortality of this singular sort that would not affect the age of the population at all are not found in actual human experience. However, there has been a tendency for persons at all ages to share some of the increased chances of survival, and the effect of reduced death rates on the age distribution has consequently been small—much smaller than the effect of reduced birth rates—in countries where both fertility and mortality have changed markedly.

As the average duration of life has risen from lower levels to sixty-five or seventy years, the most conspicuous advances in survivorship seem always to have occurred in infancy and early childhood. It is for this reason that reduced mortality has had the effect of producing a younger population, although the effect has usually been obscured by the much more powerful force of a falling birth rate that has occurred at the same time. Thus the population of the United States has actually become *older* since 1900, because of falling fertility; but falling mortality (with its tendency to produce a younger population) has prevented it from becoming older still.

The younger-population effect of reduced mortality is not an inevitable feature of all increases in length of life. The countries with the greatest average duration of life have by now about exhausted the possibility of increasing survivorship in a way that makes for a younger population. In Sweden today 95 per cent survive from birth to age thirty, compared to 67 per cent in 1870. At best, survivorship to age thirty in Sweden could approach 100 per cent. No important increase in population at younger ages would result. If there are further major gains in the chances of prolonged life in Sweden, they must occur at older ages, and if they occur, will make the population older.

Every individual inexorably gets older as time passes. How old he gets depends on how long he avoids death. President Eisenhower remarked after his retirement that he was glad to be old, because at his age, if he were not old, he would be dead.

Populations, on the other hand, can get older or younger. They get older primarily as the result of declining fertility, and younger primarily as the result of rising fertility.

The most highly industrialized countries have all experienced a decline of fertility of about 50 per cent since their preindustrial phase, and they all have older populations than they used to have. In France and the United States, for example, the number of children each woman bore declined for more than a century, reaching a minimum just before World War II. In each country during this period the population became progressively older. In fact, the "aging" of the population continued for a time after fertility had passed its minimum. Between 1800 and 1950 the median age of the French population rose from twenty-five to thirty-five years, and in the United States in the same interval the median age increased from sixteen to thirty. In both countries there has been a substantial recovery in fertility during the past twenty-five years from the low point reached in the 1930s. This rise in fertility has produced the first decrease in median age recorded in the statistics of either nation. Between 1950 and 1960 the median age in France fell from 35 to 33, and in the United States from 30.2 to 29.6.

This reversal in the trend toward an older population in the United States has been accompanied by a more pronounced reversal in the way proportions of children were changing. The long-term decline in fertility in the United States meant that the proportion of children to adults steadily shrank from about 0.85 children (under fifteen) per adult (over fifteen) in 1800 to 0.33 per adult in 1940. By 1960 the proportion had rebounded to 0.45 children per adult. In fact, the increase in the *number* of children in the population between 1950 and 1960—more than 15 million—was greater than the increase between 1900 and 1950.

The abrupt reversal of the long-term trend toward an older population has meant the first increase in the relative burden of child dependency in the history of the United States. The very productive American economy can certainly afford to support this burden, but it has not been painless. The extremely rapid increase in the number of children in the past decade has required the construction of many new schools and the training of many teachers. In some communities where foresight, willingness to pay increased taxes, or resources were inadequate, schools have been overcrowded and the quality of instruction has suffered.

The countries that have not undergone intensive industrialization have experienced no major changes in fertility, no trends of sustained decline and recovery such as occurred in France and the United States. Rather they have experienced a largely unbroken sequence of high birth rates. There has been in consequence little change in the age composition of underdeveloped areas. All have 40 per cent or more under age fifteen, only 2 to 4 per cent over sixty-five, and a median age of twenty years or less.

The age distributions of the industrialized countries on the one hand and of the preindustrial countries on the other are ironically mismatched with what each sort of country seems best equipped to accommodate. As we have noted before, the contrast in age of population is striking. In Pakistan or Mexico nearly one person of every two a visitor might encounter would be a child, and only two or three of every hundred would be old (over sixty-five); while in England only one in four would be a child and about one in eight would be old. In the industrialized countries where the proportion of the aged is so large, the importance of the family in the predominantly urban environment has diminished, and consequently the role of respected old patriarch or matriarch has nearly vanished. The wealthy industrial countries can readily afford to support a sizable component of old people but have not in fact always done so adequately. The aging of their populations has been accompanied by a weakening or a disappearance of the traditional claims of the aged on their descendants for material support and, perhaps more tragically, by a weakening or disappearance of a recognized and accepted position for old people in the family.

In the underdeveloped countries, on the other hand, the relatively few old people are accorded traditional respect and whatever economic support their families have to offer, and hence the aged are less subject to special economic and social deprivation.

Because of extremely young age distributions, adults in the impoverished underdeveloped countries must support a disproportionately large dependent-child population—twice as great a burden of dependency per adult in the working ages of fifteen to sixty-five as in typical industrialized countries—a burden these poor countries can scarcely afford. The enormous proportion of children makes it extraordinarily difficult, where incomes are extremely low, to provide adequate shelter, nourishment, and education for the young.

Moreover, the preindustrial countries can expect no relief from dependency as a result of the spectacular drop in death rates now occurring. Unless fertility declines, this drop in mortality will only make the populations younger, adding to the already extreme burden of dependent children.

In sum, it is the industrialized countries that, better able to afford a high burden of child dependency, have only half the proportion of children found in underdeveloped areas, and that, having abandoned the institutions giving a meaningful role to the aged, have four times the proportion of the elderly found in preindustrial countries.

The last question considered in this brief survey of the age of populations is the past trend in age distribution from man's origin to the present, and what alternative trends may possibly develop in the future.

The human population as a whole has always been and is now a young population, consisting of at least 40 per cent children, and having a median age of no more than about twenty years, because the over-all human birth rate has always been about 40 per 1,000 or higher. It is almost certain that until perhaps two hundred years ago all sizable national or regional populations likewise were young, with about the same age characteristics as the population of the world.

These statements can be made with confidence, even though no reliable records of the age distribution of the world, or of world birth rates, or even records of many national populations exist for most of man's history. We can be confident that the world's population has always been young because until the last two centuries it was not possible for any population to achieve low mortality for any sustained period, and any population with a low birth rate would therefore have become extinct.

It is simply not possible for a population to have a birth rate much below its death rate for a prolonged period, as can be shown by the following example. The population of the world has grown from about one-quarter billion to about three billion since the time of Julius Caesar—it has been multiplied by about twelve. But the average annual rate of increase has been very little—about 1 per 1,000 per year. If the world birth rate has averaged 40 per 1,000 (a reasonable guess), the world death rate by logical necessity has averaged 39 per 1,000. A world birth rate only two points lower (38 instead of 40 per 1,000) would have led to an annual *decrease* of 1 per 1,000, and the current population would be only one twelfth instead of twelve times the population of Caesar's day. A birth rate of 35—that of England or the United States in 1880—would have reduced the 250 million of two thousand years ago to less than one hundred thousand today.

The industrialized countries have been able to reduce their birth rates without having their populations shrink drastically because they first reduced their death rates. Beginning in the late eighteenth century some countries made preliminary steps in the improvement in living conditions and sanitation that has continued until today, and in the latter half of the nineteenth century there began the remarkable development of modern medicine and public health that so greatly extended the average duration of life in the industrially more advanced countries.

In the past few decades modern medical techniques and public health methods have been introduced into the underdeveloped countries, causing an extraordinary drop in death rates, and since birth rates have not changed, the growth of world population has sharply accelerated so that it is now 2 per cent per year.

Just as it is not possible for a population to maintain for long a birth rate much below its death rate, because such a population would shrink to extinction, it is not possible to maintain for long a birth rate much *above* a death rate, because then the population would grow to a physically impossible size. For example, had the current 2 per cent rate of growth existed since the time of Caesar, the population of the world would have been multiplied by about 135 quadrillion instead of twelve, and there would be more than 30,000 times the entire world's current population on each square mile of land area on the earth. Starting with today's three billion persons, it would take only about 650 years for a 2 per cent rate of increase to produce one person per square foot, and about twice that long to produce a total that would outweigh the earth.

In short, the present combination of a high world birth rate and a moderate and rapidly falling death rate can only be temporary. The only combinations that can long continue are birth and death rates with the same average levels.

If man chooses to continue the high birth rate that he has always had, the human population will remain a young one—but in the long run it can remain young only by returning to the high death rate and short average life it has always had. Sustained geometric increase is impossible.

If, on the other hand, mankind can avoid nuclear war, and bring the fruits of modern technology, including prolonged life, to all parts of the world, the human population must become an old one, because only a low birth rate is compatible in the long run with a low death rate, and a low birth rate produces an old population. In fact, if the expectation of life at birth of seventy years—now achieved or exceeded in many industrialized countries—becomes universal, the average number of children born per woman must decline to about two from five or more in the underdeveloped areas, slightly more than three in the United States, and some two and a half in Europe. Such a decline in fertility would give the whole world as old a population as any country has had to date—only about 21 per cent under fifteen, at least 15 per cent over sixty-five, and as many persons over thirty-six as under.

A world population with the age composition of a health resort is a mildly depressing prospect. Such a population would presumably be cautious, conservative, and full of regard for the past. A young, vigorous, forward-looking population perhaps appears more attractive, but in the long run the world can keep its youth only by tolerating premature death.

We find at the end, then, that although the birth rate determines how old a population is, the death rate determines what the average birth rate in the long run must be. If prolonged life produces by its direct effects a younger population, it is nevertheless compatible only with an older population.

SUGGESTIONS FOR FURTHER READING

L. Dublin and A. Lotka. "On the True Rate of Natural Increase." *Journal of the American Statistical Association.* Vol. 20, No. 151, September 1925, pp. 305–39.

A classic article in which the interrelations of fertility, mortality, growth, and age distributions were presented with the ingenious invention of a new concept, "the stable age distribution."

United Nations. "The Cause of the Aging of Populations: Declining Mortality, or Declining Fertility?" *Population Bulletin* No. 4, December 1954, pp. 30–38.

Ansley J. Coale. "How the Age Distribution of a Human Population Is Determined." *Cold Springs Harbor Symposium on Quantitative Biology*. Vol. 22, 1957, pp. 83–88.

    Two short articles, the second somewhat technical, explaining the respective roles of fertility and mortality in shaping age distributions.

Ansley J. Coale. "Population and Economic Development," in *The Population Dilemma*, edited by Philip M. Hauser. Englewood Cliffs: Prentice-Hall, 1963, pp. 46–69.

    Includes a discussion of the significance of age distributions for economic development.

Fertility

Introduction

As one considers the basic elements in the population formula, it is difficult to escape the conclusion that fertility will be the most crucial factor in determining the demographic future of both individual countries and the world. What happens to fertility will determine more than anything else whether the growth rate of the world will be slowed. An increase in mortality could, of course, act to reduce the world's growth rate, but such a circumstance is distasteful to contemplate, and not really very likely to occur, given the present state of knowledge about medicine, food production, and transportation. Migration obviously cannot do much to solve world population problems, unless great advances are made in the reclamation of lands that are presently unsettled and uncongenial to habitation, or interplanetary travel and migration somehow become a reality much more quickly than expected.

In general, the key to the demographic future would seem to rest with fertility. The fertility trend of the next third of a century will certainly influence the nature of man's life on earth, and it is for this reason that experts and laymen alike are intensely interested in it. With regard to the underdeveloped countries of the world particularly, there is a great interest in what can be done, and in what is being done, to curb the generally high fertility rates.

It is for these reasons that our selections in this section tend to focus largely on fertility control as it applies, though not exclusively, to the underdeveloped countries of the world. While there are some aspects of fertility in the United States which might have been given more attention, we have tended to favor those issues that are more directly related to the high-fertility societies of the world, or are concerned with more universalistic issues.

The first two papers in this section have a general or universal applicability. The first of these is an extraordinarily useful paper by Kingsley Davis and Judith Blake which provides an analytic scheme that greatly facilitates the consideration of the relationship between sociocultural factors and fertility. The authors advance a definitive list of twelve factors as "intermediate variables" through which social structure and culture must necessarily operate if they are to influence fertility. The analytic scheme proposed in this paper has an elegance and utility that is unmatched by anything else in the comparative sociology of reproduction.

The second paper in this section, written by social anthropologist Mary Douglas, uses ethnographic data from four societies to demonstrate a fundamental point about population control by societal groups. Douglas refutes a hypothesis that asserts that populations (through a kind of inherent wisdom) will reach an optimum size relative to their natural resources. She does so by describing the resources, social customs, and population-control policies of several different societies, and arriving at the conclusion, by a careful ordering of the evidence, that the limited *social* resources of a society (particularly prestige) bring about population control more readily than limited natural resources. Douglas concludes her paper by pointing out the implication of her thesis for the societies of the world interested in controlling population growth.

The paper that follows, "Culture and Human Fertility in India," by T. J. Samuel, uses a somewhat different but still social frame of reference to discuss the fertility of India. The key concept in Samuel's analysis is social stability. The cultural elements of Indian life which lead to social stability "at the expense of social progress" seem to explain much of the fertility behavior of the Indian people. Samuel supports his position with historical-ethnographic data and more recently acquired data coming from special surveys of the Indian population.

In the next paper several such surveys are described by Thomas and Shirley Poffenberger. They utilize the results of a survey of Indian men and women, and compare them with the results of a study of male vasectomy in the United States. The Poffenberger paper is complementary to that of T. J. Samuel, since it provides additional data on the cultural features of Indian society which affect the acceptance of fertility-control techniques. Furthermore, the paper represents a useful frame of reference which allows the authors to make systematic comparisons from one culture to another.

Judith Blake's paper "Demographic Science and the Redirection of Population Policy" deserves a careful reading not only for the empirical data it offers on the fertility desires and motivations exhibited by Europeans and Americans, but also for the implications that she draws from the data regarding population-control policies. This is a careful and well-documented study of population, and the policy conclusions that are ultimately reached deserve very serious consideration. Blake begins her analysis by contrasting the two prevailing modes of viewing the relationship between economic development and fertility in the underdeveloped countries. Essentially, one school of thought holds that economic development must come first, with fertility declines following, while the alternate argument emphasizes that as long as high fertility remains unchecked, economic development can never be realized. Blake rejects the former position on both theoretical and practical grounds, and she concludes on the basis of the latter position that primary and immediate efforts should be made in the area of fertility control. Blake argues that since the only alternative control of the population growth rate in underdeveloped countries prior to economic development would be higher mortality rates, the only acceptable position is to turn to fertility control. If fertility control is the objective, then, Blake urges that it be based on a firm empirical foundation, not on intuitive assumptions. The major assumption that Blake attacks with empirical data is "that high birth rates in developing countries are today primarily a result of unwanted births."

On the basis of actual and desired fertility data, coming from societies in all parts of the world, Blake questions the effectiveness of fertility-control programs that are based solely on education about birth-control methods and propaganda on the desirability of a small family. She sees clearly that societies around the world have developed institutional structures that virtually ensure that people will desire children, and the evidence emerging from European countries is that they will desire as many children as they can afford. This being the case, it is not enough for a population-control policy to provide education and propaganda; it is also necessary that considered and deliberate changes be made in the institutions of the society. In particular, psychological alternatives must be found for the satisfactions that are currently being provided by marriage and family life. Since this kind of suggestion invades the nearly sacrosanct institution of the family, it must be made clear that no one is advocating a wholesale rejection and abandonment of the family; rather we must begin to examine the nature of its present supports and the impediments to alternatives. This is one paper on population control policies which takes seriously what social scientists have long been saying: social structure and culture exert a profound influence on fertility.

The final two papers in this section are summary evaluations of the research that has been done to educate people about birth-control methods and to improve their use of available methods. While Berelson is not unaware of the importance of social structure, his paper "On Family Planning Communication" focuses on the process of getting information (and techniques) of birth control to a population. For this reason it complements the paper by Blake, which emphasized the necessity of changing the institutional supports for high fertility.

The final paper in this section, J. Mayone Stycos' "Obstacles to Programs of Population Control—Facts and Fancies," deals with some of the practical and political problems that have hindered actual programs. Stycos has participated in several major studies of family planning in the Caribbean area. He first reviews some of the attitudes and beliefs held by the political and social elites in high-fertility countries which impede the development of effective population programs, and then turns to some of the characteristics of birth-control programs which by their very nature reduce the effectiveness of attempts to control fertility. Stycos offers a number of concrete suggestions for changing the character of fertility-control programs and thus improving their effectiveness.

The papers in this section concern themselves largely with the social and cultural foundations of high fertility, and the quest for effective fertility-control strategies and programs. This pattern clearly reflects the most pressing problem of population today, but we should perhaps remind ourselves that thirty years ago the important issue might have been declining fertility and the possibility that national populations would fail to reproduce themselves.

It is encouraging to recognize that the problems that concern the writers of these papers have received the serious attention of demographers for less than twenty years. It will be evident from a reading of these papers that we have already learned a great deal about why high fertility rates prevail in many countries. In particular, the importance of social structure and culture in the production of high fertility is demonstrated repeatedly. Furthermore, it will be clear that successful fertility-control programs must utilize this knowledge in two ways: First, some part of fertility-control programs must work to change the social structure (and culture) directly. Second, programs that are aimed toward education in fertility-control techniques must take cognizance of the prevailing characteristics of traditional social organization and culture.

18

Social Structure
and Fertility:
An Analytic Framework

Kingsley Davis
Judith Blake

A striking feature of underdeveloped areas is that virtually all of them exhibit a much higher fertility than do urban-industrial societies. This well-documented but insufficiently analyzed fact is known to be connected with profound differences in social organization as between the two types of society, and is therefore significant for the comparative sociology of reproduction. The clarity and importance of the contrast, however, should not be allowed to obscure the equally important fact that underdeveloped areas themselves differ markedly in social organization, and that these differences appear to bring about variations in fertility. Though the demographic statistics of backward regions have generally been so poor as to place in doubt the validity of reported differences, there are cases in which the evidence is reliable (e.g., as between Puerto Rico and Jamaica, or Arab Palestine and Ceylon). Of equal interest are the cases in which societies with differing social organization have the same level of fertility, for they may reach this common result by quite different institutional mechanisms. All told, ample opportunity exists for the comparative analysis of social structure as it affects fertility. In view of the bearing of future population trends on economic development, the pursuit of such analysis has a practical as well as a theoretical significance.

The present paper represents an attempt to set forth and utilize an analytical framework for the comparative sociology of fertility. It first pre-

Reprinted from *Economic Development and Cultural Change*, 4, no. 3 (April, 1956), pp. 211–35, by permission of the authors and the University of Chicago Press. Copyright © 1956 by the University of Chicago Press.

sents a classification of the intermediate variables through which any social factors influencing the level of fertility must operate. It next tries to show, in broad outline, how some types and elements of social organization, acting through these variables, appear to enhance or depress societal fertility. Our hope is that as more sociological and demographic information becomes available, the theories advanced can be refined further and tested empirically.

THE INTERMEDIATE VARIABLES

The process of reproduction involves three necessary steps sufficiently obvious to be generally recognized in human culture: (1) intercourse, (2) conception, and (3) gestation and parturition.[1] In analyzing cultural influences on fertility, one may well start with the factors directly connected with these three steps. Such factors would be those through which, and only through which, cultural conditions *can* affect fertility. For this reason, by way of convenience, they can be called the "intermediate variables" and can be presented schematically as follows:

I. Factors Affecting Exposure to Intercourse ("Intercourse Variables")

    A. Those governing the formation and dissolution of unions in the reproductive period.[2]

        1. Age of entry into sexual unions.

        2. Permanent celibacy: proportion of women never entering sexual unions.

        3. Amount of reproductive period spent after or between unions.

            a. When unions are broken by divorce, separation, or desertion.

            b. When unions are broken by death of husband.

    B. Those governing the exposure to intercourse within unions.

        4. Voluntary abstinence.

        5. Involuntary abstinence (from impotence, illness, unavoidable but temporary separations).

        6. Coital frequency (excluding periods of abstinence).

II. Factors Affecting Exposure to Conception ("Conception Variables")

        7. Fecundity or infecundity, as affected by involuntary causes.

        8. Use or non-use of contraception.

            a. By mechanical and chemical means.

            b. By other means.[3]

        9. Fecundity or infecundity, as affected by voluntary causes (sterilization, subincision, medical treatment, etc.).

III. Factors Affecting Gestation and Successful Parturition ("Gestation Variables")
   10. Foetal mortality from involuntary causes.
   11. Foetal mortality from voluntary causes.

It is clear that *any* cultural factor that affects fertility must do so in some way classifiable under one or another of our eleven intermediate variables.[4] Hence the latter provide a framework in terms of which the relevance of cultural factors to fertility can be judged. In fact, attempts to explain causal relationships between institutions and fertility without such a framework have led to inconclusive and confused writing on the subject.[5] The cultural factors, or "conditioning variables," are presumably many, and no effort is made here to classify them; but the "intermediate variables" offer a means of approach to selecting and analyzing these factors.

It is also clear that *each* of the eleven variables may have a negative (minus) or a positive (plus) effect on fertility. If by examining all societies we could find the range of influence of a given variable, any effect more negative than the midpoint of this range would be on the minus side, and any influence more positive would be on the plus side. If, for example, a society uses contraception successfully, it has a *minus* value with respect to variable number 8; if it uses *no* contraception, it has a plus value on this variable. The value of each variable refers to how it affects fertility in each case; so a positive use of something (e.g., contraception, abortion, abstinence) may mean that it has a "minus" fertility-value.

One cannot say, as is frequently implied in the literature, that some of these variables are affecting fertility in one society but not in another. *All* of the variables are present in *every* society. This is because, as mentioned before, each one *is* a variable—it can operate either to reduce or to enhance fertility. If abortion is *not* practiced, the fertility-value of variable number 11 is plus. In other words, the absence of a specific practice does not imply no influence on fertility, because this very absence is a form of influence. It follows that the position of any society, if stated at all, must be stated on all eleven variables.

Societies differing in their social organization do not necessarily have different fertility-values with respect to all the variables. On some of the variables they may exhibit quite similar values. A nomadic tribe may have the same age at marriage as a settled agrarian village; a primitive group may practice the same rate of abortion as an industrial society. Two contrasting societies are not likely, however, to manifest similar values for all the variables; they are not likely to do this even when their general fertility level is practically the same. The actual birth rate depends on the net balance of the values of all the variables. Though societies which generate a high fertility tend to be predominantly on the plus side, no society has the highest plus value on all eleven variables; and societies with low fertility turn out to be amazingly positive on a number of them.

It should, of course, be mentioned that cultural influences affecting our eleven variables do not necessarily represent rational attempts to govern fertility. Many fertility consequences stemming from socio-cultural conditions (especially in underdeveloped regions) are by-products, being unanticipated and unrealized by members of the society. Surely by now social scientists know that they cannot confine their attention only to rational actions or treat nonrational actions as somehow defying systematic analysis. The requirements of a given society can be met just as well, and just as ill, by an unintentional level of fertility as by an intentional one.

INSTITUTIONAL PATTERNS AND THE INTERMEDIATE VARIABLES: A PRELIMINARY ANALYSIS

From the standpoint of comparative sociology, an important question is how the fertility-values of our intermediate variables distribute themselves in different kinds of societies. A preliminary generalization is that underdeveloped societies tend to have high fertility-values for numbers 1, 2, 8, and 9 on the list; they *may* have high values for 3a, 3b, and 11; and they often have *low* values for 4 and 10. As for the remaining variables—5, 6, and 7—it is hard to prove that there are any consistent differences between pre-industrial and industrial societies. If this generalization is roughly accurate, then it becomes meaningful to re-group the eleven variables as follows:

THE INTERMEDIATE VARIABLES ACCORDING TO THEIR VALUES IN PRE-INDUSTRIAL SOCIETIES

Usually High Values	*Usually Low Values*
1. Age of entry into unions.	4. Voluntary abstinence.
2. Permanent celibacy.	10. Foetal mortality—involuntary.
8. Contraception.	
9. Sterilization, etc.	

High or Low Values	*Indeterminate*
3a. Time between unstable unions.	5. Involuntary abstinence.
3b. Post-widowhood celibacy.	6. Frequency of coitus.
11. Foetal mortality—voluntary.	7. Involuntary sterility.

In attempting to analyze in a preliminary way how different institutional patterns affect the variables, we shall find it convenient to follow the order just given.

Number 1. Age of Entry into Unions

In beginning with age of entry into unions, we are dealing with one of the variables governing exposure to intercourse. It should be noted that these particular variables, however favorable they may be to fertility in themselves, may be counteracted in practice by other factors governing conception and gestation. For example, even though sexual unions begin early, pregnancy or childbirth may be prevented. This is often the case when the sexual union is not a marriage. Many societies, even though they permit pre-marital intercourse, strongly forbid illegitimate pregnancy.[6] With respect to marital unions, however, reproduction is specifically sanctioned, indeed expected. As already mentioned, there may be, in addition, non-marital unions in which reproduction also normally occurs. Consequently, in dealing with age of entry into unions, we shall separate those unions in which off-spring normally appear (including both marital and non-marital types) from those in which reproduction is so strongly condemned that it is infrequent. We shall now deal with the first general class (paying attention mostly to marriage itself), leaving until later the discussion of non-reproductive sexual unions.

Since in pre-industrial societies the age of entry into reproductive unions is generally young, the question must be raised as to why the fertility-value of this variable is usually positive when on certain other variables it is often negative. From a broad functional standpoint, the explanation stems from high mortality. Not only does a high death rate normally prevail in underdeveloped societies from year to year, but there is always the danger of a sudden catastrophic rise in mortality. Early marriage therefore represents the maximum possible hedge against the threat of failure in population replacement. Entering a union at a young age does not commit one irretrievably to a large family, because all other means of reducing fertility come *after* this point. If a particular union is resulting in progeny that are too numerous under current circumstances, this eventuality can be obviated by abstinence, contraception, abortion, or infanticide. These means, precisely because they come later, can be utilized at a time closer to the actual impingement of new individuals on the resources of those responsible. If, on the other hand, the age of entry into unions is late, the potential fertility that is lost can never be recovered. The threat of mortality, from a societal standpoint, has reference not only to the potential offspring, but also to the parents themselves. Early formation of unions helps to guarantee that the young adults will achieve at least some reproduction before they die.

This broad functional explanation does not, however, enlighten us concerning the specific institutional mechanisms by which early marriage is insured. These can best be understood in terms of family and kinship organization (involving rules of residence and rules of descent) and the control of property. Such mechanisms apply most clearly to formal marriage, although they may apply as well, though in lesser degree, to informal reproductive unions.

From the standpoint of kinship organization, an essential distinction is that between a joint household and/or clan system, on the one hand, and an independent nuclear family organization on the other. When the clan is the unit controlling the property (whether the latter consists of herds or land), the question of inheritance does not normally arise, because the clan is immortal. When the joint family is the controlling unit, the question arises only when the joint family divides; the joint family, however, does not divide when the offspring marry, but rather, at the earliest, when the father dies. Thus, in societies having a joint household (and *a fortiori* in those having a strong clan organization), marriage is in no way made contingent on the possession of separate property by the newly married pair.

Furthermore, with strong clan or joint-household control (or both), marriages are usually arranged by the elders, who are often motivated to make the arrangements early in the lifetime of the prospective mates, i.e., before puberty. Religious prescription may require this result, and the economic exchanges involved in betrothal may be structured in such a way as to yield an advantage to the parents who marry their daughter early. If the system is one of patrilocal residence, for example, a grown daughter remaining in her parental home is an anomaly. Not only does her presence run counter to the normal division of labor by sex, which assumes the complementarity of husband and wife, but she must adjust to the wives of her brothers coming into the household. Add to this fact that the daughter, as a prospective spouse, is most in demand by other families when she is young, first because she then has a greater potential fertility ahead of her, and, second, because she is more attractive sexually and fits more easily into a subordinate status in her husband's parental home. If, then, there is a substantial brideprice or groomprice at marriage, the girl's kin stand a better chance of a favorable bargain if they marry her off early. This may help them in procuring wives for their sons.

In societies having neither a strong clan nor a joint family, the forces leading to early marriage may be overbalanced by others. The Irish family, for instance, has long been organized in terms of neolocal residence and hence marital rather than filial solidarity. This being true, land had to be obtainable or marriage postponed. During the greater part of the eighteenth century land was scarce and could not be subdivided because the economy was predominantly pastoral. Consequently, an obstacle to early marriage "was the difficulty of acquiring a settlement *upon which a new family might depend.*"[7] Later, during the sixty years before the Famine, when the potato

became the staple food and the economy shifted from pastoralism to cultivation, couples could get property at marriage by subdivision of the land,
thus removing temporarily the main obstacle to early marriage. But with the
crisis of the Famine, the futility of progressive subdivision led to the Land
Purchase Acts stipulating that the loans which transformed tenants into
owners were granted only on condition that no subdivision would take
place. Since the annuities ran for 35 years, this represented some restraint on
subdivision.[8] A more powerful restraint was the fact that, once the tenants
became owners, they grew unwilling to subdivide in behalf of their sons.
The tendency was to retain only one son on the paternal land, the remainder
of the children being dispersed, partly through migration abroad. The independent nuclear family was maintained, but the son who remained at home
could not establish such a family until the father was willing to resign both
authority and property. As a result the average age at marriage in Ireland
became extremely advanced, reaching 29.1 for women by 1926.[9]

Lest our characterization of Irish family organization as neolocal appear surprising, it should be noted that although the Irish have been interpreted as having a joint household and patrilocal residence,[10] the opposite
seems to be true. Even if one or two sons remain at home, the resulting
menage is not what is ordinarily called a joint household; because in Ireland
marriage implies the independence of the son. When the son brings a bride
into what was the paternal homestead, he brings her into a home that has
been redefined as his, no longer his father's. The father has relinquished
both ownership of the farm and authority over the son. As long as the father
continues to own the land, the son who remains at home cannot marry because the land is necessary for the "match."[11] If marriage occurs, therefore,
the fact that the parents are still in the home is merely adventitious—they
have entered "the age grade of the dying."[12] Significantly, if irreconcilable
conflict develops in the shared household, it is the parents, not the son and
his wife, who must leave. "The bond between them [husband and wife] is
stronger than that between son and parent."[13] Thus in Ireland the fact of
sharing a house with the parents is not a reflection of the joint family ideal
but of the force of circumstances. The fact of a common menage is socially
defined in such a way as to comply with the ideal of a neolocal and independent nuclear family.

This independent nuclear family organization is neither unique to Ireland nor modern in development. In Northwestern Europe the custom of
impartible inheritance (e.g., by primogeniture or ultimogeniture) was
found in many areas during the Middle Ages. In some sections it was apparently customary for the old people to give their land to the heir before
they died. Surrendering their authority, they expected only their keep off
the land. The heir's marriage was contingent on the land being turned over

to him; if his sisters and brothers stayed on, they could claim their keep but not the privilege of marriage.[14] The principle of no holding, no marriage,[15] operated to advance the average age beyond what it otherwise would have been. Furthermore, the notion of the independence of the nuclear family also manifested itself in the master-apprentice relationship within the medieval guilds; for marriage often did not occur until an adequate guild status had been acquired by inheritance, purchase, or dower.[16] There is thus evidence that European society has long emphasized the marital rather than the filial bond as the basis of family organization, with a consequent tendency to delay marriage.[17]

The emphasis on marital rather than filial solidarity, on neolocal rather than patrilocal residence, which appears to have delayed marriage in Ireland and Northwestern Europe, contrasts sharply with the forces operating to precipitate marriage in an extended family system. In a truly joint household the authority of the elders continues *after* marriage; the marital bond is therefore subordinate to the filial bond and does not require economic independence on the part of those getting married. Such a family pattern is well known as the ideal one in traditional China, India, Bantu Africa, and many other peasant or primitive cultures. In the Chinese case, the father maintains his tutelage over the married son and his control over the familial property until death. He consequently need not fear the marriage of his son as a threat to his authority, and therefore, unlike the Irish father, has no motive (at least in this regard) for postponing such marriage. On the contrary, to the extent that his son brings a wife into the house and has children, the old man's authority is extended. Indeed, it is only by the marriage of his son that the patriarch can fulfill *his* filial obligation to *his* father.[18]

Number 2. Extent of Permanent Celibacy

If late marriage can have a minus effect on fertility, so can permanent non-marriage. In both cases, if this effect is to be produced, there must be either continence outside of marriage, or the use of means to prevent intercourse from resulting in childbirth. In practice, non-marriage usually does produce a low rate of reproduction among the unmarried, because, as mentioned already, marriage in all societies is the preferred institutional arrangement for having children. It seems wise, therefore, to discuss "celibacy" primarily in terms of non-marriage, and to consider sexual continence only in so far as it illuminates that factor.

Although permanent non-marriage is obviously a more potent factor than mere postponement of marriage, it actually occurs less frequently and hence has less negative influence on fertility. Only rarely can a population be found where more than 20 per cent of the women complete the reproductive period without ever having married. Ireland is an extreme case, with 26.3% of its women aged 45–49 in 1946 still single.[19] If we assume that these women, had they married, would have had the same completed fertility as those who did, then their proportion represents an estimate of the loss of fertility due to non-marriage (excluding illegitimate births).[20] Thus the loss due to permanent non-marriage seems, even in the extreme case, scarcely to exceed one-fourth. Such a loss in fertility is greatly exceeded by that due to late age at marriage. For example, in Switzerland (where the data are readily available), if all women in 1941 who had ever married by ages 40–44 had married at ages 15–19 and had subsequently manifested the same age-specific fertility as those who had actually married then or did marry at some point prior to age 40, the reproduction would have been 75% greater than it actually was![21] In other words, the gain in fertility if late marriage had been eliminated would have been approximately three times the gain (25%) if permanent non-marriage had been eliminated.

It is mainly in urban-industrial societies that the proportion of women never marrying by the end of the reproductive span exceeds 10%. In India in 1931 it was only 0.8%; in Ceylon in 1946, 3.4%; and in Malaya in 1947, 3.3%. Thus the underdeveloped areas generally show a very high plus value for fertility with respect both to variable number 1 (age at marriage) and variable number 2 (proportion ever married), whereas industrial societies often show rather low fertility-values on these.

We thus have to answer two questions: Why do all societies generally make less use of non-marriage than of late marriage in depressing fertility? Why do underdeveloped peoples make less use of *both* of the mechanisms than do industrial societies? Let us attempt to answer these two questions in order.

Given the low fecundity of the human species, no society can hope to replace itself unless either a majority of its women participate in reproduction or its mortality is rigorously controlled. Since most of man's history has occurred under conditions of heavy mortality—conditions which still prevail for many of the world's people—all viable societies have evolved social mechanisms that lead the majority of women to participate in reproduction. Their participation is organized through the institution of marriage, which links sex and reproduction to the care and socialization of children. This institution is in turn supported by its articulation with the rest of the social order. The marital relation thus becomes a general norm in terms of which the hopes and expectations of virtually all individuals are channelized. If for some reason the pressure of mortality is relaxed, the norm still continues in effect. Not only do normative systems change slowly, but there still remains the necessity for a family organization in terms of which reproduction and child-rearing are provided for. Thus individuals continue to anticipate marriage as a normal and important part of life, an event more easily postponed than forgone altogether.

In any case, an increase in non-marriage would not reduce fertility unless either coitus outside of wedlock were successfully banned or contraception and abortion were freely used. If the latter were readily available, they could be used *within* marriage, and the consequent reduction in marital fertility would obviate the necessity of denying marriage to a substantial portion of the population. If contraception and abortion were not readily available, non-marriage would be an effective brake on fertility only at the price of permanent sexual celibacy. Everything we know about human society indicates that this price is so high that no population is willing to pay it.

Since no society has ever attempted to incorporate permanent celibacy as a widespread custom, we have no conclusive evidence as to what it would do to a social system. We can, however, obtain some clues by examining countries in which permanent celibacy has appeared to an unusual extent and by examining organizations which have enjoined it as a rule. We can also say something on purely theoretical grounds concerning what it might do if utilized as the chief means of reducing fertility to a modern level. Limitations of space prevent our giving a complete treatment along these lines, but something can be said about each of them.

Because Ireland has an unusually late age at marriage and a high proportion who never marry, together with a strong prejudice against coitus outside of marriage, it provides the main example of a rather extensive practice of celibacy.[22] Has this adjustment exacted a price? To answer such a question is difficult. A puritanical attitude toward sex cannot be listed as a consequence, because this is part of the celibacy itself. That the Irish avoid reproduction outside of marriage is shown by their low illegitimacy rate—2.8% of all live births in 1921–1930 and 3.3% in 1931–1940.[23] However, such descriptions as we have suggest that a great amount of attention, community effort, and personality conflict go into controlling sexual expression. Having a social system that emphasizes the marital bond and the nuclear family, the Irish cannot completely segregate unmarried females, as is done in Moslem countries. The young people must have some chance to participate in courtship and mate selection. But, given this system, the Irish seem to make an unusually strong effort to control sexual behavior. For a country not living under a dictatorship, the official censorship of literature and ideas is exceptionally rigid, and has as its main purpose the suppression of material pertaining to sex and reproduction.[24] Furthermore, the data on mental illness, which show a high rate for Ireland, indicate a possible consequence of such repression.[25] There appear to be few features in Irish life that compensate for whatever is lost through celibacy. Ireland has, for example, the lowest level of living of any nation in Northwestern Europe. All told, there is some ground for the hypothesis that Ireland is paying a price for its unusual degree of celibacy.

Celibacy as an *organizational* rule has been almost solely applied to religious personnel. Among those few religions which have adopted such a rule for their clergy, our evidence is most readily available for the Roman Catholic priesthood. As is well known, the application of the rule in this case encountered great difficulties. It required nearly nine centuries before the edict of non-marriage itself could be enforced with relative success. Priests were first commanded to separate from their wives and remain continent in 385 A.D. After that date there were periods when the ban against marriage could be safely ignored by priests, followed by periods when the Church was militantly purging its married clergy. Pope Gregory (Hildebrand) encountered such obstacles in enforcing the rule of non-marriage that he ordered the laity to withdraw their obedience from all members of the clergy who disregarded the papal canons on simony and incontinence. By so doing, he undermined a basic principle of the Church—clerical immunity—and thus as early as 1074 directly laid one of the foundations of the Reformation. Only by placing the sacrament of marriage in a lower position than that of the religious vow (Lateran Council of 1123) did the Church finally settle the issue of clerical marriage, although in practice such marriages occurred with some frequency after that—as late as the nineteenth century in some parts of Latin America, for example. In periods when the ban against marriage was being enforced, the Church still had to deal with sexual incontinence among its priests and nuns. "Solicitation" (the seduction of female penitents), concubinage, and other violations were so common as to cause chronic public scandal. In some areas priestly concubinage became, for long periods, a customary practice, and the sons of priests received preferment.[26] We can thus see that the enforcement of celibacy even for that small fraction of the population represented by the clergy was anything but easy.

If we imagine a society in which celibacy is institutionalized and becomes a norm rivaling marriage, we can see that the result would be paradoxical and impossible. Should the celibate class be large enough to reduce the birth rate to a modern level without other means, it would have to contain at least half the population. For individuals on such a scale to be induced to make the sacrifice of celibacy, they would not only have to be firmly controlled (perhaps segregated from the rest of the community and thus divorced from the temptations of everyday life), but would also have to be ideologically indoctrinated, and, above all, socially rewarded. If the rewards were great enough to recruit people for the numerous celibate portion of the population, this class would inevitably occupy the top of the social ladder. But the celibate class would be too big to be an elite. Furthermore, the sheer fact of celibacy would not represent in itself a contribution to the productive capacity of the society. If the celibate population were given useful tasks to perform, the variety of functions would necessarily be great; and if all these received an indiscriminately high reward, some celibates would be receiving this return not because of their productive contribution, but because of their celibacy. In this way, seeking to give half or more of its population advantages that at best only a few can be given (and doing so regardless of productive merit), the society would suffer an intolerable economic and social burden.[27]

After this analysis of the relatively minor role of permanent celibacy in fertility limitation, we are now ready for our second question: Why are late marriage and non-marriage more frequent in industrial than in pre-industrial societies?

Perhaps non-marriage occurs more often in industrial societies because these societies depend less upon kinship and the family as bases of social organization. The fact of being or not being married affects less the individual's economic chances. In pre-industrial societies, where the family is a productive unit, marriage has a high value for the individual. Also, where the partners to marriage are self-selected by a competitive process of courtship, as in modern countries, there tends to be a substantial proportion who are not successful in attracting a suitable mate.

The greater postponement of marriage in urban-industrial nations can be similarly explained. The necessity of lengthy training for skilled positions in an industrial economy, the often lengthy trial-and-error process of courtship, the necessity of economic self-sufficiency on the part of the newly married couple—all are conducive to marital postponement.

But in neither type of society is non-marriage likely to be as important a depressant of fertility as late marriage, because marriage remains the institutional norm in both cases. Wedlock may be postponed with some equanimity, but individuals who actually never marry have, in most cases, hoped that this would not be their fate. In Ireland, for example, clerical celibacy is certainly valued, but not permanent celibacy among laymen.[28]

Once again let us note that neither the postponement nor the total abjuration of marriage necessarily implies sexual celibacy. Hence no industrial society today is required to use either method as a dominant means of controlling fertility, because other less drastic, less sacrificial methods are available. It is clear that marital postponement, non-marriage, and abstinence within marriage, if they are effective in limiting fertility, all have a common feature—sexual denial; and all share the difficulties that this entails.

Number 8. Use or Non-Use of Contraception

Whereas the "intercourse variables" have a negative effect on fertility only through abstinence, neither the conception nor the gestation variables require this drastic behavior by the individual or the institutionalization necessary to insure such behavior. With the "conception variables" (of which the use or non-use of contraception is one), the pleasure of intercourse is not forgone. The individual, thus released from paying a heavy appetitive penalty for the decision not to have children, is much freer to decide this issue in terms of his economic and social interests alone.

With reference to contraception in particular, its apparent efficiency might lead one to expect a widespread use of it as a depressant of fertility. Yet we have already stated that this is one of the three variables which almost universally have a strong plus fertility-value in pre-industrial societies. Why, then, do these societies so widely exhibit the *non-use* of contraception? To answer this question, we must consider separately the two types of contraception.

8a. Contraception by chemical or mechanical means. In many primitive and peasant cultures the idea of chemical and mechanical contraception is known and attempts are made to apply it. Yet, even in situations motivating the individual to limit his fertility, this is *not* usually the means adopted, simply because the technology of underdeveloped societies cannot supply effective methods. In the absence of a knowledge of reproductive physiology, people in these societies have little sense of even the kind of instrumentalities to look for. Similarly, there is not enough knowledge of chemistry to give command over materials. The methods, therefore, tend to be hit or miss, with magic rather than science playing a prominent role. Lack of experimental technique leads one method to be valued as highly as another.[29] Even the methods that would actually accomplish the purpose of contraception are apt to be clumsy, sexually unsatisfactory, and unhealthful, e.g., insertion of an okra-like seed pod in the vagina (Bush Negroes of British Guiana); insertion of rags or finely chopped grass (Bapindas and Bambundas in Central Africa); insertion of dung (Egypt and other societies).[30] Furthermore, granted that a really satisfactory method is hit upon, such as possibly the use of a douche containing lemon juice or a decoction of the husks of mahogany nut (Martinique or Guiana),[31] the materials are likely to be available only in one locale or in certain seasons of the year. Thus the technology and economy of pre-industrial societies have not been equal to the task of providing a chemico-mechanical contraceptive that would be at once cheap, satisfactory, effective, and readily available.

8b. Contraception without chemical or mechanical means. Clearly such methods as withdrawal, intercourse without penetration, and various heterosexual "perversions" do not depend on scientific and technological progress. They are known and practiced in one form or another in nearly all societies.[32] Yet they seem to be insufficiently employed to represent a major control over fertility. They may be so employed in a few primitive societies, but apparently not in the civilizations such as those of China, India, and the Near East, where huge population aggregates are found. For the most part, it seems, they are employed in extra-marital relations or in those cases where premarital intercourse is permitted but premarital pregnancy forbidden. But it is doubtful that such practices represent an important contribution to fertility control in whole societies. Numerous societies —some with a good share of the world's people—either do not permit the ordinary female to engage in premarital intercourse, or have such a young age at marriage that such intercourse would play a small role in any case. As for extra-marital relations, those societies which permit them under certain circumstances are not particularly concerned about the woman's becoming pregnant, because biological paternity is not stressed. Only those societies branding adulterous children as illegitimate would condemn the married woman's pregnancy by another man than the husband, and these would be societies which restrict extra-marital intercourse. For these reasons, to have an independent and significant effect on fertility, non-mechanical contraceptive methods would have to be used *within* marriage. We are therefore forced to ask why such methods are not more widely used within wedlock in pre-industrial societies.

The reader should recall that any society with a high mortality must in general motivate its members to view legitimate reproduction favorably. Under this pressure the cultures in question, as already pointed out, are so organized as to maximize fertility values in the early stages of the reproductive process—e.g., by early marriage. Although intercourse is one step later, it is still so early as to involve a risk of inadequate fertility. If conditions subsequently make children undesirable, measures can still be taken after conception.

An additional consideration is that the physical burden and danger of childbearing, and the responsibility for nourishing and rearing the child, fall mainly on the mother. If therefore there is a wish to avoid childbirth, this wish is apt to be hers rather than her husband's. It happens, however, that the non-chemico-mechanical methods of contraception are the ones requiring the cooperation and partial frustration of the male. Since he is not under the pressures that affect his wife in this matter, he may be reluctant to aid her in avoiding pregnancy.

The social insulation of the two sexes is often carried so far that communication between them is difficult. This insulation is particularly observable in regard to sexual behavior, which tends to be surrounded by taboos and rituals. As between husband and wife, sexual intercourse, by virtue of being the special bond and therefore the focus of anxiety and conflict between them, may be the topic they discuss with least freedom. Thus the cooperation necessary for contraception is made difficult.

In such terms we can understand why the available methods of contraception receive scant use in underdeveloped societies. Which of the considerations mentioned plays the greatest role is hard to say, but the fact should be emphasized that not all the reasons for limiting births are predictable at the time of intercourse—particularly in simple societies that live close to the environment and are threatened by quick catastrophe. The individual couple may, therefore, as we shall see later, limit fertility *after* rather than *at* the time of intercourse.

Number 9. Voluntary Control over Fecundity

Like chemical and mechanical contraception, satisfactory control of fecundity is beyond the technical capacity of pre-industrial societies. Neither the reduction nor the enhancement of fecundity by harmless medical measures appears possible in such cultures. Operations on the male external genitalia can be performed, such as subincision and castration, but these are either too drastic to be harmless or have little effect on fecundity.[33]

We may conclude, then, that pre-industrial societies are plus on variable number 9. But so are industrial societies. The latter may have even more of a plus fertility-value on this variable than simple societies because they can, and usually do, forbid sterilization and, at the same time, foster medical treatment for sterility, thus *enhancing* the fecundity of partially sterile couples.

Although modern science makes harmless sterilization possible, it has not yet been used, except in Puerto Rico, as a popular method of avoiding children.[34] The Puerto Rican case suggests, however, that sterilization may in the future become more widely diffused in underdeveloped areas. If the operational technique were improved to the point where it could be easily reversed—so that it could be used for the spacing, as well as limiting the total number, of children—it might become the principal means of reducing fertility in backward areas.

Number 3a. Time between Unstable Unions

Any negative effect on fertility from variable 3a is a function of both the rate of dissolution of unions and the time lost between them. If unions are stable, or if they are unstable but no time is lost between them, fertility will not be affected adversely.

With reference to *marital* unions, pre-industrial societies seem generally to have a low rate of dissolution. True, there are certain exceptions to this rule. Some of the Islamic peoples show a tendency toward marital instability, and in some primitive societies the clan or joint household takes such precedence over the nuclear family that the latter tends to be somewhat unstable.[35] On the whole, however, the institutional structure of pre-industrial groups buttresses marriage in such ways as to give it considerable stability.

When a society has a significant proportion of informal unions which it regards as inferior to legal marriage but in which reproduction is nevertheless expected (e.g., "consensual unions" in Latin America and "common law" unions in the British West Indies), one of the features of such unions is that they tend to be unstable. In such cases the woman may wait some time before entering a new union, and the fertility lost may be substantial. For a small sample of women in Jamaica (where around 70% of the births are illegitimate) the reduction in fertility due to the instability of unions was approximately 37%.[36] The informal type of union arises as an institutional form from various historical causes. In societies that have been disorganized by Western contact, they may appear abundantly, and legal marriage itself may become unstable.[37] In other instances where the social order has grown largely out of a former slave class, informal unions may.be both more numerous and more unstable than legal marriages.[38]

With reference to premarital unions, there is every evidence that in the many societies where these are permitted they are, as a rule, highly unstable, amounting in many cases to adolescent promiscuity. However, there is ordinarily little time lost between such liaisons; few societies permit reproduction in them; and, given a young age at marriage, most such unions occur at an age when adolescent sterility seemingly reduces the number of conceptions.

It follows that pre-industrial societies generally have a plus fertility-value with respect to variable number 3a, but the exceptions are more numerous than was the case with the other variables so far considered.

Number 3b. Post-widowhood Celibacy

What effect the high rate of widowhood found in pre-industrial societies has on fertility depends on the institutional position of the widow. In many such societies she loses little time from exposure to intercourse, because she soon marries again. In other pre-industrial cultures, however, the widow either must wait for a protracted period or is subject to a distinct prejudice against remarrying at all. An important problem in analyzing the institutional impingements on fertility is the discovery of why some societies take one course in· this regard and others take the opposite course.

If we study those societies in which remarriage occurs universally and soon, we find that they are the ones requiring the widow to marry a kinsman of the deceased husband (levirate). Such societies are usually primitive, practicing a shifting cultivation, hunting, or pastoral pursuits, and are characterized by strong clan or lineage organization. Marriage involves substantial economic exchanges and, if the system is patrilineal and patrilocal, these are weighted in favor of the bride's lineage (brideprice). The woman brought into the clan or lineage as a wife is conceived as belonging to this clan, which has paid the brideprice; her children, who are automatically members of the husband's lineage, represent her contribution in return for the cost of procuring her. When the woman is widowed, the lineage retains control over her, not only because a price has been paid for her, but also because her children must remain with the lineage. If she still is fecund, the lineage feels it would be losing potential children if she did not remarry. But remarriage to an outsider would be unsatisfactory, because the children of that union would belong to another lineage. Hence the remarriage must be within the clan. Since in the exchanges cementing the first marriage, the husband's nearest relatives bore the main cost, it is natural that his close kin (notably his brothers) should have first claim on the widow. If the deceased husband has no actual brothers, one of his "classificatory brothers" can be substituted. In anticipation of her possibly entering a leviratic union, a woman's relation with her husband's actual and classificatory brothers is often one of privileged familiarity. The term for "husband's brother" may be the same as that for "husband." The social structure clearly demonstrates that the clan is thinking of the widow in terms of her potential production of children. Among the Nuer, for instance, even if the widow should take as a lover a person outside the clan (she cannot legally marry outside), the children are viewed as the descendants of the dead husband and therefore as members of his, not the lover's, clan.[39]

In many societies, on the other hand, the widow is forbidden to marry a close relative of the deceased husband. These seem to be cases in which the clan, however important it may once have been, has receded in economic and political significance, seemingly as a result of technological advance and greater class stratification. The economy is that of a more stable agriculture in which the same land is intensively cultivated year in and year out. Under such circumstances the joint household acquires more independence and more significance as an economic unit than it seems to have in most primitive societies. The distinction between relatives in different households thus takes precedence over their solidarity as members of the same lineage or clan. To be sure, the woman marrying into the joint household may do so in terms of some form of economic exchange, but this exchange is between individual households rather than clans. The widow and her children accordingly belong to the deceased husband's household. Remarriage to one of her dead mate's brothers or other close male relatives, however, would be structurally inappropriate, because the joint household is always subject to dissolution and must be so organized as to minimize the complications of such dissolution. Unlike the clan or lineage, which is immortal and indefinitely expandable, the household is a residential economic unit which can easily grow too large for its immediate resources. With stable agriculture, the household must be near the land it works. If its membership increases, it must ultimately break up because the land required for sustenance will be too distant. When the household does break up, usually at the death of the male head, it does so by the separation of its nuclear families.[40] Accordingly, even when the nuclear family forms part of a joint household, it is visualized not only as a separate unit but also as one that may in the future have its own independent residence. A widow's remarriage to one of her husband's relatives within the household would conflict with this idea of potential independence. It would inextricably merge two nuclear families. It would require polygyny and would emphasize the solidarity of the sibling relationship rather than the father-son relation so central to the independent joint household.

Stable agrarian societies not only forbid the widow to marry within the circle of her husband's kin but also often frown on her marrying anyone at all. This additional prejudice seems likewise to be explicable in structural terms. For the widow to marry outside would require that some agency make a match for her, because marriages in traditional agrarian societies are arranged by persons other than the parties to the union. However, her family of orientation is no longer responsible for her. The family of her deceased husband is restrained from taking the responsibility for several reasons. It would, in seeking a mate for the widow, have to treat her as a daughter, which might interfere with the rights of the actual daughters. Furthermore, since she is a widow and is older, she has become less valuable than upon her first marriage, so that it is difficult to get her married at a social level reflecting favorably on the family's prestige. If the widow has children, her marriage outside the immediate kin would require her separation from them. It is thus understandable why traditional agrarian societies, especially where the joint household is normally preferred, should exhibit a prejudice against widow remarriage. Such unions certainly do occur, particularly in the lower classes, which cannot carry out the joint family ideal, but the prejudice may be strong enough to prevent a high proportion of widows in the upper classes from remarrying.[41] In India the caste controls reinforce those of the joint household in preventing widow remarriage. Since such unions are thought to lower the caste's prestige, and since marriage is endogamous within the caste, both parties to a remarriage are condemned. For this reason the reduction of fertility due to widow agamy is probably greater in India than in any other country, especially because of the early age at marriage and the high mortality there.

Number 11. Voluntary Control over Foetal Mortality

Underdeveloped societies have few means for *lessening* foetal mortality, but they do have readily available means, through abortion, for *increasing* such mortality. In fact, abortion is widely practiced in pre-industrial societies, being the individual's principal means of limiting fertility.[42] Since medical measures to avoid foetal mortality do not, at least as yet, have as much influence on fertility as voluntary abortion can and does, we can say that whether a society has a plus or minus fertility-value with respect to variable 11 depends primarily on the extent to which it practices abortion. Accordingly, some pre-industrial societies are on the "plus" side (forbidding abortion and practicing it little) but many others are on the "minus" side (practicing abortion to a considerable extent). If we grant that interference with conception is less hazardous to health than interference with pregnancy, an important question for us is why abortion is so much more frequently used in underdeveloped societies than contraception.

In answering this question, one can point to the following considerations: (a) as compared to mechanical and chemical means of contraception, abortion is technically simple.[43] (b) In contrast to such non-chemico-mechanical methods as *coitus interruptus* or *coitus inter femora,* abortion is not applied at the time of intercourse and does not require cooperation between man and woman. It is a woman's method and can be practiced without the man's knowledge. (c) Unlike contraception, it is completely effective. (d) Once an undesired pregnancy has occurred, the need for abortion is certain, whereas at the time of intercourse there is always the chance that pregnancy will not eventuate anyway. (e) Although a child may be desired at the time of intercourse, subsequent events may alter this attitude, at which time abortion rather than contraception is a remedy.

A note on infanticide. Although infanticide is not dealt with as an integral part of our analysis because it does not affect fertility, one should note that it is virtually a functional equivalent of abortion in controlling family size, and that it too is practiced widely in pre-industrial societies, much more so than contraception. The rationale for its use is much the same as that for abortion, but it does differ from the latter in at least three respects. First, infanticide allows the progeny to be selected by sex, as shown by the custom of *female* infanticide. The logic of this practice is exemplified by the Netsilik Eskimos:

> The most glaring consequence of the struggle for existence is manifested in the way in which they try to breed the greatest possible number of

boys and the fewest possible girls . . . girls are killed at birth, if they have not already been promised to a family where there is a son who some day is to have a wife . . . They hold the view that if a woman is to suckle a girl child it will be two or three years before she may expect her next confinement . . . A hunter must take into consideration that he can only subject himself and his constitution for comparatively few years to all the strain that hunting demands . . . Now if he has sons, they will as a rule be able to step in and help just when his own physique is beginning to fail. Thus it is life's own inexorability that has taught them the necessity of having as many sons as possible. Only by that means may they be certain that they will not need to put the rope around their own neck too early; for it is the common custom that old people, who can no longer keep themselves, prefer to put an end to their life by hanging . . .[44]

Olga Lang discusses the persistence of the immemorial custom of female infanticide in China. The hospital records used for her study "contained matter-of-fact references to infanticide made by Chinese social and medical workers indicating that it was taken for granted. Much more often, however, infant daughters have not been killed outright. What happens is that the small amount of food available for the family is unequally distributed: the son gets the larger share and the daughters are practically starved. Hence the frequent epidemics have taken a heavier toll of girls than of boys."[45] Much the same could be said of India.

Second, infanticide also allows the offspring to be selected according to physical status, weeding out those with deformities, bad health, or unacceptable physical or racial characteristics.[46] Third, it can be practiced when the circumstances of birth are considered to be abnormal and ritualistically taboo. Twins, children born with feet first or with teeth, infants whose mothers died at their birth,[47] and offspring born on unlucky days are typical victims.[48] Fourth, whereas abortion may injure the health of the mother, infanticide obviously does not.

A *disadvantage* of infanticide may seem to be that since a child has already been born, a living person is being killed. However, the newborn child is often not viewed as a member of society until he has passed through some sort of ceremony (*amphidromia* in ancient Greece, presentation of the child to the father in China) which defines him as such. The destruction of the child is therefore viewed psychologically in much the same light as abortion.

Number 4. Voluntary Abstinence within Unions

Abstinence within unions is practiced much more, on the average, in preindustrial than in industrial societies. The effect of such abstinence on fertility, however, depends on the circumstances; for there are at least four types of restriction—post-partum, occasional, gestational, and menstrual. The first two types tend to limit fertility, while the last two, if they have any effect at all, tend to increase it.

Post-partum abstinence occurs in nearly all societies, including our own. The amount of time involved, however, varies greatly—all the way from one to two weeks in some societies to two to three years in others. Many pre-industrial societies insist upon abstinence for an arbitrary period of time after birth, usually for several weeks or months. In a few instances the duration of abstinence is fixed by some developmental stage of the child—e.g., when the baby first crawls, sits up, walks, or cuts its teeth. In many cases the taboo on coitus extends through the lactation period, which may last two to three years.[49] Not all of the time involved, of course, represents a loss of fertility, because ovulation is often delayed or occurs sporadically for a time after parturition. It is only when the period of abstinence extends to two months or more that a loss of fertility can be assumed, although even then it may not be quite commensurate with the amount of time covered. These longer periods, though found frequently in primitive and peasant societies,[50] are not customary in industrial countries.

Long post-partum taboos on intercourse obviously help to space out children, but this is not the reason usually given in communities that practice such taboos. Instead, a violation of the taboo is viewed as being magically dangerous to the child or the parents.[51] Such notions probably lead to the observance of the abstinence rules. In addition, it should be noted that in many instances the male has access to another wife (if he is polygynous) or to a concubine or other available woman. The social structure may encourage observance of the taboo in another way. When, as in India, the wife customarily goes to her parents' home to bear each of her first two or three children and stays there for a few months after the confinement, the taboo is enforced with ease. Thus the fact that 80% of Indian villagers in one study reported post-partum abstinence of six months or more indicates a significant loss of fertility from this cause.[52] Doubtless similar or greater losses occur in many other agrarian societies.

The "occasional" restrictions on sexual intercourse are those occurring in connection with regular holidays and special ceremonies, tabooed days of the week, and important communal tasks (war, economic undertakings, etc.).[53] The exact amount of time lost to reproduction in this way has seldom been calculated, but the Indian field study just cited found that the average number of days of avoidance for religious reasons was 24 per year in a rural village, while in a middle-class housing project it was 19.[54] If these days occur sporadically, they hardly represent much loss of fertility, because they are practically comprised within the normal frequency of intercourse; but in many societies the abstentions extend over substantial periods. "The natives of the Mortlock Islands, a part of the Caroline group, proscribe any sexual intercourse in time of war; a man who violated the rule would die a sudden death. During the fishing season, which lasts for six to eight weeks, every Yap fisherman is subject to many restrictions . . . Women are very strictly tabooed to him . . ."[55]

In contrast to post-partum and "occasional" tabooes on coitus, gestational abstinence obviously cannot diminish fertility. The only question is whether it may slightly *increase* fertility. Most societies proscribe intercourse during some part, but seldom during all or even the major portion, of the gestation period. Only seven of the primitive groups in Ford's sample extended the taboo to the greater part of the period.[56] Usually it is toward the end of the pregnancy that the prohibition applies. If intercourse during the later stages occasionally induces miscarriage or causes puerperal infection, as is sometimes claimed,[57] then the taboo may enhance fertility, but only slightly.

Similarly, the almost universal prohibition of coitus during menstruation can have little or no negative effect on fertility. Such abstention, when fertilization is least likely, tends to concentrate sexual activity in the more fertile part of the menstrual cycle. In some pre-industrial cultures the taboo is extended for a few days after the menstrual flow has ceased (as among the ancient Hebrews), which has the effect of concentrating coital activity still more directly on the days when conception is most likely.

On the whole, primitive and peasant societies appear to have a greater fertility loss through intra-marital abstinence (variable number 4) than do industrial societies. They have considerably more post-partum and "occasional" abstinence, and the effect of these in inhibiting reproduction is not fully counterbalanced by the fact that underdeveloped societies also occasionally have longer menstrual and gestational taboos (which may slightly enhance fertility).

The Other Intermediate Variables

There remain four variables—number 10 (which usually has a low fertility-value in non-industrial societies) and numbers 5, 6, and 7 (which seem indeterminate in their values). All four of these variables appear not to be clearly determined by institutional patterns in different cultures. If there is any difference in their fertility-values as between one type of society and another, the difference seems to be more a function of the general level of living than of the specific institutional structures. Perhaps one clue to this circumstance lies in the fact that three of the four variables (10, 5, and 7) are defined as involuntary in the sense of not being under control and hence not amenable to motivational determination. The other variable (number 6, frequency of coitus), though subject to individual control, is possibly too private and too linked up with organic capacity to be culturally controlled.

With respect to number 10—foetal mortality from involuntary causes— we have said that the fertility-value is generally low in pre-industrial societies, because the data available indicate that stillbirth rates are greater in such societies. However, the conclusion is tentative, because adequate comparative information does not exist for miscarriage rates.

Number 5—involuntary abstinence—presumably varies according to several disparate factors. In so far as health or sickness may be involved, the non-industrial peoples would probably exhibit a higher degree of such abstinence. The same inference might be drawn with regard to impotency, except that this condition is often caused by psychological determinants which may be more prevalent in industrial cultures. Another cause of involuntary abstinence, the separation of couples due to migration, would seem to vary according to the particular historical circumstances of the society. Except under conditions of European contact, indigenous groups apparently have little individual mobility. Clearly, these divergent influences affecting involuntary abstinence can run counter to each other. It is therefore difficult to claim, for this variable, any consistent overall differences between societies. We are also handicapped by an almost total lack of data, for no comparative information has been collected with this issue in mind.

Variable number 6—frequency of intercourse—possibly favors fertility more in underdeveloped than in industrial societies. But at best the evidence for this view is indirect, drawn solely from a few advanced societies where coital frequency appears greater among the manual than among the sedentary classes. Such direct evidence as we have supports no view at all. Average figures on "coital frequency" given in the literature, usually stated as so many times per week, are ambiguous, because it is unclear whether they mean *every* week or only those weeks when coitus is not impossible because of sickness, absence, menstrual or other taboos, etc. Also, the comparative frequency figures cited in the literature are fantastic, showing variations from one society to another that are wholly inexplicable.[58] We have found no reliable evidence that the average frequency of intercourse for comparable age groups varies significantly as between one society and another, and certainly none which indicates that this is a significant factor in inter-societal variations in fertility.

With respect to variable number 7 (involuntary sterility) we again have little evidence. The hard conditions of life in pre-industrial societies may give rise to a considerable amount of low fecundity or absolute sterility—particularly in the latter part of the woman's reproductive span; and in given instances, after contact with highly civilized peoples, venereal disease may have a pronounced effect of this sort. On the other hand, the nervous tension and artificial modes of life in urban-industrial populations may possibly tend to lower fecundity to some extent.

Patently, the comparative fertility-values of the four intermediate variables just discussed are unknown. Not only is evidence lacking, but there is no sound line of reasoning by which the behavior of these variables can be linked up with specific institutional patterns. At most, there may be some connection in each case with the general level of living. The evidence for this is best with respect to number 10, but the other three must be left for the time being as indeterminate.

CONCLUSION: THE GENERAL PATTERN

Any analysis of institutional factors in fertility must first explain the well-known fact that underdeveloped societies in general have a higher rate of reproduction than industrial societies. The explanation, in brief, is that the pre-industrial peoples, in the face of high mortality, have had to develop an institutional organization which would give them sufficient reproduction to survive. However, analysis at this level does not carry us very far. In order to study the effects of institutional factors, one needs to break down the reproductive process itself so as to distinguish clearly the various mechanisms through which, and only through which, any social factor *can* influence fertility. In trying to do this, we have found eleven "intermediate variables." When analysis is made along those lines, it can be seen that the generally high fertility of underdeveloped areas does not mean that these areas encourage high fertility in every respect. As we have seen, they do not have high plus values on *all* the intermediate variables. Why, then, do they have low values in some respects and not in others?

It is possible to discern a systematic difference between underdeveloped and developed societies with reference to the eleven variables. In general, the pre-industrial societies have high fertility-values for those variables farthest removed from the actual moment of parturition and which, therefore, imply an overall outlook favorable to fertility. To a much greater degree than industrial societies, they tend to encourage early exposure to intercourse—exhibiting a far younger age at marriage and a higher proportion married. They thus lose little potential fertility by delaying or avoiding the formation of unions. After unions have been formed, these societies tend to enjoin more abstinence than industrial societies do (and therefore have lower values on variable number 4), but such "sexual fasting" arises from religious and magical motives rather than as a deliberate fertility-control measure, and it does not appear to be great enough to have a substantial negative effect on fertility.

Underdeveloped societies also have high fertility-values for the conception variables. They practice little contraception and virtually no sterilization. Consequently, the tendency is to *postpone* the issue of controlling pregnancy until a later point in the reproductive process, which means that when a couple wishes to avoid children, those methods nearest the point of parturition—abortion and infanticide—are employed. These have the advantage, in societies living close to privation, of being nearer to the actual moment when the child must be supported.

Industrial societies, on the other hand, exhibit low fertility-values for those variables involving the early stages of the reproductive process, especially age at marriage, proportion married, and contraception; and they manifest high fertility-values for the variables in the later stages, especially infanticide. It follows that for many of the variables the two types of society exhibit opposite values. This is true for age of entry into unions, permanent celibacy, voluntary abstinence, contraception, and (if included as a variable) infanticide. It is not *necessarily* true of the time spent between or after unions, of sterilization, or of abortion; and it, of course, is not true of those variables characterized as "indeterminate"—involuntary abstinence, frequency of coitus, or involuntary infecundity. But the general contrast is sufficiently clear to require explanation.

A key to the position of the industrial societies lies in the fact that, as compared to pre-industrial cultures, they have achieved their lower reproduction, not by acquiring low fertility-values for *all* the intermediate variables, but by singling out particular ones as the means to that result. They took those means of reducing fertility which involved the least institutional organization and re-organization and which involved the least human cost. In the secular decline of the birth rate they relied more heavily on the mere postponement of marriage than on non-marriage. They relied less on abstinence, which makes heavy demands on the individual, and more on contraception and abortion, which do not. They dropped infanticide altogether and, in the later stages, tended to reduce abortion. In other words, they have undertaken to lower fertility, not primarily by extending further the negative effect of the variables by which fertility was lowered in the pre-industrial stage, but by using readily available institutional mechanisms with respect to marriage and by employing the possibilities of their advanced technology for conception control. Marital postponement was easily extended in the early and middle stages of industrialization because the basis for it already existed in Western society and because contraception and relatively safe abortion freed those who married late from the necessity of premarital celibacy. Gradually, in the late stages of industrial development, contraception has gained such predominance that it has made low fertility-values on the other variables (including abortion and late marriage) unnecessary.

NOTES

1. Although the physiologist sees more steps in the process, these can all be subsumed under the three headings given here. We are concerned only with the steps in reproduction as they may be socially recognized and utilized.

2. Since sexual intercourse is not confined to wedlock, the term "sexual union" seems preferable to "marriage." A union is here defined as any heterosexual relationship in which either actual intercourse occurs or orgasm is produced for at least the male partner. Every society has a type of union (marriage) in which reproduction is expected, approved, and even enjoined. At the same time every society runs the risk of unions in which reproduction is condemned, either because they lack the legal form of marriage or because they violate one or more institutional taboos (adultery, incest, caste or class endogamy, etc.—see K. Davis, "The Forms of Illegitimacy," *Social Forces*, Vol. 18, October 1939, pp. 77–89). Between the fully approved and the strongly proscribed unions, there may be other types which have a lesser grade than marriage but in which reproduction normally occurs. Such unions may be frequent, in some cases representing the majority of reproductive unions. Any satisfactory sociological analysis of reproduction must keep straight the different types of unions.

3. Means of contraception other than mechanical and chemical include the "rhythm" method (which can also be classed as voluntary abstinence), withdrawal, simulated intercourse without penetration, various "perversions," etc.

4. The reader will note that our list of variables does not include infanticide or child care. The reason for this omission is that our analysis is focused on factors affecting fertility strictly defined. Infanticide does, of course, affect family size and natural increase and may serve as an alternative to factors affecting fertility. It

is therefore discussed briefly at a later point.

5. For instance, Frank Lorimer, *Culture and Human Fertility*, Paris, 1954, by failing to make clear the ways in which fertility *can* be affected, gives in some ways a confused picture of how it *is* affected. The reader may wish to compare our framework with a half-page outline of direct and indirect factors affecting fertility given by Raymond Pearl at the end of an article on "Biological Factors in Fertility," *Annals of the American Academy of Political and Social Science*, Vol. 188, November 1936, p. 24.

6. Among the 250 societies for which he had information, Murdock found that, apart from incest taboos, "premarital relations are fully permitted in 65 instances, and are conditionally approved in 43 and only mildly disapproved in 6, whereas they are forbidden in only 44. In other words, premarital license prevails in 70 per cent of our cases. In the rest, the taboo falls primarily upon females and appears to be largely a precaution against childbearing out of wedlock rather than a moral requirement." George P. Murdock, *Social Structure*, New York, 1949, p. 265. On p. 5 the author gives slightly different figures, but the majority of his societies still permit premarital sexual relations.

7. K. H. Connell, *The Population of Ireland, 1750–1845*, Oxford, 1950, p. 89 [italics ours].

8. See Elizabeth R. Hooker, *Readjustments of Agricultural Tenure in Ireland*, Chapel Hill, 1938, esp. pp. 55–57, 106, 151, 208.

9. A. M. Carr-Saunders, *World Population*, Oxford, 1936, p. 91. *Cf.* James Meenan, "Some Causes and Consequences of the Low Irish Marriage Rate," *Journal of the Statistical and Social Inquiry Society of Ireland*, 86th session, 1932–33, pp. 19–27.

10. E.g., Conrad M. Arensberg and

Solon T. Kimball, *Family and Community in Ireland*, Cambridge, 1938, p. 80.

11. Arensberg and Kimball, *op. cit.*, pp. 107–122.

12. *Ibid.*, p. 123.

13. *Ibid.*, p. 128.

14. George C. Homans, *English Villagers of the Thirteenth Century*, Cambridge, 1942, Chs. 9–10.

15. Josiah C. Russell, "Demographic Values in the Middle Ages," *Studies in Population*, George F. Mair, ed., Princeton, 1949, p. 104.

16. Josiah C. Russell, *British Medieval Population*, Albuquerque, 1948, pp. 163–164.

17. Of course, not every society with neolocal residence shows a retarded age at marriage. In a primitive economy with high mortality, where no formal training or other obstacles to adult status must be hurdled, and where scarcity of persons rather than scarcity of land is the felt need, independent nuclear families may be formed by early marriage, e.g., the Netsilik Eskimos, Fox Indians, Andaman Islanders, Ruthenians.

18. Marion J. Levy, Jr., *The Family Revolution in Modern China*, Cambridge, 1949, pp. 168–170. When the family head dies there is the problem of one of the sons assuming authority over the others. It is precisely at this point that the joint household often dissolves; but if it survives this crisis, as it may, it does so because of the past institutionalization of relative age as a factor in authority.

19. Other cases of high proportions never married are Sweden (1945) 20.9%, Switzerland (1941) 20.1%, England and Wales (1931) 16.8%, Belgium (1930) 13.3%.

20. Differences in mortality and possible fecundity as between married and unmarried women may introduce a small but probably not serious error into this estimate.

21. This calculation excludes nonmarriage as a factor, because the women who had never married by age 40–44 were subtracted from the women under consideration in each age group. In other words, 21.4% of Swiss women at ages 40–44 had never married. But the remaining 78.6% had married at various ages. If this 78.6% had all married at ages 15–19 and had from that age experienced the same age-specific fertility as those ever married at each age, their total fertility would have been 76% greater. Stated in terms of the potential fertility lost by late marriage, the figure is approximately 64%. The calculation is rough, because the data refer to 1941 and thus do not represent a true cohort analysis; but a refined calculation on a cohort basis should yield rather similar results.

22. David Glass, *Introduction to Malthus*, New York, 1953, pp. 27–54, shrewdly notes that Ireland is the only country which has come close to following Malthus' rules of conduct—"moral restraint" and no birth control. In other countries of Northwestern Europe, such as Sweden and Norway, a late age at marriage does not imply sexual abstinence, not only because illegitimacy is more tolerated but also because contraception is more freely practiced.

23. *Ibid.*, p. 37.

24. For attitudes toward sexual behavior see Arensberg and Kimball, *op. cit.*, Ch. 11; and also such literary and popular sources as Frank O'Connor, "Ireland," *Holiday*, Vol. 6, December 1949, p. 40; Seán O'Faoláin, "Love among the Irish," *Life Magazine*, Vol. 34, March 16, 1953, pp. 140–157. Regarding censorship, the following passage from O'Faoláin is pertinent: ". . . Our censorship of books and publications, instigated by the clergy and submitted to, willy-nilly, by everybody, is a symbol of this fear of sex . . . In the 150 close-packed pages of the official register of books and periodicals banned by the Irish Censorship Board we find the names of almost every single Irish writer of note, some for one book, some for several. The banning is done in secret. There is no appeal to the courts of law. . . ." See also an article, "Irish Challenge Censors' Methods," *The New York Times*, August 14, 1955, where it is pointed out that the Irish Censorship Board "has banned books by the most reputable Irish authors, including Sean O'Casey, Liam O'Flaherty, Sean O'Faolain, and Ireland's most brilliant short story writer, Frank O'Connor. Nobel prize winners have even come under the interdict . . . many works of worth are condemned on a few isolated marked passages, while the general tenor of the book is ignored . . . Even the works of Roman

Catholic authors approved by the church authorities in Britain have not escaped the five Irish Roman Catholic Censors."

25. In 1949 the proportion of hospital beds devoted to mental cases was 57% in Ireland, whereas it was only 49% in the United States. The rate of mental patients per 100,000 population in 1948 was 603 in Ireland as contrasted to 382 in the United States. Adventitious circumstances seem not to account for this result. Though Ireland has a larger percentage of persons in the advanced ages than does the United States (24.7% at ages 50 and over as against 22.4% at these ages in the United States), she has a higher proportion under age 30. The fact that Irish medical services are less developed than in this country suggests that the comparison understates the difference in mental illness. In 1949 Ireland had only one hospital bed per 1,000 inhabitants, whereas the United States has 9.6, so that a higher proportion of mental cases in Ireland may never appear in the statistics.

26. For the history of clerical celibacy in Europe, see Henry C. Lea, *History of Sacerdotal Celibacy in the Christian Church*, London, 1932, and *A History of the Inquisition of the Middle Ages*, Vol. 1, New York, 1888, pp. 31–32; Alexander C. Flick, *The Decline of the Medieval Church*, New York, 1930, Vols. 1–2, *passim*; J. R. Tanner *et al.* (eds.), *Contest of Empire and Papacy*, Vol. 5 of *Cambridge Medieval History*, New York, 1926, esp. pp. 11–14, 40, 61–62, 73, 695; Eileen Power, *Medieval English Nunneries*, Cambridge, 1922, Ch. 11; Geoffrey Baskerville, *English Monks and the Suppression of the Monasteries*, New Haven, 1937, pp. 261–266; Joseph McSorley, *An Outline History of the Church by Centuries*, St. Louis, 1944, pp. 83, 154, 206–207, 237; H. J. Schroeder, *Disciplinary Decrees of the General Councils*, St. Louis, 1937, p. 193. For Latin America, see J. Lloyd Mecham, *Church and State in Latin America*, Chapel Hill, 1934, p. 48; Mary Watters, *A History of the Church in Venezuela, 1810–1930*, Chapel Hill, 1933, p. 211; Gilberto Freyre, *The Masters and the Slaves*, New York, 1946, pp. 446–452.

27. Of course, a society could be imagined in which half or more of the women were forced to be celibate, the rest of the people living in polyandrous marriage. But such a speculation would evoke more paradoxes than that already sketched. A society capable of such deliberate organization could scarcely be expected to use celibacy alone as its means of controlling fertility. With other less drastic means available, the end would hardly justify the means.

28. Arensberg and Kimball, *op. cit.*, p. 69.

29. Norman E. Himes, *Medical History of Contraception*, Baltimore, 1936, pp. 53–54, 99. See also Clellan S. Ford, *A Comparative Study of Human Reproduction*, New Haven, 1945, pp. 40–42.

30. Himes, *op. cit.*, pp. 10, 18–19, 63.

31. *Ibid.*, p. 17. Also see M. Soors, "La denatalité chez les Mongo," *Zaïre*, Vol. 4, May 1950, pp. 525–532.

32. Himes, speaking of Europe, says that "*coitus interruptus* is doubtless the most popular, widely diffused method of contraception . . . and has been for centuries . . . [It] is probably nearly as old as the group life of man." *Op. cit.*, pp. 183–184. He also cites numerous primitive tribes in which *coitus interruptus* is practiced. I. Schapera, writing of the Kgatla of Bechuanaland, says: "The commonest method of contraception locally practiced is *coitus interruptus* . . . It is widely employed not only by married people, but also by unmarried lovers." Sometimes the woman, by moving her hips so as to extrude the penis just before ejaculation, accomplishes *coitus interruptus* without the male's cooperation. *Married Life in an African Tribe*, New York, 1941, pp. 222–223. *Coitus inter femora* is practiced in many societies, particularly by the Bantus in Africa. Girls may wear special girdles designed to avoid penetration. C. Daryll Forde, *Marriage and the Family among the Yakö of South-Eastern Nigeria*, London, 1941, p. 14. Bantu tribes, permitting sexual relations but not pregnancy before marriage, teach (or did teach) their young people how to have intercourse without penetration, the unbroken hymen in some tribes being regarded as an important index of virginity, insisted on at marriage.

Alfred C. Kinsey *et al.* found "petting to climax" to have been practiced by 24% of the male sample (blown up to represent the U.S. male population) by age 21, and by 50% of college-educated males. The cumulative incidence among females was less but still substantial, being 24% for the college-educated at age 20. *Sexual Behavior in the Human Male*, Philadelphia, 1948, pp. 531–542, and . . . *in the Human Female*, 1953, p. 270.

33. Castration is so drastic that it is apparently never used with enough frequency to affect group fertility. Subincision, the splitting of the penis in such a way that the semen is expelled from the lower part rather than through the glans, seemingly has little effect on fecundity, depending in part on the position assumed during intercourse. Also the practice has a very limited distribution even in primitive society and seems unknown in more advanced pre-industrial societies. Among the Australian aborigines, where it is found, opinion differs as to its effects. German theorists, according to Himes, have generally held that the operation lowers fertility and is so intended. Modern anthropologists, on the other hand, have denied both these contentions. Himes himself believes it may have nome negative effect of this kind. *Op. cit.*, pp. 41–51.

34. See J. M. Stycos, "Female Sterilization in Puerto Rico," *Eugenics Quarterly*, Vol. 1, June 1954, pp. 3–9.

35. See Ralph Linton, *Study of Man*, New York, 1936, Ch. 10. Murdock, *op. cit.*, p. 3, criticizes Linton for holding that in some societies organized on a "consanguine" basis the nuclear family plays an insignificant role, but the fact is that in such cultures marital instability may have little disorganizing effect. See K. Davis, "Children of Divorced Parents," *Law and Contemporary Problems*, Vol. 10, Summer 1944, pp. 700–710.

36. Judith Blake, "Family Instability and Reproductive Behavior in Jamaica," *Current Research in Human Fertility*, Milbank Memorial Fund, New York, 1955, pp. 26–30.

37. Margaret Mead, *Changing Culture of an Indian Tribe*, New York, 1932, pp. 14–15, Ch. 10. Schapera, *op. cit.*, Ch. 10; *Migrant Labour and Tribal Life*, London, 1947, pp. 183–189; and "Cultural Changes in Family Life," *The Bantu-Speaking Tribes of South Africa*, London, 1937, pp. 380–385. The literature covering the impact of Western culture on native peoples is so enormous that one could document indefinitely the tendency of such contact to produce illicit sexual unions and instability in such unions and in marriage.

38. T. S. Simey, *Welfare and Planning in the West Indies*, Oxford, 1946, *passim*. F. M. Henriques, *Family and Colour in Jamaica*, London, 1953, *passim*. G. W. Roberts, "Some Aspects of Mating and Fertility in the West Indies," *Population Studies*, Vol. 8, March 1955, pp. 199–227. R. T. Smith, "Family Organization in British Guiana," *Social and Economic Studies*, Vol. 1, February 1953, pp. 87–111.

39. E. E. Evans-Pritchard, *Kinship and Marriage among the Nuer*, Oxford, 1951, pp. 112–123.

40. For mention of the joint household's vulnerability to change and its consequent fissive tendency, see Murdock, *op. cit.*, p. 36.

41. Levy, *op. cit.*, p. 46, points out that although the Chinese gentry have always frowned on widow remarriage, the peasants have usually practiced it. In fact, if a peasant widow was young and lacked grown sons, remarriage was inevitable. As the peasantry is said to comprise as much as 80% of the population (p. 44), widow celibacy is hardly characteristic of China as a whole, although gentry patterns set the ideals for the entire society. Olga Lang, without distinguishing between gentry and peasantry, says that remarriage is frowned on. *Chinese Family and Society*, New Haven, 1946, p. 53. She says (p. 126) that poor men often marry widows because they are easier to get than virgins. Any divorcee or widow can find a husband if she is willing to marry beneath her status. With regard to the absence of anything like the levirate in China, it is interesting to note that Miss Lang says (p. 21) that "early in the feudal period, under the Chou dynasty (ca. 1027–256 B.C.), the clan began to divide into economic families." Today, even in the South, where clans are of some importance, they have no real authority in family matters. The strongest clans in Central and North China lack the essential of clan life, a fair amount of common property (pp. 177–178).

42. Ford, *op. cit.*, pp. 50–51, found that most of his tribes took cognizance

of abortion. In eleven it was specifically stated to be forbidden, and in eight it could be inferred to be forbidden; in 21 it was permitted to the young girl who finds herself pregnant, and in 4 this could be inferred to be the case; and in 12 a married woman was allowed to practice abortion if she believed that she had become pregnant through an adulterous intrigue. Himes regards abortion as widespread in primitive societies (*op. cit.*, p. 52). A recent study of George Devereaux, *Abortion in Primitive Society*, New York, 1955, pp. 25–26, cites cases of tribes where abortion is quite frequent.

43. Premature labor can be induced by killing the foetus. This can be done by beating, pressing, or massaging the abdomen; by drinking poisons or strong emetics or laxatives; by piercing the foetus or amniotic sac with sharp reeds or instruments; or by wearing a tight belt. See Ford, *op, cit.*, p. 52; Devereaux, *op. cit.*, pp. 27–42.

44. Knud Rasmussen, *The Netsilik Eskimos*, Copenhagen, 1931, pp. 139–140.

45. Lang, *op. cit.*, p. 150.

46. Hutton Webster, *Taboo: A Sociological Study*, Stanford, 1942, pp. 59–61.

47. *Ibid.*, pp. 59–65.

48. Linton, *Study of Man, op. cit.*, pp. 194–195, with reference to the Tanala of Madagascar. In a letter to W. Lloyd Warner quoted by Himes, *op. cit.*, p. 8, Linton says: "I do not think that there was any idea of limiting population in it [infanticide], but the losses were severe. In at least one tribe all children born on three days in each week were killed."

49. Clellan S. Ford and Frank A. Beach, *Patterns of Sexual Behavior*, New York, 1951, p. 219.

50. Webster, *op. cit.*, pp. 67–71.

51. Ford and Beach, *op. cit.*, p. 219.

52. C. Chandrasekaran, "Cultural Patterns in Relation to Family Planning in India," *Proceedings of the Third International Conference on Planned Parenthood, 1952*, Bombay, p. 78.

53. Ford, *Comparative Study of Human Reproduction, op. cit.*, pp. 28–29. Webster, *op. cit.*, pp. 132–139.

54. Chandrasekaran, *op. cit.*, p. 78.

55. Webster, *op. cit.*, p. 134.

56. Ford, *op. cit.*, p. 48.

57. *Ibid.*, p. 49.

58. Thus Ford and Beach report as an apparent fact that "the Aranda of Australia have intercourse as often as three or five times nightly, sleeping between each sex act," and that for Chagga men "intercourse ten times in a single night is not unusual." Nothing is said about how these bizarre statistics are gathered, or about what age groups in the population are being considered. The authors say simply, "it is reported that" or "it is not unusual that," etc. Such reports are all the more questionable since societies apparently with a similar level of living are said to have extremely different figures—some at "once a week" or "once or twice a week"—without any explanation of why they should be so low and others fifteen or twenty times as high. *Op. cit.*, pp. 78–79.

19

Population Control
in Primitive Groups

Mary Douglas

This paper is about four human groups which attempt to control fertility. The first are the *Pelly Bay Eskimos,* who regularly kill off a proportion of their female babies. The next are the *Rendille,* camel herders in the Kenya highlands. They postpone the age of marriage of women, send numbers of their women to be married to polygamists in the next tribe, kill off boys born on Wednesdays or boys born after the eldest son is old enough to have been circumcised. The third are the *Tikopia,* inhabitants of a small Pacific island measuring three miles across, isolated by 700 miles of sea. They used to use abortion, contraception, infanticide and suicide migration to keep their population down.

These are all groups who by their way of life would be counted as primitive peoples, within the usual range of an anthropologist's interest.

I will also mention a fourth group who restrict their numbers by only allowing the eldest son in each family to contract marriage and correspondingly maintain a large proportion of their female population in barren spinsterhood. These are the *Nambudiri Brahmins* of South India—by no means either poor, or illiterate, or primitive in any sense. I plan to use these examples as a basis for considering Wynne-Edwards' hypothesis that in primitive human groups social conventions operate homeostatic controls on population.

Wynne-Edwards' thesis is as follows. He asks how a balance is maintained between population density and available resources; what holds back the latent power of increase so that critical resources are not over-exploited? The problem stated thus includes an assumption that the normal distribution of a species is optimum. Wynne-Edwards actually goes so far

Reprinted from the *British Journal of Sociology,* 17, no. 3 (April–June, 1966), pp. 263–73, by permission of the author and the publisher.

as to say that normally the habitat provides what he calls "the best possible living" to species higher up the chain. I quote:

> Where we can still find nature undisturbed by human interference . . . there is generally no indication whatever that the habitat is run down or destructively over-taxed [each species affords] the best possible living to species higher up the chain that depend on it for food. [Pp. 8–9.]

His question is about restraint in the midst of plenty. What prevents predators at each point from so multiplying that they over-exploit their own resources?

His answer is inspired by the analogy with homeostasis in physiology. Physiological systems have controls which regulate the internal environment of the body and adapt it. If it can be established that population homeostasis parallels physiological homeostasis, then much behaviour that is apparently functionless can be explained by its contribution to population control. There appear to be density-dependent brakes which impose a ceiling on natural increase. It is important to the argument that the relevant ceiling is *not* imposed by starvation or by predators or natural hazards. Rather it is imposed by otherwise inexplicable aspects of social behaviour. For example:

(*a*) Territorial behaviour limits the number of territories occupied in the food-gathering area and deprives redundant males of feeding or breeding facilities.

(*b*) Communal roosting has a function in providing a display of numbers.

(*c*) Hierarchy is a way of cutting off the tail of the population "at the right level," by excluding certain sections from feeding or breeding.

Finally, the analogy with physiology suggests that the higher species would exhibit more complex adaptations and that population homeostasis would tend to reach the greatest efficiency and perfection in human groups.

Wynne-Edwards extends his argument to human groups by citing enthusiastically a very early work of Professor Carr-Saunders (*The Population Problem*, 1922). There is indeed a remarkably close parallel between the approaches of the two authors. In so far as he discusses primitive human populations, Carr-Saunders' argument is as follows.

He starts with the premise that in any human society there will be a theoretical optimum size for the population (that will give the highest return of goods per head). If the density is greater or less than this desirable density, then the average income will be less than it might have been. He goes on to assume that this desirable optimum is actually attained in primitive populations, where it has been observed that the members live in evident enjoyment of satisfactory resources, relatively free from want and disease. To account for this achieved optimum he looks for controls on population. He supposes that starvation is not an acceptable means of limiting numbers, because it makes social conditions unstable, and notes that anyway primitive people are better able to withstand hunger than we are (p. 231). The controls that interest him are imposed from within, social conventions which decrease fertility or increase elimination. Restricted territory, infanticide, head-hunting, such customs are in common use and the degree to which they are practised may be such as to approximate to the optimum number (p. 230). It is only fair to say that Carr-Saunders' book was written a long time ago. None of his other distinguished studies of world population repeats this argument. The anthropological reports which he quotes are out of date and the argument now sounds very naïve. I started out with the intention of exposing its fallacies, presented anew by a zoologist. However, if one could adapt the argument to avoid certain inherent difficulties, I would find myself in some measure of agreement with the youthful Carr-Saunders.

The main difficulty with the Wynne-Edwards/Carr-Saunders thesis is that it is so protected from contradictory evidence as to be irrefutable. Wynne-Edwards only expects his thesis to apply where "nature is kind and reliable." The negative instances which he cites in chapter 20 are said to occur in highly variable environments and so to be compatible with the thesis which is framed for steady environments (p. 470). Carr-Saunders has the corresponding idea that savages are generally found to live in comfort and ease.

These assumptions make it difficult to select relevant data for testing the thesis in its extensions to human groups. Are we expected to limit ourselves to savage communities which live in comfort and ease? This could be a very big restriction. What standards of comfort are we to apply, our own or theirs? Peoples whose population is obviously controlled by disease or starvation are to be excluded from the discussion. But there are degrees of starvation. Do we exclude the many peoples who face an annual hungry season between harvests or those who expect a famine every five years, or every ten or twenty years? In short, a principle of selection that conforms to these requirements eludes me. I therefore propose to include any primitive populations for whom good information exists.

The next difficulty with their approach is that under-population is not seriously considered. This omission enables them to take the actual given population at any time as the optimum.

If a zoologist tells me that the concept of under-population is not relevant to animal groups, I would accept it, but it is highly relevant to human demography because there are many classes of activity which require a minimum number of participants. Much anthropological evidence suggests that primitive populations are prone to *under*-population and that the latent power of increase, far from being a threat to the resources, is not sufficient for the people to realize the full possibilities of their environment. If this were also true of animal populations it would destroy the assumption on which Wynne-Edwards' problem and solution are based. There would be no problem to solve about internal social controls if in fact it could be shown that external controls, in the form of predators and external dangers, kept the population at each point in the chain down well below the level at which it could threaten to over-exploit its food resources. But this is in fact frequently the case with human groups.

Now for a word about the danger of taking actual human populations at any given time as being at optimum size or density. It is about as defensible as if a town planner were to take the actual size of towns to be the optimum, without analysis or evidence. Thus Carr-Saunders infers from the immensely long pre-historic period through which mankind existed without attaining high densities that some kind of social controls must have operated to produce the optimum size (pp. 239–40). Again he argues that the existence of restrictive practices such as infanticide imply that the relevant populations are at an optimum size. It is as absurd as for the town planner to infer from the existence of parking meters that the traffic flow is optimal.

The idea of an optimum human population is too complicated to be inferred from such evidence. An optimum density or size can be defined in relation to the demands upon a particular resource. An optimum size in relation to land, for example, would be such that an additional unit of population would not proportionately increase the yield of the land per head, and a subtracted unit of population would more than proportionately increase its yield per head. Such a concept is not always very relevant to actual densities. For example the Ndembu, a Lunda tribe in Zambia, living at a density varying from 3–6 per square mile, grow cassava as their staple crop. Cassava is very easy to grow. It does not require labour-intensive methods. The Ecological Survey of Northern Rhodesia calculated that, cultivating cassava with traditional Ndembu techniques, their tribal area would be capable of supporting a population of up to 18 per square mile. Only near that point of density would the idea of the optimum for cassava cultivation become relevant. At the present density more or less units of human population would not affect the *per capita* yield. In actual fact the Ndembu are not likely to crowd together at the highest densities which their land permits for cassava-growing. Though cassava is their staple, their bread and butter as it were, they are not all that interested in cassava. They are passionately interested in hunting. Game is scarce in their region and the search for it causes them to move their villages when an area is hunted out. It would be nice to think that their actual low density represents the optimum for their hunting economy. But I see no reason for such optimism. They could as likely be *over*-populated from the hunting point of view as to have struck a happy equilibrium between their demands on critical resources.

Here is another big difference between human and animal populations when we are thinking of optimum densities. For the animal population it makes sense to make the calculation in terms of critical resources and to recognize that the critical resource is not necessarily food; it may be nesting room or some other necessary amenity. But for human behaviour it can be more relevant to take into account the ceiling imposed by the demand for champagne or private education than the demand for bread and butter.

The shift that has to be made between the zoologist and the sociologist is a shift from the idea of a particular optimum (a size or density related to a particular resource) and a general optimum (a size or density related to the satisfaction of all kinds of demands—including demands for luxuries and leisure).

I give an example of a people who are under-populated from two angles, economic and social. They are the Western Shoshone, Indians native to Eastern California, who used to live by gathering grass-seeds and nuts. All the year they wandered from one floristic zone to the next as the seeds and berries ripened, but they wintered near the juniper pine nut crops, wherever they happened to be gathering these when the winter fell. Some of the Shoshone tribes lived at a density of *2 to the square mile* in permanent villages. These are the lucky ones. They could sally out for short foraging trips and return to their fixed base. They could get to know each other, hold elections, have winter festivals and organize deer and rabbit drives. Others were much more sparsely scattered at *1 person to 2 square miles*. Though they tried to come back to the same place each autumn, it was not certain who would be spending the winter together. But at least they could have a festival and could organize a rabbit drive when the others arrived. The least fortunate in the most arid zones were living at a fantastic sparsity of *1 person to 30 square miles*. They could never be sure of seeing the same party again from winter to winter, had few festivals and fewer rabbit or deer drives. According to the accepted standards of their own culture they were obviously *under*-populated. It is dubious whether these rabbit drives they had to forgo for lack of numbers are to be counted as a critical resource from a strictly economic or physiological point of view. The protein intake of rabbit meat would be very slight and, anyway, their staple was probably not deficient in vegetable protein. The needs which were not met because of low density were social and cultural. But once we admit such resources are relevant to the idea of optimum population we are a long way from both Wynne-Edwards and Carr-Saunders. I am going to argue that it is the demand for oysters and champagne, not for the basic bread and butter, that triggers off social conventions which hold human populations down.

In the absence of any reliable means of calculating a general optimum density I shall take a position close to that implicitly adopted by Carr-Saunders. I shall try to assess what the people living in a particular culture would seem to regard as their optimum size, having regard not only to their demographic policy, but also to the pattern of goals which they appear to set themselves.

Now we come to the final and serious difficulty with the homeostasis theory of human population, which is that it visibly *does not* work. If it did we would not be worrying about a population explosion in India, Mauritius, Egypt, etc.

There are many examples of primitive peoples who hectically recruit newcomers when their basic resources are visibly running down. The Lele in the Congo were aware of deforestation and erosion, yet each village was more anxious to maintain or increase its *relative* size than to relate size to total resources. Other examples abound of political competition to increase numbers in face of economic pressures to reduce them. What is needed is an account of how population stability is achieved and under what conditions it breaks down. My argument is that human groups do make attempts to control their populations, often successful attempts. But they are more often inspired by concern for scarce social resources, for objects giving status and prestige, than by concern for dwindling basic resources.

Now I am ready to examine the four cases I started with.

First, the Netsilik Eskimos of Pelly Bay. In the 1920's they were an almost isolated group of 54 people. Though their area was rich in game, their life was one of great hardship, endurance and hard-taxed ingenuity. Rasmussen said that there was scarcely any country on earth so severe and inclement for man. These Eskimos were at a special disadvantage because of their low mobility in winter. They had no driftwood. In the short time between thaw and freeze they travelled by kayak, but in winter their sledges, made of old sealskin tents, folded and frozen stiff, or of blocks of ice, were heavy and difficult to move. They kept dogs, not for traction but for locating seals. They went sealing, caribou hunting and fishing in groups or singly, according to the seasonal cycle. Dr. Asen Balikci, from whose researches I take this account, considers that in order to survive at all in their environment these people have to show great ingenuity and flexibility. In 1923 Rasmussen noted 38 cases of female infanticide out of 96 births for 18 marriages. Their hunting and fishing economy places great emphasis on the division of labour between the sexes and a man without a woman is at a disadvantage.

Rasmussen was struck by the social difficulties and friction caused by competition for women, often resulting in fighting and killing. He was inclined to argue that the Pelly Bay Eskimo practised female infanticide to a pitch which endangered the survival of the group. However, the more recent anthropologist in the area, Dr. Balikci, argues convincingly that the practice is a more flexible and sensitive instrument of demographic policy than was at first supposed. Decisions to kill a new-born infant were taken in the family. If the first-born were female it might possibly be saved, for fear of bringing bad luck on later births, but generally a family was reluctant to take on the charge of rearing a girl, especially if it had a daughter already. A man needed sons to hunt and fish for him when he was past his prime, but rearing a girl would benefit only her future husband. A girl child would not be killed if a future husband would betroth her, or if her grandmother were willing to adopt her as security for old age. So the supply of girls was not simply related to the pressures felt by their own parents. The young men who could not find a wife in their own group had another resource. They could marry girls from another Eskimo group living to the west who did not practice such a high degree of infanticide. Furthermore, although the disparity of the sexes was very marked in infancy, the balance was nearly even for the adult population. The mortality of adult men in hunting accidents, drowning, suicide and fighting was much greater than for women. Thus, Balikci argues, this group, driven to the edge of survival by harsh conditions, in practising female infanticide was contributing to its own survival and making a more or less successful attempt to control the balance of the sexes. Here we have an instance of infanticide genuinely used as an instrument of demographic policy.

According to my general thesis this type of population control in the interests of bare survival is rare. More usually there is prestige rather than subsistence at stake.

The next human group I discuss are the Rendille, a tribe of 6,000 camel herders in Kenya (Spencer). The Rendille live on the meat and milk of herds of sheep, goats and camels. They cannot keep cattle because of the aridity and the rough terrain. Camels anyway give two to three times as much milk as a cow, in the wet season, and give adequate supplies in the dry season when a cow gives none. They can survive with water only once every ten days to two weeks, and in the wet season they need no water. They can travel forty miles a day and so can exploit vegetation in distant areas.

Rendille are aware that their population is limited to the size of herd that can feed it. Each herd requires a minimum number of people to manage it successfully. Smallpox in the 1890's reduced the human population to a too low level of manpower, so they lost stock. The great limitation of camels in these conditions is that the herds increase very slowly. Rendille believe their camels to be a fixed resource. A static stock population cannot support an increasing human population. Rendille are very different from their neighbours, the cattle-owning Samburu, who believe their herds can expand faster than human populations and that a poor man can grow rich in his own lifetime. Rendille have a problem of over-population in relation to camels. They deal with it by several measures:

1. By emigration. One third of the Samburu cattle herders are descended from emigrant Rendille, and Rendille still emigrate to this day.

2. By monogamy. A man is not obliged to help his sons to marry a second wife. A herd is not divided and goes only to the eldest son.

3. By late age of marriage for women. A slight excess of women is created by the Rendille custom of monogamy and met by allowing the neighbouring Samburu to marry their female surplus.

4. By killing off boys born on Wednesdays or after the circumcision of the eldest brother, ostensibly to avoid jealousy between brothers.

In this case a shortage of a critical resource, camels, is met with restraints on population. Again this is a fair case for Wynne-Edwards' general thesis.

If we go on like this, collecting positive instances of successful population control, we finally confront the main question—why do people *not always* practice population control? Why do populations explode? Why do some groups continue to welcome new recruits when crucial resources are visibly running down?

The answer lies in defining more precisely what are the conditions in which a resource is recognized as crucial and limited enough to provoke population policy.

We note that the Rendille camels are in the control of the elders. The whole society is under rigid social constraints, the elders have the whip hand against the juniors, their curse is feared, discipline is tight. In other words, the crucial scarce resource is the basis of all prestige in their society. It happens to be their bread and butter, but at the same time it represents caviar and champagne and all the symbols of status rolled into one.

The next example is the island of Tikopia. In 1929 there were 1,300 inhabitants. This group was fully conscious of pressure on resources, as well it might be, 700 miles from the nearest big island and needing to produce all its own food. Strong social disapproval was felt for couples who reared families of more than two, or at most three children. Their population policy was aimed at steady replacement. It was exerted by contraception, abortion, infanticide, and they talked of an ancient custom of pushing out to sea undesirables such as thieves. They lived on fish, root crops (taro and yams) and tree crops (breadfruit and coconuts). Even at the apparently dense population of 1929 they did not seem to feel pressure on land; particularly their rules about lending and borrowing garden land for root crops were very free and easy; they were much more strict about orchard land and particularly coconuts, which produced the cream which made all the other food palatable. Men would fight about orchard land, but not about garden land. In 1952 and 1953 two typhoons in succession produced a famine. Their villages and trees were wrecked and salt spray retarded the growth of their root crops. By this time the population (influenced by missionaries and administration) had relaxed its grip on itself and had increased to 1,750. During the famine there were 89 deaths, but only 17 attributed to starvation. There would have been a higher mortality if relief supplies had not been sent in from the government. The anthropologist Raymond Firth, who was there in 1929 and also in 1952, gives a fascinating account of the Tikopian reaction to the famines. He considers whether it was famine or fear of famine, which seemed to have occurred every twenty years or so, which actually kept the population down to its size at any given point. But the number of deaths from the 1952 famine is so small, and even those from a 1955 epidemic (only 200), that he did not incline to this Malthusian interpretation. Instead it seems that when they were sedulously restricting their population it was supplies of coconut cream that they had their eye on, not supplies of roots and cereals. Without food of good quality they did not like to hold feasts; without feasts they could not contemplate religious ceremonies; without ceremonies social life came to a standstill. They would exclaim, "Tikopia does not exist without food . . . It is nothing . . . There is no life on the island without food." The anthropologist remarks, "These expressions alluded not so much to biological survival as to sociological survival" (p. 84). In making their estimate of how many months it would take to recover from the damage of the first typhoon, when they reckoned that it would be a year at least before the island was on its feet again, there was talk of people putting off to sea in despair. One very old man with experience of previous famines said, "They say they will die, but they will not die. They will dig for wild yam roots which will not be exhausted and they will go and search for early yams and for wild legumes" (p. 57). Summing up the native attitudes, Firth concluded,

> Tikopia did not appear to be concerned with a balance between population and food supply in terms of mere subsistence. They would seem always to have been interested in quality as well as quantity of food, and indeed their estimate of the prosperity of the land is basically affected by this (p. 54).

My last example illustrates the oysters and champagne factor in population control even more clearly. The Nambudiri Brahmins belong to one of the richest land-owning castes in Southern India. They are rich and very exclusive. To maintain their social and economic advantage they avoid dividing their estates, but allow only the eldest son to inherit and to administer it on behalf of his brothers (in the same way as the Rendille camel herders). The other sons are not allowed to marry at all. For each married couple only one son and one girl are likely to be allowed to marry. The other sons console themselves with women of another caste, but the other daughters are kept all their lives in the strictest seclusion (Yalman). Only a very rich community could afford to seclude and condemn to sterility a large proportion of its women, and such a ruthless course must presumably be justified by the value of the prize, in this case maintaining a social and economic hegemony.

To conclude, it seems that population homeostasis does occur in human groups. The kind of relation to resources that is sought is more often a relation to limited social advantages than to resources crucial to survival. In the graded series which I have developed from the hard-pressed Pelly Bay Eskimos to the luxuriously settled Nambudiri Brahmins, the Rendille are important. Their camels are no luxury, but necessary for sheer survival, but I would suggest that the impetus for restrictive policies comes from the great social advantages which accrue to the older men who hold rights in camel herds.

This approach has the possibility of explaining the many cases in which population homeostasis does not appear to work. The argument is that policies of control develop when a smaller family appears to give a relative social advantage. The focus of demographic inquiry should therefore be shifted from subsistence to prestige, and to the relation between the prestige structure and the economic basis of prosperity. A small primitive population which is homogeneously committed to the same pattern of values and to which the ladders of social status offer a series of worthwhile goals which do not require large families for their attainment is likely to apply restrictive demographic policies. Such a people would be the ritualistic and feast-loving inhabitants of Tikopia. In a stratified population it is in those sections which are most advantageously placed in relation to power and prestige in which policies of population control are spontaneously applied. Such a people would be the rich and exclusive caste of Nambudiri Brahmins.

When social change occurs so rapidly that the prestige structure is no longer consistent, we should expect population explosions to occur. Or if the whole traditional prestige structure is broken as a result of foreign oppression or economic disaster, again we would expect that the social controls on over-population would be relaxed. This happened in Ireland between 1780–1840. It is often said that the Irish population made such a remarkable increase in this period because of the adoption of the potato as a cheap form of food. But elsewhere in eighteenth-century Europe the potato did not oust other staples (Salaman), and it is unfashionably Malthusian to argue that populations respond directly to increase in the means of subsistence. It is more plausible to adopt my general argument here and to suppose that the ruin of the native Irish society by the penal laws and the ruin of its foreign trade by English tariffs were the cause of the population increase. Similarly, to go further back into English history, the misery caused by the Enclosures and the Poor Laws would have a similar effect and help to produce the manpower for the Industrial Revolution.

It follows that there is a message here for the countries whose prosperity is threatened by uncontrolled population increase. In those countries we see the well-educated and well-to-do actively preaching family limitation and setting up birth-control clinics as a social service for the teeming poorer classes. They encounter resistance and apathy from the milling poor of the Caribbean, the outcastes of India, the landless labourers of Egypt and Mauritius. Their failure spurs them on to more enthusiastic propaganda. But if they would succeed, let them first look to their prestige structure. What hope of advance does their system of social rewards offer to those to whom they preach? Have the ladders of high prestige enough rungs to reach into the most populous sections of the community? If the prestige structure were adjusted, propaganda would be more effective or perhaps not be necessary. For given the right incentives some kind of population control would be likely to develop among the poor as it apparently has amongst those who seek to administer the demographic policy.

BIBLIOGRAPHY

Balikci, Asen, "Infanticide in the Netsilik Area," forthcoming in *J.R.A.I.*

Carr-Saunders, 1922, *The Population Problem.*

Firth, Raymond, 1957, *We the Tikopia;* 1939, *Primitive Polynesian Economy;* 1959, *Social Change in Tikopia.*

Rasmussen, K., 1931, *The Netsilik Eskimos,* Report of the Fifth Thule Expedition, vol. 8.

Salaman, S., 1949, *The History and Social Influence of the Potato.*

Spencer, Paul, 1965, *The Samburu.*

Turner, V. W., 1957, *Schism and Continuity.*

Steward, J., 1938, *The Basin Plateau Indians.*

Wynne-Edwards, V. C., 1962, *Animal Dispersion in Relation to Social Behaviour.*

Yalman, Nur, 1963, "Female Purity in Ceylon and Southern India," *J.R.A.I.*

20

Culture and
Human Fertility
in India

T. J. Samuel

The social structure and value systems of societies, primitive, agrarian or industrial, have an important bearing on the fertility levels of its people. A study of the different cultures and their levels of fertility at different stages of development have shown that while certain cultures promote the attainment and maintenance of high fertility levels, certain others try to keep it low.

In recent years several theories have been formulated in an attempt to discover the cultural factors that have a specific relationship to human fertility in non-industrial societies.

The extensive researches of Carr-Saunders led him to the conclusion that the "evolution of human culture brought a universal tendency toward the maintenance of an 'optimum population' appropriate to the resources of each area and the economic technology of its occupants."[1]

Another theory propounded by some of the American demographers, primarily based on their study of agrarian societies in Asia, says that societies with a high rate of mortality follow certain cultural practices which would ensure a high rate of fertility. "Their religious doctrines, moral codes, laws, education, community customs, marriage habits and family organization are all focussed toward maintaining high fertility."[2]

The Institute of Human Relationship at the Yale University has put forth the theory that "if people are to reproduce, social life must offer enough rewards (promises of security, prestige and approval) for bearing children to outweigh the punishments (the pain, suffering and anxieties connected with childbirth) involved in reproduction."[3]

Reprinted from the *Journal of Family Welfare*, 9, no. 4 (June, 1963), pp. 45–53, by permission of the author and the publisher.

Some anthropologists of modern times approach this problem on the basis of the theory that "various elements of the culture of any society must interact to provide an adequate basis for some degree of social stability. They have tried to examine the functions of social institutions and their relation to other factors in the society."[4]

Among the above mentioned theories, the fourth one emphasising "social stability" seems to be applicable to the Indian society. The Indian culture seems to be one which puts a premium on "social stability" at the expense of social progress. This social stability was achieved through the caste system, the joint family system, respect for religion, customs and traditions, and by its peculiar attitudes toward women, sex and children.

The Hindu culture, which aimed at social stability, influenced the reproductive pattern of this sub-continent in various ways. There were and still are some forces which promote high birth rates and certain others which try to keep it low. The following are some of the cultural factors which promoted high fertility.

In a society where joint family was the rule, the joint family, rather than the individual, was and still is to a certain extent the primary unit in the Hindu society. Hence, marriages are arranged by the family and the sexual behaviour of the individual is very much influenced by his membership in the joint family. More often than not, a member of the extended family does not have to search bread for those whom he breeds. The birth of a child is always welcomed, particularly so if it is a boy, for he adds to the strength of the family and the prestige of the head of the family as one with a large number of dependents.

The great law giver of the Hindus, Manu, suggested four different stages through which a member of the Hindu society has necessarily to pass, one of which being *grahasthashrama* (householder), thereby making marriage almost obligatory for everyone. The religious motive behind universal marriage becomes clear when one understands the meaning of the word *putra,* or son. "The Sanskrit word for son, *'putra,'* means literally one who saves from *puth* or hell, the hell into which all parents without sons fall."[5] The keenly felt necessity for a son resulted in early and universal marriages followed by high fertility rates.

Another reason for early marriage was the respectability attached to virginity. It was considered "safe" to arrange the marriage of a girl before anyone got even a chance to suspect her virginity. It was also believed that "the father or guardian incurs the sin of destroying an embryo at each appearance of menses as long as the girl is unmarried after puberty."[6]

Yet another reason for early marriages was the notion that "no maiden could be considered pure if she feels love for a man other than the one to whom she might get married. If she does so, it is a sin."[7]

Moslem invasions of the 12th and 13th centuries also promoted the practice of early marriage, because married women were seldom carried away by the invaders.

Thus early and universal marriage became a significant characteristic of the Hindu society. A proverb prevalent among some of the caste Hindus of Kerala in South India says that "a girl should be given away in marriage even to a *Paraya* (an untouchable) after she is sixteen."[8]

The status of women in the society has its impact on reproductive rates. The ancient scriptures of the Hindus say that "marriage is not for lust but for domestic life and progeny, so that the Aryan mode of life may be continued for ever."[9] In Rig Veda, the great scripture of the Hindus, the bridegroom prays to the god Indra to "make the bride the mother of good and lucky children, bless her to get 10 children and make the husband the 11th one."[10] The purpose of life for a woman came to be looked upon as bearing children and looking after the husband. Women of India tried to do their best in both these roles assigned to them. This determined the particular status of women in India, which was very much a factor contributing to the high fertility rate.

The status of women in the modern Western culture stands in marked contrast to the one mentioned above. "The evidence collected from younger housewives makes it abundantly clear that the awakening of women, which has inspired a desire not only to have a share in life's social pleasure, but to participate in activities outside their homes, has been an influential factor in the limitation of families."[11]

Lack of opportunity and social opprobrium attached to free mingling between the sexes has affected the sexual behaviour and reproductive pattern of the Hindus. The definition given to adultery in some of the old writings included "addressing other men's wives in lonely places, offering them presents, romping with them, touching their ornaments and dress, sitting with them, touching them improperly, etc."[12] This definition of adultery may be compared to the value systems of advanced countries in the West, where men and women mingle freely, especially in the years that intervene between puberty and marriage. At the same time, the Western culture imposes sanctions on maternity out of marriage. The free availability of contraceptives coupled with the desire for sexual pleasure enables them to become familiar with contraceptives, which could be of much help later, in their married life.

There were certain factors in Indian culture which applied brakes on high fertility. Despite early marriages, the practice of the consummation of marriage taking place at a later date and the fewer chances of establishing sexual relations in the early years of marriage due to the strict surveillance of the elder members of the family, headed by the mother-in-law of the bride, were of some importance. To have a child soon after marriage was frowned upon. All this reduced the prospects of early childbirth.

According to the principles of the *Varnashramadharma,* or the caste system, the social status of an individual is irrevocably decided at his birth and there is no freedom to marry outside the caste in which one was born. The caste system, by its insistence on endogamy, tended to lower fertility rates very often and helped to keep them there. "By the rigid division of the society into water-tight compartments, it remained a hindrance to the attainment of sexual parity as the deficiency in one caste cannot be remedied by the superabundance in another."[13] This led to the practice of the dowry system and even to the infanticide of girls, both of which had a depressing effect on fertility, the former by postponement of marriages owing to financial difficulties and the latter by reducing the number of females in the total population.

Apart from the lowering of fertility due to the lack of sexual parity, the ban on widow remarriage, so effectively enforced by the customs and traditions of certain castes like the Brahmins, has been a major factor in lowering the levels of fertility among these castes. In 1952, while the number of children below 6 years of age per 1,000 married women in the age group of 14–43 was 967 for Brahmins, it was 1,075 for tribal people and 1,033 for *panchamas* (untouchables).[14] Assuming the rate of miscarriages and infantile mortality were the same for all castes, this difference in fertility on the basis of the caste can be explained by the number of widows among the different castes per 1,000 married women. For Brahmins it was 235 while it was only 119 for tribal people and 127 for the *panchamas*.[15]

The sexual behaviour of the Hindus is also influencd by religious rules which lay down as to when a husband should meet his wife physically. A study made by WHO in Delhi and Mysore shows that the Hindus observed sexual abstinence during certain periods. Avoidance of coitus during religious festivals was reported by 50% of the persons interviewed.

> The phase of the moon plays an important role here. New moon days, full moon days, and *Ekadashi,* i.e., the eleventh day after the new or full moon, were mentioned by some. Some mentioned the avoidance of coitus on Sunday, Monday and Saturday. The days when a man had a shave and a bath, days of solar and lunar eclipses, days of sowing the fields were also mentioned in some cases. The number of days of avoidance for religious reasons mentioned by individuals ranged from 2 to 120 per year in Ramanagaram (Mysore) and from 1 to 79 in Lodi colony (New Delhi).[16]

Abstinence is reported to have been invariably practised during the period of lactation for 3 to 6 months.

Fertility levels of religious minorities like Moslems, Christians, and Parsis show some variations from that of the Hindus.

The orthodox Moslems believe that the primary purpose of human life is the generation of new life. Mohammed is recorded as having said, "Marry and generate."[17] While the Hindus emphasise the need for *a son*, the Moslems want to see that their women are *richly fruitful*. Perhaps this difference in outlook explains partly the higher fertility noticed among the Moslems of India. The child-woman ratio of all women between 15 and 39 years of age was 770 per 1,000 for Moslem women, whereas it was only 678 for the Hindus.[18] Partly this higher fertility of Moslems is due to their lower economic status; but to a greater extent, the cultural factor is found to be responsible. The use of contraceptives was found to be less prevalent among the Moslems than among the Hindus.

In the urban areas of Uttar Pradesh 40% of the wives among the Hindus with a monthly income of Rs. 500 per month used contraceptives. Among the Moslems in the same income group, it was only 14.9%. In the income group of Rs. 100–300 per month, no Moslem woman used contraceptives, but 12.4% of the Hindus used them.[19]

Paradoxical though it may seem, when one has in mind the fertility of Christians in the West, the Indian Christians are found to be much more fertile than the non-Christians. The Christians in India have inherited from the Hindus some of their cultural characteristics. The Hindu preference for a male child is one of them. The ancient Christian community of Kerala in South India used to welcome the news of the birth of a male child with great joy. "Women would slam the wooden bolts of the doors backwards and forwards and grind coconut shells in a mortar to make noise, as well as made the *kurava* sound (a shrill sound made with fingers moved up and down in the mouth)."[20] But if a female child is born, the family will look like a bereaved family.

Practices like early marriage and universal marriage and extended families are also retained by the Christians. However, they do not ban widow remarriage, and practise abstinence on religious grounds. "The Indian Christians, therefore, stand in the vanguard of a trend that is seemingly coming to characterise the population of the entire peninsula."[21]

The Parsis of India have shown a reproductive behaviour which is conspicuous by its resemblance to the reproductive behaviour of the people in the West. "The balance between births and deaths in the whole community has been small and fluctuating above and below the zero point during the last half century."[22] While 85% of the Hindu men and women between 15 and 19 years of age were married in 1931, among the Parsis only 18% were married. More than 89% live in towns and they are seen in the forefront of most industrial ventures in India. Ethnocentric values have not influenced them to become more prolific in reproductive behaviour.

The motivations for bearing children seem to be quite different in India as compared to the West. According to a survey conducted in Mysore, the motivation for getting children in the case of 22.3% of the women was "to be taken care of in old age"; 14.1% wanted children "to ensure family survival," 15.5% wanted "a son," and among the rest some wanted children to "avoid community criticism," some for "household help," and some to "follow the community pattern."[23]

These motivations are, in most cases, completely at variance with the system of motivations prevalent in the Western society, where children are wanted just for their own sake, because care in old age is provided by old-age pensions, "ensuring family survival" does not cause too much worry, the "community" is too busy to criticise the childless couple, and "household help" is ensured by machines.

The net effect of the impact of Western culture on India's fertility level has been, by and large, neutral. On the one hand, the new culture released certain forces like the weakening of the caste system, tolerance of widow remarriage, less orthodox attitude to abstinence during religious festivals, less rigorous control on the young bride by the mother-in-law, etc., which have the effect of raising the level of fertility. It also introduced some counter-vailing forces such as break-up of the joint family, higher age at marriage, greater freedom for women, change in attitude toward sex and motivation for children, etc. So far, these forces have been equally balanced in their effect on fertility. The birth rate (estimated), which remained at 39.9 in 1950, fell only to 39.1 in 1958.[24]

Recent investigations concluded in various parts of India show that the Indian culture offers little resistance to family planning. Even as late as in 1945, while the members of the Royal Commission on Population in Britain were of the view that "to attempt a house-to-house questioning on a national scale was to foredoom the enquiry to failure,"[25] statistical investigations on a house-to-house questioning basis regarding sexual behaviour have been surprisingly successful in India.

Statistics collected from all over India show that 55 to 80% of the population are in favour of family planning. Among the rest, some do not find it necessary to look beyond their noses and be troubled by something which is not of immediate concern to them, while the rest equate contraception with abortion and thus do not want any knowledge of it.[26] There are only very few who quote religious reasons.

Owing to the non-availability of contraceptives, their unsuitable nature and their high prices, the use of contraceptives is found to be very limited so far. According to a survey in Bombay, only 0.1% in the rural areas practise contraception.[27] In some villages around Delhi, only 0.05% of married females used birth-control techniques.[28] And 0.05% of married couples were found to be practising family planning in a Kerala village.[29]

The strong feeling against destruction of life makes abortion as a family-planning technique unacceptable in Indian culture.

However, Indian culture does not react against sterilization operations as a method of birth control. In recent years, sterilization operations have received a great boost. In the state of Madras, for which statistics are available, the number of sterilization operations conducted in the first 10 months of 1961 were much higher than the combined total of the five preceding years.[30] Unlike in Puerto Rico and Japan, the majority undergoing sterilization operations in India are males. "The surprising phenomenon in India is the willingness of men to undergo vasectomy when they decide to limit further births."[31]

The ancient Indian culture based on social stability is slowly but steadily giving way to a new one motivated more by "social progress" than "social stability," under the influence of the Western culture, and with the initiative provided by enlightened political leadership that stands for democratic institutions.

NOTES

1. A. M. Carr-Saunders, "The Population Problem," as quoted by Frank Lorimer and Others in *Culture and Human Fertility,* UNESCO (1954), p. 15.

2. *Loc. cit.,* p. 17.

3. *Loc. cit.,* p. 17.

4. Frank Lorimer and Others, *loc. cit.,* p. 20.

5. Abbe J. Dubois and H. K. Beauchamp, *Hindu Customs and Ceremonies,* Third Edition, Oxford (1906), p. 206.

6. K. M. Kapadia, *Marriage and Family in India,* Oxford University Press (1958), p. 139.

7. S. V. Ketkar, *The History of Caste in India,* Amraoti, India (1909), p. 32.

8. T. J. Samuel, "Report on an Attitude Survey in a Kerala Village," *The Journal of Family Welfare,* Bombay, Vol. VII, No. 1 (1960).

9. S. V. Venkateswara, *Indian Culture through the Ages,* Longmans Green and Co., London (1948).

10. S. Chandrasekhar, *Population and Planned Parenthood in India,* G. Allen & Unwin, London (1955), p. 55.

11. L. S. Florence, "Britain and Her Birth Rate," *The Economic Journal,* London, January, 1946.

12. S. V. Ketkar, *loc. cit.,* p. 150.

13. Jathar and Beri, *Indian Economics,* Vol. 1, Oxford University Press (1942), p. 101.

14. Kingsley Davis, *Population of India and Pakistan,* Princeton University Press, Princeton (1951), p. 73.

15. Kingsley Davis, *loc. cit.*

16. C. P. Blacker, "The Rhythm Method, Two Indian Experiments," *Eugenics Review,* London, Vol. XLVII, p. 96.

17. The Population Council, *Population: An International Dilemma,* 230 Park Ave., New York 17 (1958), p. 33.

18. Kingsley Davis, *loc. cit.,* p. 188.

19. J. N. Sinha, "Differential Fertility and Family Limitation in an Urban Community of U.P.," *Population Studies,* Vol. XI, 1957–58. London, 1958.

20. L. W. Brown, *Indian Christians of St. Thomas* (1956), p. 185.

21. Kingsley Davis, *loc. cit.,* p. 188.

22. C. Chandrasekharan, as quoted by Frank Lorimer and Others, *loc. cit.,* p. 186.

23. C. Chandrasekharan, "Fertility Survey in Mysore State, India," *Current Research in Human Fertility,* Milbank Memorial Fund, New York (1955), p. 18.

24. U.N. Demographic Year Book, 1960.

25. Papers of the Royal Commission

on Population Studies, Vol. I, as reported in *Population Studies*, Vol. XV, No. 1.

26. N. V. Sovani and Kumudini Dandekar, *Fertility Survey of Nasik, Kolaba and Satara (North) Districts,* Publication No. 31, Gokhale Institute of Politics and Economics (1955), Ch. V.

27. *Ibid.,* p. 108.

28. S. N. Agarwala, "A Family Planning Survey in Four Delhi Villages," *Population Studies,* Vol. XV, No. 2, November 1961.

29. T. J. Samuel, *loc. cit.*

30. R. A. Gopalaswami, "Family Planning, Advantages of Sterilization," *The Hindu Weekly Review,* Dec. 25, 1961.

31. M. C. Balfour, "Family Planning in Asia," *Population Studies,* Vol. XV, No. 2, November 1961.

BIBLIOGRAPHY

BOOKS

1. Frank Lorimer and Others, *Culture and Human Fertility,* UNESCO (1954).

2. Abbe J. Dubois and H. K. Beauchamp, *Hindu Customs and Ceremonies,* Third Edition, Oxford (1906).

3. K. M. Kapadia, *Marriage and Family in India,* Oxford University Press (1958).

4. S. V. Ketkar, *The History of Caste in India,* Amraoti, India (1909).

5. S. V. Venkateswara, *Indian Culture through the Ages,* Longmans Green & Co. (1948).

6. S. Chandrasekhar, *Population and Planned Parenthood in India,* G. Allen & Unwin (1955), London.

7. Jathar and Beri, *Indian Economics,* Oxford University Press (1942).

8. Kingsley Davis, *Population of India and Pakistan,* Princeton (1951).

9. The Population Council, *Population: An International Dilemma,* 230 Park Ave., New York 17 (1958).

10. L. W. Brown, *Indian Christians of St. Thomas,* Cambridge University Press (1956).

11. C. Chandrasekharan, *Current Research in Human Fertility,* Milbank Memorial Fund, New York (1955).

12. *U.N. Demographic Year Book* (1960), U.N.

13. N. V. Sovani and Kumudini Dandekar, *Fertility Survey of Nasik, Kolaba and Salara (North) Districts,* Poona (1955).

PAPERS

1. L. S. Florence, "Britain and Her Birth Rate," *The Economic Journal,* London, January, 1946.

2. C. P. Blacker, "The Rhythm Method, Two Indian Experiments," *Eugenics Review,* London, Vol. XLVII (1955).

3. J. N. Sinha, "Differential Fertility and Family Limitation in an Urban Community of U.P.," *Population Studies,* London, Vol. XI, 1958.

4. Papers of the Royal Commission on Population Studies, Vol. I, as re-ported in *Population Studies*, Vol. XV, No. 1 (1961).

5. S. N. Agarwala, "A Family Planning Survey in Four Delhi Villages," *Population Studies*, Vol. XV, No. 2, November 1961.

6. R. A. Gopalaswami, "Family Planning: Advantages of Sterilization," *The Hindu Weekly Review*, Madras, Dec. 25, 1961.

7. M. C. Balfour, "Family Planning in Asia," *Population Studies*, Vol. XV, No. 2, November 1961.

8. T. J. Samuel, "Report on an Attitude Survey in a Kerala Village," *The Journal of Family Welfare*, Bombay, Vol. VII, No. 1 (1960).

21

A Comparison of Factors Influencing Choice of Vasectomy in India and the United States

Thomas Poffenberger
Shirley B. Poffenberger

Since studies have found the vasectomy to be a highly satisfactory method of controlling birth in India and the United States, a comparison of some of these findings may be of value to persons working professionally in fields related to population control. The comparisons made in this paper are based largely upon samples studied by the authors in the states of California and Gujarat during the years 1960–64. Information was collected from a California surgeon relative to 2,000 voluntary vasectomy cases. Some of these cases were followed up by interviews and questionnaires. Indian samples studied in Gujarat included 53 women who had just undergone tubectomy and three men vasectomy in a rural government-sponsored "camp," 61 cases of vasectomy arranged by a private but free factory clinic in a major urban center of the state, and 46 randomly sampled nonoperated men in two Gujarat villages. (The Indian and U.S. studies are reported in seven papers. See references 5, 6, 8, 9, 10, 11, 12.) We have also drawn upon other research reports (1, 2, 7) and materials resulting from acquaintance with family planning officers (medical doctors) and social workers engaged in this work during the past two and one-half years of travel and residence in India as well as insights gained by the authors in three years of intensive study of a Gujarat village.

Faced with the problem of comparing even a limited behavior such as having a vasectomy in cultures as diverse as India and the United States caused us to think in terms of some sort of framework. We have therefore outlined (Fig. 1) a frame of reference that we believe may be useful in com-

Reprinted from the *Indian Journal of Social Work*, 25, no. 4 (January, 1965), pp. 339–51, by permission of the authors and the publisher.

paring not only India and the United States, but other cultures or subcultures, as well as individuals within a subculture. A comparison of the factors which motivate or stand in the way of adoption of vasectomy (or any method of birth control) may aid in the development of a more exact body of knowledge needed in the field of population control. In the preliminary conceptualization presented here, each factor affecting adoption of the vasectomy is considered as a *dimension* which theoretically can be placed at some point on a continuum from low to high. For example, a dimension such as "desire to have a son" would rate moderately high in the U.S. but would rate very high in India. It is obvious that while we have some preliminary data on how the two cultures may be rated on the various dimensions, much more research is needed before we will be able to rate with any degree of confidence. It is hoped that this paper may stimulate such cross-cultural research.

CONCEPTUALIZATION FOR CROSS-CULTURAL COMPARISONS

Regardless of the culture, it is assumed that a person will show interest in vasectomy only if he does not want additional children. This *primary motive* (a degree of desire to terminate fertility) is determined in part by the overall culture in which the person lives and in part by the more personal aspects of his family life. Assuming this primary interest in birth control, *secondary motivation* (a degree of desire to have a vasectomy) is influenced by various kinds of communications with elements in the culture. These communications are both *institutionalized* and *interpersonal*. The first includes the officially expressed position of the political and religious institutions of the culture as well as of organized medicine. The second of these would include local beliefs, attitudes of individual's friends, neighbors and others in his subculture who may or may not have undergone vasectomy.

Availability of the operation may be visualized as a complex of factors which to varying degreees enable the person to present himself for surgery or cause him to delay or completely avoid this final action. Availability of the surgeon at the time when he is ready to take action, factors related to transportation, cost, and inconvenience in regard to loss of work time are all part of the complex which deters or accelerates a man in his progress toward vasectomy. When factors motivating him toward sterilization become sufficiently greater than those motivating him to avoid it, he undergoes the operation (action).

The individual's *response* to the total vasectomy experience becomes *feedback*. In interpersonal situations the satisfaction of operated persons is

**FIGURE 1.   A Conceptualization of Vasectomy Adoption
Based upon a Comparison of U.S. and Indian Samples**

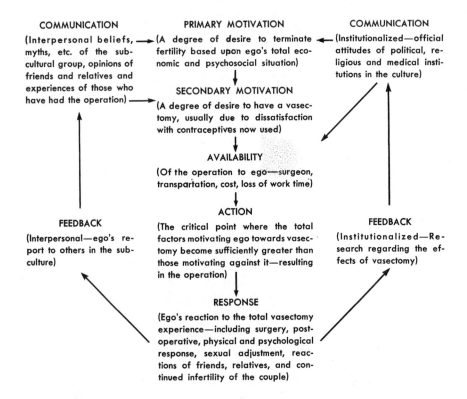

communicated directly by them or indirectly by others who know of their experiences to candidates for vasectomy. Personal advice and gossip are transmitted to a greater or lesser extent depending upon individual inclination to reveal reactions to others. When the vasectomy experience has been interpreted positively, there is a tendency to let others know about the benefits of the operation—in some cases to the point where he may become an active propagandist who propels others toward surgery. When his experience is interpreted negatively, he may disclose his dissatisfaction to others and become an active negative propagandist—whether or not his complaints are justified.

Institutionalized feedback occurs through research reports which may influence official policy; these reports may have originated in the same culture or in another culture as a result of the research conducted by governments or private agencies, or by individuals studying problems related to population control.

Primary Motivation

The desire of an individual to terminate fertility is based upon his total economic and psychosocial situation. In comparing India and the United States, it must be kept in mind that 80 percent of Indian men are rural and oriented to the joint or extended family, where conformity to group norms is stressed. Even in urban areas, the importance of the extended family stands in stark contrast to the importance placed upon the individual in predominantly urban-suburban U.S. society. The close face-to-face interaction of village life, where the most intimate matters of a family are known to the other villagers, must be compared with the relative anonymity of life even in the suburban United States. Whatever action most Indians take is considered primarily in terms of what effect it will have upon members of the extended family and caste group—no matter what may be their own personal desires. If a man goes against the mores of the group, not only his own status is affected, but that of his family as well. While U.S. studies have shown an inclination for Americans to yield to the opinions of others, it is hypothesized that the tendencies of Indians to yield may be considerably higher, particularly in rural areas.

The importance placed upon bearing children can be rated as higher in India than in the U.S. This is particularly true regarding sons. In a random sample of 1,250 couples between the ages of 21 and 43 years in Gujarat's capital city of Ahmedabad (pop. 1,250,000), over 91 percent reported that they would not consider family planning until they had a son (7). The same study found that 66 percent of the sample would not consider family planning regardless of how many children they had. This contrasts sharply with the general acceptance of family planning in the U.S., in spite of disagreements about the moral and legal aspects of particular methods. Apparently this feeling was not based on any moral or religious ground, but upon Hindu fatalism—that one should not or cannot obstruct the "course of nature." Of the 1,250 couples, 5.8 percent were reported as actually practicing some method of birth control.

Those who work in the villages find less motivation to control pregnancy. This is particularly true of lower caste, low-socioeconomic-status families, where children are employed in agricultural work which adds their wages to the family income. In spite of the declining infant death rate in India, a village mother may still have nearly as many children die as survive between birth and adolescence. By contrast, in the United States, there is relatively little fear of infant or childhood death, sons are not required from a ritualistic standpoint, and the small nuclear or unitary family is valued. Perhaps a partial comparison of U.S. and Indian primary motivation as well as secondary motivation might be given by comparing the Indian factory workers (9) who were sufficiently motivated to have a vasectomy with those factory workers in the U.S. who had undergone the operation (5,6,10,11). In the Indian factory sample, the average number of children fathered by the men at the time of vasectomy was 4.5, while in the U.S. the mean was 3. The Indian men's mean age was 37.1 years at the time of the operation, whereas the mean age of the U.S. workers was 31. There was a tendency for Indian fathers in both village and urban samples studied to realize the advantage of family planning only after they had had a large number of children. In the two villages in Gujarat (12), of those men 36 years of age and over, 47.5 percent had five or more children. When asked the number of children desired, 38 percent said they would like three or fewer children, while only 19.5 percent said they would like five or more. Of those men under 36 years of age, 26 percent said they would prefer five or more children.

For a variety of reasons, then, primary motivation or desire to limit birth cannot be rated as high in India as in the United States. This is not to indicate that there is not real interest in birth control on the part of a large segment of the population. Studies have found, however, that even when some motivation is present, the people seem unable to act upon it, at least in terms of using contraceptives. A follow-up study in Madras State of 40,000 women who had been given contraceptive information (because of initial interest on their part) found that only 4 percent had actually used a contraceptive after the information had been given (2). In the highly motivated Baroda factory workers who had undergone vasectomy, less than one-third indicated that they had ever used contraceptives in spite of the fact that these were readily available at the factory family planning clinic (9).

The reasons behind the lack of use of contraceptives in India are many and varied. Both in the cities and in the villages, the crowded conditions of living are difficult to imagine for one who has not seen them. The number of people who must share one room makes privacy almost impossible. Sexual intercourse may be hurried—or, in the case of village people, it may take place in the fields instead of in the home. Private lavatory facilities are usually absent and water has to be carried in pots or vessels on the wife's head. Bathing takes place outside the house in the public view. The soiled garments are left on while washing takes place. After the bath is completed, clean clothing is put on and the wet garment is dropped from underneath. In this way the body is covered during bathing but the effectiveness of the bath is obviously minimized by the procedure. Soap is not often used because of cost and because of the belief that it is harmful to the skin and clothes. The relationship of the husband and wife tends to be formal and the wife may find great difficulty in talking with him about such things as family planning and contraceptives. In the joint family, the mother-in-law to a large extent determines the action of the wife. Since the mother-in-law would probably know of any use of contraceptives, it would not be possible to use them without her approval.

Aside from the difficulty of use, we found an attitude of "disgust" on the part of the men in two villages (12). Also, this feeling was expressed by some urban workers who remarked that condoms were "dirty" and "unnatural" to the point of "nausea." One man reported that he believed he would become diseased if he used a condom (9). This attitude toward contraceptives may not be easy to change. Besides, the use of the condom was associated with visits to prostitutes, according to some comments.

Of those who are strongly motivated and will try contraceptives, there tends to be dissatisfaction for the same reasons as we found in the United States. Of the 31 percent of the Baroda factory sample who had used contraceptives, all indicated dissatisfaction with them, as did the U.S. sample. Half of the Baroda group said the contraceptives they used had failed to prevent conception. This appeared to be due to misunderstanding and perhaps partly to the quality of the contraceptives. One man's obvious lack of understanding was evident in the remark that he had taken his wife for "injections" to prevent pregnancy, while another said that his wife had taken some foam tablets orally (9).

In the U.S. sample, nearly 50 percent of the husbands thought the wife had become pregnant while they were using contraceptives (5,10). In the U.S. sample, a frequent reason given for dissatisfaction with contraceptives was that they interfered with mutual sex pleasure—a reason not given in the Indian sample.

Before examining secondary motivation, one more point may be made regarding methods of control. In India, as in the U.S., abortion is illegal. The study by Kinsey *et al.* in the U.S. has demonstrated that abortion is frequently resorted to by both married and unmarried women (4, pp. 66, 119). Of the Kinsey sample of pre-marital pregnancies that ended before marriage, 89 percent were induced abortions. Between one quarter and one fifth of the married women had had an induced abortion at one time or another. There is evidence that this is also the case in India. In a recent news report it was stated that in Madras State, about 30 percent of rural and urban pregnancies were aborted, largely with the aid of village barbers' wives who also serve as midwives (13). In our "intensive study" village (of twenty families) near Baroda, two mothers recently attempted abortions. The reasons are: one woman does not want another child at this time because her eldest daughter is also pregnant and she said she would feel shame having a child at the same time as her daughter. The second woman has such strained relations with her mother-in-law that she is fearful that she would not take care of her husband and children during her confinement period. In both situations the husbands have indicated their interest in having the wife abort because they feel that additional children will be a greater economic burden. This apparent willingness to have abortion on the part of the village women may be due to the fact that it is something known and understood by them. Many women have had spontaneous abortions, and when they have an unwanted pregnancy, it is logical for them to hope for this type of termination. When it does not occur, they consider possible ways to induce it. In spite of the law, it is our understanding that it is not difficult to find a doctor who will perform an abortion if the family can pay for it. Of course, the state of health of many Indian village women is so poor that abortion may be judged as necessary to save the life of the mother. However, while abortions by qualified doctors may be available for some, they are not performed in the public clinics, and as a result, village women and the poorer urban women must either have them performed by unqualified persons or induce them themselves.

Secondary Motivation

We have seen that for a variety of reasons, primary motivation or desire to limit birth cannot be rated as high in India as in the U.S. When we add to this the problems of using contraceptives in India as compared with the U.S., the findings regarding lack of effectiveness of typical family planning methods are understandable. The programs in India that have been most effective so far have stressed sterilization. It seems that while primary motivation in India is too low to bring about effective and prolonged use of contraceptives under Indian conditions, it may be sufficiently strong to cause a sizable number of men to have a vasectomy (or females a tubectomy). The success of such states as Madras and Maharashtra, where a combined total of 157,186 vasectomies were reported to August 1963, indicates the possibility of relatively successful programs throughout India, provided a similar scheme of monetary reward is used (3). The importance of fee payments was indicated in Madras, where the number operated each month in Madras City dropped from 3,000 to 200 when payments were no longer made. In spite of the record of these two states, there is little reason to believe that Indian men in general are more ready to have vasectomies than men in other countries. In fact, in Gujarat State, we find almost total initial rejection of the vasectomy on the part of village men, and experiences in other parts of India indicate that this may be the usual reaction. Details of this rejection will be given later in the paper. It is not that vasectomy will be easily sold, but that in spite of hard resistance, it still seems to have the most promise of any method yet used in the attempt to slow down the population increase. In general, it is our feeling that it would be easier to motivate U.S. men than Indian men to undergo vasectomy.

Availability

The willingness of surgeons to perform vasectomy and the number who are available are major factors in the number of men who have the operation. In India, most surgeons will perform the operation since there is no fear of illegality, whereas in the United States, the fear of illegality and the attitude of medical associations cause many to shy away from performing vasectomy. Availability of surgeons is a problem in India because of the low ratio of medical personnel to population, and the lack of monetary reward for this surgery. The operation is performed by many surgeons as a public service or for small fees from the government. Candidates for vasectomy are not often able to pay a fee for surgery, and they may not find a surgeon willing to perform vasectomy free of charge, except in a government camp. In the U.S., the ratio of surgeons to population is more favourable and performing the vasectomy is profitable.

In India, transportation is no problem where camps are provided, but this is dependent upon government help. In the United States, the person may have to travel independently some distance to undergo surgery by a private surgeon, but transportation is seldom a problem.

In both cultures, time away from the job may be a deterrent factor keeping the person from final action. In India, as in the U.S., it is possible in private surgery to undergo vasectomy on the weekend and return to work the following Monday, thus not losing any work time; however, since the weekend is not necessarily a "work break" for the farmer in rural areas, the sterilization camp appointment may not be convenient for him.

Cost and inconvenience are related factors which add weight to decision-making in both cultures. If female sterilization is a possibility, the cost of the wife's hospitalization is considered not only in monetary terms, but in relation to her absence and ability to undergo surgery. Baroda factory workers remarked that their wives couldn't be spared from the home for the hospitalization period and that they were concerned that there might be unforeseen medical costs in case the wife had any complications. Since in the U.S. culture most of the couples were denied a choice of sterilization operations, this decision did not have to be made except in a very few cases where the wife's ill health might have made her a candidate for tubectomy —which would be a more expensive operation, considering hospital costs and surgery fee. Absence of wife from the village home, because of the presence of more adult females, may be less of a problem for the rural husband than the urban husband in India.

Actual cost of surgery in India may be nothing, and in some instances the male is paid to have the vasectomy. For some men this rupee payment may be a strong motivating factor.

In the United States, once the person has learned of a surgeon who will perform the operation, he can usually have it performed immediately. In India, the time of the year may be a deterrent to action. Since in much of India the summer and monsoon seasons have been found to be a poor time for any surgery, this may mean that a sterilization camp will be planned only once a year in a given area. Some operated men have said that they would have undergone the vasectomy a year or more before and that to their regret the wife had become pregnant because of this delay.

In Gujarat State, as in most states, while vasectomy is encouraged, limitations of facilities and staff may make it as difficult or more difficult to have a vasectomy as in the U.S. In general, we would rate India little higher in availability than the U.S.

Response to Vasectomy

Repeated studies have found almost complete satisfaction on the part of those who have undergone the operation both in India and the United States, and it is these men who are most effective in convincing others of its advantages. In every study, however, there are a few men who have had either physical or psychological difficulties that leave them less than fully satisfied with the result. In future studies such dissatisfied men and their wives should have closer scrutiny in order to better understand which persons should be discouraged from having a sterilization operation. If fewer potentially negative patients undergo this surgery, the present small percentage of dissatisfaction may be almost completely eliminated.

We have little Indian or California data on the physical effect of the operation itself; what we have indicated that most men regarded the pain as slight and the aftereffects as minor. In the California interview study, however, some of the men reported concern about discoloration of the genital area and some "drainage" of the wound. Some time after the operation these concerns were forgotten, but one of the respondents thought that men should be warned of possible short-term aftereffects to reduce anxiety if they did occur (10). In any case, it must be recognized that these men did not give fully positive reports to others regarding the operation during this relatively short period of concern, and it may be stated that some of the misconceptions regarding vasectomy are communicated at this time.

In the Indian factory sample, some men blamed the vasectomy for physical conditions obviously not related. One man said, "I enjoy sexual relations as I did before the operation, but I feel bodily weak since the operation. This may be due to the fact that I take less food now than before." He went on to say, "The operation seems to have had some bad effect upon my wife. She was menstruating regularly and was in good health before the operation. Now she is menstruating irregularly and does not feel healthy. I consider this to be a defect in the operation" (9). The Indian sample, to a greater extent than the U.S. sample, associated with the vasectomy changes in health such as weight gains or losses and increase or decrease in physical vigour. Since misconceptions both before and after the operation are related to educational level, this is to be expected.

Results of the vasectomy seem to differ in the U.S. and India relative to increased satisfaction. In the Indian factory sample, most men reported no change in sexual enjoyment, while only 15 percent reported an increase in enjoyment (9). This finding is supported by that of Phadke in a follow-up study of 655 cases in Bombay, where he found less than 12 percent reported improvement in sex enjoyment. In his sample, again, most men reported no change (2). In contrast, in the U.S. sample, 70 percent of the men and 80 percent of the wives were reported as having increased sex enjoyment following the operation. This was found to be particularly true of the 19 percent Catholic men and 24 percent Catholic wives in the sample who showed significantly greater increase in sex desire, frequency and pleasure in comparison with the Protestant group (5). Several reasons can be offered regarding these differences. In India, few couples had evidently been using contraceptives before the vasectomy, whereas dissatisfaction with their contraceptive was common with the majority of the U.S. couples studied. The interference of the diaphragm with sexual satisfaction was frequently mentioned. Also couples in the U.S. are more likely to think of sex as a pleasurable activity and expect a degree of satisfaction from it that is not expected by the Indian couple. This may be particularly true of the American wife, who has been conditioned to think of sexual satisfaction as equally as desirable for herself as for her husband. In India sexual satisfaction of the wife is more likely to be secondary to the satisfaction of the husband. In addition, the crowded living conditions mean that sexual intercourse must in most cases be completed quickly, omitting the foreplay thought to be necessary by American couples.

The Catholic-Protestant differences noted in the California study may be explained on the basis of release from guilt of using contraceptives on the part of Catholic women. While the Catholic sample did express some guilt about having the vasectomy, the constant reminder of breaking faith related to use of a contraceptive was removed.

Communications Regarding Vasectomy

The political, religious and medical institutions of a society may take formal positions regarding vasectomy and propagandize their views. In India, there is full support by the government and organized medicine. There seems to be no question regarding its legality, nor is there organized objection on the part of any major Indian religion. In the United States, vasectomy seems to be still regarded officially by the medical associations as mayhem, the legality of the operation is still questioned, a major religion is strongly opposed, and the government has taken a hands-off policy toward population control in general (11). Positive institutional communication regarding vasectomy would certainly be rated high in India as compared with the U.S. Even in our village sample, the men were aware that the government encouraged vasectomy, while in the U.S. sample some believed they had broken the law by having undergone the operation. In the U.S., hesitancy to have a vasectomy and to some extent shame and guilt (where religion is involved) after having it are related to the official positions of the institutions, while in India they are largely determined by more personal factors.

More significant than the official view are the communications to the individual from his primary group. The beliefs and myths and misconceptions of his subcultural group must be examined to determine their role in positive or negative motivation, since the individual's status depends upon how his associates view him and his action. In India, the attitude of the extended family and the caste, as pointed out previously, have a high order of significance in the Indian village, and even in the urban area, relatively more so than the person's family and subcultural group in the United States.

In the villages studied, attitude toward vasectomy was certainly not positive (12). Thirteen percent of the men sampled said they thought that a vasectomy might be acceptable only under certain extreme conditions of poor health. The rest were strongly opposed, even though they knew that the government favored such a program. A list of some of the more frequently stated beliefs regarding vasectomy may give some idea of the degree of misinformation most villagers held. Seventy percent either believed that intercourse would not be possible after the operation or were not sure that it would be possible. Over 30 percent thought that it involved castration as in the case of a bullock or of members of a semi-religious order of castrates found in Gujarat. One man said the operation would encourage one to have sexual intercourse, thereby causing him to lose strength through loss of semen (a frequent belief of village people). If, because of poor health, a sterilization operation was considered necessary for a couple, the female operation was more highly approved (41 percent). However, there was strong objection even for female sterilization on the part of the rest of the sample, some associating it with prostitution.

The greater willingness to permit women to have the operation seemed related to the general belief that it was the duty of women to suffer. In the village sample one man said, "Not a single male is prepared to be operated, but then, fifteen women are prepared." When asked why, he remarked, "The male does not have to suffer physical pain at the time of pregnancy while the female does, so she is prepared. Males have to suffer economically" (12).

Women who underwent sterilization operations in a rural Gujarat camp indicated that they had done so to spare their husbands pain. Fear of pain for the male was given as a reason by the wives who were dominated by their mothers-in-law and told that it was the wife's duty to submit to sterilization. One wife remarked that her mother-in-law had told her she didn't want her son to be hurt (8). It might be expected that in India, where the male is protected by the female, the vasectomy operation would not have as general an adoption as female sterilization. Sterilization statistics in Gujarat indicate that two female sterilizations are performed for every male operation (3).

In the Indian factory group, 23 percent said they had feared disapproval or opposition if it became known that they planned to have a vasectomy (9). They believed that people would make filthy jokes or ridicule them. The frequent concern about what one's family would think was indicated by a man who said, "I feel ashamed to tell about such things to an adult son or old mother." However, the fact that 69 percent of the sample reported later family approval indicates that urban groups would be more easily convinced of the value of vasectomy than would rural ones. In the U.S. sample, some evidence of shame was indicated by several respondents who did not want their friends and particularly their children to know that they had had the operation (10). But in general, the evidence we have indicates that shame regarding vasectomy would be rated considerably higher in India than in the United States. Even so, in both the U.S. and India, it is evident that a feeling of shame on the part of operated males may keep many from communicating with others about the vasectomy. On the other hand, the majority of both the California sample and the Indian factory workers indicated that they either had or would tell others about its benefits. The shame factor was most evident in relation to family members or peers who might cause one embarrassment. In work situations, where the operated male was away from his family, he seemed more willing to talk freely about it. One Baroda factory worker said, "I recommended the operation to a friend of mine working in the factory. Now he is operated and finds himself very happy. Whenever someone comes to me for advice, I tell him about the advantages of the operation. At present, I am persuading my barber to undergo the operation, as he is very poor and has many children. I recommend the operation on the ground that it is absolutely harmless, as it does not affect your sexual relations. On the contrary, you enjoy them more after the operation. Moreover, the operation improves the health of the husband as well as of the wife" (9). In the U.S., as in India, it is this kind of heart-felt testimonial that is most effective in determining the final action of others.

Feedback

Perhaps the most significant finding in all of the studies is the importance of positive feedback in motivating men toward vasectomy. In the California study we found that the surgeon performed 191 vasectomies in 1956 and 638 in 1961. This increase was the result of communication by men who were satisfied with the operation to others who are interested. The importance of personal communication among Gujarat village women was suggested by interviews with operated females who remarked that the women we saw waiting outside their ward were relatives and friends who had accompanied them to see if they recovered and how they felt—before they agreed to have the tubectomy themselves (8).

Feedback can be negative as well as positive, and those who are not satisfied with the operation can be a strong influence in deterring persons from undergoing sterilization. In the study of two villages it was reported that a man who had the vasectomy regarded the operation as painful. One of the men interviewed said, "It [vasectomy] is painful." Another said, "Don't go because I've suffered." Another person in the same village had evidently talked to the same man or another who was not satisfied with the hurried conditions of the vasectomy camp. He said, "In camps for family planning the doctor does not take care so there is possibility of pain, but if a special doctor is there, it does not pain." In the two villages, most of the men either thought the operation would be painful or did not know. Only 21 percent thought it would not be painful (12). These reports of negative experiences are likely to be believed more readily than the expression of positive experiences, since they support the prejudices of the men. The importance of maintaining high standards in operative procedure is obvious, but under field conditions in India it is difficult. As a result we would expect a greater number of men dissatisfied with the operation in India than in the U.S.

Failure of the vasectomy to prevent conception may be greater in India than in the U.S. One Baroda surgeon working in an urban family planning clinic disclosed that only about one in ten men returned for a sperm count. In the camps there is even less possibility for follow-up checks. Rare cases of multiple vas or other reasons for failure are not detected until pregnancy does occur. Probably a more frequent cause of apparent failure has nothing to do with the husband's vasectomy. Among some lower castes, extramarital relations are not unusual, and when the wife becomes pregnant, the surgeon may be confronted with the accusation of operative failure. We know of more than one case where in such instances the doctor has played the role of the gentleman and taken the responsibility. This seems to happen with enough regularity that some surgeons prefer to perform tubectomy to "protect the wife." In our village one man gave as his reason for not wanting the vasectomy that he feared his wife might become pregnant by someone else. He pointed out that if he had the vasectomy it would be known to the village that his wife had been sleeping with another man. Our tentative information indicates that the husband may not have been as concerned about his wife having sexual intercourse with another man as he was with the shame of having it discovered. If he could call the baby his own the situation would not be nearly as serious.

Since a number of men in the Indian samples have remarked that the female is highly sexed, the possibility of a wife's extramarital relations might be a frequent concern.

SUMMARY AND CONCLUSION

Vasectomy adoption in the U.S. and in India have been compared in terms of the following factors based upon studies done by the authors in both countries: (1) primary motivation or desire to terminate fertility, (2) secondary motivation or desire to have a vasectomy, (3) communication from the culture regarding vasectomy, both institutionalized and interpersonal, (4) availability of the operation, (5) action or the point of operation, (6) response of the individual to the operation, and (7) feedback of the individual's feelings about the operation to the culture.

Primary motivation can be rated higher in the U.S. than in India. The factors contributing to minimal desire for family limitation in India include the belief that it is contrary to nature, that one should have a large number of children, particularly boys, and that it is an economic advantage to have many children, particularly in the case of lower caste agricultural workers. In India those who wish to limit family size are confronted by considerably greater difficulties than are found in the U.S. Availability and cost of contraceptives, negative attitudes toward contraceptives, family crowding and lack of privacy, insufficient lavatory facilities, inability of husband and wife to discuss family planning, and mother-in-law domination are all factors in preventing effective usage. Of those who have tried contraceptives, dissatisfaction with the method used was a major factor in both the U.S. and India in motivating the man toward a vasectomy. Perhaps to the same extent as in the U.S., abortions are used in India to control birth. Spontaneous abortion is a natural phenomenon well known to Indian village women and an induced abortion may seem little different. In any case, it may be that in rural areas abortion is not rejected to the same extent as are contraceptives.

While two states in India had considerable success in the number of vasectomies performed, the indication is that Indian men are at least as reluctant as men in the U.S. to have the operation. While the institutions of the Indian society such as government and medicine give their full support to vasectomy programs and propagandize for them, the communication from the primary group tends to be negative. In spite of government propaganda, urban men as well as village men tend to regard the vasectomy as a painful operation that may result in impotency. If sterilization must be performed, it is believed that sterilization of the wife is to be preferred, and the women agree with this position. While some fear does exist on the part of U.S. men regarding the vasectomy, these fears are less firmly rooted. In spite of the fact that vasectomy is encouraged in India, limitation of facilities and staff may make it as difficult to have the operation as in the U.S., where the medical profession is officially opposed to performing it as a method of birth control.

Response of those who have had a vasectomy in India, as in the U.S., is generally positive. However, the necessity for performing large numbers of operations under "camp" conditions in India may cause a greater percentage of dissatisfaction. In both cultures both negative and positive experiences are important as feedback that encourages or discourages men to undergo vasectomy. The generally almost total positive response to the operation in both India and the U.S. indicates that voluntary vasectomy is one of the most effective and satisfactory methods of family planning yet used in either culture.

REFERENCES

1. Agarwala, S. N., *Attitude toward Family Planning in India.* Bombay: Asia Publishing House, 1962.
2. Blacker, C. P., "Voluntary Sterilization: Transition throughout the World," *Eugenics Review,* 54 (Oct. 1962), pp. 143–62.
3. *Family Planning News,* 4 (Dec. 1963), p. 239.
4. Gebhard, P. H., *et al., Pregnancy, Birth and Abortion.* New York: Harper, 1958.
5. Landis, J. T., and Poffenberger, Thomas, "The Marital and Sexual Adjustment of 330 Couples Who Chose Vasectomy as a Form of Birth Control," unpublished manuscript.
6. Landis, J. T., and Poffenberger, Thomas, "Population Control—The Vasectomy," unpublished manuscript.

7. Patel, Tara, "Some Reflections on the Attitude of Married Couples towards Family Planning in Ahmedabad," *Sociological Bulletin*, 12 (Sept. 1963), pp. 143–62.

8. Poffenberger, Shirley, and Poffenberger, Thomas, "Interview Report of Fifty-six Sterilization Cases Performed at a Rural 'Camp,'" *Journal of Family Welfare*, 9 (Sept. 1962), pp. 1–7.

9. Poffenberger, Shirley, and Sheth, D. L., "Reactions of Urban Employees to Vasectomy Operations," *Journal of Family Welfare*, 10 (Dec. 1963), pp. 7–23.

10. Poffenberger, Thomas, and Poffenberger, Shirley, "Vasectomy as a Preferred Method of Birth-Control: A Preliminary Investigation," *Marriage and Family Living*, 25 (Aug. 1963), pp. 326–30.

11. Poffenberger, Thomas, "Two Thousand Voluntary Vasectomies Performed in California: Background Factors and Comments," *Marriage and Family Living*, 25 (Nov. 1963), pp. 469–74.

12. Poffenberger, Thomas, and Patel, H. G., "The Effects of Local Beliefs on Attitudes toward Vasectomy in Two Indian Villages in Gujarat State," *Population Review*, 8 (July 1964), pp. 37–44.

13. Verghese, B. G., "A Go-Ahead State in Many Ways Is Madras," *Times of India*, March 21, 1964.

22

Demographic Science
and the Redirection
of Population Policy*

Judith Blake

In recent years informed laymen as well as professional demographers have become increasingly convinced that poor but densely settled countries must achieve a successful demographic revolution and a rapid one. Although consensus on this goal is nearing unanimity, persons equally committed to it are frequently in disagreement about how it is to be achieved. In fact, policy aimed at reducing rates of population growth in developing countries has become bipolarized. One group tends to say that decreases in family size will occur only as an end-product of advanced economic and social development which, in due time, will lead to a desire for fewer children. The other group is inclined to bypass the institutional setting of reproduction entirely and to assume that education and communication respecting birth control will eventually reduce births to a level consonant with low mortality. Yet these approaches do not appear to be adequate either in fact or in theory when taken alone, or even in some combination. Consequently additional strategies designed to solve the dilemma of population growth are needed. This can be seen by examining each position and the objections to it.

The development school of thought emphasizes that motives for a transition from high to low birth rates such as occurred in presently industrial countries were contingent not only on declines in mortality, but also

Reprinted from the *Journal of Chronic Diseases*, 18 (1965), pp. 1181–1200, by permission of the author and the publisher. Footnotes have been renumbered.

* Research for this paper was conducted at International Population and Urban Research, Institute of International Studies, University of California, Berkeley, under a grant from The Equitable Life Assurance Society. The author wishes to thank Kingsley Davis for his criticism and suggestions.

on changes in the social and economic organization that previously had led individuals to desire numerous births. Without such changes (and in spite of mortality declines) individuals would have continued to attach independent importance to institutionalized roles, activities, and goals that directly or indirectly provided the motivational underpinning for many offspring. Hence, it is claimed, changes similar to the industrial and urban revolutions of the Western world must occur in developing countries if their family structures are to alter and a wish for drastically curtailed reproduction is to evolve. Policy must therefore be directed at accelerating overall social and economic development which, in turn, will indirectly affect the family and reproduction. The most that can be expected by way of directly reducing family size is to spread birth control knowledge and means among crucial groups (such as educated urban elites) where desires for smaller families may already exist.

This position is, however, clearly open to objections of both a scientific and practical nature. For instance, it can be argued that social structures are far less tightly integrated than the theory just outlined presupposes. Since all societies have visible lines of cleavage, strain, and vulnerability, important social changes can occur without a complete socio-economic revolution. Particular sectors of the population such as the young, the females, the peasants, or the outcastes may be so chronically dissatisfied that they are eager to experiment if the opportunity arises. In actual fact, many developing countries have undergone enormous, if piecemeal, changes in recent years. These changes have typically been accelerated by the importation of technical knowledge and assistance, the rapidity and influence of which should not be underestimated.[1] We therefore hesitate, on purely empirical grounds, to assume that these societies do not have their own internal sources of motivation for change, and that these cannot be stimulated to an unprecedented degree by close contact and co-operation with more modern societies.[2] From a practical standpoint, the objections to exclusive reliance on the "development approach" center on the appalling dilemma it poses. If birth rates will not decline markedly prior to industrialization and modernization, what will happen if the latter are effectively slowed down, as seems to be the case, by the very malady they are supposed to cure—population growth itself? A shift back to higher levels of mortality is of course the answer, and it is one that few people are willing to accept without a struggle.

Many thoughtful persons have therefore been led to advocate demographic strategies that are more directly geared to affecting reproduction. Unfortunately, so little systematic thought and analysis have been devoted to the presuppositions involved and the possible alternatives available that this more direct population policy has fallen into what appears to be an intuitively "obvious" course of action. The assumption is made that high birth rates in developing countries are today primarily a result of unwanted births. On this assumption, population policy in developing countries has recently taken the form of an intensive planned parenthood campaign for contraceptive education and distribution. Such policy seems to have gone beyond a modification of the sociological and economic assumptions of the "development" approach to the pole of ignoring them altogether. It is therefore hardly surprising that this extreme course of action is not leading to marked reductions in birth rates and rates of population growth among the illiterate rural masses that predominate in developing countries.[3] In fact, because family size desires are so substantial in these countries, primary reliance on inhibiting the births that are in excess of these desires may have little effect on birth rates under conditions of relatively high mortality, and no effect on present population growth rates if mortality declines. This dilemma requires some systematic consideration.

In countries like India mortality is declining enough to provide a high rate of demographic increase—as far as we know, over 2 per cent annually. But even so, mortality remains shockingly high, and improvements may be sporadic. Although surveys show that Indians normally desire 3–5 children, it is still true that in India many births are required to guarantee this result. Presumably Indian parents want their children to survive at least through their own reproductive periods. This dependency of birth-reducing motives on confidence in mortality improvements is widely recognized as a principal reason for the lack of success to date of family planning programs.[4]

But even if continuously spectacular improvements in mortality were to be made and births were proportionately reduced, population growth rates would remain high unless the *desired size of the planned families* was itself greatly curtailed. Developing peoples may not wish to have an unlimited number of offspring, but survey data gathered so far do not turn up excessively modest family-size desires either. For example, available data on ideal family size in India show that the mass of the people on the average prefer about 4 (presumably surviving) children.[5] But high proportions (30–45 per cent) either refuse to answer the question or are not asked it, often because they do not wish even to consider limiting births. The averages may therefore have a downward bias, although a countervailing tendency for subfecund couples to refuse to answer may also exist. In Latin America, the 4-child preference has also been found in a large study of Santiago, Chile; and in Taiwan, Freedman and his colleagues have found 4 children to be the ideal.[6] In all these cases, such an average typically means that close to 60 per cent of the respondents consider 4 *or more* children to be ideal. To be sure, these desires represent a wish for a family of only moderate size, and in general the ideals are lower than the actual number of births, but for reducing population growth under conditions of low mortality the desires are not low enough. They are on the whole somewhat higher than the actual family size of the overseas European countries (the United States, Canada, Australia, and New Zealand) and these countries have been experiencing population growth rates which, if continued, will result in a doubling of their populations every 30–40 years. Family-size aspirations such as those among peoples who characteristically marry and reproduce even earlier than overseas Europeans will, if realized in practice, result in higher rates of population growth (at comparable mortality levels), because the mean length of a generation is shorter, thereby allowing more generations to be squeezed into a given unit of time.

Can family planning programs solve this dilemma by introducing not only contraceptive means but more modest family-size desires? In answer we can only say that to date we have no compelling reason to believe that developing peoples will ever be merely propagandized or "educated" into wanting really small families—slightly more than two children on the average—regardless of the level of mortality. It does not seem as if their desires for larger families will succumb to flipcharts, flannelboards, message movies, group leaders, or "explanations" about the "advantages" of few children. As we shall see, this expectation is so discontinuous with our existing knowledge of the institutionalization of reproduction as to be virtually incongruous.

Have we then exhausted the alternatives available for reducing population growth by means of direct policy? The answer is, I think, that we have not yet begun to explore them. But if we are to bring them to light, we must review what is already known of reproductive motivation through research concerning family-size declines and present levels in industrial countries. In doing so we shall find that an analysis in terms of the social and economic factors affecting reproduction does not necessarily only result in indirect choices for population policy such as economic development. This type of analysis is just as capable of generating possibilities for direct action regarding family size.

HISTORICAL PERSPECTIVES ON FAMILY SIZE

Concomitant with improved mortality, the desire for smaller families among Western industrializing peoples appears to have resulted from a complex of factors (among them urbanization, increased opportunities for social mobility, separation of work from residence, compulsory education, child labor laws) that diminished the economic utility of offspring (as income producers and security in old age), leaving simply their noneconomic utility for parents to take into account. This complex not only decreased the range of utilities but augmented the costs of children, both direct and indirect. Parents had to undergo increased direct costs such as those for compulsory education, food, recreation, and space in crowded urban circumstances. They also suffered an extension of indirect or opportunity costs since expanding economies offered them unprecedented opportunities for upward mobility and investment, and a modern, urban, middle-class way of life opened up virtually unlimited non-domestic avenues of recreation and interest.[7] This account amounts to a delineation of how modernizing and urbanizing societies affected the family and its articulations with socio-economic structure, and how couples reacted by altering the number of their "hostages to fortune."[8]

In utilizing this outline of Western experience for clues as to the determinants of very modest family-size ideals, we must, however, be wary of two potential fallacies: the *particularistic fallacy* and the *economic fallacy*. The particularistic fallacy occurs when one turns one's attention entirely to the associations between particular variables—urbanization, education, social mobility—and declining family-size goals, instead of utilizing the associations to trace out the basic and more general mechanisms involved. Thus our real concern seems to be with factors making children less and less useful to parents and increasingly expensive (both directly and indirectly). The exact nature of these factors will necessarily vary between historical periods and among societies, although we may expect to find some recognizable patterns and repetitions. But we must be sensitized to search for this common element of decreased utilities and increased costs in a wide diversity of events. Otherwise, we are operating in demography as epidemiologists did prior to bacteriology—we mistake the vector for the agent.[9]

On the other hand, although the framework of utilities and costs outlined above is reasonable as far as it goes, it becomes very limited in its applicability if we are led to assume that the *noneconomic* utilities of offspring are somehow not very important or meaningful, as is implied when we say that children have become mere "items of consumption." If we fall into this line of reasoning, then we are expecting the theory to explain some of the most social aspects of human motivation, without giving these aspects independent status in the formulation. Thus, as the theory is stated in the "economic development" school of thought, the family plays an almost completely passive role in the formulation. It is assumed throughout that the family is acted upon and that it only indirectly affects individual calculation regarding familial investment. Yet one can readily point out that the family has powerful sources of resistance to its own demise. Socialization is not simply "a function" that the family "performs" for "the society";

it is a primary mechanism of indoctrination and control. Individuals who are socialized in families will be likely to want families themselves, to enforce norms and sanctions regarding families, and to take pleasure in acting out familial roles. This means that the family complex is itself a goal—the utilities represented by children are not merely economic or affectional, but socially structured in a powerful manner. Moreover, societies with long familial traditions have powerful sanctioning and ideological systems which help to keep parents from being discouraged by direct reproductive costs, or distracted by indirect ones. It is hardly surprising, therefore, that in its purely economic form the theory led social scientists to extreme conclusions. The idea arose that the desire for children was on the way to disappearing altogether from Western societies, and this expectation made the subsequent "baby boom" a source of never-to-be-forgotten embarrassment.

Unfortunately, the lesson of the reproductive renaissance seems to have concluded with the rediscovery that social institutions like the family are adaptive to change and hence (without direct intervention) are neither transformed readily nor obliterated rapidly. The relevance of family-size declines up to the "baby boom" is not extended to an analysis of possibilities for further declines in family size—that is, from moderate to small numbers of offspring. This disjuncture is due primarily to the inability of the theory, when stated in purely economic terms, to deal with variability within the moderate to small family range. Such variation is categorized as short-term fluctuation, and no long-term institutional determinants of small families are postulated.[10] This truncating of the theory is, moreover, buttressed by the fact that long-term and widespread institutional influences leading to small families may well not actually exist in any major societies today. Even if this is the case, it does not argue against the scientific and practical advantages of extending the theory to logical closure. In fact, even if it appears that modern industrial societies typically generate desires for a moderate, rather than small family, this very fact should give us some insights into the types of factors that to date *prevent* families from stabilizing at few children. Let us examine, then, one of the principal existing differences in fertility among modernized countries—the family-size differential between Western Europeans and overseas countries (the so-called "frontier" countries).

FAMILY SIZE VARIATIONS
AMONG MODERNIZED PEOPLES—
WESTERN EUROPE AND THE OVERSEAS COUNTRIES

For some years the overseas or "frontier" countries (the United States, Canada, Australia, and New Zealand) have been exhibiting a noticeable

TABLE 1.   Ideal Number of Children. Selected Western European and Overseas European Countries at Various Survey Dates, 1936–1960

Country	Date	Av. Ideal No. of Children	% Saying 4+
Austria	1960†	2.0	4.0
Belgium	1952*	2.64	25.0
Finland	1953*	2.84	22.0
France	1944*	3.17	34.0
	1945*	2.92	24.0
	1946*	2.70	20.0
	1947*	2.77	23.0
	1947*	2.88	23.0
	1959–60†	2.77	16.9
Italy	1951*	2.80	19.0
Netherlands	1947*	3.66	46.0
	1960†	3.3	38.7
Norway	1960†	3.1	25.0
Switzerland	1960†	2.9	22.4
Great Britain	1938*	2.94	25.0
	1939*	2.96	29.0
	1944*	3.00	33.0
	1947*	2.84	25.0
	1952*	2.84	26.0
	1960†	2.8	23.2
Sweden	1947*	2.79	22.0
West Germany	1950*	2.21	11.0
	1953*	2.28	11.0
	1958‡	2.6	12.0
Australia	1947*	3.79	64.0
Canada	1945*	4.06	60.0
	1947*	3.91	55.0
	1960†	4.2	70.1
United States	1936*	3.17	34.0
	1941*	3.42	41.0
	1945*	3.61	49.0
	1947*	3.37	43.0
	1949*	3.91	63.0
	1953*	3.33	41.0
	1960†	3.6	50.6

*Stoetzel, J.: Les attitudes et la conjuncture démographique: la dimension idéale de la famille, Proc. Wld. Pop. Conf., 1954 (Papers), Vol. VI, p. 1019. United Nations, New York, 1955.

†Glass, D. V.: Family limitation in Europe: a survey of recent studies, in Research in Family Planning, p. 244. Ed. by Kiser, C. V. Princeton University Press, 1962.

‡Freedman, R., Baumert, G., and Bolte, M.: Expected family size and family size values in West Germany, Pop. Stud. **13**, 141, 1959.

difference from Western Europe in family-size ideals and desires, as well as in actual family size itself. Table 1 indicates that with the possible exception of the Netherlands, Western Europeans for whom we have data consider 2–3 children "ideal," whereas respondents in the frontier countries are more inclined to place their ideals at 3–4 offspring. Moreover, the difference in proportions replying in terms of 4 or more children between the two sets of countries is quite striking.

Turning to recent trends in actual family size we must rely on a series of age-adjusted birth rates (in this case we have used gross reproduction [GRR] to document the trends since the fifties [Table 2]). It is not yet possible to bring together recent cohort data on family size for a large number of the countries in question. The overall contrast between the frontier and European countries constitutes about a one-child difference in favor of the overseas group (remembering that the GRR refers to girls only and that the differentials must therefore be roughly doubled). This difference between period data from the two sets of countries seems to be a continuation of earlier trends that were beginning to show up in marriage cohort data from censuses around 1950 (Table 3).

Are there dissimilarities between the two sets of countries that may lead to long-term stabilization of the family-size differential? If this is the case, Western Europe may contain significant clues to the institutionaliza-

TABLE 2.   Recent Gross Reproduction Rates for Western European and Overseas European Countries

Countries	1955	1956	1957	1958	1959	1960	1961
Western European countries							
With rising rates							
Austria	1.08	1.17	1.20	1.23	1.26	1.28	—
Belgium	1.16	1.18	1.19	1.22	1.26	1.24	—
West Germany	1.03	1.08	1.12	1.12	1.16	1.17	—
Netherlands	1.48	1.48	1.50	1.51	1.54	1.52	1.58
Norway	1.33	1.37	1.37	1.38	1.39	1.38	—
Switzerland	1.10	1.12	1.14	1.14	1.15	—	—
England and Wales	1.08	1.15	1.19	1.22	1.23	1.29	—
With stable rates*							
Denmark	1.24	1.26	1.24	1.23	1.21	1.24	—
France	1.31	1.30	1.32	1.31	1.34	1.33	—
Sweden	1.09	1.10	1.11	1.08	1.08	1.06	—
With falling rates							
Finland	1.42	1.37	1.38	1.29	1.31	1.29	—
Overseas European countries							
Australia	1.59	1.61	1.66	1.67	1.68	1.68	1.73
Canada	1.86	1.87	1.91	1.89	1.92	1.90	1.87
New Zealand	1.82	1.84	1.89	1.93	1.95	1.97	2.03
United States (whites)	1.67	1.72	1.76	1.73	1.73	1.72	—

Source: *Pop. Index* **29**, 196, 1963.
*This category also used for cases of no discernible trend.

TABLE 3.   Number of Live Births per 100 Marriages Existing at Census Date by Duration of Marriage—Around 1950

Countries	Census Year	Number of Years after Marriage			
		0–4	5–9	10–14	15–19
Western European countries					
Lower than overseas European					
Belgium	1947	69	146	182	...
France	1946	84	169	211	231
West Germany	1950	73	137	178	214
Great Britain	1946	57	134	182	209
Norway	1950	81	174	217	240
Switzerland	1950	81	182	221	237
Higher than overseas European					
Finland	1950	106	210	274	320
Netherlands	1947	72	200	275	322
Overseas European Countries					
Australia	1947	66	164	225	271
United States	1950	79	168	220	253

Source: United Nations: *Recent Trends in Fertility in Industrialized Countries*, p. 60. ST/SOA/Series A/27. New York, 1958.

Belgium: Includes families headed by a widow or widower, but excludes divorced couples.

France: First marriages only. Includes marriages where the woman was widowed or divorced at the age of 45 or over. All children born alive to the woman, including children born before marriage.

W. Germany: Federal Republic of Germany excluding Berlin. Including stillbirths. Excludes marriages where the couple was separated, e.g., the husband was missing or a prisoner of war.

Gt. Britain: First marriages only. Excludes marriages where the woman was 45 or over at marriage. Includes marriages where the woman was widowed or divorced at 45 or over. All children born alive to the woman (including children born before marriage). Adjusted for understatement of childlessness.

Norway: Excluding marriages where the woman was aged 45 or over at marriage.

Switzerland: All legitimate and legitimized children born alive.

Netherlands: First marriages only.

Australia: Excluding marriages where the couple was permanently separated, legally or otherwise.

U.S.A.:   White women married once and husband present who were aged 15–49 at date of census.

tion of the small family as a way of life. Indeed, Freedman has suggested that analysis of the institutional settings for this difference may provide just such guidance.[11] Still, before we embark on such a mammoth undertaking, let us consider how reasonable it is to assume that the differential is at all stable. It is initially sufficient to deal with one set of countries alone. If these promise to be unstable, there is no need to go further. We shall start with Western Europe because it offers the nearest hope for clues to small family desires.

First, to judge from actual period data (see Table 2 on GRR), fertility is rising somewhat among the European countries that previously experienced the very lowest rates, and it appears to be stabilizing among others

TABLE 4.   Mean Number of Children Expected and Desired, by Occupation and Education of Head of Family. West Germany, 1958

	Mean Number of Children Expected	Mean Number of Children Desired (Good Conditions)
Occupation of family head		
Professional	2.5 (37)	2.9 (37)
Businessman	2.1 (167)	2.7 (176)
White-collar workers	2.1 (305)	2.7 (314)
Officials	2.1 (136)	2.7 (145)
Skilled laborers	2.1 (581)	2.6 (598)
Unskilled laborers	2.3 (304)	2.8 (887)
Education of family head		
Elementary school	2.2 (1429)	2.7 (1491)
Secondary school, or high school without *Abitur*	2.0 (220)	2.7 (228)
High school with *Abitur*, or university	2.3 (59)	2.9 (62)

Source: Freedman, R., Baumert, G., and Bolte, M.: Expected family size and family size values in West Germany, Pop. Stud. 13, 145, 1959.

like Denmark.[12] Second, the average "ideal" number of children given by Europeans (like the ideals given by Americans) is typically in excess of actual behavior or of expectations. The excess is particularly marked when the question refers to the number desired under better financial or living conditions if these were available. Finally, both ideal and actual family size in some European countries have been showing either a U-shaped or a direct linear relationship with socio-economic status.

The Discrepancy between Fertility Ideals and Expectations or Behavior

The discrepancy among modernized peoples between the number of children they say they consider "ideal" and the number they personally intend to have, or in fact do have, has been noted in the literature for many years. In his 1954 summary of existing European survey data on "ideal" family size, Stoetzel was struck by the discrepancy between actual European fertility in the reporting countries and "ideal" fertility.[13] A recent study in West Germany that found the same type of excess of ideals over actualities was fortunately designed so that an explicit analysis of the differences in reply to three related questions was possible. These were (1) the number of children actually expected; (2) the "ideal" size of the average family in Germany; and (3) the number of children personally desired "if financial and other conditions of life were very good." German respondents expected fewer children than they considered ideal for "average Germans," and they desired for themselves (under good conditions) more children than they

TABLE 5.   Ideal Family Size by Economic, Occupational, and Educational Levels, Selected European Countries, 1939–1958

Country	Date	Economic Level			
		Impoverished	Poor	Middle Class	Rich
West Germany	1950	2.18	2.20	2.14	2.33
	1953	2.34	2.30	2.21	2.35
	1958	2.8	2.6	2.4–2.5	2.6
France	1944	——2.92——		——3.72——	
	1946	2.54	——2.77——		3.15
	1947	2.70	——2.90——		3.27
United Kingdom	1939	3.00	——2.90——		3.07
	1947	2.92	2.79	2.93	2.89
	1952	3.10	2.79	2.81	2.92
Sweden	1947	2.72	——2.89——		3.41

Country	Date	Occupational Level						
		Farmers	Farm Laborers	Laborers	Clerical	Officials	Industry-Commerce Staff	Free Professions
West Germany	1950	2.88	2.20	2.03	2.11	2.37	2.23	2.08
	1953	2.71	2.44	2.17	2.23	2.49	2.31	2.44
	1958	——2.9——		2.5–2.6	2.6	2.6	2.6	2.8
Belgium	1952	——3.45——		2.25	2.44		2.69	2.80
Finland	1953	3.10	2.65	2.71	——2.98——		——3.15——	
France	1944	——3.74——		2.70	——2.80——		——2.95——	
	1945	——3.15——		2.60	——3.03——		2.78	3.34
	1947	——3.33——		2.67	——2.79——		2.94	3.32
	1947	——3.09——		2.73	——2.76——		2.87	3.47

Country	Date	Educational Level		
		Primary	Secondary	Higher
West Germany	1950	2.26	2.18	2.22
	1953	2.26	2.31	2.42
	1958	2.6	2.5	2.7
Finland	1953	2.75	3.16	3.24
France	1947	2.77	3.15	3.35

Sources: Stoetzel, J.: Les attitudes et la conjuncture démographique: la dimension idéale de la famille, Proc. Wld. Pop. Conf. 1954 (Papers), Vol. VI, p. 1019. United Nations, New York, 1955.
   Data for West Germany, 1958, from Freedman, R., Baumert, G., and Bolte, M.: Expected family size values in West Germany, Pop. Stud. **13**, 145, 1959.

thought the average German family should have, and hence more than they expected.[14] The German study is particularly valuable in presenting these data by socio-economic indicators (Table 4). At all nonfarm occupational levels there is a discrepancy between expected and desired family size. Although the professional class desires the most children, the discrepancy for them is the smallest because they expect the most as well. On the other hand, most other nonmanual workers desire over 25 per cent more children than they expect to have. The stability of this gap for most of the population comes out clearly when we look at the data broken down by educational level.

These data suggest that among Western European populations that have been experiencing very low fertility since the Second World War or before, there is what we might call a latent child hunger that would be satisfied under more favorable financial and living conditions. Moreover, it is of interest that in desiring or idealizing more children than they expect to have, Western Europeans are similar to Americans.[15] The Europeans apparently do not have some stabilized low fertility ideology that their recent behavior expresses. Let us now test the idea that Europeans would desire and have larger families under what they conceive to be better conditions by looking at European ideal and actual family-size data according to socio-economic indicators. If the hypothesis has any validity we should find that the better situated Europeans both idealize and are beginning to have larger families than less fortunate groups.

Differential "Ideal" and Actual Fertility among West Europeans

As far back as the late 1940s and early 1950s, when systematic data on ideal family size in selected European countries begin, there have been noticeable exceptions to the inverse relationship between these ideals and socio-economic status. Table 5 shows that many of the highest socio-economic groups express a family-size ideal of around 3 children. Among different educational levels and nonfarm occupations, the data indicate a positive association between social advantage and family-size goals. On the economic variable, Sweden and France evince a direct relationship with familial ideals, and Britain and Germany a U-shaped one—the middle-income groups have the lowest reproductive ideals. It seems possible that West Europeans of the upper strata have for many years desired a family of relatively modest size. In fact, some upper-status European groups come close to idealizing the same number of children as was found for Americans of all classes in the Growth of American Families Study—3.3 (minimum) or 3.5 (maximum).[16]

The pertinence of these differentials in reproductive ideals is suggested by the recent trends in *actual* fertility for selected European countries (where we have data), which show the same types of variation with status indicators. Special studies in Great Britain, Sweden, and the Netherlands indicate that the family size of the better educated is "clearly above the

average rates for these countries."[17] In Britain, Norway, and the Netherlands, the professional class no longer has the lowest fertility. The latter is
found among civil servants and other white-collar employees.[18]

It thus seems unlikely to us that Europeans are on the road to permanent adjustment of family size at approximately two children. Like Americans they typically desire at least two, and there is an apparent backlog of
motivation for more under better circumstances. That this desire is meaningful seems to be illustrated both by the very recent upturn in period rates
and by the larger families desired and achieved among higher socio-
economic groups.

Hence the one-child difference between European and frontier countries may be due not to some fundamental differences in reproductive or
social and economic goals, but to the fact that Europeans have, during the
past 25 years, experienced a heavier dose of the cost factors involved in
reproduction than the overseas countries. Although Europeans operated
within the same modern context as other industrialized people (that is, they
were subject to the modern costs of child rearing, plus the need to maintain their own positions and assure themselves of security later in life), they
underwent a relatively long period of deprivation during which the realization of these goals was very difficult. No one factor can necessarily be
said to be crucial. But differences in *per capita* income between Western
Europe and the overseas countries have long been unfavorable to Europe,
and Europe suffered the principal devastations of war and its aftermath.
Moreover, it is more densely settled. There are apparently fewer opportunities for social mobility, and more clogging and insufficiency of channels
of mobility such as education. It hardly seems surprising in terms of existing
theory that the frontier peoples should feel more carefree about having an
extra child or two than do Europeans, since they have enjoyed unprecedented wealth, a halcyon period of suburbanization, high rates of social
mobility, and a great expansion of educational opportunity.

POPULATION POLICY AND
THE SMALL FAMILY PATTERN

Nowhere in the world to date, therefore, has modernization alone had an
abiding and drastically downward effect on family-size desires. Peoples of
the wealthy overseas countries have sustained a prolonged boom in births
not merely because of intrinsic demographic factors (age structure, shifts
in age at marriage, or changes in the age patterning of childbearing), but
because they have come close to realizing their wishes for families of 3–4
children. Europeans seem clearly to be attempting to bridge the gap between their desires for a moderate-size family and their modest achieve-

ments of the last quarter of a century. Yet it is certainly true that the modern world exacts the high direct and indirect costs for reproduction that have been attributed to it.

Why do adults buck the pressures against childbearing to the extent that they do? To understand this paradox it seems necessary to return to the noneconomic utilities of children as powerful forces outweighing the impact on direct and indirect costs. Although it cannot be denied that modernization has brought about many changes in family organization, the complex of roles and goals we call the family is still a major focus of individuals' expectations and activities. This means, by definition, that children are high on the list of adult utilities. Offspring are not simply outlets (and inlets) for affection, they are the instrumentalities for achieving virtually prescribed social statuses ("mother" and "father"), the almost exclusive avenues for feminine creativity and achievement, and the least common denominator for community participation—to give but a few examples.[19] Parents (and potential parents) are thus motivated to create and respond to seemingly superficial arguments for an extra child or two. Childhood mortality risks, desires for a boy, for a girl, for companionship for the youngest—such reasons prevail because parental motivation is already socially structured toward having children. This structuring blunts the sense of deprivation in things forgone (the indirect costs of additional offspring). It even permits the rationalization of direct costs, particularly if the latter are the sort that the children rather than the parents suffer— outgrown and worn clothing, educational limitations, crooked teeth, congenital defects that have a high probability of occurring—the list is not difficult to lengthen. That parental rationalization does not carry the day in modern societies is testimony to the strong social pressures for "doing a good job" at parenthood, and the aforementioned difficulty of finding outside sources of relief from the costs of this privileged status.

This analysis clearly begs the further question of why individuals are still so oriented toward achieving familial statuses in such a seemingly nonfamilial world. One suggested answer is that the family as a social group has certain attributes uniquely suited to the individual's needs in a modern, urban, mobile society.[20] This view is certainly stimulating as far as it goes, but to understand the family's unique powers we must pay some attention to the types of control mechanisms that channel the quest for satisfactions in the direction of children (and not something else) and families (and not some other social groupings). In a sense, the answer has already been suggested. A strong parental orientation is readily perpetuated through a prolonged period of youth socialization. Beyond this, the de facto primacy of the family provides mechanisms for excluding viable alternative affiliations and satisfactions. Implementation of such alternatives—even popular discussion of them—is ridiculed, or at the worst branded "immoral." Insofar as such alternatives are thrown open for consideration at all, it is typically with reference to clearly disadvantaged or despised choices (celibacy, prostitution, homosexuality, the "Don Juan" complex), descriptions of which make traditional family roles seem overpoweringly advantageous by contrast. The family thus seems to be uniquely well suited to modern life in part because functional rivals (competing roles, satisfactions, and activities) are effectively relegated to the sidelines.

It seems therefore that a stabilized reduction in the family-size desires of both prosperous and poor countries will require a significant lessening of involvement in familial roles. Otherwise, policy is bucking a motivational syndrome that has a built-in "righting reflex" in the face of antinatalist blows. The family complex may bow to depression, stoop to war, and shrink into an urban apartment, but until nonfamilial roles begin to offer significant competition to familial ones as avenues for adult satisfaction, the family will probably continue to amaze us with its procreative powers.

Yet policy directed at reducing rates of population growth has to date failed to come to grips with this predicament. It has either enjoined institutional changes, such as economic development, that are once removed from the family, or it has taken off towards purely technical and instrumental considerations respecting birth control. In neither case is there direct manipulation of family structure itself—planned efforts at deflecting the family's socializing function, reducing the noneconomic utilities of offspring, or introducing nonfamilial distractions and opportunity costs into people's lives. In neither case is there genuine leadership out of the demographic dilemma posed by declining mortality.

The question may well be raised, however, as to whether we have other than purely theoretical reasons for believing that direct policy affecting family structure would also affect family-size desires and their implementation. For example, would deflection from important familial roles lead individuals to desire smaller families? A full answer to such a question will require a wide variety of research endeavors. But, fortunately, demographers and sociologists have already devoted fairly intensive study to this problem in their research on female labor-force participation and family size.

FAMILY SIZE AND WORKING WIVES

From the standpoint of the theory discussed in this paper, the employment of women outside the home constitutes one of the most likely sources of a desire for small families. Such employment will often entail satisfactions alternative to children (companionship, recreation, stimulation, and creative activity), or the means to such satisfactions in the form of financial remuneration. Forgoing employment will frequently be experienced as a cost—one of the costs of having children. Thus employment is a means of introducing into women's lives the subjective awareness of opportunity costs involved in childbearing—an awareness that traditional feminine roles and activities are well designed to circumvent.

In actual fact, female labor-force participation has long been known to bear one of the most impressive relationships to family size of any variable —typically in Western countries it has been equaled or exceeded in strength only by Catholic–non-Catholic religious affiliation. An inverse relationship between the labor-force participation of married women and their family size has been suggested by census data for Western Europe and the United States for many years.[21]

Recently, Collver and Langlois found a high negative association of fertility with women's participation in work (other than domestic service). For 20 countries of varying modernization levels (having data available) the Pearsonian correlation was −0.60. The regression equation shows that the number of children per 1,000 women declined by 7 for each 1 per cent increase in the work participation rate.[22] Jaffe and Azumi contrasted the smaller families of both Puerto Rican and Japanese wives employed outside the home with the families of wives not in the labor force or engaged in cottage industry. Among Puerto Rican women it was possible to control for women's educational levels and the relationship was still maintained.[23]

Furthermore, family-size ideals, desires, and expectations have also been related to women's work behavior. In a number of American studies it was discovered that the longer the work experience of fecund wives since marriage (holding constant age of wife or duration of marriage or both), the smaller the family size expected.[24] The difference in desired or expected family size between wives who have had no work experience and those having "much" (5 years or more) is about one child—a difference as great as is typically found between Catholics and non-Catholics, and usually greater than any other single difference.[25] A recent study in West Germany revealed a similar association.[26]

Although this association between married women working and family size is generally acknowledged to be one of the strongest, most persistent over time and space, and most theoretically reasonable, questions must be raised about the nature of the causal relationship. It seems clear by now that the relationship is not due simply to the fact that involuntarily infecund or subfecund wives are more inclined or able to work. The association holds among fecund wives. However, from none of these studies is it clear whether the small-family ideal is solely a *result* of labor-force participation by women (a result of their becoming socialized to earning their own living, a nondomestic way of life, etc.), or whether the *intention* of working precedes the desire for small families (or coincides with it in youth), before either family experience or intensive work experience is undergone. Fortunately, data now being analyzed at the University of California, Berkeley, allow us to examine this very point, because the sample was drawn from high school and college students who were asked about both their work intentions after marriage and their family-size ideals.[27] As may be seen from Table 6, whether girls intend to work for any prolonged period of time outside the home after marriage exerts approximately as important an influence on their family-size desires as does their religious affiliation—probably the other single most important influence we will be able to show. The importance of most socio-economic variables other than religious affiliation is relatively slight.

These data should serve to illustrate that already existing research on

TABLE 6.   Mean Number of Children Desired and Percentage Distribution of Children Desired, by Work Intentions after Marriage and Selected Social and Economic Characteristics

(Gallup study of high school and college students, 1961. White females only.)

Selected Characteristics	Mean Number Desired	Percentage Distribution— Desired Number of Children				No.
		0–1	2–4	5+	Total	
Work intentions after marriage:						
Does not intend to work	4.1	2.2	67.8	30.0	100	270
Intends to work:						
Until family	3.8	1.3	79.9	18.8	100	149
1–2 years	3.7	0.8	82.0	17.2	100	239
3 years	3.5	1.6	79.5	18.9	100	127
4 years	3.4	2.1	87.5	10.4	100	48
5 or more years	3.3	6.9	81.0	12.1	100	173
Occupation of household head:						
Professional and business	3.6	2.2	81.0	16.8	100	417
Clerical and sales	3.8	1.4	75.0	23.6	100	148
Skilled	3.8	4.4	69.6	26.0	100	135
Semi-skilled and service	3.7	1.8	81.8	16.4	100	171
Laborers (nonfarm)	3.5	0.0	84.6	15.4	100	26
Farmers/farm laborers	4.3	5.1	70.9	24.0	100	64
Education of household head:						
<8 years	3.5	1.8	85.5	12.7	100	55
8–11 years	3.6	3.4	77.7	18.9	100	238
H.S. graduate	3.7	3.0	74.7	22.3	100	305
Some college	3.9	0.6	77.7	21.7	100	152
College graduate	3.4	3.1	80.1	16.8	100	131
Professional, etc.	3.6	2.7	78.5	18.8	100	149

TABLE 6 (Continued)

Selected Characteristics	Mean Number Desired	Percentage Distribution— Desired Number of Children				No.
		0–1	2–4	5+	Total	
Religious affiliation:						
Catholic	4.3	1.6	61.3	37.1	100	248
Protestant	3.5	3.0	81.8	15.2	100	664
Jewish	3.3	0.0	94.0	6.0	100	50
None	3.4	4.8	83.3	11.9	100	42
Region of country:						
East	3.7	1.7	76.0	22.3	100	346
Midwest	3.8	3.5	73.9	22.6	100	310
South	3.5	3.6	79.6	16.8	100	225
West	3.5	1.3	86.7	12.0	100	158
Age:						
14–15	3.8	0.7	75.7	23.6	100	148
16–17	3.7	2.7	76.9	20.4	100	333
18–19	3.5	3.5	78.9	17.6	100	142
20–21	3.6	3.0	78.8	18.2	100	363
22–23	3.7	1.1	79.1	19.8	100	91
Grade:						
H.S. sophomore	3.6	2.8	78.1	19.1	100	320
H.S. senior	3.7	2.6	76.2	21.2	100	302
College junior	3.7	2.0	80.7	17.3	100	249
College senior	3.5	3.3	88.9	7.8	100	234

one of the possible means of reducing the noneconomic utilities of children, and increasing the opportunity costs in childbearing, shows considerable promise for reducing family size. From the standpoint of population growth, the potential influence of policy designed to deflect women from family participation lies not only in the direction of reducing family-size desires, but of lengthening the period between generations through later marriage and delayed childbearing. Further, policy designed to increase feminine labor outside the home will often involve few direct governmental outlays, but rather merely the abolition of legal restrictions and informal barriers. Even actual investment in such policy (for example, in-service training for women) would have social and economic functions, rather than solely helping to reduce family size. Finally, work in factories and other organized situations outside the home makes women readily (and inexpensively) accessible to all types of educational influences, including (in developing countries) those that will help them to reduce infant and child mortality as well as undesired fertility.

In view of the advantages just cited, it is surprising that a country like

India (where impressive amounts are being invested in family-planning campaigns) is not taking advantage of this structural means of influencing family-size motivation. If anything, the cumulative effect of governmental policy has been one of discouraging rather than encouraging the employment of females. While trends in long-term employment of women in India are difficult to evaluate, there does seem to have been a decided decrease in the proportion of all women classified as working in census reports during the first half of the century.[28]

SUMMARY

To date efforts at curtailing population growth in developing countries have been bipolarized into the "economic development" approach on the one hand and the family-planning approach on the other. The first sees decreases in family size as the long-range resultant of a complete socio-economic overhauling which, in turn, leads to a desire for fewer children. The second overlooks the institutionalization of reproduction entirely and assumes that education and communication regarding birth control will eventually reduce births to a level in keeping with low mortality. Neither approach seems to be practical taken alone, nor do they even appear to be adequate in combination. Population growth is clearly impeding economic development in many poor countries, rather than itself being reduced through the modernization process. Family-planning programs are not lowering birth rates among the mass of the people in such countries, and their failure is understandable in view of their superficiality. We are thus led to ask whether additional types of direct action for reducing family size cannot be incorporated into population policy.

In answer, we have taken the position that the limitation of alternatives is more a function of insufficient thought and analysis than actual circumscription of choice. For example, theory and research accounting for declining family size in Western societies is as relevant for direct action concerning reproduction as it is for indirect action respecting family size (such as economic development). It is instructive to analyze the present-day preference in industrial societies for approximately *three* children from the standpoint of the institutional barriers to further declines. We then see that the purely economic assumptions concerning the utility of children discount too readily the importance to individuals of the noneconomic benefits involved in reproduction. These far exceed simple affectional or companionship elements, since they are built into the achievement of familial statuses and the success of marriage. When one analyzes further why modern, urban, mobile individuals are so familially oriented, one cannot discount the advantages of the family group in a modern world. But one must also take into account the strong social controls which isolate individuals from alternative roles and satisfactions and, hence, bolster their intense feelings of dependency on the family, and *a fortiori* on having children.

It would thus appear that policies expressly related to family roles, and opportunities for legitimate alternative satisfactions and activities, constitute the crux of future reduction in family size because they directly assault the motivational framework of reproduction. Moreover, many of these policies for influencing the family do not depend on prior economic development; they can be implemented concomitantly with modernization strategies. Regardless of the level of development, policy can undermine the utilities found in offspring (thereby allowing a sense of increased costs to prevail) and can structure itself in terms of crucial existing foci of change in the society. We have used female labor-force participation as an example because it met both of these criteria—a lessening of family involvement on the part of a disadvantaged (and hence potentially revolutionary) group. Numerous additional facets of policy come to mind, one such being rigidly compulsory education of children which would remove them as potential economic utilities (even as household help on anything but a token level), all the while effectively putting intellectual barriers between them and the past generation. Regardless of the specific paths taken by population policy, its designers cannot afford to overlook the lesson already available to them in the substantial family-size desires and actualities to be found in presently industrial countries. Modernization and birth control alone will clearly not bring family size into line with modern levels of mortality unless this reproductive institution is itself modified to make the small family a way of life.

NOTES

1. For a discussion of the multiphasic theory of demographic change, see Davis, K.: The theory of change and response in modern demographic history, *Pop. Index* 29, 345, 1963.

2. See, for example, Davis, K.: Fertility control and the demographic transition in India, in *The Interrelations of Demographic, Economic and Social Problems in Selected Underdeveloped Areas*, p. 65. Milbank Memorial Fund, New York, 1954.

3. Bogue, D. J.: Some tentative recommendations for a "socially correct"

family planning communication and motivation program in India, in *Research in Family Planning*, p. 503. Ed. by Kiser, C. V. Princeton University Press, 1962.

4. See, for example, *Research in Family Planning*, p. 528. Ed. by Kiser, C. V. Princeton University Press, 1962. Although the direction of the relationship is not made clear, Edwin D. Driver presents for Central India some suggestive data on births and child mortality. He shows that the larger the number of births in a family, the larger the proportion of children who have died. Doubtless some of this associa-

tion is due to the independent effect of high fertility on child mortality as well as to the fact that large families will have older children who may have lived out a normal adult span for India and then died. The ages at death were not recorded. See Driver, E. D.: *Differential Fertility in Central India*, Chap. VI. Princeton University Press, 1963. For a discussion of the "realization lag" respecting mortality, see Leibenstein, H.: *Economic Backwardness and Economic Growth*, p. 166. Wiley, New York, 1957.

5. See, for example, Driver, E. D.: *Differential Fertility in Central India*, Chap. VI. Princeton University Press, 1963. In this study 30 per cent of the couples had no interest at all in limiting the size of their families. This percentage ranged from 23 per cent for couples where the wife was under 25 to 38 per cent where she was 45 or more. The data on ideal family size were only obtained from the couples interested in limiting. See also United Nations: *The Mysore Population Study*, Chaps. 9–12. United Nations, Population Studies No. 34, 1961; Dandekar, V. M., and Dandekar, K.: *Survey of Fertility and Mortality in Poona District*, Chap. 7. Gokhale Institute, Poona, 1953. Close to one half of respondents in both urban and rural districts answered in terms of "any number" or that they "could not say."

6. Tabah, L., and Samuel, P.: Preliminary findings of a survey on fertility and attitudes toward family planning in Santiago, Chile, in *Research in Family Planning*, p. 289. Ed. by Kiser, C. V. Princeton University Press, 1962. Out of 1970 respondents only 12 did not answer, and 14 said "an unlimited number." See also Freedman, R., *et al.*: Fertility trends in Taiwan: tradition and change, *Pop. Stud.* **16,** 232, 1963.

7. This highly generalized statement of the elements in declining family-size goals may be found in Leibenstein, H.: *Economic Backwardness and Economic Growth*, Chap. 10. Wiley, New York, 1957. Other statements of the same basic ideal by sociologists and demographers have usually been in terms of particular features of modernization—urbanization, educational levels, social mobility, etc.—and have seldom attempted to differentiate

clearly among utilities, direct costs, and opportunity costs. See, for example, Notestein, F. W.: The economics of population and food supplies, *Proc. 8th Int. Conf. Agricultural Economists*, p. 13. Oxford University Press, London, 1953; and Notestein, F. W.: Population—the long view, in *Food for the World*. Ed. by Schultz, T. W. University of Chicago Press, 1945. For recent efforts to document the important role played by opportunity costs, see Banks, J. A.: *Prosperity and Parenthood*. Routledge & Paul, London, 1954; and Davis, K.: *Pop. Index* **29,** 345, 1963; and Davis K.: Population, *Sci. Am.* **209** (Sept.), 63, 1963.

8. The theory also accounts for other related adjustments, such as delayed marriage and nonmarriage, but these need not concern us here. The phrase "hostages to fortune" is Francis Bacon's, from *Essays or Counsels, Civil and Moral* (1625).

9. This in effect has been one of the principal criticisms of so-called "demographic transition theory," namely that it represents a more or less unweighted and nonspecific collection of associations between broad social trends and fertility (as well as mortality) with little attempt to assess common factors and their actual connection with fertility. See Van Nort, L., and Karon, B. P.: Demographic transition reexamined, *Am. Sociol. Rev.* **20,** 523, 1955.

10. For example, Leibenstein, H. (*Economic Backwardness and Economic Growth*, p. 169), only discusses the theory with reference to the demographic revolution up to the point of achieving some undefined level of relatively low fertility. He says, "This point refers to the stage at which per capita output is quite high, considerably beyond the subsistence level, and where the economy has overcome the major obstacles to sustained growth. Usually, this is a point at which the gap between mortality and fertility rates closes gradually. In this situation the business cycle is likely to be a signficant determinant of economic and social phenomena. Since we are not concerned, in this essay, with short-time fluctuations, we shall not enter into an analysis of fertility determinants under such circumstances."

11. See Freedman, R., *et al.*: Expected family size and family size values in West Germany, *Pop. Stud.* **13,** 136 and 142, 1959; Freedman, R.: American stud-

ies of family planning and fertility: a review of major trends and issues, in *Research in Family Planning*, p. 216 and p. 226. Ed. by Kiser, C. V. Princeton University Press, 1962.

12. See, for example, the discussion by Pressat, R.: Tendences récentes de la fécondité en Europe occidentale, *International Population Union Conference*, Paper No. 93 (mimeo), 1961.

13. Stoetzel, J.: Les attitudes et la conjuncture démographique: la dimension idéale de la famille, *Proc. World Population Conf.* 1954 (Paper), VI, p. 1019. United Nations, New York, 1955.

14. Freedman, R., et al.: *Pop. Stud.* 13, 141, 1959. The differences between the expected number and the number desired under good conditions are not accounted for merely by the fact that couples expecting to be childless actually desired some children. For example, the percentage expecting 3 or more children was 31.9, but 49.5 per cent would have desired that many if conditions were good.

15. For a discussion of the Growth of American Families Study data on this topic, see Freedman, R., Whelpton, P. K., and Campbell, A. A.: *Family Planning, Sterility and Population Growth*, p. 220. McGraw-Hill, New York, 1959. Also, similar findings have been reported for the Detroit Area Study and for the Indianapolis Study. See Freedman, R., et al.: Ideals about family size in the Detroit Metropolitan Area, 1954, *Milbank Mem. Fd. Q.* 33, 187, 1955; Pratt, L., and Whelpton, P. K.: Social and psychological factors affecting fertility. XXX, *Milbank Mem. Fd. Q.* 34, 1245, 1956.

16. The average "minimum" and "maximum" figures come from using the lower and upper limits of answers giving a range of children—i.e., "2 or 3" or "3 or 4." See Freedman, R., et al.: *Family Planning, Sterility and Population Growth*, p. 220 and p. 226. McGraw-Hill, New York, 1959.

17. Johnson, G.: Differential fertility in European countries, in *Demographic and Economic Change in Developed Countries*, p. 53. (National Bureau of Economic Research.) Princeton University Press, 1960.

18. Johnson, G.: In *Demographic and Economic Change in Developed Countries*, p. 59; and Wrong, D. H.: Class fertility differentials in England and Wales, *Milbank Mem. Fd. Q.* 38, 37, 1960.

19. A systematic account of the noneconomic utilities of children would be well worth considering. For instance, they allegedly prevent marital boredom and premature aging and "stodginess," as well as providing couples with a "common interest" and topics of conversation with their own parents. The further one extends the list, the more one becomes aware of how explicitly the marital institution is structured in terms of reproduction.

20. For instance, Freedman says, ". . . I suggest that with all its loss of functions, the family in a highly mobile, specialized society continues to have a unique set of core functions. It is, in the first place, the only continuing primary group that a man takes with him in his travels in space and in society. It is the unit which specializes in nonspecialized relationships in a highly specialized society. It is, therefore, the only social unit which can provide dependably the emotional support and stable orientation man needs in a kaleidoscopic, mobile, specialized world . . . The family performs a correlated and equally important function in serving as the center which organizes the impersonal socialized services of the economy and the society for consumption on a personal basis by its members. This important function increases the family's strength as a source of nonspecialized orientation and emotional support." See "Comment" on Johnson, G. Z.: Differential fertility in European countries, in *Demographic and Economic Change in Developed Countries* (National Bureau of Economic Research), p. 74. Princeton University Press, 1962.

21. These data for married women during the 1930s and 1940s have been summarized by the United Nations (U.N. Population Division: *The Determinants and Consequences of Population Trends*, p. 88. Pop. Stud. No. 17 (ST/SOA/Ser. A 17), New York, 1953.

22. Collver, A., and Langlois, E.: The female labor force in metropolitan areas; an international comparison, *Economic Development and Cultural Change* 10, 381, 1962.

23. Jaffe, A. J., and Azumi, K.: The birth rate and cottage industries in under-

developed countries, *Economic Development and Cultural Change* 9, 52, 1960. The authors say, "What implications can be drawn from these findings? First, it is clear that cottage industries are not an unmixed blessing, even if it can be proven —which is doubtful—that they are economically advisable. By maintaining high fertility levels together with relatively low levels of worker productivity they simply help perpetuate a system of rapid population growth together with a rate of economic growth which at best barely manages to keep abreast of population growth. Traditional forms of social and family relationships are maintained (one of the important elements involved in sustaining traditionally high fertility levels) and no or little progress is made toward transforming the entire socio-economic structure into that of a rapidly growing modern economy . . . From the population viewpoint, perhaps the most desirable industries to be introduced into an underdeveloped country would be those using large quantities of female labor away from home, in modern factories, stores, offices, etc. If enough women were so occupied the birth rate would be lowered considerably." See also Jaffe, A. J.: *People, Jobs and Economic Development,* Chap. 10. Free Press of Glencoe, 1959. The same type of relationship between women working and family size is suggested by data from a survey on fertility and attitudes toward family formation in Santiago, Chile. See Tabah, L., and Samuel, P.: In *Research in Family Planning,* p. 281. Ed. by Kiser, C. V. Princeton University Press, 1962.

24. Pratt, L. V., and Whelpton, P. K.: Social and psychological factors affecting fertility. XXX. *Milbank Mem. Fd. Q.* **34,** 1245, 1956; also Ridley, J. C.: Number of children expected in relation to nonfamilial activities of wife, *Milbank Mem. Fd. Q.* **37,** 277, 1959; Freedman, R., Goldberg, D., and Slesinger, D.: Current fertility expectations of married couples in the United States, *Pop. Index.* 29, 377, 1963.

25. Freedman, R., *et al.: Pop. Index*

29, 384, 1963. The 1955 and 1962 studies have shown that the difference between the religious groups contrasts with increased length of wifely work experience. In the 1962 study, wives with at least 5 years' experience evinced a Catholic–non-Catholic difference of 0.6 in expected family size, those with no such experience since marriage showed a difference of 1.2—double the other figure.

26. Freedman, R., *et al.: Pop. Stud.* **13,** 145, 1959.

27. The data are from the Gallup Youth Study, 1961. Their analysis is part of a project being conducted by the author and Kingsley Davis at International Population and Urban Research on family formation attitudes in the United States. This project utilizes survey data from a variety of agencies. I wish to thank Glen Elder for allowing us to make use of some of his tabulations.

28. A recent study of female employment in India claims that "the number of working females declined from 43 million in 1911 to 40.7 million in 1951, while the female population during the period increased from 149.9 million in 1911 to 173.4 million in 1951." In other words, there was a decrease of about 2.3 million working females as against an increase of 23.5 million in the female population (*Women in Employment,* 1901–1956, p. 10. A Joint Study by the Labour Bureau, Simla, and the Labour and Employment Division, Planning Commission, Government of India, August 1958). See also Labour Bureau, Ministry of Labour, Government of India: *Economic and Social Status of Women Workers in India,* p. 12. Ganga Printing Press, Delhi, 1953; Sengupta, P.: *Women Workers of India,* p. 26. Asia Publishing House, Bombay, 1960; Gokhale, R. G.: *Summary of Workmen's Records.* The Millowners Association, Bombay, 1941, and *The Bombay Cotton Mill Worker,* The Millowners Association, 1957, as quoted in James, R. C.: Discrimination against women in Bombay textiles, *Ind. Labour Relations Rev.* 15, (Jan.), 211, 1962.

23

On Family Planning Communication

Bernard Berelson

I

Just a year and a half ago, I first came into direct professional contact with the world population problem, when the Population Council asked me to see if material from the communication field could be applied to the family planning being developed around the world. All I can do is to summarize where I have come out after 18 months of trying to do the job. For mnemonic purposes I put my tentative conclusions under ten headings, and these ten points are necessarily compressed—perhaps overcompressed and oversimplified.

Our task is to learn how the birth rate in the so-called underdeveloped areas of the world can be brought down, through voluntary contraceptive actions of the couples involved, by a substantial amount and in a short period of time. Just to indicate order of magnitude, by "substantial amount" and "short time" I mean something like ten points off the birth rate in five years or fifteen points off in ten years—say, move from a birth rate of 45 to 35 in five to seven years. Can that be done? And if so, how? *Whatever answer we get from our studies, that answer must be realistically applicable to the society as a whole or to large segments of it.* "Realistically applicable" means that the recommended program must be practicable when gauged against the resources in money and in personnel that are available for the task. So we are searching for efficient means and not simply effective ones. Finding out that you can lower the birth rate in a little corner of the society at an expenditure, in money or in personnel, of ten times the amount you

Reprinted from *Demography*, 1, no. 1 (1964), pp. 94–105, by permission of the author and the publisher.

would have available to do it across the society as a whole constitutes an advance but is far short of the knowledge we need.

When the problem is put this way, it is hard to think of a greater challenge to social research. What we are up against is nothing less than trying to change the behavior of couples in societies just emerging from a traditional state, where most actions are specified by social custom and cultural arrangements of long standing—behavior requiring sustained action by pairs of people on a matter of the utmost privacy and delicacy, plus the complications provided by one of man's strongest drives, sex.

The array of obstacles to be overcome before achieving success is impressive: illiteracy; ignorance of family planning methods, purposes, and consequences; inertia and apathy, both general and specific; peasant resistance to change; costs to both the society and the individual; dispersal of population; lack of communication between husband and wife, both general and specific; the personalized character of the subject; the desire for children and/or for sons for political, economic, and status reasons; occasional moral, religious, or ideological objections; early marriages and high marriage rates; lack of alternatives available to women; occasional ineffectiveness of the simpler (hence more usable) contraceptive methods that discourages at the outset; lack of trained personnel for action programs; little differential fertility as a lever to start with, that is, few small-family models; lack of an adequate system of distribution of supplies; remote and problematic rewards for successful action; invisibility of social support, deriving from the privacy of the practice. These are some of the salient obstacles that have to be overcome. On the other hand, we can take heart from some favoring factors: pressure from the sheer struggle for subsistence, which gives a motive; governmental support, or at least permissiveness; general social change in a direction favorable to fertility limitation; improved contraceptive methods; and, finally, a widely professed interest in family planning, especially among the high-parity couples (though as a leading demographer once reminded me, that finding is based on an abstract answer to an abstract question).

I have found the following statement by Frank Notestein a dramatic way of thinking about the problem of effecting family planning, as against effecting some other health innovations of benefit to the society. "Consider what would happen," he once suggested, "if malaria were as welcome as children—if a majority of young couples felt that they had really not justified their existence until they had undergone four or five attacks of malaria, which, moreover, they thoroughly enjoyed; if their fathers, mothers, mothers-in-law, uncles and aunts were constantly urging them to become exposed to the disease as soon as possible; if each new onslaught were welcomed with approbation by the whole community; and if to avoid this attractive disease, each deviant couple had to spray its own home with DDT acquired somewhat furtively."

Now for the ten points I wish to make.

II

1. Three Factors

I've come to think that there are three factors, or clusters of factors, that are involved in the effective spread of family planning. Our job is to learn as much as we can about each of the cells in the matrix that these three factors, together, make up. They are (*a*) the nature of the society, from traditional to modern or modernizing; (*b*) the nature of the contraceptive method, from hard to easy; (*c*) the nature of the communication approach.

a) Nature of the Society. In a rough way, we can order societies, communities within societies, and individuals within communities from the most traditional to the most modern, or modernizing. By traditional we refer to much of the so-called underdeveloped countries, the countries that give an inferior role to women, that have a low level of literacy, that have little industrial development, and mainly an agricultural subsistence economy. By modern or modernizing, we mean an approximation to the present conditions in Western Europe or Japan—high literacy, high degree of industrialization, and so on. This can get terribly complicated, but I think for our purposes it does not need to be. Generally speaking, some countries are more modern than others, some communities are more modern than others (for example, the cities within the underdeveloped countries are usually more modernized than the rural areas), and some individuals are more modernized, by this definition, than others (for example, the better educated). And in general we know pretty well that family planning, like any innovation, goes better at the modern end of the continuum—where there is more flexibility, more fluidity, less hold of custom, more literacy, more exposure to new ideas, more ideas around, more innovating leaders as models, and so on. *We need not do more studies to find out that family planning will do better at this end than at the other end, but we do need to know how far down this continuum we can have some effect and at what cost.*

b) Contraceptive Methods. We might also order contraceptive methods on a continuum, but, for present purposes, it is sufficient to dichotomize them. Let us simply classify them into "hard" and "easy" on the basis of whether or not sustained motivation or repetitive action is required. By "hard" I mean those contraceptives that require sustained motivation and repetitive action, usually before the very act of intercourse itself. It is relatively hard to teach or to use the rhythm method, diaphragm, condom, foam tablets, etc. By "easy" I mean the newer methods of contraception that, in one way or another, bypass this problem of sustained motivation and repetitive action. To a certain extent the oral pill does this. It does require some amount of sustained motivation; but it doesn't require action prior to the sex act itself and it's a relatively easy act that one member can do privately. But it does require supplies—thus you have the whole logistics problem—and it does require regularized attention and "doing something."

The newly developed intra-uterine devices are more nearly ideal from the communication and motivation standpoint, although all of the bio-medical evidence is not yet assembled. The devices are inserted into the uterus by a simple action that takes only a few minutes. They are, so to speak, a one-shot contraceptive method. If accepted and retained, this device works indefinitely, so far as we know. So far it has remained in some uteri for a year or two years without any problems. This device bypasses the tremendous problem of sustained motivation which I think is close to being a key to the effectiveness of any program. If the couple does not want to have children for the next year or so or longer, it can accept this device and from then on nothing needs to be done. It is reversible; if the device is removed, the women can become pregnant immediately. It has many of the characteristics of what people call the ideal contraceptive. These comments are not made as a sales talk for intra-uterine devices. The only point I want to make is that with regard to the implementation of family planning programs we are in a completely different situation if we have at least some methods to offer that do not require sustained, repetitive actions, especially just before or as an interruption to the sex act.

c) The Communication Approach. By this I mean the way in which informational and educational programs are put into the field. Before expanding on this point, let me first note that *at any given point in time the first two of the three factors are pretty well fixed:* the society and the technology are given, and there is not much you can do about them but accommodate your program. *The communication approach, however, is not given.* That is up to us. There are a large number of ways by which we can think of taking this program to the people. We can choose to go to the people directly or to work through the community leaders. We can choose to make family planning part of a total program of socio-economic improvement or we can choose to try to organize communities for family planning specifically. We can choose to make extensive use of mass media or we can try to inform people through small group discussions, or both.

One of the most useful choices we can make is in deciding where to concentrate our efforts and what methods we will advocate. Perhaps this point can be made more clearly if we construct a cross-tabulation of the first two factors and then consider the alternative communication approaches that could be made. The simple fourfold accompanying tabulation may be used to represent the first two factors.

Type of Methods	Type of Society	
	"Traditional" Societies	"Modern" Societies
"Hard" methods	Impossible	Possible
"Easy" methods	Possible	Possible

Some people think it isn't worth going into family planning in the most "traditional" communities because you must introduce many other changes before you can effect family planning. They assert that you need to have some small amount of literacy, to free the women from their low status, to get industrialization going, to start community development, to succeed in getting the adoption of improved agricultural practices, before you can get family planning to take root. In other words, they believe that most or all of the basic elements of modernization must already be present before a communication program can have any significant effect. This is an important research question. Can we do anything at all about family planning at the traditional end of the continuum? If research shows that very little can be accomplished here, then it may well be that we should not try —because we don't have enough resources anyway. If research supports this conclusion, we should concentrate our efforts toward the modern end of the continuum—and every society does have communities and groups and individuals at that end of the continuum.

The type of society may influence the methods we choose to communicate. It may be, for example, that in the traditional societies the "hard" contraceptive methods are very difficult to get adopted—perhaps impossible. The type of society may also influence the type of communication approach we should use. For a full scientific understanding we need to ask and answer, by research, all of the combinations of questions provided by the model. But we can't do this. It is impossible to undertake all the studies needed to accomplish this, but at least it is useful to keep this matrix in mind, and to see where various studies fit and what we are learning about the traditional types of society as against the more modernized types. We need to ask ourselves a question like "Does the same amount of effort or cost give us twice as much success in one type of community as it does in another, given the same methods and the same approach?" If so, that's an economic fact that the administrators of family planning programs can take into account in deciding how they should allocate their total effort.

In this connection *a question of extreme importance is whether family planning can move ahead of the general modernization of society.* My personal opinion (and I think it is pretty clear that I'm in a minority on this) is that it can. My feeling is that in the general movement of modernization the various components don't move ahead in direct synchronization according to a single unvarying pattern. A 10 percent improvement in education doesn't become a 10 percent improvement in agricultural innovation (or any other fixed ratio). The components are uneven and do not progress in any set pattern. So *something has to be in front, and why not family planning?* I think that given present motivation among the high-parity couples (where professed desire for fertility limitation is generally strong), given an easy and effective contraceptive, and given a reasonable system of information and services, then family planning can indeed be effective even in the "traditional" societies—well in the lead of the modernizing movement. But, as we said, that is a research question and one of the things we ought solidly to know in order to guide the administrative organization of these programs.

Basic research on this question is needed to attain the goal of *feasibility,* mentioned in the introductory remarks. We ought to tie our studies to realistic administrative decisions that the policy makers will have to make. In doing this we should be, so to speak, researching the future, because the future is going to be different from the past and the present. The future is going to have more easy methods, and whether that future is three years from now or five or seven or ten, it certainly is coming. In any case, studies always take a long time to do; if we start a study today, we won't get the results (especially on this matter where you have to wait for the birth rate to respond) for two years or more.

With respect to the various methods of communication approach, it is my suspicion that our research is going to show that *any* reasonable approach is about as effective as any other. Given some information about methods and given the supplies, couples who are motivated to fertility control, usually by high parity, will undertake the practice. Couples who are not so motivated probably cannot be influenced to adopt family planning by direct communication under any circumstances, in the short run. If this is so, then the cheapest approach to the high-parity, favorably disposed, and widely scattered minority is the best one, at least at this time. These remarks should make it clear why I regard the factor of method as being so important. There's an inverse relationship between the amount of motivation required for doing family planning and the ease of the method available. If there is an easy method available—one that requires no sustained action, little learning or skill, and that is very effective, cheap, non-troublesome, non-bothersome, not unaesthetic, and so on—then you don't need very much motivation. But if you have something that requires persistence, skill, learning, that needs supplies, that costs money, that's unpleasant, that's objectionable to one or the other partner, then you need a great deal of motivation to keep that up. Usually there isn't that much motivation available, immediately. If you get enough motivation, of course, you can use almost anything and reduce the birth rate successfully. Historically, Western Europe did. Western Europe brought down the birth rate before any of these devices were available. But it took a very high level of motivation, and it also took a long time. With easier methods, we should be able to get faster results with much less motivation, and in traditional societies.

2. Short Run

To make sense in talking about the implementation of family planning, we have to put a time scale on it. Most family planning programs and research have a short-run (five to ten years) time scale in mind. What can we do in five to ten years? We should be doing research on both long-run and short-run time scales. But we need to emphasize achieving success quickly, because if we don't reduce fertility in the next ten years, the problem is going to be much worse in the next twenty years and so on, becoming progressively worse. We need to have an effect as soon as possible.

With regard to the long time period, here again I think I hold a somewhat deviant position. Many people feel that this is a terribly complex, complicated and difficult problem, and it is. However, I want to warn against accepting a cliché that academicians who aspire to do something of practical use often state. This is the claim that you need *full* understanding based on a long-run program of "basic" research before you can successfully deal with a social problem of this sort. This is a useful cliché for some purposes, but let's be clear that it is a cliché. We regularly take action successfully on all sorts of social problems without having full knowledge of "how it works." So let's not feel that we have to understand the world population problem in any complete sense before we can act on it. In the intra-uterine device, incidentally, we have a very good example of this point. It is almost the most effective contraceptive method there is. Yet as of today the bio-medical people do not know its exact mode of operation: scientifically, they don't know *how* it works. But we can use it to great effect, nevertheless.

Similarly, we don't have to have a full understanding of motivation and communication for family planning in order to be able to get a successful program going. We don't have to understand all there is to know about the cultural, personal, social, situational, economic factors, and so on. Fifty years from now maybe we'll understand what we were doing that was effective, but we can do a lot without having complete understanding. From a long-run point of view that demands complete and detailed knowledge it is a very complicated problem; you have to understand everything before anything can be done. This calls for tremendous amounts of basic research. On the short time span you don't need that much knowledge or so much research. In the short run, you recognize that there are some people who are more highly motivated for family planning within any particular society and some who are less motivated or not motivated at all.

As I read the literature, there are two factors that strongly correlate with motivation and that go a long way toward explaining its level. One is *social-economic* status—class, educational level, standard of living, and so on. I think that almost every study will show that the better-educated people are more receptive to family planning than the lesser educated; the wealthy more than the poor; those in higher occupations more than those in lower occupations. The second factor is *high parity*. By high parity I mean three or four children, of whom at least one is a son. The studies all show that if you ask people a question such as "Are you in favor of birth control?" or "Would you want to practice birth control?" the curve of acceptance goes up with parity. Couples with no children or only one child have very little interest, those with two children are beginning to be a little interested, and by the time you get to those with three or four children (including a son or two) you have high motivation. Those people are ready to learn about family planning, and my view is that in the short run, the best thing we can do with our limited resources is to satisfy the existing motivation. To put it in marketing terms, the thing to do is to exploit the existing market instead of trying to expand the market. You can't exploit the existing market fully anyway, because there are not enough resources. So this is the most efficient thing to do in terms of allocation of scarce resources.

Exploiting the existing market is the strategic thing to do for another reason; it is the best way to spread the market, to make family planning more in demand. Let those who are strongly motivated "sell" the idea of family planning to those who are only mildly motivated. Gradually the practice will infiltrate the entire population. To get a program started, we must develop a body of social support via satisfied users. Bringing family planning promptly to the few who are motivated now is probably the best thing that can be done to spread awareness, interest, and desire to try it. Now this means "skimming the cream" in a motivational sense—that is, deliberately planning a communication program that will influence only 20 to 35 percent of the society within a reasonably short time.

3. Implementation, Not Persuasion

As I mentioned, I came to this post as an alleged specialist in persuasion, but I quickly persuaded myself that persuasion wasn't the problem. In a way this is an amusing situation. The experts in communication say that the important thing is to get easy methods; this redefines the problem as a bio-medical one. Yet the doctors go out into the field, and they come back saying it is completely a motivational problem. They report, "We gave people the method and they wouldn't use it, so why don't you fellows in motivation get their motivation higher?" Everybody is pointing the finger of responsibility at somebody else.

The major need, in my opinion, is to furnish information to the people who are uninformed but interested. A great deal more emphasis needs to be placed on the *administrative* and *organizational* aspects of family planning services. If there is one deficiency in this field that is more serious than any other, I think it's neither lack of an ideal method or inadequacy of our persuasion techniques. *It is a general lack of adequate implemental machinery.* We don't have family planning administrators who know how to furnish services efficiently to great masses of population. We don't have a cadre of people who can organize a governmental program, for example, and apply it to a large population and run it successfully. I believe that the desire for fertility control (motivation) is high enough to give us a good, strong beginning in most of the nations of the world—if we could satisfy it properly. Information is low; practice is lower; we don't have the network of administration and organization to take this program into the field. We need to build it.

4. Bureaucratic Timidity

There is one important exception to the comments just made concerning persuasion. Persuasion is needed at one point in the society: governmental officers are badly in need of it, especially very high government officers. The people themselves, I think, need less persuasion than the public servants (especially at the elite level) who have utimate responsibility for family planning programs. There are programs where the response of the general citizenry seems very gratifying but where the expansion of the programs to larger populations is inhibited by lack of support—real support as against verbal expression—at governmental levels.

There may be two good methods of persuading government leaders. Getting the true demographic situation and its implications brought to the attention of responsible governmental officers is one of the best things we can do at this point. Another avenue is to conduct surveys of attitudes toward family planning which measure desire for information and service, and bring them to official attention. Public presentation of the facts showing both how essential it is to the nation's future and how strongly the people sense the need for family planning and would welcome it in their own lives can encourage them to take a stand. If there is to be any success, it will require that responsible government officers get behind the family planning programs in sufficient force to carry them out fully. If the people running them are always concerned about how their superiors are going to react or are handicapped by recognizing ambivalence in support or are frustrated by the usual difficulties, then the already hard problem becomes harder still.

To make this specific, let's take an example. A major resource for the spread of family planning in most countries—and a neglected one—is the men under draft in the armed services. Most countries have large numbers of young men aged seventeen to twenty-five who must spend two years or so in the armed forces. After military service they go back to their villages or their homes in the towns and cities. Now wouldn't it be the most natural thing, if you were seriously interested in effecting family planning, to have a major educational and informational program for those young men before they go back? They are at the beginning of their own marital careers; they are going back into the whole stream of the society; they're going back in sufficient numbers to reinforce one another when they are back in the villages; they are, in a sense, a captive audience. While they are in service there are other kinds of instructional and informational programs for them, for example, literacy programs. Why shouldn't they all be made literate about family planning in order that they could begin to spread the idea and support it back home? In order to do that you obviously have to get strong support at the highest levels of the armed forces. There are no extraordinary problems that need to be solved to carry out this program; we know how to do it. What is needed is permission and genuine support, i.e., the opportunity to put efficient programs like this into effect.

Very prominent in the elite that needs persuasion is the medical profession. The medical community is an indispensable partner to this whole enterprise. The plain fact of life is that in almost all countries family planning is seen as a health problem. The medical community will make it a health problem, and you can't get anywhere with family planning without the help and cooperation of medical men. They should be involved in these programs from the outset, and thoroughly.

5. Mass Media as Legitimators

What is the role of the mass media in family planning? By mass media I mean newspapers, radio, pamphlets, and so on. (Television doesn't exist in most of the developing countries.) Here let me quote a paragraph or two from something I wrote earlier:

With regard to objectives, the job of the mass media is twofold but the second task is unappreciated or insufficiently appreciated. The one task of the media, the one that is strongly recognized, is to generate interest, provide information, change attitudes, stimulate action; that is, to do all those things that a program of information and education is supposed to do. All of us believe, I suppose, that people should be allowed to make their own decisions in matters affecting their own welfare and involving how they will spend their time and money, but they should make them on the basis of good and full knowledge. The media are supposed to provide that knowledge. Although the term is suspect in some academic circles, we call this the "rational" use of the media. The other function the media can play with respect to a new idea or a new practice is to help make it look *legitimate*, to help make it familiar and acceptable. This is a most important and worthy task, and if anything perhaps more effective than the rational action function. The job is to develop the perception of social support for an innovation within the community. How can that be done? By spreading the perception that "other people like me are doing it and deriving benefit from it." This is something the mass media can do, and it is critical for the acceptance of almost any conceivable program. It is neglected, I fear, relative to the rational use of the media.

If one generalization emerges as much as any from the communication studies done on change of opinion over the past years, it is that people are strongly influenced in attitudes and behavior by other people, by their direct personal contacts, and by their perception of what they consider the others consider the right thing to do. In short, the job of the media is, in this sense, both rational and social. What this means in practical terms is that, when devising informational and educational material, we remember that in addition to the content itself, one should include material to show that this is socially acceptable and personally beneficial behavior—that doing what is suggested is taken for granted as a natural part of a good and wise life by people as close to the subjects of the informational program as one can honestly get. The very massiveness of the mass media can promote this image of social acceptability. The job of the media, then, is not simply to spread information but to spread a sense of social rightness, even righteousness, about the practice.

This needs to be underlined because it is so important for the developing nations. It's difficult for some of us to appreciate how novel family planning can seem to a population that hasn't been particularly concerned with it. And with anything that is novel, people aren't quick to pick up the innovation unless they know that it is approved or taken for granted by the people around them or the people whom they esteem.

In this regard, family planning has a handicap which most of the innovations do not have. If you can develop a better way to raise rice and get twice the yield as traditional methods, the benefit is tangible and quickly visible. But family planning is invisible. It is private in the sense of being personal, and it's also private in that it isn't talked about very much; it isn't a "normal" topic of conversation. As a consequence, it needs to have social support built up much more than most innovations. This is one job the mass media can do. The mass media can combat what the sociologists call "pluralistic ignorance," a situation where people favor an idea but think everyone else is against it, and so are afraid to speak or act in an approving way. The media might be able to turn that around, and if so they will have done an important job.

6. Communication Not Refined

In my opinion, one doesn't need a highly refined, a highly nuanced presentation of the case for family planning. In helping to design a communication program for Taiwan, I reviewed the literature to see what principles and what theories should be incorporated in these materials. After a while I came to feel that this search was a little silly. The messages we have are few in number; they are not difficult ideas, and they seem to be pretty much the same the world over. The people need to be told "what" (the elementary facts about the physiology of reproduction), "how" (contraceptive methods), and "why" (the rationale *for themselves*). How many reasons can there be for practicing family planning? The number is not infinite. There are only about five or so important ones. Whether you have a blue cover on the leaflet or a red cover doesn't make any significant difference.

We can be misled in thinking about communication if we generalize from our experience in this country. We live in a very atypical situation. We're bombarded by communications all the time. Some people want us to buy Gleem toothpaste, some Crest, and some Colgate: so whether the package is red or green might really make a difference to the people who like red better than green. We live in a highly competitive communication situation and every little refinement might make a percent difference in the market, which could make a great deal of difference on the profit side.

But on this topic and in the areas we're mostly concerned about, there isn't that kind of competition from the communication media. Quite the contrary; there is hardly any mass communication at all, so that anything you say is attractive just by virtue of the fact that it is novel. It has a kind of entertainment value, a stimulus value, just from the fact that it is there, that it exists. Once we've told the basic story of "what," "how," and "why," with some personalizing humor and a little entertainment, once we've done that and repeated it ingeniously, then we've just about done what we can so far as the sheer communication context is concerned—plus, of course, doing what we can to build the message into the social framework.

7. Success Is Not "Success"

Here I want to make a plea for realism. What is success in this field? Let me emphasize that you are successful if you can move a relatively few people. That's what success is. Success in family planning can never consist in getting an entire community to accept this practice, certainly not in our short run of five or ten years.

Let's start with the following enlightening, and sobering, set of data. Let us imagine that we start to promote family planning in a given community, and the target population is all married women from ages fifteen to forty-five. This is equal to 100 percent. When you go into the community, this is what you find: (a) First, x percent are already using something, so that's fine; you don't have to worry about them, except that what they're using might be less effective than what you think you have to offer. (b) Then, y percent are sterile, or think they are, so they're not available for your program. (c) Z percent are pregnant or lactating. If they are pregnant, they don't need family planning, at least not now; and if they are lactating, they think they don't. Now if you add up these figures—the total varies, of course, from population to population—they can amount to as much as half the population, and seldom less than a third, unavailable before you begin. (d) Then there is the group who positively want more children now, or who want a son (typically people of low parity). And how many are they? Perhaps another quarter. So as many as three-fourths of the married women may be out-of-bounds with respect to the program before we begin. One-fourth of the initial 100 percent are what you might call currently eligible at any given interval of six months or a year. So, if we can be successful in getting our message adopted by 50 percent of the currently eligible (a very high return), that means we would get only 12.5 percent of the original target. In this example, success, very great success, would be 12–13 percent. We'd be satisfied with about one-half of that, or 6 percent. Now the point of what I am saying is that 6 percent is success, it isn't failure; 6 percent of the 100 percent is success, not failure, in building family planning practice.

In a way there's a certain arrogance in our implicit notions, sometimes explicit, that people should give us pieces of their attention, their minds, their time (sometimes their money) precisely when and because we are sure we have something good for them. I say with a sincere feeling that what we have is indeed good for them, but I still find it humbling to keep in mind Thoreau's observation that "When I see someone coming toward me with the sole aim of doing me good, I run for my life." People have their own lives to live, and they are being bombarded from all sides by other people who are also convinced, no less firmly than we, that they have something essential to offer. Even if everyone were willing to give serious attention and serious efforts to all of these opportunities (a dreadful vision in itself), there may not be enough attention to go around. And this is part of the reason why we have to settle with a small fraction and call it success.

As realists with a difficult task, let us maintain professional expectations lest we start blaming the people for being blind to our attractive wares. They are the ultimate judges of the attractiveness. It is not unrealistic to assume that for the first few years of new family planning programs, success will be far closer to 1 percent than 100 percent of the couples. But as I suggested earlier, this proportion of initial success, if not infinitesimal, has a built-in chain reaction of its own. Happily, from our standpoint, this chain reaction is not only quite effective but also free. Less than complete success, then, may be a cause for regret but certainly not for despair or disillusionment.

8. Cost

I'm coming to believe that we are moving from one slogan to another. The former slogan was "It can't be done." There were a lot of early failures in trying to effect family planning, and people in the field said, "If we could only get a success somewhere to point to!" The Singur project was one success; we think we now have others in Singapore, Ceylon, Taiwan. So I think we are moving from that slogan to the current slogan, "We can do it but it costs too much." I think that we do have successes to point to, but they are too expensive. We have to find ways to spread birth control more cheaply. The newer methods will help, and so will the mass media, and so will word-of-mouth, but beyond that I have little more to suggest.

9. Place of Research

Where does research come in? Briefly, my feeling is, again thinking of this short-run period, that basic research, as it would be defined by many a sociologist or psychologist or anthropologist, is not warranted, because it will not yield enough results to be helpful in the short run. Doing academic studies on family structure, or community power structure, or innovative personalities, or communication networks, I think is not going to pay off with results in time to be useful. I think that the role of research is the applied role. I don't use that term invidiously. I'm proud to be an applied social researcher. The research needed is primarily in the evaluational role, appraising the results: "How much effect are we actually having in what we are doing, at what effort, how and why?"

Let me give an example that I think is a fair one. The noted psychologist Carl Hovland, at Yale, became famous for doing experimental studies on communication effects. He studied communication effects by laboratory experiments carefully controlled, very nicely done—and without doubt he was a major figure in this field. One of his studies, done during the War, was a so-called one-sided, two-sided argument study. It was devoted to the question "In trying to persuade people, should you present only one side of the argument or should you present both sides—the argument against your position as well as those favoring it?" Hovland did a whole series of experiments on one-sided and two-sided persuasion. The results were quite clear: (a) with people who initially disbelieve what you are trying to tell them it's better to give them the two-sided argument so that they know that their arguments were taken into account and answered; (b) educated people want two-sided argumentation more than uneducated people. Now how can we apply the Hovland experiments to family planning? In my opinion we cannot make much use of them. In the first place, on ethical grounds you should present both sides. You don't have the right to put together materials like this, certainly not for another society, and just present a one-sided case as though the other side didn't exist. Secondly, just on the basis of common sense and any experience at all in the field, you recognize that while these people may be illiterate and may be uninformed, they are by no means unintelligent. If you don't speak to their concerns, you might just as well not speak at all. So you have to use the two-sided approach on both ethical grounds and common-sense grounds.

What I think we need from research is the careful evaluation of results. From the standpoint of the scientist, you do research only where you don't know the answer, you want the answer, and you'll accept the answer, whatever it is. That's what research ought to be. Once you have stated the question and you have gone through the inquiry with proper methods, you are committed as a scientist to accepting the results, however they turn out, whether you like them or not. In this field, I think there is one result that research can give that will never be acceptable, certainly not to the administrator and not even to the scientist, and that is a negative answer. No amount of research showing that family planning cannot be done is going to stop the effort from going forward. There is just too much importance attached to it, too much investment in doing it—economic, social, psychological. But research can never give a fully negative answer anyway. What research can do is to eliminate needlessly futile efforts. If we do research in connection with the three factors of my first point, we can narrow the range of the worthwhile and delineate the realm of failure and the impracticable.

10. Direct Approach

How then should we go about implementing family planning, in the short run? My answer is, "The way to do it is to do it." We shouldn't back off and say that we have to have endless basic research before we know how the family structure ties in to the community leadership. There are so many limitations on what you can do in the field anyway. You don't have a *tabula rasa;* you have only a few limited choices you can make. The best thing to do is to move into a situation, set up as reasonable an experiment as you can to test the elements of choice you do have. Set up the implementational machinery, train the family planning administrators and field workers, and start operations. Adjust your efforts as the appraisals come in, remembering that if you get 6 percent you've had a success, not a failure, and continue. Keep a sharp, common-sense eye on the effort as you proceed, and keep yourself free to shift gears as the terrain indicates. Get the implementational machinery and start. Experiment as much as you can; see what works and what doesn't; hope that the bio-medical people will produce an ideal contraceptive before you are very far down the road. *And evaluate the results firmly as you go.*

III

My concluding impressions, then, are (1) that in the typical traditional community of the underdeveloped countries there is a wide range of motivation for and saliency of family planning; (2) that a substantial group at the lower end of the range cannot be motivated, at least not in a period of five years or so, but groups at the other end, especially the high parities, are ready now, a group representing from one-fourth to one-third of the community; (3) that given methods of good effectiveness and not too much bother, such people will use family planning with satisfactory consistency, enough to make some difference in the birth rate; (4) that the best way to motivate new users is to satisfy the motivation that already exists, that is, the best way to spread the market is to exploit the available market; (5) that the people are ill informed about family planning but by no means unintelligent about this or other matters affecting their lives closely; and (6) that given this state of affairs, any reasonable program of communication plus supplies will do about as well as any other; certainly it will not require a high degree of nuance and refinement in the campaign to distinguish between success and failure.

24

Obstacles to Programs of Population Control— Facts and Fancies

J. Mayone Stycos

Because the size, distribution and rate of increase of population are closely related to questions of national power and economic development, population has long been a topic of interest for most nations. The science of demography, moreover, has a long and distinguished history within the social sciences. It is all the more surprising, then, that until the past few years scientific research on motivational aspects of demographic problems has been virtually nonexistent. In a science dealing with three of the most basic human events and processes—birth, death, and migration—psychological, social, and cultural factors have been all but ignored as objects of scientific inquiry. It is probably fair to say, even now, that we know more about what people expect, want, and do with respect to planting wheat or purchasing TV sets than with respect to having babies.

Part of the explanation lies in the fact that demographers have tended to ignore or minimize certain types of data. The field has recruited many of its personnel from economics, actuarial science, and statistics, disciplines highly suspicious of "soft" data collected in the area of attitudes and opinions; and has relied almost exclusively on the "hard" data provided by national censuses and vital statistics. Since these data are not collected primarily for social scientists, and since they are subject to a number of inadequacies, an important aspect of the role of demographer is ingenuity at upgrading data (often from poor to fair) by conceptual and statistical manipulation. In a sense demographers have been seduced by the enormous volume of free data provided them by national governments and

Reprinted from *Marriage and Family Living*, 25, no. 1 (February, 1963), pp. 5–13, by permission of the author and the publisher.

have been lulled into asking limited questions of these data, rather than raising new questions which can only be answered by collecting other types of information. Demographers tend to be disdainful, on the one hand, of the social scientist who collects superb original data on his Sociology 101 students, and on the other, of the grand theorist who requires little empirical data for reaching conclusions.[1]

With respect to fertility research there have been special obstacles. Demographers are part of a general culture which has regarded the sexual sphere as an intensely private and personal affair. As most social scientists, demographers have not only been members of the middle class, the major bastion of restrictive sexual norms, but in their very role of social scientists have perhaps been overly sensitive to taboos in the sexual sphere. Inquiry into sexual matters has, until recently, been largely within the confines of the psychiatrist's couch, and it is of interest that it took a zoologist (Kinsey) to crack the myth that *normal* people will not talk about their sexual behavior to a social investigator.

Fortunately, for the field as a whole, if not for population experts in particular, practical exigencies have forced demographers to stick their necks out in a way rarely demanded of social scientists.[2] They have been repeatedly asked to *predict* future population, and more recently, are being asked what to do about it. On both counts the field has been found deficient, and this discovery has in large measure been responsible for a rather sudden spate of motivational studies in a wide variety of countries.

As is usually the case in the early stages of research, the studies have been generally marked by an absence of theoretical sophistication and by a failure to build in comparability with investigations of a similar nature done elsewhere. Nevertheless, they have provided an invaluable baseline of information from which a number of crude hypotheses is emerging. It is not the objective of this paper to summarize or evaluate these studies in any systematic fashion. Rather, these studies will be drawn upon, along with the personal experience of the writer, to outline some of the real and mythical obstacles in the way of planned programs of fertility control.

At the most general level, the explanation for a durable demographic gap (a discrepancy between low death rates and high birth rates) goes something like this. Until recently, most underdeveloped areas had very high death rates, perhaps forty or more per thousand population. In order to survive, such societies *had* to have comparably high birth rates. Any cultures which did not develop mechanisms for maintaining high fertility in the face of high mortality have disappeared. Consequently, customs such as early marriage emerged and survived along with various beliefs and values emphasizing the desirability of maximum fertility. The introduction of fertility control techniques into such societies runs counter, therefore, to some of the most basic customs and values, and can be expected to meet with considerable resistance or indifference.

At the same time, good health and long life are almost universal values, so that modern technology for saving lives is readily accepted. Moreover, unlike birth control, many public health measures do not require individual commitment, but can be carried out by draining swamps, improving sewage disposal, purifying the water supply, etc. Consequently, death rates can be expected to decline rapidly wherever the technological means are made available.

This general explanation is quite plausible and may even be valid. However, the well-known fact that fertility can be expected to decline very slowly by "natural" means would seem to argue the necessity for public programs to speed up the process. Why have so few governments in areas of high growth rates introduced such programs? Obviously, democratic governments are reluctant to introduce policies they believe contrary to the values of the majority of the people; but this would not be so serious a consideration for totalitarian societies, or for democracies where opposition parties are weak. In order to understand the typical reluctance of governments, it would be useful to discuss in some detail the attitudes of the elite and of the masses toward population growth and fertility control.

ELITE ATTITUDES

We can discuss reasons for the reluctance of governments to introduce family planning programs under three major headings: (1) ideas about population and population control closely related to nationalism; (2) naïve faith in the "demographic miracle"; (3) erroneous theories about the causes of high fertility.

Nationalism

Throughout the world, underdeveloped societies are experiencing waves of nationalism. Perhaps an essential condition of significant economic development, it is actively fostered by national leaders. Several common ingredients of nationalism present obstacles to programs of fertility control.

Pride in Numbers. A large population, while not guaranteeing international power, is probably a necessary condition of power. Giant armies and industries both require large population bases, and the total national product of a nation is greatly influenced by the sheer weight of numbers. Chinese leaders have even suggested maximizing their population size to guarantee survival in strength following an atomic decimation. Mixed with such more or less rational beliefs are more sentimental notions. Leaders of the new nation Nuvela become passionately convinced that there is something valuable in being a Nuvelian. More of a good thing—more Nuvelians for the world—emerges as a goal or at least as a vague feeling obstructing policies for reduction of numbers. Low birth rates may even be viewed as a sign of the decadence of nations surfeited with "civilization" and approaching cultural senescence. Views similar to these have been current among leaders in nations as disparate as Mexico and the Soviet Union.

Anticolonialism. An almost invariable aspect of nationalism is the channeling of aggressions toward a common scapegoat, usually the foreign country which has historically exercised the greatest degree of political or economic control. Any lever for pinning responsibility on this country for a host of local ills will receive maximum exploitation. If the suggestion of a population control program can be in any way linked to the "imperialist" nation, an unusually powerful and effective anticolonialist charge can be advanced—that the colonial power wishes to "do away with" Nuvelians or at least inhibit their growth, a subtle and insidious form of genocide.

Faith in Economic Policies. The new government also wishes to show that its past backwardness was due to the economic and political policies of the imperialist nation. Freed of such tyrannical shackles, its new program of economic and social reform can provide adequately for its present and future population. Admission of a population problem may sound like an admission of programmatic defeat. Marxist ideology, and to a large extent Roman Catholic ideology, regard "population problems" as smoke screens concealing inadequacies of the economic and social system; but the argument has great appeal (as well as a certain amount of truth) in areas where neither Marxism nor Catholicism reigns.

Where democratic forms of government are emerging, the party in power is wary of population programs, since many of these same arguments used against the colonial powers can be used against it by the opposition party. Within the West Indies, cleavages of color (black versus white), ethnicity (East Indian versus colored West Indian), and class (rich versus poor) have variously been used by politicians when family planning programs have been publicly discussed. In addition to charges of genocide, admission of a population problem by the majority party has been used as evidence of the inadequacy of the party's reform policies. In China, a major governmental program of family limitation was short-lived, partly because orthodox groups regarded it as an admission of weakness of the nation's economic policies. In other communist countries, birth-control programs are carefully labeled as maternal health programs.

Population Pressure as an Instrument of Nationalism. Population growth is typically viewed as a phenomenon which is not influenced but which influences other things. In its most extreme form it has been used as a rationale for territorial expansion, as in the case of Japan, Italy, and Germany prior to World War II. Currently, underdeveloped nations use population growth to justify the necessity for new markets, the need for more foreign aid, etc., and to stir up national enthusiasm for expensive programs of education, social and medical services, and industrialization. Programs for more houses, jobs, land, schools, and hospitals are intrinsically more appealing than programs for fewer babies. The former programs become even more appealing if it can be shown that there are more babies every day who need and deserve such services.

The Demographic Miracle

It is common knowledge that Western countries once had high fertility and that following their industrial revolution fertility declined to "modern" levels. Faced with high birth rates and high rates of population growth, many leaders of underdeveloped areas place their trust in the magic of economic development. If we invest in schools, factories, and cities, they argue, the population problem will take care of itself. The argument is subject to at least two important limitations.

First, demographers do not know exactly why or how fertility rates have declined. In the absence of such knowledge there is no guarantee that what happened in one set of societies in the past will happen to a quite different set in the future. Indeed, under certain conditions, improved economic circumstances and the breakdown of traditional patterns can cause increases in fertility. For example, such changes might bring about greater marital stability to nonlegal unions which now have decidedly lower fertility than more stable legal unions; or, as in India, the breakdown on taboos on the remarriage of widows could lengthen the average reproductive period. A growing body of evidence indicates that fertility did in fact increase among western nations in the early periods of industrialization, as a result of such changes as increased and earlier marriage and reduced maternal mortality.

Second, mortality in the Western nations declined much more rapidly than fertility, and closure of the ensuing "demographic gap" took some nations up to two hundred years. It was during the industrial revolution that Europe's great population increases occurred. Because of modern medical technology, mortality among contemporary underdeveloped nations is declining far more rapidly than has ever been the case in the past, with little indication that fertility will show a similarly accelerated decline.[3] Even assuming that the decline will occur eventually, how long can a society afford to wait when annual rates of increase are such that the population will double in thirty or forty years?

Another comfortable belief about the population problem stems from the theories of Josue de Castro. In the *Geography of Hunger*, de Castro popularized the notion that protein deficiency accounts for the high fertility of the lower classes. Despite the disrepute with which this theory is regarded by demographers, it has captured the imagination of many of the educated elite in a number of countries. It has the familiar twin advantage of simplicity and of avoidance of the real problem. With economic development the population will eat better and therefore bear fewer children. No direct attack on the problem is necessary.

Elite Theories about Lower-Class Fertility

Upper-class explanations for the high fertility of lower-class groups are similar in most societies with which the writer is acquainted. It is argued that the lower classes want many children or it is argued that they do not care how many they have. Religious values are also viewed as major obstacles to fertility control. In addition, the lower classes have certain needs such as an unusually high drive for sexual relations which are uninhibited by a sense of morality or social responsibility. In the face of such values and biological drives, birth-control programs are doomed to failure, and might even increase the immorality of these classes. In any event, the problem should be attacked more directly by teaching "self-control," reducing sexual frequency by state-provided avenues for sublimation, and the reduction of illegitimacy by legal, religious, and social pressures.

The Desire for Large Families. Because the typical couple in underdeveloped areas in fact produces a large family, it is tempting to conclude that this is the desired state of affairs. The available evidence, while not entirely satisfactory, would suggest the contrary. When asked to name the ideal number of children, or when asked whether or not they want more children, lower-class women in societies as different as Peru, Lebanon, Puerto Rico, Jamaica, and India do not regard the question as meaningless, and do not favor very large families. Three or four children is generally seen as the ideal number, and most women who have four children do not want any more.

Religious Values. The major religions of the East do not contain explicit ideologies with respect to fertility control. While there are certain aspects of the philosophy of such faiths which encourage the having of large families, respondents in surveys rarely cite religious objections to family planning; and it is generally agreed that religious ideology is not a major factor in resistance to population control for non-Christian religious groups.

While the Catholic religion strongly and explicitly condemns most forms of birth control, and while the Church as an organization can be highly influential in the determination of international, national, and local policies with respect to population control, the weight of the evidence suggests that its impact on attitudes and behavior of individual couples is small. Studies comparing Catholic and non-Catholic beliefs and behavior with respect to family planning have been conducted in countries where Catholics are in the majority (Puerto Rico), minority (Jamaica), or evenly balanced (Lebanon). In none of these areas is there any significant difference in attitudes or behavior with respect to family planning.[4] Such results almost invariably astonish national leaders, who tend to assume that the teachings of the Church are followed by its members.

Sex Relations and Fertility. Just as it is tempting to deduce attitudes from behavior, so it is tempting to deduce a high frequency of sex relations from high fertility, since sex relations are a necessary antecedent to fertility. The temptation is made all the more attractive by the generally condescending and patronizing attitudes of the upper classes toward the lower classes. The latter are variously viewed as "children," as primitive or animal-like, or as amoral or immoral. Thus, biological urges are stronger and inhibitions are weaker than among the upper classes. Finally, lacking electric lights and civilized means of diversion, the lower classes retire early. The entire complex is expressed in a saying, "Procreation is the poor man's recreation."

Again, the available evidence, while unfortunately limited, points in the opposite direction. First, there is no assurance that high sexual frequency increases fertility; indeed, there is a current plausible hypothesis suggesting that it inhibits it because of lower sperm counts per act of coitus. Second, there is no reason to believe that lower-class sexual frequency is higher than that of the upper class and, because of malnutrition and fatigue, it may well be lower. In limited studies in the United States, Lebanon, and India, lower educational groups have not been found to have higher sexual frequencies than better educated groups. Third, the notion that night baseball will substitute for sex seems somewhat naïve. Lest the reader think we are building straw men, let us recall the advice of the ex-Governor General of Ceylon:

> "He who goes to bed early to save candles begets twins," said Viscount Soulbury . . . Ceylon's former Governor General quoted this ancient Chinese proverb to illustrate what he considers the cause for the alarming increase in Ceylon's population. He said he had advised Ceylon's Prime Minister to introduce electric lighting to the villages to counter the population rise . . . "There has been a lot of glib talk about family planning," said the Viscount, "but that was not very easy—electric lights are the solution."[5]

Such notions are not limited to Europeans. In an opening speech to an international Planned Parenthood Conference, Prime Minister Nehru announced, "I was told only today about the possible consequences of, let us say, electricity going to a rural area . . . the period for which they can work or amuse themselves or do other things is enormously lengthened and thereby, indirectly perhaps, it affects even this family planning business."[6] A vice-president of India has publicly commented that "Sex is the only indoor sport open to us, and large families are produced. It is the poor people that produce large families and not the rich ones."[7] In recommending the rhythm method for India's masses, another high-ranking Indian official pointed to its salutary effects on "self-indulgence": "The task is essentially that of educating the individual in a manner which will enable him to sublimate his sexual urge into channels of activity which are productive of gain to the community . . . instead of yielding without even a thought of self-restraint to the desire of self-indulgence."[8]

Illegitimacy and Promiscuity. A frequent phrase heard in the West Indies is "irresponsible paternity," referring to the common pattern of having children out of wedlock. The fact that a large proportion of children are born illegitimate in the West Indies leads the middle classes to make a causal connection with high fertility rates. Religious leaders and social reformers appear to view males as casting their seeds indiscriminately throughout the female population. The young are therefore exhorted to marry as a curb to irresponsible paternity and high fertility. In point of fact, most illegitimate births are the produce of common-law or consensual unions rather than of promiscuity. Moreover, if the young entered legal unions as recommended, there is good reason to believe that their fertility would show marked increases, since they would be changing from transitory relationships to more permanent ones. In short, the relation between legitimacy and fertility in the West Indies, and perhaps in many regions of the world, is the opposite of what is usually assumed.

PROGRAMS OF FERTILITY CONTROL

If middle-class notions have deflected attention from the real problems and solutions, they have also profoundly affected the programs of fertility control where these have occurred in underdeveloped areas. This is the case because private programs are largely controlled by urban middle-class women, and because the basic philosophy and methods of such programs have been borrowed from American and British experience. The latter programs were formed by crusading middle-class women battling simultaneously against the shackles of puritanism and the tyranny of men. What have been the implications of this historical background and how appropriate are western patterns for nonwestern countries?

The Dominance of Feminism. As most voluntary organizations, planned parenthood groups have been led by women. Unlike most voluntary organizations, however, they adopted explicit and implicit female policies because they were part of the whole movement to emancipate the woman. Specifically, they were aimed at freeing the woman from the pain and drudgery of childbearing and child rearing as well as from the consequences of male sexual exploitation. It is no surprise, therefore, that a major intent of the movement, perhaps only partly conscious, has been to wrest control of fertility from males and give it to females. We say "wrest control" since there is overwhelming evidence that insofar as western fertility declines are due to contraceptive techniques, these techniques have been predominantly male methods. In their almost exclusive concern with female methods and female audiences, planned parenthood groups have been swimming upstream.

In underdeveloped areas, the emphasis may be even more misplaced, since male dominance in general and specifically in the sexual sphere is much more marked than in the modern western societies. In justification of its position, planned parenthood advocates repeat their plaints about the irresponsibility of males and the lack of male motivation for controlling fertility. However, in western nations of low or moderate fertility the evidence is against this hypothesis; and in underdeveloped nations, while the evidence is scanty, male sentiments favoring small families do not seem markedly different from female and in certain aspects may be stronger. Interestingly enough, a major reason for the scantiness of the evidence is that the typical survey concentrates on females and never elicits the opinions of the male.

The Clinical Approach.   Partly because of the medical orientation of Margaret Sanger, and primarily because of the legal difficulties under which the movement in this country has labored, a very strong medical bias dominates the Planned Parenthood movement in the United States. Among other things, this has meant a concern with "maximum protection" methods and concentration on the individual case rather than a mass approach utilizing less effective but simpler techniques. It has meant the clinical system which waits for patients to come to it, and it has meant examination rooms, case histories, and white coats. It has also meant a highly conservative attitude toward abortion, sterilization, publicity, and nonmedical personnel.

While a good case can be made for the tactical necessity for medical sponsorship in puritanical nations, no such necessity exists in most underdeveloped areas, a fact which makes examination of the efficacy of the clinical system quite relevant.

An important limitation of birth-control clinics is that they are not used. In England, according to a recent national sample, only 6% of those who have used birth control have ever received family planning advice from a clinic.[9] In Japan, where over 800 health centers include family planning, an experienced observer estimates that: "Of the families utilizing birth control in Japan, not more than 10% have received instruction or material from government services."[10] In Puerto Rico, despite the existence of an extensive network of birth-control clinics for two decades, less than one in ten families has ever obtained birth-control materials from a clinic. In less developed areas, wherever clinics exist they show pitifully small case loads.

The explanations of clinical services probably lie on several levels, only some of which have to do with the clinics *per se*. For the time being let us enumerate three.

(1) The methods typically offered by the clinics are not those most popular with most people. Neither abortion nor male contraceptives are ordinarily offered in private or public clinics.

(2) The clinical atmosphere discourages many women and all but the most stouthearted of men. On the one hand, it is too public in the sense that to be seen there may be embarrassing. On the other hand, the intimate private examination and case-history rituals frighten and embarrass many women in cultures where female modesty is an important value.

(3) Being underpublicized, clinics are not known about by large groups of the population. The very people who most need their services are least likely to know about them. Moreover, the clinics' emphasis on child *spacing* and on the advantages to health of family limitation are not the most effective appeals in underdeveloped areas at this time. Among lower-class and peasant populations, the having of children is the most natural thing in the world. Women do not become concerned until they have four or five children and then want to *stop* having children for reasons that have less to do with health than with economics.

The Chimerical Contraceptive. Hardly a planned parenthood conference goes by without at least one speaker accounting for the failure of birth-control programs in the following terms: "Because of crowded living conditions and the absence of privacy, and due to the lack of running water and sanitary facilities, a cheap, simple contraceptive must be developed appropriate for use under such conditions." In the light of the number of bodily and household functions which are daily performed without running water in lower-class houses, we feel that the concern over this matter is somewhat excessive. Further, one can only conclude that the same lower-class ingenuity which manages such "prodigious" sexual frequencies in the face of such strong needs for privacy could also deal with the "problem" of privacy for birth control. Curiously, while the middle class ascribes sexual attitudes and behavior to the lower class different from its own, it projects its own attitudes with respect to needs for privacy and sanitary facilities. This is not to say that simpler contraceptives are not desirable; it is merely to point out that inadequacies in organization, educational techniques, and basic approach should not be concealed by fanciful explanations for programmatic failure.

A cheap, safe, and relatively simple contraceptive will soon be generally available in the form of an oral pill. It will prove more popular than any other female method, but whether it will solve by itself the kind of problems outlined below is questionable. As well phrased by one writer, ". . . the governments of underdeveloped areas that have launched such programs seem to have fallen into the 'technological fallacy' which has long marked Western thinking in this area. They have adopted, in other words, a kind of blind faith in the gadgetry of contraception. . . ."[11]

SOME REAL PROBLEMS

We have discounted a number of popular explanations for the failure of birth-control programs. Are there no real problems? There are, and they are at least as numerous as the fallacious ones. Let us summarize a few.

Ignorance. Wherever studies have probed lower-class knowledge of sexual physiology, including the United States, the degree of ignorance has been startling. Maintained by strong taboos on discussion of sexual matters in many countries, this basic ignorance extends to the area of modern contraceptive techniques. While it is generally known that *something* can be done, only vague notions exist about *what*. "Birth control" or "family planning" is often confused with abortion, with the permanent stopping of childbearing, or with something done by prostitutes to avoid pregnancy or by men to avoid venereal disease. In the light of such ignorance and misinformation, it is little wonder that people stay away from clinics, the functions of which must seem mysterious and faintly nefarious.

Indifference. In the absence of information about contraceptive means, commitment to small family goals should not be expected to be strong. While we have seen that the average woman wants only three or four children, in studies conducted by the writer high proportions of these same women say they have *never thought of the matter before.* In the absence of information on means, questions on ideal size must be interpreted carefully. Most of these women would probably reply positively if asked whether they would like to own Cadillacs—but lacking the remotest chance of doing so, they have never seriously considered the matter before. Desiring three children may be in the same category for women ignorant of anything but sexual abstention as a contraceptive technique.

Ambivalence. While women or men may express sentiments generally favorable to small families, it is not difficult to get them to admit favorable sentiments toward large families as well. Because of the fear of high infant mortality, the need for support in old age, and the emotional satisfaction of children, parents can simultaneously favor small and large families. Moreover, in the absence of knowledge for achieving small families, large ones are achieved and are *post hoc* likely to be rationalized as a good thing, especially in public situations.

Late Motivation. Analysis of the data from almost any birth-control clinic in the world will show that the average woman seeks family planning assistance only after she has had several children. Sample surveys also disclose that women become seriously interested in birth control only after several births and then want to *stop* having children. However, contraceptive activity at this late date tends to be relatively inefficient because of lack of experience and because sexual patterns have become fairly routinized and difficult to change. Thus, even if birth control is introduced at this point, its impact on fertility is relatively minor.

SOLUTIONS

The initial and perhaps major hurdle of programs for fertility control in underdeveloped areas is the elite ruling classes. These groups must be informed about the gravity of the population problem, disabused of comfortable beliefs about the problem taking care of itself, and educated concerning the values, attitudes, and behavior of the lower classes in the population. The programs, themselves, should be government sponsored rather than private for several reasons. Private programs cannot marshal the economic and human resources necessary to make a major impact on the birth rate. Moreover, the prestige of government backing is highly important in an area which is characterized by ambivalent attitudes. Finally, and perhaps most important, such programs should be taken out of the hands of do-gooding amateurs and put in the hands of professionals. While medical aspects and personnel may be included in such a program, basic policies and administration should be turned over to nonmedical professionals—social scientists, community development experts, and communications media specialists.[12] What might the broad outlines of such a program be?

(1) It would give at least as much attention to males as to females, and possibly more attention. Given the fact of male dominance and the fact that fertility declines have historically been accomplished by means of male contraceptive techniques in many countries, males cannot be ignored. Moreover, because of their generally higher literacy, prestige, sophistica-

tion, and range of social relationships, they would be not only accessible to more new ideas, but more effective disseminators of these ideas.

(2) Far more resources, and probably the bulk of them, should be put into nonclinical systems of education and contraceptive distribution. Normal retail channels should be maximized by education and subsidization of key shopkeepers, druggists, healers, midwives, barbers, etc. Most of these would be dealing with men in the normal atmosphere of economic transaction rather than the strange world of the clinic. Insofar as possible, local organizations should be formed, with volunteer and paid workers serving as agents for distribution of materials and ideas. Extension workers, home economists, and community development and public health personnel should receive special education programs.

(3) The mass media, especially the printed word, should be given much more emphasis than is usual in such programs. Experimental programs in Puerto Rico and Jamaica have shown pamphlets to be as effective as personal visits or group meetings in getting people to adopt birth control. In Japan, according to recent studies, half of the women knowledgeable about birth control learned of it through magazines, nearly 20% through newspapers, and nearly 10% through books.[13] Even in nations of high illiteracy, written materials can be utilized with much greater effectiveness than is usually supposed.

(4) Every effort should be made to reach young couples with the object of initiating contraceptive practice at an early date for child-spacing purposes. Relatively simple techniques such as coitus interruptus should be encouraged, and with no great expectations of high individual effectiveness. This will have the advantages of effecting a significant reduction in fertility on a mass basis and of preparing couples for more efficient but difficult contraceptive techniques after they have as many children as they desire.

(5) Particularly with younger couples, the reputedly deleterious effects to health of rapid childbearing should be ignored or minimized, and social and economic disadvantages of excessive childbearing stressed.

(6) For women and men who have had all the children they desire, sterilization facilities should be provided. Female sterilization in Puerto Rico has enjoyed enormous popularity, and in India and Puerto Rico male sterilizations, especially where subsidized, are gaining rapidly. Legalized abortion programs similar to the Japanese should receive careful consideration. Programs such as these, which are often viewed as immoral or at least "drastic" in western eyes, do not appear so to many other populations, where they tend to be considered safer, more efficient, and less troublesome than contraception. At the very least, such programs could be

viewed as interim measures until efficient contraceptive practice becomes widespread.[14]

CONCLUSIONS

The population problem in many underdeveloped areas is serious and can be expected to grow worse. Slowing the rate of population increase is no substitute for economic development, but can make possible, assist, or accelerate that development. Programs of fertility control are entirely feasible but face major obstacles in elite attitudes and beliefs about population dynamics and lower-class culture, as well as in the dominance of ideas about family planning programs imported from the United States and England. There are also problems associated with informing and motivating the mass of the population, but, in the writer's opinion, these are less serious than those of informing, motivating, and activating ruling groups into creating careful and intelligent programs. Given the seriousness of the consequences of continued population growth in underdeveloped areas, optimism about the possibilities of fertility control programs is a necessity—and *cautious* optimism is justified.

NOTES

1. The very insularity of the demographer has in some ways produced salutary results not unlike those produced among artists working in a highly limited medium. In addition to milking with great imagination every drop of significance out of unimaginative data, demographers have been impelled to make various sorts of assumptions about human attitudes and behavior which, although often unrealistic, have allowed the development of very elegant and useful mathematical models.

2. Prediction is usually less hazardous in other branches of the social sciences. The predictions are often not quantified, as is necessarily the case in demography; or there is little danger that adequate data will be collected to test the accuracy of the prediction. The extensiveness, pervasiveness, and regularity of crude population data foster both caution and constant re-examination of assumptions on the part of demographers, no small advantages in the social sciences.

3. Japan seems to be an exception, but the case may be unusual for a number of reasons, including the abortion program, the long period of industrialization, and traditional attitudes favoring family limitation.

4. Recent studies in the United States show that the completed family size of Catholics is about the same as that of non-Catholics, but that Church-approved methods (rhythm and delayed marriage) are more characteristic of Catholics, especially the better educated ones. It may be that as Catholics become more sophisticated and better educated, they become more accessible to Church teaching. In Latin America, where educational levels have been low and the number of priests few, relative to population, it is probable that Church influence will increase with economic development. There are already signs of religious revivalism in a number of countries, an additional argument against the assumption that education and economic progress will automatically bring fertility declines.

5. *News of Population and Birth Control,* London, February, 1955.

6. *The Sixth International Conference on Planned Parenthood,* London: International Planned Parenthood Federation, 1959, p. 10.

7. S. Radhakrishnan, *Third International Conference on Planned Parenthood,* Bombay: Family Planning Association of India, 1952, p. 12.

8. K. C. K. E. Raja, "Family Planning in Public Health Programs," *Third International Conference on Planned Parenthood,* p. 64.

9. R. M. Pierce and G. Rountree, "Birth Control in Britain, Part II," *Population Studies,* XV, No. 2.

10. M. C. Balfour, "Family Planning in Asia," *Population Studies,* XV, No. 2.

11. Leo F. Schnore, "Social Problems in the Underdeveloped Areas: An Ecological View," *Social Problems,* VIII (Winter 1961), p. 187.

12. In some countries there is a growing tendency to rely on demographers for shaping such programs. While a gesture in the right direction, this is basically an error. The traditionally trained demographer has little more to offer in this field than has an actuary to programmatic solutions of problems of mortality and morbidity.

13. *Family Planning in Japan* (Tokyo: Asia Family Planning Association, 1961).

14. The Japanese have been made to feel defensive and apologetic about their abortion program, which is probably the only case in the world to date of a successful mass program of fertility control.

World Population

Introduction

In this, the final section of this collection of readings on population, we have included those papers which deal with the world population as a totality. We shall begin our consideration of the world population by taking a look back through time and end by trying to look toward the future.

It often happens that factual errors creep into the popular or public domain. Exactly where they come from or how they get their credibility is unclear, but after they have been asserted by enough people who *should* know, they become accepted as fact. One such population "fact" that gets asserted every now and then—usually to demonstrate how enormous recent world population growth has been—is that "half of the people who have ever lived on earth are living now." The first paper in this section, "How Many People Have Ever Lived on Earth?" should receive wide attention, if only to counter the inaccuracy of this statement. This paper provides a tentative answer to the title question: about 77 billion people.[1] If we use this figure as a base, we can see imme-

---

[1] Using an alternative method for making an estimate, Nathan Keyfitz has arrived at a figure of 69 billion as the number of people who have lived on earth ("How Many People Have Lived on Earth?" *Demography*, 3 [1966], p. 581).

diately that the claim that "half the earth's people are now living" is grossly in error. The actual proportion is more on the order of 5 percent.

While this bit of information is of interest, the real utility of the paper in this collection is that it attempts to reconstruct the demographic history of the earth as well as it can be done today. By so doing, it provides a firm foundation upon which we can build when we try to evaluate the present demography of the earth and estimate its demographic future.

The paper by Dennis H. Wrong, simply titled "Population Myths," takes as its area of interest the world's population growth rate, but does so by attacking what the author sees as misperceptions and misguided emphases. Of course, a number of the points that Wrong makes are also contained in some of the previous papers, but the merit of this presentation is its directness and clarity. Occasionally, as when he questions whether the role of family structure has been overemphasized as a factor that deters fertility reduction in many underdeveloped countries, he is arguing counter to other papers included in this collection, and one would like to see these issues joined more directly.

The paper by Jean Mayer, "Food and Population: The Wrong Problem?" is of considerable value in a consideration of world population because the author, a noted nutritionist, combines an informed discussion of population fact and theory with his specialized understanding of food and food supply. Mayer's point is clear, and should be well considered; in any discussion of the need to control the population increase, both in individual countries and in the world, the argument should not be linked primarily to the food supply. It is Mayer's contention that the potential food supply of the earth is enormous, and available to our present and immediately foreseeable technological competence. Thus the argument for population control should not be based on grounds of an exhausted (or soon to be exhausted) food supply; for if an ever increasing number of people can be fed, albeit poorly, the argument for population control is weakened. "And yet," Mayer goes on to say, "there is a need for the establishment as soon as possible of a sound population policy for the world at large." Advocacy of population control should be based on the argument that there will surely be a shortage of "cultural" resources if the world's population growth goes on unchecked.

The same view has been forcefully expressed by one of the long-time students of population, Professor Warren S. Thompson. In an epilogue to the fifth edition of his venerable text, *Population Problems*, Professor Thompson expresses some of his personal feelings about population and population problems after more than fifty years of study:

> . . . I have never been convinced that there was any good reason to consider the attainment of a large and dense population as more desirable for man's welfare than a population of moderate size and density. For example, I cannot see how the doubling of the present population of the world will supply a better human base for the more complete development of man's personality than our present population. Indeed, if space permitted, I would argue that any increase in the density of population beyond a very modest level interposes many serious obstacles to the satisfactory development of man's inherited qualities. I cannot concede that merely because man has a large innate capacity to reproduce, he has an obligation to use this capacity to any greater extent than he decides is to his advantage. It seems to me more human for man to use the reasoning powers he possesses to attain what he judges to be a good life than to limit his achievement of such a life by the uncontrolled use of his ability to reproduce.[2]

---

[2] Warren S. Thompson and David T. Lewis, *Population Problems*, 5th ed. (New York: McGraw-Hill Book Co., 1965), pp. 570–71.

25

How Many People
Have Ever Lived on Earth?*

Annabelle Desmond

How many people have ever been born since the beginning of the human race?

What percentage does the present world population of three billion represent of the total number of people who have ever lived?

These questions are frequently asked the Population Reference Bureau's Information Service. Because of the perennial interest and because of the credence sometimes given to what would seem to be unrealistic appraisals, this issue presents an estimate prepared by Fletcher Wellemeyer, Manpower, Education and Personnel Consultant, Washington, D.C., with Frank Lorimer of American University, Washington, D.C., acting as advisor. This estimate, based on certain statistical, historic and demographic assumptions set forth in an appendix, should be regarded as no more than a reasonable guess. It assumes that man first appeared about 600,000 years ago, a date which has been proposed for the dawn of the prehistoric era. However, this date obviously is a compromise, anthropologically speaking, between varying extremes.

Since then, it is estimated that about 77 billion babies have been born. Thus, today's population of approximately three billion is about 4.0 percent of that number.

Absolutely no information exists as to the size and distribution of prehistoric populations. Presumably they were not large, nor very widely distributed. If the 600,000 B.C. date is accepted as a sound compromise, then

Reprinted from *Population Bulletin,* 18, no. 1 (February, 1962), pp. 1–19, by permission of the publisher, Population Reference Bureau, Inc., Washington, D.C.

* The research report for this *Bulletin* was prepared by Fletcher Wellemeyer, with the technical assistance of Frank Lorimer. Georgine Ogden contributed supplemental research.

only about 12 billion people—less than one sixth of the total number ever born—are estimated to have lived before 6,000 B.C.

Anthropologists and paleontologists differ by hundreds of thousands of years as to when man first walked this earth. Recent discoveries strongly suggest that the life-span of the human species might date back as much as two million years. However, this time scale has not yet been accepted by all anthropologists.

If the "beginning" actually extended a million years prior to 600,000 B.C., the estimated number of births prior to 6,000 B.C. would be 32 billion, and the estimated total number, about 96 billion.

Prior to 1650, historical population data are very scanty for every part of the world. Despite this lack of knowledge, ancillary evidence exists which reveals the general pattern of human growth. Throughout the thousands of centuries which preceded the present technological age, human survival was such a touch-and-go affair that high fertility was essential to balance brutally high mortality. The human female—a relatively slow breeder, even among mammals—had to reproduce somewhere near her physiological limit in order for the family, the clan, the tribe, and the nation to survive.

As human culture developed over the ages, the chances of survival tended to improve. When the invention of agriculture provided a more stable food supply, the base was laid for the maintenance of large populations and for their spread into new areas. However, high death rates continued to check population growth.

Until recently, at least a half of all babies born died before reaching maturity. Man's quest for some formula to avert death included magic, incantations, and prayers, but none of these had shown any efficacy against the major killers. Then, with the advance of modern science, the mortality pattern of a million years was broken.

Jenner's dramatic discovery of vaccination for smallpox was the first of a multitude of discoveries destined to defer death, especially in infancy and childhood. This brilliant application of the scientific method to biology and medicine, together with improved agricultural technology, better transportation, and the vast and complex nexus of an emerging industrial culture, set in motion forces which drastically lowered death rates and thereby greatly increased the efficiency of reproduction. In some countries, the birth rate declined also, although more slowly than the death rate. During the 19th century, the industrial countries of the West were the first to experience the transition from high to low birth and death rates. This transition took about 150 years.

These epochal changes profoundly altered the patterns of survival and population growth. In those countries of northern Europe and North America which were the first to exploit effectively the new medical discoveries, life expectancy at birth rose rapidly from 30 years to 40, then to 50, and, by 1960, to 70 years and more. Infant mortality declined drastically: now, 95 out of every 100 babies born in Western industrial countries live to reach adulthood.

Although the power to defer death is one of the greatest advances in man's long history, it has been the principal factor in the acceleration in the rate of population growth during the past century. Now, public health programs reach even the world's most remote villages, and death rates in the less developed areas are falling rapidly. But the traditionally high birth rates—so essential to offset the high death rates of even the very recent past —remain high. Thus, population growth soars.

Therefore, over the long span of history, the rate of population growth has tended to accelerate—almost imperceptibly at first; then slowly; and recently, at a rapid clip. By the beginning of the Christian era, 200–300 million people are believed to have lived on earth. That number had grown to some 500 million by 1650. Then the growth curve took a sharp upward trend. By 1850, world population was more than one billion. Today, it is over three billion.

The quickening tempo of growth is even more dramatically expressed in doubling time. It took hundreds of thousands of years for world population to reach the quarter-billion mark, at about the beginning of the Christian era. Over 16 centuries more passed before that number reached an estimated half-billion. It took only 200 additional years to reach one billion, and only 80 more years—to about 1930—to reach two billion. Population growth rates are still going up. During all of the eons of time—perhaps as long as two million years—the human race grew to its present total of three billion. But it will take only 40 years to add the next three billion, according to United Nations estimates. In certain nations and larger areas, populations will double in 25 years or even less, if growth rates remain unchanged.

This historical review traces the proliferation of the human species through three very broad time spans: Period I extends from 600,000 b.c. to 6,000 b.c.; Period II extends to 1650 a.d.; and Period III, to 1962. These time periods are chosen because the dates mark important epochs in man's cultural development.

It should be emphasized, however, that not all portions of the globe experienced simultaneously the cultural and technological advances which mark these different stages of man's history. When the first European settlement was established in Australia in 1788, the aborigines there were in the Stone Age. Even today, some tribes living in New Guinea and elsewhere still remain at that level.

PERIOD I—THE OLD STONE AGE

Period I extends from 600,000 to 6,000 B.C. It begins early in the Paleolithic or Old Stone Age and continues to the beginning of the Neolithic or New Stone Age. It is estimated that during this period numbers grew to about five million, that man's birth rate was close to 50 per thousand, and that there was an approximate total of 12 billion births.

Little, if anything, is known about population size during this hunting and gathering stage of man's existence. The total land area of the earth is approximately 58 million square miles. It seems reasonable to assume that not more than 20 million square miles could have been used successfully by the relatively few who inhabited the earth at that time. The consensus of competent opinion indicates that, on moderately fertile soil in a temperate climate, about two square miles per person would be needed for a hunting and gathering economy.

It must be assumed that there were severe limitations on man's numbers during this period, and that his life cycle and average generation were much shorter than they are today. Man existed for the most part in wandering bands in order to survive. Our ancient ancestors were completely subject to all the vagaries of the weather and the ecological cycle of the game animals on which their existence depended. Food shortages were usually endemic, and the ravages of epidemics were routine—although the wide dispersal of the population tended to localize these hazards. Nevertheless, the picture that emerges is one in which births and deaths were roughly balanced, with births perhaps holding a narrow margin.

THE LONG TIME SPAN OF PREHISTORY

Anthropologists and paleontologists are gradually putting together, piece by piece, the great jigsaw puzzle that is the history of early man. Dr. T. D. Stewart, head curator of the Department of Anthropology, National Museum, in Washington, D.C., points out that only a few fossils of humans who lived in this period have been found. Nevertheless, man's long time scale is known today with far greater accuracy than ever before, mainly because of the new radioactive dating techniques. According to Dr. Stewart, new discoveries demand new theories or that extising theories be adjusted.

The remains of *Zinjanthropus*, recently found in the Olduvai Gorge of Tanganyika by L. S. B. Leakey, curator of the Coryndon Museum, Nairobi, Kenya, which Leakey believes date back almost two million years, probably do not represent the beginning of the line. *Zinjanthropus* has been called man because he was a toolmaker, in the crudest sense. Since his physical form represents a very early stage of human evolution, it is not advisable to assume so early a beginning for purposes of estimating human population growth.

However, it is generally believed that "man" had reached the point of being able to make simple tools and to talk by a half million or even a million years ago. Though he presumably emerged much earlier, *Homo sapiens* first appeared with great force in Europe sometime between 25,000 and 30,000 years ago. Very little is known about where he came from or about his connection with the Neanderthal people, who were one of many types of man to precede him. By 20,000 B.C., he had created the first great art in human history: the magnificent paintings and other artifacts found in certain caves in southern France and northern Spain. He engraved and carved bone and ivory with faithful representations of his women and of the animals he knew so well: the mammoth, the bison, and others. These were believed to have had magic significance—to bring fertility to the clan and success to the hunter.

No birth rates or death rates have ever been found on the walls of the prehistoric caves. Thus, what is the puzzle of man to the anthropologist and the paleontologist becomes the enigma of man to the demographer. A United Nations Report, *The Determinants and Consequences of Population Trends,* published in 1953, presents a comprehensive survey of world population through the whole of man's history. Readers are referred to it for a more complete historical survey than this limited space permits. The Report states:

> That men, using tools, have been living on this planet for at least one hundred thousand years, and possibly for over a million years, is proved by various types of evidence. For example, the definitely human skeletal remains found at Choukoutien, China, in association with artificial stone and bone implements and possible indications of the use of fire, were deposited during the second interglacial period, or earlier. There is evidence, also, that several divergent types of men emerged, some of whom had specialized characteristics which place them outside the ancestral line of all living races today. The Neanderthal people, who were dominant in Europe during the last (Würm) glaciation, were apparently such a divergent race.

PERIOD II—6000 B.C. TO 1650 A.D.

Starting with the beginning of the New Stone Age, this period extends through the Bronze and Iron periods, through classical antiquity and the Dark Ages, the Renaissance and the Reformation. It is estimated that world population increased one hundredfold during the period, growing from five million to half a billion, and that about 42 billion births occurred.

It is believed that at the beginning of the era the earth was still very sparsely settled and population was widely dispersed. Vast areas of the globe were not inhabited, partly because the last glaciations had just receded.

It was during this period that man began to *produce* food instead of simply consuming what nature had laid before him. In the Near East, he had already passed the stage of the most primitive village-farming communities which grew out of the earliest agriculture with its domestication of animals. Some of these ancient communities developed into the earliest known urban settlements. The development of agriculture with its settled farming community spread to other areas of the earth during this period. Eventually, it was to change drastically man's pattern of survival and his way of life.

The earliest scene of settled village-farming communities appears to have been in the Near East. Robert J. Braidwood, professor of the Oriental Institute of Chicago and field director of the Jarmo Project, a recently studied archeological site in Iraq, says: "It is probably very difficult for us now to conceptualize fully (or to exaggerate) the consequences of the first appearance of effective food production. The whole range of human existence, from the biological (including diet, demography, disease, and so on) through the cultural (social organization, politics, religion, esthetics, and so forth) bands of the spectrum took on completely new dimensions."

Braidwood describes the hilly piedmont and intermontane regions surrounding the great "Fertile Crescent," which starts in the valleys of the Tigris and Euphrates Rivers, sweeps around to the north to touch southern Turkey and Syria, then curves south to the shores of the Mediterranean and into Egypt. One radioactive-carbon date suggests that this development was well advanced by 4000 B.C.

Sheep, goats, pigs, cattle, and some kind of horselike animal were used by those living in the area. Their plants were wheat and barley. Braidwood notes that some sort of hybridization or mutation, particularly in domesticated plants, must have taken place before certain species could have been moved to other areas. However, they seem to have moved into the Danube Valley by 4000 B.C., and into western Europe by 2500 B.C.

In other words, man was learning to utilize his environment more efficiently; thus it could support more people than ever before. But numbers were still regulated by the food-producing quality of the land. Population grew in times of plenty and declined when food became scarce and when disease decimated large populations, as it did in Europe during the Dark Ages.

During the Bronze Age, man began to use copper and bronze and to build towns, cities, and states. Kings, advanced religions, social classes, writing, and enduring monuments, such as the Nile pyramids, appeared during this period. The Iron Age brought iron metallurgy, the invention of the alphabet, the use of coined money, and the spread of commerce and navigation.

The early and great empires and cultures developed: those of Egypt, Rome, and Greece; of King Asoka in India; of the Han dynasty in China; and, later, the empires of the Mayas and the Incas in the New World. The Hindu, Confucian, Buddhist, Jewish, Christian, Moslem, and other great religions emerged.

The City—Period II

The great cities of ancient times rose in rich valleys adjacent to the Mediterranean, the Red Sea, and the Persian Gulf, along the Indus and the Nile, and along the Yangtze in China. The first great urban civilization arose about 3500 B.C. in Mesopotamia, along the Tigris and Euphrates. Another grew up in Egypt before 3000 B.C. and still another in Crete. A fourth arose along the banks of the Indus in western India, but whether this grew directly out of Neolithic beginnings or was a transplant of the Sumerian culture of Mesopotamia is a matter of dispute. Urban civilizations developed in China at a later date, and still later in some areas of tropical Central America and in Peru.

The urban societies of Mesopotamia, China, and Egypt maintained complex centralized control of soil and water resources in order to provide irrigation and to control floods. These "hydraulic" civilizations supported very dense populations with highly integrated social systems. The individual peasant was allowed a small land area which produced more food than his family needed. Such civilizations have persisted in Egypt, India, China, and elsewhere to the present day, with little change in the economic basis of life but with periodic rises and declines.

The ancient Mediterranean, Asian and American urban civilizations appear to have been isolated flowerings of human culture which culminated in "golden ages" and then declined. The archeological record abundantly reveals their wavelike nature.

The A.D. Era of Period II

The United Nations study previously mentioned states that, at the beginning of the Christian era, the world's population was likely to have been between 200 and 300 million people. Discussing the lack of historic demographic information, the Report states:

> Various kinds of evidence indicate that man's numbers became adjusted to the food-producing capacity of the land in ancient times—increasing

as it rose and declining as it fell. Unfortunately little of this evidence is of a census type, and most of the remainder does not provide a basis for estimating the number of inhabitants of an area. Large parts of the world's population were subject to some sort of census enumeration near the beginning of the Christian era, but the information available from these censuses has limited value. Roman censuses were taken for administrative purposes and were restricted to "citizens," an expanding category as citizenship rights were extended to outlying regions. Moreover, only adult males were included in some of these censuses, while all household members except "children" were included in others. Chinese censuses at about this time provided reports on total population but interpretation of the results involves many difficulties. Elaborate records were kept by the ancient Incas, but their meaning is obscure.

J. C. Russell, professor of history at the University of New Mexico, who has contributed much to the demographic history of the West, has traced the population changes within the Roman Empire from the second century A.D. to the year A.D. 543, a period he characterizes generally as one of imperial decline:

> . . . However, within the general picture there are great differences in the trends. Actually most of the decrease occurred in western Mediterranean lands: Italy, Gaul, Iberia, and North Africa, together with Greece and Egypt. In Syria the population seems to have held even while in Gaul and Britain something like recovery must have occurred at the end of the period. Eastern Asia Minor and the Slavic area probably increased markedly. The German and Scandinavian spheres apparently held even in spite of emigration. The information about the central, eastern, and northern parts of Europe is so vague and uncertain that there may have been a considerable increase in population. The general rise in temperature should certainly have reduced the semiglacial conditions of the northern countries and made them attractive for grain-growing groups.

In the second and third centuries A.D., Rome suffered two devastating epidemics which have not been identified, but their virulence suggests bubonic plague. According to Dr. Russell:

> The period from A.D. 543 to 950 probably marks the lowest ebb of population in Europe since the early Roman Empire. It covers the first great attack of the plague, the worst epidemic to strike the area with which we are concerned. Following it came the Mohammedan invasions from the seminomadic areas of the lands surrounding the Mediterranean. From the east in the tenth century the Hungarians scourged most of Europe and what they missed was visited by the terrible raids of the Vikings from the north. Some measure of the weakness of the

European population is indicated by the feeble defense put up against
these invaders by the governments of Europe. . . .

Endemic diseases such as malaria and tuberculosis were prevalent,
and the latter was particularly fatal among young people. In fact, the combination of both diseases occurred quite frequently and was highly fatal.
Dr. Russell speculates that during the periods of population decline in early
medieval Europe, much carefully tilled and drained acreage lapsed into
breeding grounds for mosquitoes; and that a period of wet, warm weather
about 800–900 A.D. greatly increased the incidence of malaria.

The span of life (extreme length of life) seems to have been around
100 years, as it is now. Those who could avoid infection were likely to live
to considerable ages. According to John Durand, assistant director in charge
of population, the United Nations Bureau of Social Affairs, the best basis for
making mortality estimates of the Roman period is a study of tombstone
inscriptions for males dying between the ages of 15 and 42. This method
corrects the exaggeration of years that humans are apt to indulge in, even
on tombstones, and allows for the underrepresentation of children's deaths.
On this basis, Durand concludes that life expectancy at birth for the whole
population of the Roman Empire was probably only about 25 or 30 years.

After the year 1000, it appears that population began to increase; and,
between 1000 and 1348, that growth was phenomenal, particularly in northern Europe. The empire of Charlemagne had already capitalized on the
upward population movement, and stronger governments began to develop
in Germany, Scandinavia, and even in Russia. The Crusades spread Christianity throughout the Middle East and brought contact between the
Moslem and Christian worlds.

Then in 1348 the bubonic plague, which seems to have first appeared
in the sixth century in Egypt, suddenly erupted in Europe in a more viru-
lent form, taking a frightful toll of lives. Russell states that "the years
1348–1350 saw a very heavy loss of life, 20 to 25 per cent in most European
countries. The decline continued with later epidemics until the population
of about 1400 was near 60 per cent of the pre-plague figures. . . ."

Between 1500 and 1700, far-ranging social, economic, and intellectual
revolutions began which formed the basis for the modern world. The era
of medieval authority was first challenged in northern Italy, at the time of
the Renaissance. This was followed by the age of discovery, with voyages
around Africa and to the New World. At the same time, the Reformation
set the stage for the revival of intellectual development in northern Europe.
For the first time since the Golden Age of Greece, the human intellect began to look at the world objectively. This led to the birth of the scientific
method: new concepts of the nature of matter, energy, and, ultimately, of

life began to capture the minds of men. Out of this intellectual revolution came powerful new insights which were eventually to greatly change man's pattern of living and dying.

In Europe about the middle of the 17th century—after the end of the Thirty Years' War and the period of peace and stability which followed —agricultural methods improved, slowly at first and then rapidly. New crops were introduced and crops were rotated; manure and fertilizers were used more generally; and the soil was cultivated more extensively. Even though these more advanced methods increased food production, the margin of plenty continued to be precarious, especially for those who lived in cities. A comparable agricultural expansion seems to have occurred in China at about the same time.

Unfortunately, little is known about population growth and decline during this period for the vast continent of Asia, particularly for India and China. M. K. Bennett, director of the Food Research Institute, Stanford University, has recognized the need for a continent-by-continent or region-by-region survey. He estimates that world population in 1000 A.D. was somewhere around 275 million, or "probably less than half of the population of Europe in 1949; . . . that there has been one century, the fourteenth [the century of the Black Death in Europe], in which world population did not increase at all, but declined. . . ."

The earlier "hydraulic" civilizations became subject to disorders which checked and, in some cases, reversed their population growth.

The Americas had an estimated population of 16 million at the time of their discovery by Columbus. Julian Steward, research professor of anthropology, University of Illinois, has estimated the population of the different regions of the American hemisphere in 1492 as follows:

North America:	
North of Mexico	1,000,000
Mexico	4,500,000
West Indies	225,000
Central America	736,000
South America:	
Andean area	6,131,000
Remainder	2,898,000
Total	15,490,000

PERIOD III—1650–1962 A.D.

If man's existence on earth is viewed as a day, this period is less than a minute. But a fourth or more of all human beings ever born have lived during this brief span.

The period brought a sixfold increase in human numbers: from an estimated half-billion in 1650 to over three billion in 1962. There were approximately 23 billion births during this period—over half as many as in the preceding 76 centuries!

World population doubled between 1650 and 1850, growing beyond the one-billion mark. It doubled again, to reach two billion by 1930, in only 80 years. Since that time, the rate of growth has accelerated steadily. Now over 50 million more people are added each year. If the current rate remains unchanged, today's population will double again in less than 40 years.

A steadily falling death rate, especially during the last century, is mainly responsible for the very rapid acceleration in population growth. It is estimated that during 1650–1750, population was growing at about 0.3 percent a year; during 1750–1850, at about 0.5 percent; 1850–1950, at 0.8 percent. Currently, the rate is somewhere between 1.6 and 1.9 percent.

This period brings man through to the modern agricultural-industrial age with its tremendous scientific and technological discoveries which have greatly speeded up the rate of social change in the Western world and which have revolutionized agriculture, industry, communication, transportation, etc. These developments have made possible the support of the mammoth populations in numerous areas of the world. However, many of those technological advances are only beginning to touch the less developed areas where living levels for over half of the world's people are only a little, if any, above what they were during much of the earlier history of the race.

For the world as a whole, the mid-17th century is a benchmark in the pattern of population growth. Then, the upward surge in the numbers of people began. Just why the response to the early stirrings of the modern age was so rapid is not entirely clear, though many of the major factors which stimulated the increase in human numbers can be recognized. In Europe, the frightful famines and epidemics that marked the Dark Ages seem to have decreased, although hunger and disease were still endemic. The discovery of the New World opened the way for great transatlantic migrations to the rich, sparsely settled lands of the Americas. To some extent, this relieved the growing population pressure in Europe and provided a new source of food for the Old World. It also gave impetus to the tremendous growth of populations of European origin—at home and in European colonies—which amounted to a ninefold increase during the period.

The development of the scientific method and the application of this new knowledge to technology stimulated the Industrial and Vital Revolutions which so greatly changed man's way of life throughout the Western world. The Industrial Revolution brought the transition from agrarian to industrial societies—a transition which is beginning only now for large areas of Africa, Asia, and Latin America. The Vital Revolution brought the Western industrial nations through the demographic transition: from high birth and death rates to low birth and death rates. . . .

WHAT IS PAST IS PROLOGUE

Since man first appeared on earth, human arithmetic has moved from a relatively simple exercise in addition to a complicated one of geometric progression. It took all of the vast reaches of time to build today's population of slightly over three billion. But it will take only 40 more years for population to reach six billion, if the present growth rates remain unchanged.

Life on this earth was a precarious gamble for *Homo sapiens* for hundreds of thousands of years. Driven by his natural reluctance to endure an early death, man ultimately discovered and then perfected the power to defer death. That he has succeeded is a notable tribute to his genius and to his humanitarian and philanthropic instincts.

It is noteworthy that the desire to control fertility has never had the emotional imperatives which brought the power over death. Only modest efforts have been made thus far to discover effective methods of fertility control which would be acceptable to the people of all cultures and religions. Less than modest efforts have been made to disseminate what knowledge is now available to all of the world's people who would benefit from that knowledge. Consequently, during the past decade of rapid death-rate decline in the less developed countries, there has been no measurable reduction in high birth rates; so population growth has increased.

Rapid population growth cannot be maintained indefinitely in any part of the world. If birth rates do not decline in overcrowded lands, death rates eventually will rise to check growth.

The gulf which exists today between the peoples of the world has widened: life is better than ever before for those who live in the Western industrial countries. But the majority of the world's people still live close to the subsistence level, in poverty and squalor reminiscent of the Middle Ages. If the demographic transition to a balance between low birth and death rates could be hastened in the less developed countries, this gulf might yet be bridged in time to avert a Malthusian disaster.

APPENDIX

The statistical and general demographic assumptions used to determine the number of people who have ever been born were provided the Population Reference Bureau by J. Fletcher Wellemeyer, an independent manpower consultant, Washington, D.C., in consultation with Frank Lorimer, American University, Washington, D.C.

The estimate was made on the basis of three time periods:

Period	Number of Years in Period	Number of Births per Year at Beginning of Period	Number of Births per Year at End of Period	Number of Births in Period
I. 600,000–6000 B.C.	594,000	"1"	250,000	12 billion
II. 6000 B.C.–1650 A.D.	7,650	250,000	25,000,000	42 billion
III. 1650–1962 A.D.	312	25,000,000	110,000,000	23 billion
Total				77 billion

To obtain the number of births at the beginning and end of these periods, certain assumptions were made regarding birth rates and the size of populations. It was assumed that at the beginning of the Neolithic era the population was five million and that the annual birth rate was 50 per thousand. The procedure assumes a smooth increase. The growth was undoubtedly irregular, but the estimates may fairly represent the net effect of the ups and downs.

By 1650, the annual number of births was estimated at 25 million, corresponding to a population of about 500 million. The 1962 world population of 3.05 billion, the number of births, and birth rate of 36 per thousand are based on United Nations estimates.

The 600,000 years' duration of the Paleolithic era is based on the assumption that manlike types were then in existence but in very small numbers. Earlier dates have been given a few species by certain authorities, but some of these dates are questionable, and the earlier species may have been considerably less than manlike. The 600,000-year period seems a reasonable compromise between extreme possibilities.

Once the number of births at the dates indicated was determined, the total number of births for each period was calculated at a constant rate of increase for the period.

The estimated rates of increase differ sharply. For the long Paleolithic period, the average annual rate of increase was only 0.02 per thousand; during 6000 B.C. to 1650 A.D., it rose to 0.6; and during 1650–1962, it reached 4.35.

For the figures derived here, the following equation was used:

$$\Sigma\, B_t = \frac{B_o e^{rt}}{r}$$

B_o is the number of births per year at the beginning of the period; t is the number of years in the period; e is the base of natural logarithms; and r is the annual rate of increase during the period.

The value of r is obtained by solving for r the equation

$$\frac{B_t}{B_0} = e^{rt}$$

where B_0 is the number of births the first year of the period and B_t is the number of births the final year of the period.

SOURCES

In the preparation of this *Bulletin*, the following sources were consulted. The reader is referred to them for additional information.

1. Bennett, M. K. *The World's Food.* New York: Harper and Brothers, 1954.

2. Braidwood, Robert J. "Near Eastern Prehistory." *Science.* 127 (3312). June 20, 1958.

3. Brown, Harrison. *The Challenge of Man's Future.* New York: The Viking Press, 1954.

4. Carr-Saunders, A. M. *World Population, Past Growth and Present Trends.* Oxford: Clarendon Press, 1936.

5. Collier, John. *Indians of the Americas.* New York: New American Library of World Literature, 1947.

6. Cook, Robert C. "World Population Growth." *Law and Contemporary Problems,* a quarterly published by the Duke University School of Law. 25 (3). Summer 1960.

7. Durand, John. "Mortality Estimates from Roman Tombstone Inscriptions." *American Journal of Sociology.* 45 (4). January 1960.

8. Huxley, Julian. *New Bottles for New Wine.* New York: Harper and Brothers, 1957.

9. Kroeber, A. L. *Anthropology.* New York: Harcourt, Brace and Company, 1948.

10. Russell, J. C. "Late Ancient and Medieval Population." *Transactions of the American Philosophical Society.* New Series 48 (part 3). June 1958.

11. *Scientific American.* Issue entitled "The Human Species." 203 (3). September 1960.

12. Steward, Julian. "The Native Population of South America." *Bureau of American Ethnology Bulletin.* No. 143.

13. Turner, Ralph. *The Great Cultural Traditions: Volume I, The Ancient Cities.* New York: McGraw-Hill Book Company, 1941.

14. United Nations, Department of Social Affairs, Population Division. *The Determinants and Consequences of Population Trends.* New York, 1953.

15. United Nations, Department of Economic and Social Affairs, Statistical Office.

    A. *Demographic Yearbook, 1960*. New York, 1960.

    B. *The Future Growth of World Population*. New York, 1958.

    C. *Population and Vital Statistics Reports* (Statistical Papers, Series A, Vol. XIII, No. 1). New York, 1961.

16. Willcox, Walter F. (editor). "Population of the Earth," by Willcox in *International Migrations*, Vol. II, Part I. New York: National Bureau of Economic Research, Inc., 1931.

26

Population Myths

Dennis H. Wrong

In recent years the rapid growth of world population has come to loom as one of the great problems of the age. Vivid and ominous metaphors like the "population explosion," the "population bomb," or the "swarming of the earth" are by now part of the familiar vocabulary of public awareness—so familiar, indeed, as to have created the impression that we have a firm understanding of the danger. Yet because population trends are inseparably related to such emotion-laden matters as the role of women and the position of the family in society, to sexual practices and moral doctrines, and to the comparative sizes of national, religious, and racial groups, there has been a general reluctance to press hard upon the conventional wisdom embodied in the prevailing metaphors. Thus the way has been left clear for a host of misconceptions to flourish about the causes and consequences and control of population growth. These misconceptions, moreover, are held both by the "optimists" who refuse to regard population growth as a profound threat to human welfare and by the "alarmists" who have for so long considered themselves voices crying in a wilderness of indifference and prejudice that they have become prone to shrill exaggerations and the brandishing of scare statistics.

Perhaps the most common of all the misconceptions concerning the so-called population explosion is that it poses a problem only to the economically underdeveloped, non-Western part of the world. Although most Americans take it for granted that their numbers will continue to increase steadily, they are not apt to regard this increase as amounting to anything so threatening as an "explosion" and are inclined to use the latter term only with reference to the larger countries of Asia. Yet the United States, as well as several other Western countries, has maintained a rate of population

Reprinted from *Commentary*, 38, no. 5 (November, 1964), pp. 61–64, by permission of the author and the publisher.

growth since World War II equaling or exceeding those of many underdeveloped areas. The American rate of increase during the past decade,
for example, has been as high as that of India and higher than Japan's.
Moreover, the comforting belief that rapid population growth is a danger
only to the underdeveloped world holds only if one adopts a thoroughly
catastrophic perspective. Continued population increase in the United
States may not threaten us with imminent mass starvation and civil disorder, but it does strain our human and material resources, and aggravate
our most serious social problems.

A second widespread misconception concerning the world population
explosion is that it has resulted from a rise in the birth rate in the countries of rapid growth. This notion stems from a confusion between postwar
American growth and the quite different pattern of growth in the underdeveloped countries. For in these latter countries the crucial factor has not
been a "baby boom" such as we experienced here after the war, but rather
a sharp drop in the death rate. In other words, while the level of fertility
has remained the same or declined only slightly, a far higher proportion
of infants is being kept alive by "death control" in the form of newly
adopted medical and public-health measures. The survival of two newborn
babies where previously only one survived is the immediate, demographically explosive consequence of the introduction of those measures, rather
than an increase in the longevity of adults. Although the effects on population increase of this decline in infant mortality are identical to those of a
rise in the birth rate, the "mindless breeding" of the "Asian masses" has
nothing to do with the issue—tasteless and irrelevant references to sex as
the "Indian national sport" notwithstanding.

But why have Asians, Africans, and Latin Americans failed to adopt
birth control to balance the effects of death control? Is the problem, as is
sometimes suggested, a matter of illiterate, superstitious, church-ridden
peasants fatalistically clinging to past customs and incapable of following
the Western example by adjusting their behavior to a new demographic
situation? Here again a misconception—and a self-righteous one—is at
work, for the demographic situation in the underdeveloped countries is
unlike anything in Western population history. In Ceylon—to take the
standard, and only slightly extreme, case—the death rate recently dropped
as much in a single year (1947) as it did over a full fifty years in the West
during the period when the latter was going through its own modernization
process. It took nearly a century of declining mortality and rapid population
growth before fertility began to decline in the West; little wonder, then,
that reproductive behavior in much of the underdeveloped world (where
mortality levels are by now only a little higher than in the West) has not
yet adjusted itself to the effects of death control. Unlike the contemporary

underdeveloped nations, moreover, the West in its time had migration out-lets to absorb part of its growth. And finally, the European states were never as large in absolute terms nor as densely settled as the major under-developed countries are today.

⌐ Still another common misconception is that the balance of power in world politics is likely to be altered by the rapid growth in the population of the underdeveloped world. In the past, this idea often inspired appre-hensions with a racist tinge (the "yellow peril" and the "black hordes"); nowadays, it more usually inspires "wave-of-the-future" rhetoric. The truth, however, is that in the nuclear age sheer numbers can no longer turn a nation into a major world power; indeed, the rapid growth of population in the underdeveloped countries actually *reduces* both their military and their industrial potential. To be sure, defenders of the view that national power in some last analysis still rests on population size insist—in an effort to adapt this thesis to the facts of nuclear technology—that only large and wealthy nations can support a considerable nuclear defense establishment. But this claim loses any plausibility it may seem to have when one considers the destructive power of even a few "old-fashioned" nuclear bombs, or when one recalls the one-sided, unbalanced patterns of economic growth which totalitarian regimes such as those of Russia and China are able to sustain in order to build up their armaments.

Does the population explosion, then, pose *no* problem to the world? Are the forebodings to which it has given rise utterly unjustified? Since the pace of world population growth has been quickened by the spread of death control rather than by an increase in human fertility, are we not en-titled to regard an extra thirty years of life as an unqualified blessing con-ferred upon us by modern technology? If death control results in a larger population, why should this be of concern to anyone except a few aesthetes, haters of crowds, and those people who (as *Time* once suggested) prefer birds and animals to human beings? The answer is that the population explosion remains a monumentally serious problem even though some of the fears to which it gives rise are groundless, and even though it is the result of a technical revolution that is beneficial in other respects. In order to grasp its true nature and dimensions, one must begin by distinguishing clearly between its long-run and short-run effects.

Looking several centuries ahead, it is impossible to escape the con-clusion that world population growth *must* eventually come to an end. One can argue, as do the "optimists," that new inventions, new sources of food, the marvels of science and technology in general are capable of achieving gains in productivity that could support a vastly larger population than at present. But to grant that this is in principle possible is a very different matter from assuming that the benefits of such technological progress will in fact be made available in a short time to all of the world's peoples. The optimists are nowhere more optimistic than in their readiness to assume that increases in productivity that are now, or will shortly become, technically *possible* are likely to be *actually* achieved in this world of wars and national and imperial rivalries. Moreover, glowing estimates of future advances in productivity usually concentrate on possible gains in food production, ignoring the fact that human beings, however well fed, also need *space*. Never ending population growth would ultimately lead to a shortage of space even if the problem of food supply were solved.

Let us go further, however, and concede to the optimists the feasibility of a hypothetical world of planetary colonization, of human settlements underground and raised above the ground, of food acquired from the oceans or grown in high-yield chemical solutions. Let us concede also that such a world might feed its much larger population *more* adequately than we are fed today on earth. Is it not obvious that even *this* world could only continue to be viable if rapid population growth were to cease? For no matter what science and technology may achieve, the time must come when only stabilization of numbers will avoid disaster.

Alarmist writers on the population problem, on the other hand, are not always clear as to the nature of the disaster they predict if population growth should continue. Frequently, they draw depressing pictures of a future in which the entire surface of the earth has been converted into a human anthill. By extrapolating present growth rates into the future, they suggest that we are heading toward such a world. Yet far more probable than the continuation of population growth to the point where we are faced with an anthill world is the cessation of growth as a result of a rise in the death rate long before such a level of density is reached. The real issue, therefore, is *how* present growth rates will be lowered: will we be forced to abandon the low mortality we now enjoy and suffer a sharp rise in the death rate, or alternatively will we cut back on population growth by learning to control our breakaway fertility? For the disaster with which the population explosion actually threatens us is not that we will one day be standing shoulder to shoulder on the earth's surface, but that we will lose our control over death and return to the kind of population stability (based on high mortality and fertility) prevailing in pre-modern societies.

In the short run, however, it is the effect of rapid growth on economic development that is the essence of the problem. Strangely, economic development and technical progress are often seen as alternatives to actions and policies designed to arrest population growth. We should, it is sometimes argued, concentrate on encouraging economic progress instead of worrying about birth-control campaigns, for economic progress will obviously permit more people to live at a higher standard of living. In its crudest form, this argument poses more food as an alternative to fewer people. But an odd distortion is involved here. Social scientists who advocate governmental birth-control policies do not see such policies as an *alternative*, but rather as a *prerequisite*, to economic development, no less essential to development than, say, the construction of dams and heavy industry. (Ansley Coale and Edgar M. Hoover have shown that at present rates of economic growth, per capita income in India would increase by nearly 40 per cent if the birth rate fell by half in one generation.)

A moderate version of the optimistic position contends that as agrarian peasant societies are modernized, population growth will be slowed up by the mass adoption of family limitation under the new circumstances of urban living, open class systems, and greater material welfare. (This, of course, is what happened when the West achieved modernization.) But high rates of population growth in underdeveloped societies may swamp and destroy all programs for economic development by diverting resources needed for capital investment to meeting spiraling consumer demands.

There is a further point of contrast between Western experience and the present situation of the underdeveloped world. Along with the faster decline in the latter's death rate, the greater density and size of its present population, and the lack of migration outlets, some sociologists and demographers have also pointed to the fact that the fertility levels prevailing today in the *tiers monde* are higher than was the case at the beginning of modernization in the West. They relate these higher levels to crucial differences between the Western family system and the so-called joint or consanguineal family systems of Asia and Africa, which are far more conducive to early marriage and to continuous childbearing through the wife's reproductive period. However, the importance of this particular difference may have been overstressed, for the underdeveloped countries possess several advantages over the West so far as prospects of succeeding quickly at fertility reduction are concerned. In the first place, they have achieved national independence in an era when a strong state, assuming full responsibilities for social welfare, has become the norm. Moreover, their traditional religions and value systems, while containing many injunctions in favor of large families and high fertility, have never made a prime doctrinal tenet of pro-natalism combined with sexual asceticism to the degree that Christianity has—and all branches of Christianity, not merely the Roman Catholic Church. Even the absence of a strong secular humanitarian and libertarian tradition which frowns upon practices like sterilization and abortion (not to speak of infanticide) is an advantage from the standpoint of attaining fertility control. Latin America, the most rapidly growing region and the one with the highest birth rates, is, of course, an exception to these generalizations, since its culture and social structure are largely an offshoot of Western civilization. Yet the very fact that it is an exception suggests that the linkage between high fertility and the joint family system may have been overstressed.

Given that modernization may be delayed and even prevented by the "premature" adoption of one of its essential features—namely, death control—the underdeveloped countries can no more afford to follow a *laissez-faire* policy with respect to population growth than they can with respect to capital accumulation and economic growth itself. But once one speaks of the necessity of state policies designed to cope with population growth, further issues arise. It cannot be assumed that "voluntary" birth-control policies on the Japanese or Indian model are the only ones likely to be adopted: the ominous possibility of man-made famines and even of direct genocide as means of reducing not population growth but existing over-population are already firmly established in the repertory of 20th-century politics. Hannah Arendt is among the few political thinkers to have recognized this danger. In *The Origins of Totalitarianism*, she contends that rapid population growth in the huge, overcrowded countries of Asia has created hordes of "superfluous" people who constitute an ever present temptation to resort to the precedent of political mass murder. And, indeed, a continuation of the pressures of rapid growth is bound to heighten the appeal of totalitarian techniques as a form of drastic demographic surgery, for totalitarianism is essentially a method of disposing of social problems by eliminating whatever and whoever makes them.

But it is by no means certain that mass genocide, demographically motivated wars, or even the milder policy of holding back death-control measures (which *may* be what China is now deliberately doing) could successfully "solve" the population problem. A temporary rise in mortality might facilitate rapid economic development, which would then lead to the adoption of family planning. But more probably, the result would be a cycle of wars, civil strife, mass bitterness, and apathy that would themselves retard or prevent economic development. It is sometimes argued that the Black Death, which carried away from one-third to one-half of the total population of Europe in the 14th century, was a necessary condition for the later emergence of the Industrial Revolution. But here again we are probably dealing with a confusion between short- and long-run considerations. Even though the Black Death was not a man-made disaster, two centuries of disorder, violence, and cultural lag intervened between its ravages and the immense release of energies we call the Renaissance and the Reformation. And most historians agree that the troubles of this period, "the waning of the Middle Ages," stemmed directly from the trauma of mass death by plague and famine. Would man-made holocausts have a lesser effect?

As for the more benign ways of lowering fertility, some of them seem almost as offensive to Western sensibilities as a deliberate increase in the death rate. Western social scientists and medical specialists have generally favored the voluntary use of chemical or mechanical contraceptives by individual couples (the method that is chiefly responsible today for maintaining the relatively low levels of fertility in the Western world itself). But it is beginning to appear that abortion and sterilization may have more appeal to some peoples as forms of birth control than the advanced contraceptive techniques of the West. Nor is it necessarily the case that "the pill"—the yet-to-be perfected oral contraceptive so often seen as the solution to population control in the underdeveloped world—will have greater appeal. In Japan, a decline of 50 per cent in the birth rate in the decade from 1947 to 1957 was achieved largely by means of abortion, which was legalized in 1948. Since 1955, the number of abortions has dropped without a concomitant rise in the birth rate, which suggests that Japanese couples are learning to substitute other methods of birth control. Whether the new methods are mainly contraception or sterilization, however, remains open to dispute. Be that as it may, it seems likely that sterilization will become the favored method of achieving an initial reduction in the birth rate in countries as dissimilar as India and some of the Latin American nations. And since the goal of anti-natalist policies in the underdeveloped world must be to achieve fertility decline *before* rather than after the achievement of full social and economic modernization, it ill behooves Westerners to frown on the adoption of methods like sterilization and abortion. The underdeveloped countries cannot afford to delay fertility reduction until they have attained the benefits of modernization, and perhaps contraceptive birth control will itself have to be viewed as one of these benefits.

The issue of whether American aid to underdeveloped countries should include advice on birth-control techniques is largely responsible for the fact that the population explosion has become a subject of public debate in this country. Formulating the problem in terms of distant and for the most part non-Christian peoples has doubtless served to moderate potentially rancorous religious differences within the United States concerning these matters. However, it has also allowed us to evade the question of whether it is desirable that the American population should itself continue to soar at its postwar rate. Among the few professional demographers who have confronted this question are Lincoln and Alice Day. Their recently published book, *Too Many Americans* (Houghton Mifflin Company), is refreshingly free from the strident alarmism that characterizes the writings of so many of the amateurs who have dealt with the subject. The Days readily concede that American population growth does not threaten us with the prospect of eventual famine or even declining living standards, for the almost universal practice of birth control among Americans provides a kind of built-in check on further growth should population pressure begin to depress standards of living. It is rather the "quality of life" that is threatened by ever growing numbers of people: outdoor recreational areas are destroyed; air and water pollution spreads; traffic jams and urban congestion become more common; and the need for centralized administrative controls to provide services to a steadily enlarging clientele reduces personal freedom. The authors might also have stressed that population growth aggravates a great many other social problems we face: unemployment due to automation; the piling up of the poor in urban and rural backwaters; the strain on educational facilities; spiraling racial tensions.

Yet the Days are surely correct in distinguishing sharply between the drastic economic impact of population growth in the underdeveloped world and its less tangible effects on the quality of life in the United States. Catholics and others who take an absolutist position on population issues may go on advancing arguments designed to minimize the role of population growth in retarding economic progress in the underdeveloped world, but the arguments will remain dubious. For when all the misconceptions are cleared away, it becomes brutally apparent that there is no alternative to a decline in population growth, and that the only ways to achieve such a decline are birth control or a relaxation of death control. It is to the credit of the absolutists that they at least draw back from insisting starkly that the latter alternative be chosen.

27

Food and Population: The Wrong Problem?

Jean Mayer

I

The problem of population control as such is not new, although it has recently acquired new and dangerous dimensions. In all early treatments of the subject, considerations of population policy were not closely linked to economic concerns and in particular to the availability of food. Plato, who undertook nothing less than the projection of an ideal city-state, in estimating, in the *Laws*, the numbers needed for the various functions of citizenship, arrived at the figure of 5,040 citizens as the desirable size, adequate to "furnish numbers for war and peace, for all contracts and dealings, including taxes and divisions of the land." It has been estimated that, with dependents and slaves, the total population of this city-state comprised about 60,000 persons. In *The Republic*, Plato further developed his concepts of population control, and in particular, described his well-known eugenics proposal for public hymeneals of licensed breeders. At all times, his preoccupation is with the quality of man and of the state; the availability of food and other resources is not considered. Aristotle similarly believes that the efficient government of city-states would be impossible if cities were too large. He was concerned with certain of the economic consequences of overpopulation, though not specifically with food. In the *Politics*, he warns that: "A neglect of an effective birth-control policy is a never failing source of poverty, which is in turn the parent of revolution and crime," and advised couples with an excessive number of children to abort succeeding pregnancies "before sense and life have begun."

Reprinted from *Daedalus,* journal of the American Academy of Arts and Sciences, Boston, Mass., vol. 93, no. 3 (Summer, 1964), pp. 830–44, by permission of the author and the publisher.

Plato and Aristotle did not go unchallenged. The Pythagoreans, in particular Hippocrates, opposed abortion. The Hippocratic oath contains the pledge: "I will not give a woman an abortive remedy." Of greater subsequent importance, the Romans almost as a body disapproved of the Greek views on population. They were not so much concerned with the quality of man and the excellence of the state as with the size of the legions and the expansion of the Empire. Cicero, in particular, in *De Re Publica*, waxes indignant at Plato for his ideas on birth control. Rome taxed celibacy and rewarded large families. Roman ideas, incidentally, were very similar to those of Confucius and his followers, also citizens of a large and expanding empire, and equally convinced that a numerous and expanding population should be promoted by wise rulers. The economic consequences of large populations were essentially ignored by the Romans; Confucius dealt with them by enunciating the rather intriguing formula: "Let the producers be many and the consumers few."

The Hebrews and the Fathers of the Church were similarly uninterested in the economic implications of population growth. Biblical and early Christian writers can, indeed, hardly be considered to have had a population policy, though their concepts of family life and of the dignity of man are as basic now as they were millenniums ago. For them, man was neither a political nor an economic unit; he had intrinsic worth as a son of God. "The Lord God formed man out of the dust of the ground and breathed into his nostrils the breath of life and man became a living being." Later God said, "Let us make Mankind in our image and likeness. . . . Be fruitful and multiply; fill the earth and subdue it." Later, Onan is killed by the Lord for having practiced coitus interruptus, and children are repeatedly designated as the gift of God, with large families particularly blessed. The prescriptions of Saint Paul are somewhat more complex: while he states that women can merit eternal salvation through bearing children if they continue to be faithful, holy, and modest, he praises virginity as more blessed than marriage, and dedicated widowhood as preferred above remarriage. The position of the Church against abortion hardens in the third century, when Saint Hippolytus opposes Pope Calixtus I for showing too much leniency towards the abortionists, and reiterates the Christian position that the fetus is a person and not, as in Roman law, a part of the mother. It is only with Tertullian, citizen of a crowded and decaying Empire, that the possible economic consequences of overpopulation are clearly stated. In *De Anima* he writes: "The scourges of pestilence, famine, wars and earthquakes have come to be regarded as a blessing to overcrowded nations, since they served to prune away the luxuriant growth of the human race." Tertullian is echoed 1,300 years later by Botero, a sixteenth-century Italian writer, who holds that man's productive powers are inferior to his reproductive powers, which do not diminish automatically when population increases. For this reason, the population of the world must be constantly checked by war and epidemics. Food limitation directly thus limits the population of the earth, which already holds as many people as it can hold. From Botero onward, concepts of optimum population size become indissolubly linked to economic considerations, and, it may be added, to economic considerations of the lowest order. Population limitation is advocated by those writers, foremost among whom is Malthus, who feel they can demonstrate that population will inevitably rise to the very margin of food production capacity, with misery and vice the only consequences. The examples chosen are often unfortunate in the light of hindsight: Malthus bases his prediction on an examination of the United States of the late eighteenth century. Lord Raffles in 1804 is appalled at the fact that Java may in time contain as many as four million people, clearly, he feels, a number representing the limit of agricultural possibilities. On the other side, mercantilist writers and rulers once again see an increase in population as a guarantee of ample manpower for production and for war, and as a test of good government. Through the nineteenth century the debate continues. Malthusians see the solution of economic problems due to overpopulation in continence and in more poverty—specifically, the repeal of the poor laws. The belief in the inevitability of starvation and the desirability of a laissez faire policy was in no small measure responsible for government inaction during the Irish famine. At the other end of the spectrum, Marx and Engels opposed Malthus as a peculiarly vicious and obsolete defender of capitalism. "Overpopulation" was a bourgeois invention, designed to justify the poverty of the working classes. Improved production and distribution, not restriction of births, was the answer. A socialistic economy could thrive under all conditions of population growth, while an economy based on scarcity and high prices required birth control to mitigate its glaring deficiencies. Oddly enough, a number of modern Catholic philosophers have held a viewpoint not very different from that of Karl Marx.

Since the mid-nineteenth century, three profound revolutions have taken place: a technological revolution, which promises to accelerate food production still faster; a demographic explosion, which is also accelerating and places the problem of population in an even more dramatic context; and changes in human attitudes, for which Assistant Secretary of State Harlan Cleveland has coined the felicitous expression "the revolution of rising expectations." It is the contention of this writer that nothing is more dangerous for the cause of formulating a sound policy of population control than to approach the problem in nineteenth-century terms; by continuing to link the need for population control to the likelihood that food supply will be increasingly limited, the elaboration of birth-control programs of sufficient magnitude will be held up for many years, perhaps many generations. We shall see that in contemporary terms, it may well be that the controversy between Plato and Cicero makes more sense than that between the neo-Malthusians and the neo-Marxists.

II

That the magnitude of the population problem has increased drastically in recent years is well publicized. Scholars have estimated that after hundreds of thousands of years of slow growth, the population of the world reached the quarter-billion mark sometime around the beginning of this era. It had doubled again, to 500 millions, by 1650. Two centuries later, it had reached the billion mark. The next doubling took 80 years, with a 2-billion population reached in 1930. It would appear that the world is on its way to the next doubling, to 4 billion in 45 years, by 1975, and a population of 8 billion may well be reached within the following 30 to 35 years unless the rates of growth are drastically decreased. The present growth rate would lead to a population of 500 billion by 2200, and give the surface of all continents a population density equal to that of Washington, D.C., at present!

This increase has been due historically not to an increase in birth rates, but to a decrease in death rates. Around 1700, life expectancy at birth of European populations was about 33 years, and had increased little in the previous three to four hundred years. By 1950, life expectancy in Western and Central Europe and in the United States had increased to 66–69 years, an increase of over 100 per cent. This decrease in mortality rates is no longer confined to populations of European stocks. In 1946, the death rate of the Moslem population of Algeria was higher than that of Sweden in 1775. In 1954, in spite of generalized guerrilla war on its territory, the death rate of this population was lower than that of Sweden in 1875. A similar telescoping of the drop in death rates is going on all over the world.

From a demographic point of view, it must be noted that a drop in the death rate, with birth rate unchanged, not only results in an increase in the rate of population growth, but also produces an acceleration in the rate of growth itself: a decline in age-specific mortality rates in ages prior to the end of the childbearing age has the same demographic effect as an increase in the birth rate. In the United States, 97 out of every 100 newborn white females reach the age of 20, 91 reach the age of 50. In Guatemala, only 70 newborn females reach the age of 20, 49 that of 50. If, within the next decade, the death rate in Guatemala fell to somewhere near the 1950 United States level—a not unlikely development—this alone would increase the number of women reaching the beginning of the childbearing period by 36 per cent, the end of the childbearing period by 85 per cent.

Generally speaking, because of the high proportion of young people in underdeveloped countries—a country like Costa Rica has twice the proportion of people under 15 that Sweden has—this drop in the death rate in the pre-childbearing period has now and will have in the next few years a gigantic effect on the birth rate. Brazil had 52 million people in 1950 and 71 million in 1960. If present rates prevail, it should have 240 million by the year 2000, or 14 times the 1900 population. With a drop in mortality in the younger age groups, the increase could be even more spectacular.

The significance of demographic trends even in this country are not generally appreciated. The United States, with a population of 193 millions, has at present one-sixteenth of the earth's population on one-sixteenth of the land area. Though a number of underdeveloped areas are piling up population faster than we are, we are accumulating about 3 million people per year, the most rapid increase in our history. The *rate* of growth seems unimpressive: 1.63 per cent per year for 1961, for example. During that same year, Western European countries grew at average rates of 0.50 to 0.75 per cent, but Asia and Latin America grew at a 2.5 per cent rate. This 1.63 per cent of 190 millions is over 3 millions; if the rate persists for 100 years, it will bring the population of the United States to one billion. Furthermore, what most of us have tended to ignore is that the so-called baby boom of the postwar era followed a period of depression and very low birth rates: from 1920 to 1933 the birth rate had fallen steadily from 27.7 per 1,000 in 1920 to 18.4 in 1933. The absolute decline in births was less steep, because the numerical base of women of childbearing age was still growing. When the birth rate started rising in the early forties, the increase was applied to the still large number of women born between 1916 and 1924. Since 1945, the baby boom that has been so publicized has actually been taking place on the basis of the shrinking group of women of childbearing age born since 1924. As of 1963, the last of the undersize groups had entered the reproducing age. In 1964, the girls born in the big postwar year of 1946 are 18. From now on birth rates must fall by a substantial amount to keep the number of births constant at 4.5 millions, 50 per cent above the 3 million figure we have come to consider a "boom" figure. . . . The sober fact is that, in this country, there were 32 million women 15 to 44′years of age in 1940 and 34 million in 1950, 36 million in 1960. There will be 43 million in 1970 and 54 million in 1980. These are not projective figures; the girls are here, now. Incidentally, even if the age-standardized national fertility rate fell immediately to its historical minimum of the thirties and stayed there—an unlikely event—the population of the United States would still reach about 420 millions in one hundred years. The reader will, I trust, give me credit for not minimizing the problem of total population either at home or for the world at large.

III

With this picture of ever increasing numbers of people, the first reaction among a portion of the public is that we are running out of *space,* that the "population density" is becoming dangerously high. This concept of "population density"—number of people per surface unit—has underlain the concept of "overpopulation" in the past. It is not very useful, except in situations where the primary resources are extractive, such as mining, the most primitive types of agriculture (independent of industry for fertilizers, machines, etc., and hence essentially dependent on area), and forestry. It also presupposes that there is no industry to absorb surplus manpower. It is a concept of dubious value where non-extractive industries are dominant and where trade is possible. The high-density band from Boston to Washington has an area of 14,000 square miles, an aggregate population of over 28 million (or over 2,000 persons per square mile), and very limited natural resources. The median family income is $6,600, or $1,000 more than for the United States as a whole. Can this area be said to be overpopulated from a *material* standpoint? To those who object that this area is part of a larger and less densely populated whole, one might point to prosperous Holland, or Belgium, or even Hong Kong, which, although trade with its hinterland is very meagre (imports from mainland China represent only 17 per cent of total imports), not only houses 3.1 million people on 398 square miles (12,700 per square mile), but has shown an unexcelled increase in national product of 7 to 10 per cent per year—a doubling of real output within ten years. The minute one argues that population density should be preserved, although perhaps in a more sophisticated form, such as density with respect to capital, one is dealing with a much more complex concept, which may lead one to the possibility that some sparsely settled countries need rapid increases in population—preferably through immigration—for optimal use of resources. The mental image of population density entertained by most people is, in any case, complicated by esthetic and social considerations, and "high density" is more likely to be ascribed to Calcutta than to Paris, to Costa Rica than to Denmark.

This leads us to the second and most popular concept: that over-population can best be appraised with respect to food resources and that the present rate of increase of the world's population is rapidly carrying us to the brink of or to actual starvation. It is my contention that this is not happening. Furthermore, I do not consider that my belief, which I will now endeavor to justify, makes me an "optimist" as compared to the legions of conservationists, social scientists, etc., who have embraced a Malthusian "pessimism." If anything, this view makes me even more pessimistic about our chances to control at any early date the world's population: limitation by famine or threat of famine is perhaps the worst method of limitation, but it would work.

IV

World War II was not a Malthusian check: in spite of the horrendous numbers of soldiers and civilians killed, in spite of the massive genocide perpetrated by the Nazis, food production was decreased much more than population: by 1945 intake per capita was 16 per cent lower than the 1934–1938 average. The creation of the Food and Agriculture Organization, a specialized United Nations agency which, during its first years, was endowed with particularly articulate spokesmen, dramatized the worldwide concern over the food situation. The difficulties inherent in getting agriculture going while industry and means of communication were not yet rebuilt led to a generalized feeling of pessimism: cereals, oils, meat, dairy herds were, in succession, the objects of great attention, the conclusion being in each case that prewar levels of production and consumption were not going to be reached for years. The chaotic state of international trade accentuated shortages, which UNRRA and various emergency agreements attempted to cope with on an ad hoc basis. And yet very quickly the situation improved. The oil shortage vanished first; while the gigantic groundnut scheme of the British government, which was supposed to mitigate it, was taking off to a very slow start, the reappearance in the channels of trade of adequate amounts of fats and oils eliminated the motivation for the scheme itself. United States production of cereals and animal products, which had grown during the war in spite of lack of abundant manpower and the diversion of the chemical industry to military purposes, had to be slowed down as surpluses started accumulating, and, with their appearance, the threat of a collapse of agricultural prices loomed. By 1952–1953, the worldwide rate of per capita production of food had overtaken prewar rates. Since then, the average rate of increase in the production of food for the world at large has been 3 per cent per year while the population has increased on the average 1.7 per cent. In document No. 8148, the Department of State estimates that if individual consumption levels remained at the 1955–1957 level, the world at large would show by 1975 an annual surplus of 40 million tons of wheat and 70 million tons of rice. (This estimate is based on the postulate that there will be no increase in rice production in Europe and North America, and no increase in wheat production in North America.) Actually, this slight but steady gain of food production over population is part of a secular trend. E. S. and W. S. Woytinski, in their monumental *World Population and Production,* estimate that since 1850 the increase in output has been more rapid than the increase in population.

This writer is a nutritionist who has worked in poor countries in Asia and Africa; he is, therefore, well aware of the widespread character of malnutrition. Caloric undernutrition is still found in many parts of the world, and not always as a result of war or civil disorder, great natural catastrophes such as earthquakes or flood, invasion of insects or other parasites and abnormally prolonged droughts; protein deficiency—kwashiorkor when it occurs without accompanying caloric deprivation, marasmus when both caloric and protein intake are inadequate—is encountered in varying degrees of prevalence among the young children of most countries of Asia and Africa and in many of Central and South America. Vitamin A deficiency is perhaps underestimated as a threat to the life—and the sight—of children of most of the same areas where protein deficiency is also seen. Riboflavin deficiency, thiamine deficiency—beri-beri in its various forms—and a number of other deficiencies are still very much with us. Still, there is no evidence that the situation is getting worse. The food balance sheets on which postwar pessimism was based are imperfect instruments: when this writer was nutrition officer of FAO, he spent considerable time attempting to gauge such unknowns as figures for wasted food at the retail level and within families; that portion of the food supply which does not move within the channels of trade—the amount of food grown by the farmer for his family—is very inaccurately known, particularly as regards fruits and vegetables, which tend to be underestimated. The nutritional standards against which available supplies are gauged are themselves being redefined. As the results of additional experimental and clinical work become available, it is realized that a number of such standards—those for protein and calcium among others—were probably unnecessarily high. Even without such reevaluation, the evolution of food balance sheets—the only instrument we have to judge the race between food and population—make it apparent that most regions do show the same slow increase of per capita supplies exhibited by the world at large. It must be recognized, of course, that many of the worst nutritional scourges of mankind have been historically due as much to ignorance and to callousness as to lack of nutrients as such. Thousands of children die of protein deficiency in areas where the proteins which would save them do in fact exist and are often consumed in sufficient amounts in the very households where infants and toddlers die for their lack: faulty understanding of the child's needs may be the main cause for his being denied some of the food consumed by his father and older siblings. As for man's inhumanity to man and its contribution to starvation, it could be illustrated by thousands of examples: from cereals being shipped from Ireland under the protection of naval guns during the famine to stocks being withheld during the Congo famine to keep prices up.

Certainly, as far as food is concerned, ours is not one world. The United States government rents 20 million acres from our farmers so that they will not grow food on them. A recent study made at Iowa State University suggests that 62.5 million acres ought to be similarly retired so that surpluses will not continue to be created in relation to the present market. Australia, Canada, New Zealand, Argentina, and France have been, or are at present, involved in similar efforts to restrict production.

Nor is this idling of food production restricted to highly developed countries. A recent study estimates that Ghanaian farmers work only an average of two hours a day in the cocoa area, the wealthiest agricultural area of the country.

It is fair to say that in most areas of the world, the race between food and population would be more favorable to the development of adequate nutrition if the rate of population growth were decreased. But I believe that there is no ground for stating in 1964 that the nutritional state of the world is getting worse. It is not. And I believe that improvement in communication, availability of surpluses in certain countries, the existence of solid international organizations, and the gradual improvement in international morality make large-scale famines—such as the Irish or the Bengali famine—less likely to occur in this era: except, perhaps, in Red China, because of its alienation from the two richest blocs of countries. (It appears, moreover, that the food situation in China has improved noticeably in the past two years, making the recurrence of famine there more remote.)

V

The present, bad as it is, is no worse than the past and probably somewhat better. But what of the future? In absolute numbers, the increase in population is likely to accelerate for some time. Can the food supply keep up? My contention is that, for better or for worse, it can and will.

First, let us consider conventional agriculture. FAO's figures indicate that 3.4 billion acres are at present under cultivation. This represents less than 11 per cent of the total land area of the world. A number of experts—Prasolov, Shantz, Zimmermann—estimate the area which can eventually be made arable at from 13 to 17 billion acres. Colin Clark, the director of the Agricultural Economics Research Institute of Oxford, uses the figure of 19 billion acres, but counts double-cropped tropical lands twice. (He considers, incidentally, that if the land were farmed as well as the Dutch

farmers work their acres today, it would support 28 billion people on a
Dutch diet; if Japanese standards of farming and nutrition were used, this
area would support 95 billion people.)

The biggest potential increase of food production does not, however,
come from the extension of the area under cultivation, but from the increase
in the use of fertilizers. The phenomenal increase in food production in
this country has actually been performed with a reduction in acreage
farmed. By pre–World War I standards of cultivation, it took one and one-
half acres to support an American. If such standards prevailed today, we
would need to add at least 40 million acres to our farm area every ten years,
or the equivalent of an additional Iowa every decade. In fact, we use the
alternative—fertilizers. One ton of nitrogen is the equivalent of fourteen
acres of good farmland. The use of between two and three hundred thousand tons of nitrogen (and corresponding amounts of other necessary elements) per decade has in fact obviated the need to discover another Iowa.
Neither is our use of fertilizers as intensive as it is in Japan (where it is well
over twice that employed here) or in Western Europe. (Incidentally, in
spite of its already high standards of cultivation, Japan is still increasing its
agricultural production at a rate of 3 per cent per year.) India, Africa, and
most of Latin America use only an infinitesimal fraction of Japanese or
Western amounts of fertilizer or use none at all. Garst has estimated that
an expenditure of ten dollars an acre for fertilizers per year would alone add
50 to 100 per cent to the low yields in underdeveloped countries. Applying
this investment to an area of 1.5 billion acres would be equivalent to adding
at least 750,000,000 acres to the crop areas of these countries, the equivalent
of a continent bigger than North America. It is interesting to note that this
primacy of fertilizers was recognized relatively late. In this country, the
recognition dates back only to World War II, and has accelerated since
the Korean conflict. In Japan, it also dates back to 1950 or thereabout. And
the leaders of the U.S.S.R. only last year realized that a large-scale increase
in fertilizer output would be easier and more rewarding than the extension
of cultivation to the "virgin lands."

There are many other advances in agriculture which have yet to be
applied on a large scale. The identification of necessary trace elements and
their incorporation into fertilizers and feeds have opened vast areas to cultivation and husbandry in Australia and elsewhere. Selective breeding of
plants and animals has permitted the development of species with superior
hardiness and increased yields, in some cases multiplied them by a large
factor. In the greater part of the world such work has hardly begun. Advances in animal health and nutrition have permitted the mass production
of milk and eggs in indoor conditioners on a scale which was unimaginable
a few years ago—the city of Los Angeles is now an important and efficient

dairy area. In some large installations, computers programmed to calculate the cheapest method of providing a diet of known energy and known content in ten essential amino acids, total protein, and other nutrients automatically set the controls which will mix basic staples providing the cheapest adequate poultry diet as they are informed of the latest commodity prices. Herbicides increase yields, pesticides prevent losses from rodents, insects, and fungi—in many underdeveloped countries one quarter of the crop is lost before it reaches the consumer. Certain methods of preservation of foods by radiation have just been approved by the Food and Drug Administration. Control of weather by seeding clouds for rain, speeding cloud formation by heating lakes by atomic energy, desalinization of brackish water by various methods are entering the realm of practical feasibility.

Powerful though these methods of "classical" agriculture are, I believe that they will, within the lifetime of most present inhabitants of this planet, be left far behind as methods of food production. The general public is still unaware of some new developments, their promise, and the extent of the means likely to be expended in the next decade in bringing the results of research to practical application. Large-scale manufacture of food from petroleum chemicals started in World War II, when the Germans manufactured synthetic fats to feed forced-labor groups. These fats did not conform to desirable standards of taste or safety (they contained a high proportion of branched-chain fatty acids not normally found in nature and probably not fully metabolized, and retained a petroleum-like odor). After the war, interest in "synthetic" fats persisted for a while during the years when it appeared that a shortage of natural fats was likely to be protracted. During the fifties, little or no work was done in this field, but recently a number of the largest international oil companies have again become actively interested, and pilot plants are now in operation. Fatty acids, triglycerides (the constituents of our common oils and fats), and fully metabolizable simpler compounds, such as 1, 3-butanediol, may soon be manufactured at very low cost for human food and animal feeds. While the promise of abundant and cheap atomic power, widely heralded for the morrow in the more immediate postwar period, has shown itself slow to be realized, abundant and cheap atomic power is coming, and it may well be that oil will be increasingly a raw material for food and plastics rather than a fuel.

As a potential source of food production, photosynthesis can be used much more efficiently in algae than in higher plants. With proper mineral fertilization and with the proper rate of removal of the finished products, one square meter may serve to support algae production sufficient to feed a man. And for a large proportion the calories produced—as much as one half

—are derived from protein; vitamins are also produced into the bargain. Several universities are working with a number of species, chlorella in particular, and again large industrial firms are yearly becoming more interested. The problems entailed in passing from the theoretically feasible to the economically feasible are formidable, but their solution is likely to be hastened for an unexpected reason. Interplanetary travel of long duration and the organization of distant stations require not only recycling of oxygen and waste water; they necessitate the fabrication of food and its integration into the recycling of oxygen, water, and excreta. Over the next two decades, an increasing fraction of the several billion dollars which the United States and the Soviet Union will spend every year for space travel is going to be channeled into life-support systems. The money spent in the aggregate on new methods of food production will probably, during that period, dwarf the cost of the Manhattan Project. In many ways, we may have in space exploration what William James called "the moral equivalent of war." We will probably also have in it the technological equivalent of war—without the corresponding losses in men and in resources. The usable "fallout" of such research is likely to be enormous. Certainly if economical harnessing of photosynthesis—through biological units or directly—can be realized under the hostile interplanetary, lunar, or Martian conditions, it should become relatively easy to put it into effect on earth. All this is no longer science fiction. It is as much of a reality as the federal income tax. Obviously, a breakthrough in this field could for centuries altogether remove food as a limiting factor to population growth.

VI

I hope I have said enough to show how dangerous it may turn out to be for the population problem to have been linked so closely to food as a number of writers have done. These have generally been conservationists and social scientists rather than agricultural or nutritional scientists, concerned—rightly—with the effects of crowding which they had observed. At the same time, not sure that the public and governments would agree with them that there was cause for concern—and action—based on these grounds, they have turned to the threat of a worldwide shortage of food as an easily understood, imperative reason for large-scale limitation of births. Had they consulted nutritionists, agriculturalists, and chemists, they might have chosen a more appropriate battleground. For if we can feed an ever increasing number of people—even if we feed them as badly as many of our contemporaries are fed—their argument fails. And yet there is a need for the establishment as soon as possible of a sound population policy for the world at large.

There is, of course, another good reason for not tying population control to food: it is that this tie eliminates from contention rich countries—and in particular surplus countries such as ours. Our population is increasing faster than it ever has; our major nutrition problem is overweight, our major agricultural problem is our ever mounting excess production. Does anyone seriously believe this means that we have no population problem? Our housing problems, our traffic problems, the insufficiency of the number of our hospitals, of community recreation facilities, our pollution problems are all facets of our population problem. I may add that in this country we compound the population problem by the migratory habits of our people: from rural farm areas to urban areas and especially to "metropolitan" areas (212 such areas now have 84 per cent of our population), from low-income areas to high-income areas; from the East and Midwest to the South and Southwest; from all areas to the Pacific Coast; from the center of cities to suburbs which soon form gigantic conurbations, with circumstances everywhere pushing our Negroes into the deteriorating centers of large cities. All this has occurred without any master plan, and with public services continuously lagging behind both growth and migrations.

Let us conclude with one specific example: 4 million students were enrolled in U.S. colleges and graduate schools in 1960. The Bureau of the Census estimates that 6 million will seek admission or continued enrollment in 1965, 8 in 1970, 10 in 1975, 12 in 1980. No one questions our ability to feed these youngsters. But are we as a nation at all prepared for a tripling of the size of our colleges and universities in fifteen years? We need a population policy and we need it soon, for the United States as well as for the world at large, not because we cannot step up food production, but because we believe, like Plato and Aristotle, in trying for excellence rather than rejoicing in numbers. Excellent human subjects will not be produced without abundance of cultural as well as material resources. We are likely to run out of copper before we run out of food, of paper before we run out of copper. We are short even in this country now of housing, of hospitals, and of educational institutions. Needs are, of course, infinitely more acute in most other areas of the world. Is it not more sensible to focus on these unmet needs, which are present for all to see, than to argue from inaccurate projections which furthermore do not support the unnecessary argument?

INDEX